WOKE, BANNED, CENSORED & CANCELLED

WOKE, BANNED, CENSORED & CANCELLED

The war on everything in culture by the politically correct, tyrannical, fascist mob

Steven D. Snyder

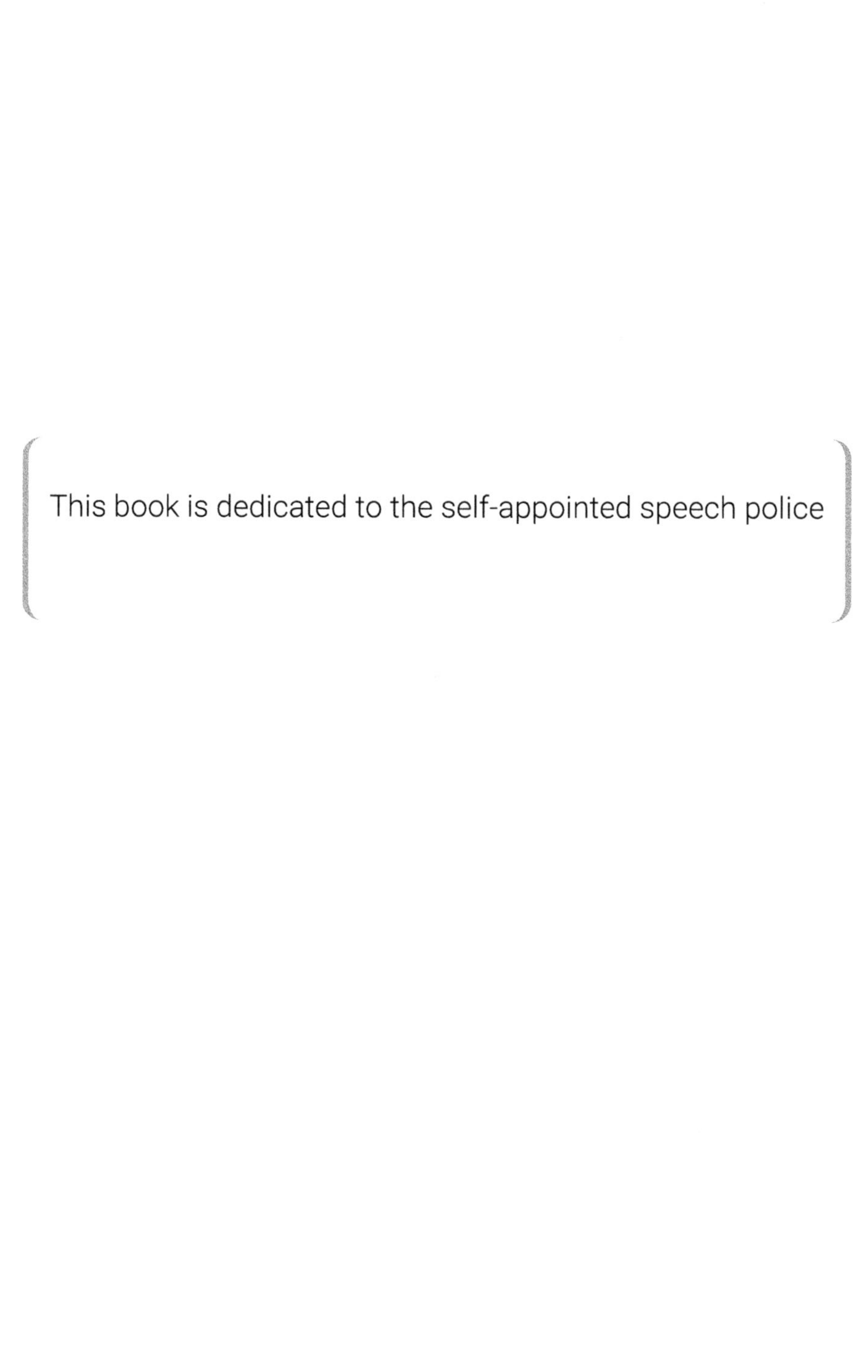

This book is dedicated to the self-appointed speech police

First Printing, 2021

CONTENTS

COMMENTARY

Before you begin reading the articles contained in this book, you might want to fix yourself a nice, stiff drink, do whatever illegal narcotic you would like to do and go scream into a pillow for an hour and a half (scheduling an appointment with your therapist and life coach is also recommended). In order to psychologically deal with the following news stories and articles laid out below, some of you might need to have electroshock therapy or even a lobotomy after reading this shit. These are 100% REAL NEW STORIES that showcase how completely fucked we are as a civilization.

Come here... Listen closely... Can you hear me now?... There is one rule that you must learn about in life...Everything is offensive. **EVERYTHING**... What am I talking about? I'm talking about the complete dismantling of our tradition, our history, our culture and our societies and it being replaced with a hell on earth utopian, sanitized, bland, faceless and controlled world and civilization.

No matter where you turn these days, there seems to be a VERY small minority of people who want to control, dominate and run every single aspect of your life. No, I am not talking about the 6'0" tall busty dominatrix with 7-inch black stilettos that I hire once a week to come to my house to punish and dominate me like the bad and "naughty boy" that I am. I'm talking about the people who want to control your entire life are from every corner of today's political world. They are Democrats, Republicans and Independents. They are young and old. They're conservative and liberal. They come from all religions. They come from all races. They come from all backgrounds. AND, they are 100% psychotic. Not "psychotic" like your ex who broke into your house to steal your clothes and to take a shit on your bed. Not that type of psycho. They're crazy and psychotic because they want to completely run, dominate and control every single aspect of your life- mostly your free speech and common sense.

What do they want? During my deep research into this topic, I discovered that they want everything. They first want to control your speech. They want to essentially control your language. The end result is that they want to control your entire life and they are doing it through language as a start. They are doing this through their "woke comedy", "woke sports", "woke education" and "woke media." They are using cancel culture, and BDS (boycott, divestment and sanctions) in order to stifle free speech and turn Grandma into a neo Nazi clansman for simply watching and enjoying the classic film, "*Gone with the Wind*."

I came to my opinion (after a few cocktails), that the politically correct, control freak Baby Boomers did this to the Millennials and Generation Z. The Baby Boomers in the 1960's and 1970's were well-meaning and they believed in peace, love, free speech, freedom and doing as many drugs in crazy sex-fueled parties in mud puddles as possible. However, as they have gotten older, a more sinister, self-righteous version of these folks have taken over every single, solitary aspect of our society. These people are nothing more than ivory tower fascists.

It is my theory that the Baby Boomers tried to coop Generation X and the Xennials (kids growing up in the 70's and mid 80's) into swallowing the blue pill of pc cancel culture, but they failed. So, what did these Baby Boomers do? They turned to the next two generations of kids and brainwashed them into believing that literally everything in life is offensive, racist, sexist, Islamophobic, homophobic, transphobic, fat-phobic, etc.

So who are these people? Studies show that these authoritarian control freaks are mostly well-to-do, wealthy, bi-costal elites living in major urban areas. Essentially, these are the people who run the high schools, colleges, universities, big corporations, the entire media complex, the Hollywood machine, the federal government and professional sports.

Now mind you, these articles show only a SMALL SAMPLE of the tyrannical bullshit that they are trying to get us to accept. These articles are only from the past two years and are a microcosm and a sample of what these people are trying to do. If I found every single article that showcased this takeover, the book would be 2,000 pages long; you wouldn't read it and if you did, you'd probably kill yourself. In the past few years, the following entities have been accused of being "offensive", "racist", "sexist", "transphobic", "Islamophobic" and wrong in our society.

These entities have been cancelled by the Nazi-like authoritarian control freak minority mob who run the country and control the narrative. The following is a **SMALL SAMPLE** list of things that these people want to ban, control, censor and cancel:

Gone with the Wind
Kindergarten Cop
To Kill a Mocking Bird
The Vagina Monologues
George Orwell Books
Dr. Seuss Books
Mr. Potato Head
Mrs. Potato Head
The Washington Redskins

The Atlanta Braves
The Kansas City Chiefs
The Chicago Blackhawks
The Little Mermaid
Names of Roads
Figures of Speech
The Motto of States
Comedy Jokes
Memes
Cheerleaders
Halloween Costumes
Idioms Referencing Meat
Pronouns
Breastfeeding
Capitalizing Words
Words in all CAPS
The American Flag
The Name of Bands
The Name of Food Products
Emojis
Mispronouncing Names
Hallmark Christmas Movies
University Mascots
Professional Mascots
Company Mascots
Logos
Statues
Monuments
The Definition of Words in the Dictionary
Clothing
The American National Anthem
Slogans
The Names of Buildings

The Names of Stadiums
Gestures
Metaphors
Analogies
Tattoos
Flags
Symbols
Icons
Board Games
Video Games
Sporting Activities
Theme Park Rides
Song Lyrics
Titles of Songs
Cartoon Characters
Superheroes
The Jungle Book
Aladdin
Flash Gordon
Fictional and Mythological Beings
Spongebob Squarepants
The Seinfeld TV Show
Elmer Fudd
Yosemite Sam
Snack, Crackle and Pop
Aunt Jemima
Uncle Bens
Paw Patrol
Chess
Cosmetics
Band Aids
Drawings
Paintings

Sculptures
Dancing
Laughing
Tone of Voice
Gestures
Dialects
Adam Sandler Movies
John Hughes Movies
Snow White
Rudolph the Red-Nosed Reindeer
Ace Ventura Pet Detective
The Cosby Show
The Lion King
James Bond Movies
The Irishman
Mary Poppins
Ronald Reagan
Margaret Thatcher
Christopher Columbus
Abraham Lincoln
Martin Luther King Jr.
Thomas Jefferson
Mt. Rushmore
Skyscrapers
John Wayne
Frank Bogert
Francis Scott Key
Saint Junipero Serra
Ulysses S. Grant
Albert Pike
The Names of Cities
The Police Department
The Military

Yoga
Fitness Centers
Andrew Jackson
Advertising
Marketing
Hawaiian Shirts
Happy Meal Toys
Lego Toys
Jesus Christ
Christmas Carols
Gingerbread Man
Santa Claus
Nativity Scenes
The Bible

This is not about Democrat versus Republican or Liberal versus Conservative. This is about everyone and is not political, or at least, it shouldn't be political. I am a hard-core Libertarian. What does that mean? Well, it means you do you and I'll do me. I won't tell you how to live your life and you won't tell me. Sure, Libertarians have their own personal and political opinions, but the main principles of Libertarianism are FREEDOM and LIBERTY. Essentially, I'm totally fine with two transgendered, gay, black, Muslim, midgets getting married while protecting their legal pot plants and legal cocaine kilos with fully automatic machine guns. Now that, my friends is **LIBERTY**...

Remind you, this is just a small sample of what is coming under attack from a group of self-righteous, bourgeois, bi-costal, virtue-signaling, wealthy and elite group of sociopaths. These people are dead serious and they are not fucking around.

I'll give you a minute to catch your breath before you begin reading these news stories. Again, the source is cited at the end of each article.

So, sit back, relax and enjoy reading about the entire culture and civilization being attacked. At the end of this, I will provide a conclusion to this book.

Enjoy...

1

The War on Literature

6 Dr. Seuss Books Will No Longer Be Published Over Offensive Images

By Jenny Gross March 2nd, 2021

The company that oversees the children's author's estate said that the titles contained depictions of groups that were "hurtful and wrong."

Six Dr. Seuss books will no longer be published because of their use of offensive imagery, according to the business that oversees the estate of the children's author and illustrator.

In a statement on Tuesday, Dr. Seuss Enterprises said that it had decided last year to end publication and licensing of the books by Theodor Seuss Geisel. The titles include his first book writing under the pen name Dr. Seuss, "And to Think That I Saw It on Mulberry Street" (1937), and "If I Ran the Zoo" (1950).

"These books portray people in ways that are hurtful and wrong," Dr. Seuss Enterprises said in the statement. The business said the decision came after working with a panel of experts, including educators, and reviewing its catalog of titles.

Mr. Geisel, whose whimsical stories have entertained millions of children and adults worldwide, died in 1991. The other books that will no longer be published are "McElligot's Pool," "On Beyond Zebra!" "Scrambled Eggs Super!" and "The Cat's Quizzer."

Mr. Geisel's stories are loved by fans for their rhymes and fantastical characters but also for their positive values, like taking responsibility for the planet. But in recent years, critics have said some of his work was racist and presented harmful depictions of certain groups.

In "And to Think That I Saw It on Mulberry Street," a character described as "a Chinaman" has lines for eyes, wears a pointed hat, and carries chopsticks and a bowl of rice. (Editions published in the 1970s changed the reference from "a Chinaman" to "a Chinese man.") In "If I Ran the Zoo," two characters from "the African island of Yerka" are depicted as shirtless, shoeless and resembling monkeys. A school district in Virginia said over the weekend that it had advised schools to de-emphasize Dr. Seuss books on "Read Across America Day," a national literacy program that takes place each year on March 2, the anniversary of Mr. Geisel's birth.

"Research in recent years has revealed strong racial undertones in many books written/illustrated by Dr. Seuss," according to the statement by the district, Loudoun County Public Schools.

The decision to stop the publication of some Dr. Seuss books helps revive a debate over classic children's titles that do not positively represent minority groups. In France, the latest in a series of beloved comic books, Lucky Luke, features a Black hero and a narrative that reimagines the role of the cowboy, drawing criticism that the book was caving to an American-inspired obsession with race.

Before he became a giant of children's literature, Mr. Geisel drew political cartoons for a New York-based newspaper, PM, from 1941 to 1943, including some that used harmful stereotypes to caricature Japanese and Japanese-Americans. Decades later, he said he was embarrassed by the cartoons, which he said were "full of snap judgments that every political cartoonist has to make."

Random House Children's Books, which publishes the Dr. Seuss books said in a statement that it respected the decision of Dr. Seuss Enterprises and the work of the panel that reviewed the books.

https://www.nytimes.com/2021/03/02/books/dr-seuss-mulberry-street.html

California school district bans 'racist' classics: 'To Kill a Mockingbird,' 'Huckleberry Finn,' 'Of Mice and Men,' and more are gone

By Sarah Taylor November 17th, 2020

Administrators at the Burbank Unified School District have determined that a variety of classic novels — including Harper Lee's "To Kill a Mockingbird" and more — will no longer be permitted for curriculum use following concerns of racism.

According to a Tuesday Newsweek report, middle school and high school English teachers will not be able to include the following books in lessons following reports of parental concerns of racism:

- Harper Lee's "To Kill a Mockingbird"
- Mark Twain's "The Adventures of Huckleberry Finn"
- John Steinbeck's "Of Mice and Men"
- Theodore Taylor's "The Cay"
- Mildred D. Taylor's "Roll of Thunder, Hear My Cry"

The outlet reported that four parents — three of whom are black — reportedly said the classic novels posed "alleged potential harm" to the district's "roughly 400 black students." One parent, identified as Carmenita Helligar, said a white student approached her black daughter and taunted her with the N-word, which the student said he "learned" from reading "Roll of Thunder, Hear My Cry." Another boy reportedly told Helligar's child, "My family used to own your family, and now I want a dollar from each of you for the week."

Helligar told the outlet, "My daughter was literally traumatized. These books are problematic ... you feel helpless because you can't even protect your child from the hurt that she's going through." Nadra Ostrom, another black parent, said that the books are problematic because there is "no counter narrative to this black person dealing with racism and a white person saving them."

The National Coalition Against Censorship sent a letter to the district urging the administration to reconsider the move. "[W]e believe that the books ... have a great pedagogical value and should be retained in the curriculum," a spokesperson for the organization wrote in the letter, which was obtained by the Los Angeles Times. Poets, Essayists, and Novelists America also crafted a petition demanding the district reinstate the use of the books.

A portion of the petition says, "Each of the books in question deal with difficult subject matter from our country's complicated and painful history, including systemic racism. Blocking engagement with these important books is also avoiding the important role that schools can and should play in providing context for why these books inspire and challenge us still today." At least one district teen created and distributed a Change.org petition calling for the district to stop the censorship.

A portion of the teen's petition states, "In a time where racism has become more transparent than ever, we need to continue to educate students as to the roots of it; to create anti-racist students. These literatures, of which have been declared 'Books that Shaped America' by the Library of Congress, won Newbury Medals, and are some of the most influential pieces, cannot disappear."

https://www.theblaze.com/news/california-school-district-bans-classic-books-racism

Michigan College Cancels 'The Vagina Monologues' Because 'Not All Women Have Vaginas'

By Tré Goins-Phillips November 15th, 2018

Leaders at a college in Michigan decided to cancel its production of "The Vagina Monologues" because it's discriminatory, given "not all women have vaginas."

The women's resource center at Eastern Michigan University put the kibosh on the famous production since it caters only to women who have the physical anatomy that accompanies the female sex, according to The Ann Arbor News.

The decision came after the resource center conducted a survey, asking respondents about "The Vagina Monologues." Those opposed to the drama said they were concerned about the fact that the production excludes some women, namely those who don't have vaginas. Due to copyright laws, the play cannot be modified to include transgender women, so the school is just scrapping it altogether.

The resource center issued the following statement on the show's cancellation:

We feel that making this decision is in line with the WRC mission of recognizing and celebrating the diverse representations of women on campus along with the overall mission of the Department of Diversity and Community Involvement, in which the WRC is housed, of supporting and empowering minoritized students and challenging systems and structures that perpetuate inequities. We truly believe that it is important to center our minoritized students and this decision is in line with this mission driven value.

Some of the survey's respondents said it's just time to give up on "The Vagina Monologues," written in 1994 by activist Eve Ensler, because the play can't fit into today's far-left feminist movement.

The resource center's email read, in part, "This created a need to ask the question: Do we still need 'The Vagina Monologues?' And, are 'The Vagina Monologues' still relevant to next-generation feminists?"

Apparently, many of the people who liked the iconic production, which is centered on stigma surrounding female anatomy, still felt it should be updated to include people who don't have female anatomy.

Other colleges, including American University and Mount Holyoke College, decided to abandon play.

American University instead created a new play called "Breaking Ground Monologues" to "broaden the focus from specifically female genitalia to multiple identities and bodies" and Mount Holyoke College decided to scrap its annual performance of the production.

https://www.faithwire.com/2018/11/15/michigan-college-cancels-the-vagina-monologues-because-not-all-women-have-vaginas/

Dr. Seuss Books Like *Horton Hears a Who!* Branded Racist and Problematic in New Study

By Sam Gillette February 28th, 2019

As Dr. Seuss' birthday approaches on March 2, a new study argues that many of the author's classic children's books are racist and problematic — and only two percent of his characters represent people of color.

"[This study reveals] how racism spans across the entire Seuss collection, while debunking myths about how books like *Horton Hears a Who!* and *The Sneetches* can be used to promote tolerance, anti-bias, or anti-racism," Katie Ishizuka and Ramón Stephens write in their February 2019 report, "The Cat is Out of the Bag: Orientalism, AntiBlackness, and White Supremacy in Dr. Seuss' s Children's Books," as part of St. Catherine University's *Research on Diversity in Youth Literature.*

They continue: "Findings from this study promote awareness of the racist narratives and images in Dr. Seuss' children's books and implications to the formation and reinforcement of racial biases in children." The study continues by explaining that some of the most iconic characters relay the troubling messages of Orientalism (the representation of Asia and Asian people based on colonialist stereotypes), anti-blackness and white supremacy. "Notably, every character of color is male. Males of color are only presented in subservient, exotified, or dehumanized roles," the authors write as part of their findings. "This also remains true in their relation to White characters. Most startling is the complete invisibility and absence of women and girls of color across Seuss' entire children's book collection."

Theodor Seuss Geisel, whose pen name is Dr. Seuss, published his first children's book in 1937, and his works are filled with problematic portrayals that coincide with the culture of pre-Civil-Rights-Movement America. For instance, in *If I Ran the Zoo* a white male is carried by three Asian characters as he holds a gun. The caption beneath the Asian males describes them as "helpers who all wear their eyes at a slant" from "countries no one can spell," according to the study. The only two characters identified as African appear in *Horton Hears a Who!*. Sporting grass skirts and wearing no shoes, "they are placed in a subservient role, carrying an animal to a White male child's zoo," Ishizuka and Stephens explain.For the researchers, these types of portrayals are deeply troubling. And they aren't the only ones saying so.

In September 2017, Cambridgeport Elementary School's librarian, Liz Phipps Soeiro, made a political statement that quickly went viral when she turned down a shipment of Dr. Seuss books from First Lady Melania Trump. "You may not be aware of this, but Dr. Seuss is a bit of a cliché, a tired and worn ambassador for children's literature. As First Lady of the United States, you have an incredible platform with world-class resources at your fingertips," the librarian wrote in an editorial for The Horn Book's reading blog, later adding. "Another fact that many people are unaware of is that Dr. Seuss's illustrations are steeped in racist propaganda, caricatures, and harmful stereotypes."

The books had been delivered as part of the National Education Association's Read Across America program, which first began in 1997 and coincides with the author's birthday. The NEA has also received criticism for associating with Dr. Seuss, since he has such a complicated history. So in 2018, for the first time in twenty years, the organization "removed all Dr. Seuss books from their annual Read Across America Resource Calendar, and featured all diverse books and authors at their RAA events," according to the study.

"I think there will always be a place for Seuss books — they are in every classroom and library in America — and in some cases, they're effective for younger readers," Steven Grant, a manager of Read Across America, told Education Week in October 2017. "That said, it's not to the exclusion of all the other great books that are out there."

While there has been a wave of criticism against Dr. Seuss and other children's books (like *Charlie and the Chocolate Factory* and *The Chronicles of Narnia)* for being racist, many readers continue to support these longtime favorites. Domenic Sarno, the mayor of Dr. Seuss' hometown of Springfield, Massachusetts, fired back at Soeiro after learning about her rejection of the books. "'One fish – two fish – red fish – blue fish' – I think her comments 'stink' and are ridiculous towards our beloved Dr. Seuss," Sarno said, according to MassLive.com. "Her comments that this is 'racist propaganda and that Dr. Seuss is a bit of a cliche and a tired and worn ambassador for children's literature' is 'political correctness' at its worst."

Scholars who spoke with Education Week have a more nuanced view. They suggested that teachers receive training in cultural sensitivity and be given access to books with diverse characters. If children do read these older books (like those by Dr. Seuss), the scholars suggested that adults approach the readings in an informed and critical way, according to the outlet.

"I don't think nostalgia is a defense. Affection is not a defense," Philip Nel, a professor of English as Kansas State University, told Education Week. "What you have to do is take a deep breath, step back, and realize that the culture in which these books live and in which these books were written is a racist culture and a sexist culture."

https://people.com/books/dr-seuss-books-racist-problematic/

Orwell Cancelled? Journalist Says "Vile" Author Aided Nazis

By Paul Joseph Watson July 8th, 2020

Despite being dead for 70 years, George Orwell may become the latest public figure to be cancelled after a left-wing journalist called him a "vile man" who aided the Nazis with his strident criticism of Stalinist Russia.

Yes, really.

"In addition to being a gov snitch, fraud George Orwell spent WWII demonizing the USSR as it defeated Nazism," tweeted Ben Norman. "As the Red Army sacrificed millions fighting Hitler, and as the Nazi regime shoved Jews into gas chambers, Orwell was writing Animal Farm. Vile man," he added. Norton followed up by denouncing the 1984 author as a "reactionary who hated communists more than fascists" before claiming Orwell "didn't actually believe in free speech. He wanted to take away the free speech of communists. Orwell was a total fraud."

Respondents pointed out that criticizing Stalinism, which killed multiple times more people than Nazism, doesn't make one a fascist enabler. "Orwell cancelled. Stop reading Orwell everybody. There is nothing you are allowed to learn from his books. Ben says," tweeted Ryan McGoverne. "This is my favorite cancellation yet. Top 10 of the last hour anyway," said Alex Boyd.

Norman was also accused of historical inaccuracies. "To believe this is to be completely ignorant of the history of WWII," remarked one Twitter user. "Stalin was completely fine with everything Hitler was doing up until the Germans invasion of USSR in 1941. Also the Red Army was not alone in defeating the Nazis."

To be fair to Norman, he does appear to be a supporter of free speech and an opponent of deplatforming. However, this once again underscores how "cancel culture" is not merely just push back on opinions considered to be "offensive". Orwell died in 1950 and his legacy as an icon of anti-authoritarianism has held firm over the last 70 years.

But just as we have seen with attempts to topple statues of Winston Churchill, George Washington and Thomas Jefferson, the woke mob is so intent on re-writing history and imposing a cultural revolution, not even some of the most seminal names in history are safe.

https://www.infowars.com/orwell-cancelled-journalist-says-vile-author-aided-nazis/

Notre Dame Students Demand to Read Fewer White Authors

By Dan Lyman November 25th, 2019

Activists at the University of Notre Dame are demanding a radical transformation of school policies and curriculum to purportedly cater to the desires of non-white, LGBT, and female students. A student group calling itself "End Hate at ND" has issued a list of demands and has held multiple campus protests in an attempt to bring about those changes. Included in the list are calls to "Decolonize Academia" and "Implement Diversity Training In Each Dorm."

"No course or program of study should have a view limited to white, western, and/or male voices," the group says. "We demand that people who are of Color, Indigenous, Black, queer, or not male are represented in the authorship of at least half course and major required readings. Diversifying the canon helps eliminate the violence of only privileging white scholarship."

The group claims, "Homogeneous spaces allow hate to fester," accusing "white people at this predominantly white institution" of allowing "slurs, prejudice, and hate speech" to occur unchecked.

Additionally, End Hate at ND is pressing for an end to "parietals," a long-standing policy which forbids students from being in undergraduate residence halls of the opposite sex late at night or during early morning hours. "Parietals effectively erase the presence of queer folks on Notre Dame's campus," the group asserts. "They help enforce heteronormativity and gender norms that propagate homophobia in the form of microaggressions, slurs, and a spirit of exclusion." Student activists have staged multiple protests where at least one attendee reportedly read aloud from the *Communist Manifesto*.

https://www.newswars.com/notre-dame-students-demand-to-read-less-white-authors/

'To Kill a Mockingbird' Pulled from Mississippi School District Reading List

By Joyce Chen October 16th, 2017

A Mississippi school district recently decided to remove Harper Lee's classic novel, *To Kill a Mockingbird*, from its eighth-grade reading list after receiving complaints that the book's language made people "uncomfortable."

"There were complaints about it," Kenny Holloway, vice president of Biloxi School District's school board, told the *Sun Herald*. "There is some language in the book that makes people uncomfortable, and we can teach the same lesson with other books."

To Kill a Mockingbird was published in 1960 and won the Pulitzer Prize in fiction the next year. It follows a series of events loosely based on Lee's own experiences growing up in Monroeville, Alabama, in the 1930s, and speaks to themes of racial inequality and discrimination in a small Southern town. The story includes instances of the "N-word" in reflection of the language used at the time, and is listed as the No. 21 most banned books in the last decade by the American Library Association.

According to Holloway, the book will still be available for students to check out in school libraries, but will no longer be used as the core text for eighth-grade ELA, the Common Core state standards for English Language Arts. The decision came as an administrative and department decision, a member of the school board told the *Herald*, and was not voted upon by the school board. When asked Thursday to confirm whether or not the controversial book had been pulled from classes, Superintendent Arthur McMillan issued a statement that read: "There are many resources and materials that are available to teach state academic standards to our students. These resources may change periodically. We always thrive to do what is best for our students and staff to continue to perform at the highest level."

Many were shocked by the decision, and voiced their thoughts on social media. Arne Duncan, who was the secretary of education from 2009 to 2015 under President Obama, tweeted, "When school districts remove 'To Kill a Mockingbird' from the reading list, we know we have real problems."

Added author Barbara Shoup in a statement to *USA Today*, "If we are going to solve the racial problems we have in our country now, we must confront the truth of how we got to where we are. ... If it is uncomfortable to read and discuss, so be it. Most things that matter deeply are." According to the *Herald*, the themes for the language arts classes in Biloxi this year are the Golden Rule and taking a stand. The initial talking points of the *Mockingbird* curriculum revolved around the idea that compassion and empathy transcend race, class and education.

https://www.rollingstone.com/culture/culture-news/to-kill-a-mockingbird-pulled-from-mississippi-school-district-reading-list-197821/

Literature

Classic literary books are being banned by these authoritarian control freaks. Why ban *To Kill a Mockingbird*? Why cancel Dr. Seuss? Every single aspect of our culture, society, and history is being destroyed because the people in power and control over our education system are ruling with an iron fist. What's next? Are we going to ban *Death of a Salesman* because it offends people who are depressed? Are we going to cancel *Frankenstein* because it is ableist? The next classics on the chopping block are:

Moby Dick- The title is offensive. It is sexist and promotes gender norms.

The Three Musketeers- It promotes violence.

The Scarlet Letter- Is sexist against women.

Romeo and Juliet- It promotes heteronormativity.

2

The War on Language

SNAFU In SF: School District Cancels Acronym, Calls It "Symptom of White Supremacy"

By Infowars.com February 2nd 2021

A San Francisco school board member is cancelling the acronym used to refer to the arts department, arguing it reinforces white supremacy. San Francisco Unified School District Art Director Sam Bass says they're doing away with the acronym "VAPA," which stands for visual and performing arts, claiming it promotes racism. "We are prioritizing anti-racist arts instruction in our work," Bass tells ABC7News.com.

Instead, Bass recommends a change from VAPA to "SFUSD Arts Department."

"It is a very simple step we can take to just be referred to as the SFUSD Arts Department for families to better understand who we are," Bass claims. The arts director alleges acronyms "perpetuate white supremacy" because they separate students based on their understanding of the English language.

"The use of so many acronyms within the educational field often tends to alienate those who may not speak English to understand the acronym," Bass insists. Bass says his anti-acronym philosophy stems from the 1999 report "White Supremacy Culture," authored by Tema Okun, who claimed, "Our culture perpetuates racism when things continue to be written down in a certain way." While the arts department acronym is getting a makeover, there's no word that terms used by the rest of the district, replete with acronyms that require an online glossary, will be changed.

One thing's certain, San Francisco is looking pretty FUBAR.

https://www.infowars.com/posts/san-francisco-school-district-cancels-acronym-calling-it-a-symptom-of-white-supremacy/

Leftist Oppression: The Thought and Language Police

By Jeff Davidson January 18th, 2021

In discussion with a liberal friend from high school, I found myself ruminating on why political correctness is so damaging to our society. Since the fraudulent 2020 election, and in particular since January 6, 2021, the Left has more blatantly dominated public discourse and is now enforcing an extreme edict of 'political correctness.' To have voted for Donald Trump is now considered a grievous sin. To take issue with the activities of BLM or Antifa is to risk ruining your career, maybe get beaten, and possibly be killed. My high school friend asked, "If I'm requesting information from someone of a certain category (ethnic, racial, religious, national, etc), aren't I more likely to be effective by acting or speaking in a way that makes him/her feel respected and equal?

Nothing Correct About It

If only political 'correctness' were confined to the view of it being appropriate and thoughtful use of language, employed to extract relevant meaning and to maintain effective relations. Unfortunately, it is a cultural battering ram employed by people who seek to:1. Silence and intimidate others2. Viciously label those who don't agree with their viewpoint 3. Belittle them for the language used, even if such language is not offensive4. Ruin their careers, if not imperil their safety5. Diminish any activity, whatsoever, that doesn't conform to such verbal fascism. Political 'correctness' (PC) advocates demand that everybody think like they do, and march on command as they direct. PC immobilizes others, such as well-intentioned government agents, from doing their jobs, protecting U.S. citizenry, and upholding the U.S. Constitution. Consider 'sanctuary cities' and the city officials within them – they are at odds with the Constitution which affords protection to U.S. citizens. Janet Napolitano, Secretary of Homeland Security in 2009, chose to employ the term "terrorism," even following despicable acts of terrorism on U.S. soil. After her initial testimony before Congress, she explained to a reporter that while she is aware of terrorism threats, she prefers to call them "man-caused" disasters. Man-caused disasters! Let that sink in...

PC is Deadly

PC is thought-control, pure and simple. It often impedes appropriate investigation into the nefarious activities of certain individuals. As such, PC can be deadly. In 2015, many individuals questioned behavior and activities of the San Bernardino, CA Islamic husband and wife who became mass murderers. The observers consciously avoided reporting them, however, due to the couple's minority status. In April 2016, the Department of Justice, under Obama, coined new terminology for convicted criminals: They now were to be cited as 'justice-involved individuals.' Youthful offenders were to be deemed 'justice-involved youth.' Such language restriction and contortion borders on lunacy. Big Brother would approve. In Orlando, FL in June 2016, the same phenomenon occurred as in San Bernardino: An Islamic mass murderer was known in advance by many others to be potentially violent and unhinged. Whoops!: 49 people died, many others were gravely injured, and the town, the state, and the nation was in shock. If the shooter employed a bomb instead of a gun, he could have murdered nearly 350 people, not "merely" 49.

Verbal Fascism

Following the Orlando massacre, the Obama Administration mandated that the Department of Justice, Homeland Security, and other agencies be barred from using the words "jihad" and "Sharia." Today, as we know too well, a single word in a single tweet that is disapproved by the 'woke' crowd might end one's career; likewise, a comment that one uttered 30 years ago. PC is the curse of our times and the go-to tool of domination. It contends that Caucasians, primarily western males, are the embodiment of oppression and that their views, behaviors, and actions are inherently wrong because they are Caucasian, western males. PC has its own vocabulary, such as "white privilege," "micro-aggression" and "mansplain." Such terms are designed to squelch the observations, experiences, rationale, and worthiness of the presumably non-conforming opposition. In PC culture, minorities can do little wrong, because they are minorities, and that the consequences of their behavior are excusable. Consider Michael Brown of Ferguson, Missouri. At age 18, he had a sealed juvenile rap sheet. It has been proven that Brown did not put his hands up and did not say, "Don't shoot," prior to his demise. Such individuals are regarded as the "continuing victims" of the Caucasian western male-dominated society. Thus, PC advocates bestow upon them a de facto life-time pass for their socially destructive behavior.

In the Distant Future

May your children and grandchildren one day live in an era when political 'correctness' has been swept out of our society.

https://politicrossing.com/leftist-oppression-the-thought-and-language-police/

Ever Had a Hard Time Understanding Someone's Accent? A Professor Says You're Guilty of 'Linguistic Racism'

By Alex Parker January 17th, 2021

Are your ears colorblind?

As you'll soon see, the answer may be hard to hear...

Have you ever had difficulty understanding someone's accent?

That is, have you ever been *racist?* According to a Michigan State University linguistics and education professor, the two are one and the same. So stop being beastly, and start understanding everyone. Per Professor Peter De Costa, when/if you don't know what someone's saying due to their consonants and vowels, you're guilty of "linguistic racism."

In a January 6 interview with MSU Today, the professor *laid it out.* First, a definition courtesy of the college man:

"Linguistic racism occurs when acts of racism are perpetuated against individuals on the basis of their language use. Victims of such racism are generally speakers of languages like Spanish or Arabic, or varieties of a language, like African American Vernacular English. These languages and variations are undervalued and seen as inferior to dominant, mainstream languages, such as standard English used predominantly by white, affluent members of society."

A deeper dive:

"These racist acts can be overt or covert in nature. On an overt level, speakers may be openly mocked by others. On a covert level, they may be told that they are unintelligible because they speak with an accent, for example." Peter says the discussion of such a sin's long been in effect, but the act itself has been kept on a "covert level." Amid his offering of information, the instructor served up a novel word. You've no doubt heard the trending term "marginalized" — a suggestion, so far as I can tell, that something isn't merely in the margin but forced there by the actions of others.

Along the same lines, meet "minoritized":

"Speakers of minoritized languages have been told to undergo accent reduction training so they can become intelligible and therefore be understood by others. These offers are masked under the guise of giving speakers "friendly advice" and framed with the supposedly good intention of helping them advance socially." Peter lamented that some who don't choose English are perniciously perceived as unpatriotic.

And xenophobia's alive and well:

"A recent example is the false labeling of COVID-19 as the "Wuhan virus" in public discourse by prominent politicians. This fueled xenophobic resentment toward people of Chinese ethnicity across the globe.

In London, for example, a young Singaporean Chinese individual was brutally attacked because of his ethnic association with the virus."

De Costa gave a couple instances of linguistically racist perpetration's:

"Acts of linguistic racism could take the form of comments like, 'Could you please repeat what you said? I don't understand your thick accent.' Or, if someone openly says only English is to be spoken in the workplace — despite the fact coworkers might be multilingual. "Another example is when someone interrupts a conversation to correct the grammar or vocabulary of minoritized speakers."

Englishsplaining?

Peter made clear the affects of linguistic racism: Shame and guilt for its victims. Among the casualties of LR: North America's tribes. "This has certainly been the case with Indigenous languages of American Indian communities, many of whom in the past were sent to boarding schools — often outside of their reservations — with the goal of erasing the home languages of American Indian youth. The sad result is that because of immense pressures from outside their respective communities, many of these speakers lost their languages and became monolingual English speakers."

But there's hope for all of you perpetrators:

"By understanding the need to correct acts of linguistic racism, people can become advocates of minoritized speakers and speak up for linguistic rights. If anyone commits acts of linguistic racism, they should be made aware; more importantly, they need to be educated about this bias and its detrimental effects. In addition, they need to explore how to create a culture of care that takes into account the socioemotional needs of minoritized speakers, with a long-term view to create an inclusive environment for these speakers, so the latter can survive and thrive linguistically."

I have but one inquiry for the educator...

What of people who can't understand the *southern* accent?

How can *they* be schooled not to be racist, *either*?

Folks from Alabama, Georgia, Tennessee, Mississippi, Louisiana, West Virginia, and Arkansas: You've all just been minoritized.

https://redstate.com/alexparker/2021/01/17/michigan-university-peter-de-costa-linguistic-racism-msu-today-n311700

Students at UK University Demand the Word "Black" be Banned From Lectures & Textbooks

By Paul Joseph Watson November, 30th 2020

Students at Manchester University have demanded that the word "black" when used as a negative expression such as the word "blackmail" should be banned because it is "divisive."

Yes, really.

The complaint was prompted by a university study surround issues affecting Black, Asian and Minority Ethnic (BAME) staff and faculty. Citing concerns of black people, the report noted that there were "linguistic concerns about Black being associated with negative expressions" such as "blackmail" and "black sheep."

After the report labeled the use of words which included "black" and "divisive and not inclusive," the university's student union demanded that "any other use of the word 'black' as an adjective to express negative connotations" should be banned in research papers, lecture slides, and books published by professors. Students claimed that such words were based on a "colonial history" and should be abolished in light of the Black Lives Matter movement.

However, Lexicographer Jonathon Green pointed out that such claims were completely erroneous given that the background environment of "identity politics" "simply wasn't there at the moment of coinage." As in America, many students have been indoctrinated to believe that one of the primary purposes for going to university is to lobby for speech and words to be banned. Back in September, Bristol University announced that it would crack down on "diet culture and fatphobia" language so as not to offend obese people and those with eating disorder.

https://www.infowars.com/posts/students-at-uk-university-demand-the-word-black-be-banned-from-lectures-textbooks/

Boston University Professor Says the Term "Legal Vote" is Racist

By Paul Joseph Watson November 11th, 2020

In another apparent attempt to delegitimize the claims of Trump supporters, Boston University professor Ibfram X. Kendi asserted that the term "legal vote" is "racist."

Kendi declared on Twitter that "The term 'legal vote' is as fictionally fraught and functionally racist as the terms 'illegal alien' and 'race neutral' and 'welfare queen" and 'handouts' and 'super predator' and 'crackbaby' and 'personal responsibility' and 'post racial.'" He went on to assert that allegations of voter fraud were inherently racist because they concern cities like Detroit, Philadelphia, Atlanta, and Phoenix, which have high black populations.

Kendi's characterization is obviously another crass effort to delegitimize claims of vote fraud, but as Professor Jonathan Turley points out, far from being "racist," the term "legal vote" is actually very close to another civil rights era term, "one man, one vote."

"The doctrine of "one man, one vote" is actually a civil rights mantra found not only in constitutional law but political movements (like this Student Non-Violent Coordinating Committee button). It is the doctrine embraced in a long series of court cases. See Gray v. Sanders, 372 U.S. 368 (1963); Reynolds v. Sims, 377 U.S. 533 (1964); Wesberry v. Sanders, 376 U.S. 1 (1964); and Avery v. Midland County, 390 U.S. 474 (1968)," writes Turley.

"The declaration of illegal votes as racist is clearly meant to paint anyone considering the current challenges as themselves racist, even before these claims are fully addressed in the courts," added Turley.

"Yet, such challenges often are filed to protect minority votes. In the 2004 election, I was working for CBS and raised whether there should be challenges in Ohio over voter suppression and irregularities targeting minority areas in the Bush/Kerry race. The very heart of our civil rights and voting rights laws is found in our political system and the integrity of our elections. Illegal voting diminishes the voice of all Americans, including minority voters."

https://www.infowars.com/posts/boston-university-professor-says-the-term-legal-vote-is-racist/

Boston prof, who got $10mn for anti-racism research from Twitter's Dorsey, catches flak after saying term 'not racist' is RACIST

By RT September 22nd, 2020

Boston University professor and anti-racism activist Ibram Kendi has called to expunge the words "not racist" from the "human vocabulary," arguing the term denies real racism. But not everyone was on board. *"We should eliminate the term 'not racist' from the human vocabulary,"* Kendi tweeted on Sunday. *"We are either being racist or antiracist. Is that clear for you? There is no such thing as 'not racist.'"*

"So what does 'not racist' mean? The term has no meaning other than denying when one is being racist. We should not have words in the dictionary that don't have definitions," Kendi doubled down, responding to a commenter, who accused him of falling into *"fallacy."*

Kendi is the author of 'How to Be an Antiracist' and director of Boston University's Center for Antiracist Research, which was funded with a $10 million donation from Twitter founder Jack Dorsey in August. Boston University President Robert Brown noted that the *"unre-*

stricted nature" of how the donation was structured gave Kendi *"endless discretion about how the income from the gift will be used over time to advance the center."*

The researcher's call to banish the term *"not racist"* for apparently failing to meet the 'woke' threshold has sparked backlash, prompting some of his critics to see distant echoes of George Orwell's dystopian novel '1984' in Kendi's demands.

"It's a beautiful thing, the destruction of words," one commenter said, quoting Orwell. Another said: *"Tyranny is the deliberate removal of nuance,"* while yet another posted a picture of a Nazi book burning, asking: *"Do you appreciate that trying to ban words, phrases and thoughts has been tried before?"* Other observers challenged the substance of Kendi's case. Writer and diversity trainer Chloe Valdary called the professor's arguments *"really silly."* Others said Kendi is creating a false dichotomy and that *"antiracism"* is, in practice, *"anti-white racism."*

Podcast host Leonydus Johnson tweeted a quote from Booker T. Washington, a black author, educator and orator who advised multiple US presidents before dying in 1915. Washington spoke of a class of black people who seek sympathy and money by *"advertising their wrongs"* and who don't want blacks to let go of grievances because *"they do not want to lose their jobs."*

https://www.rt.com/usa/501336-boston-professor-not-racist/

Democrats Pass Resolution Condemning Terms Such As 'Chinese Virus' and 'Kung-Flu'

By Amy Furr September 18th, 2020

Democrats in the U.S. House of Representatives passed a resolution Thursday condemning terms such as "Chinese virus" used to describe the coronavirus as a form of "anti-Asian sentiment," the Blaze reported.

"It passed in a mostly party-line vote of 243 to 163 with 14 Republicans voting with the Democratic majority in favor," the outlet stated.

However, all other Republicans voted against the resolution.

The Blaze article continued:

The text specifically cites the phrases "Chinese Virus," "Wuhan Virus," and "Kung-flu" as examples of "anti-Asian terminology and rhetoric" that has "perpetuated anti-Asian stigma" in the United States. It calls on lawmakers to denounce anti-Asian sentiment in any form, as well as "all manifestations of expressions of racism, xenophobia, discrimination, anti-Asian sentiment, scapegoating, and ethnic or religious intolerance."

A cluster of Republicans spoke out against the resolution and Rep. Andy Biggs (R-AZ) called it "woke culture on steroids," according to the Associated Press (AP). "Republican leader Kevin McCarthy (R-CA), said it was 'ridiculous' and a 'waste of time' as the House was about to adjourn for the week and Democrats and the White House have so far failed to agree on additional coronavirus relief," the report said. In a tweet Thursday, Rep. Grace Meng (D-NY), who introduced the legislation, said she was thankful for her colleagues' support, adding "We reject racism":

Prior to the vote, Meng said the president's use of the terms "China Virus" and "Kung Flu" were "wrong and dangerous." However, President Donald Trump told reporters in March that he did not consider "Chinese virus" a racist remark, saying he used the term to be accurate, the AP report said.

Twitter recently blacklisted Chinese virologist Dr. Li-Meng Yan's account after she claimed the coronavirus originated in China, according to Breitbart News. "Speaking with Fox News host Tucker Carlson, Dr. Yan alleged that China was covering up evidence that the virus came from a lab in Wuhan," the report said. "They don't want the people to know this truth. Also, that's why I got suspended, I got suppression [and] I am the target that China Communist Part wants to [sic] disappear," she told Carlson.

https://www.breitbart.com/health/2020/09/18/democrats-pass-resolution-condemning-terms-such-chinese-virus-kung-flu/

USC Professor Placed on Leave after Black Students Complained His Pronunciation of a Chinese Word Affected Their Mental Health

By Brittany Bernstein September 3rd, 2020

The University of Southern California has placed a communications professor on leave after a group of black MBA candidates threatened to drop his class rather than "endure the emotional exhaustion of carrying on with an instructor that disregards cultural diversity and sensitivities" following the instructor's use, while teaching, of a Chinese word that sounds like a racial slur.

Greg Patton, a professor at the university's Marshall School of Business, was giving a lecture about the use of "filler words" in speech during a recent online class when he used the word in question, saying, "If you have a lot of 'ums and errs,' this is culturally specific, so based on your native language. Like in China, the common word is 'that, that, that.' So in China it might be 'nèi ge, nèi ge, nèi ge.'"

In an August 21 email to university administration obtained by National Review, students accused the professor of pronouncing the word like the N-word "approximately five times" during the lesson in each of his three communication classes and said he "offended all of the Black members of our Class."

The students, who identified themselves as "Black MBA Candidates c/o 2022" wrote that they had reached out to Chinese classmates as they were "appalled" by what they had heard. "It was confirmed that the pronunciation of this word is much different than what Professor Patton described in class," the students wrote. "The word is most commonly used with a pause in between both syllables. In addition, we have lived abroad in China and have taken Chinese language courses at several colleges and this phrase, clearly and precisely before instruction is always identified as a phonetic homonym and a racial derogatory term, and should be carefully used, especially in the context of speaking Chinese within the social context of the United States."

The students accused the professor of displaying "negligence and disregard" in using the word and said he "conveniently stop[ped] the zoom recording right before saying the word," calling his actions calculated. "Our mental health has been affected," the group continued. "It is an uneasy feeling allowing him to have the power over our grades. We would rather not take his course than to endure the emotional exhaustion of carrying on with an instructor that disregards cultural diversity and sensitivities and by extension creates an unwelcome environment for us Black students."

The students added that the incident "has impacted our ability to focus adequately on our studies."

"No matter what way you look at this, the word was said multiple times today in three different instances and has deeply affected us. In light of the murders of George Floyd and Breonna Taylor and the recent and continued collective protests and social awakening across the nation, we cannot let this stand," the group concluded, before calling for an immediate remedy to the situation. In response, Dean Geoff Garrett apologized for the professor's use of a "Chinese word that sounds very similar to a vile racial slur in English," in an email on August 24 obtained by National Review, saying "understandably, this caused great pain and upset among students."

"I am deeply saddened by this disturbing episode that has caused such anguish and trauma," he said. The dean announced that a new instructor would immediately take over instruction for the remainder of the class. Two days later, in an email to members of the USC Marshall Graduate Student Association Executive Board, Patton apologized, explaining that he has taught the course for 10 years and had been given the example by several international students years ago.

"The inclusion is part of a deep and sustained effort at inclusion as I have reached out to find and include many international, global, diverse, female, broad and inclusive leadership examples and illustrations to enhance communication and interpersonal skill in our global workplace," he said.

"I have since learned there are regional differences, yet I have always heard and pronounced the word as 'naaga' rhyming with 'dega,'" the professor wrote. He added that the transcript of the session records his pronunciation as "naga" and that his pronunciation of the word comes from time spent in Shanghai. "Given the difference in sounds, accent, context and language, I did not connect this in the moment to any English words and certainly not any racial slur," he wrote.

"Unfortunately messages have circulated that suggest ill intent, extensive previous knowledge, inaccurate events and these are factually inaccurate. Fortunate [sic] we have transcripts, audio, video, tracking of messages and a 25 year record," he wrote. "I have strived to best prepare students with Global, real-world and applied examples and illustrations to make the class content come alive and bring diverse voices, situations and experiences into the classroom."

He said he had received positive feedback on the lesson in years past but accepted blame for failing "to realize all the many different additional ways that a particular example may be heard across audiences members based on their own lived experiences." In a statement to *Campus Reform,* USC said Patton "agreed to take a short term pause while we are reviewing to better understand the situation and to take any appropriate next steps."

According to a brief bio on the school's website, Patton is "an expert in communication, interpersonal and leadership effectiveness" who has received "numerous teaching awards, been ranked as one of the top teaching faculty at USC and helped USC Marshall achieve numerous #1 worldwide rankings for Communication and Leadership skill development."

"Professor Patton has extensive international experience, has trained, coached and mentored thousands of leaders worldwide, and created scores of successful leadership programs," the bio adds.

https://www.nationalreview.com/news/usc-professor-placed-on-leave-after-black-students-complained-his-pronunciation-of-a-chinese-word-affected-their-mental-health/

English professor's demand higher ed reject 'standard English' language, 'put some respeck on Black Language'

By Katie Craft September 1st, 2020

Several professors are teaming up to demand that colleges do away with the concept of "standard English" as Americans know it today, in favor of accommodating "Black Language."

The Conference on College Composition and Communication released a statement demanding reform of the linguistics used in higher education. The CCCC is an organization claiming to promote diversity among college campuses, by way of establishing "broad and evolving definitions of literacy, communication, rhetoric, and writing."

In its statement, the organization addressed how linguistic racism supposedly plagues higher education. The announcement, titled "This Ain't Another Statement! This is a DEMAND for Black Linguistic Justice!" cited Michigan State University English professor April Baker-Bell's assertion that "the way Black language is devalued in schools reflects how Black lives are devalued in the world . . . [and] the anti-Black linguistic racism that is used to diminish Black Language and Black students in classrooms is not separate from the rampant and deliberate anti-Black racism and violence inflicted upon Black people in society."

Baker-Bell is a self-proclaimed "teacher-scholar-activist" who touts that she coined the term "Anti-Black Linguistic Racism." The statement was signed by Bell, along with California State University-Fullerton professor Bonnie J. Williams-Farrier, Boston University Professor Davena Jackson, Michigan State University English professor Lamar Johnson, Texas Christian University gender and race studies professor Carmen

Kynard. It was also signed Teaira McMurtry, who was listed as being affiliated with the University of Alabama at Birmingham.

The professors use the term, "White Linguistic Supremacy," and suggested that English is a language stemming from racism and solely belonging to White people. The organization demanded that higher education, therefore, reject "Standard English as the Accepted Communicative Norm" and push for the education of "Black Language."

The group claimed that opposition to this point shows a disregard for "Black Lives." In the same statement, the professors upheld CCCC's statementon Ebonics. Ebonics is defined by Merriam-Webster as "African American Vernacular English" which it defines as "a nonstandard variety of English spoken by some African Americans."

"Ebonics reflects the Black experience and conveys Black traditions and socially real truths. Black Languages are crucial to Black identity. Black Language sayings, such as 'What goes around comes around,' are crucial to Black ways of being in the world. Black Languages, like Black lives, matter," states CCCC. However, instead of labeling Ebonics as a variety of the English language, this organization repeatedly identifies it as its own "Black Language." The group demanded that "teachers reject deficit descriptions and other misnomers (e.g., home language, informal English, improper speech, etc.)," and that "teachers stop using academic language and standard English as the accepted communicative norm, which reflects White Mainstream English!"

Standard English is defined by Merriam Webster as "the English that with respect to spelling, grammar, pronunciation, and vocabulary is substantially uniform though not devoid of regional differences, that is well established by usage in the formal and informal speech and writing of the educated, and that is widely recognized as acceptable wherever English is spoken and understood."

Other demands included that "teachers, researchers, and scholars put some respeck on Black Language and refrain from engaging in Black linguistic appropriation," and that "teachers respeck Black thought and how that thought manifests in Black speech and writing. That is, it might not sound like you desire it to, but remember, it sounds real right, regardless of unrelenting white supremacist socialization."

https://campusreform.org/?ID=15554&s=09

Young people don't trust anyone who uses this punctuation mark

By Hannah Frishberg August 24th, 2020

Periods may be coming to a full stop.

While older texters may consider the period an innocent symbol that a sentence has ended, digital natives consider it a triggering form of aggression. The punctuation problem ignited over social media recently, with Gen Z and millennials agreeing that ending a sentence with a period is overly hostile and, worse yet, extremely uncool. "Only old people or troubled souls put periods at the end of every sentence," wrote digital culture journalist Victoria Turk in her book on digital etiquette, "Kill Reply All."

The younger generations consider the act of sending a text a sufficient signifier of a complete thought, Turk wrote, making periods feel unnecessary and overly final. "The thing is, in a messaging conversation, a period is simply not necessary," she explained. "It's clear when you've finished your thought already, so what function does the period fulfill? As a result, using a period in messaging now looks rather emphatic, and can come across as if you're quite cross or annoyed." The difference between texts saying "That's funny" and "That's funny." may seem subtle to the sender, but many readers will interpret the latter as far less pleasant and more intense, needlessly.

Social media piled onto the sentiment, thanks to Guardian columnist Rhiannon Lucy Cosslett. "Older people — do you realize that ending a sentence with a full stop comes across as sort of abrupt and unfriendly to younger people in an email/chat? Genuinely curious," she asked in a since-deleted tweet.

Although the tweet was met with cries of ageism, her argument has a point: In a 2015 study of 126 undergraduates, researchers at Binghamton University found that texts containing periods were also perceived as insincere. "Texting is lacking many of the social cues used in actual face-to-face conversations. When speaking, people easily convey social and emotional information with eye gaze, facial expressions, tone of voice, pauses, and so on," said lead researcher Celia Klin in a statement at the time the study was released. "People obviously can't use these mechanisms when they are texting. Thus, it makes sense that texters rely on what they have available to them — emoticons, deliberate misspellings that mimic speech sounds and, according to our data, punctuation."

The period's new, aggressive interpretation can also be used purposefully, for comedic effect."While periods at the end of sentences might be on a downward slope, they can find themselves redistributed elsewhere, where they can be placed very deliberately in order to add emphasis," Turk wrote. This includes putting a period between every word, as in the example she gives: "Just. Look. How. Emphatic. This. Is."

https://nypost.com/2020/08/24/young-people-dont-trust-anyone-who-use-this-punctuation-mark/

Linguists: Young People Refusing To Use Full Stops In Sentences Because They See Them As 'Aggressive'

By Steve Watson august 28th, 2020

The world's leading language experts have noted that young people are 'fundamentally' altering written communication based on what they perceive to be aggressive or offensive. In particular, the use of the full stop, or period, in sentences is diminishing according to linguists because it has come to signify annoyance or offense.

"Full stops are, in my experience, very much the exception and not the norm in [young people's] instant messages, and have a new role in signifying an abrupt or angry tone of voice," notes Owen McArdle, a linguist at the University of Cambridge. Fellow linguist Dr Lauren Fonteyn of Leiden University said "If you send a text message without a full stop, it's already obvious that you've concluded the message. So if you add that additional marker for completion, they will read something into it and it tends to be a falling intonation or negative tone."

Professor David Crystal says that the period is perceived as "ominous" by younger people, particularly because the use of text messaging means that the end of sentences are becoming a thing of the past. Each one now has its own text message. The professor claims that the full stop is no longer the end of a sentence, but is now an "emotion marker."

"You look at the internet or any instant messaging exchange – anything that is a fast dialogue taking place. People simply do not put full stops in, unless they want to make a point." Crystal noted in his 2015 book *Making a Point*. Crystal points to a 2015 Binghamton University study that found college students perceive text messages ending in a full stop as being "less sincere" than those missing one.

During the same study, researchers discovered that exclamation points had the opposite effect, making people seem more 'sincere and engaged'. Research leader Celia Klin noted in 2015 that "When speaking, people easily convey social and emotional information with eye gaze, facial expressions, tone of voice, pauses and so on. People obviously can't use these mechanisms when they are texting. Thus, it makes sense that texters rely on what they have available to them – emoticons, deliberate misspellings that mimic speech sounds and, according to our data, punctuation."

The gradual erosion of Language was predicted by George Orwell in his classic dystopia 1984. In the novel, the all powerful Party mandates

Newspeak, which focuses on diminishing vocabulary in order to control the range of thought among the general population.

https://www.infowars.com/linguists-young-people-refusing-to-use-full-stops-in-sentences-because-they-see-them-as-aggressive/

Rutgers University Declares Grammar "Racist"

By Jeremy Frankel July 27th, 2020

The English Department at Rutgers University has now declared grammar as "racist."

As part of the never-ending Woke outrage train, proper grammar is "part of white supremacy because students of 'multilingual, non-standard academic English backgrounds' are allegedly disadvantaged," according to the Daily Wire.

The department "will change its standards of English instruction in an effort to 'stand with and respond' to the Black Lives Matter movement. In an email written by department chairwoman Rebecca Walkowitz, the Graduate Writing Program will emphasize 'social justice' and 'critical grammar,'" the Daily Wire continues, reporting from the Washington Free Beacon.

Walkowitz also stated that "[T]his approach challenges the familiar dogma that writing instruction should limit emphasis on grammar/sentence-level issues so as to not put students from multilingual, non-standard 'academic' English backgrounds at a disadvantage. Instead, it encourages students to develop a critical awareness of the variety of choices available to them [with] regard to micro-level issues in order to empower them and equip them to push against biases based on 'written' accents."

The Free Beacon added that Walkowitz continued that the department would add "workshops on social justice and writing," "increasing focus on graduate student life," and "incorporating 'critical grammar' into our pedagogy," and that "The "critical grammar" approach challenges the standard academic form of the English language in favor of a more inclusive writing experience. The curriculum puts an emphasis on the variability of the English language instead of accuracy."

Of course, to anyone with any amount of rational thought, this is absurd. But the woke Left is just hammering away at our civilization. By attempting to control the elements of language, the Left can control what we say, what we write, and what we think.

It's both stupid and nefarious.

https://bongino.com/rutgers-university-declares-grammar-racist

North Carolina mom in 'disbelief' after son, 10, punished for calling teacher 'ma'am'

By Madeline Farber August 25th, 2018

The mother of a 10-year-old boy in North Carolina is outraged that her son was recently punished for calling his fifth-grade teacher "ma'am."

"I was in disbelief," Teretha Wilson, the boy's mother, told Fox News on Saturday.

Wilson noticed her son, Tamarion, was not himself when she picked him up from the bus stop earlier this week.

"I asked him what was wrong, and he told me he got in trouble for saying 'ma'am' to a teacher. I was confused," she said. Inquiring further, Wilson asked her son to give more detail about the incident. That's when the fifth-grader at North East Carolina Preparatory School in Tarboro, North Carolina, pulled out a piece of lined paper with the word ma'am written dozens of times.

Wilson was shocked, especially when Tamarion told her that his teacher, who has not been formally identified, told him that he was required to return the piece of paper with a parent's signature.

The young boy also claimed that the teacher threatened to throw something at him during the incident, his mother said.

"He was disappointed because he felt like he had done something wrong," she said.

The next afternoon, Wilson went to the school to meet with Tamarion's teacher and the school's principal. With her she brought a separate piece of paper on which her son had written the definition of ma'am. (According to the Oxford Dictionaries, ma'am is defined as "a term of respectful or polite address used for a woman").

Wilson claims Tamarion's teacher told her that her son "was getting on her nerve when he called her ma'am" but "couldn't give me a reason of why that was bad." The teacher also claimed Tamarion knew that she wasn't serious when she allegedly threatened to throw something at him, Wilson said.

Tamarion has been placed in a different teacher's class since the incident occured.

In a statement to ABC 11, an official with the school called the situation a "personnel matter," which "has been handled appropriately by the K-7 principal."

Still, Wilson said she plans to call the school board on Monday to see "if they're really going to handle it," though she did not elaborate on what this would entail.

"This is about my child being respectful, then threatened to be hit with something. This isn't about racism, as some people have made it out to be," Wilson said, referring to some of the comments on a family member's Facebook post where she detailed the incident.

Moving forward, Wilson said she has encouraged her son to "always be respectful to [his] elders even if they don't want to be called ma'am," she said.

"Is this what happens from raising your child in a good way?" she asked.

A spokesperson for North East Carolina Preparatory School did not immediately respond to Fox News' request for comment.

https://www.foxnews.com/us/north-carolina-mom-in-disbelief-after-son-10-punished-for-calling-teacher-maam

Cursing could cost you $500 in Myrtle Beach

By ABC 30 Action News August 28th, 2018

MYRTLE BEACH, S.C. -- Some refer to Myrtle Beach as "Dirty Myrtle," but you better make sure you don't have a dirty mouth when you're there. According to WPDE, those who use profanity could pay a hefty fine or serve jail time. That's because profane language falls under the city's disorderly conduct offense. City officials say it isn't about raking in the dough but enforcing the no - as in, people shouldn't be getting out of hand.

When it comes to the fine, ultimately, courts have the final say, but your potty mouth could cost you up to $500 and/or 30 days in jail. Bryan Murphy, on behalf of Myrtle Beach Police Department, issued the following statement on the offense: A person would violate Ordinance 14-61 (b) 1 if he/she uses a language likely to provoke a violent reaction from another person. The ordinance lists several examples of the types of words which are unlawful. The penalty for conviction could include a fine and/or jail time. We encourage everyone to avoid violating this ordinance by speaking to others with the same respect and kindness he or she deserves.

https://abc11.com/cursing-could-cost-you-$500-in-myrtle-beach/4077395/

Is 'Dixie Highway' racist? The debate is growing

By Susannah Bryan January 27th, 2019

A movement to rename Dixie Highway — for some a painful reminder of a tragic, racist past — might be gaining steam in Broward County. The argument is being made by one of Broward County's youngest elected officials after she heard of a similar effort in Miami-Dade. The name Dixie harkens back to an era that glorified slavery and white supremacy, says 22-year-old Hallandale Beach Vice Mayor Sabrina Javellana. Her fellow city commissioners agree, approving a resolution in early December urging Broward commissioners to take up the cause.

Broward Mayor Dale Holness says it's an idea worth exploring and plans to bring it up for discussion early next year. "It would be good to have input from the community, to hear their voices and what their thoughts are," Holness said. "I am not opposed to renaming the street. The dilemma is some people are going to want Dixie to stay. They are going to talk about heritage also."

Javellana pitched the idea after learning of an effort by Miami-Dade Commissioner Dennis Moss to rename Dixie Highway for Harriet Tubman, an escaped slave who helped lead others to freedom before the Civil War. "Dixie was the term for the South during the Civil War," Javellana said during a Hallandale meeting on Dec. 4. "It was also a song that became the anthem of the Confederacy, with lyrics that were painting a positive imagery of slavery, talking positively of picking cotton. It's not reflective of the times we're in."

On Thursday, Javellana said she'd like to see Dixie Highway renamed Freedom Highway. In Riviera Beach, a portion of Dixie Highway is now known as President Barack Obama Highway, Javellana noted. And in Hollywood, three streets once named for Confederate generals are now known as Hope, Freedom and Liberty.

"It's part of the whole movement to take down symbols of the Confederacy," Javellana said of her attempt to rename Dixie. "I would love a Freedom Highway. That would be beautiful." The debate has not yet come up in Palm Beach County, but that could change, says County Commissioner Mack Bernard. "We're keeping an eye on it," he said Friday. "I haven't had a chance to speak to staff, the county attorney and county administrator."

Bernard says he'd want to learn more about costs and other issues before suggesting that Palm Beach County find a new name for Dixie Highway. In 2017, State Rep. Shevrin Jones, D-Hollywood, urged that cities throughout Florida rename their stretches of Dixie Highway.

"The name has divided our country," he said at the time. "There should be no recognition of it. It does not represent who we are and what we stand for as a country today." On Thursday, he said he was happy to hear Broward's mayor was taking up the cause. "I'd love to have Old Dixie Highway be a road of black history, whether it's Freedom Highway or Harriet Tubman or Barack Obama," he said.

Not everyone is on board. Hollywood resident Pat Asman fumed at her city for changing its street names two years ago and didn't take too kindly to the thought of changing Dixie either. "Come on," she said. "I'm 81 years old and that name has been on that street for years. Someone from New York must have come down here and had a problem with it. I think it's stupid. That street goes all the way through the United States. You're not going to change history. And it costs money to change those street names."

Broward Vice Mayor Steve Geller said he was not averse to the idea of coming up with a new moniker for Dixie Highway. "I do think it appropriate to rename it," he said. "But I don't want to spend years figuring out what the new name should be. Otherwise it would be known as the street with no name — and that would be bad." Other details also would need to be worked out, including how much any new street signs might cost and who would pay for them.

Jones said he had no idea.

"That's the difficult part," he said. "Before we talk about any name change, we need to find out who's going to pay for it. I'm sure the signs are expensive."

Javellana thought the county might pick up the tab. Holness thought the cities would pay. Geller, a former state senator, said it could be a combination of the state, county and cities, depending on who has jurisdiction over the road. Dixie Highway runs through seven cities in Broward: Dania Beach, Deerfield Beach, Fort Lauderdale, Hollywood, Oakland Park, Pompano Beach and Wilton Manors.

Geller shuddered at the possibility of each city coming up with its own name. "I'd hate to make it more confusing by naming it five different things," he said. Benjamin Israel, the Hollywood resident who led the charge to rename three Hollywood streets named for Confederate generals, agreed. "That can be confusing for out-of-towners," he said. "They should come up with the same name."

https://www.sun-sentinel.com/local/broward/hallandale/fl-ne-dixie-highway-rename-effort-20191227-iuj3mdirozbcdnhit5y33medwy-story.html

Rhode Island Becomes First State to Change Its Name

By Rick Moran June 23rd, 2020

The tiny state of Rhode Island announced that because some people are too stupid and too dense to understand that some words have several meanings, they will change the official name of their state.

The "official" name of the state is "The State of Rhode Island and Providence Plantations." But to those choosing to be ignorant — or those who really are — "plantations" means "a usually large farm or estate, especially in a tropical or semitropical country, on which cotton, tobacco, coffee, sugar cane, or the like is cultivated, usually by resident laborers."

But in the context as it was originally intended, "plantations" referred to a new colony. But what does context matter when there are dragons to slay? It has been decided that we should choose to remove context and substitute personal interpretation of meaning. Rhode Island General Treasurer Seth Magaziner today made the following announcement about his office's use of the state's name:

"Today, I am announcing that the Office of the General Treasurer will remove the words "and Providence Plantations" from the state's checks. We will also remove those words from our letterhead, citations, and other Office correspondence.

The Rhode Island treasurer says he talked to African American leaders who complain the word makes them uncomfortable. For African-Americans and other People of Color, 'plantations' are synonymous with centuries of race-based slavery and violence. In my discussions with African-American leaders in recent weeks, they have explained the chilling feeling they have when seeing the word "plantations" on Rhode Island government letters, citations, and checks.

Well, we can't have that — even if the black leaders are being silly.

As a student of our State's history, I know that in 1663 when 'The Colony of Rhode Island and Providence Plantations' received its Charter, the word 'plantations' was not necessarily connected with slavery. However, words and symbols can take on new meanings over time. As a Rhode Islander with Jewish heritage, I know all too well that the swastika, originally a symbol of spirituality and peace, became a symbol of profound hatred and evil.

How did the swastika make an entrance in discussing "plantations"? Yikes, he's reaching. He admits that the word has nothing to do with slavery but because some people get a "chilling feeling" when they see the word, it's gotta go. As treasurer, I hope Mr. Magaziner never has occasion to write the word "niggardly" when talking about distributing funds. If some black leaders get a chilling feeling from seeing the word "plantation," they would probably faint dead away if they saw "niggardly" in an official document.

In truth, this is not about "chilling feelings." Take 100 black people and have them read a paragraph with the word "plantation" in it and then ask how many got a "chilling feeling" by reading it? Some people wake up every morning, have their morning coffee and maybe some breakfast, and then sit down at their monitors and begin looking for something to be offended by today. They see it as their job. If they don't find anything blatantly racist, sexist, or bigoted, they twist or remove the meaning of some words to make them offensive.

They slap a hashtag on it and throw it out where so many others are eager to gang up on someone. Thus is born a Twitter meme and the makings of another scurrilous attack on someone who never intended to offend. There's absolutely no good reason for Rhode Island to change their state name. But we live in a time where there is no past, no future, only the present. And in the present, madness reigns.

https://pjmedia.com/news-and-politics/rick-moran/2020/06/23/rhode-island-becomes-first-state-to-change-its-name-n566691

Twitter blocks posts that use phrase 'illegal alien' as 'hateful content'

By Victor Skinner September 12th, 2018

The federal government, U.S. Supreme Court, and lawyers across the country use the word "illegal alien" to describe immigrants who illegally enter the country, because that's the definition in the law. But Twitter makes its own laws, and the social media giant is now blocking folks from promoting any messages with the phrase, which its moderators apparently consider "hate speech."

"1/ Twitter is not allowing us to promote any tweets including the phrase 'illegal alien(s)', citing it as Hateful Content," the Center for Immigration Studies posted to Twitter Tuesday. "However, 'illegal aliens' has been used in both federal law and by the Supreme Court."

Twitter rejected a total of four ads from the Center but provided only vague reasoning for the decision. "We've reviewed your tweets and confirmed that it is ineligible to participate in the Twitter Ads program at this time based on our Hateful Content policy. Violating content include, but is not limited to, that which is hate speech or advocacy against a protected group," according to a notice posted on the CIS website.

"All four tweets use the statutory phrases 'illegal alien' or 'criminal alien', and all of the tweets referenced law enforcement, either at the border or in the interior," CIS reports. "One of the tweets contained a powerful Daily Caller video showing illegal aliens in camouflage carrying large backpacks across the border unimpeded."

One of the tweets rejected by Twitter Ads simply stated facts put out by U.S. Immigration and Customs Enforcement. "ICE recently completed a massive multi-state enforcement operation targeting criminal aliens that resulted in the arrests of 364 individuals," it read. "Of those, 187 (51%) had prior criminal convictions and 97 had been previously removed from the United States." Others offered an opinion on immigration that runs counter to the mainstream media narrative.

"A couple in Oregon was recently killed by a drunk-driving Mexican illegal alien," another read. "Now, with the state's sanctuary law being put up to a ballot, the sanctuary law's defenders say the other side is 'seizing upon' illegal alien crime. Isn't that the point?"

"The farm which employed the illegal alien who killed Mollie Tibbetts was raided by ICE agents," the CIS posted in another rejected tweet. "ICE should do more of this – continue to focus on employers of illegal aliens who commit serious crimes. Often, those arrests lead to many more aliens found." After the ad rejections, CIS schooled Twitter with several examples of the term "illegal alien" in federal court records, as well as the definition from the Code of Federal Regulations: "Illegal alien means any person who is not lawfully admitted for permanent residence in the United States or who has not been authorized by the Attorney General to accept employment in the United States."

Twitchy points out that Twitter joins others who have attempted to censor the term "illegal immigrant" or similar descriptions of illegal immigrants in recent years. In 2013, the Associated Press advised journalists not to use the world "illegal" when referring to those who break the law by crossing the border. "Except in direct quotations, do not use the terms illegal alien, an illegal, illegals or undocumented," the AP Style Guide instructs.

Sen. Kamala Harris, a California Democrat and rumored 2020 presidential candidate, has also declared "illegal alien" offensive, stating in 2016 that "we must stop treating undocumented workers as criminals in this country," Twitchy reports.

https://www.theamericanmirror.com/blog/2018/09/12/twitter-blocks-posts-that-use-phrase-illegal-alien-as-hateful-content/

Arnold Schwarzenegger Apologizes for Using the Phrase 'Girlie Men'

By Warner Todd Huston October 11th, 2018

Arnold Schwarzenegger used to joke that only "girlie men" opposed energetic capitalism and traditional American values. But now, the former bodybuilder, Hollywood star, and California governor is apologizing for popularizing the phrase. Schwarzenegger once made a name for himself with his he-man political style, making fun of his opponents as weaklings who could not lead.

At least as early as 2004 Schwarzenegger called California Democrats "girlie men" and noted that in the next election the GOP would "terminate" them. His phrase even became the stuff of *Saturday Night Live* parody in the characters of faux bodybuilders Hans and Franz. These amusing taunts and his strongman persona eventually led Schwarzenegger to the governor's mansion in California.

But since the day he took over as the Golden State's chief executive Schwarzenegger slowly but surely started straying from the very style that so enthused his supporters. And now it seems that the "Governator" has completely abandoned his masculine terminology.

In a new interview with *Men's Health* magazine, Schwarzenegger is abjectly apologetic over his "girlie men" taunt. "At the time it felt like the right thing to do. It was in my gut. I improvised it. I called them girlie men because they weren't willing to take risks," the actor told the magazine. "They were afraid of everything," he explained. "Politicians, in general, want to do little things, so there's no risk involved."

But, today there are regrets. Schwarzenegger now says his rhetoric was counterproductive. "It was shortsighted. In the long term, it's better to not say that, because you want to work with them. If you have a little sense of history, you know that the best things are accomplished when both parties work together and start compromising like Ronald Reagan did with Tip O'Neill," Schwarzenegger told the magazine. "They argued in public and attacked each other, but with a little wink. That's why so much got done in the Reagan administration. When you can reach out across the aisle and work together, you can get much more accomplished, rather than 'girlie men' or 'fuck you' or 'it's my way or the highway.'"

Schwarzenegger also sounded like any left-wing environmentalist when asked what he would demand if he were king for a day. "Access for everyone to health care," the one-time Republican said. "And to get off the arms race and to get off [polluting]. It's inexcusable to have so much plastic floating around in the oceans."

https://www.breitbart.com/entertainment/2018/10/11/arnold-schwarzenegger-apologizes-for-coining-girlie-men/

Memes may contribute to teenage obesity, lawmakers told

By Rob Picheta October 18th, 2018

In mid-September the European Parliament passed a new copyright law that some have dubbed a "meme ban." Then Sweden's advertising watchdog ruled that the popular "distracted boyfriend" meme is sexist. Now, academics have told British lawmakers that internet memes may be contributing to the UK obesity crisis and doing harm to teenagers on a significant scale.

Memes carry dangerous health-related messages and make light of unhealthy eating habits, researchers from Loughborough University wrote in a letter sent to a British parliamentary committee. "A substantial number of individuals on Twitter share health-related Internet memes, with both positive and negative messages," they wrote, noting that many "contain inappropriate material."

A picture of an overweight child with the caption "Free food? Count me in!" was sent along with the letter as an example of a meme the researchers found dangerous.

The academics were also concerned by a meme that created a human-like body from pictures of pizzas and hamburgers, with frankfurters used for limbs and a smiley-faced potato for a face. The body was captioned "me" and placed alongside images of three well-defined bodies for comparison.

"The vast majority of sharers display little, if any, emotion when sharing these memes," the academics commented. "Just washed this chocolate bar with soap," read the caption to another image included in the letter, along with #cleaneating.

"Internet memes are generally viewed as entertaining but they also represent a body of cultural practice that does not account for the specific needs and rights of teenagers," the researchers warned. "Unhealthy lifestyles cost the NHS billions every year," they added, suggesting that "the dangers of inaccurate/inappropriate health messages" contained in memes could be a contributing factor.

Call to scrutinize memes

The letter was sent to a committee analyzing the effects of social media use on young people's health. Its authors suggested teenagers should scrutinize the underlying themes in the memes they see, rather than simply enjoying them.

"It is worrying that Internet meme content... produces a predominate sense of happiness regardless of the underlying tone or image used," they wrote.

"If Internet memes carry political, corporate or other agendas without priorities tailored to the needs of 13-16-year-olds then they have the potential to do harm on a large scale," they added. They also noted that memes "have the potential to normalize undesirable behaviors," and often "contain inappropriate material or ridicule others by race, gender, ethnicity, sexuality, body shape, religion, diet."

https://www.cnn.com/2018/10/18/health/internet-memes-obesity-intl/index.html

Kim Kardashian under fire for calling people who didn't recognize her Halloween costume the R-word

By Mariah Haas November 1st, 2018

Kim Kardashian is under fire after making an offensive comment on social media.

On Wednesday, the "Keeping Up with the Kardashians" star documented herself at her sister Kendall Jenner's Halloween party asking guests if they knew who she and best friend Jonathan Cheben were dressed up as.

“Okay guys, we are Pam Anderson and Tommy Lee,” Kardashian, 38, said according to People. “Nobody knows who we are here!" she continued. "You guys are all too f--king young. This is so sad.” Per People, in a separate video, the KKW Beauty mogul is heard telling former assistant Stephanie Shepherd: “Nobody knows who I am. Yeah! R----d."

Fans immediately took to Twitter to express their distaste with the reality star's remark.

"Kim Kardashian should know better!!! Especially as a mother just add it to the list of reasons why I can’t stand her!!! Idk why ppl especially adult women think its ok to use the word," one Twitter user wrote.

Tweeted another individual: "@KimKardashian how DARE you to used that word in any of your sentences. I bet you don't even know the meaning of it. You offend loved ones for families like mine . Your mouth is bigger than your A--. Ignorance."

"@KimKardashian Didn’t you learn from your Sister’s “MISTAKE” for using the R WORD. WHEN a Disability hits your family. I’ll remember the Kardashian’s flippant attitude towards mental disabilities your apology is BS. UR AN A--HOLE!!!" wrote another social media user. Following the backlash, Kardashian took down the video and apologized to her fans. "I want to apologize for what I said in a recent video post that is inappropriate and insensitive to the special needs community," she said in a statement to E! News. "I try to learn from my mistakes, and this is one of those times. Please know that my intention is always pure, and in this case, it was a mistake. I'm sorry."

Back in July, Kardashian's sister, Khloe, also faced backlash for using the R-word in an Instagram video.

At the time, the Good American founder was doing a morning workout with her sister Kourtney and their trainer. In the video, Khloe, 34, becomes frustrated with her older sister who was trying to sync their smartphones but seemed to be having trouble. According to Us Weekly, Khloe was heard in the video saying to her sister, "Yes, you can, you f--ing r-----d." And as Kourtney, 39, appeared to have more trouble with the devices, Khloe yelled, "Are you f---ing r-----d?"

After fans called out the reality star, Khloe took to Twitter to apologize.

"Ugh I hate that word!" she wrote. "Why did I even say that? You are a million percent right and I actually greatly dislike when people use that word! I will do better! I am sorry! much love today. "

https://www.foxnews.com/entertainment/kim-kardashian-under-fire-for-calling-people-who-didnt-recognize-her-halloween-costume-the-r-word

'Long Time, No See' Is Now Considered 'Derogatory' toward Asians

By Katherine Timpf November 6th, 2018

A student at Colorado State University was reportedly told that the expression "Long time, no see" was an example of "non-inclusive" language because it's apparently "derogatory toward" Asians.

"In a meeting with Zahra Al-Saloom, the director of Diversity and Inclusion at Associated Students of Colorado State University, she showed me an entire packet of words and phrases that were deemed non-inclusive," student Katrina Leibee wrote in the *Rocky Mountain Collegian*. "One of these phrases was 'long time, no see,' which is viewed as derogatory toward those of Asian descent." According to Leibee, "long time, no see" was not the only phrase deemed offensive. "We were told that the popular term 'you guys' was not inclusive of all genders, and we should instead replace it with 'y'all,'" she wrote. "We were told to use the term 'first-year' instead of 'freshman,' because 'freshman' is not inclusive of all genders."

"A countless amount of words and phrases have been marked with a big, red X and defined as non-inclusive," she continued. "It has gotten to the point where students should carry around a dictionary of words they cannot say." Both *The College Fix*'s Jennifer Kabbany and *Reason*'s Robby Soave have covered this story — characterizing it as an example of political correctness going too far — and I must say that I completely agree. Out here in reality-land, I'm pretty sure that no one hears the phrase "long time, no see!" and hears "I hate Asian people!" As Soave notes, the Wikipedia page for the phrase "raises the possibility that it is of Chinese or Native American origin," but an *NPR* article from 2014 — "Who First Said 'Long Time, No See' and in Which Language?" — concludes that "it is so widespread as a greeting that there's nothing to indicate the term's origins, be they Native American or Mandarin Chinese."

In any case, I'd wager that most people hear the phrase "long time, no see" and think only "This person is communicating that they have not seen me in a while" or "This person is using a common phrase sarcastically to communicate to me that we have been seeing a lot of each other lately, because I just saw him this morning and I am now seeing him again." Those are really the only two ways that I've ever used the phrase, and the only two ways that I've ever comprehended it. I don't think this is because I am ignorant and uneducated; I think it's because I'm a normal person. After all, I've never met anyone who has been hurt by the phrase "long time, no see," and I wouldn't be shocked if I lived the rest of my life without meeting one.

As a woman, I'm also so ridiculously tired of hearing that the phrase "you guys" is something that I'm supposed to find offensive because of my gender. I'm not offended by "you guys," because I completely understand that when someone uses it to address a group that includes me, they are neither excluding me nor insinuating that I am actually a man. In fact, I even often use the phrase myself — *even* to describe groups that include women, and I've yet to see a woman run out of the room in horror or burst into tears because I've done so. In my experience, women are actually stronger than that. The reason I use "you guys" is not that I'm sexist against myself and want to exclude myself, I use it because I'm from the Midwest and that's what we say instead of "y'all." What's more, I actually found Al-Saloom's suggestion to use "y'all" quite interesting, because I once covered an op-ed written by a student who alleged that the use of "y'all" by people who were not from the South amounted to "cultural appropriation." You might laugh, and you might even be right to laugh, but it's also concrete proof that even those who *devote their lives* to using the most *perfectly sensitive* language might not be able to avoid offending at least one person. So it might be better for everyone to just chill out about these sorts of things and focus instead on the real instances of racism and sexism that actually do hurt people.

https://www.nationalreview.com/2018/11/university-claims-long-time-no-see-expression-derogatory-to-asians/

Sarah Michelle Gellar Apologizes for Reminding People 'Not to Overeat' on Thanksgiving: 'Terribly Sorry that People Were Offended'

By Justin Caruso November 21st, 2018

Actress Sarah Michelle Gellar apologized to her fans Tuesday for posting a public reminder to herself "not to overeat" on Thanksgiving, saying that she's "terribly sorry" if she fat-shamed anyone. "I'm just going to pin these up all over my house as a reminder not to overeat on Thursday #thanksgivingprep," Sarah Michelle Gellar initially wrote in an Instagram caption, along with old photos of herself.

The post's caption offended many of her followers, some of whom accused the actress of promoting fat-shaming and unhealthy eating disorders. One user said that Gellar's caption was "very dangerous" and included "insensitive wording." The 41-year-old immediately buckled to the social media campaign against her, saying, "It's come to my attention that some people think I was 'fat shaming' with this post. That could not be further from my intentions."

"I love Thanksgiving and unfortunately my eyes are often bigger than my stomach, and I tend to eat so much I make myself sick. This was a joking reminder to myself not to do that," she continued. "I'm terribly sorry that people were offended by my attempt at humor. Any one that knows me, knows I would never intentionally 'shame' any one on any basis. I am a champion of all people."

The *Cruel Intentions* actress' apology may have been wholly unnecessary, however. A quick look at the comments on her Instagram page shows that there were far more comments in defending her than attacking her. As one user so succinctly put it, "You DON'T owe ANYONE an apology!!! Being disciplined and responsible with your nutrition is something to be admired."

https://www.breitbart.com/entertainment/2018/11/21/sarah-michelle-gellar-apologizes-for-reminding-people-not-to-overeat-on-thanksgiving-terribly-sorry-that-people-were-offended/

'Bringing home the bacon': Idioms referencing meat may become obsolete as veganism rises

By Olivia Petter December 3rd, 2018

You may think phrases like "bringing home the bacon" and "putting all your eggs in one basket" are harmless quirks of the English language, but they could be offending vegans and vegetarians, with one academic claiming they might end up being avoided altogether as a result.

As research shows more people are removing animal products from their diets than ever before, Shareena Hamzah of Swansea University says idioms involving animal products could be rendered obsolete because they are out of touch with the zeitgeist. Writing for *The Conversation*, the researcher explains how meat-based metaphors are a popular staple of our everyday vernacular but that an increased awareness in the environmental and ethical issues surrounding meat production "will undoubtedly be reflected in our language and literature" and that this language may no longer be so widely accepted.

"In today's reality, meat is repeatedly the subject of much socially and politically charged discussion, including about how the demand for meat is contributing to climate change and environmental degradation," she continues.

"Given that fiction often reflects on real world events and societal issues, it may very well be that down the line powerful meat metaphors are eschewed.

"The increased awareness of vegan issues will filter through consciousness to produce new modes of expression." Hamzah highlights the violent imagery proposed by popular idioms such as "flogging a dead horse" and "killing two birds with one stone" and suggests we may move to kinder alternatives such as "feeding a fed horse" or "feeding two birds with one scone".

Animal rights organization PETA has been campaigning for more vegan and vegetarian-friendly idioms for years, urging teachers not to use phrases that perpetuate violence towards animals.

"These old sayings are often passed down in classrooms during lessons on literary devices," a blog post on its website reads.

"While these phrases may seem harmless, they carry meaning and can send mixed signals to students about the relationship between humans and animals and can normalize abuse. Teaching students to use animal-friendly language can cultivate positive relationships between all beings and help end the epidemic of youth violence toward animals."

Adding to Hamzah's list of cruelty-free alternatives, PETA suggests "bringing home the bagels" as opposed to the bacon and instead of "putting all your eggs in one basket", why not try "putting all of your berries in a bowl"?

https://www.independent.co.uk/life-style/bringing-home-bacon-vegan-offensive-idom-shareena-hamzah-phrases-animals-a8664796.html

Dean at North Carolina university refers to freshmen as 'freshmores': report

By Louis Casiano December 5th, 2018

In an effort to make campus life at one North Carolina university more gender inclusive, some students are ditching the term freshman in favor of "freshmore" to describe first-year students.

Jefford Vahlbusch, dean of the Honors College at Appalachian State University, introduced the term when he came to the school two years ago, The Appalachian student newspaper reported. "We have women and men as college students, and I think having a non-gender specific way of talking about them, of addressing them, just shows that we're aware of the power of language," Vahlbusch told the paper. Vahlbusch began using the term while employed at the University of Wisconsin-Eau Claire after searching for a "non-sexist way" to describe freshmen.

"I just started using (freshmore) and encouraging students, prospective students and parents to use it, and it kind of caught on," Vahlbusch said.

"I think that certainly the "freshmore" class this year is using it more often," he added.

Vahlbusch did not immediately respond to Fox News for comment Wednesday.

https://www.foxnews.com/us/some-students-at-university-replace-frehmen-term-with-freshmore-in-bid-for-inclusivness

Teacher fired for refusing to use transgender student's pronouns

By Associated Press Dec 10th, 2018

WEST POINT, Va. — A Virginia high school teacher who refused to use a transgender student's new pronouns has been fired. News outlets report that the West Point School Board voted unanimously Thursday to dismiss Peter Vlaming after a four-hour hearing that drew an overflow crowd. The school system said in a statement that Vlaming was fired for insubordination.

Over the summer, the ninth-grade student's family informed the school system of the student's gender transition to male. The student wasn't involved in Thursday's hearing. It's not suggested that the 47-year-old West Point High School French teacher deliberately referred to the student using female pronouns in the student's presence, but in conversations with others.

Witnesses described a "slip-up" when the student was about to run into a wall and Vlaming told others to stop "her." When discussing the incident with administrators, Vlaming made it clear he would not use male pronouns, a stance that led to his suspension referral for disciplinary action. "I can't think of a worse way to treat a child than what was happening," said West Point High Principal Jonathan Hochman, who testified that he told Vlaming to use male pronouns in accordance with the student's wishes.

Vlaming told superiors that his Christian faith prevented him from using male pronouns for the student. Vlaming said he had the student in class the year before when the student identified as female. Vlaming's attorney, Shawn Voyles, says his client offered to use the student's name and to avoid feminine pronouns, but Voyles says the school was unwilling to accept the compromise.

"That discrimination then leads to creating a hostile learning environment. And the student had expressed that. The parent had expressed that," said West Point schools Superintendent Laura Abel. "They felt disrespected."

Nondiscrimination policies were updated a year ago to include protections for gender identity, but didn't include guidance on gender pronoun use, according to Vlaming's lawyer, Voyles, who notes Vlaming has constitutional rights. "One of those rights that is not curtailed is to be free from being compelled to speak something that violates your conscience," Voyles said.

Vlaming said he loves and respects all his students but when a solution he tried to reach based on "mutual tolerance" was rejected, he was at risk of losing his job for having views held by "most of the world for most of human history."

"That is not tolerance," Vlaming said. "That is coercion." Vlaming is considering a legal appeal, but said he wants to consult with his attorney before announcing further steps.

"I have to research how we would do that, what that would entail," Vlaming said. "I do think it's a serious question of First Amendment rights."

Equality Virginia, an LGBTQ-rights group, said the situation reveals the need for "statewide guidance" that will protect all students from discrimination at school.

https://www.nbcnews.com/feature/nbc-out/teacher-fired-refusing-use-transgender-student-s-pronouns-n946006

New study says that calling breastfeeding "natural" is unethical because it enforces gender roles

By Jonathon Van Maren May 2nd, 2018

Sometimes I wonder what it must be like to live in a place that is less insane than the West, and what it must be like for people who do live outside the West to watch once-great nations like the United States of America fall prey not just to bad ideas, but to *stupid* ideas that utterly defy common sense. As Laurence J. Peter once mused: "Sometimes I wonder whether the world is being run by smart people who are putting us on or by imbeciles who really mean it." The latest example comes to you from the Independent Women's Forum with this jaw-dropping headline: "Study: Describing Breastfeeding as 'Natural' Is Unethical Because It Reinforces Gender Roles." A sample:

It's "ethically inappropriate" for government and medical organizations to describe breastfeeding as "natural" because the term enforces rigid notions about gender roles, claims a new study in Pediatrics.

"Coupling nature with motherhood... can inadvertently support biologically deterministic arguments about the roles of men and women in the family (for example, that women should be the primary caretaker," the study says. The study notes that in recent years, the U.S. Department of Health and Human Services, the American Academy of Pediatrics, the World Health Organization, and several state departments of health have all promoted breastfeeding over bottle-feeding, using the term "natural."

"Referencing the 'natural' in breastfeeding promotion... may inadvertently endorse a set of values about family life and gender roles, which would be ethically inappropriate," the study says. Unless such public-service announcements "make transparent the 'values and beliefs that underlie them,'" they should quit describing breastfeeding as "natural."

So a culture that considers it perfectly ethical to abort a baby developing in the womb and pillage her corpse for research purposes apparently must reach for the smelling salts when someone calls breast-feeding natural, which it is. This is just a trojan horse for the trans activists, who have taken to inventing terms like "chest-feeding" and insisting that men can feed babies with their bodies, too. These people aren't just making war on the "natural family," they are battling against biology itself.

This sort of thing is genuinely ridiculous, and should be called out as such. Only people who spent far too much time in university could come up with this sort of post-modern drivel, which the millions of ordinary people who inhabit the West simply scoff at. Our "elites" have completely lost their grip on reality, and it is time we pointed that out as loudly as we possibly can. Thank goodness for a handful of sane men like Dr. Jordan Peterson.

https://thebridgehead.ca/2018/05/02/new-study-says-that-calling-breastfeeding-natural-is-unethical-because-it-enforces-gender-roles/

Governor's wife Jennifer Siebel Newsom to go by "first partner" in nod to gender equality

By ABC7 Staff January 7th, 2019

SACRAMENTO, Calif. (KABC) -- Jennifer Siebel Newsom, the wife of California's new governor, will go by the title "first partner," a description she feels is more inclusive than the traditional "first lady. "The title change reflects the mindset of a woman who has spent years as a passionate advocate for gender equality. Newsom is an actress and documentary filmmaker who has made two films that examine gender roles. "Miss Representation," released in 2011, looks at how the media contributes to the underrepresentation of women in positions of power and influence. "The Mask You Live In" came out in 2015 to examine the flip side of that coin - how society's definition of masculinity is harmful to men and boys. Both films premiered at the Sundance Film Festival. Last year, she announced she was working on what she considered the third film in the trilogy, "The Great American Lie." She describes the project as how some of those same issues affect broader American society. In addition, Newsom is founder of The Representation Project, which describes its mission as: "Using film and media as catalysts for cultural transformation."Gavin Newsom and Jennifer Siebel met in 2006 and married in 2008. They have four children. The governor was previously married to Kimberly Guilfoyle, a former San Francisco prosecutor and former Fox News commentator who is dating Donald Trump Jr.The Newsom family is moving to Sacramento and expects to live in the historic governor's mansion. That will mark the first time children have lived in the mansion since the 1960s. Kathleen Brown, the sister of former Gov. Jerry Brown, lived at the historic home when their father, Pat Brown, served as governor. The Newsoms will also bring two family dogs and a bunny rabbit to the mansion.

https://abc7.com/politics/governors-wife-jennifer-siebel-newsom-to-go-by-first-partner/5031744/

California State Senate Committee Bans Saying 'He' and 'She'

By Nick Givas January 23rd, 2019

Spiked Online editor Brendan O'Neill reacted to a California state Senate committee banning the words "he" and "she" during hearings and said it's an example of political correctness run amok. "It's crazy. It really shows how far the politically correct lobby are willing to go in terms of policing language," O'Neill said on "Fox & Friends" Tuesday.

"They now want to control not just hateful language and racist language, which we all agree is a bad thing, but everyday speech. 'He' and 'she.' The words that people use all the time in everyday conversation to describe men and women. They want to dig down so far into how we speak, and ultimately into how we think, that they are willing to ban the most common words in the English language." Democratic state Senate Judiciary Chair Hannah-Beth Jackson spoke about the change on Thursday, which affects her committee, and said it's a matter of gender.

"We are now a state recognizing the nonbinary designation as a gender," Jackson said. "We are using the phrase 'they' and replacing other designations so that it's a gender-neutral designation of 'they.' Basically, that's the primary reforms and revisions to the committee rules." Jackson was a victim of her own rules, however, when she referred to her old grammar teacher as a "her" instead of "them."

"We are using what my grammar teacher would have heart attack over. We are using the phrase 'they.' My grammar teacher's long gone. And I won't be hearing from her. If any of you—"

She was cut off mid-sentence from several people in the audience who corrected her and insisted she use the words "them" or "they."

"There is kind of transgender extremism at moment. Now, I'm fully in favor of trans rights. I think trans people should have same rights as everybody else. But there is this kind of trans extremism, which presumes that anyone who uses words like 'he' or 'she' is being disrespectful to trans people or disrespectful to nonbinary people," O'Neill said.

"I think it is going to spread," he continued. "We've seen similar developments in the United Kingdom, for example, where feminists who are critical of transgender politics are hounded and harassed and their meetings are closed down, simply because they think we should still have the right to talk about men and women."

https://www.dailysignal.com/2019/01/23/california-state-senate-committee-bans-saying-he-and-she/

Harvard activist group wants Board of Overseers name changed – because slavery

By College Fix Staff July 18th, 2020

A Harvard University activist group wants the name of the school's Board of Overseers changed due to the last word's connection to slavery. According to *The Crimson*, the Coalition for a Diverse Harvard noted "overseer" has "historically referred to men hired by plantation owners to violently control slaves."

The Board of Overseers is Harvard's "second-highest governing body." The coalition, which advocates "diversity, equity, and inclusion" at the school, has sought the name change for three years. Coalition board member Jane Sujen Bock said many Board of Overseer candidates "had not previously considered the ramifications of the title's link to slavery." The five candidates supported by the coalition support a name change.

As you might expect, Bock cited the current "anti-racist" atmosphere in the country as leading to a "greater push" for a new name.

From the story:

Harvard Forward, a student and alumni group working to bring attention to climate change and recent alumni representation within Harvard's governance boards, said they found the term "Overseers" to be "problematic" in a Wednesday Instagram post.

"The term 'Overseer' cannot be separated from its historical context and connotations. The continued use of a word characterized by such deep-rooted racism is a testament to Harvard's failure to confront our country's history," they wrote. Margaret "Midge" Purce '17, one of the candidates running under the Harvard Forward platform, said she believes the name should change.

"I understand what they were trying to do with it," Purce said. "I think it's tone deaf, and I think that especially now, it really resonates with people who think symbols and names matter, because they do." Jayson U. Toweh, another candidate, said the name itself is "older and antiquated," tied to discriminatory practices in the past.

As noted by *The Crimson,* Harvard previously did away with the term "master" for the heads of its residences, changing it to "faculty deans." (It took the now-deans two whole months to come up with that replacement.)

In addition, last month a quartet of students created a petition to change the name of Harvard's Mather House, named for Increase Mather, a slave owner who attended the university almost 400 years ago.

https://www.thecollegefix.com/harvard-activist-group-wants-board-of-overseers-name-changed-because-slavery/

Associated Press gives bizarre reason it's capitalizing 'black' but not 'white'

By WND News Services July 20th, 2020

The Associated Press, a U.S. wire service and news outlet, announced Monday that it will capitalize "black" when referring to the racial group in its stories, but not "white."

The AP said a statement about the change that white people have a less distinct culture than do black people, and that whites don't have the experience of discrimination based on skin color. "White people generally do not share the same history and culture, or the experience of being discriminated against because of skin color." AP's vice president for standards John Daniszewski said in the announcement. But "people who are Black have strong historical and cultural commonalities, even if they are from different parts of the world and even if they now live in different parts of the world. That includes the shared experience of discrimination due solely to the color of one's skin," Daniszewski said.

The national publication said that capitalizing white could be harmful because white supremacists often capitalize "white" when referring to people or culture, according to a report about the change posted by AP.

"We agree that white people's skin color plays into systemic inequalities and injustices, and we want our journalism to robustly explore these problems," Daniszewski said. "But capitalizing the term white, as is done by white supremacists, risks subtly conveying legitimacy to such beliefs." Daniszewski's remarks come despite several black organizations like The National Association of Black Journalists releasing guidance that "white" should be capitalized in addition to "black," AP reported.

The AP made the decision to capitalize "black" about a month ago, but released the statement Monday to clarify that they won't be capitalizing "white." The AP's guidelines are widely influential on how journalists format their writing through their release of the AP Stylebook that is adhered to by numerous news organizations.

The AP said that capitalizing "white" could cause Caucasians to abdicate conversations about racial inequality in the country, according to the announcement.

The New York Times made a similar decision July 5 and chose to capitalize only "black."

"It seems like such a minor change, black versus Black," The Times's national editor Marc Lacey said in the publication's statement to the public. "But for many people the capitalization of that one letter is the difference between a color and a culture." The Wall Street Journal, USA Today, NBC News and others have also followed the trend, according to AP.

Calls to capitalize the word "black" in writing follow nationwide demonstrations against racial inequality and police brutality after the death of George Floyd, who died after a police officer knelt on his neck for over eight minutes, video showed.

https://www.wnd.com/2020/07/associated-press-gives-bizarre-reason-capitalizing-black-not-white/

The Dictionary Adds 'White Fragility'

By L. Brent Bozell III & Tim Graham April 12th, 2019

One of strangest developments in today's Internet culture is how website dictionaries, which one might presume to be objective, have dabbled in "woke" leftist politics as a way of drawing clicks. USA Today reporter Jessica Guynn, who explains that her job is to explore how the digital world can "amplify bias and widen disparities," delighted in reporting how the term "white fragility" has been added to dictionaries as a result of racial discussions on social media.

Sociologist Robin Di Angelo, one in the endless line of perpetually bored, arrogant and/or ignorant "experts" on race, coined the term "white fragility" in 2011. It was overlooked initially (and for good reason: It's stupid). But naturally, it has picked up steam along with the political career of Donald Trump. After Trump won the presidency in 2016, the Oxford Dictionaries put the term on its short list for word of the year. Last week, it was added to Dictionary.com, defined as "the tendency among members of the dominant white cultural group to have a defensive, wounded, angry, or dismissive response to evidence of racism." For the love of God. Really?

Imagine how these politically correct lexicographers would faint at altering this term for people of color: "black fragility," "Latino fragility," "Inuit fragility." But as usual, the white majority is singled out as perpetually unaware of its skin "privilege." In 2017, the Oxford Dictionaries wrote about an instance of "white fragility" where, at diversity-training session for police officers in suburban Plainfield, Indiana, Captain Carri Weber presented an academic finding that said transgender people of color are about 2.5 times more likely to be assaulted by police than white non-transgender people. Captain Scott Arndt reacted defensively and said, "Most of the people I know have never ... accused the police of violence," and Weber replied, "'Cause of your white male privilege, so you wouldn't know." You can't win against the Thought Police. Their list of societal sins committed by white people is perpetual. Arndt then complained he was the victim of racism and sexism — hence "white fragility," his "discomfort with being told about the structural advantages that both men and white folks are more likely to have." The dictionary people lectured that white people arguing with a leftist narrative on race "takes the story away from the victims of discrimination and gives it back to the perpetrators, who then use it as a weapon to defend the unjust status quo." For expertise, USA Today turned to Aria Razfar, professor of education and linguistics at the University of Illinois at Chicago. Adding terms like "white fragility" to the dictionary is a signal the idea has "become more mainstream." Social media is accelerating the use and acceptance of this new lingo. Terms like white fragility "provide a language so that dominant society could interrogate itself and really look at itself in the mirror in terms of its relationship with non-dominant populations and oppressed groups. "The lesson?

White men can never challenge "academic data" about racism in diversity training sessions, or anywhere else. "Oppressed groups" are always presumed to have the upper hand with evidence ... because they're "oppressed." The left is always trying to stack the deck and smother debate, and crying racism is a huge favorite. The time has come, another expert told USA Today, where people are "interrogating the concept of whiteness." Somehow these people have no idea that they are driving voters right into Donald Trump's camp with their constant accusations of racism, sexism, homophobia, xenophobia and the whole dictionary of bigotries. The only way out is to renounce your whiteness. We officially declare ourselves to be American Indians (like Sen. Elizabeth Warren) and identify as oppressed.

https://cnsnews.com/index.php/commentary/l-brent-bozell-iii/dictionary-adds-white-fragility

What the cluck? PETA finds name of rural road in Idaho distasteful, asks for change

By Katy Moeller July 3rd, 2019

Chickens are friends for some people, dinner for others. Sometimes both.

But one animal rights group feels that the name of a rural road in the Treasure Valley isn't kind to poultry.

PETA sent out a news release Wednesday morning alerting Idaho media that it has written a letter to Caldwell Mayor Garret Nancolas to ask for a change to the street name Chicken Dinner Road. However, Caldwell city street maps don't include Chicken Dinner Road, which is located in rural Canyon County.

"Just like dogs, cats, and human beings, chickens feel pain and fear and value their own lives," said PETA Executive Vice President Tracy Reiman in the letter. She wants the mayor to change the name of the road to "one that celebrates chickens as individuals, not as beings to kill, chop up, and label as 'dinner.' " Susan Miller, the Caldwell mayor's assistant, told the Statesman that the mayor was in a meeting. She said she wasn't sure whether he'd be issuing a response to PETA's request.

In the letter, dated July 3, Reiman said she's not trying to "ruffle any feathers," adding that words matter and "have the power to change lives." The way the industry treats chickens is inhumane, she said, because they are "confined to crowded, filthy sheds with tens of thousands of other birds, where disease, smothering, and heart attacks are common."

It doesn't get any better from there, she said in her letter.

"Then they are violently crammed onto transport trucks for shipment to the slaughterhouse, where they're shackled and hung upside down, their throats are cut, and they're immersed in scalding-hot feather-removal tanks — often while they're still conscious," Reiman wrote. Changing the name of Chicken Dinner Road would show compassion to chickens and respect for other species, she said. She said PETA would help pay for replacing the sign.

Joe Decker, a spokesman for Canyon County, said the county has heard from a handful of residents who grew up there and don't want the name to be changed. He said county commissioners were in meetings all morning, and he's skeptical that they would change the name "based on a letter from PETA."

A road name change would be handled by the county commissioners, as long as the road isn't in Caldwell's area of impact, Decker said via email. "It would require a public hearing and we would have to notify all property owners having frontage on the affected road at least 30 days before the public hearing," Decker said. "An application and fee are also required for an unincorporated county road name change."

Why is Chicken Dinner Road named that?

How the name of the road came to be — it used to be called Lane 12 — is a story in and of itself. The tale has many versions, each with devotees, according to previous Idaho Statesman reporting. Those competing accounts initially caused Caldwell librarian Elaine Leppert in 2010 to respond to a Chicken Dinner query by saying, "I wouldn't touch it with a 10-foot pole. I wouldn't touch it with a chicken leg."

But she relented. The story's too rich to stay quiet, and its central facts are accepted by most: The titular chicken dinner was prepared in the 1930s by Laura Lamb, who lived along the then-rutted road. Other facts are less certain.

The most popular account has Lamb preparing her famous fried chicken for then-Gov. C. Ben Ross, a family friend, and asking him his opinion of the rough road he'd had to travel to reach her home. Ross told Lamb that if she could get the county to grade the road, he'd get it oiled. She did, then he did. "I've heard it was a commissioner; I've heard it was the governor," Leppert said. "My father said it was a commissioner."

That last version carries some credibility, since county commissioners are more likely than a governor to hear a plea for improving a county road. Then again, Leppert acknowledged, a governor does have clout.

According to some versions, the street name first appeared on cardboard "chicken dinner" signs placed along the route to direct the governor — or commissioner — to his supper. After the road was oiled, vandals supposedly wrote "Lamb's Chicken Dinner Avenue" on its freshly oiled surface in bright yellow letters. The name was catchy, so it stuck.

If the name of the road was ever changed, other aspects of Idaho life may be affected.

Houston Vineyards, which is located at 16473 Chicken Dinner Road, celebrates the name through its Chicken Dinner wine series. "The naming of our Chicken Dinner wines celebrates and plays off a classic Southern Idaho tale — the story behind one of the most curious road names around," Huston states on its website.

Chicken Dinner Road is also the name of an Idaho bluegrass band out of Middleton founded in 2007.

https://www.idahostatesman.com/news/northwest/idaho/article232238047.html

Colorado State University: Avoid Using the Word "America" Because It's Not Inclusive

By Paul Joseph Watson July 18th, 2019

A new "inclusive language guide" compiled by Colorado State University asserts that the word "America" is "non-inclusive" and should be avoided.

"CSU lists both "American" and "America" as non-inclusive words "to avoid," due to the fact that America encompasses more than just the U.S. By referring to the U.S. as America, the guide claims that one "erases other cultures and depicts the United States as the dominant American country." The school suggests using "U.S. citizen" or "person from the U.S." as substitutes," writes Ethan Cai.

Other words to avoid include the following:

- **Male and female/ladies and gentlemen/Mr./Mrs./Ms** (these words are gendered yet we don't know the person's gender – there are now infinite genders).

- **Straight** (when used to refer to heterosexuals, this implies LGBT people are "crooked" or "not normal," according to the guide).

- **Normal person** ("implies that 'other' people... are not whole or regular people").

- **Handicap parking** (could offend disabled people).

- **War, cake walk, eenie meenie miney moe, Eskimo, freshman, hip hip hooray!, hold down the fort, starving, and policeman** (all of these words are "non-inclusive").

"Even though these guidelines are suggested and not mandatory, they place students in the uncomfortable position of reciting politically correct talking points that they may not agree with," said Nicole Neily, president of Speech First. "Words like 'American,' 'male,' and 'female' are used every day by billions of people around the world. When these students graduate, they're in for a rude awakening!"

"The guide is not about political-correctness or policing grammar, but rather helping communicators practice inclusive language," the university claims.

That's exactly what it's about.

These are the people teaching your kids.

Good luck, America (whoops, I just committed a hate crime).

https://www.infowars.com/colorado-state-university-avoid-using-the-word-america-because-its-not-inclusive/

Update: 'Manhole' will be 'maintenance hole' as city changes municipal code

By William Lundquist July 16th, 2019 Updated: July 17th, 2019

The Berkeley City Council approved an ordinance that will eliminate masculine and feminine pronouns from the city's municipal code, changing gender-specific language to gender-neutral language.

Update, July 17: The ordinance about gender-neutral language in Berkeley's municipal code was approved at City Council on Tuesday as part of the consent calendar.

Original story, July 16: The Berkeley City Council is scheduled to vote Tuesday night on an ordinance that would eliminate masculine and feminine pronouns from the city's municipal code, changing gender-specific language to gender-neutral language.

The item proposes a revision to the grammatical interpretation of Berkeley's municipal code, which now mostly uses masculine pronouns. It would switch "he" and "she" to "they" and "them" and assume they/them indicates a single individual, "unless the context indicates the contrary." The rationale for this change states: "Amending the municipal code to include gender-neutral pronouns by eliminating any gender preference language within the municipal code will promote equality."

The measure would also change other terminology. "Manhole" would be changed to "maintenance hole," "manpower" would be changed to "human effort" and "sorority" or "fraternity" would be changed to "collegiate Greek system residence," according to the ordinance. In addition, gendered terms in the existing code such as he, she, him, her, himself, herself would be switched to specific nouns such as the architect, the attorney, the council member, the clerk, the driver and more. (See the list.)

This item originally appeared on council's March 12 agenda and was sponsored by City Council members Rigel Robinson, Cheryl Davila, Ben Bartlett and Lori Droste. Officials referred the item back to staff to be fleshed out more.

The financial implications of the change to the city code are relatively minimal, with a report by City Clerk Mark Numainville estimating it will cost $600 to get the city's publisher, Code Publishing Company, to update the code.

Before the changes are made, Berkeley will post a list with the new pronouns in every branch of the Berkeley Public Library 15 days before the ordinance takes effect.

https://www.berkeleyside.com/2019/07/16/city-council-to-consider-abolishing-gender-specific-pronouns-in-berkeley-municipal-code

San Francisco board rebrands 'convicted felon' as 'justice-involved person,' sanitizes other crime lingo

By Lukas Mikelionis August 22nd, 2019

Crime-ridden San Francisco has introduced new sanitized language for criminals, getting rid of words such as "offender" and "addict" while changing "convicted felon" to "justice-involved person."

The Board of Supervisors adopted the changes last month even as the city reels from one of the highest crime rates in the country and staggering inequality exemplified by pervasive homelessness alongside Silicon Valley wealth.

The local officials say the new language will help change people's views about those who commit crimes. According to the San Francisco Chronicle, from now on a convicted felon or an offender released from custody will be known as a "formerly incarcerated person," or a "justice-involved" person or just a "returning resident."

A juvenile "delinquent" will now be called a "young person with justice system involvement," or a "young person impacted by the juvenile justice system." And drug addicts or substance abusers, meanwhile, will become "a person with a history of substance use."

"We don't want people to be forever labeled for the worst things that they have done," Supervisor Matt Haney told the newspaper. "We want them ultimately to become contributing citizens, and referring to them as felons is like a scarlet letter that they can never get away from."

The sanitized language, though unlikely to do much to address the crime problem, may result in some convoluted descriptions of crimes in the future. The newspaper noted an individual whose car has been broken into could well be known to police as "a person who has come in contact with a returning resident who was involved with the justice system and who is currently under supervision with a history of substance use."

The board's approved new language is non-binding, with the district attorney endorsing the measure. Mayor London Breed hasn't yet endorsed the new language.

https://www.foxnews.com/politics/san-francisco-board-adopts-new-language-for-criminals-turning-convicted-felon-into-justice-involved-person

City bans calling someone an 'illegal alien' out of hate

By Rich Calder, Julia Marsh & Aaron Feis September 26th, 2019

It's now against the law in New York City to threaten someone with a call to immigration authorities or refer to them as an "illegal alien" when motivated by hate.

The restrictions — violations of which are punishable by fines of up to $250,000 per offense — are outlined in a 29-page directive released by City Hall's Commission on Human Rights. "'Alien' — used in many laws to refer to a 'noncitizen' person — is a term that may carry negative connotations and dehumanize immigrants, marking them as 'other,'" reads one passage of the memo. "The use of certain language, including 'illegal alien' and 'illegals,' with the intent to demean, humiliate, or offend a person or persons constitutes discrimination."

The directive goes on to list several examples of acts and comments that would run afoul of the restrictions, including harassing people over their accents or grasp of English, or wielding the threat of a call to Immigration and Customs Enforcement as a tool of hate. "A hotel prohibits its housekeepers from speaking Spanish while cleaning because it would 'offend' hotel guests or make them uncomfortable," reads one hypothetical.

"An Indian immigrant family complains to their landlord about mold and cockroaches in their unit. The landlord tells them to 'just deal with it' and threatens to call ICE if they file a complaint in housing court," reads another. "A store owner tells two friends who are speaking Thai while shopping in his store to 'speak English' and 'go back to your country,'" reads a third.The Commission on Human Rights made clear that the directive is, at least in part, a rebuke of federal crackdowns on illegal immigration.

"In the face of increasingly hostile national rhetoric, we will do everything in our power to make sure our treasured immigrant communities are able to live with dignity and respect, free of harassment and bias," said Carmelyn Malalis, the agency's commissioner.

The directive comes months after Mayor Bill de Blasio vocally opposed coordinated raids by ICE on the city's immigrant communities. Meanwhile on Thursday, the Mayor's Office of Immigrant Affairs announced a joint $1 million investment with the state to guarantee legal services to immigrants facing imminent deportation.

https://nypost.com/2019/09/26/city-bans-calling-someone-an-illegal-alien-out-of-hate/

Air Canada to stop announcing 'ladies and gentlemen' in recognition of gender fluidity

By Carlin Becker October 13th, 2019

Employees aboard Air Canada flights will no longer greet guests by referring to them as "ladies and gentlemen" or "mesdames et messieurs," which has been typical protocol for years, in an effort to be conscious of gender fluidity.

Flight attendants and other staff will not use the language in boarding announcements, and the company instead plans to replace the standard greetings with neutral words, such as "everybody" or "tout le monde."

"We will be amending our onboard announcements to modernize them and remove specific references to gender," a media spokesperson for the company said, also noting that Air Canada was named one of Canada's Best Div ersity Employers for 2019. "We work hard to make sure all employees feel like valued members of the Air Canada family, while ensuring our customers are comfortable and respected when they choose to travel with us." Canada has taken steps to recognize and protect its citizens who don't identify as either male or female or identify as "non-binary." In the country, gender identity and expression are protected under criminal code, and crimes motivated by such characteristics could constitute hate crimes. It is also illegal in Canada to discriminate against someone based on their gender identity.

https://www.washingtonexaminer.com/news/air-canada-to-stop-announcing-ladies-and-gentlemen-in-recognition-of-gender-fluidity

UConn students ARRESTED for 'ridiculing' speech in viral video

By Jon Street Oct 22nd, 2019

University of Connecticut Police arrested Monday two men who were allegedly seen in a viral video reciting a racial slur.

The incident occurred on Oct. 11 in the parking lot of an off-campus apartment complex. In the video, there are three men walking through the lot. An individual took the video from the window of an apartment building, according to local media reports.

The video prompted the UConn NAACP chapter to pen a letter to the editor of the campus newspaper, *The Daily Campus*, calling on officials "to fully investigate this incident and apply the proper justice." Following those calls, the university confirmed to *Campus Reform* Monday that two of the three men allegedly seen in the video were arrested under a Connecticut state statute that makes it a crime to "ridicule" certain persons.

"Any person who, by his advertisement, ridicules or holds up to contempt any person or class of persons, on account of the creed, religion, color, denomination, nationality or race of such person or class of persons, shall be guilty of a class D misdemeanor," the statute states. UConn spokeswoman Stephanie Reitz confirmed in a statement to *Campus Reform* the arrests of the men who were "heard shouting a racial slur."

"The two students both were charged under CGS 53-37, ridicule on account of creed, religion, color, denomination, nationality or race," Reitz said. "A third person had accompanied them as they walked outside of the apartments, but the police investigation determined that individual had not participated in the behavior." The two men arrested were identified in a police report obtained by *Campus Reform* as Ryan Mucaj and Jarred Karal, both 21. The police report states that Mucaj and Karal "played a game in which they yelled vulgar words" after leaving an area business.

Mucaj and Karal are scheduled to appear in court on Oct. 30. If convicted, they could face fines of up to $50, up to 30 days in jail, or both. UConn President Thomas Katsouleas released a statement reacting to the arrests, saying, "It is supportive of our core values to pursue accountability, through due process, for an egregious assault on our community that has caused considerable harm. I'm grateful for the university's collective effort in responding to this incident, especially the hard work of the UConn Police Department, which has been investigating the case since it was reported."

In a 2018 column for *Reason*, University of California at Los Angeles law professor Eugene Volokh called the statute under which the men were charged "obviously unconstitutional, because it suppresses speech based on its content (and viewpoint), and because there's no First Amendment exception for speech that insults based on race or religion." The arrests come less than one month after New York City banned the use of the term, "illegal alien," which is the legal term in the U.S. code for "any person not a citizen or national of the United States." The arrests come the same week that Massachusetts lawmakers hold a hearing on whether to impose a fine of up to $200 for using the word "bitch."

The arrests also follow *Campus Reform*'s reporting on a Knight Foundation survey that found 41 percent of college students do not believe hate speech should be protected under the First Amendment.

https://www.campusreform.org/?ID=13898

New Orleans' Dixie Beer will change its name, owner Gayle Benson says

By Ann Schmidt June 26th, 2020

Dixie Beer, from a famous New Orleans brewery with the same name, announced the company would be changing its name and the name of all its products. Dixie Brewery owner Gayle Benson -- who also owns the NFL's New Orleans Saints and the NBA's New Orleans Pelicans -- said in a statement Friday the brewery is working to find a new name in order to make "our home more united, strong and resilient for future generations."

"With inclusive input from all of our community stakeholders, we are preparing to change the name of our brewery and products that carry the Dixie brand and these conversations will determine what brand will best represent our culture and community," Benson wrote. In the announcement, Benson explained that the brewery is responding to the "critical conversations about racism and systemic social issues" that are happening across the country.

"We and our partners are committed to once again engaging in conversations with our neighbors, leaders and others to ensure that our brewery continues to be a business and brand our entire community feels represents them well and that they are proud to have as part of our culture," Benson wrote.

Benson and her late husband Tom bought the Dixie brand in 2017, according to NOLA.com. After George Floyd died while being detained by police in Minneapolis in May, protesters for weeks have called for a reckoning over racial justice in business and society as a whole.

Other than Dixie Brewery, several companies have announced they would rename or rebrand their products that are rooted in racial stereotypes, including Mars Incorporated Uncle Ben's rice, the Quaker Oats Company's Aunt Jemima brand and Conagra Brands's Mrs. Butterworth's brands.

https://www.foxbusiness.com/lifestyle/dixie-beer-name-change-gayle-benson

Twitter engineers replacing racially loaded tech terms like 'master,' 'slave'

By Stephen Shankland July 2nd, 2020

For Regynald Augustin, a Black programmer at Twitter, the impetus for change arrived in an email last year with the phrase "automatic slave rekick."

The words were just part of an engineering discussion about restarting a secondary process, but they prompted Augustin to start trying to change Twitter's use of words with racist connections. Augustin was used to seeing the term "slave" in technical contexts. "But with 'rekick' -- I was madder than I ever thought I'd be in the workplace," he said.

First on his own and then joining forces with another engineer, Kevin Oliver, he helped spearhead an effort to replace terms like "master," "slave," "whitelist" and "blacklist" with words that didn't hearken back to oppressive parts of United States history and culture. He recounted his thoughts at the time: "This has to stop. This isn't cool. We have to change this now."

No one expects that changing technical terms will end centuries of racial injustice. But some people at technology companies, including Oliver and Augustin at Twitter, are pressing for the changes that are within their reach. That includes the effort to replace racially fraught technology terms like "master" and "slave" that describe things like databases, software projects, camera flashes and hard drives.

Managers at the social network formalized the two engineers' effort in January, endorsing work to address the issue systematically across the engineering division and expanding it to terms linked to discrimination on the basis of sex, age and disabilities -- replacing "man hours" and "sanity check," for example. Oliver and Augustin detailed the effort in an exclusive interview with CNET.

Accelerated by Black Lives Matter

Such efforts have taken on new importance with the new push against racial inequality in the United States triggered by the death of George Floyd, a 46-year-old Minnesota man killed in May by a policeman pinning him to the ground with a knee on his neck. The event triggered Black Lives Matter protests around the country, legislative and policy changes, and shifts within companies.

The new Black Lives Matter energy boosted the vocabulary change at Twitter. "Everything that's happened recently has made awareness spread blisteringly fast around the company," Augustin said.

Related efforts are occurring at Microsoft's Github and LinkedIn divisions, Apple, and Google's Chrome, often as bottom-up changes rather than official positions.

Earlier, in 2018, developers of the widely used Python programming language dropped "master/slave." In 2014, the team behind the Drupal online publishing software replaced the terms with "primary/replica." In 2003, Los Angeles County asked suppliers and contractors to stop using "master" and "slave" on computer equipment.

It's complex to root out terms embedded in documentation, everyday speech and interlinked programming code and configuration files. Twitter's goal is to finish its Twitter engineering project by the end of 2021, and to publish details about what it's learned for others trying to make the same changes.

"Our code must reflect the people we serve," Oliver said.

Words matter

Changing words doesn't necessarily change the underlying concepts -- for example, in photography, what some companies still call a "master" flash still controls a "slave" flash. And sometimes people pick new words in an attempt to start fresh with neutral vocabulary, only to find the new term picks up the baggage of the old. "Water closet" becomes "toilet," which becomes "bathroom," which becomes "restroom."

But picking words carefully can make a difference when avoiding subtle or unconscious acts of discrimination called microaggressions, argues Lecia Brooks, outreach director for the Southern Poverty Law Center, a civil rights group.

"Words may mean nothing to the sender, but to the receiver it may mean something," Brooks said. "If we can become more mindful about the words that we're using, we can work to mitigate microaggressions," she said.

One common objection to changing vocabulary terms is that it's insufficient to drive real change. At Twitter, it's part of other moves to improve diversity and inclusion.

Other diversity efforts

Those efforts include donations to Black Lives Matter causes, offering advice on allyship for those who want to help, making Juneteenth a holiday for US employees, detailing its diversity and inclusion efforts during the coronavirus pandemic, offering recommended reading to better understand the Black experience in America, and advising companies about what to say and tweet about racism.

Brooks would like to see more changes at Twitter, like banishing white supremacists from its website. "If you want to remove hurtful, harmful, hateful words, you might look at removing people who use your platform in that way," she said.

In response, Twitter said, "There is no place on Twitter for hateful conduct, terrorist organizations or violent extremist groups. Because of these rules, we've permanently suspended hundreds of accounts, many of which advocate violence against civilians alongside some form of extremist white supremacist ideology."

Twitter has banned some accounts, like that of a white supremacist group posing as a left-wing antifa group inciting violence, but its rules against hateful conduct only ban accounts whose "primary purpose is inciting harm towards others." Google's YouTube banned former Ku Klux Klan leader David Duke and white supremacist Richard Spencer this week.

Out with the old words

Twitter's engineering teams are working to change terms that touch on race, sex and ability, Oliver said. Terms and recommended replacements include:

- Whitelist becomes allowlist.
- Blacklist becomes denylist.
- Master/slave becomes leader/follower, primary/replica or primary/standby.
- Grandfathered becomes legacy status.
- Gendered pronouns (for example "guys") become folks, people, you all, y'all.
- Gendered pronouns (for example "he" or "his") become they or their.
- Man hours becomes person hours or engineer hours.
- Sanity check becomes quick check, confidence check or coherence check.
- Dummy value becomes placeholder value or sample value.

Twitter's senior management is backing the effort.

"Inclusive language seeks to treat all people with respect, dignity, and impartiality," said Twitter engineering chief Michael Montano in a June 25 email to all Twitter employees. "It is constructed to bring everyone into the group and exclude no one, and it is essential for creating an environment where everyone feels welcome."

https://www.cnet.com/news/twitter-engineers-replace-racially-loaded-tech-terms-like-master-slave/

Poll: Majority of Americans Want to Re-write First Amendment to Stop "Hate Speech"

By Paul Joseph Watson October 24th, 2019

A new poll has found that a majority of Americans want to re-write the First Amendment to "reflect the cultural norms of today" in order stop "hate speech." The survey indicates "free speech is under more threat than previously believed," according to The Campaign for Free Speech, who conducted the poll. 51 per cent of Americans want to see the First Amendment rewritten while more than 60 per cent agree with restricting free speech in some way.

Nearly 60 per cent of Millennials agreed that the Constitution "goes too far in allowing hate speech in modern America" and should be done over, compared to 48 percent of Gen Xers and 47 percent of Baby Boomers. Most Millennials also support laws that would make "hate speech" a crime and 54 per cent of those support jail time for offenders. Almost 60 per cent of respondents also thought that "government should be able to take action against newspapers and TV stations that publish content that is biased, inflammatory, or false," with 46 per cent supporting possible jail time.

"The findings are frankly extraordinary," executive director Bob Lystad told the Washington Free Beacon. "Our free speech rights and our free press rights have evolved well over 200 years, and people now seem to be rethinking them." The numbers are shocking and reflect a total lack of understanding of the concept of free speech, which is that the very worst speech must be upheld for free speech to exist at all since what's considered "offensive" or "hate" is entirely subjective. The Supreme Court has ruled that so-called "hate speech" is part of free speech but the majority of Americans, and especially younger people, have no grasp of this.

https://www.infowars.com/poll-majority-of-americans-want-to-re-write-first-amendment-to-stop-hate-speech/

Facebook and Instagram ban 'sexual' use of eggplant and peach emojis

By Fox 10 Phoenix November 4th, 2019

Facebook, which has been caught in a bipartisan battle over political ads, is waging a different type of war against -- eggplants and peaches?

Back in July, Facebook and Instagram updated the company's Community Standards language regarding what type of sexual expression is allowed on the widely-used platforms. Pairing an eggplant or peach emoji with an expression of what LGBT news site Out.com calls "being horny" could qualify as "sexual solicitation." That, in turn, could get your account flagged or banned, according to adult industry news site XBIZ.

Under Facebook's Community Standards, "suggestive elements" that could get you banned -- when paired with nude imagery, sex or sexual partners, and sex chat conversations -- includes "contextually specific and commonly sexual emojis or emoji strings."

"[Content] will only be removed from Facebook and Instagram if it contains a sexual emoji alongside an implicit or indirect ask for nude imagery, sex or sexual partners, or sex chat conversations," Instagram told the New York Post. "We aren't taking action on simply the emojis."

https://www.fox10phoenix.com/news/facebook-and-instagram-ban-sexual-use-of-eggplant-and-peach-emojis

The Racist Practice of Mispronouncing Names

By Keya Roy, Zuheera Ali & Medha Kumar March 21st, 2019

When Zuheera Ali walks into a coffee shop, she stands outside the door, opens her wallet, takes out her card, figures out exactly what she wants to order, and she reminds herself: 'You're Billy. You're Billy.'

The barista doesn't believe her, of course. But they can't do anything about it.

As her co-host Keya Roy says, "You can be whoever you want because you will never see this barista again." In this episode of *RadioActive Youth Media*, Keya Roy and Zuheera Ali talk with author Ijeoma Oluo and each other about living in the United States with uncommon names. They also talk to Rita Kohli, a professor at University of California, Riverside, who has researched the effects of mispronouncing names on students of color.

Producer Medha Kumar has her name butchered constantly. Every time a teacher reads the attendance list and gets to her name, she knows they're looking at her name because they're squinting. It's one of those super awkward moments. Kumar remembers a time in second grade when she had to give a PowerPoint presentation in front of her class: "I was standing in front of my classmates and my teacher had turned on autocorrect. The first slide was just supposed to be my name, but was corrected to read 'Media K-Mart.' It was so embarrassing."

Keya Roy says she has stopped correcting her teachers when they mispronounce her name. "At some point, it's just futile," Roy says. Zuheera Ali says she was never one to let someone say her name wrong.

"My name is my identity, and allowing someone else to say it wrong is stripping me of that," she says. "I feel like as a woman of color, I'm expected to make these changes, especially when I'm at school. But asking me to make my name easier to pronounce is a very unfair way that I have to change."

Says co-host Keya Roy: "I always felt like by giving into that pressure to conform and allowing my name to be butchered, I was somehow making life easier for others...

"My name is a way to push me aside, and most of the time, the people who are doing this don't realize the damage they could be doing to my self-worth and sense of confidence."

Rita Kohli, the professor at University of California Riverside, has researched how mispronouncing names of students of color hurts them.

"We've found a lot of people feeling embarrassed — ashamed of their name, wanting to withdraw from raising their hand in class, and sitting on the edge of their seat during roll call so they can say their name before a someone else messes it up," Kohli says. "There was a lot of anxiety and fear that came along with this."

Ijeoma Oluo, author and leading voice on race in America, says her name is often used to discredit her. "People will try to — as a blatant sign of disrespect — mispronounce my name or mock my name," Oluo says. "I get that on social media all the time."

Oluo says people on social media will "deliberately, wildly misspell my name to show to other people how serious must I be taken if I don't even have what they would consider to be a serious name. It's racist at its core to think that other cultures names are invalid. It's othering and purposefully disrespectful, and it's often used as a weapon against me."

She continues: "It's my name and I won't let anyone take that from me." Research shows that having an uncommon name can cause anxiety and alienation. The racist practice of mispronouncing names has evolved from a long history of changing people of color's names to strip them of their dignity and humanity.

"The changing of people's names has a racialized history," said Kohli. "It's grounded in slavery — the renaming during slavery — renaming Americanization schools for Latinx communities and indigenous communities, and so there is a lot of history that's tied to this practice that is directly tied to racism."

This history is painful even though it seems so far in the past, Zuheera Ali says. But history is not removed for many African-Americans, many of whom don't know their ancestors' names and carry the names of slave owners. Getting someone's name right is a simple sign of respect — of them as people, and where they come from, these podcasters say. "Interrupting someone to say, 'It's Keya, not Keeya,' isn't me being irritating, it's me putting my foot down against a vehicle of racism, and then in turn, creating an environment in which owning your name is the norm, not the exception," Keya Roy says.

https://kuow.org/stories/a-rose-by-any-other-name-would-not-be-me?fbclid=IwAR3qBNjHquT4Mofi3g6yc4tDyGVLws-m7IYXX6DGm4RILyh1x02TrmbfINY

HAR no longer using 'master' to describe bedrooms and bathrooms on its property listing database

By Leah Asmelash June 25th, 2020

'Master bedroom' and 'master bathroom' replaced with 'primary bedroom' and 'primary bathroom' on HAR's Multiple Listing Service The Houston Association of Realtors no longer uses the word "master" to describe bedrooms and bathrooms on its Multiple Listing Service.

Earlier this month, HAR replaced the phrases "master bedroom" and "master bathroom" with "primary bedroom" and "primary bathroom" on its property listing database. The change came after several HAR members called for a review of the terminology.

"The MLS Advisory Group regularly reviews the terms and fields used in the MLS to make sure they are consistent with the current market environment," according to a statement HAR sent its members regarding the change. "The updates to Primary Bedroom and Primary Bath were among nine requests for review that were submitted by members and considered at the most recent meetings."

According to HAR, the topic had been raised and considered for many years.

"It was not a new suggestion to review the terminology," according to the statement HAR sent its members. "The overarching message was that some members were concerned about how the terms might be perceived by some other agents and consumers. The consensus was that Primary describes the rooms equally as well as Master while avoiding any possible misperceptions."

The associate said the change did not constitute a ban on the use of the word "master."

"You may still use the term 'Master Bedroom' or 'Master Bath' as you feel appropriate in your marketing materials and in the Public Remarks, Agent Remarks, and photo descriptions," according to the statement HAR sent its members.

https://www.click2houston.com/news/local/2020/06/25/har-no-longer-using-master-to-describe-bedrooms-and-bathrooms-on-its-property-listing-database/

Academic Wants to Ban the Insults "Nerd" and "Geek" as Hate Crimes

By Paul Joseph Watson December 18th, 2019

An academic in the UK says that the insults "geek" and "nerd" should be criminalized as hate crimes because they cause distress to people with high IQs.

No, you're not reading the Onion.

Psychology lecturer and psychotherapist Dr Sonja Falck says that "anti-IQ" insults are hate crime's last "taboo" and that they should be legally treated the same way as homophobic and racist slurs. During her research, Falck says that people being called "nerd" or "egghead" or "brainiac" contributed to them "being set apart as being different to others and feeling like they're a misfit and they don't belong."

So in other words, these individuals developed high IQs partly as a result of being taunted as "nerds," suggesting the insults actually helped them in life.

However, Falck claims that such terms cause emotional trauma and is calling for "legislative action" to treat the insults 'nerd', 'brainbox', 'geek', 'egg-head', 'smart-arse', 'dweeb' and 'smarty-pants' as hate crimes. "The N-word was common parlance in the UK until at least the 1960s. Other insulting slurs about age, disability, religion and gender identity remained in widespread use until relatively recently," said Falck.

"Society at the time turned a blind eye to their impact by passing them off as harmless banter," she added. Presumably, once "nerd" and "geek" are banned, "dumb" and "stupid" will have to be banned too.

In fact, all insults of any nature that may hurt someone's feelings should naturally result in the person who used them being locked up in a cage.

That sounds like progress to me!

https://www.infowars.com/academic-wants-to-ban-the-insults-nerd-and-geek-as-hate-crimes/

GLAAD: The Phrase 'Pillow Fight' Is Offensive To Gay People

By Paul Bois December 20th, 2019

The phrase "pillow fight" is now offensive to gay people, according to the Gay and Lesbian Alliance Against Defamation (GLAAD). As reported by Newsbusters, the LGBT activist organization criticized Politico for uttering the words "pillow fight" in reference to the argument that erupted between Mayor Pete Buttigieg and Sen. Elizabeth Warren (D-MA). "The South Bend mayor has been testing an outsider message in a field dominated by D.C. insiders, but he's been a bit sidetracked by his pillow fight with Elizabeth Warren," Politco originally wrote in its Playbook PM.

Later, Politico reported that GLAAD sent them a letter describing the use of "pillow fight" as an offensive slur. "GLAAD sent us a note yesterday about Playbook PM, noting that our use of 'pillow fight' when describing a fight between Pete Buttigieg and Elizabeth Warren may have offended people," Politico said.

Drew Anderson, GLAAD's Director of News and Rapid Response, wrote that the LGBT community generally views the phrase pillow fight as a slur.

"For women and LGBTQ people at the workplace, hearing phrases like 'dramatic,' 'over the top,' and even 'pillow fight' during office disagreements fosters negative stereotypes and diminishes a person simply because of who they are," wrote Anderson. "Disagreements happen in politics, but using these loaded terms during disputes feed into the sexist and homophobic tropes that simply have no place in our political coverage and rhetoric."

Politico subsequently apologized, claiming they never meant offense by employing the phrase, emphasizing that it meant "a fight where no one draws blood." GLAAD has been making headlines in recent days for its fight against the Hallmark Channel and its fight against author JK Rowling, who dared to say that "sex is real" regarding transgender issues.

"J.K. Rowling, whose books gave kids hope that they could work together to create a better world, has now aligned herself with an anti-science ideology that denies the basic humanity of people who are transgender," said Anthony Ramos, head of talent at GLAAD. "Trans men, trans women and non-binary people are not a threat, and to imply otherwise puts trans people at risk. Now is the time for allies who know and support trans people to speak up and support their fundamental right to be treated equally and fairly."

Prior to that, the Hallmark Channel promised that it would be working in conjunction with GLAAD in order to promote LGBTQ equality on its platform. "Hallmark will be working with GLAAD to better represent the LGBTQ community across our portfolio of brands," the company said in a statement. "The Hallmark Channel will be reaching out to Zola to reestablish our partnership and reinstate the commercials."

GLAAD originally denounced Hallmark Channel for pulling an ad that featured two lesbians kissing in response to a petition launched by the pro-family group One Million Moms. "The Hallmark Channel's decision to correct its mistake sends an important message to LGBTQ people and represents a major loss for fringe organizations, like One Million Moms, whose sole purpose is to hurt families like mine," said GLAAD President and CEO, Sarah Kate Ellis. "LGBTQ people are, and will continue to be, a part of advertisements and family programming and that will never change. GLAAD exists to hold brands like The Hallmark Channel accountable when they make discriminatory decisions and to proactively ensure families of all kinds are represented in fair and accurate ways."

https://www.dailywire.com/news/glaad-the-phrase-pillow-fight-is-offensive-to-gay-people?utm_source=facebook&utm_medium=social&utm_campaign=mjk

Transgender worker suing Nike for $1.1 million cites pronoun abuses

By Sarah Min December, 20th 2019

A transgender former Nike contractor is seeking $1.1 million in damages from the sporting goods giant for allegedly allowing gender identity-based harassment.

According to a civil lawsuit filed this week, Nike and Mainz Brady Group, a staffing firm that hired workers for Nike, discriminated against computer engineer Jazz Lyles, who identifies as transmasculine and prefers the pronouns they/them/their. The complaint was filed with Multnomah Circuit Court in Oregon.

During Lyles' tenure at Nike — from May 2017 to September 2018 — the engineer was repeatedly "misgendered" by coworkers, the complaint said. While Lyles notified management about the issue multiple times, the companies allegedly failed to implement any policies, procedures and trainings around the use of gender pronouns in the workplace. "When someone refuses to acknowledge a person's gender identity or insists on referring to them by a gender to which they do not identify (called misgendering), this causes real and significant harm," read the complaint. "This is particularly true when a person is misgendered repeatedly on a daily basis."

Nike declined to comment on the lawsuit, but said the company "is committed to a culture of diversity, inclusion and respect where everyone can succeed and realize their full potential."

Mainz Brady did not respond to requests for comment.

Nike allegedly fostered a "boys-club 'jock mentality'" work culture that was hostile to people who do not fit gender stereotypes, which the complaint said is contrary to the progressive reputation the sporting goods company enjoys with the public. In its "Be True" campaign, Nike hired transgender athletes to promote athletic wear like hoodies and sneakers.

The suit alleged that placing the burden on Lyles to educate colleagues about gender identity caused tension between the engineer and coworkers, who allegedly called Lyles "stupid" and "unstable." One colleague allegedly said, "I know I'm not supposed to call you 'she-male.'" Another coworker allegedly chose not to interact with the plaintiff. Still another colleague allegedly said she would not use Lyles' gender pronouns for religious reasons.

Despite reporting these and separate incidents to Nike and Mainz Brady, neither took action nor conducted an investigation into the matter, according to the suit.

Instead, reports to the companies allegedly resulted in retaliation against Lyles, who was told they could ask for reassignment at the expense of their career or see their work further impeded by coworkers, the complaint said. On one occasion, Lyles was removed three times by a colleague from a Slack channel the engineer required to complete certain work, the complaint said.

On another occasion, after several reports to Nike, the company held a training on proper gender pronouns for Lyles and their coworkers. But the complaint alleged that the training — conducted for the plaintiff's immediate teammates and not the entire department — was untimely, singled out Lyles and exacerbated their relationship to the team.

"Employers like Nike have a responsibility to present a safe workplace and ensure that employees respect their coworkers' gender pronouns," Shenoa Payne, the plaintiff's attorney, told CBS News. According to Payne, the misgendering lawsuit against Nike is unique, though it is not the first time the company faced a lawsuit focusing on gender. Last year, four women filed a federal lawsuit against Nike, alleging it violated state and federal equal-pay laws and fostered a work environment that allowed sexual harassment. Lyles' is seeking economic damages in excess of $195,000. The plaintiff is also seeking noneconomic damages in excess of $950,000.

https://www.cbsnews.com/news/nike-transgender-former-contractor-sues-nike-for-1-1-million-for-alleged-misgendering/

Call your animal a 'companion' instead of a pet: PETA chief says term is derogatory because it makes living things sound like a 'commodity' or 'decoration'

By Victoria Allen January 30th, 2020

Cats and dogs seem perfectly happy to be fed, watered and cuddled by doting owners. But whatever you do, don't call them pets, says the head of an animal rights organization.

Ingrid Newkirk, the president of PETA, said this is derogatory and suggests they are merely a 'commodity' or 'decoration'. The group –

People for the Ethical Treatment of Animals – has long called for owners to be renamed 'human carers' or guardians.

Yesterday, the animal rights activist, 70, from Surrey, compared calling animals pets to the treatment of women before feminism, when they were not allowed to own property or were patronizingly called 'sweetie' or 'honey' to make them seem 'less of a person'. Miss Newkirk said: 'Animals are not pets – they are not your cheap burglar alarm, or something which allows you to go out for a walk. They are not ours as decorations or toys, they are living beings.

A dog is a feeling, whole individual, with emotions and interests, not something you 'have'.' It is estimated almost 45 per cent of UK households have a pet – about 51million animals – mainly dogs.

Miss Newkirk, who once set fire to a car at a motor show and has stripped naked numerous times to publicize PETA's high-profile 'I'd Rather Go Naked Than Wear Fur' campaign, said the language used around animals is important. She wants people to describe the animals they look after as 'companions', adding: 'How we say things governs how we think about them, so a tweak in our language when we talk about the animals in our homes is needed.

'A pet is a commodity but animals should not be things on shelves or in boxes, where people say, 'I like the look of that one, it matches my curtains or my sense of myself.'

'Hopefully the time is passing for that kind of attitude.'

Some ethicists have argued that people should not keep pets at all. Last year, Dr. Corey Wrenn, from the University of Kent, said: 'Through this forced dependency and domestication, the lives of companion animals are almost completely controlled by humans. They can be terminated at any time for the most trivial of reasons, including behavioral 'problems'.' Miss Newkirk, who has written a book, called Animalkind, about animals' abilities and the need to be compassionate towards them, also wants phrases such as 'flog a dead horse' to stop being used because they refer to animal cruelty.

https://www.dailymail.co.uk/news/article-7954103/Dont-call-pet-pet-Animal-rights-charity-chief-says-term-derogatory.html

CBS Argues That Any Term With The Word 'Black' In It Is Racist

By Steve Watson March 11th, 2020

CBS News wants to reeducate America on how racist everyone is by policing their language and making them understand that the country's founding fathers were really awful bigots.

That's the overriding message that emerged from a Tuesday segment on *This Morning* where the anchors and their guests attempted to convince viewers that everyday terms with zero racial context are proof of how "the roots of racism" are deeply embedded in the US. The segment promoted a new book aimed at children titled 'Stamped From the Beginning: The Definitive History of Racist Ideas in America', by CBS News contributor Ibram X. Kendi and co-author Jason Reynolds.

Anchor Tony Dokoupil announced that "Many headlines referred to the stock market plunge yesterday as 'Black Monday,' and that is just one of the subtle and not-so-subtle ways that racism has been braided into our everyday culture." Co-host Anthony Mason then listed more terms with the word 'black' in them, ridiculously suggesting that they are all really racist.

"Terms like 'Black Monday,' 'Black Sheep,' can be freighted with a negative connotation that sometimes we don't even realize." he said, with the other co-host Michelle Miller chiming in that the terms are "baked into the vocabulary." A graphic then appeared on screen "Words With Negative Connotations: Black Monday, Black Sheep, Blackballing, Blackmail, Blacklisting."

"Yeah, and I don't think we even realize when you have a skin color and regular color and we're connoting both in a negative fashion. There are relationships between the two and I think we have to break not only the relationship, but those negative connotations." Kendi suggested.

Miller had earlier argued that children need to be reeducated about how racist the founding fathers were, saying that there are "so many misconceptions and truly lies throughout the history of what children are taught about their history."

"I hate to put it that directly, but, you know, when you go back and you look at people like a Thomas Jefferson, George Washington, these founding fathers who were so revered, how do you re-teach that?" she worried. So, just to summarise, even saying the word 'black' is now racist, terms that have no racial context, and refer specifically to the colour black are racist, and children need to be re-educated about how racist everyone is.

https://www.infowars.com/video-cbs-argues-that-any-term-with-the-word-black-in-it-is-racist/

UIllinois warns students against 'racist and xenophobic' coronavirus language

By Blair Nelson March 26th, 2020

The University of Illinois sent an email to all of its students relating to resources available online to students. In the email, the administration appeared to take a shot at the Trump administration for "racist and xenophobic language."

"All of you are valued members of our university community. It is distressing to hear racist and xenophobic language being used in national discourse about the COVID-19 pandemic," stated a campus-wide email signed by both Chancellor Robert J. Jones and Vice Chancellor of Student Affairs Dr. Danita M. B. Young.

"Such language is antithetical to the values of this university." Tweet This

"Such language is antithetical to the values of this university, and we expect everyone to treat one another with respect and dignity. Our university does not tolerate discrimination, and the stress of this moment should only strengthen our resolve to uphold our commitment to our community and our shared values." The email comes amid controversy surrounding President Donald Trump's choice to call the coronavirus the "Chinese Virus," because, as he has repeatedly pointed out, "it comes from China."

Professors are among those speaking out against this language as being "racist" toward Chinese people. Columbia University professor Marie Myung-Ok Lee responded to the president's statements by insisting that "white supremacy can be a factor even in the way that we name viruses — such as when the language around it, purportedly objective and scientific, stems from a white-centered, xenophobic perspective."

Georgia State University, shares a similar position, claiming that "the comments made by President Trump intensifies the xenophobia and racism that's become rampant against Asians and Asian Americans globally. He's fueling fears against Chinese specifically."

https://www.campusreform.org/?ID=14605

Florissant woman helps change Merriam Webster's definition of racism

By KMOV 4 Staff Jun 11th, 2020

A Florissant woman is using a different approach to make change.

While thousands of people have taken to the street to protest, Kennedy Mitchum, who recently graduated with a degree in law, politics and society, took to email. She said it all started when people would argue with her about the definition of racism and she realized the problem was in the pages of Merriam Webster's dictionary. "With everything going on, I think it's important everyone is on the same page," said Mitchum.

The dictionary defines racism as "a belief that race is the primary determinant of human traits and capacities and that racial differences produce an inherent superiority of a particular race." Mitchum said that definition was too simple and too surface level.

Get a Genuine Toyota Premium cabin air filter to start clearing out dust, pollen and more. Toyota has a great selection of Premium Cabin Air Filters that give you and your passengers a comfortable ride every time.

"So, a couple weeks ago, I said this is the last argument I'm going to have about this. I know what racism is, I've experienced it time and time and time again in a lot of different ways, so enough is enough. So, I emailed them about how I felt about it. Saying this needs to change," she said.

Mitchum is a Nerinx Hall graduate and just graduated from Drake University. She said she wasn't expecting anything from her email, but she knew she had to make an effort. "I basically told them they need to include that there is systematic oppression on people. It's not just 'I don't like someone,' it's a system of oppression for a certain group of people," Mitchum explained.

After a few back and forth emails, the editor of Merriam Webster Dictionary agreed and wrote back, "While our focus will always be on faithfully reflecting the real-world usage of a word, not on promoting any particular viewpoint, we have concluded that omitting any mention of the systemic aspects of racism promotes a certain viewpoint in itself."

Alex Chambers, the editor of Merriam Webster Dictionary, said a revision to the entry for "racism" is now being drafted. "This revision would not have been made without your persistence in contacting us about this problem. We sincerely thank you for repeatedly writing in and apologize for the harm and offense we have caused in failing to address the issue sooner. I will see to it that the entry for racism is given the attention it sorely needs," wrote Chambers. Chambers said they could not give a date on upcoming publications but that a revision should be expected in the coming months.

https://www.kmov.com/news/florissant-woman-helps-change-merriam-websters-definition-of-racism/article_30bba202-a9d9-11ea-ba9d-cb6e06fdc201.html

Language

The war on our language, in my opinion, is the worst offense from the assault orchestrated by the bi-coastal, wealthy, elite, social justice warrior, ivory tower left. By constantly lecturing people they are not allowed to say certain words or phrases, the attack on our entire system of communication breaks down. Here in the United States, we have what is called, "THE FIRST AMENDMENT." Some other countries have a similar, watered-down version of The First Amendment. Below is The First Amendment for all the Nazi speech police criticizing people for mis-gendering someone's preferred pronoun.

"Congress shall make no law respecting an establishment of religion, or prohibiting the free exercise thereof; or abridging the freedom of speech, or of the press; or the right of the people peaceably to assemble, and to petition the Government for a redress of grievances."

Perhaps these psychotic tenured professors who were once rolling around in the mud as hippies, bitching about their freedoms, should revisit this amendment and take notes.

3

The War on Sports

Vice Host Asks Jake Paul Ridiculous Question: 'Was it Racist to Knock a Black Man Out?'

By Nick Kangadis December 8th, 2020

I hope everyone's ready for the dumbest thing they'll hear and see all week. Heck, maybe all month! Vice hosts Cari Champion and race-baiting sports commentator Jemele Hill had YouTuber and boxer Jake Paul, who is white, on their program and asked him a pretty peculiar question about his recent exhibition knockout victory over retired NBA player Nate Robinson, who is black, in late November.

"Was it racist to knock a black man out?" Champion asked before stating that question was their "Question of the Week" (no joke). It apparently wasn't the first time Paul was asked the question, because he seemed pretty annoyed with the query.

"Stop asking me that," Paul responded. "I said no." After Champion repeated her question as if dumbfounded by the answer she received, she asked Paul again. Paul was not amused.

"It's a sh**ty question," Paul said. "It's a sport." If there's a chance you might not like the answer to your question, maybe don't ask the question, snowflake. Is it racist to call a black woman "snowflake?" I'm not up on what's been deemed racist in the last five minutes.Anyway, the hosts laughed at Paul's answer as if it were a foregone conclusion that it was, in fact, racist for Paul to knock out Robinson during a boxing matchup. "How does this have anything to do with race?" Paul asked after Champion kept pushing him.

Champion then followed up with advice for Paul — and presumably for white people.

"It's a fine question," Champion said. "We've gotta wake you up. You've gotta be part of this conversation." Funny how we never see a black boxer asked how if he thinks it's racist to knock out someone who isn't black. It never works the other way for race hustlers like Champion and Hill. They're always the victim.

Far-leftists like to divide people in every possible way, so it'll be interesting to see how they react the next time a black basketball player dunk on a white guy or the next time a black baseball player hits a home run off of a latino pitcher. Crickets. That's all you'll hear, which begs the question: Are the race hustlers the real purveyors of racism?

https://www.mrctv.org/blog/vice-hosts-ask-jake-paul-ridiculous-question

College athletic conference begins handing out participation trophies

By Dave Huber December 5th, 2020

Last weekend the politically correct sports world went all a ga-ga because Vanderbilt's Sarah Fuller made a kickoff in her team's football — to be clear, *American* football — game against Missouri.

With that kick, Fuller, a goalie for Vandy's women's soccer team, became the first female to appear in a major conference football match-up. The kickoff was Fuller's only action in the entire game. It went a paltry 30 yards (only 20 in the air), and would have gone out of bounds (a penalty) had not a Mizzou player stopped it.

Anyone who saw the kick and knows even a little about the sport was probably (rightly) guffawing. But not the sports/entertainment world ... and even the Southeastern Conference itself. ESPN tweeted "What an inspiration." A commentator who "got chills" at the play, said "That was pretty cool," "That was pretty awesome to see," and "What a moment." In post-game interviews, the press must have said "congratulations" more times in 40 minutes than in any time in history.

Incredibly, the SEC actually named Fuller one of its Special Teams Players of the Week for her "perfectly-executed kick." The player to share the honor actually *did* something — he ran back a punt 50 yards for a touchdown. The excuses — and that's exactly what they were — poured in for Fuller's pathetic one-time event: It was a "pre-planned" "squib" kick. A "mortar" kick. And even more laughable, an onside kick. But as Matt Walsh says, "there is no designed kick in all of football that calls for a kicker to boot it 20 yards to the sideline. And if there was such a designed kick, it's not the play you'd call when you're down 21 at the start of the third quarter."

The College Fix asked Vandy football media relations if Fuller indeed intended a "squib" kick, in addition to how far she could kick a field goal and what her tryout with the football team consisted of. The response was two links to post-game interviews.

The first doesn't address any of the queries until the very end ... sort of: A questioner states Fuller's kick was "as designed"(!) and then asks if she plans to do traditional kickoffs in the future (as in high in the air and towards the end zone). Fuller's response? She's wasn't going to "give anything out." In the second link, Fuller tells a questioner the longest field goal she "believes" she made in practice was 38 yards. (Thankfully, the questioner noted kicking a field goal in a game is a lot different than in practice.) Fuller later claims she and the other women's soccer team goalkeeper at one time were practicing kicking field goals — with a soccer ball — and that she made one from the 45-yard line.

Even more ridiculous was that Fuller felt the need to *rip her teammates* at halftime for their alleged lack of enthusiasm. A questioner (second link) asks Fuller about the etiquette surrounding such matters, and she admits the idea was all hers. She told another interviewer the following:

"If I'm going to be honest, I was a little pissed off at how quiet everybody was on the sideline," she said. "We made a first down, and I was the only one cheering and I was like — what the heck? What's going on? And I tried to get them pumped up." ... "I just went in there and I said exactly what I was thinking. I was like, 'We need to be cheering each other on. This is how you win games. This is how you get better is by calling each other out for stuff, and I'm going to call you guys out. We need to be supporting one another.'"

Joe Kinsey asks, "Do you think freshman players on the women's soccer team who've never seen the field get up and give speeches to players who've given four years to a program? Nope. Not happening." Imagine you were one of the Vandy football players sitting there in the locker room listening to Fuller. Your team hasn't won a game all season, you're currently getting smoked 21-0, and this politically correct person who "joined" the team less than a week ago is yammering at you about team spirit.

Indeed, you'll *never* hear of kickers doing such a thing in the NFL. They won't dare lecture the guys about "cheering," those who're busy grinding it out each and every play, sucking wind in the fourth quarter, all bruised and battered. And if one ever dared, he'd get a "lesson" in practice he'll never forget. I await news of some, or even just one, of Fuller's teammates who *did* take issue with this whole spectacle. That is, if they're brave enough to endure the politically correct backlash which inevitably would follow. They'd be called "misogynist," "male chauvinist" and likely would be reported to a "hate/bias" committee. After that, they'd be forced to apologize, and required to take a few workshops on "patriarchy" and "feminism."

Look at the bright side: If Joe Biden gets his way, men who identify as women soon will get full access to "sports, bathrooms and locker rooms in accordance with their gender identity." As such, maybe Vandy will get a "woman" kicker who can reach the end zone.

https://www.thecollegefix.com/college-athletic-conference-begins-handing-out-participation-trophies/

NHL's Chicago Blackhawks To Read 'Indigenous Land Statement' Before Each Home Game

By Hank Berrien November 2nd, 2020

On Sunday, the NHL's Chicago Blackhawks, marking the first day of Native American Heritage Month, announced that in deference to the Native American community, they will preface home games by reading an "Indigenous land acknowledgment."

The team said they would issue "a formal statement that recognizes the unique and enduring relationship that exists between Indigenous Peoples and their traditional territories," The Hill reported. The Blackhawks, founded in 1926, were one of the six original teams in the NHL, (along with the Boston Bruins, Detroit Red Wings, Montreal Canadians, New York Rangers, and Toronto Maple Leafs), and have won six Stanley Cups.

The team got its name from its original owner, Chicago coffee tycoon Frederic McLaughlin, who had been a commander with the 333rd Machine Gun Battalion of the 86thInfantry Division in World War I, which was nicknamed the "Blackhawk Division" after Black Hawk, a citizen of the Sauk nation. The team's name was spelled in two words as the "Black Hawks" until 1986, when the team changed it to one word because of the spelling found in the original franchise documents. NBC News added that the team released a "Land Acknowledgment" on Sunday that read:

The Chicago Blackhawks acknowledge that the team, its foundation, and the spaces we maintain, work and compete within, stand upon the traditional homelands of the Miami, Sauk, Fox, Ho-Chunk, Menominee, and the council of the Three Fires: the Ojibwe, Odawa, and Potawatomi Nations. We understand that this land holds immense significance for its original stewards, the Native Nations and the peoples of this region. We would also like to recognize that our team's namesake, Sauk War Leader Black Hawk, serves as a continuous reminder of our responsibility to the Native American communities we live amongst and draw inspiration from.

In October, a Blackhawks logo statue outside the United Center was defaced. "The Chicago Blackhawks announced earlier this year that it would not change its name despite the requests amid the protests over racial injustice. But it decided to ban fans from wearing headdresses when fans are allowed in-person again," The Hill added.

In July, the team stated that it would keep its name:

The Chicago Blackhawks' name and logo symbolizes an important and historic person, Black Hawk of Illinois' Sac & Fox Nation, whose leadership and life has inspired generations of Native Americans, veterans and the public. We celebrate Black Hawk's legacy by offering ongoing reverent examples of Native American culture, traditions and contributions, providing a platform for genuine dialogue with local and national Native American groups. As the team's popularity grew over the past decade, so did that platform and our work with these important organizations.

We recognize there is a fine line between respect and disrespect, and we commend other teams for their willingness to engage in that conversation. Moving forward, we are committed to raising the bar even higher to expand awareness of Black Hawk and the important contributions of all Native American people. We will continue to serve as stewards of our name and identity, and will do so with a commitment to evolve. Our endeavors in this area have been sincere and multi-faceted, and the path forward will draw on that experience to grow as an organization and expand our efforts.

https://www.dailywire.com/news/nhls-chicago-blackhawks-to-read-indigenous-land-statement-before-each-home-game

High School Football Players Suspended For Flying Flags to Honor 9/11 Cops & Firefighters

By Paul Joseph Watson September 15th, 2020

Two high school football players were suspended indefinitely after they carried flags onto the field honoring police officers and firefighters who lost their lives on 9/11. On Friday, the two Little Miami High School players took to the field carrying a Thin Blue Line and a Thin Red Line flag. When asked by Local 12 whether he was trying to make a political statement, senior cornerback Brady Williams, whose father is a police officer, responded, “No, not at all. I was just doing it to honor the people that lost their lives 19 years ago.”

Jarad Bentley, who carried the Thin Red Flag, told the station, “I was all for it. Because my dad is a firefighter, and if it had been him killed on 9/11, I would have wanted someone to do it for him.” However, the pair were suspended indefinitely by the school’s superintendent after disobeying an order not to carry the flags.

“We can’t have students who decide to do something anyway after they’ve been told that they shouldn’t be doing it,” said Gregory Power, who claimed the flags were expressing a “political perspective” that other families may not agree with. Power subsequently claimed he was getting “hate” messages from people who disagreed with his decision. While people are allowed and even encouraged to show deference and support at sports games for Black Lives Matter, a violent revolutionary Marxist group, honoring 9/11 victims is apparently a “political statement.” However, Williams was defiant, telling the station, “I realize that this was more than just a football team; these guys are now my brothers.”

https://summit.news/2020/09/15/high-school-football-players-suspended-for-flying-flags-to-honor-9-11-cops-firefighters/

The Trouble With Renaming the Redskins

By R.J. Petrella September 13th, 2020

Any word is a degree of separation or two from controversy. That's a reality facing the Washington Football Team, formerly known as the Redskins, as they choose a new name. Virtually anything can be found to have repugnant associations, and this poses a barrier if one is trying to cleanse a team name, or more generally the American culture, of tainted ideas or their representations. To further illustrate the point, let's look at all of the current NFL team nicknames through a post-modernist, neo-Marxist lens.

AFC East

New England Patriots

Webster defines "patriot" as "a person who loves and strongly supports or fights for his or her country." The name evokes nationalism, which is by definition exclusionary.

New York Jets

Private jets (which NFL teams use) are symbols of wealth, privilege, and gross economic inequality. In addition, the color "jet black" has often been used as a caricature or misrepresentation of a black person's skin color. See Golliwog or Pretty Little Thing ads.

Buffalo Bills

Buffalo Bill Cody was an American soldier-turned-showman, and, as documented in *Sorrow of the Earth: Buffalo Bill, Sitting Bull and the Tragedy of Show Business* by E. Vuillard, he paraded Native Americans around in his circus-like road shows, often to abuse and humiliation by audiences.

Miami Dolphins

As described in *Signs and Mysteries: Revealing Ancient Christian Symbols*, by M. Aquilina, dolphins were used in early Christian art to represent Christ. The name is thus religiously prejudicial.

AFC North

Baltimore Ravens

Odin's Raven is a Viking symbol that has been misappropriated by neo-Nazi groups (e.g., see Odin's Chosen protests in Fredericksburg, Virginia) to help propagate their messages of racism and white supremacy. See also Minnesota Vikings, below.

Cincinnati Bengals

Tigers have been symbols of imperial racism, particularly in India, where the first Prime Minister, Pandit Jawaharlal Nehru, wrote of "the tiger qualities of an imperial race," in reference to the English. Bengal is a region including part of India and Bangladesh where British colonial war policies helped bring on the famine of 1943, which killed two to three million people.

Cleveland Browns

The term "brown" or "Brown American" has been used as a term in popular culture for some South Asian Americans, Hispanics, and Luso Latinos.

Pittsburgh Steelers

As documented in the film *Struggles In Steel: A Story of African-American Steelworkers*, discriminatory work practices sanctioned by the Steelworkers' Organizing Committee kept African American steel workers in hazardous, low-paying "Negro Jobs" for decades.

AFC South

Houston Texans

"Texas" is derived from the Caddo word "Taysha," which the Spaniards spelled as "Tejas." The Caddo are a group of Native American tribes who at their height occupied much of East Texas and nearby areas, numbering upwards of 200,000 people. Exposure to European epidemic diseases led to a catastrophic decline in the population to 10,000 by the late 1600s.

Indianapolis Colts

"Colt" evokes Samuel Colt, the inventor who made the mass production of revolvers commercially viable (e.g., "Colt 45"). He was a "copperhead" — a Northerner who opposed Lincoln — and sold weapons to both sides during the Civil War. He monitored his employees' voting patterns and fired "black republicans."

Jacksonville Jaguars

Jaguars were rulers of the underworld in Mayan culture. Jaguar Paw is the hero in the Mel Gibson film *Apocalypto*, which has been accused of conveying racist messages about Mayan peoples and Native Americans more generally.

Tennessee Titans

"Grand Titan" was a title in the Ku Klux Klan hierarchy for the head of a congressional district or "Dominion."

AFC West

Denver Broncos

Bucking broncos are symbolic of rodeos, which historically marginalized blacks, Hispanics, and women. See *Gender, Whiteness, and Power in Rodeo*, by Patton and Schedlock.

Kansas City Chiefs

"Chief" is a (mostly outdated) term for leaders at various levels of tribal societies. It is often considered derogatory when used by outsiders to refer to or address Native Americans.

Las Vegas Raiders

Various confederate units that fought in the Civil War were known as "Raiders." Morgan's Raiders were cavalrymen under the command of Gen. John Hunt Morgan. Quantrill's Raiders were pro-Confederate guerillas who fought under William Quantrill.

Los Angeles Chargers

A charger is an appliance for inserting a charge of powder or shot into a gun. The term thus evokes firearms, which can be symbols of oppression.

NFC East

Dallas Cowboys

"Cowboy" is evocative of the "Cowboys and Indians" film genre, which often portrayed Native Americans as wild, irrational savages. In addition, after reconstruction, black cowboys were discriminated against, typically assigned less desirable work, and denied managerial positions. Mexican cowboys were often paid far less than white hires.

New York Giants

The Giants of Greek and Roman mythology were a superior race of men, endowed with great strength and aggression. The name thereby evokes notions of racial superiority.

Philadelphia Eagles

In the ancient world the eagle was the bird of emperors, and later the double eagle became a symbol of multiple empires, including the Holy Roman Empire. In the 1920s, the eagle was used as a symbol of the Nazi Party in Germany, and it has been adopted by modern-day neo-Nazi groups.

Washington Football Team

There is no nickname here, but George Washington owned slaves for 56 years. The word "football" itself is thought to have been used in Medieval Europe to refer to games played "on foot" by peasants, as opposed to games played on horseback by the aristocracy. In fact, the phrase "you base football player" is used as an insult in *King Lear.*

NFC North

Chicago Bears

"Bears" in the stock market are investors who bet that stocks will go down, thereby profiting handsomely while most ordinary investors (e.g., most owners of 401K plans) watch the destruction of their nest eggs. In this way, the bear is symbolic of capitalist exploitation.

Detroit Lions

The lion is a symbol of power and domination. See political criticisms of *The Lion King*. The Lion and the Sun is a symbol associated with pre-revolutionary Iran and is thought by some to represent oppressive Westernizing monarchy.

Green Bay Packers

"Packer" is a slang term for a fake penis and a derogatory term for a homosexual man.

It can also refer to a "body packer" or "mule," an individual who smuggles illegal drugs by ingesting packs full of them.

Minnesota Vikings

The Vikings were raiders and traders from southern Scandinavia in the eighth to 11th centuries. Although there is historical evidence that they were multiracial, they have been held up as symbols of white supremacy, e.g., by Nazis in the 1930s, who imagined them as their Germanic predecessors, and by modern-day white supremacists.

NFC South

Atlanta Falcons

In the ancient world, the falcon was seen as the bird of princes. The Egyptian pharaohs, who often presided over tens of thousands of slaves, were considered the living embodiment of the falcon-god, Horus. Falcons were released at their funerals.

Carolina Panthers

The name "Panthers" evokes the "Black Panthers," a political party founded in 1966 to challenge police brutality against black Americans. Use of the term trivializes that movement.

New Orleans Saints

"Saint" is a religious term that most Americans identify as Christian, thereby making it exclusionary to non-believers.

Tampa Bay Buccaneers

Buccaneers were pirates who in the 1600s and 1700s not only attacked Spanish ships in the Caribbean but also pillaged and plundered coastal areas. Use of the term celebrates violence against innocents and thereby mocks legitimate anti-establishment action.

NFC West

Arizona Cardinals

"Cardinal" is a religious term indicating a high-ranking position within the Catholic or Anglican church hierarchy, and as such its use as a team name is exclusionary to members of other religions and non-believers.

Los Angeles Rams

"Ram" has various religious connections. In the Bible, the ram is a symbol of God's provision. "Jai Shri Ram" is an allusion to the Hindu deity Ram, and the phrase has been used as a rallying cry by far-right groups in India against a Muslim minority.

San Francisco 49ers

"49er" refers to an individual who participated in the California Gold Rush of the 1840s and '50s, which had a severe impact on the indigenous peoples and environment of California. The Native American population of the region is estimated to have dropped from some 300,000 before European Americans arrived to 30,000 by 1870.

Seattle Seahawks

Skuas (sea hawks) are kleptoparasites — they wait for a gull or other bird to catch a fish and then steal it. They kill penguin chicks and other birds. More generally, hawks are swift, ferocious predators and have been often used as symbols of military might. Politically, a "hawk" is someone who is more apt to favor military aggression than peaceful negotiation.

This list isn't meant to parody the neo-Marxist, "cancel culture" point of view, which seems to be growing in popularity by the day, as much as to illustrate what's wrong with it. If every NFL team were to adopt a new nickname tomorrow, we would likely be able to repeat the above exercise with ease and similar results. And this could go on indefinitely. There was more material on this first pass, in fact, that was edited out for length.

This is no doubt part of the reason why the Washington Football Team announced in July that it will go without a nickname at least through the end of this season. The natural connectedness of ideas means that the search for links to inequitable power relationships will almost always bear fruit. So, the cost of decontamination is sterility. Just as important, the identification of these links often amounts to "biased sampling": one can always choose the worst relationships of a word, symbol, individual, or institution and present them as characteristic. Obviously, that is misleading, and the extirpation that can result is costly.

The conclusion to draw is not that every NFL team nickname is equally offensive or that our cultural symbols never need updating. But when we pledge to rid a sports league, or more broadly a culture, of its negative associations, we risk committing ourselves to the cancellation of much more than we might have at first expected.

https://spectator.org/redskins-new-name-washington-football-team/

NBA fires photographer that posted offensive meme about Kamala Harris

By Kaelan Deese August, 14th, 2020

An NBA photographer was fired following an offensive meme he posted this week on social media referencing Sen. Kamala Harris (D-Calif.), former Vice President Joe Biden's selected 2020 presidential campaign running mate.

The now-fired photographer, Bill Baptist, worked with the Houston Rockets for more than 30 years, USA Today reported. An anonymous source familiar with the matter told USA Today that Baptist had been removed from the NBA bubble at Disney property in Orlando, Fla. WNBA Hall of Fame recipient Sheryl Swoopes chimed in on Facebook about Baptist's termination, adding that he had covered photos for the Comets, as well.

"It's amazing how people will smile in your face but eventually their true colors will show. @NBA and Houston Rockets he needs to GO!!! So disrespectful. Bill Baptiste (sic) shame on You!!!"

According to a local NBC affiliate KPRC 2, Baptist posted an image that read "Joe and the Hoe." A spokesperson for the NBA told KPRC 2 that Baptist is an "independent contractor, and his services are no longer being used in Orlando." Baptist shared a statement with the local affiliate, issuing an apology for the photo he posted and saying that the photo has since been removed.

"I deeply regret posting on my Facebook page a phrase that I saw and copied from others as a sample of some people's reactions to Biden's selection of Senator Harris as his choice for VP," Baptist wrote in the statement. "The phrase I posted does not reflect my personal views at all," he added. "I should not have been so insensitive to post the statements by others. I sincerely apologize to all of those who have rightfully been offended."

https://thehill.com/blogs/in-the-know/in-the-know/512091-nba-fires-photographer-that-posted-offensive-meme-about-kamala

Martina Navratilova dropped by LGBT group over trans athletes' row

By Rob Picheta & James Masters February 20th, 2019

(CNN) An LGBT group has cut ties with tennis great Martina Navratilova after she said it was a form of "cheating" for transgender women to be allowed to compete in women's sport.

New York-based Athlete Ally, which supports LGBT sportspeople, called the comments transphobic and removed the 18-time Grand Slam winner from its advisory board and as an ambassador. Navratilova wrote in The Sunday Times that it was "insane" that transgender athletes who "decide" to become female had achieved honors "that were beyond their capabilities as men."

"Martina Navratilova's recent comments on trans athletes are transphobic, based on a false understanding of science and data, and perpetuate dangerous myths that lead to the ongoing targeting of trans people," Athlete Ally said in a statement. "Trans women are women, period. They did not decide their gender identity any more than someone decides to be gay, or to have blue eyes," the group added.

"They are women, and want to compete in the sport they love, just as any other athlete would." The move follows a flurry of criticism directed at Navratilova, a gay rights campaigner who herself suffered homophobic abuse when she came out in 1981, for her Sunday Times column.

Navratilova, who competed for Czechoslovakia and the United States, wrote that "it would not be fair" if she had to play against a transgender woman. But trans rights group Trans Actual responded on Twitter: "We're pretty devastated to discover that Martina Navratilova is transphobic. If trans women had an advantage in sport, why aren't trans women winning gold medals left, right & center?"

"Trans women don't have an advantage. Look up the changes that estrogen makes to the body," they added. Navratilova has defended her comments, tweeting to CNN on Tuesday that the controversy is "not about me and it is not about whether I was criticized or not -- you ought to talk about the actual issues I raised instead." According to current rules issued by the International Olympic Committee in 2016, trans men are allowed to compete without restriction. Trans women, however, must show that their testosterone level has been below a certain level for at least 12 months before their first competition.

'Irrational fear'

Navratilova has caused controversy for her comments on transgender athletes before.

In December she was criticized after tweeting: "You can't just proclaim yourself a female and be able to compete against women. There must be some standards, and having a penis and competing as a woman would not fit that standard." Those comments led to her becoming embroiled in an online argument with cyclist Rachel McKinnon, the first transgender woman to win a world track cycling title in October 2018.

Athlete Ally said it had reached out to Navratilova after that incident but had not heard back. "We believe that growth is possible, and we extend once again to Martina the invitation to learn from this experience," the group said Tuesday.

McKinnon reacted to Navratilova's latest comments by tweeting: "It's a wild fantasy worry that is an irrational fear of something that doesn't happen. An irrational fear of trans people? Transphobia." Navratilova rejected accusations of transphobia, adding that she deplores "what seems to be a growing tendency among transgender activists to denounce anyone who argues against them and to label them all as 'transphobes.'" She also highlighted her friendship with Renée Richards, the transgender tennis player who campaigned to be able to play in the women's US Open.

https://www.cnn.com/2019/02/20/tennis/martina-navratilova-dropped-lgbt-group-scli-spt-intl/index.html

Report: CFL's Edmonton Eskimos to Change Team Name

By Dylan Gwinn July 18th, 2020

It seems as though the Washington Redskins won't be the only North American professional football team changing their name in the near future. According to TSN, the Edmonton Eskimos of the Canadian Football League will also make a change in nickname due to concerns that the current team name is a racial slur. While the team has always claimed the name is intended to be respectful to Canada's Inuit population, there has been a strong contingent of activists who claim the name is a slur.

In 2015, an Inuit politician named Natan Obed, penned an op-ed about the team name claiming, "we are not mascots or emblems."

"In a time when we still struggle to be heard, where there is vast indifference to our socio-economic condition, where we still fight for acceptance and respect from Canadians every day, dominant society continues to use us, a minority indigenous people, as their mascots for their sports entertainment," Obed wrote

"Allowing this practice is a fundamental departure from how we wish to be treated in all other conversations we have with Canada."

Recent world events, such as the spate of protests and riots following the death of George Floyd have brought added pressure to the team. The same type of pressure that convinced the Washington Redskins to announce last week that they were changing their 88-year-old name. Like the Redskins, the Eskimos expect to announce a new name for the team, soon.

https://www.breitbart.com/sports/2020/07/18/report-cfls-edmonton-eskimos-to-change-team-name/

Atlanta Braves Remove Tomahawk Chop Statue

By Todd Starnes July 19th, 2020

As I wrote in my new book, "Culture Jihad: How to Stop the Left From Killing a Nation," there is a concerted effort to destroy American culture. Click here to read Culture Jihad – and I would really encourage to do that so you can understand how we can fight back.

From statues and monuments to paintings and books, the leftist radicals are turning our history and our traditions into a pile of rubble. The Washington Redskins decided to purge their team's name. So did the Cleveland Indians. And now comes word that the Atlanta Braves have decided to embrace wokeness. To their initial credit, they decided to keep the Braves name, but they are doing away with the popular "tomahawk chop."

And there are reports that a beautiful tomahawk chop statue outside the stadium has been taken down. "Through our conversations, changing the name of the Braves is not under consideration or deemed necessary. We have great respect and reverence for our name and the Native American communities that have held meaningful relationships with us do as well. We will always be the Atlanta Braves," the Braves wrote in a letter to ticket holders.

"As it relates to the fan experience, including the chop, it is one of the many issues that we are working through with the advisory group. The chop was popularized by our fans when Deion Sanders joined our team and it continues to inspire our players on the field. With that in mind, we are continuing to listen to the Native American community, as well as our fans, players, and alumni to ensure we are making an informed decision on this part of our fan experience."

The Braves have yet to explain why they removed the statue.

https://www.toddstarnes.com/values/atlanta-braves-remove-tomahawk-chop-statue/

Major League Baseball deems 'disabled list' too offensive

By Anthony Barstow February 7th, 2019

Say goodbye to Major League Baseball's disabled list.

The league will rename the disabled list the "injured list," according to an ESPN report, for fear the term "disabled" could offend. The rules of the "injured list" will remain the same as before, and the new moniker actually brings MLB more in line with other major North American sports leagues. The NBA has an inactive list, the NHL has the injured reserve list, and the NFL features both the injured reserve list and the physically unable to perform list.

The first official disabled list was introduced by the National League in 1915, so after 104 years, perhaps it was finally time to get with the times.

https://nypost.com/2019/02/07/major-league-baseball-deems-disabled-list-too-offensive/?utm_source=facebook_sitebuttons&utm_medium=site+buttons&utm_campaign=site+buttons

NBA teams moving away from 'owner' title

By Ethan Sears June 3rd, 2019

The NBA may be backing down from using the word "owner" due to racial insensitivity. After Golden State Warriors star Draymond Green argued against using the term on LeBron James' HBO show "The Shop" late last year, the issue gained steam, per TMZ Sports, and at least two teams have already stopped using it. "You shouldn't say owner," Green said, saying it should be changed to CEO, chairman or majority shareholder.

The Sixers have since changed the title of their owners to managing partners, and Steve Ballmer of the Clippers is listed as chairman on the team's website. "When your product is purely the labor of people, then owner sounds like something that is of a feudal nature," Jon Stewart said on "The Shop."

However, TMZ notes that there isn't pressure coming from the NBA to change the titles. "We refer to the owners of our teams as Governors," the league told TMZ in a statement, "each team is represented on our Board of Governors."

https://nypost.com/2019/06/03/nba-teams-moving-away-from-owner-title/

Navy football scraps 'Load the Clip' motto over insensitivity to those affected by gun violence

By Ryan Gaydos August 5th, 2019

Navy football dropped the "Load the Clip" motto it planned to use for the 2019 season as it was deemed insensitive to those affected by gun violence, the school's superintendent said Friday.

The slogan, which was chosen by senior captains of the football team, is insensitive to the community and inappropriate, superintendent Vice Admiral Sean S. Buck told the Capital Gazette in a statement.

"It is always my priority, part of my mission statement, for the Navy to be a good neighbor," Buck said. "The bottom line is, we missed the mark here. The initial internal football team motto selected, 'Load the Clip,' was inappropriate and insensitive to the community we call home, and for that, I take responsibility for, and apologize to not only the Capital Gazette, but the entire Annapolis community."

According to Capital Gazette, the motto was changed from "Load the Clip" after reporters started to ask Navy officials about its context amid the spate of mass shootings and the shooting that left five people dead at the newspaper's offices in June 2018.

Cmdr. Alana Garas, a Naval Academy spokeswoman, told the Capital Gazette the motto was a metaphor for gameday prep. Coach Ken Niumtalolo has said he was leery of the slogan but recognized that midshipmen have some familiarity with firearms and the slogan was intended to reflect a commitment to being prepared.

The school will now use "Win the Day" as its motto.

https://www.foxnews.com/sports/navy-football-load-the-clip-motto-scrapped

Tom Brady's popularity tied to rise in 'white rage and white supremacy,' professor says

By Ryan Gaydos September 27th 2019

It's not the six Super Bowls.

It's not the three MVP awards.

It's not the three All-Pro selections.

And it's definitely not the 14 Pro Bowl selections.

The real reason why Tom Brady is popular is because, you guessed it, white supremacy.

Kyle Kusz, a kinesiology professor at the University of Rhode Island, published a book this month titled "Making American White Men

Great Again: Tom Brady, Donald Trump, and the Allure of White Male Omnipotence in Post-Obama America." He theorized that Brady became popular due to the rise of "white rage and white supremacy," according to Campus Reform.

Brady's relationship with the media and President Trump is analyzed in the book, according to Campus Reform. The professor highlights a 2015 Under Armour commercial which depicts thousands of Tom Bradys working out and tells the audience to "Rule Yourself." Kusz says the commercial "would not seem out of place in Leni Reifenstahl's infamous Nazi propaganda film, 'Triumph des willens.'"

Kusz told Campus Reform it was the specific commercial from 2015 which drove him to analyze Brady further. "I decided to research Trump and Brady's public performances of their white masculinities and how they connect with broader debates about race and gender politics after a student in one of my classes brought the Under Armour commercial to my attention and it piqued my interest," he said.

Kusz also hammers home the point of who Brady surrounds himself with outside football, specifically with who he takes to the Kentucky Derby with each year. He told the website that because he brings mostly white teammates with him to the event it "tells a more particular story about the racial company he chooses to keep."

"It is a vision of Brady as a wealthy, white man who unapologetically enjoys, and has even made a habit out of, spending time with other wealthy white men who treasure time 'with the boys' over all others," he said. Going to the Derby, Kusz added, "suggests his performance of white masculinity shares much in common with President Trump's" because most of the Derby's attendees include elite white people.

The professor, a New York native who received a doctorate from the University of Illinois at Urbana-Champaign, also cites Brady's failure to denounce Trump and his intense diet as evidence of how his "white masculinity is repeatedly constructed."

https://www.foxnews.com/sports/tom-brady-popularity-tied-white-supremacy

No foam tomahawks on seats at Braves ballpark after comments by Cards' Helsley; other changes expected

By Derrick Goold October 9th, 2019

ATLANTA — When fans arrived Wednesday at SunTrust Park for Game 5 of the National League Division Series, one of the most important playoff games for the Atlanta Braves in more than a decade, there was something missing from their seats.

The foam tomahawks that had been placed at each seat before games 1 and 2 of this series against the Cardinals were not there this time. Rookie Ryan Helsley's comments after Game 1 about how he found the Braves' 'Tomahawk Chop' chant "a disappointment" and "disrespectful" to his Cherokee heritage prompted the Braves to consider how they promote the cheer and how they could alter their game-day practices as a result of Helsley's thoughts.

Two officials at the ballpark confirmed that the foam tomahawks were not at the seats in response to Helsley's comments and the conversations the team had as a result of them. There will be other changes during the in-game entertainment and fan interaction involving the "chop" that will be different from games 1 and 2.

"We're sensitive to it," a Braves spokesperson said. In Game 1 of the NLDS, Helsley entered the game with one out in the eighth inning. The Braves had encouraged their fans to join in the "Tomahawk Chop" chant several times throughout the game — including just before the Braves' lineup was announced — and did so again in the crucible of that late-inning moment. The cheer was not directed at Helsley, and it's doubtful Atlanta was even aware of his deep, family ties and his place in Cherokee Nation.

Helsley said he was not aware of the chant as he warmed up on the mound and only later heard it was going on. But he had heard it earlier in the game, and he was prompted by that experience to do research later that night about its origin and use in Atlanta.

The day after Helsley's comments appeared in the Post-Dispatch, the Braves issued a statement that they would "continue to evaluate how we activate elements of our brand, as well as the in-game experience." The changes Wednesday underscore that comment. Helsley got a lot of feedback from his comments, some negative and some vulgar. He also said Wednesday that he received a lot of supportive comments, suggesting that it was important that he, having been on the mound during the chant, discuss his opinion.

He did not hear personally from Atlanta officials. Helsley imagines that he will hear from the crowd during Game 5 and is unsure what will greet him if he pitches. After this story was posted, Atlanta issued a statement to the media about the changes: "Out of respect for the concerns expressed by Mr. Helsley, we will take several efforts to reduce the Tomahawk Chop during our in-ballpark presentation today. Among other things, these steps include not distributing foam tomahawks to each seat and not playing the accompanying music or using Chop-related graphics when Mr. Helsley is in the game. As stated earlier, we will continue to evaluate how we activate elements of our brand, as well as the overall in-game experience. We look forward to a continued dialogue with those in the Native American community after the postseason concludes."

Atlanta's officials have considered what they'll put on the scoreboard and the role the stadium's urging for cheers could be a part of that. Of course, the "chop" can still develop organically through the crowd, as it did when it first became part of the playoffs and ballpark atmosphere in Atlanta.

"I respect Ryan's opinion. All he's doing is trying to support his heritage," Cardinals manager Mike Shildt said. "He's sincere about his heritage and the thoughts behind it. I don't think he's got anything malicious toward it. I think he was just honest about it. And I respect that completely. ... Hels is a pro. And the hope would be, look, he was speaking out of sincerity. He wasn't speaking out of maliciousness or anything like that.

"So people can take that in whatever context they want to take it in, and how they react is how they react," the manager concluded. "But I'm sure Ryan will pitch equally good regardless."

https://www.stltoday.com/sports/baseball/professional/birdland/no-foam-tomahawks-on-seats-at-braves-ballpark-after-comments/article_c13d5386-93bb-514e-9555-98427108f8d6.html

Fox Sports 1's Marcellus Wiley Unloads on NBA Plan to Paint 'Black Lives Matter' on Courts

By Stephen Kruiser July 3rd, 2020

There are some fantastic points made here by the co-host of FS1's *Speak for Yourself,* Marcellus Wiley, on the NBA's plan to paint "Black Lives Matter" on courts when the league starts playing again. After his co-host Emmanuel Acho asks Wiley if he thinks this is a "good idea," Wiley very diplomatically, but emphatically lays out his reasoning behind why he thinks it isn't.

He first wonders "how much social space is allowed for those who don't support" whichever political idea is being freely expressed. I think we all know the answer to that one. Wiley then notes that identity politics "divides and polarizes...no matter how great the intentions are."

He then dives into the mission statement of Black Lives Matter the organization. There are a lot of people who support the "black lives matter" sentiment which can then be misconstrued as support for Black Lives Matter the organization. The latter has some very disturbing points in its mission statement and Wiley takes particular umbrage with one of them here.

It will be most interesting to see if the cancel crowd comes for Wiley now. He's been a popular fixture on sports television for years now but having a solid professional record doesn't help much once the rage mob shows up on Twitter with virtual pitchforks.

https://pjmedia.com/news-and-politics/stephen-kruiser/2020/07/03/fox-sports-1s-marcellus-wiley-unloads-on-nba-plan-to-paint-black-lives-matter-on-courts-n601246

Mike Gundy Agrees to Take $1 Million Pay Cut After Review Prompted by Backlash over OAN Shirt

By Dylan Gwinn July 3rd, 2020

Mike Gundy, the Oklahoma State football coach who faced strong backlash last month after being spotted wearing an OAN shirt, has agreed to accept a $1 million pay cut and a one-year reduction in contract length. "The changes were offered up by Mike Gundy, and I commend him for that. It was his idea to take a million-dollar pay cut," Oklahoma State Athletic Director Mike Holder said on Friday. "I think it really demonstrates his commitment to being a better coach. He wanted to make a statement that assured all the players that this wasn't just about talk, this is more about action, and that's the first step."

As ESPN reports, "In addition to the pay cut, Holder said the contract length was shortened from five to four years, his buyout was cut from $5 million to $4 million, and his guarantee dropped from 75% to 50%."

Holder hastened to add, "I want to emphasize, every one of those was offered up by Mike Gundy." The salary reduction and contract reduction come as at least a bit of a surprise. Gundy did, after all, apologize for any "pain and discomfort" he caused by wearing the OAN shirt.

In addition, the review conducted by the university did not uncover any actual instances of racism in Gundy's program. So why was Gundy further punished?

"This wasn't about a T-shirt," Holder explained. "This was about a lot of things. The missing link has been a more personal relationship with their head coach. They respect him as an excellent game-day coach, but they want more coaching on a personal level. This crosses all racial lines. To a man, our players want a better connection to Mike Gundy. They view him as a difference-maker, and they want him to help them grow as leaders.

"As uncomfortable as the last two weeks have been, I believe this experience has changed Mike Gundy and our players will be the beneficiaries," Holder said. Holder added, "All the players should be commended for having the courage to speak out. We need more of that in society, not less. That doesn't mean the players are in control." Though, given that it was a player, star running back Chuba Hubbard, who publicly criticized his head coach for wearing the OAN shirt. And, Gundy apologized for wearing the shirt despite the fact that he clearly likes the network. Coupled with the fact that the players apparently criticized Gundy enough during the school's review that administrators felt Gundy deserved even more punishment. One could be forgiven for thinking that the players are indeed, in control.

https://www.breitbart.com/sports/2020/07/03/mike-gundy-agrees-to-take-1-million-pay-cut-after-review-prompted-by-backlash-over-oan-shirt/

MLB's Cleveland Indians to Change Team Name, Mascot

By Claire Russel July 6th, 2020

The Cleveland Indians baseball team said on Sunday that the team will change its name, citing concerns over racial division and tension.

"I know in the past, when I've been asked about, whether it's our name or the Chief Wahoo, I think I would usually answer and say I know that we're never trying to be disrespectful," said the team's manager, Terry Francona, according to CNN. "And I still feel that way," he continued. "But I don't think that's a good enough answer today. I think it's time to move forward. It's a very difficult subject. It's also delicate."

The baseball team announced last week that it was considering changing its name, since its "among the most visible ways in which we connect with the community." The team had previously removed its "Chief Wahoo" logo, a caricature of a Native American that activists argued was racist. The team name, however, was in part a tribute to the success of Louis Sockalexis, a former Native American star in Cleveland, according to *Cleveland Magazine*. Despite this, the team admitted that its name does not "advance social justice and equality."

The Cleveland Indians are one of several professional sports teams featuring Native-American roots. After facing pressure from its stadium sponsor, FedEx, the NFL's Washington Redskins also announced last week that the team would undergo a "thorough review" of its name, following years of perennial complaints from left-wing activist groups. Dan Snyder, owner of the Redskins, has long defended the name despite this criticism, but the demands from FedEx and other major sponsors—including Nike—seem to have have outweighed the principle.

"This process allows the team to take into account not only the proud tradition and history of the franchise but also input from our alumni, the organization, sponsors, the National Football League and the local community it is proud to represent on and off the field," Snyder said in a statement on Friday.

https://www.libertyheadlines.com/cleveland-indians-change-name/

Charles Barkley says sports becoming woke 'circus' -- with no real results

By Brie Stimson July 11th, 2020

Sports leagues and players have turned racial justice issues into a "circus" by focusing more on who's kneeling or what message is written on players' jerseys rather than real change, basketball Hall of Famer Charles Barkley said Friday. "I think we're missing the point," the former 76ers, Suns and Rockets star told CNBC. "We need police reform, we need prison reform. ... My concern is turning this into a circus instead of trying to do some good stuff." The media contributes to the "circus" by focusing on kneeling and messages on buses and jerseys, he added.

What the country really needs, he said, is "good cops out there policing the bad cops." He pointed out that while the U.S. is a divided country, "sports used to be a place where fans could go get away from reality." The media contributes to the "circus" by focusing on kneeling and messages on buses and jerseys, he added.

What the country really needs, he said, is "good cops out there policing the bad cops." He pointed out that while the U.S. is a divided country, "sports used to be a place where fans could go get away from reality." And as fans financially struggle during the coronavirus pandemic, "they don't want to see a bunch of rich people" constantly talking about social justice issues, he said.

As more players have started to kneel for the national anthem amid Black Lives Matter protests that have swept the country, NBA players will be allowed to have anti-racism messages on the backs of their jerseys, CNBC reported. But Barkley was skeptical about how fans will respond as NBA and other games resume this summer.

"The last thing they want to do is turn on the television and hear arguments all the time. It's going to be very interesting to see how the public reacts," he said. On the coronavirus, Barkley said, "you'd have to be a fool" to think children would be safe in a classroom, adding that it's not fair to put kids in that situation -- at least until there's a vaccine. He added, however, that keeping kids out of school would "magnify" the disparity between rich and poor kids because disadvantaged children don't always have the resources such as internet to continue their education remotely.

He said he hopes NBA games can go forward soon because the economic loss - if games are canceled - would be so great. "This is a critical time in our country," he added. "I just hope we get some adults who know what they are doing and stop screwing around and dividing our country."

https://www.foxnews.com/sports/charles-barkley-says-sports-becoming-woke-circus-with-no-real-results

NFL's Washington Redskins will change name and logo, team says

By Homero De la Fuente July 13th, 2020

The National Football League's Washington franchise will change the Redskins name and logo, the team announced Monday in a statement. The new name of the team was not revealed. The announcement comes just days after the team said that a "thorough review" of the name would be conducted. The name has long been denounced by Native American groups as an ethnic slur.

"That review has begun in earnest," Monday's statement said. "As part of this process, we want to keep our sponsors, fans and community apprised of our thinking as we go forward. Today, we are announcing we will be retiring the Redskins name and logo upon completion of this review." Team owner Daniel Snyder and head coach Ron Rivera "are working closely to develop a new name and design approach that will enhance the standing of our proud, tradition rich franchise and inspire our sponsors, fans and community for the next 100 years."

Rivera told The Washington Post in an interview he was working with Snyder on a name that would honor both the military and Native Americans. Following weeks of protests denouncing racism and as the country continues to confront systems of oppression more directly in recent weeks, the Washington Redskins are the first team to announce a name change. The Major League Baseball's Cleveland Indians have also pledged to reexamine their name. The team's manager recently said he believes it's time to change the name and "it's time to move forward."

The decision to re-examine the Washington name also came amid mounting pressure from several corporate sponsors, including FedEx, who have the naming rights to the team's stadium. Other brands, including Nike and Amazon, have removed the team's merchandise from their online stores.

https://www.cnn.com/2020/07/13/us/washington-redskins-nickname-change-spt/index.html

49ers announcer Tim Ryan suspended over 'dark skin' comment about Lamar Jackson

By Elisha Fieldstadt December 5th, 2019

The San Francisco 49ers suspended radio analyst Tim Ryan for one game after he said on-air that Baltimore Ravens quarterback Lamar Jackson has an advantage in faking handoffs because of his "dark skin color with a dark football."

"He's really good at that fake, Lamar Jackson, but when you consider his dark skin color with a dark football with a dark uniform, you could not see that thing," Ryan said on San Francisco radio station KNBR's "Murph & Mac Show" on Monday. "I mean, you literally could not see when he was in and out of the mesh point and if you're a half step slow on him in terms of your vision, forget about it, he's out of the gate," Ryan continued about Sunday's game in which the Ravens beat the 49ers, 20-17.

Jackson rushed for 101 yards in the game and so far this season has rushed for 977 yards. He is close to beating the NFL single-season rushing record by a quarterback, now held by Michael Vick, who ran for 1,039 yards in 2006. Some on social media slammed Ryan's comments as racist, while others contended they were simply "dumb."

The 49ers said in a statement that Ryan would be suspended for the team's game against the New Orleans Saints on Sunday. "We are disappointed in Tim Ryan's comments earlier this week, and have suspended him for the upcoming game," the team said. "We have reached out to the Baltimore Ravens organization to extend our apologies and assure them the matter is not being taken lightly."

"We hold Tim to a high standard as a representative of our organization and he must be more thoughtful with his words," the statement added. "Tim has expressed remorse in a public statement and has also done so with us privately. We know Tim as a man of high integrity and are confident he will grow and learn from this experience."

In a statement released through the team, Ryan apologized. "I regret my choice of words in trying to describe the conditions of the game," he said. "Lamar Jackson is an MVP-caliber player and I respect him greatly. I want to sincerely apologize to him and anyone else I offended." Ryan, a former player for the Chicago Bears, has been a radio announcer for the 49ers for six seasons and prior to that was a TV analyst on Fox.

The Rev. Jethroe Moore II, president of NAACP Silicon Valley-San Jose, said he would like to meet with Ryan before he returns from suspension. "Part of his coming back should be coming to meet with members of the African American community for better understanding of how those words can be hurtful," Moore said, according to NBC Bay Area. "That includes the 49er players and actually letting them talk about how they feel about the comments."

Niners cornerback Richard Sherman, who is black, defended Ryan on Thursday and said the radio man was making a valid point — but should have chosen better words, Pro Football Talk reported.

"I understand how it can be taken under a certain context and be offensive to some, but if you're saying, this is a brown ball, they're wearing dark colors, and he has a brown arm, honestly, sometimes we were having trouble seeing it on film," Sherman told reporters.

"He's making a play fake and sometimes he's swinging his arm real fast and you're like, Does he have the ball? And you look up and (Ravens running back Mark) Ingram is running it. So it was technically a valid point, but you can always phrase things better." Former 49ers defensive lineman Dennis Brown, who has been a pre- and post-game analyst for KNBR, will take Ryan's place in the booth on Sunday, the team said.

https://www.nbcnews.com/news/sports/49ers-announcer-tim-ryan-suspended-over-dark-skin-comment-about-n1096376

WSJ: "Diversify or Die"

By Chris Menahan December 17th, 2019

The National Hockey League is too white and must "diversify or die," so says the Wall Street Journal. From WSJ, "Diversify or Die: The National Hockey League Has a Demography Problem":

The NHL, which had only 50 nonwhite players in the 2018-19 season, seemed to get the point. It kept going with 'Hockey is for Everyone' programs in 26 minority and low-income communities, and learn-to-play classes around the country.

And it sent around a policy brief co-authored by Frey and Kimberly Davis, the league's executive vice president for social impact, growth and legislative affairs, that acknowledged "hockey has a perception in some circles as being 'not for some' and 'only for others.' "

"Now, more than ever, hockey communities and its leaders must focus on the drastic demographic and cultural change that is coming. It is incumbent upon those currently in the game—for the sake of the game's future—to ensure that the sport is perceived as welcoming to all," they said.

In other words, an entity whose members are generally whiter is going to have to diversify or die.

Incidentally, the NBA is 74.3 percent black but the WSJ is not calling for their "entity" to "diversify or die." Hockey is not welcoming to all because it requires ice skates, a hockey stick, hockey pads, a helmet and an ice rink which is costly to maintain versus basketball which takes a ball and a hoop or football which takes a football, a field and perhaps some football pads. That said, their ratings have actually been going up somewhat over the past few years despite their sins against Wokism.

https://www.infowars.com/wsj-diversify-or-die/

Florida to discontinue use of "Gator Bait" chant

By Thomas Goldkamp June 18th, 2020

GAINESVILLE, Fla. -- One of Florida's most well-known cheers at sporting events will be discontinued in an effort to become part of positive change against racism, university president Kent Fuchs announced in a letter to the UF community on Thursday. The famous "Gator Bait" chant will no longer be performed by the Gator Band or anyone associated with the University Athletic Association.

Wrote Fuchs:

"While I know of no evidence of racism associated with our "Gator Bait" cheer at UF sporting events, there is horrific historic racist imagery associated with the phrase. Accordingly University Athletics and the Gator Band will discontinue the use of the cheer."

The cheer has frequently been used after a quick band intro, followed by fans chomping twice with their arms and cheering "Gator Bait." Discontinuing its use is just one of several steps Fuchs announced the university will be taking to address racism. Fuchs outlined three major areas of focus for change.

- UF will require training of all current and new students, faculty and staff on racism, inclusion and bias.
- UF's Office of Research will make available this academic year competitive grants to faculty on topics of race, equity, justice and reconciliation.
- The 2020-21 academic year will focus on the Black experience, racism and inequity. Each of our colleges will feature speakers, seminars and courses. Led by faculty, we will also reevaluate and revise appropriate elements of our curriculum, including UF Quest.

- Student Government will join in this effort by organizing programs and speakers across campus, as with yesterday's ACCENT speaker announcement.
- The UF Faculty Senate will organize Town Hall meetings and add a standing agenda item as part of their monthly Faculty Senate meetings.
- In UF's spring semester, we will devote a day to community service and learning as guided by local leaders.
- A presidential task force will document the history of UF in relationship to race and ethnicity, particularly African Americans and Native Americans.
- A second presidential task force will review and recommend values, principles and reasons for establishing and maintaining honorary namings, both historic and current. The task force will further recommend a process for individuals associated with UF to be identified and considered for future honorary namings in accordance with current values and principles, and may suggest individuals for future consideration. Ultimately there will be a process to review all historical namings to determine if they should be retained or removed.
- I am personally committed to removing any monuments or namings that UF can control that celebrate the Confederacy or its leaders.
- While I know of no evidence of racism associated with our "Gator Bait" cheer at UF sporting events, there is horrific historic racist imagery associated with the phrase. Accordingly University Athletics and the Gator Band will discontinue the use of the cheer.
- There are agriculture operations where UF has relied on prison and jail inmates to provide farm labor. The symbolism of inmate labor is incompatible with our university and its principles and therefore this practice will end.

- The chiefs of the University Police Department and Gainesville Police Department have committed with city and university leadership to review use of force policies, report their findings to the community, institute needed reforms and engage the community by including a diverse range of input and experiences.
- I am charging the university's leadership, acting within state and federal laws, to intensify our efforts in recruiting, supporting and retaining our students, faculty and employees of color, particularly Black students, faculty and staff. To promote transparency and accountability, we will publish by department and college the race, ethnicity and gender trends for faculty, staff and students and present regular reports to the Board of Trustees.
- UF will redouble efforts to support local small businesses and vendor diversity.
- UF will work with East Gainesville community leaders and residents to develop specific and sustainable programs and activities that will contribute to improving the community's educational and economic well-being.

https://247sports.com/college/florida/Article/Florida-Gators-Football-UF-to-discontinue-use-of-Gator-Bait-chant-148304677/

Former Florida State Linebacker Kendrick Scott Starts Petition To Change The Name Of Doak Campbell Stadium

By David Hookstead June 20th, 2020

Former Florida State linebacker Kendrick Scott wants the name of Doak Campbell Stadium changed. According to CollegeFootballTalk, Scott has started a petition to change the name of FSU's stadium, which is named after former university president Doak S. Campbell. He wants it renamed after former FSU star Charlie Ward.

The petition reads in part:

The stadium at FSU was named after Doak Campbell a former FSU President. While the tradition has been preserved, in reflection his non-inclusive views of blacks as a segregationist is divisive, therefore his name should be removed from a stadium that has been home to many Black football players helping to build the school and the tradition to what it has become today: a national treasure.

Should FSU change the name of their iconic football stadium? That's up for the school to decide, but this is a dangerous road to travel. Judging people from decades or hundreds of years ago by the standards of today is a very bad idea. Under that standard, very few (if any at all) historical figures will be in good standing.

The big beef here is that Campbell was a segregationist. Obviously, that's not acceptable and it's not good. However, does that mean the stadium name should be changed? If so, where does it end? Is there any ending at all or do we just purge history of anyone who did anything wrong? I'm not sure that's a journey anyone wants to take. As I said above, it's ultimately going to be up to the good people at FSU to decide what they want to do, but I can promise you that judging historical figures by the standards of today is a dangerous game to play.

https://dailycaller.com/2020/06/20/florida-state-doak-campbell-stadium-kendrick-scott-petition/

SJSU bans 'Spartan Up' gesture because it allegedly resembles 'white power' sign

College Fix Staff June 21st, 2020

San José State University has banned its popular "Spartan Up" hand gesture due to it being akin to an alleged "white power" expression, the school president announced Thursday.

As shown on the campus "Traditions" page, "Spartan Up" is made by "forming a helmet with your thumb and index finger [...] [t]he idea is to curl your remaining three fingers over the top of the 'helmet,' mimicking a feathered plume." According to *SJSU News*, SJSU Athletics Director Marie Tuite said in an email that while "Spartan Up" has "become part of the fabric and footprint of our University, when [it's] used improperly, it can be offensive to some members of our University family."

Tuite added the gesture could create "a division on campus." However, the report points out the expression's connection to "white power" is rather tenuous; in 2017 members of the site 4chan "created" the gesture as a *hoax* (the shape of the hand allegedly looks like a "W" and a "P" for "White Power") in the hope "the media and liberals would overreact" to it.

And they did just that.

"Spartan Up" became a thing back in 1990 when a former SJSU marching band director had band members, cheerleaders, and fans use it at football games during the "Procession of the Spartans." SJSU President Mary Papazian said a "working group" comprised of students and faculty "will explore and recommend new traditions to further strengthen our Spartan spirit."

From the Story:

The removal of the gesture is only part of many changes SJSU plans to enact over the next 30 days along with supporting grassroots efforts to organize activities which address institutional racism as well as any issues with the University Police Department.

"We will create an advisory board—one with a broad and diverse membership reflecting the breadth of our campus community—to begin a deep-dive with our University Police Department into the effectiveness of overall operations including policies, protocols and community engagement strategies," Papazian wrote.

But that's not all Papazian said she wants to address. The email included: broadening recruitment areas where more underrepresented students, in particular Black students, may benefit from a SJSU education, increasing the number of Black faculty, improving training for staff and management on white privilege, racial oppression and active listening and more.

Papazian "emphasized" that these measures, including eliminating "Spartan Up," are "only the beginning" of addressing systemic racism at San José State.

https://www.thecollegefix.com/sjsu-bans-spartan-up-gesture-because-it-allegedly-resembles-white-power-sign/

Patriots Rookie Kicker Justin Rohrwasser Says He'll Remove Controversial Tattoo

By WBZ4 CBS Boston April 27th, 2020

BOSTON (CBS) – An emotional New England Patriots rookie kicker Justin Rohrwasser told WBZ-TV he's going to have a controversial tattoo linked to a right-wing militia group removed.

Shortly after the Patriots drafted Rohrwasser Saturday with the 159th overall pick, photos circulated online showing a tattoo on his arm with the logo of the "Three Percenters," an anti-government group. Rohrwasser, who is 23, said he got the tattoo when he was 18, thinking it stood for support of the military. He told reporters he would cover it up. But in an interview with WBZ-TV's Steve Burton Monday night, Rohrwasser said he didn't know the real meaning of the tattoo until he was drafted and started seeing the criticism on social media. He now plans on getting it removed.

"I went on to Twitter and I saw the tweet. I saw that someone had taken a picture of me and put it with my tattoo and linking me to some horrific events, you know, obviously Charlottesville and these horrible things." Rohrwasser said none of this came up when he kicked for Marshall last season.

"Never. The first time I found out what it was linked to was on Saturday. That's why it was so surprising," he told Burton. Rohrwasser said when he got the tattoo five years ago, "it was described to me as, you know, the percentage of colonists that rose up against the authoritarian government of the British. And I was like, wow, that's such a you know, an American sentiment, patriotic sentiment and coming from a military family, I thought that really spoke to me. I always was proud to be an American. I'm very proud."

After saying Saturday he would cover up the tattoo, Rohrwasser told Burton he's going to take it another step further. "As soon as I saw what it was linked to on Saturday, it was exactly that time I knew I had to get it totally taken off my body. I said cover it up [to reporters], but I want to get it removed from my body. It's shameful that I had it on there ignorantly," Rohrwasser said, getting emotional.

"I'm sorry for all my family that have to defend me. Putting them in that compromising position is one of the biggest regrets I'll ever have, so to them, I'm sorry. I'm going to learn from this."

"No matter what, it's not who I am, hopefully you'll all find that out," he said.

https://boston.cbslocal.com/2020/04/27/justin-rohrwasser-tattoo-new-england-patriots-kicker-steve-burton-wbz-tv-interview/

NASCAR bans Confederate flag at all events and properties

By Dan Mangan June 10th, 2020

Auto racing giant NASCAR said Wednesday that it is banning the display of the Confederate flag at all of its events and properties. The announcement is sure to be controversial with a number of NASCAR fans, some of whom continue to display Confederate flags and symbols at racing events even five years after the organization asked fans not to do so. Also Wednesday, NASCAR removed its rule mandating that racing team members stand for the national anthem.

NASCAR's new outright ban on the Confederate flag comes more than two weeks after a black man, George Floyd, died when a white

Minneapolis police officer named Derek Chauvin knelt on his neck for nearly nine minutes, even after Floyd repeatedly said, "I can't breathe."

The incident ignited protests nationwide. It also triggered demands for the removal from public places of symbols of the Confederacy, the group of Southern states that started the Civil War in 1861 by seceding from the United States in a doomed, bloody effort to save the institution of enslaving black people.

"The presence of the confederate flag at NASCAR events runs contrary to our commitment to providing a welcoming and inclusive environment for all fans, our competitors and our industry," NASCAR said in a prepared statement that was issued before its race Wednesday night at Martinsville Speedway in Virginia.

Why NASCAR has a great opportunity to attract a new audience by being one of the first U.S. sports to resume live events. "Bringing people together around a love for racing and the community that it creates is what makes our fans and sport special. The display of the confederate flag will be prohibited from all NASCAR events and properties."

It is not clear how NASCAR plans to enforce the ban. On Sunday, Bubba Wallace, the only black full-time driver on the NASCAR circuit, wore a shirt bearing the words "I Can't Breathe/Black Lives Matter" before a race in Atlanta. "My next step would be to get rid of all Confederate flags," Wallace said in a CNN interview the following day.

"No one should feel uncomfortable when they come to a NASCAR race. So it starts with Confederate flags. Get them out of here. They have no place for them." Wallace also said, "There's going to be a lot of angry people that carry those flags proudly but it's time for change."

"We have to change that, and I encourage NASCAR to have those conversations to remove those flags." Before Sunday's race in Atlanta, the 40 cars on the track stopped in front of grandstands and shut off their engines. NASCAR President Steve Phelps delivered a message over driver's radio sets. "Our country is in pain and people are justifiably angry, demanding to be heard," Phelps said. "The black community and all people of color have suffered in our country, and it has taken far too long for us to hear their demands for change. Our sport must do better. Our country must do better."

"The time is now to listen, to understand and to stand against racism and racial injustice," Phelps said. "We ask our drivers, our competitors and all our fans to join us in this mission, to take a moment of reflection, to acknowledge that we must do better as a sport, and join us as we now pause and take a moment to listen."

It had been common for decades at NASCAR events, particularly in the South, for Confederate flags to be displayed by fans. But in 2015, on the heels of the slaughter in Charleston, South Carolina, of nine black churchgoers by a racist named Dylan Roof, NASCAR asked that fans not display the Confederate flag at races.

Many fans have ignored that request.

Earlier Wednesday, President Donald Trump said that he will not allow the names of U.S. Army bases that are named after generals who fought for slave-holding states of the Confederacy in the Civil War to be changed. On the same day, Trump's top economic advisor Larry Kudlow said he does not believe that systemic racism exists in the United States. NBC News reported Wednesday that Democrats in the House and Senate plan to reintroduce in both of those chambers of Congress a bill that would remove from the U.S. Capitol the statues of those who voluntarily served in the Confederacy.

https://www.cnbc.com/2020/06/10/nascar-bans-confederate-flag-at-all-events-and-properties.html

Sports

You can't even watch and enjoy any professional, collegiate, or high school sporting event without having an attack on the United States National Anthem with kneeling or other forms of protest. Watching sports without politics or any forms of political statements was previously the escape people needed. Now, politics have entered sports permanently. LeBron James likes to complain about The United States and the entire culture of the country as he hides behind his gated, multi-million-dollar mansion in Brentwood, California in a mostly all-white neighborhood; all the while, slaves in China making $.15 per hour make his $225 retail shoes.

4

The War on Fun

White privilege symposium will feature 'racial justice' board game

By Aryssa Damron October 19th, 2018

A community college will host a "white privilege symposium" today and tomorrow that will explore such topics as "constructive white conversations" and "the n!gga(er) word" as well as a "racial justice" board game. North Shore Community College's Power, Privilege, Progress: Awareness to Action event is billed as an "engaging, deep learning experience with an exchanging of ideas on the issues of privilege and power in the history of our country."

Attendees of the event will hear from keynote speakers and participate in workshops such as "The Guide for White Women Who Teach Black Boys" and "Ten Reasons Why America Can't Talk about Race." The cost of attendance is $75; students will pay $50 and North Shore Community College students will attend free. One workshop at the event will be devoted to a play-through of the board game "Road to Racial Justice," which, according to the game's website, "supports and encourages cross-cultural understanding and compassionate action in order to help create a more loving and just world." The board game was created by Kesa Kivel, "a Los Angeles-based educator, artist and activist engaged in social justice issues."

Some of the game's discussion prompts include situations such as: "The mascot for your school's football team is a person dressed up as a warlike Native American" and "Under U.S. law, farmworkers — who are mostly Latino — have no right to overtime pay, and children as young as 12 are allowed to work in the fields." One scenario the game provides for the farmworker prompt is: "Find out which stores and restaurants buy fruits and vegetables from unethical farmers, and encourage your friends and family to boycott these places."

"Players will become more aware that racism exists in many everyday situations (interpersonal and institutional), learn why the situations are racist (stereotyping, tokenism, cultural appropriation, etc.), and acquire tools to interrupt these kinds of situations," the website says of the board game. Other workshops scheduled for the symposium include "Unpacking The N!gga(er) Word," "Constructive White Conversations" and "Completely Unpacking the Invisible Knapsack: The Liabilities of White Privilege How White Privilege Hurts White Peopl [sic]."

The event's website states: "This is not about blame; it is about listening deeply, talking with each other, and increasing our awareness bringing us closer to the understanding we all desire." Laurie Carlson, listed as a contact for the event on the school's website, did not respond to requests for comment on the expected attendance at the symposium or the content of its workshops. As of Thursday evening, 22 guests indicated they are attending on the symposium's Facebook event page. The symposium is organized in part by the Privilege Institute, which states that its mission it to "equip and empower people, organizations, institutions, and communities committed to action and accountability related to issues of diversity, power, privilege and leadership." The Privilege Institute also organizes the larger White Privilege Conference, begun twenty years ago at Cornell College in Mt. Vernon, Iowa.

While costs for the event were not readily available, at least one speaker, Claudia Fox Tree, who is hosting a panel titled "Whose History Matters? A Reflection on First Nations Stereotypes and Myths," charges between $1500 and $2500 to speak in the Concord, MA area.

https://www.thecollegefix.com/white-privilege-symposium-will-feature-road-to-racial-justice-board-game/

Ubisoft Apologizes For Forcing Your Assassin's Creed Odyssey Character Into A Straight Relationship

By Eddie Makuch January 16th, 2019

Ubisoft recently generated controversy when it was revealed that the newest Assassin's Creed: Odyssey expansion, Shadow Heritage, would force players into a straight relationship for a period of time. Now, creative director Jonathan Dumont has apologized, and he also explained why it happened.

At the end of the content, Kassandra or Alexios, depending on who you're playing as, has a child in a heterosexual relationship. Dumont said in a forum post that it was important for the game to establish how "your character's bloodline has a lasting impact on the Assassins." However, Dumont acknowledged that Ubisoft "missed the mark."

"We want to extend an apology to players disappointed by a relationship your character partakes in," he explained. "Alexios/Kassandra realizing their own mortality and the sacrifice Leonidas and Myrrine made before them to keep their legacy alive, felt the desire and duty to preserve their important lineage. Our goal was to let players choose between a utilitarian view of ensuring your bloodline lived on or forming a romantic relationship.

We attempted to distinguish between the two but could have done this more carefully as we were walking a narrow line between role-play choices and story, and the clarity and motivation for this decision was poorly executed."

Players do not to need to continue this relationship in the next chapter of the DLC, Dumont added. He also said that this has been "a learning experience" for Ubisoft; he promised that Ubisoft will "do better" to make sure that player choice--which Ubisoft had hyped as one of the core tenets of the game--stays intact going forward.

The move to force players into a heterosexual relationship was especially grating for some because, as mentioned, it ran counter to what Ubisoft had promised up until this point: that you could make your own choices in regards to romantic partners. At E3 2018, Odyssey's narrative director Melissa McCoubrey stressed how the game would allow players to choose their romantic partners. "If you want to be a woman and romance a woman, you can do that. If you want to be a man and romance a woman, you can do that. If you want to be a man and romance a man and a woman, you can do that," she told Stevivor at the time.

The title of the achievement/trophy for Shadow Heritage that unlocks after the childbirth is "Growing Up," and that name is stirring controversy as well. [**Update:** the name of the achievement will be changed in a forthcoming patch, according to Kotaku]. Shadow Heritage is part of the Legacy of the First Blade paid DLC for Odyssey. In addition to new story content, it added a new Hunter ability, Rapid Fire, which allows players to fire arrows rapidly without reloading. You can watch the opening minutes of Shadow Heritage in the video embedded above.

https://www.gamespot.com/articles/ubisoft-apologizes-for-forcing-your-assassins-cree/1100-6464448/?ftag=GSS-05-10aaa0a

Dodgeball is not child's play but 'legalized bullying,' Canadian researchers claim

By Lucia I. Suarez Sang June 4th, 2019

The game of dodgeball is more than just a popular playground activity, it is a tool of bullying and oppression targeting students, a trio of Canadian researchers claim.

The researchers argue that there is a "hidden curriculum" of dodgeball that reinforces the oppression of those "perceived as weaker individuals through the exercise of violence and dominance." They claim dodgeball – which pits two teams to eliminate each other by hitting the opposition with rubber balls – doesn't actually help students. "If you practice ganging up on people, over time you'll esteem ganging up on people," David Burns, a co-presenter of the study and a professor at the Kwantlen Polytechnic, told CTV News Vancouver. "If that's what you want, then dodgeball is an excellent tool to that end."

Burns – alongside fellow researchers Joy Butler, professor at the University of British Columbia, and Claire Robson, professor at Simon Fraser University – argues that dodgeball instead teaches students to dehumanize one another and create unsafe conditions in schools. "Dodgeball is the only game where the human is the target," Butler said. "No other games focus on it."

He added: "It's tantamount to legalized bullying." The researchers acknowledged their report will be criticized by many who argue the game is fun, but they are adamant that things could be done differently. "We're not anti-competition or anti-challenge," Robson said. "These things need to be done in an educational context." Their study was presented at an education conference organized by the Canadian Society for the Study of Education in Vancouver on Monday.

https://www.foxnews.com/world/dodgeball-is-legalized-bullying-canadian-researchers-claim

Video Game Developer Ends Racism by Erasing 'OK' Hand Gesture From Call of Duty

By Paul Joseph Watson July 3rd, 2020

Video game developer Infinity Ward has officially ended racism by removing the "OK" hand gesture emote from Call of Duty: Modern Warfare.

Stunning and brave.

"After plastering "BLACK LIVES MATTER" in capitalized bold text across every loading screen and delaying the launch of Season 4 for a week seemingly failed to end racism on a global scale, it appears that Infinity Ward have removed the OK emote from the game," reports National File. The company didn't publicly acknowledge the change, but numerous Twitter users noticed the deadly hand sign's absence from the game.

Someone also created a Reddit thread to discuss the issue, but in the spirit of one of if not the most censored social networks in existence, it was swiftly locked by moderators. The notion that the 'OK' hand gesture is some kind of racist dog whistle originated as a stunt by 4chan trolls to fool the media into hysterically amplifying a hoax, which it dutifully has done for the past three years.

Although the ADL initially refused to take the bait, they later reversed their position and included the gesture in their "hate symbols" database. "Some white supremacists themselves soon also participated in such trolling tactics, lending an actual credence to those who labeled the trolling gesture as racist in nature," states the organization on its website. "By 2019, at least some white supremacists seem to have abandoned the ironic or satiric intent behind the original trolling campaign and used the symbol as a sincere expression of white supremacy."

As we highlight in the video below, other companies that helped end racism include Lego for pulling marketing of toy police stations and Uncle Bens for erasing the character of an African-American man from their products.

https://summit.news/2020/07/03/video-game-developer-ends-racism-by-erasing-ok-hand-gesture-from-call-of-duty/

Disney Fans Call to Change Splash Mountain Theme Due to Racist Inspiration

By NBC 10 Boston June 11th, 2020

Disney fans and some employees are calling for the company to change the theme of its popular Splash Mountain ride, which is based on the 1946 movie "Song of the South" that critics say is one of Disney's most racist films.

An online petition calls for the Splash Mountain ride, which has been a longtime staple at Disney World and Disneyland, to be re-themed to the 2009 Disney movie "The Princess and the Frog," which features Tiana, Disney's first Black princess. "There is a huge need for diversity in the parks and this could help fill that need," the petition reads. "Princess and the Frog is a beloved princess movie but has very little representation in the parks. Tiana could be one of the first princesses with a thrill ride, as well as giving her a much deserved place in the parks.

"The framing of the ride is such that it could be easily changed to tell the story of Tiana while not compromising too much of the ride/costing a fortune in remodeling for Disney. This change could kill two birds with one stone, remove the offensive stereotypical theming the ride currently has and bring a much needed diversity to the parks." The calls for change come as many depictions of Black life have come under fire amid the worldwide protests over racial injustice and police brutality in the wake of the death of George Floyd last month.

https://www.nbcboston.com/entertainment/entertainment-news/disney-fans-call-to-change-splash-mountain-theme-due-to-racist-inspiration/2141464/

Fun

Board games, video games, and children's physical games are all being banned and cancelled. Dodgeball is considered offensive because it "promotes bullying." Even theme park rides and attractions are coming under tremendous attack from the psychotic, tyrannical mob. In the leftist utopia they are trying to create (which is hell on earth), these authoritarian control freaks will stop at nothing to put an end to all of our fun we have in society. So, who is the arbiter and who is the rule maker for deciding what games and fun activities are now banned and cancelled? It's part of the same nameless and faceless elitist ivory tower crowd who happens to control our entire media, sports, college, big tech, government, big medicine, and corporate complexes. The main problem is that regular non-psychotic people like you and I are not in charge of these institutions. The people in charge have very nefarious, sinister, and insidious intentions with the way they are trying to control and dominate our lives.

5

The War on Logos, Mascots & Cartoon Characters

The Buccaneers embody Tampa's love of pirates. Is that a problem?

By Jamie L.H. Goodall February 5th, 2021

On Sunday, the Tampa Bay Buccaneers will take on the defending Super Bowl champion Kansas City Chiefs in Super Bowl LV at Raymond James Stadium in Tampa — the first time a team has played a Super Bowl at their home stadium. And the Buccaneers' name and logo are a true reflection of the city hosting the game, trumpeting its close association with pirate legends, like José Gaspar, namesake of an annual Tampa Festival.

When the National Football League expanded to 28 teams in 1973, the league awarded Tampa an expansion team, prompting a name-the-team contest in 1975. "Buccaneers" won, a reference to the pirates who frequented the coasts of Florida in the 17th and 18th centuries. But team executives wanted the logo to be a "classy" pirate — a cross between Robin Hood, Errol Flynn, the musketeer D'Artagnan and pirate Jean Lafitte. It was a logo the team maintained until 1997 when they switched to a more aggressive, menacing Jolly Roger.

Yet, while this celebration of piracy seems like innocent fun and pride in a local culture, there is danger in romanticizing ruthless cut-throats who created a crisis in world trade when they captured and plundered thousands of ships on Atlantic trade routes between the

Americas, Africa and Great Britain. Why? Because it takes these murderous thieves who did terrible things — like locking women and children in a burning church — and makes them a symbol of freedom and adventure, erasing their wicked deeds from historical memory. These were men (and women) who willingly participated in murder, torture and the brutal enslavement of Africans and Indigenous peoples.

Derived from the Arawak word buccan, "boucanier" initially referred to landless hunters who survived off wild game and developed a particular meat-drying technique on the islands of Hispaniola and Tortuga. Later, the term became Anglicized as buccaneer and referred to a group of Caribbean outlaws who operated much like Mediterranean pirates/privateers, who existed in a world of dubious legality. Sometimes they protected colonial interests in the West Indies with governors of Caribbean islands paying them to attack Spanish treasure ships. But most often they were considered a seafaring menace — one that gradually careened out of control, attacking any ship they felt might be carrying valuable cargo, whether it belonged to an enemy country or not.

Consider, for example, Gaspar, who died in 1821 and is still celebrated in Tampa today as the "Last of the Buccaneers." Stories say he was born in Spain circa 1756 and worked his way into a high position in the court of King Charles III. One story alleges that he kidnapped a 12-year-old girl for ransom and the judge made him choose between jail or the Spanish Navy. Choosing the Navy, he purportedly made his way into the good graces of the king due to his fabulous feats against the Barbary pirates of Tripoli and victories against many pirates in the Caribbean.

According to legend, other members of the court were jealous of his success and his new position as admiral of the Atlantic fleet. They plotted against him, accusing him of treason in 1782. Another story argues that Gaspar publicly abandoned the king's daughter-in-law for another woman. Heartbroken, she worked with the prime minister to frame Gaspar for stealing the Spanish crown jewels. Hearing that King Charles III had issued a warrant for his arrest, Gaspar escaped, stole a ship and entered into piracy, hoping to take revenge against the Spanish who had treated him so unjustly.

Another story says that at the age of 27, serving as a lieutenant on the Floridablanca, a Spanish Navy ship, Gaspar narrowly escaped a defeat inflicted on his fleet by the English. Humiliated and disappointed by Spanish governance, he decided to seek his own wealth and fame in piracy. Somehow he managed to persuade the crew to join him in mutiny and off they went pirating.

Despite the mystery and conflicting legends about his background, we know 1783 marked a turning point in which Gaspar became a pirate and established a pirate den in Charlotte Harbor on the west coast of Florida north of Fort Myers. He attacked merchant ships, accumulated immense wealth and killed all who stood in his way until he retired in 1821 at age 65. Ordering his men to disband, he promised to divide all their treasure equitably.

But on the day he was to divide the spoils, he spotted what he thought was a rich British merchant ship near the harbor. Gaspar could not resist the temptation to seize it. Unfortunately for him, it turned out to be an American warship, the USS Enterprise. Facing his own demise, Gaspar climbed to the bow of the sinking ship, wrapped the anchor's chain around his waist, and threw himself into the sea shouting "Gasparilla dies by his own hand, not the enemy's!" His crew either perished in the melee or were hanged in New Orleans. Only a few managed to escape, according to legend, one of them being John Gómez, who was supposedly the first narrator of the Gasparilla legend.

Other than Gómez's supposed recollection, there are no historical records of Gaspar. Yet that doesn't stop Tampa locals and visitors alike from celebrating his legend with a parade and a festival known as the Gasparilla Pirate Festival or Gasparillafest. It supposedly began in 1904 when Louise Francis Dodge (the society editor of the Tampa Tribune) and George W. Hardee (a federal employee) decided to promote the city of Tampa and the May Day celebration as a way to rebrand the city and attract tourists.

The only times Tampa didn't celebrate the tradition were World War I, World War II and a two-year hiatus when there was dispute over African Americans being allowed to participate. This question of who could be involved in the celebrations mattered. According to André-Marcel d'Ans, the legend and ritual of Gasparilla was "born at a time when the adventurous plundering of pioneers had just given way to a system that necessitated the peaceful cooperation of all social classes" and it "tried to open a safety valve to release the ethnic and social tensions in a city where the relations between different classes and the different ethnic groups were marked by repressive violence in which a largely Anglo elite confronted mostly Latin ... workers." In short, Gasparilla was a way to bring the multiethnic population of Tampa together in celebration.

Of course, the glamorization of Gaspar is not unusual or new. When we consider pirates, we think of swashbuckling films like "Pirates of the Caribbean: Curse of the Black Pearl" (2003), which spawned five additional films with a sixth in production. Lionizing pirates dates back at least to 1724, when Captain Charles Johnson's "A General History of the Robberies and Murders of the Most Notorious Pyrates" hit London presses. Rather than condemn piracy, Johnson created caricatures who were as charismatic as they were deadly. Other writers and artists used Johnson's work as a foundation for their own, like Lord Byron's poem "The Corsair" (1814), which sold 10,000 copies in a day. Sir Walter Scott's "The Pirate" (1821), based on the pirate John Gow, was one of his most popular novels.

So why do we celebrate individuals who were the baddest of bad guys, those whom preacher Cotton Mather once called "Common Enemies of Mankind?" Pirates were known murderers who pillaged, raped and plundered their way through the Caribbean. And they were well-known enslavers who dehumanized Africans and Indigenous people, selling them for profit.

Perhaps time has dulled us to the atrocities committed by these 17th and 18th century outlaws. Or perhaps it's the fact that if pirates of the

Golden Age were bloodthirsty, so too were the nations who opposed them. They willingly and purposefully massacred millions of African and Indigenous peoples in the name of colonization. Pirates, then, are seen as romantic heroes — the underdogs fighting the establishment — whom historian Marcus Rediker refers to as proto-democratic, egalitarian and multicultural.

Should we celebrate their complicated legacy? It's a question Tampa Bay has to contend with as we collectively contemplate other major sports mascots with dubious legacies, like their Super Bowl rivals in Kansas City.

https://www.washingtonpost.com/outlook/2021/02/05/buccaneers-embody-tampas-love-pirates-is-that-problem/

Massachusetts college scraps Colonel mascot to be more 'inclusive'

By Dean Barker September, 2nd 2020

A college in Massachusetts is cutting its Colonel mascot from its logo in order to be more "inclusive." Curry College, a private school in Milton, Massachusetts, announced in August that it would change its logo to an interlocked "CC" for the time being to replace the old logo that featured the Colonel. The decision was made over the course of a year and a half of discussions." It has become clear in a variety of ways that the Colonel mascot image has become a source of concern. In light of this, Curry College has made the decision to retire the Colonel mascot image," Curry College President Kenneth K. Quigley, Jr said of the decision. Quigley said that the college has hosted "formal and informal" discussions about the mascot and, "through the lens of inclusion and respect," retired the mascot.

"Our educational mission includes embracing difference, and continuing to create and uphold an inclusive, diverse community at Curry,"

Quigley said. Despite the change in the logo, a decision on the name itself has not yet been made.

According to the official statement, discussions will continue over the course of the next year. This will include a survey of students, faculty, alumni, etc. on their opinions of the Colonel's name and mascot. These opinions will be documented by a committee, which will recommend further procedures after releasing the survey results to the public. "Going forward, it is vital to continue to pursue discussions and make decisions that help us achieve our goal of Curry growing even stronger and closer as one community," President Quigley said. Not everyone thought the decision was a good one. Many alumni tweeted their frustration in a reply to Curry's announcement on Twitter.

Assistant Athletic Director of Communications Chris McKeon tweeted his frustration with the decision, simply saying "Such a sad day..." Quigley and McKeon did not respond to *Campus Reform's* request for comment in time for publication.

https://campusreform.org/?id=15574

This 'radical' new version of Wonder Woman looks like she's stopped battling evil and is instead fighting an ice-cream addiction

By Robin Eisenberg August 23rd, 2020

DC Comics have once again succumbed to agenda-driven identity politics and made a female superhero an overweight, badly-dressed frump. One can only hope we are scraping the bottom of the woke barrel.

Last week, DC Comics posted a variant cover of the Wonder Woman 1984 #1 partial-reprint comic. They tweeted: *"Only one word for the Wonder Woman 1984 #1 ... variant cover by Robin Eisenberg: rad."* The image exemplifies everything the comic-book industry has succumbed to in recent years - the latest example in an ongoing trend of agenda-driven identity politics, in which classic themes of heroism and sacrifice have been superseded by themes of diversity and inclusivity and the avoidance of anything that could be interpreted as problematic.

Set against a background of garish sunset hues, the Wonder Woman in this new cover has an ambiguous but diversity-approved skin-tone, barely-distinguishable lumps for breasts, and brunette hair that seems to encompass an entire constellation, but which vaguely evokes a heavy speckling of dandruff.

In place of a dynamic flowing costume, her ensemble consists of an orange boob-tube and the kind of mom-jeans worn by middle-aged mid-western chicks at Shania Twain concerts. In a spirit of body-positivity, her thighs have been rendered so large it is as if the performer Lizzo had spent the entirety of quarantine bingeing on deep-fried Mars Bars and eschewed any fitness regime beyond schlepping between the fridge and the couch.

Indeed, the only *"wondrous"* thing about this iteration of Wonder Woman is the fact she was able to persevere in searching out a *"specialist"* clothing retailer which stocked jeans in size quintuple-XL. The artist, Robin Eisenberg (whose other work has been described as akin to soft-porn, and features females with three breasts engaged in sex with other women), explained her creative choices in an Instagram post: *"Recently I was asked to create a piece inspired by Wonder Woman, in my own style, for an upcoming one-off artist collab. I love drawing aliens with realistic body types, living their lives, comfortable with themselves. So, I drew an alien character with a realistic body, wearing a more everyday version of the Wonder Woman outfit."*

First of all, why would there be any ideal correlation between aliens and realistic body types? Do we expect aliens to be relatable, body-conscious role-models in the crusade against fat-shaming? And is this a *"realistic"* body? Even Sir Mix-a-lot, composer of *"Baby's Got Back"*, would think this was over-doing it. As for the notion of *"a more realistic version of the Wonder Woman outfit,"* that can be realized by visiting Comic-Con and feasting your eyes on nerdy plus-size fan-girls who couldn't tailor a half-decent approximation of the costume on a shoe-string budget. Comic book characters are meant to be more than human, admirable, not representative, relatable and homogenized so that no one can be offended.

Naturally, Twitter went to work, lampooning the image in every way imaginable. One poster wondered whether Wonder Woman had given up fighting evil and decided to battle ice cream instead.

A succession of illustrators and graphic artists posted semi-genuine, semi-sarcastic reinterpretations of the variant cover. Some were even more slovenly than the original; others were mega-breasted and thunder-thighed parodies; yet more were hilariously trampish. All this follows a recent trend of agenda-driven identity politics, diversity and inclusivity in comics. Marvel produced the *"New Warriors"* early this year, with new characters called 'Safe-Space' and his non-binary twin-sibling, 'Snowflake.' Later, DC produced a graphic novel, Gotham High, which took the lore of Batman and bastardized it into a high-school drama featuring a teenage Bruce Wayne, whose butler, Alfred, is married to a Southeast Asian man.

The only solace we might take from such an image as the new Wonder Woman is the hope that this is as bad as it can get, a high-water mark for identity politics in entertainment. Until then, social media solidarity is all we have.

https://www.rt.com/op-ed/498638-wonder-woman-dc-comics/

Marquette's seal under fire, accused of erasing Native Americans in favor of white explorer

By Landon Mion July 21st, 2020

Marquette University students are demanding that their university change the school seal to emphasize the role Native Americans played in the early exploration of America.

But not everyone is on board with the proposal and one professor at the university said that the current seal is historically accurate. Amanda Harris, a student at the Jesuit Catholic university in Milwaukee, launched a petition on July 6 to change the university's seal, which depicts Father Jacques Marquette, the university's namesake, and a Native American guide navigating a body of water. The petition is addressed to the board of trustees.

The seal is based off a painting called "Father Marquette and the Indians." Harris said the seal's current version crops out a part of the painting that showed Marquette receiving instructions from Native Americans. "By cropping out this Native American person from the seal, it is erasing the truth," the petition states.

"The painting shows a Native American person giving Father Marquette directions. The image in the seal shows the complete opposite." Harris told *The College Fix* in an email that she decided to launch the petition after discussing the seal in one of her classes. Harris also said that recent racial controversies played a role in her activism. "I remember wondering why our seal still included that cropped out image," she said. "Since this is my last year at Marquette, I felt there was no better time than now to see if the university would be willing to change the current seal."

She said the seal's image "asserts white dominance" because it shows Marquette standing above his Native American guide. The petition states that Marquette's seal is "problematic" and does not align with the university's vision statement, which preaches the welcoming of diversity and inclusion. It has garnered about 400 signatures so far.

Even though Harris organized the petition, she said she is going to work with Native American student groups on campus to present it. "Since I am a white person who has no indigenous heritage, it is important to have indigenous students and staff to present the petition since changing the seal calls for recognizing indigenous people," she told The Fix.

She said she plans to have the Native American Student Association and Center for Engagement and Inclusion present the petition to the university as better representatives of indigenous people. But one professor at the university defended the current seal, arguing it correctly portrays Marquette's legacy.

John McAdams, a conservative professor at the university who writes about campus controversies on his personal blog, *Marquette Warrior*, criticized the petition. McAdams, who teaches political science at the university, said the seal is accurate. "The seal as it stands is quite appropriate, giving Fr. Marquette the central place, as this is 'Marquette University' after all," said McAdams in an email to *The College Fix*.

"In a broad sense, and symbolically, the seal is historically correct. Fr. Marquette was the visionary who set out on a great expedition of exploration. The Indians were just living there, and while they certainly played a helpful role, they were not the visionary explorers," the professor said.

He said he believes that the demand for a change to the university's seal is just another example of virtue signaling, citing how people often cling to "minor and inconsequential things" that have no relevance to marginalized groups. A student leader for the Young Americans for Freedom Marquette chapter told *The College Fix* that the petition misses the mark.

Chairwoman Miranda Spindt said that the painting in its entirety portrays a part of history that is no longer accepted and "Cropping it differently will not change the symbolism or address the terrible history of violence and oppression that Native Americans have faced."

"Efforts would be better spent educating students on Native American history, learning about what problems Native students are specifically facing, and most importantly having real discussion about finding solutions to those problems," Spindt said.

"That would be much more respectable than just picking a different part of an obviously misunderstood painting." In 2015, four Marquette students sat in a street near campus, demanding that the university change its seal, among other requests. *Marquette Wire* reported that the university is reviewing the seal and considering ways to update it. It did not respond to requests from *The College Fix* for comment Monday.

https://www.thecollegefix.com/marquettes-seal-under-fire-accused-of-erasing-native-americans-in-favor-of-white-explorer/

EXCLUSIVE: Calif. college calls the POLICE...over a cartoon frog

By Katie Anderson *Feb 20th, 2019*

Folsom Lake College notified the local police after finding a poster of a cartoon frog, stating that "hate has no home on our campus."

An FLC faculty member found the sheet featuring Pepe the frog on their office door earlier in February. The school informed the Los Rios, California Police Department about the incident so it would "be on heightened alert for any signs that this may be part of a larger trend or pattern," according to an email sent to the school community and obtained by *Campus Reform.*

The picture of the smirking frog appeared alongside other posters pertaining to "fascist dog whistles," Democratic Socialists of America, and a week of social justice events. FLC President Whitney Yamamura, Academic Senate President Paula Haug, Classified Senate President Lindsey Campbell, and Student Senate President Cameron Sanders co-authored the email to the campus community.

"[Pepe] has been commonly co-opted by white supremacists and others as a symbol of bigotry," Yamamura and the co-authors said in the email. "While we do not immediately know the intentions of the person(s) who posted the picture, we are treating this incident with the highest level of seriousness and have already conducted a sweep of all Folsom Lake College campuses to look for other instances of these materials."

Internet users have edited Pepe the frog to resemble people and creatures varying from President Donald Trump to a unicorn. In May 2016, Twitter trolls tricked a journalist for *The Daily Beast* into writing a piece claiming that individuals had met up for drinks and plotted morphing the over decade-old meme into a symbol for white nationalism, according to *The Daily Caller News Foundation*.

Nearly three years later, in their email about an unedited Pepe appearing on campus, Yamamura and the co-authors added that every person on campus should have a place "to study and work that is free of bigotry and discrimination." In order to accomplish that goal, the FLC president and co-authors of the email encouraged students to report any additional paraphernalia of a "hateful or bigoted nature" to staff or faculty. In the statement, Yamamura also provided an email and personal phone number to the college's Equity Officer.

The college president and the other campus leaders also discussed the importance of providing a safe environment for students, staff, and faculty, but at the same time preserving students' right to free speech.

"We believe that we can create an environment free of hateful language or symbols while still supporting the rights afforded to us in the First Amendment," the co-authors of the email said. "Folsom Lake College has always been, and must continue to be, a place for collegial and mature conversation about complex issues. As a college, we are committed to providing a safe and inclusive learning and working environment, as demonstrated from our ongoing professional development workshops and trainings related to equity and inclusion."

Campus Reform contacted several faculty members at Folsom Lake College multiple times for comment but received no response in time for publication. *Campus Reform* also reached out to the Queer-Straight Alliance group on campus, but the group declined to make a statement.

https://www.campusreform.org/?ID=11894

Cal State campus ditching 'Prospector Pete' mascot after complaints that Gold Rush hurt indigenous people

By Lukas Mikelionis April 27th, 2019

California State University's campus in Long Beach is ditching its longtime mascot amid accusations of racism and officially moving to pick either a new symbol or have no mascot at all.

The university ditched its "Prospector Pete" character in September after criticism that it was offensive to indigenous people. The supposedly offensive mascot was born when the campus opened in the 1940s, with founding President Pete Peterson's comment that he "struck the gold of education" by creating it, according to the Los Angeles Times. But students have come to see the mascot not as a tribute to their founder or to California history, but rather as a representation of the violence caused to Native Americans and others during California's Gold Rush era.

Last year, the university moved the statue of the mascot away from a prominent place on campus due to the outcry. A statement on the university website said the Gold Rush was "a time in history when the indigenous peoples of California endured subjugation, violence and threats of genocide." (Whether the NFL's San Francisco 49ers should be worried about their nickname is unknown at this point.)

The university is now asking students to vote on a new mascot, with choices including Pelicans, Sharks, Stingrays, Giraffes, Kraken (a sea monster from Scandanavian folklore), or even picking the option called "the Beach" that is sort of a no-mascot option.

Genesis Jara, president of Associated Students, Inc., told the Mercury News of San Jose that the options for students to vote on were selected from hundreds of ideas submitted by students. The final decision will rest with President Jane Close Conoley.

https://www.foxnews.com/us/cal-state-campus-ditches-half-century-old-mascot-to-replace-it-with-either-basic-moniker-or-non-mascot

MASCOT MADNESS: School spirit symbols on the chopping block nationwide

By Celine Ryan Sep 4th, 2019

Colleges and universities across the country are axing "offensive" mascots. FromW ashington, D.C. to Maine and from to Illinois to California, more and more mascots are falling prey to political correctness.

1. Colonials

Despite the school being named after an actual colonial, students at George Washington University in Washington, D.C. have launched a campaign to replace the "Colonial" mascot with one without so "deep a connection to colonization." Although the university has not officially responded to the student vote to remove the mascot that they say "glorifies the act of systemic oppression," it recently renamed a building called Colonial Center the Student Services Hub.

2. Pioneer

After failed attempts to replace retired mascot "Denver Boone," the University of Denver now has no official mascot. Until recently, the school's "Pioneer" nickname was the only remaining official unifying symbol for students. Amid controversy, the school has begun quietly removing the word "pioneer" from student ID cards and other official university documents and communication, despite insisting that it still embraces the nickname.

3. "Prospector Pete" the 49er

California State University, Long Beach's long-standing "Prospector Pete" mascot was relieved of his duties in 2018 because he represented the California Gold Rush, or as the university president put it, "a time in history when the indigenous peoples of California endured subjugation, violence, and threats of genocide."

4. Chief Illiniwek

In summer 2019, a University of Illinois commission advised the "public retirement" of the Native American mascot after critics deemed him to be offensive to indigenous peoples. Others characterized the change as an "attempt to purge" Native representation at the university.

5. Cowboys

In 2018, two dozen professors banded together to demand that the University of Wyoming cease the use of its marketing campaign slogan "the world needs more cowboys," because, as one professor put it, "the word 'cowboy' invokes a white, macho, male, able-bodied, heterosexual, U.S.-born person." The university stood its ground and continued use of the slogan, which turned out to be a success, generating a $38,000 increase in royalties over the previous year.

6. Any possible Native American mascot you haven't even thought of yet

The entire state of Maine has placed an outright ban on any mascot that "depicts or refers to a Native American tribe, individual, custom or tradition." Democrat Gov.Janet Mills called such mascots a "source of pain and anguish" for Native communities.

https://www.campusreform.org/?ID=13661

Washington Post Editor Says Texas Rangers' 'Violent And Racist' Name 'Must Go'

By Joseph Curl July 14th, 2020

A Washington Post editor said Monday that the Texas Rangers team name "must go." On the same day that the National Football League's Washington Redskins announced it would do away with its 93-year-old team name, Global Opinions editor Karen Attiah said that the Major League Baseball team must deal with "the violent and racist implications of its name."

"To know the full history of the Texas Rangers is to understand that the team's name is not so far off from being called the Texas Klansmen," Attiah wrote in an op-ed for the liberal newspaper. Attiah, who grew up in Dallas, reminisced about going to Rangers games with her father as a child, but said at the time she didn't know the Rangers "were a cruel, racist force when it came to the nonwhites who inhabited the beautiful and untamed Texas territory."

The Texas Rangers were unofficially created by Stephen F. Austin in 1823 as a statewide investigative law enforcement agency, headquartered in the capital of Austin. The Rangers stopped the assassination of President William Howard Taft and pursued such outlaws as Bonnie and Clyde. More than 120 have died in the line of duty. Attiah, who said she is part of a Ghanaian immigrant family and calls herself a "black Texan," said "the first job of the Rangers ... was to clear the land of Indian for white settlers."

That was just the start. The Rangers oppressed black people, helping capture runaway slaves trying to escape to Mexico; in the aftermath of the Civil War, they killed free blacks with impunity. "The negroes here need killing," a Ranger wrote in a local newspaper in 1877, after Rangers fired on a party of black former Buffalo soldiers, killing four of them and a 4-year-old girl. A jury would later find that the black soldiers "came to their death while resisting officers in the discharge of their duty," an unsettling echo of the justification for modern-day police killings.

The editor cited a new book, "Cult of Glory: The Bold and Brutal History of the Texas Rangers," in which author Doug J. Swanson wrote, "In service to Anglo civilization's slow march, they functioned as executioners. Their job was to seize and hold Texas for the white man."

The Post writer isn't the first to call for the Texas Rangers to change their name. After a Chicago Tribune piece last month, the team made a statement. "While we may have originally taken our name from the law enforcement agency, since 1971 the Texas Rangers Baseball Club has forged its own, independent identity," said the team statement. "The

Texas Rangers Baseball Club stands for equality. We condemn racism, bigotry and discrimination in all forms.

"To help bring about meaningful change, we are committed to listening to and supporting our communities of color. ... We go forward committed to do even more, with a renewed promise that the Texas Rangers name will represent solutions and hope for a better future for our communities," said the team.

https://www.dailywire.com/news/washington-post-editor-says-texas-rangers-violent-and-racist-name-must-go

Oklahoma student gov ditches 'Boomer' and 'Sooner' for more 'sensitive' words

By Genesis Sanchez November 19th, 2019

Students at the University of Oklahoma are working to remove the school's "Boomer" and "Sooner" nicknames out of concern that the words are offensive to Native Americans. According to the *OU Daily*, the Undergraduate Student Congress met Nov. 12 to mandate a name change for the "Sooner Freshman Council", citing the words "boomer" and "sooner" as offensive to the Native American community.

The university uses the nickname "Sooners" for its athletic teams and other purposes, as well as similar references to "Boomers." Both words, in this case, refer to groups of settlers who arrived in the late 1800s to what is now the state of Oklahoma. The decision to remove the "Sooner" name from the Freshman Council comes shortly after the Undergraduate Student Congress passed a bill in early September to execute "Indigenous Land Acknowledgment," which includes a statement that OU students are "visitors on the land" and thanks indigenous people for being generous with their land. The reading of this bill will occur before all SGA events.

"(The) motivation was just to be consistent with the indigenous land acknowledgment we had passed to be more cognizant of some of the language ... we are using in our code annotated," said Student Government Association President Adran Gibbs, who reasoned that the words "Boomer" and "Sooner" are offensive to Native American individuals. The bill asserts that the word "Sooner" is "harmful in nature to those who identify as American Indian or of Native/Indigenous descent," and that on-campus groups need to pick a more "sensitive" name within the first two weeks of fall 2020 semester.

The act passed with a roll-call vote of 19-8-7. "I think changing the name because of this takes away from the pride of being at this school. "Boomer Sooner" represents more than just indigenous people, but everyone who chooses to be part of the OU Sooner Family," OU Student McKinley Crone told *Campus Reform*.

Crone also mentioned that mascot "Sooner Schooner" is an icon on campus, and that rebranding the freshman council would be "wrong." In 2016, the OU student government rejected a similar resolution to ditch the traditional "Boomer Sooner" salute, also out of concern that the words were offensive to Native Americans. *Campus Reform* reached out to the university for comment but did not receive a response in time for publication.

https://www.campusreform.org/?ID=14011&utm_campaign=CampusWire&utm_source=hs_email&utm_medium=email&utm_content=79667234&_hsenc=p2ANqtz-_V4vG30PFPlIlUBsilj-pIO3V3bxbPrFNYMdk7KLdwUXzmWtoOwVWl3lIii-WVc5x5JxIrDEIdDSJz82eyznIB6CwKi8VQ&_hsmi=79667234

PETA Asked Georgia's Mascot to Retire. 'Uga' Isn't Going Anywhere.

By John Duffley March 31st, 2020

The People for the Ethical Treatment of Animals do a lot of great things to expose animal cruelty around the world, while simultaneously educating the public on the preservation of species everywhere. Good for them and that mission. Now, I don't personally know anyone who works for PETA, but if you do, could you let them know that trashing live mascots in the sports world is getting really, really, really, really old?

It was pouring rain in Athens when *CBS Sports* captured Uga X, the Georgia Bulldogs' iconic mascot, hanging out in his air-conditioned dog house on the sidelines of Sanford Stadium during Georgia's win over Texas A&M in 2019. Everyone was trying to stay dry, including that white English bulldog named Que. And in that moment, PETA felt the need to strike, once again condemning a live mascot tradition that first began in 1956.

In a tweet, the animal rights organization attacked the University of Georgia's use of a live mascot and included video of Uga X staying dry in his dog house.

This isn't the first time, and surely won't be the last, that PETA comes after Georgia's beloved bulldog. After Texas mascot Bevo XV lost his cool, broke through his barricade, and startled Uga X during the 2019 Allstate Sugar Bowl between Georgia and the University of Texas Longhorns, PETA demanded both the longhorn steer and bulldog retire. Neither mascot was reportedly injured in the scary incident. Time and again, PETA calls out live mascots any chance they get. They condemned Mississippi State's Jax. They condemned Oklahoma's horse-drawn Sooner Schooner. They condemned Colorado's Ralphie program. That was just over a span of two months.

What PETA didn't point out, however, is that Uga X and Reveille IX — the long-time mascot of the Texas A&M Aggies — met just hours before and had an awesome, little doggy date prior to that college football kickoff. Live mascots are treated like royalty and receive an incredible life during and after game day. It's a shame these incredible traditions and pillars of college athletics are condemned over and over, but no matter how hard PETA tries, it seems impossible that live animal mascots will ever not make public appearances and be an integral part of sports traditions everywhere.

https://fanbuzz.com/college-football/sec/georgia/peta-demands-uga-retire/?utm_source=facebook&utm_medium=agora&utm_term=cfb&utm_campaign=cfb&fbclid=IwAR08grEedujaz05LSt9MYEPfySh28PzXlAMmHn-DRJL0BgZPGbcmhsPp8K_8

New Marvel Comic Introduces 'Non-binary' Heroes Called 'Snowflake' and 'Safespace'

By Steve Watson March 19th, 2020

If there was ever any doubt that Marvel has totally lost the plot, it goes out of the window with the announcement that a new comic series will focus on a pair of twins who identify as 'non-binary' and are named 'Snowflake' and 'Safespace'. Yes, seriously. Step aside Peter Parker, the Marvel universe no longer has time for your Spidey cisness.

Geeky website *Bounding Into Comics* reports that Marvel has revived and made-over an old set of characters known as "The Warriors," labelling them the "New Warriors." Creator Daniel Kibblesmith described the series as a "story of teenage rebels." adding that "a lot of the names are about teens fighting against labels that are put on them."

Kibblesmith described how the names 'Snowflake' and 'Safespace' came about, stating that "It's this idea that these are terms that get thrown around on the internet that they don't see as derogatory — to take those words and wear them as badges of honor." Kibblesmith noted that "Snowflake" who is "nonbinary and goes by they/them."

has the super power of being able to "generate individual crystallized snowflake-shaped shurikens." (ninja stars to you and me).

"The connotations of the word snowflake in our culture right now are something fragile. And this is a character who is turning it into something sharp." the Marvel creator added. Other characters who are a part of this group include "Trailblazer", who appears to be nothing more than an obese girl with a 'magic' backpack: Another is "Screen time" an internet obsessed skinny kid who is 'patched permanently into the world wide web.'

Marvel seems intent on totally bankrupting itself by going full woke. Three years ago, Marvel VP of Sales, David Gabriel blamed poor sales on the obsession with promoting diversity and woke culture. Since then, Marvel has set about destroying many of its established characters, or altering their race and sexuality.

https://www.infowars.com/new-marvel-comic-introduces-non-binary-heroes-called-snowflake-and-safespace/

Little Devil Inside developer apologizes for 'racist stereotype' in a character design

By Nicole Carpenter Jun 15th, 2020

An indie development team apologized this weekend after a trailer shown for its upcoming PlayStation 5 game, *Little Devil Inside*, included a character model with features associated with harmful, racist stereotypes for black people.

A trailer for *Little Devil Inside* appeared on Sony's PlayStation 5 reveal event last Thursday, showcasing the quirky indie game from South Korean developer Neostream Interactive. The stream, called The Future of Gaming, showcased a number of next-generation games that'll be released on PS5 — *Little Devil Inside* is among them, and was immediately popular on social media for its aesthetic.

However, shortly after the trailer debuted, some viewers noticed racist character design for some enemies shown briefly. People on social media began pointing this out, including Twitch streamer LordBalvin, that the character design appeared to be based on racist depictions of black people in media. Neostream apologized over the weekend and vowed to change the design.

"I was so excited for *Little Devil Inside*," LordBalvin wrote on Twitter. "But then I noticed these enemy types." He continued: "So — this game is developed by an indie team in Seoul called Neostream, it's not a Sony game. It's not up to me to decide the intentions here, it could just be a tone deaf character design. But this shows you need some insight from indigenous and/or black people in the room." Neostream business development director John Choi told Polygon in a statement that the "racist stereotype ... was absolutely not intended." Choi apologized, and said the developer will adjust the design.

Choi said the characters were designed to be "protectors/guardians of a particular mystic region in the world of *Little Devil Inside*." The developer didn't reference real "African and/or Afro-American human tribes," and instead focused on "creating colorful masks."

Choi said Neostream will "remove the dreadlocks," "change the bold lips," "change skin tone," and "tweak the dark blower so it looks less like a joint." He added that the team will also consider changing the design of the characters entirely — and noted that this scenario will not happen again. Sony has not responded to Polygon's request for comment. *Little Devil Inside* does not yet have a release date.

https://www.polygon.com/2020/6/15/21291436/little-devil-inside-racist-stereotype-character-design-update-sony

Land O' Lakes drops 'racist' Native American image from packaging after nearly 100 years

By Alexandra Deabler April 16th, 2020

The farmer-owned dairy cooperative, which produces butter, cheese and other milk products, has dropped the Native American maiden image from its packaging, opting instead for just a landscape. The logo, which has been the company's label for nearly 100 years since it was founded in Minnesota in 1921, has been called "racist" and criticized for its use of the "butter maiden."

The new label was announced in a press release from Land O' Lakes in February, though it made no specific mention of removing the Native American image from all products. The press release shared "the new packaging will show up in a variety of ways, including through a new front-of-package design that features the phrase 'Farmer-Owned' above the LAND O LAKES brandmark," as well as include pictures of farmers and co-op members on the label.

"As Land O'Lakes looks toward our 100th anniversary, we've recognized we need packaging that reflects the foundation and heart of our company culture—and nothing does that better than our farmer-owners whose milk is used to produce Land O'Lakes' dairy products," said Beth Ford, President and CEO, Land O'Lakes, in the press release."As a farmer-owned co-op, we strongly feel the need to better connect the men and women who grow our food with those who consume it," Ford said.Many on social media are celebrating the move, criticizing the company for using the image of a Native American woman, named Mia, for its branding in the first place.The packaging is expected to be fully rolled out across all products by the end of 2020.

SJWs Complain That Orcs Are 'Racist', Draw 'Soft, Queer' Versions To Combat 'Colonial Portrayals'

By Gabriel Keane April 29th, 2020

As a white, male, Christian author of significant historical repute, it seemed inevitable to many that Tolkien and his legacy would be assailed by Woke Twitter. This week, the topic of orcs became a trending topic on the platform. The woke brigade went on to attack the unrelated "Dungeons and Dragons" fandom and related games for its portrayal.

Some even went as far as to claim orcs are a direct, "dehumanizing" allegory for "black and brown people." The accusations of racism were quickly debunked, and the trending topic was quickly capitalized on by fantasy fans, who used the hashtag to steer the conversation in a positive, non-political direction.

Many of the users trying to rationalize their opinion that Tolkien's works and DnD are riddled with hidden "racism" later deleted their tweets. One of the accounts that was later set to private mode after backlash posted orc fan art in an attempt to "diversify and humanize" the fictional species.

"It's important to know how orcs were made to fit into pre-existing racist and colonial ideals, and how that has tainted their portrayal. I think by diversifying and humanizing the, we can keep the good parts and toss out the racist trash. So here, have some soft, queer orcs," the caption accompanying drawings of lesbian orcs taking selfies read.

Another user said the art was unnecessary, since orcs are already "cute" and "gay."The discussion on Twitter appears to have died down by Wednesday, presumably as the woke brigade searches for another historical, fictional, or video game-related fandom to assail with cries of racism.

https://nationalfile.com/sjws-complain-that-orcs-are-racist-draw-soft-queer-versions-to-combat-colonial-portrayals/

'Snap, Crackle, Pop' Determined To Be Racist

By Rick Moran Jun 17th, 2020

Fiona Onasanya, a Black Lives Matter activist and former member of the UK parliament, claims that Kellogg's Rice Krispies is a racist cereal because it has "three white boys" as mascots.

Now *that's* "systemic racism"!

If Ms. Onasanya had stopped there, she would simply be dismissed as a fool and that would have been that. But in her eagerness to prove racism, Onasanya doubled down on her charge and, in the process, proved she is an ignorant fool.

It's an idiotic point, even if it were true. It isn't. Much mirth ensued. Onasanya's online attack quickly drew ridicule from users on Twitter who made sure to point out that the beloved characters of Snap, Crackle, and Pop are also the brand champions for Cocoa Krispies, the chocolate flavored Rice Krispies. Another responded to Onasanya's attacks with "Elves Lives Matter." Kellogg's told the Daily Mail in a statement that it "stands in support of the black community."

"We do not tolerate discrimination and believe that people of all races, genders, backgrounds, sexual orientation, religions, capabilities and beliefs should be treated with the utmost dignity and respect," the company said, going on to note that the Coco Pops monkey is also the same character representing the white chocolate cereal. "The monkey mascot that appears on both white and milk chocolate Coco Pops, was created in the 1980s to highlight the playful personality of the brand."

Anyone who sees their entire existence through the lens of race — including the brand of cereal that children of all colors and hues enjoy — is in serious trouble and desperately needs help. I could say the same about most Black Lives Matter activists whose paranoid rantings about police wanting to kill black people is beyond delusional.

As for Ms. Onasanya, she has a "checkered past," to put it delicately. Ms Onasanya, who was jailed for three months in January 2019 after she was convicted of lying to police about a speeding ticket, says that there is little difference between Coco Pops and sister brand Rice Krispies beyond their colour and flavour.

The former Peterborough MP revealed she has emailed Kellogg's UK office for clarification on why Rice Krispies have 'three white boys' as a mascot whereas chocolate-flavoured Coco Pops is represented by a monkey. Sometimes, a monkey is just a monkey. And three little elves flitting over a bowl of Rice Krispies are sometimes just three little elves flitting over a bowl of Rice Krispies. Not everything is a metaphor in life, just like everything isn't a conspiracy. Only the weak-minded and naive believe otherwise. I'll say this; they will have to pry my Rice Krispies from my cold, dead hands.

https://pjmedia.com/news-and-politics/rick-moran/2020/06/17/snap-crackle-pop-determined-to-be-racist-n542693

Univ. of Virginia Vows to Change 'Racist' Logo Over Minuscule Detail

By Michael Barnes June 17th, 2020

'There was no intent to cause harm, but we did, and for that I apologize to those who bear the pain of slavery in our history...' University of Virginia officials backpedaled on a proposal to incorporate the iconic serpentine walls into the sabres in its logo. / PHOTO: University of Virginia via YouTube

(Michael Barnes, Liberty Headlines) Nothing appears to be off-limits in the current political climate, where anything can be construed as offensive and thus canceled—not even the handle of a 200-year-old sword. The University of Virginia found itself on the receiving end of cancel-culture on Monday after activists accused the school of promoting slavery through its new university logo design.

The logo features a large gray V with an orange outline with two sabers underneath. But the handles on the sabers have grips reminiscent of slavery, critics alleged. When the logo was unveiled in April, the grips were shaped to reference "the design of the serpentine walls found on the Grounds," according to the school.

The serpentine walls were built two hundred years ago and served as a signature feature of the historic campus. But since they were built with the help of slave labor, they are now considered racist, even though the walls were torn down and replaced in the 1950s. Carla Williams, the university's athletic director — who also happens to be black — apologized and said the logo would be altered to nix the slavery connotation.

"There was no intent to cause harm, but we did, and for that I apologize to those who bear the pain of slavery in our history. As such, we have redesigned the logos to remove that detail. All other aspects of the logos will remain the same," Williams said in a news release. "Over the last few weeks, I have worked to better educate myself and that education will continue," she added.

The University of Virginia was founded in 1819 by Thomas Jefferson, author of the Declaration of Independence and the nation's third president. Jefferson's plantation home, called Monticello, is located a few miles away.

Kirt von Daacke, a radical history professor at the University of Virginia, and co-author of the 2019 book "Educated in Tyranny: Slavery at Thomas Jefferson's University," accused Jefferson of constructing the old walls to hide slave laborers from public view.

https://www.libertyheadlines.com/uva-change-logo-slavery/

PepsiCo to drop Aunt Jemima name, criticized for racist history; Uncle Ben's under review

By Martinne Geller June 17th, 2020

(Reuters) - PepsiCo Inc (PEP.O) will change the name and brand image of its Aunt Jemima pancake mix and syrup, it said on Wednesday, dropping a mascot that has been criticized for a racist history.

The logo of the more than 130-year-old brand features an African American woman named after a character from 19th century minstrel shows. The offensive caricature is rooted in a stereotype of a friendly black woman working as a servant or nanny for a white family.

Separately, Mars Inc said it was evaluating possible changes to its Uncle Ben's brand of packaged rice, which feature a white-haired African-American man named after a Texas rice farmer. The brands had been called out on social media in recent days, amid widespread protests over racism in the United States after the death of George Floyd, a black man, in police custody in Minneapolis.

A TikTok video called "How To Make A Non-Racist Breakfast" by user @singkirbysing, in which a woman pours the pancake mix down the sink, got over 109,000 views on Instagram since Tuesday when it was posted.

"We recognize Aunt Jemima's origins are based on a racial stereotype," Kristin Kroepfl, vice president and chief marketing officer of PepsiCo-owned Quaker Foods North America, said in a statement. "As we work to make progress toward racial equality through several initiatives, we also must take a hard look at our portfolio of brands and ensure they reflect our values and meet our consumers' expectations."

Mars said it had "a responsibility to take a stand in helping to put an end to racial bias and injustices" and that "one way we can do this is by evolving the Uncle Ben's brand, including its visual brand identity."

"We don't yet know what the exact changes or timing will be, but we are evaluating all possibilities," a spokeswoman said in an emailed statement. Some observers lauded the moves, but said they were slow to come. "Brands built on racist imagery have been living on borrowed time," said James O'Rourke, management professor at the University of Notre Dame's Mendoza College of Business. "This move by Quaker Oats, while welcome, is decades late in coming."

Quaker did not announce a new pancake-syrup name or logo, but said packages without the Aunt Jemima image would start appearing in the fourth quarter of 2020. PepsiCo also announced on Tuesday a set of initiatives worth more than $400 million over five years to support black communities and boost black representation at PepsiCo.

https://www.reuters.com/article/us-pepsico-race-aunt-jemima-idUSKBN23O1V1

Black Lives Matter Targets Paw Patrol for 'Depictions of "Good Cops"'

By Joel B. Pollak June 10th, 2020

The Black Lives Matter movement is targeting *Paw Patrol*, the popular children's cartoon on the Nick Jr. channel, because it shows a positive view of police, according to the *New York Times*.

The show actually attempted to support the Black Lives Matter movement on "Blackout Tuesday," in common with the Nickelodeon network as a whole. However, the show's tweet amplifying "melanated voices" was met with an avalanche of criticism and mockery. The *Times* reported on Wednesday (original emphasis and links): It was only a matter of time before the protests came for "Paw Patrol."

[L]ast week, when the show's official Twitter account put out a bland call for "Black voices to be heard," commenters came after Chase. "Euthanize the police dog," they said. "Defund the paw patrol." "All dogs go to heaven, except the class traitors in the Paw Patrol." As the protests against racist police violence enter their third week, the charges are mounting against fictional cops, too. Even big-hearted cartoon police dogs — or maybe *especially* big-hearted cartoon police dogs — are on notice. The effort to publicize police brutality also means banishing the good-cop archetype, which reigns on both television and in viral videos of the protests themselves. "Paw Patrol" seems harmless enough, and that's the point: The movement rests on understanding that cops do plenty of harm.

Cops can dance, they can hug, they can kneel on the ground, but their individual acts of kindness can no longer obscure the violence of a system. The good-cop act is wearing thin.On Tuesday, Paramount announced the cancelation of the decades-old *Cops* reality show, and other shows are also being targeted as the "woke" protests continue.

https://www.breitbart.com/entertainment/2020/06/10/black-lives-matter-targets-paw-patrol-for-depictions-of-good-cops/

Logos, Mascots and Cartoon Characters

Mascots and the culture of teams are also under attack. The following teams have been under attack for their mascots:

The Atlanta Braves
The Chicago Blackhawks
The Kansas City Chiefs
The Tampa Bay Buccaneers
The University of Illinois Fighting Illini
The Florida State Seminoles

Yosemite Sam and Elmer Fudd get banned because they have firearms. SpongeBob SquarePants gets cancelled because he's racist. Mascots and mascot-themed events are now banned because literally, everything is offensive.

6

The War on Race

San Francisco Chronicle Op-Ed: Bernie Sanders "Manifests" White Privilege, Male Privilege, Class Privilege

By Evan James February 1st, 2021

An op-ed in the *San Francisco Chronicle* (paywalled) asserts that socialist Bernie Sanders is a manifestation of "white privilege, male privilege, and class privilege." The piece, published in the *Chronicle*'s "open forum" part of their opinion section, was penned by Ingrid Seyer-Ochi, a former professor and principal who now teaches at a high school in the San Francisco Unified School District. Seyer-Ochi begins her op-ed by describing how she "processed the Capitol insurrection" with her high school students and then the inauguration of Joe Biden two weeks later. "We saw diversity, creativity and humanity, and a nation embracing all of this and more," she wrote.

But then Bernie Sanders came out of nowhere with his "puffy jacket and huge mittens, distant not only in his social distancing, but in his demeanor and attire." An image of Bernie looking grumpy and uninterested while sporting a mask and those mittens spread like wildfire, quickly becoming the basis for a barrage of memes over the next several days. Despite Seyer-Ochi's best efforts to focus with her students on "gender" and the "possible meanings" of the clothing worn by Kamala Harris, **DR.** Jill Biden, et al, Bernie and his mittens just kept on distracting her.

"And there, across all of our news and social media feeds, was Bernie: Bernie memes, Bernie sweatshirts, endless love for Bernie. I puzzled and fumed as an individual as I strove to be my best possible teacher. What did I see? What did I think my students should see? A wealthy, incredibly well-educated and -privileged white man, showing up for perhaps the most important ritual of the decade, in a puffy jacket and huge mittens," she wrote.

Lest anyone think she's comparing Bernie with the "white supremacist insurrectionists" at the Capitol on January 6, Seyer-Ochi says she does not mean to "overstate the parallels" between the two. BUT, she adds, "he manifests privilege, white privilege, male privilege and class privilege, in ways that my students could see and feel." And there it is. Bernie was "manifesting privilege when seemingly no one else did." Seyer-Ochi claims she "struggled" to explain it to her undoubtedly aghast students.

"I am beyond puzzled as to why so many are loving the images of Bernie and his gloves," she says. *"I don't know many poor, or working class, or female, or struggling-to-be-taken-seriously folk who would show up at the inauguration of our 46th president dressed like Bernie. Unless those same folk had privilege. Which they don't."*

And once again, the line between satire and reality has entirely blurred. It's nothing short of a tragedy that people like Seyer-Ochi are teaching your children. Homeschool if you can!

https://bigleaguepolitics.com/san-francisco-chronicle-op-ed-bernie-sanders-manifests-white-privilege-male-privilege-class-privilege/

Multiracial Whiteness

By John Hinderaker January 21st, 2021

At the American Spectator, "Cockburn" writes about "The terrifying scourge of 'multiracial whiteness.'"

[T]here's a small problem. Somehow, on their way to launching a neo-fascist takeover of the United States, the white supremacists ran out of whites. Simply looking at video of the Capitol riot, or looking at the FBI's wanted images afterwards, makes it obvious that the mob of Trump die-hards were multiracial. The two most famous members of the Proud Boys, America's premier 'white nationalist' group, are an Afro-Cuban and a Samoan. 'Stop the Steal' organizer Ali Alexander identifies as black and Arab. And of course, there are November's famous exit polls, which showed that Joe Biden was carried to the White House by improving on Hillary Clinton's support with white voters, while faltering with Hispanics and blacks.

Yikes! When you read those facts a few too many times, you start to wonder: what if the white supremacists aren't white supremacists? Fear not, though! The Washington Post is here to explain all the bad think away. Over the weekend, the paper ran a piece by NYU history professor Cristina Beltrán: 'To understand Trump's support, we must think in terms of multiracial Whiteness.'

Multiracial...whiteness? Aren't those antonyms? Not at all, you fool. Beltran's WaPo piece is a marvel of intellectual confusion. It probably exemplifies all too well the low level of instruction in today's universities. Yes, Trump's voters — and his mob — are disproportionately White, but one of the more unsettling exit-poll data points of the 2020 election was that a quarter to a third of Latino voters voted to reelect Trump.

How dare they? I don't know, maybe they liked their rising incomes. Of course, mundane details like rising wages and near-zero unemployment are of no interest to liberals. And while the vast majority of Latinos and an overwhelming majority of African American voters supported the Biden-Harris ticket and were crucial to its success, many Black and brown voters have family and friends who fervently backed the MAGA policy agenda, including its delusions and conspiracy theories.

Weird how when liberals talk about delusions and conspiracy theories, they never mean the Russia collusion hoax. Or the plot to pilfer the mailboxes, and so on. I call this phenomenon multiracial whiteness — the promise that they, too, can lay claim to the politics of aggression, exclusion and domination. Whoa! So "whiteness" refers to a "politics of aggression, exclusion and domination"? Who knew? Silly non-critical race theorists thought it just referred to an ethnic group. But, given that definition, are Twitter, YouTube, Facebook, Amazon, Apple and Microsoft now "white"? Is there anyone else in our society so dedicated to aggression, exclusion and domination?

Rooted in America's ugly history of white supremacy, indigenous dispossession and anti-blackness, multiracial whiteness is an ideology invested in the unequal distribution of land, wealth, power and privilege — a form of hierarchy in which the standing of one section of the population is premised on the debasement of others. Multiracial whiteness reflects an understanding of whiteness as a political color and not simply a racial identity — a discriminatory worldview in which feelings of freedom and belonging are produced through the persecution and dehumanization of others.

Multiracial whiteness promises Latino Trump supporters freedom from the politics of diversity and recognition. For voters who see the very act of acknowledging one's racial identity as itself racist, the politics of multiracial whiteness reinforces their desired approach to colorblind individualism. In the politics of multiracial whiteness, anyone can join the MAGA movement and engage in the wild freedom of unbridled rage and conspiracy theories.

To call this bullshit is an insult both to bulls and to excrement. Does this woman have students? God help them. Multiracial whiteness offers citizens of every background the freedom to call Muslims terrorists...

Of course, no one has ever said that all Muslims are terrorists, but many have noted that some terrorists are Muslims. That makes us all "white," apparently.

...demand that undocumented [i.e., illegal] immigrants be rounded up and deported...

Actually, that is what the laws of the United States demand, and the president's duty under Article II of the Constitution is to take care that the laws be faithfully executed. But I suspect that the Constitution is not a document with which Ms. Beltran is well acquainted.

...deride BLM as a movement of thugs and criminals...

While no one disagrees with the innocuous slogan "Black lives matter," the BLM organization does in fact consist largely of thugs and criminals, as last summer's riots demonstrated.

...and accuse Democrats of being blood-drinking pedophiles.

Heh. I haven't heard that one before. Maybe she just mixed it in to see whether we were paying attention. Personally, I am not aware of any blood-drinking Democrats. There is more insanity at the link, but you can't read it without paying the Washington Post, which you shouldn't do. The bottom line is that an ideology so confused as to denounce its philosophical opponents as "white," regardless of their skin color, is not going to last long.

https://www.powerlineblog.com/archives/2021/01/multiracial-whiteness.php

Lady Gaga: 'When You're Born in This Country, We All Drink the Poison That Is White Supremacy'

By David Ng September 17th, 2020

Pop superstar Lady Gaga has made the baffling claim that people who are born in the United States are all fed white supremacy ideology. The *Chromatica* singer added that she supports the social justice activism taking place around the country and hopes that it will continue to grow.

In a lengthy *Billboard* interview, Lady Gaga said that she is trying to learn and unlearn things that she's been exposed to her entire life.

"When you're born in this country, we all drink the poison that is white supremacy," she told the magazine. "I am in the process of learning and unlearning things I've been taught my whole life." The Grammy and Oscar-winning star said that she hopes social justice activism continues to grow "louder."

"Social justice is not just a literacy, it's a lifestyle," she said. "What do I think about [posting] a black square? I think everybody has a different feeling about a black square. Do I think there's such a thing as performative activism? Yes. Do I think there's been true activism that's been very important and needed? Yes. Do I believe Black lives matter? Yes. Do I believe this is going to get louder? Yes. Do I believe it should? Yes."

At the same time, Lady Gaga called out performative activism and other forms of virtue signaling. "I call that the Lindseys: the girls that protest and are taking pictures of themselves like, 'Look at me protesting!'" The singer said she wouldn't add social justice elements to her live performances just for the sake of it. "To say that I would do it to make my show relevant? Absolutely not. I would do it to make my show right. I would do it to make my show good."

Lady Gaga's comments on race echo those she made in June when she recorded a message for YouTube's "Dear Class of 2020" event. The singer said the "racist seeds" of America have become "trees that grew prejudice branches and oppressive leaves and mangled roots that buried and entrenched themselves deep within the soil."

In May, Lady Gaga posted a lengthy screed to social media in which she attacked President Donald Trump as a "racist." The pop star wrote that President Trump "offers nothing but ignorance and prejudice while black lives continue to be taken. We have known he is a fool, and a racist, since he took office. He is fueling a system that is already rooted in racism, and racist activity, and we can all see what is happening."

Lady Gaga recently appeared at the MTV Video Music Awards in August during which she performed in a series of eccentric masks and urged people to wear masks in response to the coronavirus. "I might sound like a broken record, but wear a mask. It's a sign of respect," she said during one of her several acceptance speeches.

https://www.breitbart.com/entertainment/2020/09/17/lady-gaga-when-youre-born-in-this-country-we-all-drink-the-poison-that-is-white-supremacy/

Nasdaq Wants To Push Companies To Hire Fewer White, Straight Men

By Justin Danhof January 6th, 2021

Wall Street has always hated Main Street. Never before, however, has it been so open and brazen in wielding that animus. Take, for example, Nasdaq's recent pronouncement that it plans to delist any company from its exchange that won't appoint board members based on how they look, whether they have sex with the "right" people, or identify as a letter in the LGBT lexicon.

Nasdaq's dictate is wholly unconstitutional, panders to minority groups and women, and would financially strain many American businesses. Still, it's pushing forward anyway because it thinks no one will have the courage to stand up and stop it.

Specifically, Nasdaq is seeking permission from the U.S. Securities and Exchange Commission (SEC) to delist any American company from its platform unless the company puts two "diverse" individuals on its board of directors. One position *must* be given to a female. And one position *must* be given to a racial minority or a member of the ever-broadening definition of LGBT.

This is the definition of racism and sexism, which are illegal in U.S. employment, but it's also the state of play in corporate America: Follow the leftist political directives of the Wall Street and Davos crowds, or lose the ability to finance your business in the public marketplace. Where can we begin to unpack this wholly backward plan, and how did we get here?

For starters, this scheme has precisely nothing to do with financial performance. In its petition to the SEC, Nasdaq doesn't claim minority or female board membership leads to increased corporate performance. It simply cites debunked studies claiming that such board diversity is "positively associated" with better financial performance. This confuses causation with correlation, a logical fallacy known as *post hoc ergo propter hoc* ("after this, therefore because of this").

Nowhere does Nasdaq say that financial performance improves *because* a company increased the surface-characteristic diversity of its board, only that in some cases, financial performance improved after a diverse board member was added. You could just as easily conduct a "study" showing that companies that instituted Pizza Fridays or Ice Cream Wednesdays saw improved financial performance after the fact. For such a study to have any validity, it must show that the first action *caused* the subsequent result. In short, Nasdaq failed to prove its work.

Yet it gets worse. Another likely illegal aspect of Nasdaq's plan is that a company can bypass the minority requirement by appointing to its board a white male who identifies as LGBT. It is entirely against the law, however, to ask any job applicant for his or her sexual orientation.

So, if a company complies with Nasdaq's demands, and ends up with a board comprised of one female and the rest all white males, the company just potentially (and publicly) outed one of those men LGBT. Surely not every single member of those groups wants that information made public.

Let's be clear-eyed about what Nasdaq is doing, beyond expressing its ideological commitment to identity politics. It is trying to set up a system similar to tenure for professors in higher education. Whatever its possible noble origins and designs to protect academic freedom, tenure has become nothing more than a means to blackball conservative academics from college campuses.

The left has been so successful at blocking conservative thought in academia that, according to the National Association of Scholars, "faculty political affiliations at 39 percent of the top-tier liberal arts colleges ... are Republican free — having zero Republicans ... and 78.2 percent of the academic departments ... have either zero Republicans or so few as to make no difference." This is exactly what is already occurring in corporate boardrooms and what Nasdaq is trying to accelerate.

A 2019 survey conducted by Barron Public Affairs compared the ideological makeup of the board members of the Fortune 100 companies with any prior political experience. In the Fortune 1-10, the split was 100 percent Democrat and 0 percent Republican.

Among the financial companies in the Fortune 1-100, the split was 83 percent Democrat and 17 percent Republican. Nasdaq is trying to fast-track the left's complete takeover of corporate America by ensuring that board seats are now rewarded to leftists — thereby keeping any businessmen with conservative or traditional values out of the club.

Because in today's environment no CEO would dare challenge the liberal mob, Nasdaq expects its request will go unchallenged. Therefore, it's up to the Americans who prioritize business success over virtue signaling to do something about it.

And you can. The SEC is accepting public comments regarding Nasdaq's request until January 4, 2021. We at the Free Enterprise Project just submitted our comment blasting Nasdaq's gambit. You can submit your comment here. Don't let the mob win.

https://thefederalist.com/2021/01/06/nasdaq-wants-to-push-companies-to-hire-fewer-white-straight-men/

Pentagon Training Manual Singled Out "White, Heterosexual, Christian" Men

By Todd Starnes September 8th, 2020

In 2013, I received a controversial 600-plus page manual used by the military to train its Equal Opportunity officers teaches that "healthy, white, heterosexual, Christian" men hold an unfair advantage over other races, and warns in great detail about a so-called "White Male Club."

"Simply put, a healthy, white, heterosexual, Christian male receives many unearned advantages of social privilege, whereas a black, homosexual, atheist female in poor health receives many unearned disadvantages of social privilege," reads a statement in the manual created by the Defense Equal Opportunity Management Institute (DEOMI).

The manual, which was obtained by the *Todd Starnes Radio Show*, also instructs troops to "support the leadership of people of color. Do this consistently, but not uncritically," the manual states. The Equal Opportunity Advisor Student Guide is the textbook used during a three month DEOMI course taught at Patrick Air Force Base in Florida. Individuals who attend the training lead Equal Opportunity briefings on military installations around the nation.

The 637-page manual covers a wide range of issues from racism and religious diversity to cultural awareness, extremism and white privilege. I obtained a copy of the manual from an Equal Opportunity officer who was disturbed by the course content and furious over the DEOMI's reliance on the Southern Poverty Law Center for information on "extremist" groups.

"I'm participating in teaching things that are not true," the instructor told me. He asked not to be identified because he feared reprisals. "I should not be in a position to do that," he said. "It violates Constitutional principles, but it also violates my conscience. And I'm not going to do it – not going to do it."

DEOMI instructors were also responsible for briefings at bases around the country that falsely labeled evangelical Christians, Catholics and a number of high-profile Christian ministries as domestic hate groups. I contacted the Pentagon as well as the DEOMI multiple times for comment on this story, but so far they have not responded to my requests.

DEOMI opened in 1971 in response to the civil rights movement. It's responsible for Equal Opportunity/Equal Employment Opportunity education and training for military active duty and reservists, according to its website. The subject of white privilege emerged in a 20-page section titled, "Power and Privilege."

"Whites are the empowered group," the manual declares. "White males represent the haves as compared to the have-nots." The military document advises personnel to "assume racism is everywhere, every day" and "notice code words for race." They are also instructed to "understand and learn from the history of whiteness and racism."

"Assume racism is everywhere, everyday," read a statement in a section titled, 'How to be a strong 'white ally.'"

"One of the privileges of being white is not having to see or deal with racism all the time," the manual states. "We have to learn to see the effect that racism has." On page 181 of the manual, the military points out that status and wealth are typically passed from generation to generation and "represent classic examples of the unearned advantages of social privilege."

"As such, the unfair economic advantages and disadvantages created long ago by institutions for whites, males, Christians, etc. still affect socioeconomic privilege today," the manual states. The guide also points out that whites are over-represented and blacks are underrepresented in positive news stories, that middle class blacks live in poorer neighborhoods than middle class whites and that even though there are more white criminals than any other race, the news coverage of black criminals is about equal to the news coverage of white criminals.

The military manual goes into great detail about a so-called "White Male Club."

"In spite of slave insurrections, civil war, the 13th, 14th, and 15th amendments, the women's suffrage movement leading to the 19th amendment, the civil rights movement, urban rebellions and the contemporary feminist movement, the club persists," the document states. DEOMI states that "full access to the resources of the club still escape the vision of equitable distribution."

The military also implies that white Americans may be in denial about racism. In a section titled, "Rationalizations for Retaining Privilege and Avoiding Responsibilities," the military lays out excuses white people use. "Today some white people may use the tactic of denial when they say, 'It's a level playing field; this is a land of equal opportunity,'" the manual reads. "Some white people may be counterattacking today by saying political correctness rules the universities or they want special status."

DEOMI points out that if "white people are unable to maintain that the atrocities are all in the past, they may switch to tactics to make a current situation seem isolated." They said some of the ways whites may claim to be victims include saying things like, "I have it just as bad as anyone else," "They're taking away our jobs," or "White people are under attack."

The military concludes the section by urging students to "understand and learn from the history of whiteness and racism" and "support the leadership of people of color." I called former Congressman and Lt. Col. Allen West (ret.) to get his take on the manual. In a nutshell – he wants a congressional investigation.

"This is the Obama administration's outreach of social justice into the United States military," he told me. "Equal Opportunity in the Army that I grew up in did not have anything to do with white privilege."

West said he is very concerned about the training guide. "When the president talked about fundamentally transforming the United States of America, I believe he also had a dedicated agenda of going after the United States military," he said. "The priorities of this administration are totally whacked." West said the DEOMI manual reminded him of a similar program inflicted on the military by President Clinton.

"They came down with a new training requirement called, 'Consideration of Others Training,'" he said. "The soldiers were supposed to sit around and go through vignettes and talk about their feelings." I truly wish the Pentagon and the DEOMI would return my telephone calls. I'd like to know how teaching soldiers, airmen and sailors about white privilege and fomenting racial division helps them protect our nation from the enemy.

https://www.toddstarnes.com/values/pentagon-training-manual-singled-out-white-heterosexual-christian-men/

University hosts separate orientation for black freshmen

By Drew Van Voorhis September 7th, 2018

Incoming freshmen at George Mason University recently had the opportunity to attend another orientation created specifically for black students. The event was called the "Black Freshman Orientation." Hosted by the Black Student Alliance, the additional orientation occurred on August 25 at the university. It has become an annual event there.

Incoming black freshmen at GMU did not have to attend the Black Freshman Orientation, and if they decided to attend, they still were required to go to the university's regular orientation as well, according to the university. As for the Black Freshman Orientation, it aimed to help new students feel welcome at the public, Virginia-based university. "This event is dedicated for the incoming freshman who identify as black or are supporters of black people. The Black Freshman Orientation will offer ways to be involved at Mason not only with the black organizations but also mason as a whole. This event allows incoming students for an outlook on how the Black Community at Mason is like," a Welcome 2 Mason website about the event states.

On a separate website, GMU Campus Labs, it described the event as a chance to network. "The Black Freshman Orientation is a Black Student Alliance event that occurs annually at the beginning of the school year. This year, the Black Student Alliance will be collaborating with other on campus organizations to make the experience even more valuable and enriching for all who attend," it stated.

"This event is exclusively for the freshman class at George Mason University. At this event, the freshman class will be able to get the ins and outs of GMU, learn how to navigate the campus, as well as learn about the different resources and organizations available to them on campus," the website states.

Michael Sandler, director of strategic communications at George Mason University, told *The College Fix* that while the Black Student Alliance did hold this event, it was open for any student to attend. "The university also has over 300 student organizations that sponsor a variety of events throughout the year. Many student organizations hold welcome back activities as we get close to the beginning of the fall semester. Mason's Black Student Alliance, one of our student organizations, did sponsor a welcome event during the first week of the fall semester, which was open to all," Sandler told *The Fix.*

Black Student Alliance at GMU did not respond to an inquiry from *The College Fix* for comment. George Mason University is not the only school to host such an event. Many universities across the nation each year host a variety of welcome back events designed especially for black students.

https://www.thecollegefix.com/university-hosts-separate-orientation-for-black-freshmen/

Ad Agency Darkens Skin of Students in School Photo to Promote 'Diversity'

By Paul Joseph Watson September 12th, 2018

Students in Lyon, France posing for a school photograph had their skin artificially darkened by an ad agency in order to promote "diversity" in the United States. Planning to establish a branch in the U.S., the Emile-Cohl school posted an image of the smiling freshmen students to Twitter. However, the students themselves drew attention to the fact that darker skin had been photshopped onto some of their faces, in a few cases making them look like completely different people.

After the school began receiving criticism over the manipulated image, they blamed the ad agency that provided the photo, before suspending access to their own website, severing a contract with the agency and issuing an apology. A spokesman for the school denied "any intention to manipulate reality" and pointed the finger at the ad agency for deliberately manipulating the photo in a bid to amplify a message of diversity for a U.S. audience.

Twitter users reacted with scorn. "White guilt and self-hatred has gotten out of control. This is a mental illness," said one. "Madness," added another. Maybe if the ad agency had just used an image from Sweden, they wouldn't have felt the need to manipulate it.

https://www.infowars.com/agency-darkens-skin-of-students-in-school-photo-to-promote-diversity/

University of Denver hosts 'White Privilege Symposium'

By Adam Sabes Oct 31st, 2018

The University of Denver will host and sponsor the annual "White Privilege Symposium," (WPS) which is set up to "examine patterns, cultures, and systems that contribute to identity, power, and privilege," on Friday and Saturday.

The symposium will feature breakout sessions such as "Anti-Racist Allyship: Avoiding The Pitfalls," "Colleagial Check-In for POC: Needing Connection While Managing Whiteness," "Colored White: A Discussion On White Identity," "White Accountability," and more, according to the symposium website,

"White Accountability" will explain why white people need to check their privilege in order to stop racism.

"Helping white people understand the difference between accountability and blame and challenging white people to use this knowledge to check their own white [privilege] and to dismantle the systems of racism that permeate this country," is the stated purpose of the session. Another workshop titled "Similar but Separate" seeks to explain the difference between black and brown women to the audience.

"We will explain the differences of black and brown women in Colorado," that description states. "Many people believe black and brown women experience the same inequalities; however we do not."

The "Anti-Racist Allyship: Avoiding the Pitfalls" workshop even criticizes the "good progressive or liberal" who considers themselves an "anti-racist ally."The description asks progressives and liberals, "what happens when you are challenged, to think of yourself and your work differently?"

"Quite often, POC find ourselves disappointed, shocked, and saddened by how frequently the 'ally,' especially the white ally, reveals themselves to be anything but," it explains. "How are folks engaged in this work really problematizing their own white fragility, defensiveness, tokenization of POC, etc., and how can you become an even better ally/accomplice?"

When *Campus Reform* asked the University of Denver what the university is doing to sponsor the program, the school said it is letting the WPS use university space. If members of the community disagree with the content in the symposium, they are encouraged to come and discuss the issue, the school told *Campus Reform*.

"The University of Denver brings together people and communities with diverse and opposing viewpoints and we invite members of our community to engage in civil discourse regardless of subject. We strive to create an inclusive environment that fosters the intellectual growth of our students, alumni, and the greater, global community," the school told *Campus Reform*. "Within that environment, we encourage each individual to engage in respectful discourse and the critical examination of ideas. Freedom of expression is crucial to the mission of the University of Denver." The UD Graduate School of Social Work is sponsoring the WPS as well as The University of Colorado-Denver.

https://www.campusreform.org/?ID=11467

White liberals more likely to 'patronize' minorities than conservatives, study finds

By Valerie Richardson November 28th, 2018

White liberals present themselves as less competent when addressing minorities, while conservatives use the same vocabulary no matter what the race of their audience, according to a newly released study. Yale and Princeton researchers found that white Democratic presidential candidates and self-identified liberals played down their competence when speaking to minorities, using fewer words that conveyed accomplishment and more words that expressed warmth.

On the other hand, there were no significant differences in how white conservatives, including Republican presidential candidates, spoke to white versus minority audiences. "White liberals self-present less competence to minorities than to other Whites — that is, they patronize minorities stereotyped as lower status and less competent," according to the study's abstract.

Cydney Dupree, assistant professor of organizational behavior at the Yale School of Management, said she was surprised by the findings of the study, which sought to discover how "well-intentioned whites" interact with minorities.

"It was kind of an unpleasant surprise to see this subtle but persistent effect," Ms. Dupree said. "Even if it's ultimately well-intentioned, it could be seen as patronizing." The study flies in the face of a standard talking point of the political left — that white conservatives are racist — while raising questions about whether liberals are perpetuating racial stereotypes about blacks being less competent than whites.

The paper, which is slated for publication in the Journal of Personality and Social Psychology, first examined speeches by Republican and Democratic presidential candidates to mostly white and mostly minority audiences dating back 25 years. Ms. Dupree and Princeton's Susan Fiske analyzed the text for "words related to competence" such as "assertive" and "competitive" and "words related to warmth" such as "supportive" and "compassionate."

"The team found that Democratic candidates used fewer competence-related words in speeches delivered to mostly minority audiences than they did in speeches delivered to mostly white audiences," said the Yale press release. "The difference wasn't statistically significant in speeches by Republican candidates."

Ms. Dupree noted that Republicans also gave fewer speeches to minority audiences. The researchers then set up an experiment in which white liberals were asked to respond to hypothetical individuals named "Emily" and "Lakisha."

"Liberal individuals were less likely to use words that would make them appear highly competent when the person they were addressing was presumed to be black rather than white," said the release. "No significant differences were seen in the word selection of conservatives based on the presumed race of their partner."

Ms. Dupree said the "competence downshift" could indicate a greater eagerness by white liberals to connect with those of other races. "My hope is that this work will help include well-intentioned people who see themselves as allies but who may be unwittingly contributing to group divides," said Ms. Dupree. "There is a broader need to include them in the conversation."

https://www.washingtontimes.com/news/2018/nov/28/white-liberals-patronize-minorities-downplaying-co/

University hosts 'critical look at whiteness' forum

By Drew Van Voorhis December 3rd, 2018

SAN MARCOS, Calif. — The Christian cartoon "VeggieTales" is racist because the villains are vegetables of color. The NFL is racist since most players are black and most coaches and owners are white. White women advance white supremacy when they support President Donald Trump.

These are some of the arguments made by students at a "Whiteness Forum" held at Cal State San Marcos on Thursday that aimed to take a "critical look at whiteness," according to organizers. The two-hour event took place in a large multipurpose room, with more than a dozen poster board projects lined up in a circle around the room for viewers to review. The forum is a result of Professor Dreama Moon's Communications 454 class titled "The Communication of Whiteness," with the annual event serving as a showcase of students' final projects for the class.

Walking into the room, a large digital overhead screen read "The Annual Whiteness Forum," and at each station students stood by their projects to talk about their whiteness studies. Various titles for projects included "White Avoidance," "Civilized vs. Uncivilized," "Kill the

Land, Kill the Indian," "White Women's Role in White Supremacy," "Gun Ownership and Racial Bias" and more.

One project argued the NFL is to blame for its role in white supremacy, as most football players are black, yet most coaches, who many times were previous players, are white. It also noted that an even higher majority of team owners are white.

Another project suggested that the children's Christian television show, "VeggieTales," perpetuates racial stereotypes. A female student who worked on the project said in an interview that the accents of the evil characters tend to sound ethnic, such as Latino, while the good characters sound white.

"When kids see the good white character triumph over the bad person of color character they are taught that white is right and minorities are the source of evil," the project stated. Still another student project stated that white supremacy is caused in part by the media, since white shooters are simply called shooters on the news, yet minority shooters are often called terrorists.

And a flier handed out with the "White Women's Role in White Supremacy" project shows a picture of women supporting President Trump flanked by pictures of women in the KKK. As the afternoon event unfolded at the public university, several hundred people — mostly students — came into the room and viewed all of the different presentations.

Some students were also offered extra credit by other professors to attend the Whiteness Forum, such as Professor Gloria Pindi, who teaches critical intercultural communications and women and gender studies at the university. A student in Pindi's class who attended the event for the extra credit also told *The College Fix* that he felt the forum accomplished just the opposite of promoting the notion of equality for all. "I feel like the university system [leaders] are a bunch of hypocrites, they're talking about stopping racism and promoting equality for all, yet they have no problem bashing white people," the student said, adding he is half-Mexican. "They're trying to make people feel guilty for being white."

https://www.thecollegefix.com/university-hosts-critical-look-at-whiteness-forum/

American University Students and Staff Call for Minority-Only 'Spaces' on Campus to Promote Inclusion

By Alana Mastrangelo Dec 11th, 2018

American University students and administrators are pushing for "spaces" on campus designated for "students of color," claiming that it will promote diversity and inclusion at the university.

Students and staff at American University (AU) are calling for "the creation of more spaces for students of color," so that minority students can have an area on campus where they can go to be separated from the rest of the campus body, in the name of "diversity and inclusion," according to the university's student newspaper.

AU students are criticizing the university's Hub for Organizing Multiculturalism and Equity (HOME) for being "marketed to students of all backgrounds rather than to students of color."

"HOME doesn't provide people with a sense of security, with a sense of belonging, when everyone from all types of affinity groups can be there," said Othniel Malcolm Andrew Harris to AU's student newspaper.

As it currently stands, any student can apply on AU's website to request access to HOME, as long as they agree to "the mission and goal of continuing to foster a sense of community and belonging for our communities of color and allies."

The Director of the University Center, Michael Elmore, suggested that students are currently unable to walk around on campus while simultaneously enjoy living under the principles of "basic respect, basic agreement on civility and human rights," which is why HOME is necessary.

HOME was created in response to a racial incident that occurred on campus in 2017, as well as in reaction to a survey conducted on campus in which 34 percent of black respondents reported that they did not feel welcomed on campus.

It is not clear, however, why students and staff felt that the proper response to a racial incident and unfavorable survey results is to promote apparent segregation throughout the campus community. AU's student newspaper goes on to say that many students also called for the university to "create a black house" in response to racist incidents on campus.

The idea behind a "black house" is to provide a living-learning community for black students, which would be followed up with a survey gauging students' interests in potentially implementing a similar layout within "AU's inventory of housing."

The Director of Diversity, Equity, and Inclusion for Student Government, Rafael Cestero, noted that providing a "space" for one minority group, could lead to "every single other minority group" demanding their own segregated space as well. Elmore stated, however, that the university has a "Center for Diversity and Inclusion" which consolidates "a plethora of identity-based offices" into one center, adding that the idea behind this center is to "organize diversity" under one single umbrella. One could surmise that diversity on campus already exists under one single umbrella — the university itself — and that installing race-based segregated spaces and housing for the sake of diversity may be counterproductive, especially in an environment where students should be focusing on preparing themselves for careers, not ostracism.

https://www.breitbart.com/tech/2018/12/11/american-university-students-and-staff-call-for-minority-only-spaces-on-campus-to-promote-inclusion/

Missouri school ponders white-only racism workshop

By Eduardo Neret Jan 27th, 2019

A Missouri school is considering a segregated safe space for white students to talk about their racism and white privilege. Vincent Flewellen, chief diversity officer at Webster University in St. Louis, has plans for a new program based off a book, titled, "Witnessing Whiteness: The Need to Talk About Race and How to Do It." The local Young Women Christian Association (YWCA) began the "Witnessing Whiteness" program, which requires participants to be white. If brought to Webster University, the workshop would launch in late 2019.

"I have not had an opportunity to fully explore the possibility. Should we move to bring the program onto campus, it would not be before August of this year," Flewellen said, according to Webster University's student newspaper, the *Webster Journal*.

Flewellen most recently brought a "Witnessing Whiteness" program to Washington University in St. Louis. He spoke about the program during a 2018 interview with NBC and said that he wants white people to stop calling the police on black people "just because they're gathering in a park." Additionally, he told NBC that he hopes white people who participate will "find their voice and are able to speak to, call out and stand up against racism."

According to the YWCA chapter's Racial Justice Director Mary Ferguson, there are currently 16 "Witnessing Whiteness" groups that meet regularly and approximately a dozen more that could begin meeting this year. Ferguson also formerly served as an adjunct professor at Webster University from 1997 to 2009.

"It was important to us that we had a group where people of color wouldn't be on the spot, wouldn't be asked to teach, wouldn't be asked to listen to white people as they struggle to understand racism," Ferguson told NBC. "White people would not be as forthcoming if they were in a mixed group," Ferguson told the *Webster Journal*.

The YWCA's website states that members of "Witnessing Whiteness" will explore the "history and construction of white racial identity," "white culture and values," "manifestations of white supremacy and privilege," and "activation of white solidarity and accountability."

The website also has a document that explains the reasoning behind creating a "white space." Some of the reasons listed are: "people of color shouldn't always have to be the ones to educate white people about racism and oppression," "white people need to unlearn racism," and "it's a place where white people can begin to build a new culture of white anti-racism."

Campus Reform reached out to Flewellen, Webster University, the Student Government Association at Webster University, and the YWCA about the Witnessing Whiteness program but received no response in time for publication. If Webster University decides to implement the "Witnessing Whiteness" program, it wouldn't be the first time a university has done so. In September, the University of Maryland-College Park announced a white student only support group called "White Awake." The name of the group was later changed to "Anti-Racism and Ally Building Group" in response to the backlash. And, in May, the University of Colorado-Colorado Springs announced that it would end its affiliation with the "Unmasking Whiteness" conference.

https://www.campusreform.org/?ID=11802

Minority students offered no-whites 'safe space' racial healing circle

By Drew Van Voohis March 12th, 2019

San Diego State University is set to host a "Racial Healing Workshop" for minority students and faculty later this month that aims to help students and professors of color get through college and career life.

"This intimate one and a half hour Racial Healing Workshop catered to students and faculty of color will be led by well-known professional Dr. Cheryl E. Matias," state the student organizers of the event, the Marriage and Family Therapy Association, a recognized student organization under the College of Education.

"She will provide a safe space for students and faculty of color to discuss issues that impact persons of color in higher academia," the event's online description states. "Dr. Matias will facilitate group healing and she will provide tools to help POC [people of color] navigate racialized spaces such as higher education and professional fields." Called "Taking Back Our Truths: Healing Circle," it is scheduled for March 22 at the public university's student union building.

The healing circle takes place after a connected event on campus called "Taking Back our Truths: Deconstructing Whiteness in Academia and Embracing Racial Justice and Healing workshop." This too will be hosted at San Diego State through the student therapy association and is the first part of the association's racial healing activities. According to the deconstructing whiteness workshop's online description, Matias will give a one hour research-driven lecture on whiteness in higher academia and the negative impacts it has on people of color.

"This workshop will raise awareness about the challenges that universities face in attracting, supporting and retaining students and faculty of color. In addition, the research-driven lecture will also provide tools for white identified faculty who work with students of color to help raise consciousness about allyship in academia and professional fields," the event's website states.

Reached for comment by *The College Fix,* La Monica Everett-Haynes, a university spokesperson for SDSU's Office of the President, said that despite the way in which the event description is written, white people are allowed to attend the racial healing circle if they want.

"The event is in no way barring white students, faculty and staff from participation," she said. She also stated that the deconstructing whiteness workshop may help reduce discrimination and racism at the school. "The event is designed to connect students and faculty of diverse backgrounds to understand the experiences of people from minoritized backgrounds. Those who attend will discuss issues of race and identify tools necessary to help students and faculty to work collaboratively and to support one another in ways that may help reduce instances of discrimination and racism," Everett-Haynes wrote.

"[SDSU's student] groups regularly host programs and events collectively to explore and dialogue about discipline-specific topics related to careers, community engagement and service, philanthropy, spirituality and religion, race, class, cultural traditions and numerous other topics and interests. Participation in such programs and events is optional, not mandatory," Everett-Haynes said. "This type of interaction helps to honor SDSU's vision and mission to support a diverse and inclusive campus climate, which benefits us all, not merely specific groups."

Cheryl Matias and the Marriage and Family Therapy Association did not respond to an inquiry from *The College Fix* for comment. Healing circles are not new to San Diego State. In 2016, it hosted a "Healing Circle" to help students process their confusion, anger and fear over Donald Trump's election and develop ways to stand against "injustice."

Editor's note: *After publication, Everett-Haynes contacted* The College Fix *to state that white people are allowed to attend racial healing workshop if they like. This article has been updated to reflect this. The article has also corrected Everett-Haynes' name and clarified that the deconstructing whiteness and racial healing workshops are two parts of one overall event.*

https://www.thecollegefix.com/minority-students-offered-no-whites-safe-space-racial-healing-circle/

Liberal NY college students demand administrators deal with 'racist white professors,' provide free detergent

By Greg Norma March 14th, 2019

Students at a New York college routinely ranked as one of the most liberal in America are accusing administrators of not being progressive enough – unless they accept a long list of demands, including taking teaching duties away from "racist white professors" and providing laundry detergent -- and softener -- for all.

The wide-ranging declaration that emerged this week at the $54,440-a-year Sarah Lawrence College comes as bands of students have been marching around campus, chanting outside the president's home and participating in sit-ins over their beliefs the school has "not implemented sufficient strategies to dismantle systematic oppression to be sustainable or safe for marginalized people in an increasingly dangerous political climate."

"If the College does not accept these demands, it will no longer be hailed as a progressive institution, but instead remembered for its inability to truly embody its self-proclaimed progressive ideology and support all students against an international rising tide of white supremacy and fascism," reads a press release from the Diaspora Coalition student group. The group, which describes itself as "students who can speak to the injustices imposed on people of color by this institution on a daily basis", is demanding that, among other requests:

- "All campus laundry rooms are to supply laundry detergent and softener on a consistent basis for all students, faculty and staff."
- "Students of color should not be forced to resort to racist white professors in order to have access to their own history. It is crucial that the College offer courses taught about people of color by

people of color so that students may engage in and produce meaningful work that represents them authentically."

- "When dining options are closed on campus, the College must provide free meals for students staying on campus, including vegetarian, gluten-free, vegan, halal, and kosher options."
- Students from the Diaspora Coalition and "at least three faculty members of color" are allowed to conduct a tenure review surrounding the position of politics professor Samuel Abrams – who they describe as "an anti-queer, misogynist and racist who actively targets queer people, women and people of color." They also want Abrams to publicly apologize for writing an op-ed for the New York Times last year.

In the piece, Abrams says he surveyed around 900 college administrators and "found that liberal staff members outnumber their conservative counterparts by the astonishing ratio of 12-to-one." He also says Sarah Lawrence's Office of Student Affairs "was organizing many overtly progressive events — programs with names like 'Stay Healthy, Stay Woke,' 'Microaggressions' and 'Understanding White Privilege' — without offering any programming that offered a meaningful ideological alternative."

Students met with Sarah Lawrence President Cristle Collins Judd and Daniel Trujillo, its Dean of Studies and Student Life, on Wednesday night. A Twitter account that appears to be run by students, providing updates on the protests, posted that the "Dean of Studies says he will sign the agreement to work together!" But the group then added: "As we have not come to an agreement with admin., the occupation will CONTINUE!"

Judd, in a statement put out earlier this week, likened the protests to similar ones held at the school in 1969 and 1989, noting that "it is incumbent upon the College to grapple with these issues to support the inclusion and well-being of all students. "I believe collaboration from all parties is the best means to move these efforts forward, and this will require us to develop the most effective process for working with students as well as faculty and staff," she added.

But Judd also pushed back on the "inappropriateness of demands related to the work and tenure" of Abrams, whom she has stood by during the op-ed uproar. In November, she said "academic freedom is a fundamental principle at Sarah Lawrence College" and that "Professor Abrams has every right, and the full support of the College, to pursue and publish this work." It is not clear when the protests will end, but the students want to make one thing certain – that they aren't punished by faculty for participating in them. Their last written demand: "It is our hope that faculty and staff value our voices outside of the classroom and support students' right to protest without repercussion."

https://www.foxnews.com/us/liberal-new-york-college-students-demand-administrators-deal-with-racist-white-professors-and-provide-free-laundry-detergent

KU offers 'angry white male' course

By Grace Gottschling April 3rd, 2019

The University of Kansas is offering a course on angry white men and the role of "dominant and subordinate masculinities" as they connect to "rights-based movements of women, people of color, homosexuals and trans individuals."

"Angry White Male Studies" (HUM 365), which is being offered during the fall 2019 semester, will explore "the deeper sources of this emotional state while evaluating recent manifestations of male anger" in Europe and America from 1950 to present, according to the course description.

The course is cross-listed under both the Humanities department and the Women's, Gender and Sexuality Studies department at KU and is an option to satisfy a Humanities course requirement. Christopher E. Forth, the Dean's Professor of Humanities and Professor of History at KU, is listed as the course instructor. Forth has considerable history studying masculinities and European cultural history and has "Cultural History, Gender and Sexuality, the Body and the Senses" listed as teaching interests. *Campus Reform* reached out to both Forth and KU for comment but did not hear back in time for publishing. If and when a comment is received, the article will be updated.

https://www.campusreform.org/?ID=12058

Leftist Council Member Says Cleaning Feces Off Seattle Streets With a Power Washer is Racist

By Paul Joseph Watson September 5th, 2019

A leftist council member recently tried to stop feces being cleaned off the streets of Seattle with a power washer, arguing that it was racist.

Yes, really.

The problem centers around King County courthouse in downtown Seattle, where homelessness is surging and a tent city has sprung up in a nearby park. Several courthouse employees and two jurors have been assaulted. The area is also littered with fecal matter, leading King County Sheriff John Urquhart to ask the county to order a daily power wash of the sidewalks, which "reek of urine and excrement."

However, leftist Council member Larry Gossett pushed back against the proposal, arguing that it was racist because power washing "brought back images of the use of hoses against civil-rights activists."

That's right. Because high pressure water hoses were once used over 50 years ago to oppress civil rights activists that means streets in 2019 should remain smothered in shit. What's next? Maybe we should just let fires burn endlessly because someone might get offended at the sight of a hose. As we previously reported, Seattle parks are becoming no-go areas for the general public because of spiraling problems with aggressive homeless people and trash. As we highlight in the video below,

San Francisco also has a monumental poop problem and power washers seems to be losing the battle.

https://www.infowars.com/leftist-council-member-says-cleaning-feces-off-seattle-streets-with-a-power-washer-is-racist/

German Scientists Conclude Term 'Race' is Racist

By Deutsche Welle September 12th, 2019

Following the 100th anniversary of the death of the "German Darwin," researchers have distanced themselves from the classification of humans into races. Scientific decency should preclude using the term "race," they say. Scientists at the University of Jena in eastern Germany have called for the term "race" to no longer be used, saying there is no biological basis for the classification of humanity into races.

"The primarily biological justification for defining groups of humans as races — for example based on the color of their skin or eyes, or the shape of their skulls — has led to the persecution, enslavement and slaughter of millions of people," the scientists wrote in the Jena Declaration.

"However, there is no biological basis for races, and there has never been one. The concept of race is the result of racism, not its prerequisite," they continued.

The hierarchical categorization of groups of people based on their biological traits — for example, eye color, skin color, or skull shape — infers evolutionary relationships between species, which scientists in Jena now call a form of racism.

The Jena Declaration, composed by Martin S. Fischer, Uwe Hossfeld and Johannes Krause of the Friedrich Schiller University Jena, and Stefan Richter from the University of Rostock, was presented at the 112th annual meeting of the German Zoological Society in Jena at an event titled "Jena, Haeckel, and the question of human races, or how racism creates races."

This year marked 100th anniversary of the death of Ernst Haeckel, who was seen by many as Germany's answer to Darwin. He was a well-known German zoologist and evolutionary biologist who some say contributed to Nazi biology. Through Haeckel's allegedly scientific classification of human "races" into a "family tree," he "made a fateful contribution to a form of racism that was seemingly based on science," the scientists wrote.

Scientific research on genetic variations of human beings shows that "instead of definable boundaries, genetic gradients run between human groups," say the scientists. "To be explicit, not only is there no single gene that underpins 'racial' differences, but there is not even a single base pair." This research carries added weight in Germany where during the Nazi era, eugenics, a set of beliefs and practices aimed at ostensibly improving the genetic quality of a human population, and racial hygiene, were used extensively in order to further the National Socialist ideological tenet of maintaining a pure master race that was biologically superior to other races.

The President of Jena University, Walter Rosenthal, admits that while simply removing the word "race" from shared vocabulary will not prevent racism, "as academics we can help to ensure that racism is no longer able to invoke us as a justification." In the Jena Declaration, the group of scientists drew a link between current forms of racism and "seemingly scientific disciplines" like racial hygiene or eugenics.

"Designating 'the Africans' as a supposed threat to Europe and attributing certain biological characteristics are also in the direct tradition of the worst racism of our past. So, let us ensure that people are never again discriminated against on specious biological grounds," the scientists write.

https://www.infowars.com/german-scientists-conclude-term-race-is-racist/

Whites need not apply: Campus sci-tech symposium to only feature scholars of color

By Brittany Slaughter September 16th, 2019

An upcoming science and technology symposium slated to take place at Williams College promises a unique feature: it will showcase "new" voices in the field, and those voices will only come from scholars of color.

"New Voices in Science and Technology Studies: A C3 Symposium," set for early November at the private Massachusetts-based liberal arts university, invited scholars to submit papers if they represent a "historically underrepresented group." The call for papers specifies that means either "African Americans, Alaska Natives, Arab Americans, Asian Americans, Latinx, Native Americans, Native Hawaiians, and other Pacific Islanders."

Part of the application process asked applicants to write a couple sentences proving themselves as a member of a "historically underrepresented group." Yet the application also provides an equal employment opportunity statement that people from all backgrounds are welcome.

Chosen scholars will receive a $500 honorarium and be hosted by Williams College as they present their papers to the audience, organizers state, adding "we aim to create an inclusive, intellectually enriching experience for all involved, including the visiting speakers and the faculty and students of Williams."

Williams College Associate Professor of Political Science and Chair of Science and Technology Studies Laura Ephraim is the point of contact for the event. For the last three weeks she has ignored repeated phone calls and emails from *The College Fix* seeking comment on the event.

Williams College's media affairs office and several faculty members in the Science and Technology Studies program at the school also ignored repeated requests for comment. The only person at the college willing to return numerous requests for comment was an administrative assistant in Science and Technology Studies who said they were unsure who could help *The College Fix* with its questions.

Promotional materials for the symposium state: "The Science & Technology Studies Program at Williams College invites papers on any topic concerned with science and technology and their relationship to society for a day-long symposium showcasing the work of early-career scholars (ABD or recent PhD) from historically underrepresented groups."

As for the science and technology program at Williams, it is an interdisciplinary social sciences field, its website states. "The Program in Science and Technology Studies (STS) aims to provide students with an interdisciplinary framework through which to appreciate the complex interactions between science, technology and society, and with which to analyze and understand the ways science and technology give shape to, and are in turn given shape by, society, culture and history," the website states.

The program also works on "critical dialogue" issues. "The STS Program furthermore serves as a forum in which students from all divisions are invited to partake in critical dialogue on a range of pressing issues: scientific controversies, expert knowledge, innovation and socio-historical transformation, politics and policy, media and communication infrastructure, public understanding of science and technology, and philosophical questions," according to its website.

https://www.thecollegefix.com/whites-need-not-apply-campus-sci-tech-symposium-to-only-feature-scholars-of-color/

University Bans White Students From Attending Anti-Racism Meeting

By Paul Joseph Watson October 10th, 2019

The University of Sheffield Student's Union in the UK has banned white people from attending a meeting about anti-racism.

Yes, really.

The SU announced that it would hold focus groups on "how we can create an anti-racist Students' Union" as part of an effort to shift from a "non-racist to an actively anti-racist" stance.

However, no white people are allowed to take part. "Please note that these sessions are only open to black and minority ethnic (BME) students," states the announcement. Banning people from a meeting about racism because of their skin color is...what's the word? Oh yeah, racist. The controversy follows a similar farce at the University of Edinburgh where white people were banned from asking questions at an event called Resisting Whiteness.

"We will not be giving the microphone to white people during the Q&As, not because we don't think white people have anything to offer to the discussion but because we want to amplify the voices of people of colour," stated promotional material for the event.

https://www.infowars.com/university-bans-white-students-from-attending-an-anti-racism-meeting/

Popular chess channel hit by YouTube's racial justice algorithm

By JD Rucker June 30th, 2020

A story came across my virtual desk last night that seemed relatively innocuous. The author who sent it to me must have felt the same because the story was very short. Nevertheless, I watched the video referenced in the article and realized the story was much more important than I originally thought.

A popular chess podcast with nearly 700,000 subscribers on YouTube called “agadmator’s Chess Channel” posted a video telling of how during a livestreamed podcast, his video was removed by YouTube for breaking community guidelines. The communication they sent him said he had seven days to review the video and decide if he wanted to appeal the decision. He didn’t need seven days as he knew he hadn’t said anything that went against the guidelines. He said he doesn’t even swear on his podcast, let alone say anything that YouTube should deem illegal, so he instantly sent in his appeal. The response from YouTube was instant as well: Appeal rejected over “Harmful or dangerous content.”

Again, this is a chess podcast that analyzes games. He had no idea what in the world he could have said that would have driven such a response, but he knew for certain based on the speed of the reply that it was not reviewed by a human. AI was behind his video being taken down and his appeal being denied.

It seems clear to me, as I noted in the latest episode of Conservative News Briefs, that the AI flagged some supposedly racist remark like “white knight takes black pawn” and assumed it was against Black Lives Matter or something. And while that may seem like a minor technology flaw, it exposes the reality we face in America today, that as long as we rely on Google, YouTube, Facebook, and Twitter as our primary Big Tech companies through which to spread the message, that message will always be a potential victim to some skewed AI. Racial justice technology is on the rise, folks.

Of course, I’m also a hypocrite. I use YouTube because the competitors don’t have the same reach. I have a Parler account, but I’m still on Twitter as well. I don’t do much on Facebook and I’m no seeking an alternative. As for Google, I’ve been on DuckDuckGo for a while.

Big Tech is the biggest long-term threat to patriotism, conservatism, and common sense. The Cultural Marxists are popping up in every aspect of American life. We need to try harder. We need to fight smarter.

https://noqreport.com/2020/06/30/popular-chess-channel-hit-by-youtubes-racial-justice-algorithm/

'Blackface' Pumpkins Pulled From Bed Bath & Beyond After Complaints Of Racism

By TooFab Staff October 24th, 2019

Bed Bath & Beyond has stopped selling black jack-o-lanterns amid complaints the decorations are a form of blackface.

The backlash first arose after a local law firm in Nyack, New York placed the pumpkins -- painted black with white eyes, nose and mouth -- on their front porch as part of a Halloween display. Some residents found the pumpkins harmless, but NAACP regional director, Wilber Aldridgewhich, said the decorations showed "an extreme lack of sensitivity."

"By now I would believe everyone [would] know that anything in Black face is offensive -- Equally as offensive is that a retail store would have such an item in [their] inventory for general purchase," read a statement from Aldridge. "It wasn't about the pumpkin itself, but what was done to the pumpkin. When you proceed to put the white eyes and the white mouth, now you have crossed the line because it then goes into having blackface," Aldridge told News 12. The criticism prompted Ferick, Nugent, MacCartney Law to remove the display within 48 hours.

"We understand that someone complained about them and so once we got word of that we immediately took them down," Mary Marzolla, a partner at the law firm, told the news outlet. She said the pumpkins -- personalized with the names of the partners of the law firm -- were not meant to be offensive.

"We represent people of all colors and faiths, and we would never do anything to exclude anyone from any community," Marzolla explained. Her associate, Alak Shah, backed her claims. "It's just nothing I take offense to personally, but since it did offend someone we took proactive steps to take it down," he said.

After News 12 contacted Bed Bath & Beyond about the controversy, the item was removed from its website. "This is a sensitive area and, though unintentional, we apologize for any offense caused. We immediately removed the item from sale," the company said in a statement.

Social media blew up in response to the news, as users noted the decorations were tossed, yet politicians -- such as Canadian Prime Minister Justin Trudeau -- known to wear blackface in the past remained in office.

https://toofab.com/2019/10/24/blackface-pumpkins-pulled-bed-bath-beyond-racism/

Brown University Students Push To Abolish All Prisons, Says They're Racist and Unjust

By Jack Davis November 23rd, 2019

A group of Brown University students wants to abolish prisons in the name of justice.

"The end goal is to not have prisons as any form of incarceration," student Grace Austin, a member of the group called RailRoad, said at a teach-in called "Prison Abolition 101" held early this month, according to The Brown Daily Herald. "Punishment at any stage doesn't guarantee any kind of growth," she said. Fellow student Aida Sherif said the prison system is about punishment and not justice. "Prisons were founded in the ideas of punishing the poor, punishing people of color," Sherif said. "I don't see it as an institution that can ever fully break away from those foundations."

RailRoad's vision "is a world where the Prison Industrial Complex in all of its forms has been destroyed and built in its place are systems of accountability that allow for healing and growth," according to the group's "about" section of its Facebook page.

The group's thinking is aligned with comments from Democratic Rep. Alexandria Ocasio-Cortez of New York, whose recent tweet condemning prisons was posted on the group's Facebook page.

"Mass incarceration is our American reality. It is a system whose logic evolved from the same lineage as Jim Crow, American apartheid, & slavery. To end it, we have to change. That means we need to have a real conversation about decarceration & prison abolition in this country," Ocasio-Cortez tweeted last month.

Her call for prison abolition was not popular on Twitter. The Brown students suggested that there could be alternative institutions for justice that are not prisons, which one student said are not essential. "Our society is constructed in a way that would have us believe prisons are absolutely necessary," Sherif said while presenting at the event. "People perceive it as crazy, unreasonable, dangerous, too radical. Abolition is not anarchy."

The student group wants the Ivy League college to adopt what it called "fair chance" hiring practices that would include saying it does not discriminate based on anyone's conviction history. Students also want the college to hire individuals who have been in jail.

"If people aren't totally on board with the issue of mass incarceration and prison abolition in general, then they may not necessarily be as convinced about fair chance hiring," student Leah Shorb said. "Anything that is interrupting the cycle of incarceration is abolitionist to me as long as it's not further entrenching the system of incarceration."

https://www.westernjournal.com/brown-university-students-push-abolish-prisons-says-racist-unjust/

Law school student interrogated by FBI, expelled over 'It's Okay to be White' flyers

By Victor Skinner December 11th, 2019

A student who posted "It's Okay to be White" flyers outside of a building at the Oklahoma City University of Law was expelled and interrogated by the FBI Joint Terrorism Task Force.

The Oklahoman reports:

OCU Police Director Bill Citty said the male student was already on suspension from the law school, 800 N Harvey, and was not allowed to be on school property. The student violated the terms of his suspension when he posted the flyers on the door and exterior of the law school building the night of Oct. 31, Citty said.

Jim Roth, the school's dean, sent the perpetrator a letter informing him of his expulsion in mid November. The culprit, who remains anonymous, was serving a prior suspension for his Tinder profile, which stated a preference for a girl who "hasn't been with a black guy."

"You have violated the terms of your suspension, which prohibited you from entering campus grounds. The University is in possession of evidence clearly demonstrating that you entered University grounds on or about October 31, 2019," Roth's letter read. "Based on a preponderance of the evidence, pursuant to the terms of your suspension, and according to University policy, you are hereby expelled from Oklahoma City University School of Law, effective immediately."

The letter reiterated the student's ban from campus and threatened legal action if the student ever comes back. Roth also issued an ironic public statement praising students who ripped down the posters and notified school officials. "Despite what the intentions of that message may have been, the message reminds me of one fact that I know our community embraces – it's okay to be EVERYBODY," he wrote. "Exclusion and hate will not be tolerated here. You are accepted at OCU Law no matter how you pray, what you look like, or who you love. And you always will be."

That message, the student said, doesn't apply to white students who aren't ashamed of their skin color. The student told The Red Elephants' Vincent James he was interrogated by an agent with the FBI's Joint Terrorism Task Force, who confirmed the posters were not a crime. The agent also told the student, who was dressed up for Halloween when he posted the flyers, there is no possible way for law enforcement to positively identify him from surveillance video, even if it was illegal.

"He basically said no crimes were committed, we just got to make sure you're not a threat," the student said. "Both the FBI and the Oklahoma City Police said ... we have no reason to open an investigation, we're not considering you a suspect of any crime, but the campus police, the private police they have at the school, I guess if they wanted to they could press trespassing charges."

National File contacted another "It's Okay to be White" activist for another perspective on the debacle, which he claims is an illustration of the double standard for racism in America. "My only thoughts on this incident are that the response was draconian and hysterical (but sadly predictable) and should serve as a wake-up call to anyone who does not want to live under totalitarianism. The people who want to ruin this young student's life for refusing to hate himself are evil," the unidentified activist said.

"The response also clearly demonstrates a racial hatred and paranoid fear of white people deeply rooted in the establishment media, academia and government, not only in the US but across the West," he said.

"If you replaced the word 'white' with any other group and put up a flyer saying 'It's Okay to be (another group),' there would likely have been no police attention or media coverage," he said. "This law student who was expelled is essentially a martyr. He sacrificed years of study, large sums of money and part of his reputation and future to warn people about this totalitarian threat."

https://www.theamericanmirror.com/blog/2019/12/11/law-school-student-interrogated-by-fbi-expelled-over-its-okay-to-be-white-flyers/

The White-Guilt Cult

By Kyle Smith June 18th, 2020

Amidst nationwide Black Lives Matter protests, a black man and woman are seated on a park bench while a white woman wearing a sweatshirt that reads "LOVE" takes to her megaphone. "We repent on behalf of, uh, Caucasian people," she says. A small crowd of white people comes to kneel before the two seated black folks, who are co-pastors of a local church. Some of the kneelers wash the feet of the black people. A white man with an English accent solemnly intones, "It's our honor to stand here on behalf of all white people, . . . repenting, Lord, for our aggression, Lord, repenting for our pride, for thinking that we are better, that we are above." Police officers join the ritual. Several people start audibly weeping, or keening, as the speaker continues. Roughly a dozen people join in the gesture and kneel before the black couple. "We have put our necks, put our hands, our knees, upon the necks of our African-American brothers and sisters, people of color, indigenous people," says the English man. "Lord, where we as a church, a white church, have used you as a persecution towards black people, Lord, as we've burnt crosses, as we've burnt churches, . . . we've used it as a weapon against people of color."

It's been coming for some time, this transmutation of white guilt into a cult, a religion that borrows from and intersects with Christianity but substitutes its own liturgy. In the Nineties, liberal white Hollywood filmmakers began to nourish a fantasy that black people were imbued with magical powers, and they built stories around angelic or Christlike black redeemers who stood apart from and above this fallen race we call humanity. Will Smith in *The Legend of Bagger Vance*, Cuba Gooding Jr. in *What Dreams May Come*, and Michael Clarke Duncan in *The Green Mile* served as spiritual and/or actual caddies to troubled white men, guiding them toward salvation.

Today those "magical negro" films, as Spike Lee dubbed them, get ridiculed by the critical intelligentsia, but the same impulse is visible in different form. White people continue to have difficulty perceiving blacks as individual human beings, instead conferring on blackness a holy quality. Fallen white people can get closer to the divine by showing due deference in any way they can. Books that promise to assist white people with the project of metaphorically scourging themselves — *White Fragility*, *How to Be an Antiracist* — bounded up the best-seller lists. Black Americans report, with more annoyance than appreciation, that white friends are calling them nervously, seeking absolution.

The original sin in the White Guilt Cult, the New Church of Anti-Racism, is to be, "uh, Caucasian people." Parker Gillian, a young black college graduate in Chicago who is in no need of financial support (she grew up in affluence, she told the *Washington Post*), says that someone from work texted out of nowhere to ask, "What's your cash app?" and then pinged $20 into her account, unasked. "It is so exhausting being everybody's one black friend right now," tweeted a comedian named Sarah Cooper. Black people observing such displays by their white acquaintances can be forgiven for wondering: Is it really a friendship if one party is groveling, throwing money, and begging to wash the other party's feet? If anything, the Great Awokening's response to the George Floyd killing seems to be bolstering racial barriers rather than eradicating them. By making a religion of anti-racism, white people carry on with the longstanding project of "othering" black folks.

Anti-racism is the most critical element of a broader new Woke Orthodoxy whose other elements include environmental apocalypticism, feminism, and a severing of sexual identity from genetic indicators. Settling on a term for the new religion will take some time. Wesley Yang's suggestion (seconded by Ross Douthat) of "the Successor Ideology" is clunky, anodyne, and a bit euphemistic given the righteous, roiling fervor and unnerving credulousness that define the cult. As Dmitri Solzhenitsyn writes in National Review Online, a YouTube prankster named "Smooth Sanchez" who walks the streets of New York demanding that white people kneel before him and declare their privilege receives surprising compliance, even as he signals his charlatanry by referring to George Floyd as "George Foreman."

Ben Shapiro notes astutely that the new woke religion rushes in to fill a "God-shaped hole" in secular hearts. Devotees immerse themselves in the sacred texts of Ta-Nehisi Coates and Ibram X. Kendi (né Ibram Henry Rogers of Queens), books designed to make white wokesters writhe with a kind of ecstatic anguish. Indoctrination in early childhood is taken up as a parental duty (Kendi's new board book for toddlers, *Antiracist Baby*, is a hot seller), parishioners engage in ritualistic incantation of sacred phrases ("Hands up, don't shoot," "I can't breathe"), and there are mass displays of penitential self-abasement. All over the country, guilty white crowds have gathered to reenact the circumstances of George Floyd's horrifying death. Scores, even hundreds, of parishioners in the new faith prostrate themselves on the ground, hands behind their back, repeating "Mama" and "I can't breathe." Sometimes police officers joined these displays, kneeling or prostrating themselves for the sanctified period of time: eight minutes, 46 seconds. Floyd's death is a kind of new Crucifixion, his final words the new "My God, my God, why have you forsaken me?"

The new clergy consists of black thought leaders (Coates, Kendi, Stacey Abrams) and those white people who loudly proclaim themselves allies and proselytize for the organizing dogma, which is that everything is racist. Those who question orthodoxy are kept at bay, derided as "conservatives" who are "arguing in bad faith" if not actual racists. "For example, one is not to ask 'Why are black people so upset about one white cop killing a black man when black men are at much more danger of being killed by one another?'" wrote John McWhorter in his 2015 essay "Antiracism, Our Flawed New Religion." "The answers are flabby but further questions are unwelcome," McWhorter added. The much-promised "conversation on race" consists of repeating points in the catechism to enhance their power — phrases such as "I must do better," "white privilege," "systemic racism," "white supremacy," "allyship."

"There is more dogmatism in this ideology than in most of contemporary American Catholicism," writes the Catholic columnist Andrew Sullivan. "And more intolerance. Question any significant part of this, and your moral integrity as a human being is called into question." As the fierceness of old religions fades, a corresponding desire for a new righteous fury rises. The fervor sweeping through the South (but not just the South) to pull down statues seen as blasphemous to the new faith loudly echoes the 16th-century rampage through the monasteries that burned icons and laid waste to stained glass. Each successive wave of iconoclasm will take more and more historical monuments until either the new Reformation ends or all blasphemous iconography has been destroyed, with the logical endpoint being Mount Rushmore, with its quintuple heresy: Washington and Jefferson held slaves, Teddy Roosevelt is damned as a racist, the land the monument sits on was seized from indigenous peoples, and the sculptor, Gutzon Borglum, was friendly with the Ku Klux Klan.

https://www.nationalreview.com/magazine/2020/07/06/the-white-guilt-cult/#slide-1

Kristen Bell Will No Longer Voice Mixed-Race Character in Apple's 'Central Park'

By Will Thorne June 24th, 2020

Kristen Bell will no longer voice the mixed-race central character of Molly Tillerman in the forthcoming Apple animated series "Central Park." The decision to re-cast the role was announced via a lengthy statement from the show's creative team, which said that "casting of the character of Molly is an opportunity to get representation right – to cast a Black or mixed race actress and give Molly a voice that resonates with all of the nuance and experiences of the character as we've drawn her."

Bell also released her own statement, saying that her voicing the character "shows a lack of awareness of my pervasive privilege."

"Casting a mixed race character w/a white actress undermines the specificity of the mixed race & Black American experience," Bell's statement read. Creator Loren Bouchard previously addressed the casting during a panel in Jan., at which point there was clearly no intention to re-cast the role. "Kristen needed to be Molly; we couldn't not make her Molly. But then we couldn't make Molly white and we couldn't make Kristen mixed race so we just had to go forward," Bouchard said at the time.

News of the re-casting comes mere hours after Jenny Slate announced that she was stepping away from voicing a biracial character on Netflix's "Big Mouth." Read the full statement from Bouchard, Josh Gad, Nora Smith, Halsted Sullivan and Sanjay Shah below:

"Kristen Bell is an extraordinarily talented actress who joined the cast of Central Park from nearly the first day of the show's development – before there was even a character for her to play – and she has since delivered a funny, heartfelt, and beautiful performance.

But after reflection, Kristen, along with the entire creative team, recognizes that the casting of the character of Molly is an opportunity to get representation right – to cast a Black or mixed race actress and give Molly a voice that resonates with all of the nuance and experiences of the character as we've drawn her. Kristen will continue to be a part of the heart of the show in a new role but we will find a new actress to lend her voice to Molly.

We profoundly regret that we might have contributed to anyone's feeling of exclusion or erasure.

Black people and people of color have worked and will continue to work on Central Park but we can do better. We're committed to creating opportunities for people of color and Black people in all roles, on all our projects – behind the mic, in the writers room, in production, and in post-production. Animation will be stronger for having as many voices, experiences, and perspectives as we can possibly bring into the industry. Our shop and our show will be better for respecting the nuances and complexity around the issue of representation and trying to get it right."

"Central Park" is currently five episodes into its first season run. It voice cast also includes Josh Gad, Leslie Odom Jr., Kathryn Hahn, Tituss Burgess, Daveed Diggs and Stanley Tucci.

https://variety.com/2020/tv/news/kristen-mixed-race-character-central-park-apple-1234648875/

UK University Says Complaining About Everything Becoming a Race Issue is a Racist Microaggression

By Paul Joseph Watson January 15th, 2020

The University of Sheffield in the UK is to pay its own students to patrol thought crimes, one of which is the common complaint that everything is becoming a race issue, which the university considers to be a racist microaggression.

Checkmate, bigots. "A university is to hire 20 of its own students to challenge language on campus that could be seen as racist," reports the BBC. "The University of Sheffield is to pay students to tackle so-called "microaggressions" – which it describes as "subtle but offensive comments."

According to the university, examples of these microaggressions include;

- "Stop making everything a race issue"
- "Why are you searching for things to be offended about?"
- "Where are you really from?"
- "I don't want to hear about your holiday to South Africa. It's nowhere near where I'm from"
- "Being compared to black celebrities that I look nothing like"

In other words, pointing out that people play the race card to avoid having to defend their opinions and that 'offense' culture is out of control is now itself a subtle form of racism. You've got to hand it to them; Not only have they seized control of language, they've also banned your ability to question why they're doing so.

"Sheffield University is paying students to spy on their peers and report any "microaggressions," comments Andrew Doyle. "One example they give is "Why are you searching for things to be offended about?" Given this sinister Stasi-like initiative, that's a very good question."

https://www.infowars.com/uk-university-says-complaining-about-everything-becoming-a-race-issue-is-a-racist-microaggression/

Discriminatory chalk prompts frustration among students, university condemnation

By Tiffany Huang March 27th, 2020

Discriminatory chalk writing that appeared late Wednesday night sparked frustration and fear among UW-Madison's Asian and Asian-American community — and prompted the university to again emphasize its stance against racist actions.

"It's from China, #ChineseVirus" and "F*** the Chinese Government" was chalked on the sidewalk in front of Walgreens on State Street and Bascom Hill. Signs were washed off by a group of students the following morning. Students started raising the issue of discrimination against Asian and Asian-American communities in February after UW-Madison announced its first case of coronavirus.

One month later, incidents like this demonstrate blatant discrimination occurring in Madison alongside Pres. Donald Trump's choice of calling COVID-19 the "Chinese Virus." It is unclear who wrote this and exactly when it happened. However, Muyang Deng took photos of the chalk and shared them in the Chinese international student group chat around 2 a.m. Thursday.

Julia Tan, who is a member of the group chat, was shocked by the images Deng sent. “This is not acceptable and it is very terrifying. If I were still on campus now, I would be so scared to leave my apartment,” Tan said.

However, Tan — who is originally from Beijing, China — is one of the few international students who has a stable extended family in the country where she can stay off-campus and continue her academics. Most international students’ only permanent home in the US is on UW-Madison's campus, and they are unable to get back to their families during this pandemic.

There have been 81 bias reports so far in 2020 — 47 of those were made by Asian American and Asian international students at UW-Madison, according to the assistant director of Bias Response Jenna Friedman.

Tao Zhou, who is a senior studying economics with a certificate in photography and video production, shared the most recent incident on Instagram. “This is not okay. I’m calling for non-discrimination in this global crisis on campus, because no matter who you are, we are all in this together. We should send love and care more about each other, instead of hate,” Zhou captioned her post. Other students are reposting the images and urging the university to do the same on their official social media accounts to raise awareness of anti-Asian discrimination and hate.

The university has apologized to Zhou, personally, that she and other fellow students have had to endure racism such as this. “No one person, country, or ethnicity created this pandemic—disease does not discriminate,” Chancellor Blank stated in the email to all students and faculty. “We want to be clear that racist behaviors or stereotyping of any kind are not tolerated at UW–Madison—no matter if we are online, passing others in public, or quarantined at home.”

In addition to Blank's email, the university hosted a virtual town hall in response to the current campus climate Thursday afternoon. Approximately 350 people logged on for the town hall hosted by the Dean of Students Office, in partnership with the Multicultural Student Center, International Student Services and the Division of Diversity, Equity and Educational Achievement.

During the town hall, students shared concern about the growing racism and xenophobia that targets the Asian and Asian-American community — particularly those who perceived as being of Chinese or East Asian descent — and they questioned the action UW-Madison plans to take to address the issue and foster a more inclusive community.

"We are here for students and here to let them know that [any discriminatory] behavior is not tolerated at UW-Madison," Dean of Students Christina Olstad said. "We can do better than this." Professor Cindy Cheng from the Asian-American Studies Program also used the meeting to urge the Asian and Asian American communities to remember to create love and support for each other and themselves.

Students are encouraged to file a bias incident report and employees can file a complaint with the Office of Compliance if they experience harassment or discrimination. There are also free university mental health resources, including SilverCloud for anxiety and stress management; the Center for Healthy Minds for resilience and mindfulness training; and LifeMatters through the Employee Assistance Office for employees seeking assistance with life, work, family and well-being.

The Division of Diversity, Equity & Educational Achievement will host another virtual town hall meeting Friday afternoon from 12 p.m. to 1 p.m. in support of Asian and Asian-American students, faculty and staff members. This is a chance for everyone to hear university community members, voice concerns regarding the campus climate, ask questions and share experiences.

https://www.dailycardinal.com/article/2020/03/discriminatory-chalk-prompts-frustration-among-students-university-condemnation

NHS Nurses' Haka Dance Blasted as "Cultural Appropriation"

By Paul Joseph Watson April 20th, 2020

A now deleted viral video in which NHS workers in the UK performed a modified version of the haka, a ceremonial dance in Maori culture, has been condemned as "cultural appropriation." The video received over 600,000 views on Twitter before it was removed, presumably in response to claims that it was racist.

In the clip, nurses from the Tavistock Day Case Theatre in England performed the iconic dance while wearing white headbands and black face paint. At the end of the video, one of the nurses screams, "This is the message we wish to affirm, you'll never beat us we hate you, you germ. Together we'll triumph with the strength from within. Mankind will destroy you, mankind will win."

However, despite following a trend of other dancing videos by health professionals which have been labeled both "cringe" and "courageous" by viewers, the haka version was deemed to have crossed the line of political correctness.

Maori cultural advisor Karaitiana Taiuru said the video was "absolutely offensive and degrading" and that the nurses were "re-enacting blackface" by painting black streaks on their faces. "What appears to be headbands is reminiscent of the culturally appropriated Maori dolls and a cultural stereotype that all Maori wear headbands and have facial tattoo," said Taiuru.

"There is no reasonable excuse why any semi-educated person with access to the internet, from anywhere in the world, to not know that mocking another person's culture is offensive," he added, arguing that the video was "blatant cultural abuse that is verging on being racist."

Taiuru also suggested that the performance may be a violation of the Haka Ka Mate Attribution Act of 2014. "There appears to be a fixation with many people in the UK with Maori culture and what appears to be an inherited colonial perceived right to appropriate Maori culture with marketing of food and beverages and more so in particular to mocking the Haka," complained Taiuru.

https://www.infowars.com/nhs-nurses-haka-dance-blasted-as-cultural-appropriation/

Gregg Popovich: 'Embarrassed as a white person'

By Associated Press June 7th, 2020

SAN ANTONIO – San Antonio Spurs coach Gregg Popovich said he's "embarrassed as a white person" that George Floyd could die in such a "nonchalant" manner. The 71-year-old Popovich addressed Floyd's death in a video released Saturday by the Spurs as part of the team's #SpursVoices social media series.

Floyd was in handcuffs when a Minneapolis police officer pressed his knee into his neck as he pleaded that he couldn't breathe. Derek Chauvin is charged with third-degree murder and second-degree manslaughter. "In a strange, counterintuitive sort of way, the best teaching moment of this recent tragedy, I think, was the look on the officer's face," Popovich said. "For white people to see how nonchalant, how casual, just how everyday-going-about-his job, so much so that he could just put his left hand in his pocket, wriggle his knee around a little bit to teach this person some sort of a lesson -- and that it was his right and his duty to do it, in his mind...

"I think I'm just embarrassed as a white person to know that that can happen. To actually watch a lynching. We've all seen books, and you look in the books and you see black people hanging off of trees. ... But we just saw it again. I never thought I'd see that, with my own eyes, in real time.

"It's like the neighborhood where you know there's a dangerous corner, and you know that something's going to happen someday, and nobody does anything. And then a young kid gets killed and a stop sign goes up. Well, without getting too political, we've got a lot of stop signs that need to go up -- quickly -- because our country is in trouble. And the basic reason is race."

Popovich said white people must help lead the charge for change. "We have to do it. Black people have been shouldering this burden for 400 years," Popovich said. "The only reason this nation has made the progress it has is because of the persistence, patience and effort of black people. The history of our nation from the very beginning in many ways was a lie, and we continue to this day, mostly black and brown people, to try to make that lie a truth so that it is no longer a lie. And those rights and privileges are enjoyed by people of color, just like we enjoy them. So it's got to be us, in my opinion, that speak truth to power, and call it out, no matter what the consequences. We have to speak. We have to not let anything go." Popovich has led the Spurs to five NBA titles and is a three-time coach of the year. He's set to coach the United States in the Tokyo Olympics.

https://www.click2houston.com/sports/2020/06/07/gregg-popovich-embarrassed-as-a-white-person/

Prof blames 'white Christian nationalism' for death of George Floyd

By Leo Thuman June 8th, 2020

A professor at the University of Vermont has attracted attention with controversial tweets, in which she suggested that white Christians are broadly culpable in the recent death of George Floyd, a black man killed in police custody.

In response to the recent killing of George Floyd by Minneapolis police, Ilyse R. Morgenstein Fuerst, who is an Associate Professor of Religion at the University of Vermont, tweeted that "white Christian nationalism is the thing we're all watching," adding that nationalism and white Christianity are "inextricable from the anti-Blackness murdering" victims of police brutality.

"White Christian nationalism is the thing we're all watching—it's inextricable from the anti-Blackness murdering folks." This hasn't been the only charged statement Fuerst has posted to social media in recent days regarding current protests and riots.

On June 1, she retweeted a photo of President Donald Trump holding a bible in front of the desecrated Saint John's Church in Washington, D.C., adding her own profane commentary. Fuerst also shared tweets from other users comparing law enforcement's handling of recent riots with the Communist Chinese government's 1989 assault on peaceful protesters in Beijing's Tiananmen Square.

Fuerst, whose research and teaching focuses on Islam, has commented on current events in the past, both on social media and in traditional publications. In the wake of the 2016 presidential election, she wrote an article in *Religion & Politics*arguing that the president's rhetoric on the campaign trail was tied to crimes against American Muslims. Fuerst has taught at UVM for eight years. In addition to being a professor, she serves as Associate Director of the institution's Humanities Center. She did not respond to *Campus Reform*'s request for comment in time for publication.

https://www.campusreform.org/?ID=15001&utm_campaign=CampusWire&utm_medium=email&_hsmi=89203773&_hsenc=p2ANqtz--4yuIRtGssHg0b6j8OJysPPkmtwB1AVEil-rxjqQIzHg8Yj8ua9BWq6FtiP8hRJp5b_BpII0USJA844jhjZ_khopZtwRw&utm_content=89203773&utm_source=hs_email#.XuA9bFC3bKo.facebook

Democrats Seek To Outlaw Suburban, Single-Family House Zoning, Calling It Racist And Bad For The Environment

By Luke Rosiak December 23rd, 2019

Democrats in Virginia may override local zoning to bring high-density housing, including public housing, to every neighborhood statewide — whether residents want it or not.

The measure could quickly transform the suburban lifestyle enjoyed by millions, permitting duplexes to be built on suburban lots in neighborhoods previously consisting of quiet streets and open green spaces. Proponents of "upzoning" say the changes are necessary because suburbs are bastions of segregation and elitism, as well as bad for the environment.

The move, which aims to provide "affordable housing," might be fiercely opposed by local officials throughout the state, who have deliberately created and preserved neighborhoods with particular character — some dense and walkable, others semi-rural and private — to accommodate people's various preferences. But Democrats tout a state-level law's ability to replace "not in my backyard" with "yes, in your backyard."

House Delegate Ibraheem Samirah, a Democrat, introduced six housing measures Dec. 19, coinciding with Democrats' takeover of the state legislature in November. "Single-family housing zones would become two-zoned," Samirah told the Daily Caller News Foundation. "Areas that would be impacted most would be the suburbs that have not done their part in helping out."

"The real issues are the areas in between very dense areas which are single-family zoned. Those are the areas that the state is having significant trouble dealing with. They're living in a bubble," he said. He said suburbs were "mostly white and wealthy" and that their local officials — who have historically been in charge of zoning — were ignoring the desires of poor people, who did not have time to lobby them to increase suburban density.

In response to a question about whether people who bought homes in spacious suburbs have valid reasons, not based on discrimination, for preferring to live that way — including a love for nature and desire to preserve woods and streams — he said: "Caring about nature is very important, but the more dense a neighborhood is, the more energy efficient it is."

He said if local officials seek to change requirements like setbacks to make it impossible to build dense housing in areas zoned to preserve a nature feel, "if they make setbacks to block duplexes, there'd have to be a lawsuit to resolve whether those zoning provisions were necessary." He wrote on Facebook, "Because middle housing is what's most affordable for low-income people and people of color, banning that housing in well-off neighborhoods chalks up to modern-day redlining, locking folks out of areas with better access to schools, jobs, transit, and other services and amenities."

"I will certainly get pushback for this. Some will call it 'state overreach.' Some will express anxiety about neighborhood change. Some may even say that the supply issue doesn't exist. But the research is clear: zoning is a barrier to more housing and integrated communities," he continued. He tweeted Sunday that that would include public housing. "Important Q about new social/public housing programs: where are we going to put the units? Under current zoning, new low-income housing is relegated to underinvested neighborhoods, concentrating poverty more. Ending exclusionary zoning has to be part of broader housing reform," he said.Tim Hannigan, chairman of the Fairfax County Republican Committee — in one of the areas Samirah represents — said that urban Democrats were waging war on the suburbs.

"This could completely change the character of suburban residential life, because of the urbanization that would develop," he told the DCNF. "So much of the American dream is built upon this idea of finding a nice quiet place to raise your family, and that is under assault."

"This is a power-grab to take away the ability of local communities to establish their own zoning practices ... literally trying to change the character of our communities," he said. He said suburbs were not equipped to handle the increased traffic, and "inevitably it will just push people to places where they feel they'll get away from that, they may move to West Virginia to get their little plot of land." Minneapolis became the first city to eliminate single family zoning in December 2018, after a push by progressive advocacy groups promoting "equity." Austin, Texas, and Seattle soon followed suit.

But those cities were amending zoning codes that have always been the domain of local governments. Oregon passed state legislation blocking local governments' single-family zoning in July, CityLab reported.

It quoted Alex Baca, a Washington, D.C., urbanist with the site Greater Greater Washington, saying that single-family zoning is a tool for wealthy whites to maintain segregated neighborhoods and that the abolition of low-density neighborhoods is necessary for equity. CityLab acknowledged that "residents might reasonably desire to keep the neighborhoods they love the way they are," but said that implementing the law at the state level makes sure that those concerns can be more easily ignored.

"By preempting the ability of local governments to set their own restrictive zoning policies, the state policy would circumnavigate the complaints of local NIMBY homeowners who want to block denser housing," it wrote.

While he implied that suburbs are prejudiced, Samirah himself has a history of anti-Semitic comments. "I am so sorry that my ill-chosen words added to the pain of the Jewish community, and I seek your understanding and compassion as I prove to you our common humanity," he said in February. He interrupted a speech in July by President Donald Trump in Jamestown, Virginia, and said, "You can't send us back! Virginia is our home." His father is Jordanian refugee Sabri Samirah, who authorities banned from the U.S. for a decade after the Sept. 11, 2001 attacks, in part because of his membership in the Muslim Brotherhood, the Chicago Tribune reported in 2014.

https://dailycaller.com/2019/12/23/virginia-house-zoning-environment/

Race

Perhaps one of the most disgusting things that we are now being inundated with is the war on race. Why can't we all just get along? I'll tell you why. It's because you can control people if you pit them against each other via race. You can't control a group of people who don't see race and who all get along with each other. It's ok for person "X" to say "Y" about person "Z." However, person "Z" is not allowed to say "Y" about person "X." Follow the logic? Me neither. The same rules Martin Luther King Jr. urged us to judge each other based on our character and not the color of our skin have totally gone out the window. Everything is racist. Everything is tribal. Everything is offensive. Everything is "cultural appropriation." And we are all divided based on race, sex, genitalia, and class from the ruling mob. The ruling mob does not want to see equality, integration and people living together, loving each other. They want us all divided and at each other's throats because that allows them to control us like chess pieces in their sick game. Can't we all just get along and love one another? No... Your owners will never allow it.

7

The War on Music

Rapper Tom MacDonald's "Fake Woke" Hit Removed from Apple Store in Left-Wing Censorship Move

By Richard Moorhead February 11th, 2021

Big Tech is now censoring music that criticizes the hypocrisy and stupidity of the political Left. Apple removed Tom MacDonald's "Fake Woke" from the Apple Store sometime on Wednesday night. The smash hit criticizes anti-white prejudice on the part of the cultural left, cancel culture, censorship, political intolerance, and the violence of the Black Lives Matter street terror movement.

View the music video for MacDonald's smash hit on YouTube, before it's purged from the Silicon Valley platform. "*Cancel culture runs the world now, the planet went crazy Label everything we say as homophobic or racist If you're white, then you're privileged, guilty by association All our childhood heroes got Me-Too'd or they're rapists*" "*They so fake woke, facts don't care 'bout feelings They know they won't tell me what to believe in They so fake woke, same old safe zones They so fake woke, facts don't care 'bout your feelings*"

Apple may claim that the song was removed for licensing or royalty purposes, but it's abundantly clear why Fake Woke was actually removed. It's very rare for Apple to remove music from the Apple Store after it's featured there. MacDonald, a Canadian rapper and professional wrestler, secured the top spot on Billboard Charts' "Emerging Artists" lists on the coattails of the song.

Censorship of music is a defining feature of many totalitarian regimes throughout history, anxious to shut down creative expression that defies the official state ideology. Liberals now have Big Tech monopolies to do their dirty work for them.

https://bigleaguepolitics.com/rapper-tom-macdonalds-fake-woke-hit-removed-from-apple-store-in-left-wing-censorship-move/

Vox Accuses Beethoven's Fifth of Being a 'Symbol of Superiority and Importance' For Wealthy White Men

By Brittany M. Hughes September 16th, 2020

According to Vox, Beethoven's iconic Fifth Symphony is now a "symbol of exclusion" because white men think it's a "symbol of their superiority and importance."

No, I'm not kidding. Progressives are now so woke, they haven't slept in years and are starting to hallucinate. Beethoven's Fifth Symphony starts with an anguished opening theme — dun dun dun DUNNNN — and ends with a glorious, major-key melody. Since its 1808 premiere, audiences have interpreted that progression from struggle to victory as a metaphor for Beethoven's personal resilience in the face of his oncoming deafness.

Or rather, that's long been the popular read among wealthy white men who embraced Beethoven and turned his symphony into a symbol of their superiority and importance. For others — women, LGBTQ+ people, people of color — Beethoven's symphony may be predominantly a reminder of classical music's history of exclusion and elitism. One New York City classical music fan wrote in the 1840s, for example, that he wished that "all women shall be gagged by officers duly licensed for the purpose before they're allowed to enter a concert room."

Wow. One lone, random classical music fan from over 150 years ago said a sexist thing. Remind me to be offended.

Let's dissect this just a bit, if we may. The authors - Nate Sloan and Charlie Harding, at least the latter or which is a white man by his profile picture – claim, without offering any evidence or supporting information whatsoever, that "wealthy white men" have "turned [the] symphony into a symbol of their superiority and importance."

Now, given that Sloan and Harding have offered exactly zero proof to back up this assertion, I have to ask: are there any wealthy white men out there who feel this way? I'm asking in all seriousness. If the above statement describes you, let me know. Because I've been to plenty of live music concerts that featured this symphony and I have yet to see one rich Caucasian dude hearing Beethoven's Fifth and going, "Ohhhh yeah, listen to that Aryan authority right there, that's the stuff." Why? Because beyond the musical brilliance of Beethoven's work, it's a classical symphony. That's it. That's literally all it is.

And yet, because they have nothing better to do with their time than see racism and "homophobia" in everything so they can pen a thousand-word blog about it for their so-woke-they're-insomniacs audiences, Sloan and Harding accuse Beethoven, his symphony, its supposedly "wealthy white male" audience and concert halls of "exluding" gays, blacks and women. How? By suggesting that these communities aren't welcome in concert halls.

Which, again, is about as baseless and nonsensical a claim as you can make. Then, seeming to realize there's nothing more to write on that shallow subject, the authors then pivot to a new argument, suggesting that Beethoven's symphony is so great and so famous that it's become a "symbol" of exclusion because it sets an impossible standard of popularity for new composers to compete with.

Yeah, try and wrap your brain around that idiocy. Beethoven's Fifth is famous and, therefore, symbolizes how black folks are marginalized in white society. That's the parallel they saw.

What sad, terrible lives.

https://www.mrctv.org/blog/vox-accuses-beethovens-fifth-being-symbol-superiority-and-importance-wealthy-white-men

University Marching Band 'Founded on Basis of Racism' Votes to Dissolve Itself

By Ben Ziesloft September 16th, 2020

The Columbia University Marching Band will disband "unanimously and enthusiastically" due to "racism, cultural oppression, misogyny, and sexual harassment." An announcement posted to the group's Facebook page, begins with a "TW," or "trigger warning," and explains that more than 20 band members met on Sept. 12 to discuss anonymous social media postings that accused individual marching band members of "sexual misconduct, assault, theft, racism, and injury to individuals and the Columbia community as a whole."

The band then unanimously decided that it would "dissolve" itself and would "no longer serve as a Columbia spirit group."

"With this decision, the current Band attempts to take responsibility both for harm directly caused by present Band members and for injuries which occurred at other times in the Band's history," the band stated. The marching band says that its club structure was "founded on the basis of racism, cultural oppression, misogyny, and sexual harassment." They hope that the band's dissolution "will provide relief to the present suffering of the Columbia community and time to heal from the decades of harm caused by this organization."

On Sept. 3, the band detailed anonymous posts made on the Columbia Confessions Facebook page that accused unnamed students of wrongdoing.

In addition to its statement, the band publicized a form to collect feedback "on any and all issues and concerns ranging from incidents with specific bandies to group-wide problems."

"We also do not tolerate any racist, sexist, transphobic, or otherwise harmful behavior, and we absolutely do not condone personal theft," read the form. "We fully apologize for any pain or injury the band has caused, and we are working to atone for this pain."

Campus Reform reached out to Columbia University and the marching band and will update this article accordingly.

https://www.infowars.com/university-marching-band-founded-on-basis-of-racism-votes-to-dissolve-itself/

Why it might be time to finally replace 'The Star-Spangled Banner' with a new national anthem

By Lyndsey Parker June 24th, 2020

In an increasingly anti-racist era when problematic iconography — ranging from Aunt Jemima and Uncle Ben to even the *Dukes of Hazzard* General Lee car and country band Lady Antebellum's name — is being reassessed, revised or retired, America's national anthem, "The Star-Spangled Banner," seems to be striking a wrong note.

Last week, protesters in San Francisco toppled a statue of the song's composer, Francis Scott Key, a known slaveholder who once said that African Americans were "a distinct and inferior race of people, which all experience proves to be the greatest evil that afflicts a community." This week, Liana Morales, an Afro-Latinx student at New York's Urban Assembly School for the Performing Arts, refused to sing "The Star-Spangled Banner" at her virtual graduation ceremony, explaining to the *Wall Street Journal*, "With everything that's happening, if I stand there and sing it, I'm being complicit to a system that has oppressed people of color." Instead, Morales performed "Lift Every Voice and Sing," a hymn widely considered to be the "Black national anthem."

So, is it time for this country to dispense with "The Star-Spangled Banner" and adopt a new anthem with a less troubling history and a more inclusive message? Historian and scholar Daniel E. Walker, the author of *No More, No More: Slavery and Cultural Resistance in Ha-*

vana and New Orleans and producer of the documentary *How Sweet the Sound: Gospel in Los Angeles*, says yes.

"The 53-year-old in me says, we can't change things that have existed forever. But then there are these young people who say that America needs to live up to its real creed," Walker tells Yahoo Entertainment. "And so, I do side with the people who say that we should rethink this as the national anthem, because this is about the deep-seated legacy of slavery and white supremacy in America, where we do things over and over and over again that are a slap in the face of people of color and women. We do it first because we knew what we were doing and we wanted to be sexist and racist. And now we do it under the guise of 'legacy.'"

Activist and journalist Kevin Powell, author of the new book *When We Free the World*, says it's important to understand the song's racist legacy, starting with Key's bigoted background. "'The Star-Spangled Banner was written by Francis Scott Key, who was literally born into a wealthy, slave-holding family in Maryland," explains Powell. "He was a very well-to-do lawyer in Washington, D.C., and eventually became very close to President Andrew Jackson, who was the Donald Trump of his time, which means that there was a lot of hate and violence and division. At that time, there were attacks on Native Americans and Black folks — both free Black folks and folks who were slaves — and Francis Scott Key was very much a part of that. He was also the brother-in-law of someone who became a Supreme Court justice, Roger Taney, who also had a very hardcore policy around slavery. And so, all of that is problematic. And the fact that Key, when he was a lawyer, also prosecuted abolitionists, both white and Black folks who wanted slavery to end, says that this is someone who really did not believe in freedom for all people. And yet, we celebrate him with this national anthem, every time we sing it."

"Francis Scott Key, he was a big-time guy in terms of the American colonization of society," adds Walker. "This was not just a person who just lived *in* the time period. This is a person who helped *define* the time period." In fact "The Star-Spangled Banner," based on a poem Key wrote about his eyewitness account of the War of 1812, originally featured a little-heard third stanza that was blatantly racist: "No refuge could save the hireling and slave/From the terror of flight or the gloom of the grave/And the star-spangled banner in triumph doth wave/O'er the land of the free and the home of the brave." While that version of the song is rarely performed today, Powell has been aware of it for years, and, like Morales, has therefore refused to sing the anthem since he was in high school in the 1980s, when he first learned of its history.

"I grew up in hip-hop," says Powell, who used to write for *Vibe* magazine, "and I remember how people would criticize hip-hop for being violent. Yet 'The Star-Spangled Banner' is *riddled* with violence. How are you criticizing a rap song for being violent, but when we get to kindergarten, we are literally teaching children violence through song? I said, 'I can't participate anymore.' So I stopped a long time ago.'"

While Powell may have known about the national anthem's problematic background at quite a young age, Walker understands that many people have only recently become aware of Key's abolitionism or his song's horrific third stanza. "People just don't know history, and everybody's guilty of this. I mean, if I wasn't a historian, I wouldn't know these things. And it took getting a PhD to learn certain things! And I am still learning things every day," says Walker. "There are students of mine, who are white, who say to me, 'I'm so upset that I got sugarcoated history my whole life. I feel cheated. And once I found this out, then I don't want to have a part in it.' Those are the people you see in these rallies. They're saying that they want to live in a world where those vestiges are gone because they have no reason to be here. And that we need to be about redemption in a society — that if we have wronged someone, we can go back and do our best to fix that. And this one is pretty easy to fix."

All this being said, Powell doesn't pass judgement on the many Black artists who've performed "The Star-Spangled Banner" at high-profile events in the past — though he predicts that many artists will start refusing to sing it in the near future, in a movement similar to Colin Kaepernick and his supporters taking a knee during the anthem in recent years.

"The issue is *not* Black people's patriotism. I mean, there's very few folk that are as patriotic as African-Americans," says Powell. "The way I look at it is, I think what Jimi Hendrix did with 'The Star-Spangled Banner' at Woodstock, or the way that Marvin Gaye reinterpreted it and made it a soul song, or Whitney Houston singing it at the Super Bowl in 1991, it became something that belonged to all people, not just folks that thought we should just blindly sing this song. And that's what we do: take these opportunities to perform it because it's a way to showcase one of the greatest gifts to the world, which is music."

So, if "The Star-Spangled Banner" goes the way of the Confederate flag and *Gone With the Wind*, what should America's new national anthem be? Whatever it is, Walker says there should be a formal "vetting process" to make sure the next anthem doesn't have a terrible past; Powell, for his part, suggests John Lennon's "Imagine," which he says is "the most beautiful, unifying, all-people, all-backgrounds-together kind of song you could have."

But what about "Lift Every Voice and Sing"? That song, written as a poem by James Weldon Johnson in 1900, set to music by his brother J. Rosamond Johnson in 1905, and first publicly performed as part of a celebration of Abraham Lincoln's birthday by Johnson's brother John, was dubbed "the Negro national hymn" by the NAACP in 1919. In more recent years, it has been referenced in Maya Angelou's 1969 autobiography *I Know Why the Caged Bird Sings* and Spike Lee's 1989 film *Do the Right Thing*; it was also performed in 1972 by Kim Weston as the opening number for the Wattstax festival and by Beyoncé during her celebrated 2018 Coachella set.

"["Lift Every Voice and Sing"] took on a life of its own, because I think when you think about 1900, it's same kind of ruthless, tragic, white supremacy, white nationalism, and terrorism — the lynchings of black people openly, almost like as if it was a Super Bowl of white folks posing with pictures of dead black bodies hanging from trees, quite literally. And so this song comes out of the tradition of slave plantations, of what became known as spirituals. It was a way for us to make ourselves feel good and empowered in spite of everything that was going on around us. And over time absolutely became the official national anthem for Black America."

Regardless of whether or not "Lift Every Voice and Sing" could ever officially become the anthem for all of America, Walker thinks its lines like "Sing a song full of the faith that the dark past has taught us" are fitting, and he's glad that it's at least being considered as an alternative. "I do like that there's more attention to the fact that there is a thing called 'Lift Every Voice and Sing,' that people are rediscovering it kind of like with Juneteenth," Walker says. "I guarantee you, we had way more people celebrating Juneteenth this past week, knowing what it was, than we'd ever had in American history.

"The difference between then and now, is I — probably like most people — thought that there was no power to be able to change anything, because so many times when women and people of color say something, somebody either pats you on the back and says, 'It's not that bad,' or tells you really be quiet, because if you want to move forward, you shouldn't be a troublemaker," Walker continues, speaking of the current climate and the national anthem debate. "And so I think you've got generations of that because patriarchy and racism and income inequality put people of color and women in those positions. So we just go ahead and sing ["The Star-Spangled Banner"] because we don't want to be the person who's sitting down when everybody else is standing up, don't want to be the person who doesn't have our hand over our heart. We don't want somebody ask, 'What's wrong with you?' where you are in a compromised position already, and they're questioning, 'Are you an American or not? Go back to Africa if you don't like it here!' But I think right now, the great thing is that people who have advocated for this in the past and have not been heard are able to double-back now."

"If you really love your country, if you really are patriotic, then you criticize and challenge your country to be better and do better, not just reinforce things that actually may not be true for all people in the country. ... *That* is what democracy is," Powell sums up. "If there's a tradition that hurts any part of the society — sexist, patriarchal, misogynistic — then it's time to just throw it away."

https://www.yahoo.com/entertainment/why-it-might-be-time-to-replace-the-star-spangled-banner-with-a-new-national-anthem-023741108.html

Univ. of Texas Drum Major Says 'The Eyes of Texas' Represents 'Invisible Form' of Racism, Refuses to Play Song

By Warner Todd Huston August 17th, 2020

The University of Texas student has joined those who claim that the song is irredeemably "racist."

"It's not ultimately about the song, it's about ingrained, institutionalized racism that frankly, in invisible form, takes the image of a school song," Morales said, according to the *Dallas Morning News*. "Removing our alma mater is the first step to realizing the oppression that the Black students face on campus and off-campus." The student went on to say that she has been won over by detractors who say the school's 117-year-old song is racist, and no longer serves the school.

"If the one thing that unites us all is a song, I feel like we're missing the real values of the university and the institution that we love so much," Morales added. "It's about the community that brings us all together. There can be any reason for that, but 'The Eyes of Texas' is no longer synonymous with community."

Morales also opposed UT President Jay Hartzell's recent decision to keep the song. "I think President Hartzell made a very, I don't want to say uneducated, but out of all the ways to respond to it, that was not the way to do it," Morales exclaimed. "Coming from a white man that is the president of this University, it's inappropriate for him to say, 'Let's reclaim this song.'" The school website explains Hartzell's decision to keep the song and defends the tune saying, "Embracing the song's meaning today should not stop us from seeing its complicated past, and acknowledging the many ways that people see the song."

The song's music was based on the minstrel song, "I've Been Working on the Railroad," which mimicked black railroad workers. The school song's writer, one-time school chief William Lambdin Prather, took the earlier tune and added the new lyrics that would become, "The Eyes of Texas." To compound matters, Prather's song was introduced to the school in 1903 through a minstrel show performed by whites in blackface makeup.

This history has caused woke students to rebel against the more than one-hundred-year-old school song, and, as HookEm.com noted, resistance to the song has been growing, especially among the school's athletes.

https://www.breitbart.com/sports/2020/08/17/univ-of-texas-drum-major-says-the-eyes-texas-represents-invisible-form-racism-refuses-play-song/?utm_source=facebook&utm_medium=social

Ohio radio station stops playing 'Baby It's Cold Outside' after listener expresses concern over song's lyrics

By Mariah Haas November 30th, 2018

A radio station in Ohio has pulled "Baby It's Cold Outside" from its lineup after a listener expressed concern over the holiday song's lyrics. According to Fox 8, WDOK Christmas 102.1 removed the tune after one listener called the radio station and suggested it's not appropriate to play the 1940's classic in 2018. "It wasn't really our decision," WDOK host Desiray told the outlet. "It's the decision of our listeners."

"People might say, 'Oh, enough with that #MeToo,' but if you really put that aside and listen to the lyrics, it's not something I would want my daughter to be in that kind of a situation," she continued, explaining that the "the tune might be catchy, but let's maybe not promote that sort of an idea."

According to Fox 8, the Cleveland radio station said they conducted a poll on its website with the majority of voters in favor of removing the song. However, the results were not visible online, Fox 8 reported.

A separate poll on the radio station's Facebook page did show results and they were quite different: 92 percent out of more than 600 voters were in favor of playing the song while 8 percent thought it was inappropriate. The 1944 song, written by Frank Loesser, has sparked debate over the years on whether or not its lyrics are problematic. In the tune, which has been covered by many artists since its debut, a female sings: "I really can't stay," to which a man responds: "But baby, it's cold outside." In another part of a song, a woman is heard singing lines like "Say what's in this drink?", "The answer is no" and "I've gotta get home."

https://www.foxnews.com/entertainment/ohio-radio-station-stops-playing-baby-its-cold-outside-amid-me-too-movement

Princeton a cappella group yanks 'Little Mermaid' song over consent concerns

By FOX 29 December 5th, 2018

PRINCETON, N.J. (AP) -- An all-male a cappella group at an Ivy League university has pulled a Disney movie song from its act following a student newspaper column that suggested the lyrics helped promote "toxic masculinity."

The Princeton University Tigertones have performed "Kiss the Girl," a song from "The Little Mermaid," for years. During the performances, a female audience member would be brought onstage to decide whether or not a man from the crowd could kiss her. Noa Wollstein, who wrote the column, claimed the song's message is misogynistic and that too many women have been pulled on stage for unwanted encounters.

In a response published in the newspaper, the Tigertones' president apologized to anyone made uncomfortable by the tradition. He said the group won't perform the song until it can find a way to do so without offending any audience members.

https://www.fox29.com/news/princeton-a-cappella-group-yanks-little-mermaid-song-over-consent-concerns

Kesha Rids the World of 'Rich, White, Straight Men' on New Track

By Emily Zemler June 4th, 2019

On her latest track, Kesha wants to know "What if rich, straight white men didn't rule the world anymore?" The singer's new song, "Rich, White, Straight, Men," released to YouTube as a surprise for fans, takes on modern political and social concerns.

The thumping, punk-laced pop song tackles inequality as Kesha imagines a new world, singing, "And if you are a boy who loves a boy/ You'll get a wedding cake and all/And if you are a lady and you do your lady work/Then you will make as many dollars as the boys/Not just two thirds." She also invokes children's tune "Twinkle, Twinkle Little Star," reimagining the lyrics as: "Twinkle, twinkle little star/How I wish the world was different/Where who you love and who you are/Was nobody's fucking business."

Kesha's last full-length album, *Rainbow*, dropped in 2017. She released a documentary about the recording, *Rainbow – The Film,* last year, detailing how making the album felt like a life-saving experience. "Making *Rainbow* the album was such a therapeutic process and given the opportunity to turn it into a three dimensional piece of art has helped me find even deeper healing and catharsis," the singer said in a statement. She added, "I hope this film inspires others to never give up even if you feel full of hurt or lost, because after the storm comes a rainbow."

https://www.rollingstone.com/music/music-news/kesha-rids-the-world-of-rich-white-straight-men-on-new-track-844010/

Rock band Confederate Railroad fires back at Illinois state fair after being removed from performance lineup

By Julius Young July 9th, 2019

A Southern rock band called Confederate Railroad is firing back after it was barred from performing at an upcoming state fair in Illinois over its name and use of the Confederate flag.

Formed in 1987 in Atlanta, Ga., Confederate Railroad was tapped to play the Du Quoin State Fair on Aug. 27 in Du Quoin, Ill. as part of "90s Country ReLoaded Day," the New York Post first reported, citing local media. In a statement to Fox News, the band confirmed they have been removed from the show by the Illinois Department of Agriculture because of the name of the band.

"This was very disappointing as we have played this fair before and enjoyed it very much," read the lengthy statement by lead singer Danny Shirley. "The outpouring of support from Confederate Railroad fans, fans of other acts, and the public in general, has been both overwhelming and very much appreciated. I would also like to thank the actors, athletes and fellow country music artists who have spoken out in support."

The statement continued: "Live concerts are how we pay our bills and feed our families. I would never want to see another act lose a payday because of this. Please go out to hear these two great bands. As I have said many times onstage, I am by no means a saint but, I am a man of faith and I have faith that God will see us through this as well as whatever comes next!" Shirley wrote.

The band's response came after their performance cancelation was first addressed by the fair's manager, Josh Gross, in a statement provided to the Du Quoin Weekly, the Southern Illinoisan reported. "The Illinois Department of Agriculture has removed Confederate Railroad from our 2019 Du Quoin State Fair Grandstand lineup," Gross said. "While every artist has a right to expression, we believe this decision is in the best interest of serving all of the people in our state."

When reached for comment by the Southern Illinoisan, the state Department of Agriculture declined to iterate when the band was initially booked, whose decision it was to pull the act or why Confederate Railroad was removed from the lineup, according to The New York Post.

Fellow musician and country music legend Charlie Daniels was one of many to voice their displeasure with the State Fair's decision to ax the rock group, writing in a tweet on July 5, "This political correctness thing is totally out of control."

"When a fair cancels the Confederate Railroad band because of their name its giving in to facism [sic], plain and simple and our freedom disappears piece by piece. Sick of it," read the tweet. A Facebook group has since been created over the band's treatment and had garnered nearly 2,800 members as of Tuesday. Among others irate over Confederate Railroad's cancelation is Oak Ridge Boys member Joe Bonsall, who summoned the man upstairs to help with his disbelief.

"I have played the @DuQuoinFair many times over the decades ... however, I must say that canceling @ConfederateRR JUST because their name is CONFEDERATE RAILROAD is a crock of crap!!! These are good men singing good songs... God please help us all ..." wrote the singer and banjo player who provided a local newspaper clipping detailing the banishment.

However, all is not lost for fans of Confederate Railroad, as the Southern Illinoisan reported that other venues in the region are working to book the rock and country band for a makeup show. "To me, this isn't about getting people to our business. If whoever else in Southern Illinois ends up bringing them in, I won't be mad. This is about Southern Illinois proving a point," Joe McKinney, the manager of entertainment at the local Field of Dreams event venue, told the news outlet.

"This choice was made by a select few up north who are offended, instead of what the majority want, and the band was completely disrespected."

https://www.foxnews.com/entertainment/rock-band-confederate-railroad-illinois-state-fair

Taylor Swift Slams Scooter Braun & Calls His Supporters the 'Definition of Toxic Male Privilege'

By Robyn Merrett & Brianne Tracy December 13th, 2019

On Thursday, Swift, 30, delivered a moving speech, in which she bluntly called out Scooter Braun and slammed the people who tried to hush her as the "definition of toxic male privilege" after she was honored with the first-ever *Billboard* Woman of the Decade award. Swift passionately explained at *Billboard*'s Women in Music awards that in addition to the continuous and unfair plight women face when trying to break into the music industry, there's a new shift that has "affected me personally."

"That is the unregulated world of private equity coming in and buying up our music as if it's real estate," Swift said.

In June, Swift publicly slammed Braun for acquiring her music catalog from her former label Big Machine. Their feud continued when Swift accused Braun of blocking her from performing her old songs. "This just happened to me without my approval, consultation or consent," Swift said in her speech Thursday. "After I was denied the chance to purchase my music outright, my entire catalog was sold to Scooter Braun's Ithaca Holdings."

"To this day, none of these investors have ever [contacted me] or my team directly to perform their due diligence on their investment in me to ask how I might feel about the new owner of my art, my music... my handwriting," Swift continued, adding "Of course, Scooter never contacted me or my team to discuss it prior to the sale or even when it was announced."

"I'm fairly certain he knew exactly how I would feel about it though and let me just say that the definition of toxic male privilege in our industry is people saying, 'But he's always been nice to me' when I'm raising valid concerns about artists and their rights to own their music. Of course, he's nice to people in this room, you have something he needs."

"The fact is that private equity is what enabled this man to think, according to his own social media posts, that he could 'buy me.' Well, I'm obviously not going willingly." Despite her struggles, Swift said she found comfort in the many women who have stood by her during this difficult time. "Yet, the most amazing thing was to discover that it would be the women in our industry, who would have my back and show me the most vocal support at one of the most difficult times."

"I will never ever forget it. Like, ever," Swift added. During her speech, Swift also called for more women to be in more executive roles, A&R meetings and in recording studios. "We have to prove we deserve this," Swift said of the battles women in music face, adding that over the last 10 years she's watched as women are "measured up to each other" and pit against each other — something she wants to end.

Despite there being a long road ahead, Swift made sure to point out the strides made in the music industry. "I've seen forward steps in our awareness, in our inclusion and ability to call out unfairness and misconduct," Swift said.

Swift also paid homage to the plethora of new female faces in music like Megan Thee Stallion, Lizzo and fellow *Billboard* Women in Music honoree Billie Eilish, who was honored with Woman of the Year. In November, Braun broke his silence on his feud with Swift saying during a Q&A moderated by Variety, "I just think we live in a time with toxic division and people thinking that social media is the appropriate place to air out on each other and not have conversations."

The record executive, who declined to mention Swift by name, went on to say that the ideal solution would be to discuss the issue privately. "What I'll say is, people need to communicate and when people are able to communicate I think they work things out," he continued. "I think a lot of times things are miscommunicated, but I believe that people are fundamentally good."

Swift's call to action comes at the 2019 Billboard Women in Music Awards after she revealed she's finally aligned herself with a "generous label" amid her feud with Braun and Big Machine. In PEOPLE's Dec. 16 cover story, Swift — who is honored as one of four People of the Year — reveals exactly why it's been so important for her to speak up about injustices in the industry, and how she's feeling more supported than ever by her new musical home.

"One of the feelings of pride and contentment and gratitude that I had when *Lover* came out was this sense of being so thankful that after so long of being denied the rights to music that I had made and created, I finally felt like I was in a place where I had aligned myself with generous people," says the 10-time Grammy winner, whose first six albums were all released under Big Machine. "The label that I'm at now, the team that I have now, there's not a single person in that sphere that wants to deny me of what I created, and that feels really good."

When Swift signed her new contract with Universal Music Group, the label agreed to pay their artists a "significant portion" of money they earn from Spotify shares. "It's a hugely important thing to me as an artist because that's our pension plan. That's our thing that we get to leave to our kids," she said. "That's what we should be able to have as creators and writers."

Despite any backlash the superstar may face when she speaks out, Swift said it would be disingenuous of her to stay silent. "I'm just gonna always speak up for things if I think it's a discrepancy in the narrative of the music industry. If I think that the industry isn't bringing certain things to light that I think new artists should know about, if I'm in a position to speak about it — which thankfully I am — and somebody who's younger who's signing a record deal can learn from that, then that's a good day."

https://people.com/music/taylor-swift-slams-scooter-braun-billboard-women-in-music-toxic-male-privilege/

Leftists Now Want Beatles' 'Penny Lane' Road Renamed in UK Over False Racism Accusations

By Warner Todd Huston June 18th, 2020

Fake News leftists have begun to claim that England's Penny Lane, the famous road from the Beatles song, is "connected to slavery" and now the cancel culture wants the street eliminated. Several days ago, vandals spray-painted over the iconic Penny Lane street signs in Liverpool sparking the call from uninformed leftists to have the famed street renamed. Why? Raaaaacism, of course.

Despite a complete lack of any proof whatever, liberals have recently begun claiming that Penny Lane is named after a British slave trader named James Penny, a man who died in 1799. Penny had a slave dealing empire including ships and a home port in Liverpool. But even though liberals have been making the claim for several years, even the International Slavery Museum has not been able to uncover any proof that the street's name is linked to the slave trader.

So far, the only facts that have come to light is that there was a slave trader named James Penny in Liverpool, and there is a street called Penny Lane. But the fact that the two exist is no proof at all that they are linked. The street is most well-known because of its links to the Beatles, not because of any mythical links to slavery.

The song was mostly penned by Paul McCartney and it tells the story of various sights and characters McCartney recalls from his youth in Liverpool. The song was originally set to appear on The Beatles legendary album *Sgt. Pepper's Lonely Hearts Club Band*, but was instead released as a double A-side single with "Strawberry Fields Forever."

Many locals are furious at the left-wing loons who have begun defacing the city's Penny Lane street markers. After all, a tidy portion of Liverpool's income is derived from Beatles fans making pilgrimages to see Penny Lane and take photos there.

As the BBC reported:

City tour guide Jackie Spencer, who runs Blue Badge Tour Guides, said she was "absolutely livid".

"It's pure ignorance," she said.

"We've researched it and it has nothing to do with slavery. James Penny was a slave trader, but he had nothing to do with the Penny Lane area." Local resident Emmett O'Neill, who has helped clean the paint from the signs, said he thought it was "an idiotic act".

"If you want something removed, there's ways and means," he said.

"Defacing Penny Lane signs isn't going to change a lot [and] it's the wrong way to go about things." Liberals don't care about what is right, nor are they interested in facts or truth. They only care about their agenda.

https://washingtonsent.wpengine.com/leftists-now-want-beatles-penny-lane-road-renamed-in-uk-over-false-racism-accusations/

Country band Lady Antebellum changes name to Lady A because of slavery reference

By Jessica Napoli June 11th, 2020

Fox News Flash top entertainment and celebrity headlines are here. Check out what's clicking today in entertainment. The country band Lady Antebellum announced on Thursday that it changed its name to Lady A.

The decision, which the Grammy-winning group announced on Twitter, comes "after much personal reflection" and conversations with "closest black friends" as Antebellum refers to a period of time "which includes slavery." Band members, Hillary Scott, Charles Kelley and

Dave Haywood, said in a statement they are regretful and embarrassed for not taking into consideration the word's associations with slavery.

The statement said that they chose the name after the antebellum-style home where they shot their first band photos, and it reminded them of Southern styles of music. But they said in recent weeks, their eyes have been opened to "blindspots we didn't even know existed" and "the injustices, inequality and biases black women and men have always faced." The band said it is deeply sorry for the hurt this has caused and for anyone who felt unsafe, unseen or unvalued.

https://www.foxnews.com/entertainment/country-band-lady-antebellum-changes-name-to-lady-a-because-of-slavery-reference

Music

You know things are really fucked up in society and culture when the Christmas classic, "Baby It's Cold Outside" gets cancelled from being played on air, and Cardi B's "Wet Ass Pussy" is played instead. The American national anthem is under attack as "racist." Hard rock is under attack because it promotes "toxic masculinity." University songs and marching band tunes are being banned as well. With the entire system under attack, it does seem like music is under a vicious assault. You can't even watch the Grammy Awards without being inundated with leftist, communism, totalitarianism propaganda. Welcome to the new world where a small group of sociopaths control what we listen to and the music norms of society.

8

The War on Movies

SJWs are Mad Robert Downey Jr. Used 'Blackface' in Tropic Thunder: Oscar-nominated role fails the woke litmus test

By Lionel Du Cane April 30th, 2020

People on Twitter are mad that the man who played Tony Stark donned "blackface" in his performance of the 2008 satirical comedy Tropic Thunder. Of course, many things fail to pass the bar for wokeness these days as seemingly innocuous things are deemed problematic.

Even much-loved Robert Downey Jr has been vilified for wearing "blackface"–a huge no-no in today's hypersensitive public arena–in a movie that was released twelve years ago. One tweeter reminded social media, "Remember that time Robert Downey jr did full blackface and nobody said ANYTHING," to which other commenters, less than impressed, tore apart a tweet accused of chasing clout.

"Might as well put 'please give me likes & attention,'" replied one account. A second tweeter wrote: "If you watched the movie you'd know why." Another account jokingly tweeted about "woke teenagers" coming to the groundbreaking realization that a childhood favorite actor may have to be the latest victim claimed by so-called "cancel culture." One social media user tweeted: "I hate that teenagers tend to discover Twitter before they discover Google." To which another person wittily replied: "I hate that teenagers discover the internet before a healthy relationship with their parents."

"Wait till they find out he got OSCAR NOMINATED for it," remarked a third person. A fourth person wrote: "I didn't know about RDJ (Robert Downey Junior) before watching that movie, so I genuinely thought he was a black guy. You can probably imagine that the reveal that he was actually white was damn surprising to me."

Picking apart one of the cancel culture tweets, one account tweeted: "'I can't find an apology either????' Lol. They're so used to people cowering to their screeching cancel culture that it's actually surprising to them when somebody doesn't do it." Many other social media users took to Twitter to pick apart a one-dimensional narrative of Robert Downey Jr simply using blackface for racist end–thus deserving to be canceled.

The general sentiment indicated frustration toward "woke" culture for indiscriminate cancellations of anybody who fails to toe the line. Others blasted blackface critics for never having watched the movie before passing judgement. Last year, people were upset with Pennywise–the demonic nightmarish entity assuming the form of a clown that eats children from Stephen King's classic, *It*–for not being enough of an LGBT ally.

https://nationalfile.com/sjws-are-mad-robert-downey-jr-used-blackface-in-tropic-thunder/

'Uncle Tom' Blacklisted by Hollywood

By Larry Elder January 21st, 2021

Actor Ben Affleck once explained why he found it difficult to watch Republican actors on screen. "It's...hard," explained Affleck, "to get people to suspend disbelief. ... When I watch a guy I know is a big Republican, part of me thinks, I probably wouldn't like this person if I met him, or we would have different opinions. That (expletive) fogs the mind when you should be paying attention and be swept into the illusion."

This likely explains why "Uncle Tom," the documentary on which I worked as executive producer, gets no love from the lists of best documentaries of 2020. A critical and financial success by any measure, the gross earnings of "Uncle Tom," so far, exceed seven times its cost and counting. It recently became available on iTunes, Amazon Prime and Walmart online, as well as on store shelves.

Former CBS reporter Sharyl Attkisson recently wrote about the film's snub with the headline: "Censored: Larry Elder's 'Uncle Tom' film." But the Hollywood trade publications Variety and Hollywood Reporter? Silence.

The Chicago Tribune's John Kass, a political writer, wrote a piece headlined "What Frightens the American Left: Larry Elder's New Documentary 'Uncle Tom.'" Kass writes: "Is there anything more frightening to the American political left and their high media priests of the woke world than Black Americans who think for themselves and refuse to kneel? ... And so, they are demeaned by Democratic politicians and either ignored outright or marginalized as race traitors, sellouts and 'Uncle Toms.' It's a way to humiliate them, shut them up, and cancel them. And the party's handmaidens of the media play along. But that's one reason why Larry Elder's stunning new film, 'Uncle Tom: An Oral History of the American Black Conservative,' is so important, especially now."

Each of the following three year-end lists of "best" documentary films of 2020 ignores "Uncle Tom," despite an IMDb viewer rating higher than *any* on the lists -- in most cases, *far* higher. (IMDb, the Internet Movie Database website, assigns films a rating, from one to 10, based on viewers' reviews.)

First, Polygon's list: 1) "Dick Johnson Is Dead," 7.5 (IMDb rating); 2) "Bloody Nose, Empty Pockets," 7.3; 3) "Welcome to Chechnya," 7.9; 4) "Collective," 8.4; 5) "You Don't Nomi," 6.7; 6) "The Go-Go's," 7.5; 7) "Mucho Mucho Amor," 7.2; 8) "I Am Greta," 5.2; 9) "Mayor," 7.5; 10) "City Hall," 7.3.

Next, Paste Magazine's top-25 list, listed alphabetically, without rankings, contains some of the same films, but many others are not on the first list. The new additions are: "76 Days," 7.1; "David Byrne's American Utopia," 8.3; "The Annotated Field Guide of Ulysses S. Grant," N/A; "Boys State," 7.7; "City So Real," 7.4; "Crip Camp," 7.8; "Epicentro," 6.8; "Feels Good Man," 7.6; "Fireball: Visitors from Darker Worlds," 7.0; "The Grand Bizarre," 6.7; "Heimat Is a Space in Time," 6.8; "The History of the Seattle Mariners," N/A; "I Walk on Water," 6.7; "Malni -- Towards the Ocean, Towards the Shore," 6.2; "The Metamorphosis of Birds," 7.8; "The Painter and the Thief," 7.6; "Sunless Shadows," 7.3; "Time," 7.2; "Vick," 7.4.

Finally, there's IndieWire, an independent film website whose 2020 "best of" list (unranked and listed alphabetically) also ignores "Uncle Tom." The films on its "best of" but not already listed above include: "All In: The Fight for Democracy," 6.3; "Athlete A", 7.7; "Gunda," 7.4; "The Mole Agent," 7.6; "The Social Dilemma," 7.7. Not a single film on these three lists achieved an IMDb rating of 8.5 or more. Not one. "Collective" registered the highest at 8.4. How did "Uncle Tom," again, shut out on *all three lists*, rate on IMBD? 8.9. Not a typo: 8.9. Finally, of the last 10 Oscar winners for Best Documentary, none has a higher IMDb rating than "Uncle Tom." None. Only one matched its 8.9 rating. See you at the Academy Awards?

https://townhall.com/columnists/larryelder/2021/01/21/uncle-tom-blacklisted-by-hollywood-n2583458

Under pressure, Hallmark rolls out gay-themed Christmas movie

By Steve Jordahl November 20th, 2020

In a move that surprised no one, the family-friendly Hallmark Channel caved to pressure from homosexual activists and is including homosexual characters in a Christmas-themed movie. The Christmas House, which premieres Nov. 22, follows "husband" Brandon Mitchell and fellow "husband" Jake who are seeking to adopt a child during the holiday season, ET Online reported.

Brad Harder, the actor portraying Brandon, told ET it was an "honor to make a little history" at the Hallmark Channel. Monica Cole of One Million Moms says she saw it coming. Hallmark executives began feeling the pressure last year, she recalls, when powerful LGBT groups pushed for more "inclusive" content after the channel, owned by Crown Media, stirred up their anger by caving to Cole's group over a TV ad. In a two-week tug-of-war, Cole and One Million Moms had convinced Hallmark to pull a Zola ad featuring kissing lesbians only to watch the other side howl in protest. Hallmark reinstated the ad and apologized for the "hurt and disappointment" it had caused.

Pinknewscom, an LGBT website, reported last year that Hallmark drew the wrath of the "LGBT community" by caving to One Million Moms. With those activists now angry, they also protested that the cable network was rolling out 40 Christmas films but not would include a "queer lead character." Hallmark executives promised to change that and hence The Christmas House" was written and produced.

LGBT website The Advocate mocked Cole last year for describing the cultural conflict as a "war for the soul of man," but that is how many view the ongoing culture fight. The orthodox belief in the world's three biggest religions is that homosexuality is sinful because God created men and women to marry and have children. That ongoing fight, in which Cole and her group win and lose ground every day, now includes a win for the other side at the Hallmark Channel after the company's CEO, Bill Abbott, said he was "open" to homosexual characters in the channel's line-up of Christmas movies.

"The Hallmark Channel has done a 180 in 12 months or less, unfortunately," Cole tells OneNewsNow. "The once-wholesome, family-friendly channel is no more." That is because Hallmark is learning, she adds, that the other side celebrates a win but always demands more.

https://onenewsnow.com/media/2020/11/20/under-pressure-hallmark-rolls-out-gay-themed-christmas-movie

Academy announces inclusion requirements set to take full effect in 2024

By Nate Day September 8th, 2020

The Academy of Motion Picture Arts and Sciences has announced a set of requirements for films to be awards-eligible in an effort to increase representation and inclusion in Hollywood.

Just before the #OScarsSoWhite controversy's fifth anniversary, the Academy is limiting Best Picture award nominees -- beginning with 2024's slate of entries -- to those that can meet requirements that "encourage equitable representation on and off screen" by ensuring more people of color fill positions on a film set from the starring role to interns and everything in between, as outlined in a press release published online.

To be eligible for the award in 2022 and 2023, productions must submit a confidential Academy Inclusion Standards form, however, meeting the thresholds will not yet be a concrete requirement. "Academy governors DeVon Franklin and Jim Gianopulos headed a task force to develop the standards that were created from a template inspired by the British Film Institute (BFI) Diversity Standards used for certain funding eligibility in the UK and eligibility in some categories of the British Academy of Film and Television (BAFTA) Awards, but were adapted to serve the specific needs of the Academy," explained the release. "The Academy also consulted with the Producers Guild of America (PGA), as it presently does for Oscars eligibility."

All other award categories will be held to their current eligibility requirements. Submissions to the best picture category from other entries such as "animated feature film, documentary feature [or] international feature film" will be evaluated separately. Two of the four following standards must be met in order to qualify for eligibility for the best picture award beginning with the 96th Oscars.

On-screen representation, themes and narratives

The first requirement requires that at least one of the following criteria be met, including hiring "at least one of the lead actors or significant supporting actors" that belongs to a marginalized population -- Asian, Hispanic/Latinx, Black/African American, Indigenous/ Native American/Alaskan Native, Middle Eastern/North African, Native Hawaiian or other Pacific Islander or another "underrepresented race or ethnicity."

Similarly, 30% or fewer "secondary and more minor roles" must be occupied by women, people in the LGBTQ+ community or a "racial or ethnic group," as well as those "with cognitive or physical disabilities, or who are deaf or hard of hearing." The first standard also requires that story lines focus on the same underrepresented groups.

Creative leadership and project team

This standard dictates that a number of behind-the-scenes professionals must come from such underrepresented populations as well. At least two "creative leadership positions and department heads" must be filled by those belonging to underrepresented groups, including the "casting director, cinematographer, composer, costume designer, director, editor, hairstylist, makeup artist, producer, production designer, set decorator, sound, VFX supervisor and/or writer."

Additionally, at least six other crew positions must be filled by those belonging to underrepresented groups. Such "positions include but are not limited to first AD, gaffer, script supervisor" and more. Production assistants are excluded.

Industry access and opportunities

"The major studios/distributors are required to have substantive, ongoing paid apprenticeships/internships inclusive of underrepresented groups ..." the release explained.

Such positions must be available in several departments: Production/development, physical production, post-production, music, VFX, acquisitions, business affairs, distribution, marketing and publicity.

"Mini-major or independent studios/distributors" are required to have two such apprenticeships or internships in the "production/development, physical production, post-production, music, VFX, acquisitions, business affairs, distribution, marketing [or] publicity" departments. Additionally, the film's "production, distribution and/or financing company" must offer "training and/or work opportunities for below-the-line skill development" to people belonging to underrepresented populations.

Audience Development

Perhaps the most straightforward, but demanding, of the standards, "audience development" requires a studio or company to have "multiple in-house senior executives from" the outlined underrepresented groups.

https://www.foxnews.com/entertainment/academy-inclusion-requirements-2024

Blade Runner & HAL 9000 racist? 'Whiteness' of artificial intelligence 'exacerbates racial inequality,' new study suggests

By Aly Song August 6th, 2020

A University of Cambridge study examining the depiction of artificial intelligence in film, television, Google searches, images, and voices, suggests it is yet another area that showcases racism.

While most would likely assume a machine cannot have a race, the researchers said that they do indeed have *"racial identities"* influenced by *"real world"* stereotypes. These *"racial identities"* can be found in both the fact that AIs and depictions of AIs have caucasion features and also typically talk in *"standard white middle-class English,"* including voices given to smartphone technology. The study suggests *"black di-*

alects" have been avoided because they are deemed *"too controversial or outside the target market."*

Because society has *"for centuries, promoted the association of intelligence with white Europeans,"* the researchers argue that artificial intelligence and machines are given white characteristics to feed into the racial biases of both users and creators.

The study has a fairly broad definition for what it considers artificial intelligence, as it cites 'Star Wars' character Jar Jar Binks as an example of such racial inequality. The character's Caribbean dialect, according to the research team from Cambridge's Leverhulme Centre for the Future of Intelligence (CFI), demonstrates the bias of the creators. The *"orientalized"* nature of 'Flash Gordon' alien villain Ming the Merciless is also cited as showing racial stereotypes.

More traditional examples of artificial intelligence in pop culture, like 1982's 'Blade Runner,' are also pointed to in the study, published in the Philosophy and Technology journal.

"Androids of metal or plastic are given white features, such as in 'I, Robot.' Even disembodied AI — from HAL 9000 to Samantha in 'Her' — have white voices," co-author Dr. Stephen Cave said. *"Only very recently have a few TV shows, such as 'Westworld,' used AI characters with a mix of skin tones."*

These characteristics are used to *"justify colonialism and segregation,"* according to the researchers. If *"white voices"* in machines and think pieces on Jar Jar Binks sound far-fetched, the study does try to present a real-world consequence to this perceived bias: these depictions in AI "exacerbate racial inequality" and make it more difficult for non-white people to get into and ahead in tech.

"In cases where these systems are racialized as white, that could have dangerous consequences for humans that are not," Dr. Kanta Dihal, lead researcher in the study, said. *"The perceived whiteness of AI will make it more difficult for people of color to advance in the field."*

https://www.rt.com/usa/497287-cambridge-artificial-intelligence-racist/

Seth Rogen Says He's "Actively trying to make less things starring white people"

By Infowars.com August 4th, 2020

Actor and comedian Seth Rogen says there's too much white in Hollywood and he's actively working to make things "less white" in his upcoming films.

Speaking to *Entertainment Weekly*, the "Pineapple Express" star said he's taking race into mind when choosing starring roles, and is employing an affirmative action-style hiring process that will ensure diversity among film staff. "I mean personally, I think I am just actively trying to make less things starring white people. And if I'm succeeding or I'm not, I'm very much looking to have a far more diverse group of writers and directors and actors that we generally work with, because that group is not incredibly diverse, you know?" Rogen told *EW*.

"So that's how I've been trying to deal with it, is just to actively take as they would say, anti-racist measures to assure that some work is doing done to acknowledge that Black people are very marginalized in American society," Rogen stated.

Of course, discriminating or being prejudiced against a particular racial group, in this case white people, is the very definition of racism. Now, imagine if Rogan had said he's "just actively trying to make less things starring black people."

https://www.infowars.com/seth-rogen-says-hes-actively-trying-to-make-less-things-starring-white-people/

Kindergarten Cop Is Canceled, Likened to Birth of a Nation

By Nick Gillespie August 4th, 2020

It's come to this: *Kindergarten Cop*, a banal 1990 comedy-action movie starring Arnold Schwarzenegger as a police detective who masquerades as a teacher, has been canceled and likened to the explicitly racist silent film *Birth of a Nation.*

Kindergarten Cop was slated to kick off Portland's Northwest Film Center's Cinema Unbound Drive-in Theater on August 6 until critics led by local author Lois Leveen said the PG-13 movie promoted a "school-to-prison pipeline," according to the *Willamette Week.*

In an email to *Willamette Week,* Leveen likened the Schwarzenegger vehicle to *Birth of a Nation* and *Gone With the Wind*:

It's true *Kindergarten Cop* is only a movie. So are *Birth of a Nation* and *Gone With the Wind*, but we recognize films like those are not 'good family fun.'...They are relics of how pop culture feeds racist assumptions. Because despite what the movie shows...in reality, schools don't transform cops. Cops transform schools, and in an extremely detrimental way. The Northwest Film Center wouldn't tell the *Willamette Week*'s Matthew Singer "how much influence Leveen's comments had on its decision, but the organization did respond to her tweets directly in announcing the cancellation." *Kindergarten Cop* has been replaced by a second showing of *John Lewis: Good Trouble*, a documentary about the recently deceased congressman and civil rights leader. Other films in the series include *Fast Times at Ridgemont High*, *Creature from the Black Lagoon*, *Xanadu*, *Pee Wee's Big Adventure*, and *The Shining*.

It's a good thing that "cancel culture" doesn't exist or otherwise this would be deeply disturbing, wouldn't it? This sort of skirmish is the predictable and regrettable outcome of the politicization of everything and a totalist approach to cultural production and consumption that assumes audience members are either slack-jawed dullards who are effectively programmed by what they watch or ultra-sensitive flowers shredded by every imaginable slight. Either way, madness lies. Or maybe just a new episode of *Portlandia*.

https://reason.com/2020/08/04/kindergarten-cop-is-canceled-likened-to-birth-of-a-nation/

People Are Re-Watching Adam Sandler Movies And Finding Him Too Aggressive

By Jess Hardiman August 13th, 2019

There are many trademarks to an Adam Sandler movie. Along with cameos from his many celebrity mates, slapstick fight scenes, deadbeat sidekicks (usually played by Rob Schneider), you've also often got animals doing amusing things - like that walrus vomming all over its zookeeper in *50 First Dates* or the talking bulldog in *Little Nicky.*

However, perhaps the most recognizable trope of them all is Sandler himself - who's created a bit of a reputation for always portraying some waster who doesn't really give a shit. Through films like *Happy Gilmore, The Longest Yard, Billy Madison* and *Big Daddy*, Sandler has created a long-running persona that is eccentric, outlandish, loud, and, more importantly, that absolutely hates the world.

That's something that modern audiences are picking up on, noting in particular that his characters can actually come across as pretty aggressive sometimes. One person tweeted: "What's that Adam Sandler movie where he plays the aggressive nice guy who gets the girl in the end?"

After someone suggested *50 First Dates"*, she replied: "It's supposed to be a joke, the answer is literally all of them." Another person also tweeted: "I really hate Adam Sandler. His acting is way wayy too aggressive. He's just always angry and blabla. Ah!"

Mind you, it's actually when Sandler isn't being his loud, shouting self that people seem to worry most. Almost a year ago he appeared on The Graham Norton Show, when viewers took to social media to comment on how subdued he seemed. "I can't figure out if Adam Sandler is stoned, drunk or just terrible at interviews," one person tweeted.

"Adam Sandler looks pissed - anyone agree??" another added. Others picked up on his slightly awkward behavior with fellow guest Claire Foy - after he placed his hand on her knee, before she batted it off, laughing.

One viewer said: "Adam Sandler has no social awareness of how awkward he seemed to be making Emma Thompson and Claire Foy." Someone else wrote: "Felt very uncomfortable watching Adam repeatedly put his unwanted hand on the knee of Claire Foy & the wonderous Emma T."

A representative for Foy later said that no offence had been taken, telling the *Metro:* "We don't believe anything was meant by Adam's gesture and no offence was caused to Claire." Reps for Sandler also said: "This is completely ridiculous. It was a friendly gesture." They added that Sandler had acted in a similar way with Dustin Hoffman during a recent interview in the US.

https://www.ladbible.com/entertainment/film-and-tv-people-are-re-watching-adam-sandler-movies-and-finding-him-aggressive-20180922

Molly Ringwald finds some John Hughes movies 'problematic' in a post #MeToo world

By Rachel McRady Oct 2nd, 2018

The 1984 John Hughes flick "Sixteen Candles" has long been hailed as a coming-of-age classic, but in light of the #MeToo and Time's Up movements, a lot of the story's plot has been seen as problematic by both fans and now star Molly Ringwald.

The 50-year-old actress opened up to NPR about the film more than three decades later, saying that while she had some problems with the film at the time, becoming the mom of a teenage daughter has also changed her perspective on it.

"Everyone says and I do believe is true, that times were different and what was acceptable then is definitely not acceptable now and nor should it have been then, but that's sort of the way that it was," Ringwald said of the '80s. "I feel very differently about the movies now and it's a difficult position for me to be in because there's a lot that I like about them."

The film features male love interest and lead Jake Ryan (Michael Schoeffling) talking about the possibility of "violating" his unconscious girlfriend, Caroline (Haviland Morris), and later shows Caroline not remembering having sex with Ted (Anthony Michael Hall) after Jake sends her home with him.

Ringwald also noted that it's important to her not to criticize or "appear ungrateful" to late director John Hughes, who is known for "Sixteen Candles," "The Breakfast Club," "Ferris Bueller's Day Off" and more classics, but added, "But I do oppose a lot of what is in those movies."

The '80s icon insists that she was concerned about some of the film's content even back when they were making it, saying, "There were parts of that film that bothered me then. Although everybody likes to say that I had, you know, John Hughes' ear and he did listen to me in a lot of ways, I wasn't the filmmaker. And, you know, sometimes I would tell him, 'Well, I think this is kind of tacky' or 'I think that this is irrelevant' or 'this doesn't ring true,' and sometimes he would listen to me, but in other cases he didn't."

Ringwald notes she was cautious about crossing a line with the director at the time. But just because she finds parts of "Sixteen Candles" problematic doesn't mean that Ringwald is opposed to all of the Hughes' films she made.

"Having a teenage daughter myself, I know that it's not always easy to get teenagers to talk. But these films or to break through that," she said. "There's something that really touches teenagers, especially "The

Breakfast Club I feel like sort of gives them permission to talk about their feelings — says that teenagers' feelings really matter." This isn't the first time Ringwald has spoken up in light of the #MeToo movement. Last October, she penned a piece for The New Yorker discussing her own sexual harassment at the age of 13.

https://www.foxnews.com/entertainment/molly-ringwald-finds-some-john-hughes-movies-problematic-in-a-post-metoo-world

Kristen Bell says 'Snow White' kiss sends controversial message about consent

By Christian Gollayan October 18th, 2018

Kristen Bell is getting candid with her kids about Disney's princesses in the age of #MeToo. The 38-year-old actress and mom of Lincoln, 5, and Delta, 3, told Parents magazine that she had a serious conversation with her kids about the infamous kissing scene in "Snow White."

"Don't you think that it's weird that the prince kisses Snow White without her permission? Because you cannot kiss someone if they're sleeping!" she told the magazine. Bell, who's played a Disney princess herself as the voice of Anna in "Frozen," also spoke to her children about Snow White's naivete. "Every time we close Snow White I look at my girls and ask, 'Don't you think it's weird that Snow White didn't ask the old witch why she needed to eat the apple? Or where she got that apple?' I say, 'I would never take food from a stranger, would you?' And my kids are like, 'No!' And I'm like, 'Okay, I'm doing something right,'" Bell said.

She's not the only actress who's questioning Disney movies. Keira Knightley recently told Ellen DeGeneres that her 3-year-old daughter, Edie, is "banned" from watching "Cinderella" and "The Little Mermaid." The 33-year-old actress said the 1950s Cinderella character "waits around for a rich guy to rescue her. Don't! Rescue yourself. Obviously!"

And when it came to "The Little Mermaid," Knightley questioned the film's message about relying on a "prince charming."

"And this is the one that I'm quite annoyed about because I really like the film, but 'Little Mermaid,'" she said. "I mean, the songs are great, but do not give your voice up for a man. Hello."

https://nypost.com/2018/10/18/kristen-bell-says-snow-white-kiss-sends-controversial-message-about-consent/?utm_source=NYPFacebook&utm_medium=Native&utm_campaign=NYPFacebook

Rudolph the Red-Nosed Reindeer' called 'seriously problematic' for bullying, racism, homophobia

By Dave Urbanski November 29th, 2018

The beloved Christmas movie, "Rudolph the Red-Nosed Reindeer," has been called out as "seriously problematic" for its displays of bullying, racism, homophobia — not to mention verbal abuse, sexism, bigotry, lack of acceptance, and even exploitation of workers.

That's what a video courtesy of the Huffington Post declared Wednesday, even calling the protagonist "Rudolph the Marginalized Reindeer" in its opening montage. "Viewers are noticing the tale may not be so jolly after all," the video's text noted, "and they're sharing their observations online."

"The holiday TV classic 'Rudolph The Red-Nosed Reindeer' is seriously problematic," the text of the Huffington Post tweet reads. The clip flashed screenshots of a couple of tweets that take issue with the Rudolph storyline, with one calling it a "parable on racism & homophobia w/ Santa as a bigoted exploitative prick" and another accusing "Santa's operation" of being "an HR nightmare" that's "in serious need of diversity and inclusion training."

Verbal abuse

“Former fans are pointing out Rudolph’s father verbally abuses him,” the video text indicates, showing a clip of Donner forcing his son Rudolph to wear a fake nose over his red schnoz in order to gain "self-respect."

"You'll like it and wear it!" he hollers at Rudolph.

Bullying

Everybody knows from the Rudolph song that the other reindeer called him names and laughed at him — but in the movie, even the reindeer coach piles on: “From now on, gang, we won’t let Rudolph join in any reindeer games, right?”

Bigotry

When a doe shows interest in Rudolph despite his red nose, she gets the big 'ol stop sign from her "bigot" father who says "no doe of mine is going to be seen with a red-nosed reindeer."

Sexism

When Rudolph's mom wants to join Donner in search for their son who ran away in shame, he refused and said "no, this is man's work."

Lack of acceptance

Besides the terrible time Rudolph endured from others, the movie features an "outcast" elf who wants to be a dentist — and who gets berated ("you'll never fit in!") for such a thought. Not to mention all those misfit toys.

Exploitation of workers

“In the end, Rudolph & friends learn the bitter truth...” the video text says before noting yet another tweet screenshot which declares the movie teaches that “deviation from the norm will be punished unless it is exploitable.”

This writer's perspective

For some reason the video leaves out the other part of the movie where characters come to realize the error of their ways — at least in the lack of acceptance department — and Rudolph emerges as the hero.

https://www.theblaze.com/news/2018/11/29/rudolph-the-red-nosed-reindeer-called-seriously-problematic-for-bullying-racism-homophobia?utm_content=buffer58c99&utm_medium=social&utm_source=facebook.com&utm_campaign=theblaze

Netflix's *Bird Box* Is Really About How White People Don't Want to See Racism

By Michael Harriot December 27th, 2018

If you haven't seen or read the viral social media discussions of the Netflix thriller *Bird Box*, you're missing one of the greatest race allegory movies that has ever been released in the last part of December 2018. It's about how white people suddenly realize racism is spreading across the world and they can only escape its wrath if they refuse to acknowledge it because...

Wait. You think it's a monster movie? Don't be silly. One of my favorite pastimes is dissecting the themes of movies and TV shows and then theorizing what the movie or show is *really* about. For instance, John Boyega plays Nat Turner in the *Star Wars* reboot, *The Force Awakens*. He's a slave (Stormtrooper) who leads a rebellion that eventually destroys the plantation (The Death Star) and defeats the slavemaster (Kylo Ren).

I must admit that horror isn't my favorite genre, but I try to inject some suspense into viewing scary movies by pulling for the villain. I find it admirable how Freddy Krueger overcame obvious skin problems and dedicated himself to protecting Elm Street from gentrification. I believe Chucky is just a misunderstood little doll who can be a little boisterous at times.

So when I started watching *Bird Box*, I was pulling for the invisible monster because I immediately recognized that the movie was a parable about white America's willingness to ignore white supremacy. I even tweeted an entire thread about it, here. So, if you have seen the movie, or even if you haven't, please allow me to break down the subtext of the movie *Bird Box.*

The movie stars Sandra Bullock who plays a character called "White Privilege." Miss Privilege is very sad because she has lived a very hard life. She grew up on a beautiful horse farm with her sister in California, which is just like living in the projects except that she hated her father. She really doesn't say why she hates her father, but white people *always* hate one of their parents for some bullshit reason like missing their third-grade Christmas play or making them clean their room.

For some reason, the only thing Caucasians hate more than cleaning their rooms is gluten. I still don't know what gluten is, but I think someone should make a horror movie starring Kate Winslet about a girl who awakens to find gluten sprinkled all over her room, leading to a moral crisis. That shit would win an Oscar because Winslet is great at looking wistful while contemplating a moral dilemma.

Anyway, Ms. Privilege is pregnant. Somehow she makes it through most of her pregnancy while doing the backbreaking work of creating oil paintings while her sister rides prized horses all day. One day, White Privilege's sister tells her about this never-before-seen problem called "racism." They watch a little bit of news about this racism thing, but they don't worry about it because no one where they live is racist.

Then, during a trip into town to visit the doctor, they discover racism is everywhere and its spreading quickly. Things have gotten so bad that when people discover racism, they immediately become depressed. Privilege's sister immediately kills herself, leaving our heroine surrounded by this invisible monster. Luckily, because of her privilege, she finds a house where people are hiding from racism. It is filled with white people and a couple of black men who are some of the "good ones."

Soon, the white people realize they can become immune to racism by ignoring it. They figure out that if you just don't look at racism, it won't make you feel bad. So they quickly decide they would never acknowledge the existence of racism, which would prevent them from being attacked.

In the movie, Lil' Rel plays a character who has studied racism for years. He tries to explain to everyone that racism has existed since the beginning of time, but no one will listen to him because he's not educated, he's just some dude who works at a grocery store. The only thing the uneducated black guy is good for is helping them get some food from his grocery store. He helps them get through the bad neighborhood that is torn apart by racism. When they get to the store, they discover that there are some crazy people who have looked directly into the eyes of racism. Lil' Rel eventually dies saving them from a guy who was trying to tell them about racism, but that guy spent time in the criminal justice system, so he was *obviously crazy.*

But instead of listening to the self-taught black man or the crazy people, Miss White Privilege discovers that a little birdie will tell her when racism is near. So she finds some birds that were going to be sold as chattel and keeps them caged up for the purposes of keeping racism away. Of course, the birds want to be free, but they must remain in a box because... after all, how else would the white people survive?

In the movie, Trevante Rhodes plays a Tom (Bruh, that's *literally his name).* Tom is very handsome and very resourceful. Even in the apocalypse, Tom finds a way to keep his edge-up fresh as he tries to saves all the white people from racism. Ultimately, even though one of their best friends is black, Tom can't prevent the white people from seeing racism. Soon racism takes over everything, creating a white supremacist world.

Donald Trump made a cameo appearance as "Gary." Gary Trump's shenanigans killed most of the cast (even the old white people) because after they let him in, he gained their trust and then forced them to look racism squarely in the eyes. Luckily, Tom saves the children and then, and only then, Tom fucks Sandra Privilege, because she's the last woman on earth. Because of their uncle Tom, the white children learn that they can ignore racism, too. They learn how to listen to everything else in the world *except* the whispers about white supremacy.

Uncle Tom dies keeping the children safe from people trying to tell them about white supremacy, and the entire White Privilege family decides that the only thing that will protect them from white supremacy is a safe space. So they take a journey to find this oasis where white supremacy doesn't exist.

The journey consists of a lot of falling down. There has to be a scene with a white woman falling down to get horror movie certification. White people in horror movies have weak ankles and terrible balance. But even when they fall, the racism monster that traveled across the world somehow can't catch them. Then, there comes a point when Miss Privilege has to decide which kid is going to look at racism. It's repeated throughout the movie. But when the time comes, Sandra tells the kids: "Fuck that, it's too dangerous. Matter fact, ain't no one looking!"

And somehow they find this beautiful oasis where racism doesn't exist. There's only one problem:

Racism still exists.

No one kills racism. They don't even escape racism. The only reason that this compound is protected from the supremacy of whiteness is that the people who live there *literally can't see race!* The ones who can see race must *still* ignore racism because racism still rears its ugly head.

The only thing that protects the sighted people from the racism monster is that they have a bunch of birds. And the birds aren't even free. They just think they are free because the white people gave them a bigger bird box. The birds are still slaves, they just don't know it! But everyone lives happily ever after in a post-racial society where the problem of white supremacy is solved simply by walking around with blinders on.

See? I told you.

https://www.theroot.com/netflixs-bird-box-is-really-about-how-white-people-dont-1831345159

People Are Saying Ace Ventura: Pet Detective Is 'Transphobic'

By Ladbible March 8th, 2019

There are many things in life that don't translate particularly well through the decades. But while sometimes that can be something as trivial as a bad 80s perm, at the other end of the spectrum it can relate to a much bigger issue.

Some people re watching *Friends*, for instance, have argued there are moments in the hit comedy series that are homophobic, misogynistic or transphobic. The latest slice of cult entertainment from yesteryear under scrutiny? *Ace Ventura: Pet Detective,* the zany Jim Carrey flick released back in 1994. "Do you know what I made the mistake of doing yesterday? I watched *Ace Ventura: Pet Detective* with my eight-year-old and my 10-year-old," Rogan said.

"I didn't realize how transphobic that fucking movie is." Rogan then discussed the main plot twist - in which a detective, played by cisgender woman Sean Young, is revealed to be transgender.

"All the cops are throwing up... It's off the charts," he added.

"Everyone is freaking out. It is so insanely transphobic."

Rogan's guest, Bari Weiss, added: "When I saw that movie, I was 10. Transphobia was not a thing. Now it is a thing. That's good. That's good news." Many others seem to agree on Twitter, too, with one writing: "Have you ever rewatched a movie from your childhood and realized shit is not only unfunny but hella offensive? Wtf? Why was I allowed to watch *Ace Ventura*?"

Another Twitter user also said: "At the very least it's homophobic. Ventura re-enacts the shower scene from *The Crying Game* - a film about a transwoman - as a response to having kissed a man he thought was a woman. And it's played for laughs. Grim."

Someone else wrote: "It's base level comedy with no intelligence to it. I don't think it's either trans or homophobic as such but it's touching the edges of being offensive. I do believe there's a difference. You can offend without hating something." Another person commented: "*Ace Ventura: Pet Detective* is one of the most problematic movies ever made. Transphobic: this goes without saying. The dolphin's name is Snowflake: the alt right's degrading name for people who fight for social justice issues. Makes fun of mental illness: mental hospital scene."

A third added: "Oh wow the end of *Ace Ventura: Pet Detective* is super transphobic." Some others have defended the movie, with one person tweeting: "So people that are just now watching *Ace Ventura: Pet Detective* for the first time are saying it's too offensive. Yeah it is because that's what we did then. We watched offensive shit without getting fucking offended like a bunch of bitches... End rant."

Another argued: "The character played by Sean Young was not trans. He was a man hiding as a woman to exact his revenge. Lighten up, it wasn't about gender discrimination."

But Joe Rogan isn't the only person who's previously spoken about the potential transphobia of the movie. Trans model Munroe Bergdorf has also previously spoken out about the negative impact of watching the film as a child. She said on Instagram: "As an eight-year-old, I remember watching the film *Ace Ventura: Pet Detective*, starring comedian Jim Carey, at a classmate's house after school.

"Sorry to ruin the ending if you haven't seen it (don't bother) - it ends in the movie's villain being caught, stripped to her underwear and exposed as in fact 'a man'. Then to add insult to injury, everyone in the room starts vomiting as they have all engaged in sex with her.

"Seeing a scene like this including a trans person, played by a cis woman - it may seem trivial to some but I carried that 'punchline' throughout my adolescence, it made me feel guilty and confused about who I truly was, so I pushed my true self into my subconscious and tried to be someone I was not. "Fast forward two decades and I am so proud to be doing my bit for transgender visibility in the media. I'm by no stretch of the imagination a perfect person, but none of us are."

https://www.ladbible.com/entertainment/film-and-tv-people-are-saying-ace-ventura-pet-detective-is-transphobic-20190307

Pleasant Plains administrators respond to concerns over movies in classrooms

By Amanda Henderson March 12th, 2019

SPRINGFIELD, Ill. (WICS/WRSP) — Outrage from Pleasant Plains parents over movies being shown in classes that they call inappropriate. But the school said the parents knew what their students were signing up for.

"'Shawshank Redemption,' 'Blade Runner' and 'One Flew Over the Cuckoo's Nest,'" said Gregg Good, a concerned guardian. Movies and their themes are often credited for inspiring young minds, but sometimes they can be seen otherwise.

"I don't think education needs to run parallel to society," said Patti Good, a concerned guardian. In an elective class at Pleasant Plains High School called Film and Fiction, students are able to analyze and discuss the films they watch. Some of which carry an R-rating, which not everyone is happy with. "What is the justification for why an R-rated movie must be shown? There are literally tens of thousands of other movies in the repertoire out there that could highlight the pillars of film and fiction that the teacher could use as support in their curriculum," said A.J. Good, a concerned citizen.

Some of the controversial movies include "Bladerunner," "Shawshank Redemption" and "In Cold Blood." Movies the school said they outline in a parental permission slip for the course.

"School administration has to actually approve this as well," said Gregg. As for why Patti doesn't just take her student out of the class? "It's going to be hard for her to pick up another class," she said. That and that permission slip, she said she did not receive it until three weeks into the course, which is already well into the semester. "It wasn't in the course description. I sat without student and with the guidance counselor when we signed up for her classes and it was never mentioned," said Patti.

Now, the whole family wants to see a change. "Nothing above a PG-13 movie gets shown. That's what we're looking for," said Gregg. Students do have the option to not watch the R-rated movies and complete an alternative assignment. But Patti said she does not want her student to be isolated. She and her husband Gregg also said they don't approve of the movies being shown as they promote ideas such as suicide and foul language that they fear could shape the minds of the students watching them.

When speaking with Pleasant Plains CUSD 8 Superintendent Matt Runge, he tells us that there is a parental consent form for the class. The elective course is only available for junior and senior level students and it is an opportunity to watch the movies with an adult to explain the themes. To his knowledge, there has been no push back prior to this year. It will be mentioned at the school board meeting next Monday and there will be a decision on whether or not to amend the policy to show R-rated movies.

https://newschannel20.com/news/local/pleasant-plains-administrators-respond-to-concerns-over-movies-in-classrooms

Jordan Peele on Making Movies After 'Us': "I Don't See Myself Casting a White Dude As the Lead"

By Chris Gardner & Seth Abramovitch March 26th, 2019

Hot off the record-breaking success of his latest high-minded horror flick, the writer-director advised Hollywood improv students on ego, marijuana use and why minority actors will always star in his films.

On Monday, as the town buzzed about new box office records set by *Us*, the film's 40-year-old director, Jordan Peele, was not whiling away the hours in a Universal lot bungalow fielding congratulatory calls from studio execs. Peele was on a cramped stage in East Hollywood at improv mecca Upright Citizens Brigade Theatre, the starriest guest yet for the school's new conversation series.

There was a sense of familiarity hovering over the proceedings. No surprise, as Peele got his start in improv before landing on *MADtv* in 2003, then achieving sketch-comedy stardom with Comedy Central's *Key & Peele* in 2012.

Peele gave the standing-room-only audience — a diverse set of 20-something improv students, aspiring storytellers and fans — about an hour and 20 minutes of his time in a wide-ranging conversation that covered his hugely successful career, his marijuana dependence (a double-edged sword), the making of *Get Out*, inclusive casting and his favorite *Twilight Zone* episode.

The audience gave Peele a raucous standing ovation when he entered the room, a conquering hero dressed down in dark denim jeans, black Nikes, an Aviator Nation hoodie and a T-shirt with Corey Feldman's face on it, for some reason.

UCB co-founder and moderator Ian Roberts, who executive produced *Key & Peele*, began by mentioning *Us*' $88 million global box office haul — the "second-biggest opening for an original live-action film," he noted. Added Peele: "That's after *Avatar*. The stats get cooler when you say the thing that beat me."

"The best way to end this great weekend is with you guys," Peele told the crowd of 200. The moderator asked Peele when he first recognized his earliest glimmers of talent. That would be when Peele was in fifth grade doing a stint at TADA! Youth Theater in New York City. He recalled feeling a "burning sensation in my gut" that was hotter than his shyness. Peele was cast in a show that proved to be "the first win in a long career of wins and losses."

From an early age, Peele showed natural skill at drawing, painting and other visual arts. "But the performing part came out of nowhere," he recalled. "It surprised everyone." No one more so than his single mother. "When I was 7, I did an impression of Ronald Reagan and my mom gave me great feedback," he said, before launching into that wobble-headed impression with a raspy, *"Hello."*

He credited his skill with impressions and, later, improv to his ears. The art of listening, he said, is something that continues to inform and elevate his work. "Nothing is more important," Peele insisted. "The more you are armed with what you take in, the more ammo you have. ... Directing for me is about hiring the right people, listening to them and helping them do the best job possible."

Peele said he's also learned how to listen to his ego — and to turn down the volume. "You have to shelve it," he said. "You have to check it constantly. It's so easy for it to come out and rear its ugly head." That can happen anywhere from the set of a $20 million horror film to the humble improv stage. "The ego is deceptive and it will screw you up," he said, adding that when it comes to performing, the "honest response" will always get the biggest laugh.

He name-checked Steve Martin and Martin Lawrence as major influences in comedy; in directing, he listed Tim Burton ("the aesthetic and the fact that he was telling these fairy tales about 'the other'") and Ridley Scott ("*Alien* and *Thelma & Louise* were two really important movies for me — very different, but perfect"). In high school, he knew he wanted to be a director, but rather than go to NYU to study film, he picked private liberal arts school Sarah Lawrence College in Yonkers, New York.

"The day I didn't go to NYU, I said maybe [directing] wasn't for me," he recalled. In the end, Sarah Lawrence wasn't for Peele, either. He dropped out after two years in order to study improv and sketch comedy, noting a dearth of black performers in those fields, a hole he intended to fill. "I knew I had to leave," Peele said. "But it's not a classically lucrative industry, so it's not like I can recommend that black people get into it because it doesn't pay." The line drew weary laughter.

He moved to Chicago and studied at Second City, where he met Keegan-Michael Key. The two brought their talents to Los Angeles and landed on their feet with gigs on *MADtv*. Toward the end of his contract on the Fox sketch show, Peele said he was offered his dream gig: a spot in the cast of *Saturday Night Live*. It was around the time that then-Senator Barack Obama was "becoming a thing," he explained, and Peele did an uncanny impression of the future president. But *MADtv* producers wouldn't let him out of his contract, ending his *SNL* dreams.

He locked himself in a room and started smoking a lot of weed, plotting his revenge, "like a comic book supervillain," he explained. Then it hit him: "I wanted to be a producer," he realized. "These producers are making these decisions about art and comedy and they don't know anything about art and comedy. I want to be a producer and bring my artistry and they'll all be sorry."

Peele decided he first had to "be great" and gave himself "seven to eight" years to get there. So he started developing multiple projects simultaneously to see what stuck. *Get Out* was one of those early scripts. "Every two weeks I'd go, 'What the fuck am I doing? I'm writing a movie where a black man is victimized and all the white people are evil and I'm trying to get the audience to have fun,'" he recalled. "But if you *could* make that fun ... that's what brought me back."

He eventually finished the script. Producer Sean McKittrick bought the thriller spec on the spot, to Peele's utter surprise. That turned to shock when McKittrick said he was on board with the idea of Peele directing it himself.

Budgeted at $5 million, the film became a cultural phenomenon, earning north of $250 million worldwide and winning Peele an Oscar for best original screenplay. He saw his status in Hollywood change almost overnight. With the success of *Us*, he's now well on his way to joining the rarefied ranks of blockbuster auteurs like Christopher Nolan and personal hero Scott.

Fame is still something he's figuring out. "I don't envy someone who gets famous overnight," Peele cautioned. "The hardest part is being recognized. I used to think that being in the public eye gave you power. But all of a sudden, they have the power and can come up to you an hour into dinner."

But there are other kinds of power, and Peele plans on wielding his judiciously. One way is to keep putting black faces on the screen in leading roles. "The way I look at it," he explained, "I *get to* cast black people in my movies. I feel fortunate to be in this position where I can say to Universal, 'I want to make a $20 million horror movie with a black family.' And they say yes."

It's a formula he's not interested in messing with.

"I don't see myself casting a white dude as the lead in my movie. Not that I don't like white dudes," he said, nodding over to his moderator pal Roberts. "But I've seen that movie." The line drew loud applause and shouts of agreement. "It really is one of the best, greatest pieces of this story, is feeling like we are in this time — a renaissance has happened and proved the myths about representation in the industry are false."

During an audience Q&A, a woman asked Peele to name his favorite episode of *The Twilight Zone*, seeing as he's taking over from Rod Serling for CBS All Access' planned reboot of the sci-fi anthology series.

Peele cited "The Monsters Are Due on Maple Street." The story centers on what happens to a neighborhood when they fear aliens have landed in their town. "It points out the ugliness and flaws of humanity," Peele explained. "That's what I like to do with my stories. The real monsters are within us. When people get together we are the greatest monster we've ever known."

https://www.hollywoodreporter.com/rambling-reporter/jordan-peele-says-i-dont-see-myself-casting-a-white-dude-as-lead-us-1197021

Will political correctness kill classic movies?

By Christian Toto May 12th, 2019

"The Hustle," a gender-swap remake of 1988's "Dirty Rotten Scoundrels," rails against the patriarchy between sight gags. "Avengers:

Endgame" shoehorns a minor gay character into the story as a super-virtue-signal. "Long Shot" shows Seth Rogen apologizing for the United States bombing Japan to help end World War II.

Even older films, and the stars who made them great, are now seen through the PC prism. Just ask the estate of John Wayne. The legendary star got pummeled a few months ago, decades after his passing, for a racially insensitive Playboy interview in 1971. Some critics demanded that his name be stripped from John Wayne Airport in Orange County, Calif.

Singer Kate Smith's film career is dwarfed by her radio, TV and stage accomplishments. Yet Smith's recording of two 1930s songs deemed racist convinced two professional sports teams — the New York Yankees and the Philadelphia Flyers — to strip her iconic rendition of "God Bless America" from their programming.

It's easy to imagine the culture attempting to do something similar to films that don't mirror today's cultural mores. Molly Ringwald, who brought some of John Hughes's best films to life, turned on her collaborator last year, saying that his films weren't "woke" enough in our "Me Too" era.

Those films primarily hit theaters in the 1980s. So what about older films? Would any modern studio greenlight 1974's "Blazing Saddles," the Mel Brooks farce teeming with racial and sexual humor?

What about James Bond's early adventures, in which 007 treated female characters in a sexist fashion? Even a comedy classic such as 1959's "Some Like It Hot," featuring two men dressed in drag, could be insensitive given modern mores.

Could problematic films eventually be pulled from home video and streaming services? Sound hysterical? It's currently in vogue to tear down statues that don't align with current groupthink. So why would pop culture artifacts be spared?

In fact, it's already been done. Two years ago, a Memphis theater nixed a screening of the 1939 classic "Gone with the Wind" because of its "insensitive" content.

Disney's Oscar-winning "Song of the South" won't be seen on the company's forthcoming streaming platform. The 1946 film's antiquated, and some say racist, portrayal of black life turned the movie into cultural poison. It's never made it to home video, and that's unlikely to change in the near future.

The effort to wipe clean questionable content is happening elsewhere, too. The work itself doesn't have to be "problematic" if the performer in front of the camera is. Bounce TV yanked reruns of "The Cosby Show" following star Bill Cosby's conviction on rape charges.

When comedian Louis C.K. admitted to pleasuring himself in front of a series of women without their consent, he lost more than his FX series "Louie." HBO announced it had expunged all C.K.-related programming from its service, including stand-up specials and his series "Lucky Louie."

His 2017 film "I Love You, Daddy" never hit theaters as intended following his revelation. More than a year later, the film can't be found on home video or streaming outlets, despite rave reviews from its festival run. The film's star, Chloe Grace Moretz, even argued against the film's release. "I think it should just kind of go away, honestly," the millennial actress told the press.

Her age matters because her peers represent a potent part of the PC movement. Just ask any conservative speaker chased off campus by students frightened by unfamiliar viewpoints. Woody Allen's historic film career may be over, and not because of his age or any health woes. Allegations of child abuse against his daughter Dylan Farrow, while never proven, finally caught up with the "Annie Hall" superstar. Amazon refused to release Allen's latest work, "A Rainy Day in New York," citing Allen's Me Too statement in court.

One highly controversial film, and its collective shunning, predates the current PC mania. The 1915 drama "Birth of a Nation" glorified the KKK and dehumanized black slaves, among other revolting elements. Cultural critics marvel at some of its artistic achievements, given the technical constraints of the era, but its content makes any public display cultural dynamite.

Is that the best way to deal with art? Wouldn't a screening of the film, followed by an informed dialogue on its place in culture and how the real KKK used it as a recruiting tool, be more illuminating? Audiences could process the material on their own terms along with the vital context. That's the key word missing from PC-themed conversations — "context." Without it, PC scolds too often win the day.

Hughes couldn't have imagined his plucky teen comedy would one day be shamed by its star. And there's a chance movies like "Long Shot," "The Hustle" and "Avengers: Endgame" may one day be seen as "problematic," too, in ways we can't imagine now. Who knows how we'll handle art that doesn't fit the current zeitgeist by then?

https://thehill.com/opinion/technology/443282-will-political-correctness-kill-classic-movies

BEWARE: 'Lion King' Is 'Fascistic,' 'White Supremacist,' Says WashPost

By Gabriel Hays July 11th, 2019

Well, it was bound to happen. One of the woke writers at *The Washington Post* found something political to nitpick about Disney's remake of *The Lion King*. Rather than let everyone enjoy one of childhood's great classics, Dan Hassler-Forest tried to burst the bubble, pointing out how it's a "fascistic story" that "incorporates the white supremacist's worldview."

Good grief.

Hassler-Forest claimed that the very fact that there is a lion king, is a problem. It means there is a whole strata of animal subjects under his rule, and that is just not ok. On Wednesday, the world's biggest Negative Nancy wrote, "But as nostalgic as 'Circle of Life' may make us feel, this bombastic scene is also a painful reminder of the film's ideological agenda: It introduces us to a society where the weak have learned to worship at the feet of the strong."

At least in *The Lion King* Mufasa actually protects the fauna he rules over. If Hassler-Forest's got a problem here, wait til he watches a Nat Geo special on the hierarchical murderous goings-on in the animal kingdom ... wait ... "animal kingdom?" My word, there's no escape.

He continued, saying that "'The Lion King' offers us a seductive worldview in which absolute power goes unquestioned, and where the weak and the vulnerable are fundamentally inferior." In the budding socialist, all-inclusive culture that our author seems to want so bad, the fact that Simba or Mufasa have any authority is a no-go. Forget the fact that their peaceful stewardship of Pride Rock is the only thing that keeps the hyenas at bay.

Nevermind. That's where the real propaganda lies — in seeing Simba and Mufasa's benevolent rule as a good thing. It's just a mirror to our own racist and class-ist society. He wrote, "With the lions standing in for the ruling class and the 'good' herbivores embodying society's decent, law-abiding citizens, the hyenas transparently represent the black, brown and disabled bodies that are forcefully excluded from this fascist society."

But, yeah, that's right. *The Lion King,* which takes place in Africa with only animal characters, is specifically depicting a white supremacist society. The author added, "[B]y using predator-prey relationships to allegorize human power, the film almost inevitably incorporates the white supremacist's worldview, one in which some groups of people are inherently superior to others."

And if you think that's far-fetched, well, imagine Pride Rock to be a pretty clear metaphor for the very bastion of fascism itself, Trump Tower: "Doubling down on Disney's historical obsession with patriarchal monarchies, it places the audience's point of view squarely with the autocratic lions, whose Pride Rock literally looks down upon all of society's weaker groups — a kind of Trump Tower of the African savanna."

And don't try to tell Hassler-Forest that it's "just a movie." He's been prepped for that argument. He wrote, "As in every fable, a variety of cute and cuddly figures stand in for human societal organizations." He added, "Mapping our internalized social hierarchies onto the pristine and 'neutral' world of the animal kingdom renders these power dynamics natural, common-sense and desirable."

So, if you take your kids to see *The Lion King* this weekend, well then you're promoting fascism. Ok? And if you use your grill this Saturday, there's going to be a massive carbon footprint and that's a weapon of fascism. And if you — yeah we get it. Way to ruin the fun, *Washington Post.*

https://www.newsbusters.org/blogs/culture/gabriel-hays/2019/07/11/beware-lion-king-fascistic-white-supremacist-says-washpost

James Bond's Wife Will Refuse To Take His Name, Phrase 'Bond Girl' Banned From Set

By Paul Bois November 11th, 2019

According to leaks reported by The Daily Mail, the upcoming James Bond sequel "No Time to Die" will be the secret agent's wokest outing yet. Among other things, Bond will have a wife who refuses to take his surname.

"The script has Bond marrying Dr Madeleine Swann — the psychologist played by French actress Lea Seydoux who first appeared in 2015's 'Spectre.' But she refuses to take her new husband's name," the Mail reported. "The morning after their wedding, Bond wakes sleepy-eyed and says 'Good morning, Mrs. Bond,' to which she replies: 'Don't you mean Ms. Swann?'"

On top of that, a source close to production told the outlet that the phrase "Bond Girl" was banned from the set while filming.

"The phrase 'Bond girl' was outlawed from the set," the source said. "The women in this film are all strong, brave and fiercely independent.

These women are not helpless girls who jump into bed with Bond — their reactions are very different from what people might think. Bond tries his usual seduction techniques but they fail miserably. It's very funny."

The Daily Mail also reported that James Bond will be driving an electric car, but that rumor has been debunked multiple times in the past several months. "We have no idea where that rumor came from," said car manufacturer Aston Martin. "The three cars for the new Bond film were decided ages ago, well before that rumour emerged."

The phrase "Bond Girl" was also not the only thing reportedly outlawed from the "No Time to Die" set; plastic water bottles were also nowhere to be seen. "Crew members were given reusable water bottles which they filled from taps, saving an estimated 230,000 single-use plastic water bottles," The Daily Mail continued. "More than 11 tons of packaging waste was also recycled, while producers sent 30 tons of food waste and biodegradable packaging to 'anaerobic digestion,' in which micro-organisms break down material, producing a gas that can be used to generate electricity."

Amid reports, however, that James Bond will be ushered into the #MeToo age, screenwriter Phoebe Waller-Bridge recently attempted to clarify that she had no intention of turning the iconic spy into some feminist superhero.

"They were already doing that themselves. They're having that conversation with themselves the whole time," she told BBC Radio 4's The Today Programme. "They were just looking for tweaks across a few of the characters and a few of the storylines."

"[My involvement] was much more practical. Just, 'You're a writer, we need some help with these scenes.' And you come up with some dialogue for these characters," she continued. "There's been a lot of talk about whether or not [the Bond franchise] is relevant now because of who he is and the way he treats women. I think that's [nonsense]. I think he's absolutely relevant now. It has just got to grow. It has just got to evolve, and the important thing is that the film treats the women properly."

Last week, actress Lashana Lynch, who will reportedly make history as the first black woman to play 007, told The Hollywood Reporter that the makers of "No Time to Die" worked hard to usher James Bond into the #MeToo age. "Everyone was really responsive to having her be what I wanted," Lynch said of her character. "You're given a fresh perspective on a brand-new black woman in the Bond world."

"I didn't want someone who was slick. I wanted someone who was rough around the edges and who has a past and a history and has issues with her weight and maybe questions what's going on with her boyfriend," she later added. Lynch even suggested to Waller-Bridge the possibility of a scene in which her character is on her period. "We had one conversation about her maybe being on her period in one scene, and maybe at the beginning of the scene — and I spoke to Cary about this — throwing her tampon in the thing," said Lynch.

https://www.dailywire.com/news/report-james-bonds-wife-will-refuse-to-take-his-name-phrase-bond-girl-banned-from-set?utm_source=facebook&utm_medium=social&utm_campaign=mjk

Hallmark Channel Under Assault by Race Hustlers and LGBTQ Cult, 'Too White'

By Megan Fox December 29th, 2019

Every Christmas season, it appears we have to endure listening to the race hustlers and the gay patrol complain about the one channel left in America that does not partake in envelope-pushing. The Hallmark channel really is the last known entertainment that does not engage in the culture wars by pushing "diversity" for the sake of pleasing the agitators and instead focuses on its demographics; white moms and grandmas. But these days, being white and enjoying things white people like is a cause for concern and mockery. I'm white, and a mom, and Hallmark doesn't particularly appeal to me except in the sense that I know I can turn it on and not be concerned that my children will be exposed to the clown world morality that is on every other channel. It's safe.

The Hollywood Reporter penned an article called "Hallmark Channel Struggles to Give Diversity a Home For the Holidays." In it, author Lesley Goldberg takes aim at white people liking to watch other white people as if it's some kind of mortal sin. "While other networks are viewing the holidays with an eye toward inclusion, Hallmark is delivering the dream of a white Christmas, just like the one's audiences used to know." I doubt Goldberg would ever complain about the lack of diversity on Black Entertainment Television (which, by the way, I happen to think is a great idea and caters to a specific audience that likes what they do. What a concept!)

As bad as the acting generally is on the Hallmark channel, the stories are blissfully devoid of any toxic cultural stew pushing politics with every line. There was a time in America where television censors would never allow any sex scenes as graphic as what you would see on Cinemax after dark but today it's old hat to have to watch people groaning and panting (and swearing) at 7 pm on NBC. It's gross. As a result, I've given up cable and only subscribe to online services with access to movies and shows the cultural elites now call "unwatchable." I've completely lost the desire to watch any new programming.

In an article from 2017 in the Walrus entitled "The Unwatchable Whiteness of Holiday Movies," Hallmark fans give reasonable explanations for why they like the channel. But in a culture that values offensive sex acts, profanity, and violence overall, the Hallmark channel is doomed. The diversity activists will never be satisfied until everything white people like is canceled, including white people themselves. And they will eventually get their wish because white people in America will become a minority in the not-too-distant future. Meanwhile, however, whites are still the majority population. Even so, if that majority wants to watch entertainment that represents them or doesn't include a constant assault on morality and decency, they're relegated to one cheesy channel that plays nothing but sappy Christmas movies most of the year. But when the social justice soldiers get done with Hallmark, they won't even have that.

The sustained campaign against the Hallmark channel will work, as illustrated with the channel's CEO, Bill Abbot, signaling that they are open to gay stories. It's only a matter of time until the panting and groaning comes to Hallmark. "While the film and TV industries, among others, are embracing inclusion onscreen, in the executive ranks and among writers, producers and directors, Abbott says Hallmark is 'open' to doing any type of movie — including with gay leads (which it currently lacks, too)," says Goldberg.

This leads me to believe that Hallmark is not interested in pleasing its base of "moms and grandmas" and will instead try to please the outrage mob that doesn't watch their channel. That reminds me of the current Chick-fil-A controversy where after years of standing up to the agitating gay mob, it caved to please people who don't patronize their business. *Get woke, go broke,* the saying goes. It remains to be seen whether there will be a financial hit to the companies who go to the dark side capitulating to protesters instead of customers. Gillette didn't do so well but still seems to be sticking with their new corporate policy of bending over for clown culture, ranting against toxic masculinity. Perhaps these companies don't want profits. Perhaps the people directing these boards are more invested in shifting our culture leftward, profits be damned.

All I know is that I don't care if Hallmark gets woke. It's terrible writing anyway. I have an entire library of classic movies starring Cary Grant and Maureen O'Hara and Dorris Day to enjoy whenever I want. The censors can't stop the signal now that everything is digital. If nothing worthwhile ever gets made going forward, we will always have old Hollywood, and that's more than enough for me.

https://pjmedia.com/news-and-politics/megan-fox/2019/11/29/hallmark-channel-under-assault-by-race-hustlers-and-lgbtq-cult-too-white-n70751

Scorsese's 'The Irishman' Blasted For Not Giving Anna Paquin Enough Lines

By Paul Bois December 2nd, 2019

Even though the point of Anna Paquin's seemingly endless silence in Martin Scorsese's "The Irishman" was to reflect her character's brewing hatred and disgust for her own father (Robert De Niro), feminists are now ripping the film for not giving her more lines.

Writing for The Guardian, Beatrice Loayza said Paquin's lack of lines in the movie represents "a troubling trend in Hollywood," arguing her character amounted to more of a "symbol than an actual person."

"A practically mute, moral spectre judging her father's criminal lifestyle from the sidelines, she appears only a handful of times – less than 10 minutes in total," Loayza writes. "Within these boundaries, Peggy is disconcertingly diminished: Paquin speaks six words in a movie that clocks in at three-and-a-half hours. There may be a potency to such intentional restraint within the film's elegiac trappings, yet circumscribing Peggy as Frank's moral conscience remains doggedly frustrating. Is she more of a symbol than an actual person?"

"In any case, women in The Irishman are moral reminders and checks on an inward looking all-male reality," she continues. "So much of The Irishman's final act has us yearning for Peggy's final thoughts, for Paquin to take the stage once and for all in some sort of cathartic fashion. But we get no such closure, condemned like Frank to a dreary purgatory of what could have been."

Rebecca Laurence, editor of BBC Culture, writes: "Anna Paquin is such a great actress, I was waiting for her to speak more than a line and... it didn't happen."

"Just saw The Irishman and there is much to say but the most important thing is that Martin underused Anna Paquin SO much my head is spinning," said one Twitter user. After enough controversy, people took to Twitter to defend Scorsese's treatment of Paquin's character, arguing her few lines packed an emotional punch that even the best Shakespearean monologue couldn't deliver.

"Anna Paquin in THE IRISHMAN. I'm sincerely confused by people who think she's wasted or has nothing to do in the movie. She is the moral core. She has one line in the movie, I believe, one word uttered. And it's f***ing devastating. An ice pick to the heart," wrote one Twitter user.

"If you honestly don't understand why Anna Paquin's character is (mostly) silent in THE IRISHMAN...well, I don't want to say you're watching movies wrong. But, you're watching movies wrong," argued film critic Chris Evangelista. Rumors even began to spread that Martin Scorsese ordered Anna Paquin to play the role, which the actress emphatically denied. "Nope, nobody was doing any 'ordering'. I auditioned for the privilege of joining the incredible cast of [The Irishman] and I'm incredibly proud to get to be a part of this film," she tweeted.

Actor Robert De Niro came to the film's defense as well, telling USA Today that Paquin's role was "perfect."

"She was very powerful and that's what it was," De Niro said. "Maybe in other scenes, there could've been some interaction between Frank and her possibly, but that's how it was done. She's terrific and it resonates." The social justice warriors put Scorsese in their crosshairs this past October when a reporter at the Rome Film Fest asked him why his films have so few female characters. He immediately shot the question down, saying it was not even a "valid point."

"That's not even a valid point. That's not valid. I can't. ... That goes back to 1970. That's a question that I've had for so many years. Am I supposed to?" said Scorcese. "If the story doesn't call for it. ... It's a waste of everybody's time. If the story calls for a female character lead, why not?"

Director Quentin Tarantino faced a similar accusation from the press with the debut of his latest hit film, "Once Upon a Time in Hollywood," when a reporter questioned him as to why Margot Robbie's character had so few lines. When he rebuked the line of questioning, TIME published an article in which two reporters actually watched all of Tarantino's films to count the number of lines women characters spoke, accusing him of subtle misogyny.

https://www.dailywire.com/news/scorseses-the-irishman-blasted-for-not-giving-anna-paquin-enough-lines?utm_source=facebook&utm_medium=social&utm_campaign=dwbrand

New 'Purity Test' Tool to Scan Hollywood Scripts For 'Diversity Bias'

By Paul Joseph Watson February 20th, 2020

Major Hollywood studios are set to use a new tool that scans movie & TV scripts and flags up any examples where "diversity" is not portrayed positively in a chilling new development that has echoes of Soviet realism.

Called 'Spellcheck for Bias', the tool was developed by the Davis' Institute on Gender in Media and USC's Viterbi School of Engineering. It is set to be implemented by Universal Pictures, DreamWorks Animation, Focus Features and NBC Entertainment within the near future.

"The tool supposedly breaks down diversity in material such as scripts and advertising briefs by scanning for mentions of LGBTQ, race, and disabilities, and then identifying how positively such things are portrayed," writes Zachary Leeman. 'Beetlejuice' actress Geena Davis has also partnered with Universal Filmed Entertainment Group to use the program "to police gender roles in scripts."

Are we entering into an era where movies will not just be given age ratings, but also political correctness scores, with films that don't hit diversity quotas being restricted from enjoying widespread theatrical release? "Instead of broadening their horizons and opening their gates to more filmmakers and scripts, they'd rather invite in a police-state like tool that feels like a discarded bit from George Orwell's '1984.' Forced diversity is not diversity at all — we've seen how it works out at the box office — and an app developed by people trapped in the very same industry they are trying to fix sounds more like a swing for headlines than real change," writes Leeman.

Running art through an Orwellian purity test before it can be allowed to be seen. Where have we seen that before? Throughout the course of the Soviet empire, dictators mandated that 'socialist realism' be the prescribed style of idealized art.

This meant that every sculpture, statue and painting had to conform to an established aesthetic in order to "educate citizens on how to be the perfect Soviets." In order to entrench loyalty to the Communist Party and advance a utopian image of Soviet society, "The purpose of socialist realism was to limit popular culture to a specific, highly regulated faction of emotional expression that promoted Soviet ideals." While Soviets were subjected to a mono-culture designed to ensure fealty to a political dictatorship, westerners are being subjected to 'woke' politically correct speech codes and social engineering to ensure fealty to the new cult of diversity.

https://www.infowars.com/new-purity-test-tool-to-scan-hollywood-scripts-for-diversity-bias/

Mary Poppins branded 'racist' by US academic over soot scene

By Jack Shepherd Sunday February 3rd, 2019

An American academic has criticized *Mary Poppins* for projecting racial stereotypes, saying Dame Julie Andrews's character wears "blackface" during one scene.

Writing for *The New York Times*, Professor Daniel Pollack-Pelzner – a gender studies professor at Linfield College, Oregon – sharply criticizes the scene where Mary Poppins joins Dick Van Dyke's chimneysweep Bert to dance on a rooftop. The pair both get covered in soot as the dance number "Step in Time" is performed.

Pollack-Pelzner says that, while the scene may be comic, the author of the *Mary Poppins* books, PL Travers, often associated chimney sweeps' blackened faces with racial caricatures. He points to one scene in *Mary Poppins Opens the Door* in which a sweep reaches out to a woman with his darkened hand, to which she replies: "Don't touch me, you black heathen." Later, the sweep approaches a cook, who uses the slur for black South Africans "Hottentot" to describe the character.

"The 1964 film replays this racial panic in a farcical key," Pollack-Pelzner writes. "When the dark figures of the chimney sweeps step in time on a roof, a naval buffoon, Admiral Boom, shouts, 'We're being attacked by Hottentots!' and orders his cannon to be fired at the 'cheeky devils'.

"We're in on the joke, such as it is: these aren't really black Africans; they're grinning white dancers in blackface. It's a parody of black menace; it's even posted on a white nationalist website as evidence of the film's racial hierarchy."

After the article appeared online, many fans of the films responded vehemently, one person calling the piece "ridiculous" while another calling it "manufactured controversy".

Pollack-Pelzner responded with a post reading: "The chief reason I wrote this article was the hope that a Disney exec would read it, take another look at the forthcoming *Dumbo* remake, and ask if there was anything just a little bit racist they might want to rethink before it hits the big screen.

"Here's one thing I've learned about the alt-right, after I wrote this article and received a zillion hate messages in response: they sure like *Mary Poppins*!"

https://www.independent.co.uk/arts-entertainment/films/news/mary-poppins-racist-blackface-soot-controversy-dick-van-dyke-julie-andrews-disney-a8760771.html

Hollywood Hires Private Investigators To Root Out Racist Past Posts From Celebrity Newcomers

By Kira Davis June 22nd, 2020

The cultural guillotines are beginning to drop left and right and it looks like Hollywood is trying to get ahead of the bloody game by outing their own players before someone else can do it for them. In recent weeks, Bravo – a reality show power player led by Andy Cohen – has fired several stars after their social media feeds were discovered to contain what the network describes as racist posts. Page Six reports that the popular show "Vanderpump Rules" had to let go of two stars but it isn't just Bravo...the axe is dropping all around town.

The move comes after a spate of celebrities were recently fired over resurfaced racist posts. Last week, Bravo fired "Vanderpump Rules" stars Brett Caprioni and Max Boyens for offensive tweets, and on Wednesday the network canned "Below Deck Mediterranean" star Peter Hunziker for a racist Instagram post. Meanwhile, the CW fired Hartley Sawyer from "The Flash," and MTV let go "Teen Mom's" Taylor Selfridge for similar offenses (although Selfridge claims she quit).

Now comes word that some Hollywood studios are hiring private investigators to comb through the public utterances of current and upcoming stars to root out any future surprises. Now we're told that several networks have hired California-based firm Edward Myers & Associates in an attempt to root out offensive posts from on-air and production talent before they're made public and embarrass their bosses.

According to sources, letters have gone out to stars alerting them that the firm, run by Myers — who has worked as an investigator for LA County's "hardcore gang division," which handles the most difficult gang murders, and for Jeff Bezos' private security chief, Gavin de Becker — will begin its probe soon.

On his Web site, Myers describes himself as an "investigation and risk assessment specialist" and offers services such as "surveillance and counter-surveillance," as well as "intelligence gathering." Myers may be probing some TV classics, including “Dating Naked,” “Jersey Shore,” “RuPaul’s Drag Race,” “Teen Mom,” “Game On,” “Vice” and “Love & Hip Hop.” No word on whether CBS’s “Magnum, PI” is among those being vetted.

The standard of personal perfection this is setting up is alarming. In fact, we may see some sort of residual rollback of social media and its importance when it comes to young Hollywood. The issue here isn’t the current “witch hunt” nature of problem, the issue is that we’ve re-defined the word “racism” to the point of nearly having no meaning whatsoever. Some people (not all, but some) are only being insensitive or ignorant, not blatantly racist. As a fan of trashy reality tv I know it is ignorance and egotistical insensitivity that makes for fascinating television. I’m not tuning in to the “Real Housewives” franchise because I want to see the boring lives of good people. If people aren’t allowed to make mistakes or even be offensive at times, there is no entertainment value. Not just that, we don’t get to see anyone overcome or be better versions of themselves. We are only left with their failures and failure is often not the end of the story. Any good story has an arc but if the “bend” is simply erased then so is the arc altogether, and then so is the story.

Perhaps Hollywood will just ‘woke’ themselves right out of being one of the most powerful industries in the world. We’ll see. Until then, get a social media deleting service for your kids. For a small monthly fee you can set them to only keep the content of the last year or two years or five years or whatever you decide. It looks like the progressives are going to make it as hard as possible for your kids to ever mature, so give them as much privacy as you can in our digital age

https://www.redstate.com/kiradavis/2020/06/22/hollywood-hires-private-investigators-to-root-out-racist-posts-celebrity/

Gone With the Wind Removed From HBO Max, Will Return With Disclaimer

By Dave Nemetz June 9th, 2020

HBO Max has temporarily removed the classic film *Gone With the Wind* from its movie library following a number of calls to do so, in light of the ongoing global protests for racial equality. When the film returns, it will carry a disclaimer.

In a statement, the streamer said, "*Gone With the Wind* is a product of its time and depicts some of the ethnic and racial prejudices that have, unfortunately, been commonplace in American society. These racist depictions were wrong then and are wrong today, and we felt that to keep this title up without an explanation and a denouncement of those depictions would be irresponsible. These depictions are certainly counter to WarnerMedia's values, so when we return the film to HBO Max, it will return with a discussion of its historical context and a denouncement of those very depictions, but will be presented as it was originally created, because to do otherwise would be the same as claiming these prejudices never existed. If we are to create a more just, equitable and inclusive future, we must first acknowledge and understand our history."

ScreenRant first reported the news of Gone With the Wind's removal from the HBO Max archives. The film, released in 1939, won ten Oscars and became one of the top-earning movies of all time, and was prominently featured in HBO Max's initial advertising push. But its romantic depiction of Civil War-era America and whitewashing of slavery is seen as problematic by many modern-day viewers, especially in light of the current social unrest regarding racism and police violence.

Oscar-winning screenwriter John Ridley (*12 Years a Slave*) called for *Gone With the Wind* to be removed from HBO Max for the time being in a *Los Angeles Times* op-ed published this week, calling it "a film that, when it is not ignoring the horrors of slavery, pauses only to perpetuate some of the most painful stereotypes of people of color." Others joined Ridley online in asking that the movie be shelved.

HBO Max is not the only network changing its programming in light of the public outcry surrounding the protests: Paramount Network officially cancelled the police docuseries *Cops* after a more than three-decade run, and A&E Network has pulled new episodes of *Live PD*. HBO Max has also removed all guns from its new *Looney Tunes Cartoons* series, apparently in response to U.S. gun violence.

https://tvline.com/2020/06/09/gone-with-the-wind-removed-hbo-max-protests-racism-slavery/

Movies

When you ban the film *Gone with the Wind*, you know things are really fucked. The Academy Awards (The Oscars) are essentially irrelevant now. They used to be the most coveted award in Tinsel Town. The biggest night for movies and art has now been turned into racial quotas, gender quotas, and skin pigmentation quotas. Who cares what color your skin is or what genitalia you have between your legs? We should award these winners and nominees based on their artistic creativity and achievement, not their arbitrary outward appearances. How racist is that? Again, the people at the top who are making all these calls are in fact the REAL racists. We don't go to see Morgan Freeman or Bruce Willis movies based on their skin color. We go because they are amazing actors who make excellent films. We go and see Meryl Streep and Angela Bassett act in films, not based on their sex, but based on them being both AMAZING actresses. Again, when every single aspect of our society and culture is under attack, you know that these totalitarian masterminds are going to be coming after movies. The movies in my opinion peaked in the 1980s and since then it has been a slow and painful downward decline into the abyss of hell. Even 1980s movies are being cancelled because they "promote gender stereotypes" or are "racist." Really? I didn't know *E.T.*, *Back to the Future* and *Gremlins* were racist and offensive. Hold onto your butts, folks, because this is going to get a lot worse. A LOT WORSE...

9

The War on Television

SpongeBob' is a 'violent,' 'racist' colonizer, says University of Washington professor

By Nate Day Oct 11th, 2019

"SpongeBob SquarePants," which celebrated its 20th anniversary on Friday, has millions of fans around the world, but one University of Washington professor is clearly not among them.

For a recently published academic journal, the professor, Holly M. Barker, wrote an article "Unsettling SpongeBob and the Legacies of Violence on Bikini Bottom," in which she offers a different take on the affable sea sponge. "SpongeBob Squarepants and his friends play a role in normalizing the settler colonial takings of indigenous lands while erasing the ancestral Bikinian people from their nonfictional homeland," the article reads.

Barker calls SpongeBob's colonization of Bikini Bottom "violent" and "racist," and also claims that the cartoon is guilty of the "whitewashing of violent American military activities" against natives of the Pacific.

Barker's beliefs come from the idea that the show is set in a version of the real-life Bikini Atoll in the Marshall Islands. During the Cold War, natives of the area were relocated and the American military used the zone for nuclear testing. The area remains uninhabitable to this day. That history has given rise to fans' theory that Bikini Bottom is inhabited by creatures who owe their mutation to that testing.

Barker stated that as an "American character" allowed to inhabit an area that natives had no choice but to leave, SpongeBob showed his privilege of "not caring about the detonation of nuclear bombs."

Barker also points out the cultural appropriation of Pacific culture, with Hawaiian-style shirts, homes in the shapes of pineapples, tikis and Easter Island heads, and the sounds of a steel guitar perpetuating stereotypes of the region. Even the theme song, according to Barker is problematic, as it denounces the area as one full of "nautical nonsense." Barker understands that the writers likely didn't have colonization in mind when creating the show, but she's upset by the lack of acknowledgment that "Bikini Bottom and Bikini Atoll were not (the writers') for the taking."

Other issues for Barker: a perceived imbalance between male and female characters, and the name "Bob" representing an everyman rather than a culturally appropriate character

In the article, Barker claims that because of these themes, children have "become acculturated to an ideology that includes the U.S. character SpongeBob residing on another people's homeland." The article concludes with this: We should be uncomfortable with a hamburger-loving American community's occupation of Bikini's lagoon and the ways that it erodes every aspect of sovereignty."

The journal in which the article was published is called "The Contemporary Pacific: A Journal of Island Affairs," and it is designed to publish pieces on "social, economic, political, ecological and cultural topics." A rep for Nickelodeon did not immediately respond to Fox News' request for comment. Fox News' attempts to reach Tom Kenny -- who voiced SpongeBob Squarepants -- were unsuccessful.

https://www.foxnews.com/entertainment/spongebob-violent-racist-colonizer

Elmer Fudd will not have a gun in 'Looney Tunes' reboot

By Marina Pitofsky June 6th, 2020

In a new series based on the beloved "Looney Tunes" cartoons, the classic character Elmer Fudd will no longer carry a gun.

The new series "Looney Tunes Cartoons," which premiered last week on the streaming service HBO Max, will feature the cartoon's characteristic violence – using sticks of dynamite, booby traps and the iconic anvils and bank safes dropped onto characters, The New York Times reported last week. However, Peter Browngardt, the series executive producer and showrunner, told the outlet, "We're not doing guns."

"But we can do cartoony violence — TNT, the Acme stuff. All that was kind of grandfathered in," Browngardt told the outlet. Elmer Fudd is regularly foiled trying to hunt Bugs Bunny on the show. In the new series, the character will carry a scythe.

However, comics artist Johnny Ryan, who worked on the show, noted to the Times that he believes "We're going through this wave of anti-bullying, everybody needs to be friends, everybody needs to get along."

"'Looney Tunes' is pretty much the antithesis of that," he said. "It's two characters in conflict, sometimes getting pretty violent." The reboot will not be the first in the entertainment world to eliminate guns from its production. In 2016, the cast of the musical "Hamilton" chose not to use guns during its performance at the Tony Awards in the wake of the mass shooting at Pulse nightclub in Orlando, Fla.

https://thehill.com/blogs/in-the-know/in-the-know/501503-elmer-fudd-banned-from-having-a-gun-in-looney-tunes-reboot

Sky warns viewers Jungle Book, Aladdin and Flash Gordon have 'outdated language and attitudes which may cause offence'

By Hana Carter June 19th, 2020

SKY Cinema has warned viewers that The Jungle Book, Aladdin, Dumbo and Aliens have 'outdated values', as broadcasters axe tv shows and films that do not fit today's narrative.

Subscribers received a disclaimer from the media giant that some of its content has "outdated attitudes, languages and cultural depictions which may cause offence today." Sixteen films have been issued with the warning, these include: Breakfast at Tiffany's, The Goonies, Aladdin, Dumbo, Gone With The Wind, Lawrence of Arabia, Tropic Thunder, The Jazz Singer, The Littlest Rebel, The Lone Ranger, Balls of Fury, The Jungle Book, Flash Gordon and The Last Samurai.

The remakes of Aladdin, The Jungle Book and Dumbo were issued the disclaimer but were removed shortly after, with Sky claiming it was a mistake. The 1992 version of Aladdin came under fire for its use of Orientalist stereotypes and the casting was questioned as Aladdin, Princess Jasmine and the genie were voiced by white actors.

The original Dumbo animation has been accused of containing racist stereotypes of African Americans in the form of the black crows who used jive-like speech patterns. The main bird was named Jim Crow, the name of the racist segregationist Jim Crow laws of the time.

He was also voiced by a white actor. The 1939 classic romance Gone With The Wind, set during the American Civil War and Reconstruction, has been issued with a disclaimer. This comes after HBO Max removed the film from its options because of its 'racist depictions'.

Not all the movies tagged with warnings are old films, some, like The Lone Ranger, were made as recently as 2013. The broadcasting corporation came under fire for putting a warning on Alien, with some feeling that it discredits a film with a 'strong female lead'.

One person wrote: "This is nuts. I'm guessing this is true and not a wind up. Sky Cinema warnings on films, even Disney ones." Another added: "Seeing some accounts expressing outrage and confusion over these disclaimers on Sky Cinema. Y'all know Vasquez was played by a white woman in brownface, right?"

"Good on Sky Cinema for putting this content warning on," said one person. A Sky spokesperson said: "Sky is committed to supporting anti-racism and improving diversity and inclusion both on and off-screen. "We constantly review all content on Sky's owned channels and will take action where necessary including adding additional information for our customer to allow them to make an informed decision when deciding what films and TV shows to watch."

This comes as Little Britain and Come Fly With Me have been removed from Netflix, BBC iPlayer and BritBox after controversy over the use of blackface characters. Both series starring Matt Lucas and David Walliams are no longer available to watch on the online streaming sites amid the Black Lives Matter protests. An iconic episode of Fawlty Towers that coined the phrase "Don't mention the war" from the streaming site UKTV.

The streaming service which is owned by the Corporation, have decided to take down the episode that also features racial terms. This is the latest "classic" British TV show to be removed from a streaming service owned by the BBC, as broadcasters continue to re-assess old British television content.

A spokesperson for UKTV repeatedly refused to clarify why the programme had been removed, or whether the decision was permanent: "We aren't commenting on individual titles.

"However, we regularly review our programmes, and make edits, add warnings and make schedule changes where necessary to ensure that our channels meet the expectations of our audience." The episode in question showed John Cleese as Basil Fawlty yelling the famous phrase while goose-stepping around a Torquay hotel.Ant and Dec issued an apology this month for 'impersonating people of colour' on Saturday Night Takeaway.

https://www.thesun.co.uk/news/11908094/sky-warns-viewers-outdated-language-and-attitudes/

'VeggieTales' is 'racist' and 'dangerous' for children, California students claim

By Caleb Parke December 15th, 2018

A group of students at a California college's "Annual Whiteness Forum" labeled the Christian children's cartoon "VeggieTales" as "dangerous" and promoting racial stereotypes for making the villains colored.

The forum at Cal State San Marcos is a project from Professor Dreama Moon's class titled "The Communication of Whiteness." Students called various things racist, including the NFL, women who support President Trump, and the popular animated cartoon that started in 1993 and always ended with Bob the Tomato and Larry the Cucumber's tagline, "Remember kids, God made you special and he loves you very much," the College Fix reported.

A female student made the claim that by humanizing vegetables, the creators of VeggieTales were using the children's programming to promote racial stereotypes by making the villains racial minorities. "When supremacists aim to taint the way children think of people of color, it will work," the poster titled "Children in the Church" reads. "Whiteness in the Bible isn't just seen as 'power' it's seen as 'good,'" it continues. "When kids see the good white character triumph over the bad person of color character they are taught that white is right and minorities are the source of evil." The female student who headed up the project reportedly said the evil characters sound ethnic or Latino, while the good characters sound white.

Just to be clear, the good guys, Bob and Larry, are red and green respectively, both of which are colors. Eric Metaxas, a best-selling author and former "VeggieTales" writer and narrator, gave his take on the forum.

"All vegetables are part of one race, even though they are of many colors. They are all descended from the same parents — the Adam and Eve of vegetables, who foolishly ate a forbidden fruit (irony?) and screwed everything up for all vegetables descended from them," Metaxas told PJ Media. "At least I'm pretty sure that's the story."

https://www.foxnews.com/entertainment/veggietales-is-racist-and-dangerous-for-children-california-students-claim

The Politics of HollyWeird: Dumbo and Peter Pan Racist?

By Kelli Ballard October 23rd, 2020

Four Disney classics just got branded with an advisory label, which reads:

"This program includes negative depictions and/or mistreatment of people or cultures. These stereotypes were wrong then and are wrong now. Rather than remove this content, we want to acknowledge its harmful impact, learn from it and spark conversation to create a more inclusive future together." So, why exactly are these movies being targeted? Some were first aired a half-century ago, but the woke culture has deemed these classics as harmful to minorities and other groups. Here are four shows and the reasons for the advisory label:

The Aristocats

Released on Dec. 24, 1970, *The Aristocats* tells the story of Duchess (voice by Eva Gabor) and her three kittens who are left an inheritance by their owner. The butler, however, wants the fortune for himself and abandons the cats in the country. An alley cat comes to the rescue and they go on an adventure to find their way home and reclaim their inheritance. Along the way, they meet an alley cat jazz band, and this is where the disclaimer comes into play, especially regarding Siamese cat Shun Gon:

"The cat is depicted as a racist caricature of East Asian peoples with exaggerated stereotypical traits such as slanted eyes and buck teeth. He sings in poorly accented English voiced by a white actor and plays the piano with chopsticks. This portrayal reinforces the 'perpetual foreigner' stereotype, while the film also features lyrics that mock the Chinese language and culture such as 'Shanghai, Hong Kong, Egg Foo Young. Fortune cookie always wrong."

Peter Pan

Released Feb. 5, 1953. This iconic story about a boy who wouldn't grow up follows Peter Pan as he takes the three Darling siblings to Never Land and the many escapades they embark upon. The watchdogs found issue with one particular scene, where Peter and the Lost Boys dance with the natives. According to the disclaimer: "It shows them speaking in an unintelligible language and repeatedly refers to them as 'redskins,' an offensive term." The group "engage in dancing, wearing headdresses and other exaggerated tropes, a form of mockery and appropriation of Native peoples' culture and imagery."

Dumbo

Released on Oct. 23, 1941. No, it's not the name of the movie that has caused such an uproar. The poor circus elephant with the overly large ears was teased mercilessly and dubbed Dumbo for his looks. However, it was the crows, who befriended the young elephant and gave him wise advice, who catch the flak for being racist. "The crows and musical number pay homage to racist minstrel shows, where white performers with blackened faces and tattered clothing imitated and ridiculed enslaved Africans on Southern plantations," the warning explains. The leader of the birds also has the insulting name of Jim Crow, which "shares the name of laws that enforced racial segregation."

A recurring theme with the disclaimers is that white people voiced the characters depicted as blacks or other nationalities. Something that was very common at the time. In *Dumbo*, most of the crow gang were voiced by African Americans, except for 'ole Jim Crow. Their song, *When I see an Elephant Fly*, was actually performed by the Hall Johnson Choir, an all black band, which was also very rare for the time.

Swiss Family Robinson

Released on Dec. 10, 1960. Who can't relate to the Robinsons, who fled the reign of Napoleon so that they could live off the land, without the cruelty and politics governing their lives? Although the plan had been to go to New Guinea, the family instead landed on a deserted island and had to forge a whole new life and deal with its dangers. The pirates that attacked the Robinsons are getting shamed now for being "portrayed as a stereotypical foreign menace." Condemning the characters for wearing "yellow face" or "brown face," the disclaimer also mentions the top knot hairstyles, robes, overdone facial make-up and jewelry as "an exaggerated and inaccurate manner," further saying it reinforces "their barbarism and 'otherness.' They speak an indecipherable language, presenting a singular and racist representation of Asian and Middle Eastern peoples."

https://www.libertynation.com/the-politics-of-hollyweird-dumbo-and-peter-pan-racist/

Disney+ removes 'Peter Pan,' 'Dumbo' from children's profiles due to negative stereotypes

By Alexx Altman-Devilbiss Tuesday March 9th, 2021

(WPDE) — Disney+ has removed several movies from children's profiles on its service due to negative stereotypes.

The Walt Disney Company previously showed content warnings on the films for "negative depictions and/or mistreatment of people and cultures" in October but has now removed access to the films for children under 7. Adults can still view the movies on their Disney+ accounts with the content warnings. Some of what Disney has said about each of the movies at the "Stories Matter" section include:

"Dumbo" (1941): "The crows and musical number pay homage to racist minstrel shows, where white performers with blackened faces and tattered clothing imitated and ridiculed enslaved Africans on Southern plantations. The leader of the group in Dumbo is Jim Crow, which shares the name of laws that enforced racial segregation in the Southern United States."

"Peter Pan" (1953): "The film portrays Native people in a stereotypical manner that reflects neither the diversity of Native peoples nor their authentic cultural traditions. It shows them speaking in an unintelligible language and repeatedly refers to them as 'redskins,' an offensive term. Peter and the Lost Boys engage in dancing, wearing headdresses and other exaggerated tropes."

"Swiss Family Robinson" (1960): "The pirates who antagonize the Robinson family are portrayed as a stereotypical foreign menace. Many appear in 'yellow face' or 'brown face' and are costumed in an exaggerated and inaccurate manner with top knot hairstyles, queues, robes and overdone facial make-up and jewelry, reinforcing their barbarism and 'otherness.'"

"The Aristocats" (1970): "The (Siamese) cat (Shun Gon) is depicted as a racist caricature of East Asian peoples with exaggerated stereotypical traits such as slanted eyes and buck teeth. He sings in poorly accented English voiced by a white actor and plays the piano with chopsticks."

The content warning displays on the films says:

"This program includes negative depictions and/or mistreatment of people or cultures. These stereotypes were wrong then and are wrong now. Rather than remove this content, we want to acknowledge its harmful impact, learn from it and spark conversation to create a more inclusive future together. Disney is committed to creating stories with inspirational and aspirational themes that reflect the rich diversity of the human experience around the globe."

https://newschannel9.com/news/entertainment/disney-removes-peter-pan-dumbo-from-childrens-profiles-due-to-negative-stereotypes

BREAKING: Lucasfilm caves to WOKE MOB and fires Gina Carano from Mandalorian

By The Right Scoop February 10th, 2021

Lucasfilm just went woke today and fired Gina Carano (Cara Dune) from the Mandalorian after the left went into an uproar over some recent social media posts:

Here's the statement Lucasfilm made:

"Gina Carano is not currently employed by Lucasfilm and there are no plans for her to be in the future. Nevertheless, her social media posts denigrating people based on their cultural and religious identities are abhorrent and unacceptable."

According to Variety, here are the 'offending' posts:

Carano shared several offensive posts on her Instagram stories Tuesday night, including one that likened contemporary political differences to the treatment of Jews in Nazi Germany.

"Jews were beaten in the streets, not by Nazi soldiers but by their neighbors...even by children," Carano wrote Instagram. "Because history is edited, most people today don't realize that to get to the point where Nazi soldiers could easily round up thousands of Jews, the government first made their own neighbors hate them simply for being Jews. How is that any different from hating someone for their political views." The post originated on a different Instagram account.

Another photo on Carano's story featured a person with several cloth masks covering their entire face and head. The caption said "Meanwhile in California." Both posts were removed from Carano's Instagram story Wednesday afternoon. Other posts, including a quote saying "Expecting everyone you encounter to agree with every belief or view you hold is fucking wild" and one saying "Jeff Epstein didn't kill himself," remained.

Many people on Twitter began using the hashtag #FireGinaCarano, tagging accounts for Disney, Disney Plus, "Star Wars" and Lucasfilm and requesting that Carano be dropped from "The Mandalorian." What a joke. There is nothing at all wrong with her posts! In fact she makes a great point about hating someone for their political views!

But you see why Lucasfilm fired her right? "Many people on Twitter began using the hashtag #FireGinaCarano..." Lucasfilm caved to the woke mob on Twitter and Carano has to pay with her job. It's absolutely ridiculous and completely unfair.

https://therightscoop.com/breaking-lucasfilm-caves-to-woke-mob-and-fires-gina-carano-from-mandalorian/

New 'Saved by the Bell' Pushes Woke Gender Agenda

By Elise Ehrhard December 7th, 2020

On Nov. 25, NBC's Peacock network premiered its new reboot of the popular 1990s sitcom *Saved by the Bell.* Rebooting old favorites has become a trend in Hollywood, with writers increasingly relying on famous brands from decades ago and updating them with more diverse casts and woke themes. This has included remakes of sitcoms like Charmed, books series like The Babysitter's Club and kids' cartoons like She-Ra.

Usually, the reboots are unoriginal in their re-imagining and just "make it new" by throwing in contemporary left-wing obsessions with LGBTQIA (particularly trans), race, and radical feminism. The new *Saved by the Bell*, set at fictional Bayside High, is no exception to this rule.

Original cast members Mario Lopez and Elizabeth Berkley return in their roles as A.C. Slater and Jessie Spano. Slater is now the football coach and Jessie is a school counselor. Mark Paul Gosselaar and Tiffany Thiessen, who played Zack and Kelly in the original, also return for a few select episodes. They are now the governor and first lady of California.

As governor of California, Zack cut funding to lower-income schools in California and sent the low-income students to high-income schools like Bayside. Minority students from a low-income school named Douglas High join the wealthy, entirely white students at Bayside to teach them all a thing or two about privilege.

Of course, each episode takes digs at white characters for the color of their skin. In the second episode, there is even a clueless Bayside mom whose name is literally "Joyce Whitelady." She is patronizing to the minority students and hands them a welcome gift bag with a pregnancy test in it.

In a later episode, the school principal erroneously thinks 30 misplaced iPads were stolen. Former Douglas student Aisha confronts fellow former Douglas student, Devante, about stealing them. She thinks he stole the iPads because he used to steal stuff at Douglas. Instead of just telling her he did not do it, he accuses her of wanting to look good in front of her "little white friends." Oddly, nobody seems bothered that he never faced any consequences for stealing at Douglas. Throughout the series, the minority students from Douglas are always educating and enlightening their clueless and often dumb, white Bayside friends.

Aisha becomes the star quarterback on the Bayside football team. When Coach Slater is worried about making her the starting quarterback, Jessie tells him, "A woman can do anything a man can." Actually, male athletes after puberty have greater muscle mass and strength than females. Conversely, men do not have the female superpower of carrying a baby in the womb and giving birth. We are different. That is okay. Women do not need to prove anything by trying to compete physically with men.

Propagandizing women to think they are the same as men and should compete with other men in sports leads to disappointment. The recent farcical kick by Vanderbilt's Sarah Fuller is a textbook example of this. Yet the viewer is supposed to pretend that Aisha is the best quarterback Coach Slater has ever had. This is almost as bad as the trans agenda pretending that biological males competing with females in sports is "progress."

Speaking of which: unsurprisingly, *Saved by the Bell* has a trans character. The Disney star Josie Totah, previously from Mindy Kaling's comedy Champions, announced in 2018 that he was a male-to-female transgender. He plays transgender student Lexi, the most popular "girl" in the school. Lexi has a crush on the straight male football player, Jamie. Lexi and Jamie reveal their attraction for each other and kiss at the end of the series. The viewer is supposed to pretend this is a male-female kiss. Actually, it is a homosexual relationship between two biological males, one of whom is taking hormones, dressing up in girl's clothes and "acting" female. Lexie will never have the chromosomes or biological parts of a woman no matter what surgeons do. It is an insult to biological woman to pretend otherwise.

When the series is not insulting girls with the trans agenda, it is emasculating boys. The male football players put on a "feelings helmet" whenever they are struggling with emotions and cry it out. When two boys are fighting over a girl, Coach Slater tells them that is "toxic masculinity."

The whole series, rather than trying to recapture what made the 1990s version popular decades ago, uses nostalgia from the original to push contemporary radical left-wing agendas. Nothing can save this new *Saved by the Bell.*

https://newsbusters.org/blogs/culture/elise-ehrhard/2020/12/07/new-saved-bell-pushes-woke-gender-agenda

CBS pledges *Survivor, Big Brother* casts will now be 50 percent people of color

By James Hibberd and Dalton Ross November 9th, 2020

CBS announced a new diversity pledge Monday that will have a visible impact on its staple of reality shows: All future casts will contain at least 50 percent Black, indigenous and people of color. That means hits like *Survivor*, *Big Brother*, and *Love Island* will be far more diverse starting with the 2021-2022 season.

"The reality TV genre is an area that's especially underrepresented, and needs to be more inclusive across development, casting, production and all phases of storytelling," said George Cheeks, president and chief executive officer for the CBS Entertainment Group. "As we strive to improve all of these creative aspects, the commitments announced today are important first steps in sourcing new voices to create content and further expanding the diversity in our unscripted programming, as well as on our network."

The move follows several *Survivor* contestants speaking out about the lack of diversity in the long-running show's cast. Over the summer, contestants including Sean Rector (season 4, *Survivor: Marquesas*) and Jolanda Jones (season 10, *Survivor: Palau*) formed a group called The Black Survivor Alliance with the goal of "bringing light to our collective experience with implicit bias and racism on and off the show" and had a series of meetings with CBS executives and host and executive producer Jeff Probst about the show being more equitable and inclusive. The BSA was one of two groups of former Black contestants to hold meetings with the network and producers.

In an interview with EW, Rector suggested his outspoken criticism of the show's diversity issues was one reason he never appeared on the show again for one of its *All-Stars* seasons. "If you don't think racism and implicit bias exists, tell me why [*Survivor: Marquesas* winner Vecepia Robinson] has been completely ignored and has NEVER received an inquiry call or invite to even play in a season with all previous winners?," Rector wrote. "(Please miss me with the 'she was boring or not great TV' BS). Subsequently, ten seasons later, Earl Cole, a Black man, finally won and like my sis Vecepia and *Marquesas*, was largely ignored by showrunners ... Television, specifically the *Survivor* franchise, has a responsibility and the power to represent a more just and equitable playing field as a benchmark of real progress for ALL people, and not some concession of perceived power or standing that had to be compromised by one group to another."

Other contestants like *Survivor: Edge of Extinction's* Julia Carter (season 38), *Survivor: Cagayan's* J'Tia Taylor (season 28) and Jones have likewise recently spoken out in Ross' *Quarantine Questionnaire* series of interviews with past contestants. (Below, the cast of 2017's *Heroes vs. Healers vs. Hustlers).*

"My edit, and that of so many other Black people, caused me to organize the BSA and move to end systematic racism on *Survivor*," Jones says. "Of the seasons I watched, the one that makes me the saddest, makes me cry and breaks my heart, is season 14, where there were three Black players, Earl Cole, Cassandra Franklin, and Dreamz Herd, as the finalists. The systematic/systemic racism, implicit bias, and microaggressions shown throughout the editing but especially during the final Tribal were so hard to watch. The thickness of the racism could be cut with a knife ... 'diverse' does not mean the majority of the cast is white with a mixture of other races."

Added Carter: "Many people do not realize the impacts that [diversity] has on the game. When you truly diversify the cast (and I don't mean just a sprinkle of each race in every season), you even the playing field and allow every castaway a real opportunity to connect with more individuals, find allies, and win the game. Seasons like *Cook Islands* and *Fiji*, in which there was racially equal casting, should be the norm, not the exceptions."

Agreed Taylor: "Lazy, crazy, workhorse, and sidekick are the typical ways that *Survivor* portrays African Americans, which is disproportionally negative. We are heroes, nerds, beauties, and so much more in real life. And I'd like to see that on *Survivor."*

Big Brother has likewise had controversies over racial issues over the years, particularly in 2019, due to remarks made by white contestants on the show. Also, just in general, more than any other broadcaster CBS has come under fire in recent years for a lack of diversity. In 2017, for example, the network's entire new fall lineup consisted of six scripted shows all staring men – five of which were white men.

Since then, the network has announced a series of changes both behind the scenes and in front of the camera, with this reality TV casting goal as the latest move. Over the summer, for example, CBS announced it will allocate a minimum of 25 percent of its future script development budgets to projects created or co-created by Black, indigenous and people of color (a goal that will also now apply to unscripted shows), and also set a target for its writers' rooms to be staffed with a minimum of 40 percent of same (a goal which increases to 50 percent in 2022). The network's scripted cast diversity has also improved with series such as *Bob Hearts Abishola, The Neighborhood, All Rise, SWAT* and *FBI.*

https://ew.com/tv/cbs-reality-series-casting-representation/

Actresses America Ferrera, Issa Rae Portray Hollywood as Racist at Emmys: They Said 'Sound More Latina'

By David Ng September, 29th 2020

Actresses America Ferrera and Issa Rae portrayed the Hollywood television industry as bigoted towards ethnic minorities during the 72nd Emmy Awards on Sunday, calling out industry gatekeepers who demeaned and insulted them at the start of their careers.

America Ferrera said during a recurring Emmy segment dedicated to highlighting diversity in Hollywood that a casting director once asked her to change her accent during an audition. "Can you do that again but this time sound more Latina," the casting director allegedly said.

"I am a Latina and this is what I sound like," Ferrera replied. The *Ugly Betty* star said the experience fueled her desire to create more opportunities for "little brown girls to fulfill their talent and their dream." Issa Rae, who stars in HBO's *Insecure*, said that a series pitch with a white male executive turned sour when he tried to lecture her on what black people want to see on TV.

"He's this executive who's not black, telling me what black people like," Rae recalled during Sunday's Emmys. "It just became very clear to me that he didn't get the show... Why does he get to tell me what gets to be on TV? Why does he get to tell me what people like me want to see?"

She added: "For me, that moment was the motivation I needed to keep doing what I was doing, to kind of bet on myself." Rae concluded with a laugh: "You know, one of us got fired after that."

https://www.breitbart.com/entertainment/2020/09/20/actresses-america-ferrera-issa-rae-portray-hollywood-as-racist-at-emmys-they-said-sound-more-latina/

When Black People Appear on *Seinfeld*

By Lauren Michele Jackson August 3rd, 2020

White sitcoms have of late united, disavowing the misbegotten race play of television's recent past. Contrary to prior negligence, shows such as *Scrubs* and *30 Rock* have pulled episodes featuring blackface from streaming platforms as a way of making amends. Even episodes like *It's Always Sunny in Philadelphia*'s "Dee Reynolds: Shaping America's Youth," which cracks wise about the absurdities of racial performance, got the ax. I was something akin to relieved upon my *Seinfeld* rewatch to find Michael Richards's scorched visage, grinning like Sambo, still intact on the episode "The Wife."

Exorcisms are boring these days — that is, exorcisms of a PR sort, which give the impression that race arrives only when we perceive it and evaporates with every redacted slur. After all, the American sitcom, like so many national institutions, has an earned reputation for segregation. There are the vaunted Black classics and then there are the shows that are containers for white stories, which present an urbanscape — usually New York City — whose multiculturalism goes unseen.

But Black people have never been nonexistent, or invisible, in the white sitcom. They have been invisible only in the way that Black people who service the margins of white world-making must be. In a genre whose conventions (and hilarity) thrive on white ridiculousness, Black people, relegated to the smallest of parts, exist to rein in the free play of whites, reminding viewers how safely deviant the main cast can be. No show exhibits this effect as quietly as the one that crested in lockstep with the '90s culture wars, the quintessential sitcom and, in one woman's opinion, the greatest — *Seinfeld.*

I speak of certain characters often deprived of a name:

The Florist (Lionel Mark Smith in "The Gum"); the Agency Rep (Victoria Dillard, "The Old Man"); the Orderly, who bars George from his fiancée's cousin's delivery room (Charles Emmett, "The Seven"). There are the two Walters — Walter (Wayne Wilderson) and Other Walter (Mark Daniel Cade) — who saddle Elaine with too much cake ("The Frogger"); the co-producer of *Scarsdale Surprise* (Tucker Smallwood), who arrives with a threat to take Kramer's Tony away ("The Summer of George"); all the people George stalks, desperate for a friend to call "Black" ("The Diplomat's Club"), some of them with names, such as Joe (Robert Hooks) and Remy (Diana Theodore), a father and daughter who've already made the mistake of letting this nebbish into their lives and onto their now-juice-stained couch ("The Couch").

Black people on *Seinfeld* play a very particular role, defining the social edges of "very," or too much. A thankless job, to be sure. There's no glory in it or, it seems, much fun. I am charmed, though. They foil the Black bestie type, the sidekick destined to enliven a white protagonist's script and social life with idioms and shade. All the bombast, wackiness, and camp belong in the domain of the four protagonists — Jerry, George, Elaine, and Kramer, plus a rotating circle of co-conspirators. The conceit of *Seinfeld* resides in its middle-class sympathies; its normcore aesthetic invites the assumption that its characters are conventional, living and moving about in a world held together by the titular character's observational joke style. In truth, the group is selfish and deranged, delicious micromenaces to normalcy and etiquette who nonetheless enter and leave each episode with their worlds intact. When white characters run wild on *Seinfeld,* Black people are cops. They exist as agents of public decency next to whom our main characters appear all the more indecent.

Consider "The Diplomat's Club," in which George compels Mr. Morgan (Tom Wright) to take a Polaroid with him — a naked attempt to brownnose his Black boss and preempt an impending staff reorganization in the Yankees front office. Shouldering up next to the unenthused supervisor, George tells Mr. Morgan he resembles the boxer Sugar Ray Leonard. "Yeah, you must hear that all the time," George adds, grinning and missing Mr. Morgan's quiet stupefaction. "I suppose we all look alike to you. Right, Costanza?" he responds, giving a neutral half-smile in time for the flash of the camera, while George flounders in the wake of his faux pas. He looks for solidarity among his colleagues — all white — who file out of the room on cue. As many plots with Mr. Morgan demonstrate, George is unfit for work, unfit, therefore, for adulthood, and unfit for life.

Like plain white walls in a room full of rubber balls, these Black figures are ready and waiting to absorb and repel the zany energies of characters we care about. In "The Alternate Side," George fills in for Sid (Jay Brooks), whose car-parking gig literally crashes and burns under George's control. "Moving cars from one side of the street to the other don't take no more sense than puttin' on a pair of pants," Sid tells George upon his return. "My question to you is, Who's putting your pants on?" In "The Airport," Elaine slips into first class from coach and stumbles into an open window seat. Caught out of turn by the composed Black flight attendant with a French twist, she pleads and bargains and pouts and shouts — Julia Louis-Dreyfus cycling through more facial expressions than I can count, as physically comic in face as in body. The stewardess sends her back whence she came, gently rolling her eyes while Elaine jerks the dividing curtain to and fro.

Seinfeld isn't alone. *Friends*, the sitcom most frequently judged for its lack of black characters, stations its black actors on the mundane edges of urban life — with the exception of Charlie (Aisha Tyler), a brief fling for Joey and Ross, and Kristen (Gabrielle Union), an even briefer fling. In "The One Where Emma Cries," Chandler mistakes the name of his boss, Elaine (*Fresh Prince*'s O.G. Aunt Viv, Janet Hubert), and misgenders her daughter. He fumbles in classic Chandler form, talking well past the point of no return; she stares back at him with reproach. Like most black people who speak within the course of the show, she flies under the radar. With appearances so minor, the demographics of the show might as well round-up to white.

And yet, black characters play a significant role precisely because they are true strangers — estranged by city planning and the color line — for these main casts to bump up against. Those frustrated with the sweeping whiteness of shows that presuppose a New York City state of mind — from the mundane (*How I Met Your Mother*) to the iconic (*Girls*) — must grant that they are not unlike the way white residents, transplants or not, experience the city, moving alongside and in between darker people whose lives are not worth their curiosity.

This feature — or bug — of America's sitcoms complements another brainchild of broadcast media: the crime procedural. Within the recent waves of redress regarding what has been shown on TV, actors and viewers are revisiting "copaganda," mass culture's long-standing infatuation with avatars of justice. "TV has long had a police's-eye perspective," Kathryn VanArendonk wrote in June. "Order, a police-imposed status quo, is good; disruption is bad." But in the crime television we call meaty and good — *Justified, True Detective, Mindhunter* — white people are so synonymous with order that their chaos is justified. In stories in this vein, Black authority — the Black mayors and Black principals and Black police chiefs — appears backward, playing by the rules to the detriment of what's important, or at least intriguing. The second season of *Big Little Lies* is haunted, for example, by Merrin Dungey's Adrienne Quinlan, the principal detective chasing the murderer of an abuser. We observe her parallel in another Black character, Bonnie (Zoë Kravitz), whose goody two-shoes affect is overwhelmed by her co-stars' capriciousness.

The sitcom takes itself much less seriously than that. The highs are higher, and the stakes are lower. *Seinfeld* is never absent stereotypes, not with its penchant for ethnicized characters. But here, only the cherished have the privilege of genuine buffoonery. Disruption is good. Scenes are engineered to be stolen by the over-the-top white in the room, to whom the scene always belonged in the first place.

There are notable reversals: Rebecca DeMornay, the charity representative played by Sonya Eddy, whose vacillating delivery commandeers the comedy whenever she appears. In "The Muffin Tops," she lambastes the philanthropic aim of Elaine and Mr. Lippman's tops-only muffin bakery, calling the remainders they'd donated to a homeless shelter "just stumps." In a later episode, when George seeks to recoup the cost of an art book he never wanted, Ms. DeMornay is there, advising he remove himself and his "toilet book," acid in tone. Her unruly performance is magnetic.

The show's most audacious Black presence materializes in the character of Jackie Chiles (Phil Morris). Jackie gets his start in "The Maestro" as the can't-lose lawyer in pursuit of a settlement over the latte that burned Kramer in the previous episode. In their initial meeting, Kramer's patented jitters are somewhat subdued; he is cautious, contrite even, in the face of Jackie's staccato timing. The oddness of their coupledom persists throughout the series. Kramer thwarts his lawyer at every turn, yet Jackie earns the laughter, as unhinged as the capital-*W* Wackiest character in the cast. They team up in "The Abstinence" against the tobacco companies after Kramer's in-unit smoking lounge wreaks havoc on his face — "Jackie's cashing in on your wretched disfigurement," Jackie says with glee.

In "The Finale," an undisguised clip show, past encounters parade into the courtroom with all the subtlety of a final act. Represented by Chiles, naturally, the four leads are on trial for violating a rural county's "Good Samaritan" law. The prosecution (interracial co-counsels) calls "character witnesses" to establish a "pattern of antisocial behavior that's been going on for years." The quartet is convicted; the show could end no other way — just deserts for the delinquents. Yet this is no crime procedural, and the show is not over. Jerry, George, Elaine, and Kramer stroll to their cell, and their bit resumes. "We'll be out in a year and then we'll be back," Jerry says, shrugging. Conversation picks up. Consequences fall away. It is just the four — white and unfazed.

https://www.vulture.com/2020/08/seinfeld-rewatch-close-read.html?utm_source=pocket-newtab

Netflix responds to claims that they changed the artwork of shows based on viewers' race

By Tom Skinner October 23rd, 2018

Netflix has denied changing the artwork for their films and programmes based on a viewers' race after some claimed they were deceiving black users with the use of 'intrusive' and 'manipulative' advertising.

The streaming platform generates suggestions of TV shows and movies for individual users based on personal viewing habits. Netflix began offering the personalised artwork to users in December last year after research indicated that this was the biggest influence on users deciding what to stream.

However, some subscribers found that the promo images used for certain content have been manipulated to reflect their ethnicity.

Netflix's promo shots for 2004's *Love Actually* and the Kelsey Grammer-starring *Like Father* have been shared as examples of the alleged advertising tactic.

Some viewers are finding that the poster for the Richard Curtis romcom features Chiwetel Ejiofor alongside Keira Knightly – even though the former only appears as a minor character. One Twitter user posted a screenshot from her Netflix account, which showed two black actors on the poster for *Like Father* – despite them having around "10 cumulative minutes of screen time [and] 20 lines between them, tops."

"Other Black Netflix users: does your queue do this?" Stacia L Brown asked her Twitter followers. "Generate posters with the black cast members on them to try to compel you to watch?" Brown then posted another shot showing a number of similar promos, although she added: "None of those are quite as weird as the Like Father one, btw." The algorithms were described as "beyond deceptive" by the editor of editor of *MelanMag.com* – a lifestyle magazine for women of colour.

"In their keenness to cater to black audiences, Netflix has overstepped the mark with this issue," Joy Joses told *Sky News*.

"It's beyond deceptive to think that I am being manipulated based on my so-called algorithm choices," she said. "It really is an own goal though, as audiences have caught on." She added: "Why don't they give us more of what we want instead – black leads in big budget productions? In every other sphere, clear signage is the rule. Why should it be different with film and TV promotions?"

Speaking to *The Guardian*, *The Receipts Podcast*'s Tolani Shoneye described the apparent move as "intrusive" and "the dark side of marketing".

"I noticed it a while ago with a Zac Efron film that I'd already seen, but Netflix kept showing me it as a Michael B Jordan movie," she added. Netflix have now denied the claims. "We don't ask members for race, gender or ethnicity so cannot use this information to personalise their individual experience," a spokesperson for the company told *Newsbeat.*

"The only information we use is a member's viewing history. Reports that we look at demographics when personalising artwork are untrue."

"In terms of thumbnails, these do differ and regularly change. This is to ensure the images we show people are useful in deciding which shows to watch," they added. "We are always trying to learn from our members and looking for ways to improve how we personalise the service over time."

https://www.nme.com/news/tv/netflix-accused-of-deceiving-black-users-with-manipulative-personalised-artwork-2392085

'Seinfeld' is the latest TV classic to offend millennials over jokes about 'Soup Nazi,' same-sex relationships

By Brian Flood January 3rd, 2019

"Seinfeld" might offend young people, not that there's anything wrong with that. Millennial-focused website Bustle is taking heat for publishing a listicle that examines all the reasons why "Seinfeld" would be a little too edgy in the modern climate of policing everything that isn't deemed politically correct.

Comedian and author Tim Young told Fox News that the article is "ridiculous," and that it blows his mind how desperate people are to be offended, with the attack on "Seinfeld" the latest example. "Seinfeld," which aired from 1989-1998, is widely considered one of the best programs in television history — but Bustle doesn't exactly feel that way.

Angelica Florio's piece, headlined "These 13 jokes from 'Seinfeld' are offensive now – Yes, that includes the 'Soup Nazi,'" was published on

New Year's Eve and claims that watching the classic sitcom in 2019 will "hopefully" make viewers realize how much times have changed.

"Hopefully most people can agree that comedy, even 'edgy' comedy, doesn't need to alienate marginalized groups in order to make people laugh," Florio wrote. "Thanks to more modern understandings of what political correctness entails — and why being PC is important — it's less common these days to find jokes like the offensive ones that often played out on 'Seinfeld.'"

The Bustle reporter went on to condemn the "Soup Nazi" because, according to Florio, "using the term 'Nazi' to label someone as a joke doesn't sit so well anymore."

"It's not the fault of 'Seinfeld' that the media 20 years later gave constant attention to a small group of radicals and gave them outsized importance. It's also not 'Seinfeld's' fault the media has made the term "Nazi" meaningless because it uses the label on anyone to the right of Nancy Pelosi," Daily Wire reporter Ashe Schow wrote in a piece criticizing the Bustle article.

"The entire point of 'Seinfeld' was to show four terrible people interacting in a world full of kind, thoughtful people."— Tim Young.

"The entire point of Seinfeld was to show four terrible people interacting in a world full of kind, thoughtful people. The humor was in how terrible they were. After all, they ended up in jail at the end of the series for violating a good-Samaritan law when they chose to laugh at an obese man getting carjacked rather than help him," Young said. Other "Seinfeld" jokes the Bustle article considers taboo include calling a Native American an "Indian Giver," Kramer accidently burning the Puerto Rican flag, Japanese businessmen sleeping in Kramer's dresser drawers, Jerry mistakenly getting someone deported and "a whole episode's worth of bad jokes" when a reporter thought Jerry and George were gay.

Young pointed out that the episode in which main characters are thought to be in a same-sex relationship was actually a groundbreaking episode for the gay community. "It won a GLAAD award for its positive outlook on gay and lesbian relationships in the media as the script and interactions of the cast never mocked being gay," Young said. "Rather, they took extra precaution in creating the line 'not that there's anything wrong with that' to show that it's ok and normal to have a same-sex relationship, just that 'it wasn't them.'"

The Bustle reporter also has an issue with storylines such as George staring at a woman's cleavage, Jerry not understanding why liking Chinese women could be considered racist, Kramer referring to someone as a "fat little mental patient," George seeking a woman who can't speak English and a storyline based on illegally parking in a handicap spot.

While Young thinks the entire article is absurd, he also doesn't think it's particularly original. "The first thing I thought when I saw this article was that it was a rip off of a Fine Brothers Entertainment video on YouTube entitled 'Do Teens & College Kids Think Seinfeld Is Funny? | Does It Hold Up?' Which has a million views and was given 130k dislikes and only 14k likes," Young said. "They knew this was clickbait to egg on Americans who disagree with them."

https://www.foxnews.com/entertainment/seinfeld-is-the-latest-tv-classic-to-offend-millennials

Game of Thrones Keeps Killing Off Entire Immigrant Populations, and It's a Problem

By Kyle Munzenrieder April 29th, 2019

On last night's *Game of Thrones*, the priestess Melisandre sauntered in at the last possible minute to light up the Arakhs of the Dothraki in flames. It offered both the assembled forces of Winterfell and the audience at home a brief glimmer of hope before the next 60 or so minutes of horror-film-meets-battle-scene tension, and resulted in a clever cinematic trick. The swift extinguishing of that flame, like a city skyline experiencing a rolling blackout, telegraphed the pure carnage that awaited without zooming in on the details.

Narratively, however, it also literally represented the end of what was left of Daenerys's 100,000-plus Dothraki horde. Presumably, there are the woman and children and possibly a few rogue hordes of Dothraki still left in Essos, but unless the show pulls a trick of "Oh, we actually have some more Dothraki over here, you just couldn't see them! It was dark!" this may have been their send-off from the show. It was an abrupt end to an entire group whom we were introduced to in the very first episode, and a people we've spent more time with and understand better than many of the populations of the actual Seven Kingdoms. (What is even happening in, say, the Reach, lately?) And it points to a worrying problem.

Where once it seemed like *Game of Thrones* had something to say on the topic of immigration and the introduction of new populations to the staid old continent of Westeros, I'm no longer sure it's interested in such heady ideas anymore. It continues to burn up entire ethnicities like kindling in the fire of expensive battle scenes, revealing that it only introduced them in the first place to populate its numerous bloodbaths. Entire peoples with proud, interesting histories have been given the send-off of a random red-shirt cadet in *Star Trek*.

Game of Thrones first started teasing that it had something big to say about the impact of borders on humans with the Wildlings, or as they preferred to be known, the Free Folk. The group was hated by many in Westeros simply because they had been hated for years; it was tradition. And while we now know that there was actually a very good reason why the wall had gone up in the first place, most of the characters in the show didn't believe that White Walkers and other assorted supernatural threats beyond the wall existed. Most of them had come to believe that wall was simply there to keep the Free Folk out. The show then spent several seasons humanizing the Free Folk, tracking the peace they eventually came to with the Northerners and exposing centuries-old bigotries as nonsense in the process. Indeed, some of the biggest, purest romantic storylines on the show were between Free Folk and Westeros citizens. It wasn't hard to see the show grappling with what Westeros would look like if it came to recognize the Free Folk as equals. An eighth kingdom perhaps? A spot on the small council? In some ways, the show might still attempt that, but it's not like it has that many Free Folk left to work with. The only major named Free Folk who are still alive are Tormund Giantsbane, Gilly, and baby Samwell. How much of the population is left beyond that is up for debate. Most of them have now been killed at least twice on the show, first by the White Walkers, and then as Wights.

Then there are the Unsullied. We're left to assume that at least a good chunk of them have somehow survived the Long Night and will fight in the upcoming Last War, but it's not entirely clear if the show has any larger plan for them outside of "dudes who will die for Daenerys" (granted, that's about half of the show's cast at this point, but still).

Grey Worm is by far their most prominent member, and should Daenerys sit on the throne, he and Missandei (another Essos native, though the only Naath native featured on the show) could very well become a Westeros power couple. You have to figure Grey is on the shortlist for leader of the Queensguard, and Missandei a candidate for a small council seat. Yet should they survive, they've already decided they want to retire back to the beach of Missandei's native Naath. From a character perspective, that's nice for them, but thematically, unless they change their minds, it means that two of the most potentially powerful postwar characters have placed themselves outside of the answer of what would a Westeros with immigrants in positions of power would look like. Sure, some of the Unsullied may survive the battle against Cersei and her rented Golden Army (yet another force of foreigners whose fate seems simply to die in battle), but as that population can't reproduce to form a lasting society in Westeros, there are certain themes their fate won't be able to directly address.

It's odd, because not only have so many outsiders died to protect the people of the Seven Kingdoms, but some the most prominent characters have foreigners to thank for the skills, experiences, and magic they've learned from both Essos and the Free Folk. So it sits a bit awkwardly that there are very few Free Folks or immigrants from Essos left to share in the rewards and the power structure that emerges afterward.

Given a few thousand more years, maybe the White Walkers, had they survived, could have figure out how to man boats (or at least fly an ice dragon) over to Essos, but for the most part, so many people died for a threat their people didn't directly face.

This may also be a result of the show getting ahead of the books. The author George R. R. Martin has suggested that ultimately, he's more interested in exploring what the victors do with their power and responsibilities after they win a war than he is in the war itself. His future books may imagine what a Free Folk–run eighth kingdom would look like, or what would happen if some Dothraki survived and decided they had every right to bring their wives and children over and set up a new home within the Seven Kingdoms. It makes sense that the HBO show killed off the horde, because it made a great visual spectacle, but the literary version would find more satisfying material to answer the question of what would become of surviving Dothraki.

The show could still find some way to address these themes and questions that once seemed so central. Unfortunately, it's killed off so many immigrants and foreigners that it's left itself very little to work with.

https://www.wmagazine.com/story/game-of-thrones-battle-immigration-problem/

'The Simpsons' Will No Longer Have White Actors Voice Non-White Characters

By Denise Petski June 26th, 2020

Fox's venerable animated series *The Simpsons* has released a statement on casting for non-white characters that will affect the voices of such popular Black characters on the show as Carlton Carlson and Dr.

Julius M. Hibbert. "Moving forward, *The Simpsons* will no longer have white actors voice non-white characters," the series said Friday.

The Simpsons' new policy follows an announcement by *Family Guy* veteran Mike Henry earlier on Friday that he will no longer voice the black Cleveland Brown character on Fox's long-running animated hit. Earlier this week, two white actors, Jenny Slate of Netflix's animated series *Big Mouth*, and Kristen Bell of *Central Park* on Apple TV+, said that they will stop voicing the mixed-race characters in those shows.

Additionally, several live-action comedies, including *Scrubs* and *30 Rock*, have pulled episodes featuring blackface from their streaming platforms, and amid a nation dealing with controversial depictions of race on TV and film.

On *The Simpsons*, Hank Azaria has been the voice of the black cartoon character Carlton Carlson. He also was known for voicing Apu, a character which has long been criticized for portraying a racist depiction of an Indian immigrant. Azaria announced in January that he would no longer voice the character. Harry Shearer voices the black character Dr. Julius M. Hibbert, one of several characters he voices, including Mr. Burns, Waylon Smithers, Principal Skinner, Ned Flanders, Reverend Lovejoy and Kent Brockman.

https://deadline.com/2020/06/the-simpsons-will-no-longer-have-white-actors-voice-non-white-characters-1202971437/

Hulu Axes Episode of 'The Golden Girls' for the Dumbest Reason

By Matt Margolis June 28th, 2020

The popular streaming service Hulu has removed an episode of *The Golden Girls* featuring a scene that *Variety* describes as featuring "a scene with characters in blackface."

Except the characters aren't in blackface. They're wearing mud masks—a common cosmetic facial treatment. "Mixed Feelings," episode 23 in season 3 of the sitcom, aired in 1988. In the episode, Michael (Scott Jacoby), the son of Dorothy (Beatrice Author), plans to wed a much older Black woman, Lorraine (Rosalind Cash). Dorothy is critical of their age difference and Lorraine's family disapproves of their daughter marrying a white man, so the two families attempt to stop the marriage.

Lorraine's family arrives as Rose (Betty White) and Blanche (Rue McClanahan) are testing out a new mud face treatment. The two greet the family with their masks still on, saying to them "This is mud on our faces, we're not really Black."

Thank you for being a snowflake, Hulu. There's nothing offensive about this scene. Blanche and Rose are not wearing blackface, for crying out loud. In fact, in the context of the scene, it is quite clear that writers of the episode were very much aware of how offensive blackface is and found a way to take an innocent situation and make comedy out of it. Is it worth being so sensitive and politically correct that we're gonna start censoring content that isn't even racist? What does removing the episode do except prove that the management of Hulu, and anyone who took the time to complain about the episode, is just a delicate snowflake offended by everything?

https://pjmedia.com/culture/matt-margolis/2020/06/28/hulu-axes-episode-of-the-golden-girls-for-the-dumbest-reason-n583563

Television

You know society is completely fucked when *VeggieTales* is considered "racist." Let that sink in. A group of academic Nazis are proclaiming a fruit and vegetable cartoon series for children is racist. I'll let your blood pressure get back down to normal for a minute.........

Even the wildly popular iconic *Seinfeld* TV series is under attack from the fascist mob. The golden age of television basically ended after Seinfeld departed. Throughout the 70s, 80s, and 90s, it seems there were no radical and politically correct agendas being force fed down people's throats. We had wholesome sitcoms like *Roseanne*, *Family Matters*, *The Cosby Show*, and *Cheers* with relatively few hidden political agendas. In present times, these ivory tower masterminds throw a racist and sexist woke agenda down our throats to push their narrative. Everything is about race and not art or acting. Everything is about gender and not art or acting. Everything is about forcing political platitudes and extremely politically correct euphemisms down our throats. You literally can't watch any TV series or TV news broadcast without an agenda being forced upon you. Welcome to the "Shitty Age of Television." It's not going to get any better folks. Even as an actor, I will tell you that you should turn off your TVs and go outside to enjoy your day. Don't feed the beast.

10

The War on Broadway

Wave of criticism smashes Lin-Manuel Miranda as leftists declare 'Hamilton' to be 'problematic'

By Paul Sacca July 5th, 2020

The circular firing squad of progressivism has taken aim on one of its former darlings. Leftists loved the musical "Hamilton" when it hit Broadway in January 2015. Democratic leaders, including Bill and Hillary Clinton, Bernie Sanders, and the Obama family, flocked to see Lin-Manuel Miranda's musical over the years. The musical is based on founding father Alexander Hamilton but with a modern twist and heavy influence of hip-hop. Flash forward to 2020, and now the progressives say the founding fathers should solely be remembered for being slave owners, and all of their achievements have been nullified by many leftists. Some progressives not only declare that the founding fathers should no longer be admired, but they call for their statues to be ripped down. Now, there are people who want to cancel the "Hamilton" musical because it is based on the founding fathers. Many of the harsh critics are the same people who made the musical into a cultural leviathan.

"Hamilton" was trending on social media this weekend as the film-version made its debut on Disney Plus. There was also an undercurrent of leftists saying that "Hamilton" is "problematic."

"Are y'all ready to talk about how problematic Hamilton is? Lin Manuel Miranda created a piece of work that used hip hop (a genre created by black people) to tell the story of colonizers and slave owners," one Twitter user wrote.

"As much as I love the show, it and it's writer are deeply problematic," another wrote. "I've intentionally or unintentionally ignored these things for years, but I'm trying to fix this now so I can fully contextualize and understand Hamilton and it's effect as a whole."

"Hamilton is deeply problematic in concept and so is Lin Manuel Miranda to some degree," another person tweeted.

"I mean I think the fact that a musical like Hamilton (which is deeply problematic and nationalist) has to exist in order for non-white actors to have a space on Broadway is just very indicative of how non-white stories will never be able to thrive on this elitist medium," another person said.

"Reminder for all y'all Hamilton watching mofos: Hamilton was a racist slaveowner, and casting POC as white bigots isn't the reclamation you think it is," read a tweet that had nearly 60,000 likes. "It's a romanticized telling of a white man's plights, so none of y'all better be stanning the founding fathers AGAIN."

Ajamu Baracka, a self-described "international human rights activist," blasted Miranda.

"Lin-Manuel Miranda is a Puerto Rican Uncle Tom who instead of fighting for independence makes feel-good revisionism for white liberals. He is pathetic," Baracka said.

In May, Miranda and "Hamilton" creator Jeffrey Seller were forced to apologize because people criticized them for not supporting Black Lives Matter sufficiently and not speaking enough about police brutality and the George Floyd protests.

"We spoke out on the day of the Pulse shooting. We spoke out when Vice President Mike Pence came to our show 10 days after the election. That we have not yet firmly spoken the inarguable truth that Black Lives Matter and denounced systematic racism and white supremacy from our official 'Hamilton' channels is a moral failure on our part," Miranda said in a video. "As the writer of the show, I take responsibility and apologize for my part in this moral failure."

"'Hamilton' doesn't exist without the black and brown artists who created and revolutionized and changed the world through the culture, music and language of hip-hop," he added. "Literally, the idea of the show doesn't exist without the brilliant black and brown artists in our cast, crew and production team who breathe life into this story every time it's performed."

"It's up to us and words and deeds to stand up for our fellow citizens," he concluded. "It's up to us to do the work to be better allies and have each other's backs."

Seller apologized by saying, "I'm not a politician. I'm not an activist. I'm not an expert. I'm a theater producer. But what I realize today is most importantly I'm an American citizen, and silence equals complicity and I apologize for my silence thus far."

The cancel culture mob comes for everyone.

https://www.theblaze.com/news/hamilton-problematic-lin-manuel-miranda-criticism

Broadway

Broadway has always had an artistic, leftist slant. Previously we could deal with it. Now you know society is truly in the shitter when *Hamilton* comes under attack as being "offensive" and "racist" by the Nazi, fascists, and their woke leftism. I expect the following musicals to come under attack soon too:

Cats- Promotes animal abuse and captivity.

Death of a Salesman - Pushes ageism and makes light of serious mental health issues.

Guys and Dolls - Sexist name. And what about the other 66 genders?

Chicago - Sexist towards women.

The Book of Mormon - Pushes a racist, white, Caucasian society.

The Phantom of the Opera - Promotes bullying towards the trans-abled community.

To Kill a Mockingbird - Racist.

Rent - Anti LGBTQ and homophobic.

West Side Story - Racist.

Oklahoma! - Racist and supports colonization.

You get the point. The cancers of wokeness and political correctness are literally permeating every single aspect of our society. It's going to continue unless we say no and vote with our dollars. By boycotting people, places, and things that are trying to destroy our culture, it will just continue on and on.

11

The War on Statues, Buildings & Monuments

Brown University Cultural Leftists Demand Destruction of Classical Roman Emperor Statues on Campus

By Richard Moorhead November 22nd, 2020

Left-wing racial ideologues at Brown University in Rhode Island are demanding that the school destroy two classical statues of iconic Roman emperors, claiming that the works of art represent "white supremacy."

Amanda Brynn, Justin Han, Sam Kimball, Junaid Malik, Olivia Mayeda, and Kelley Tackett, six undergraduate students affiliated with "Decolonization at Brown," are demanding that the school destroy two classical-style statues of Roman emperors Augustus Caesar and Marcus Aurelius.

They claim in a blog post that the statues "*were brought to our campus with the goals of upholding the ideal of the 'perfect' white form, white civilization, white supremacy and colonialism — ideas that we believe are incompatible with Brown today.*"

"*This is not just about monuments. It is also about the kinds of people and histories that students at Brown today are taught to idealize.*" They're demanding that the classical statues, which appear to be replicas of famous Renaissance and ancient art, be replaced with pieces created by "artists of color."

Marcus Aurelius was Roman emperor in the 2nd century in an era of peace and prosperity for the ancient civilization, and is known for documenting the philosophy of stoicism in literature that has been studied for millennia. Ironically, classical-style statues have been targeted for destruction on cultural grounds before. The Vandals, a Germanic tribe that warred with the Roman Empire in its era of decline, associated their name with property damage and barbaric behavior through their frequent destruction of cultural statues.

The stringent ideologues detest the glories of western civilization, and would destroy the cultural inheritance of the American legacy before it is passed to future generations. Their own liberal fanaticism will fade from history as an uncreative and empty religion, whereas the legacies of great men will endure.

https://bigleaguepolitics.com/brown-university-cultural-leftists-demand-destruction-of-classical-roman-emperor-statues-on-campus/

DC Mayor's Commission Wants to 'Rename, Remove' 153 Statues, Buildings, or Monuments in Nation's Capital… Including the Washington Monument

By Staff Writer, September 2nd, 2020

Of the 1,330 named properties in Washington, D.C., 153 were identified as "problematic" – nearly 12 percent. To identify a building, landmark, street name, or other property as warranting offense, members of the District of Columbia Facilities and Commemorative Expressions (DCFACES) committee considered factors such as the honoree's "involvement in systemic racism" or "support for oppression."

The entities targeted by DCFACES, established by Bowser in July, were far-reaching. For example, DCFACES "recommended the Federal government remove, relocate, or contextualize" eight statues and memorials including the Washington Monument, a Benjamin Franklin statue, and a Christopher Columbus fountain:

Seven government buildings including one named after Francis Scott Key and 12 parks, fields, or playgrounds including three named after U.S. Presidents were identified as requiring a renaming. An additional nine residential buildings and campuses including three named after U.S. Presidents along with 21 public schools such as one named after the inventor of the telephone Alexander Graham Bell were also targetted by DCFACES.

To remedy the alleged injustice – "that more than 70% of assets named in the District of Columbia are named for white men, many of whom were not District residents" – DCFACES insisted Bowser "ensure future assets, especially and including those recommended for renaming by this Working Group, include more women, people of color and LGBTQ Washingtonians."

And Bowser, who notoriously renamed the street outside the White House to "Black Lives Matter Plaza," welcomed the suggestions, stating she "wanted to thank the chairs and members of the DCFACES working group, the committee staff, and the residents who participated in this process for their commitment to building a more inclusive Washington, DC."

"The recommendations in this report will guide us as we move forward in advancing these shared DC values," she emphasized. Meanwhile, Bowser's city teems with Chinese Communist Party propaganda and adversarial capital, emboldens radical, violent Antifa and Black Lives Matter rioters, and boasts record-high crime levels.

https://thenationalpulse.com/news/dc-mayor-wants-to-remove-washington-monument/

California Students Call to Remove Ronald Reagan, Margaret Thatcher Busts

By Arik Schneider August 6th, 2020

A petition at Chapman University calls for the removal of busts depicting Ronald Reagan, Margaret Thatcher, and other prominent conservatives. With more than 700 signatures, the petition demands that the university remove and replace the "problematic" conservative icon depictions. "There are a handful of busts displayed around Chapman University's campus that do not reflect the ideals of the University," the petition reads. "In order to create a safer and more inclusive environment for Chapman's marginalized students and community, we feel the busts of Ronald Reagan, Albert Schweitzer, Margaret Thatcher, Milton Friedman, and Ayn Rand need to be removed and replaced."

"During these times of reckoning with serious injustice in the U.S. we are asking for your support and for the Chapman Administration to hear our demands," the petition continues. It goes on to include a letter that will be sent to the university's administration "once this petition has been shared enough."

The letter states, in part, "While some believe the removal of busts and statues equates to erasing history and hiding past mistakes, we believe their removal provides opportunity for deeper understanding and engagement in history. We believe the removal provides not only a display of allyship but also a hopeful opportunity for educating students on the ways these historical figures abused their power to mistreat others."

"[W]e hope this transforms into an opportunity to recognize our history and the ways certain historical figures have abused their power at the expense of marginalized groups," the letter concludes. The petition suggests replacing the current busts with busts of Angela Davis, Malcolm X, Harvey Milk, Nelson Mandela, Princess Diana, John Lewis, Cesar Chavez, James Baldwin, and Dolores Huerta.

Chapman College Republicans said in response to the petition, "This reckless removal of history is dangerous, especially for a University whose job is to educate in an attempt to better their students and their futures. For a school that has put so much effort in pushing for diversity, the removal of these statues would be proof that Chapman University takes no pride in intellectual diversity of their student body."

Pointing out that "diversity comes in multiple forms," including diversity of thought, the group said, "We conservatives do not push to remove parts of history that we do not like. we expect the same in return. When you remove history you cannot learn from it, you repeat people's mistakes and we cannot better ourselves. There are many conservatives on campus who support the Republican Party and Ronald Reagan who feel they are unable to speak out about their beliefs in fear of being shunned by unaccepting members of the student body."

Chapman College Republicans President Justin Buckner further told Campus Reform, "the main reason we felt it was necessary to speak out on this issue was that the petition claimed the statues on campus did not represent the ideals of the University, which is not true."

"The removal of Ronald Reagan," Buckner continued, "one of the most pronounced modern-day conservative voices in American history, would symbolize that anyone who believes in modern-day conservatism has no place on our campus. We want everyone to have representation and feel welcomed at Chapman University, regardless of your political beliefs."

https://www.infowars.com/california-students-call-to-remove-ronald-reagan-margaret-thatcher-busts/

Chicago removes Columbus statue from Grant Park in dead of night

By Brie Stimson July 24th, 2020

Workers arrived under cover of darkness early Friday to remove a Christopher Columbus statue from Chicago's Grant Park – a week after rioters clashed with city police as they attempted to tear the statue down. The statue was being removed partly to de-escalate tensions between protesters and police as unrest continues in the nation's third-largest city, the Chicago Tribune reported.

Chicago Mayor Lori Lightfoot made the decision to remove the statue -- as well as another Columbus one in Little Italy earlier Thursday, according to FOX 32 in Chicago. Videos and still images posted on social media showed the statue draped in a cloth as a crane pulled up to dislodge the statue from a pedestal before driving off.

Where the statue would be stored – and whether it will return anytime soon – wasn't immediately known. The statue was removed around 3 a.m. Friday after hours of tense arguments between proponents of its removal and supporters of the statue, FOX 32 reported. "This statue coming down is because of the effort of Black and Indigenous activists who know the true history of Columbus and what he represents," neighbor Stefan Cuevas-Caizaguano told the station. The decision to remove the statue is a reversal for Lightfoot who has said in the past that taking down Columbus monuments erases history, the Tribune reported.

Last Friday, multiple police officers were injured and several arrests were made during a tense protest in which demonstrators tried to pull down the statue, FOX 32 reported. Protesters filed at least 20 complaints of police brutality and activist Miracle Boyd said an officer hit her in the face, knocking at least one of her teeth out, according to the Tribune.

Some Italian Americans in the city, who see Columbus as a figure of pride, have reportedly been opposed to the removal of the statue.

"The Italian American community feels betrayed," Pasquale Gianni of the Joint Civic Committee of Italian Americans, said in a statement, according to WLS-TV in Chicago. "The Mayor's Office is giving into a vocal and destructive minority. This is not how the Democratic process is supposed to work." Columbus statues across the country have been targeted by protesters over his treatment of Indigenous people.

https://www.foxnews.com/politics/chicago-removes-columbus-statue-from-grant-park-in-dead-of-night-reports

Founding Fathers under attack: Students demand Thomas Jefferson statue removal

By Sergei Kelley Mar 29th, 2019

Students at Hofstra University protested a statue of Thomas Jefferson on Friday at the second annual event, titled "Jefferson Has Gotta Go!"

The statue has been the center of controversy on the campus and has been defaced with "DECOLONIZE" and "Black Lives Matter" signs and stickers. According to a media advisory sent by the Jefferson Has Gotta Go (JGG) campaign, the protest was held at Hofstra Breslin Hall. Organizers included "students of Hofstra University, staff from Planned Parenthood of Nassau County, and supporters of Hempstead community."

The group gathered on campus to "expose the culture of bias and discrimination," as stated in the media advisory, and to demand "the statue of Thomas Jefferson is removed." Hofstra College Democrats "want the statue to be removed and [we] stand with the Jefferson Has Gotta Go Campaign," the group's president, Brynne Levine, told *Campus Reform*.

Former College Democrats executive board member Miranda Pino also professed her support. "JGG isn't just about a statue," she told

Campus Reform. "Yes, the removal of the statue is important, but it is about what the statue represents: a legacy of racism and bigotry on college campuses."

Further demands from JGG, stated in its media advisory, include "an online, bias reporting system, an online complaint receipt program, and mandated, comprehensive, cultural competency training."

The University's Board of Trustees and Hofstra University President Stuart Rabinowitz have yet to be persuaded to go along with the demands. "President Stuart Rabinowitz has refused to remove our campus sculpture of Thomas Jefferson at the will of the board of Trustees," JGG stated in its media advisory. The university president responded in June 2018 after the first protest, announcing the statue would remain and that he would create a task force "to consider further dialogue and education about our founding fathers, the Atlantic slave trade and Western expansion; to think about what freedom and equality mean at the University."

Hofstra University did not respond to a request for comment in time for publication. The protest came just hours after George Washington University students voted to ditch the school's mascot, "George the Colonial," named after another Founding Father, George Washington.

https://www.campusreform.org/?ID=12043

Univ. of Wisconsin-Madison Students Demand Lincoln Statue Be Removed

By Rick Moran June 27th, 2020

Lincoln is one of our most misunderstood and complicated presidents. The Great Emancipator once sent an emissary to Belize to see if the U.S. government could purchase land and move all the freed slaves there. The man who saved the union suspended constitutional rights, oversaw the military occupation of Kentucky and Maryland, and ignored decisions by the Supreme Court.

But Abraham Lincoln freed the slaves and saved the union. That got his face on Mount Rushmore and gave him the loving admiration of historians.

Now, University of Wisconsin-Madison students just don't think that Honest Abe was woke enough. So they're demanding his statue on campus be removed. Their reason is astonishingly stupid: "Just because he was anti-slavery doesn't mean he was pro-Black," says the president of the black student union, Nalah McWhorter.

"He was also very publicly anti-Black," said Nalah McWhorter, the president of the Wisconsin Black Student Union. "Just because he was anti-slavery doesn't mean he was pro-Black. He said a lot in his presidential campaigns. His fourth presidential campaign speech, he said that he believes there should be an inferior and superior, and he believes white people should be the superior race."

It's a not-often-taught fact about Lincoln, but it's true. It is part of why she and the rest of her organization are pushing to get him removed, and Lincoln isn't the only one.

There are anecdotes galore about Lincoln's casual, nauseating racism. He mused aloud in a cabinet meeting that maybe some of the freed blacks were smart enough that they could learn how to read — even vote. He saw black soldiers as cannon fodder for white troops. Until September of 1862, he was willing to accept the Southern states back in the union — slavery and all.

He was, simply put, a man of his time. UW-Madison Chancellor Rebecca Blank said in a statement to News 3 Now the university is continuing work on creating a diverse and inclusive campus, but she added she supports keeping the statue of Lincoln.

"Like those of all presidents, Lincoln's legacy is complex and contains actions which, 150 years later, appear flawed," she said. "However, when the totality of his tenure is considered, Lincoln is widely acknowledged as one of our greatest presidents, having issued the Emancipation

Proclamation, persuaded Congress to adopt the 13th Amendment ending slavery and preserved the Union during the Civil War."

McWhorter not only doesn't understand history, but she also has no reverence for it.

"For them to want to protect a breathless, lifeless statue more than they care about the experiences of their black students that have been crying out for help for the past 50, 60 years, it's just a horrible feeling as a student, as a black and brown student on campus," she said.

Can't you do both? Can't you protect a statue and care about blacks at the same time? But these kids don't think that way. There's no nuance. There are no gray areas — only black and white. It comes from an education system that doesn't offer alternatives. There are good guys and bad guys and we should judge them not by the standards of their own time, but by our standards. Pointing out that Lincoln doesn't live in 21st-century America and would have no clue what McWhorter or any other activist is talking about doesn't seem to faze her.

There are old photos of S.A. Brownshirts burning books by Jewish authors on college campuses across Germany. The only problem was that the ignorant kids were burning books by everyone of any religion, any political persuasion, just to see the bonfire grow.

It's this kind of mindless barbarism that's at work in Madison and elsewhere. They're not going to stop until the bonfire is so large it consumes us all.

https://pjmedia.com/news-and-politics/rick-moran/2020/06/27/uw-students-demand-lincoln-statue-be-removed-n583086

Wasteful, damaging and outmoded: is it time to stop building skyscrapers?

By Rowan Moore Jul 11th, 2020

If no one ever built a skyscraper ever again, anywhere, who would truly miss them? I ask, because the engineer Tim Snelson, of the design consultancy Arup, has just blown a hole in any claim they might have had to be environmentally sustainable. Writing in this month's issue of the architecture magazine *Domus*, he points out that a typical skyscraper will have at least double the carbon footprint of a 10-storey building of the same floor area.

He is talking about the resources that go into building it, what is called its "embodied" energy. Tall buildings are more structurally demanding than lower ones – it takes a lot of effort, for example, to stop them swaying – and so require more steel and concrete. In London, which is mostly built on clay as opposed to Manhattan's rock, they require ample foundations. Snelson also mentions "in-use" energy consumption and carbon emissions – what is needed to cool and heat and run lifts, which he says are typically 20% more for tall than medium-height buildings.

If all this might seem pretty obvious, it's good to have calculations to attach to a hunch. And tall buildings are still sold on the basis that they are good for the environment. Mostly the argument is about density – if you pile a lot of homes or workplaces high on one spot, it is said, then you can use land and public transport more efficiently. There's some truth in this, but you can also achieve high levels of density without going above 10 or 12 storeys.Every now and again you get a one-off skyscraper design that makes play of its environmental features. The Gherkin, where cooling air was to flow through spiralling internal atria, was an early example. Strata SE1, the south London tower with three wind turbines at its top was another. Often these don't perform as promised. Even when they do, they're fighting to overcome the self-inflicted environmental handicap of being tall buildings in the first place.They have got away with it in part because embodied energy hasn't until recently been paid as much attention as energy in use. It has been deemed acceptable – by the building regulations, by architects, by the professional media – to rip untold tonnes of matter from the earth and to pump similar tonnes of greenhouse gasses into the atmosphere, in order to produce magical architectural devices that might, if all their wizardry were to function as promised, pay back some of their carbon debt some time in the next century. By when it might be too late.There's another meaning to "environment", which describes personal rather than global surroundings. In this respect, it's a bit of mystery why towers are thought desirable: you typically progress from a windy and inhospitable plaza to a soulless lobby, to a long lift ride, to another lobby, to a flat that has to be fortified and sealed against strong winds, to a balcony (if you're lucky) with a similarly embattled relationship to nature. Good design can mitigate at least some of these deficiencies, but good design is weirdly hard to find in new tall buildings.

Skyscraper apartments are sold on the view, with prices rising the higher you go up a building, which can indeed be spectacular. But this visual buzz goes with a range of sub-optimal physical experiences, which have been made that much less attractive by the spread of a virus that seems to thrive in air-conditioned and enclosed spaces. Architecture is not just about things you can see.

Meanwhile, towers continue to be built. An annual survey by the independent organization New London Architecture has found that in the capital 525 buildings of 20 stories or more are in the pipeline – either under construction, approved or going through the processes of planning applications. Other British cities, including Manchester, Liverpool and Bristol, have succumbed to the belief that there is something glamorous about this well-worn and old-fashioned building type.

In Jeddah, Saudi Arabia, a concrete stump stands in the desert that may or may not turn into the world's first kilometre-high tower, its progress having been stalled by the arrest on corruption charges of its patron, Prince Alwaleed bin Talal, in 2017. If it is ever completed, it will not be a sign of economic dynamism, as might have been said of the 20th century's skyscrapers in New York and Chicago, but of the ability of a few members of an authoritarian society to accrue vast wealth for themselves.

In Britain, tall buildings are signs of failed planning, which finds it hard to discover the space for more sustainable and humane ways of building homes. In Gulf states (and indeed in Britain, to the extent that dirty money often goes into tower projects), skyscrapers often indicate corruption. What they are not are markers of progress.

Tim Snelson puts it well: "While the collective progression of civilisations over centuries is still largely measured by the ability to build bigger, faster and taller, we have come to the point where we must put the limits on ourselves and apply our forces to the challenge of building sustainably, above all else, or risk destroying the very future that will hold our legacy." Quite so. And why, really and truly, would you want to live in one of these things?

https://www.theguardian.com/artanddesign/2020/jul/11/skyscrapers-wasteful-damaging-outmoded-time-to-stop-tall-buildings

Black Student Union Demands Lincoln Statue Come Down

By Todd Starnes July 1st, 2020

The Black Student Union at the University of Wisconsin is calling for the removal of a statue honoring President Abraham Lincoln – the man who freed the slaves and reunited a fractured nation.

"For him to be at the top of Bascom (Hill) as a powerful placement on our campus, it's a single-handed symbol of white supremacy," Black Student Union president Nalah McWhorter said in an interview with the *Wisconsin State Journal*.

The statue, which was erected in 1906, is a beloved icon on the Madison campus. Students traditional rub Lincoln's left shoe for good luck. The Wisconsin State Journal reports that Lincoln is considered a patron of the university because he signed the Morrill Land Grant College Act in 1862.

"The Morrill Act provided federal aid to land-grant colleges, and allowed UW-Madison to buy 933 acres for less than $2 per acre," the newspaper reports. The Black Student Union says the statue also needs to be removed because some of the donors were allegedly racist.

They also alleged in an Instagram post that while Lincoln freed the slaves, he was not "pro-black." Folks, it's never going to end – they are going to completely eradicate American history — good and bad.

https://www.toddstarnes.com/campus/black-student-union-demands-lincoln-statue-come-down/

Boston Taking Down Lincoln Emancipation Statue After Unanimous Vote

By Tré Goins-Phillips July 1st, 2020

With a unanimous vote, the Boston Art Commission voted Tuesday to get rid of the Emancipation Memorial commemorating President Abraham Lincoln's signing of the proclamation that ended slavery in America.

The statue, first erected in 1879, is a replica of the monument in Washington, D.C., that depicts Lincoln standing with a freed slave in the process of standing up as shackles fall from his arms. The inscription at the base of the statue, which was paid for by freed slaves and dedicated by the beloved abolitionist Frederick Douglass, reads: "A race set free and a country at peace. Lincoln rests from his labors."

Boston Mayor Marty Walsh (D) issued a statement in support of the decision to remove the Boston-based replica of the Emancipation Memorial, which follows weeks of peaceful Black Lives Matter protests and violent riots that led to the destruction of public and private properties in cities across the country.

"As we continue our work to make Boston a more equitable and just city," he said, "it's important that we look at the stories being told by the public art in all of our neighborhoods."

He went on to say: After engaging in a public process, it's clear that residents and visitors to Boston have been uncomfortable with this statue and its reductive representation of the black man's role in the abolitionist movement. I fully support the Boston Art Commission's decision for removal and thank them for their work.

The petition calling for the statue of the Great Emancipator to be taken down garnered more than 12,000 signatures.

"I've been watching this man on his knees since I was a kid," wrote the petition's creator, Tory Bullock. "It's supposed to represent freedom but instead represents us still beneath someone else. I would always ask myself, 'If he's free, why is he still on his knees?' No kid should have to ask themselves that question anymore."

But, as the woman in the video above explains of the original memorial in Washington, D.C., that is not at all what the statue depicts.

"That man is not kneeling with two knees with his head bowed," she said. "He is in the act of getting up. And his head is up — not bowed — because he's looking forward to a future of freedom. People have said, 'Well, he's chained to Mr. Lincoln.' With a closer look, you'll see that, while there's a shackle on his right hand, he's holding the end of a broken chain, which means he has taken to his freedom. He now realizes that he's free."

"So I say leave it," the woman added. "Let it stand."

During his dedication of the original statue on April 14, 1876 — 11 years after Lincoln's assassination — Douglass delivered a powerful dedication in front of then-President Ulysses S. Grant, members of the U.S. Congress as well as justices of the U.S. Supreme Court.

"Let it be known everywhere," he declared, "[that] we, the colored people, newly emancipated and rejoicing in our blood-bought freedom, near the close of the first century in the life of this Republic, have now and here unveiled, set apart, and dedicated a monument of enduring granite and bronze, in every line, feature, and figure of which the men of this generation may read, and those of after-coming generations may read, something of the exalted character and great works of Abraham Lincoln, the first martyr president of the United States."

https://www.faithwire.com/2020/07/01/boston-taking-down-lincoln-emancipation-statue-after-unanimous-vote/

NYT Targets Mount Rushmore: Indigenous Land, KKK Ties, Slave Owner Presidents

By Hannah Bleau July 1st, 2020

The *New York Times* has set its sights on Mount Rushmore as protesters demand the removal of historic monuments in the name of racial justice, citing its location on "Indigenous land," the sculptor's purported ties to white supremacy, and two of its subjects' slave ownership.

"Mount Rushmore was built on land that belonged to the Lakota tribe and sculpted by a man who had strong bonds with the Ku Klux Klan. It features the faces of 2 U.S. presidents who were slaveholders," the *New York Times* wrote, linking to a news article detailing complaints against American landmark:

The *Times* piece lists three broad grievances with Mount Rushmore, beginning with the sculptor, Gutzon Borglum, who was previously involved in "an enormous bas-relief at Stone Mountain in Georgia that memorialized Confederate leaders."

"It was eventually completed without him, but Mr. Borglum formed strong bonds with leaders of the Ku Klux Klan and participated in their meetings, in part to secure funding for the Stone Mountain project," the *Times* wrote, adding that Borglum "also espoused white supremacist and anti-Semitic ideas, according to excerpts from his letters included in 'Great White Fathers,' a book by the writer John Taliaferro about the history of Mount Rushmore."

It is not just the sculptor critics take issue with but the faces featured in the landmark located in South Dakota's Black Hills. Their grievances even extend to Abraham Lincoln, signer of the Emancipation Proclamation:

Critics of the monument have also taken issue with the men whose faces were etched into the granite. Mr. Borglum chose Washington, Jefferson, Lincoln and Roosevelt, he said, because they embodied "the founding, expansion, preservation and unification of the United States."

But each of these titans of American history has a complicated legacy. Washington and Jefferson were slaveholders. Roosevelt actively sought to Christianize and uproot Native Americans as the United States expanded, Professor Smith said. "He was a racist," he added.

And although Lincoln was behind the Emancipation Proclamation — a move some have characterized as reluctant and late — he has been criticized for his response to the so-called Minnesota Uprising, in which more than 300 Native Americans were sentenced to death by a military court after being accused of attacking white settlers in 1862.

The *Times* piece also laments the location of the landmark, writing that it is "built on land that had belonged to the Lakota tribe." It goes on to quote Nick Tilsen, a member of the Oglala Lakota tribe and leader of the Indigenous activist group NDN Collective, who stated that Mount Rushmore "needs to be closed as a national monument, and the land itself needs to be returned to the Indigenous people."

Gene A. Smith, a professor of U.S. history at Texas Christian University, told the *Times* that the U.S. could "attempt to make amends for our greediness and our unjustified taking of their land" by issuing reparations to tribes.

The piece comes as protesters vandalize and, in some cases destroy, historical monuments in cities nationwide. Trump last month signed an executive order protecting monuments from rioters, noting that the behavior exhibited by violent protesters is "not the behavior of a peaceful political movement."

"They're tearing down statues, desecrating monuments, and purging dissenters," Trump said in a statement. "It's not the behavior of a peaceful political movement; it's the behavior of totalitarians and tyrants and people that don't love our country."

Some have speculated that Mount Rushmore would become the next target of activist wrath due to the upcoming Independence Day celebration at Mount Rushmore. It is taking place July 3, and the president will be in attendance.

The Democrat Party this week tweeted and subsequently deleted an attack on Mount Rushmore and Trump, accusing him of "holding a rally glorifying white supremacy at Mount Rushmore–a region once sacred to tribal communities":

About 7,500 people are expected to attend the celebration on Saturday. Meanwhile, South Dakota Gov. Kristi Noem (R) has vowed to protect the monument radical leftists who wish to see its removal:

"The President looks forward to taking part in the Independence Day festivities, hosted by Governor Noem, and celebrating the greatest country the world has ever known capped off with a magnificent fireworks display above the great faces of Presidents George Washington, Thomas Jefferson, Theodore Roosevelt, and Abraham Lincoln," White House Deputy Press Secretary Judd Deere told Breitbart News.

https://www.breitbart.com/the-media/2020/07/01/nyt-targets-mount-rushmore-built-on-indigenous-land-features-slave-holding-presidents/

Columbus Removes Christopher Columbus Statue Outside City Hall Named After Columbus

By Tristan Justice July 1st, 2020

Columbus, Ohio, removed a statue of its namesake explorer Christopher Columbus outside City Hall Wednesday morning as the community succumbs to a woke reckoning on race, condemning the very leader it memorializes as a genocidal European imperialist.

According to ABC6 WSYX, crews arrived to bring down the statue in the early morning hours by order of the mayor, who announced last month the monument would be removed as early as possible. Democratic Mayor Andrew Ginther said the Columbus Art Commission had been tasked with replacing the Columbus statue with public artwork that more accurately represents the community, as if the Ohio capital were not named after the legendary explorer who changed world history.

"For many people in our community, the statue represents patriarchy, oppression, and divisiveness," Ginther said. "That does not represent our great city, and we will no longer live in the shadow of our ugly past."

After Ginther joined the Jacobin mob trying to rewrite American history by purging the statue, an online petition to rename the city to "Flavortown" picked up more than 118,000 signatures, many of them likely from nonresidents.

The Columbus statue was a gift from the people of Genoa, Italy, in 1955 and stood tall on the steps of City Hall for decades before the 21st-century woke revolution brought about its demise. Between 1991 and 2014, the city was also host to a replica of the ship on which Columbus sailed across the Atlantic, the Santa Maria, which operated as a museum docked in the Scioto River. The ship was built to commemorate the 500th anniversary of the Columbus voyage but was dismantled due to city construction projects on the river combined with high-cost repairs needed to keep it afloat, according to Columbus Monthly.

Statues of Columbus have also become a prime target of demonstrators around the country. Protesters toppled one statue in Richmond, Virginia, and beheaded another in Camden, New Jersey.

https://thefederalist.com/2020/07/01/columbus-removes-christopher-columbus-statue-outside-city-hall-named-after-columbus/

Denmark's Little Mermaid statue vandalized with 'racist fish' graffiti

By Associated Press July 4th, 2020

The famed statue of Hans Christian Andersen's Little Mermaid, one of Copenhagen's biggest tourist draws, has been vandalized with the text "racist fish."

The words were tagged on the stone on which the oft-attacked 1.65-meter (5.4-foot)-high bronze is sitting at the entrance of the Copenhagen harbor. No one has taken responsibility for the act. The statue was created in tribute to the Danish storyteller Andersen. It has long been a popular target for vandals, who have blown her off her perch, beheaded her and painted her.

The bronze is based on a mythical sea king's mermaid daughter who, according to the Hans Christian Andersen tale, falls in love with a prince and longs to become human.

Last month, a statue in Copenhagen of a Danish missionary who was key to the colonization of Greenland, was doused with red paint and the words "decolonize." It was not known whether the two cases of vandalism were linked. Statues and monuments around the world are being reconsidered in light of racial justice demonstrations following the death of George Floyd in Minneapolis.

Rights activists on Thursday accused Danish officials of being unable to recognize racism after authorities said the killing of a biracial man by two white men was not racially motivated.

https://www.foxnews.com/world/denmark-little-mermaid-statue-vandalized-racist-fish-grafitti

USC to remove John Wayne exhibit after student protests over racist comments the actor made decades ago

By Tomás Mier July 10th, 2020

USC's School of Cinematic Arts will remove an exhibit dedicated to John Wayne after students called for its removal last year because of racist comments the late actor made in a 1971 Playboy magazine interview, the school announced Friday.

Citing a push to promote "anti-racist cultural values," Evan Hughes, the assistant dean of diversity and inclusion, announced the change in a letter to the school's community. "Conversations about systemic racism in our cultural institutions along with the recent global, civil uprising by the Black Lives Matter Movement require that we consider the role our school can play as a change maker in promoting antiracist cultural values and experiences," Hughes said in the statement. "Therefore, it has been decided that the Wayne Exhibit will be removed."

In December, the school said it would not remove the exhibit and instead create a space exploring the American West, according the Daily Trojan. A few months before, students protested the Wayne exhibit, stating that by keeping it, the school was "endorsing white supremacy." Wayne attended USC in the late 1920s, where he played football.

The protests were prompted after comments Wayne made in the Playboy interview resurfaced. The popular actor made bigoted statements against Black people, Native Americans and the LGBTQ community. "I believe in white supremacy until the blacks are educated to a point of responsibility," he said in the interview. "I don't believe in giving authority and positions of leadership and judgment to irresponsible people."

He later said that although he didn't condone slavery, "I don't feel guilty about the fact that five or 10 generations ago these people were slaves." He also felt no remorse about the subjugation of Native Americans. "I don't feel we did wrong in taking this great country away from them," he said. "There were great numbers of people who needed new land, and the Indians were selfishly trying to keep it for themselves."

On June 26, Orange County's Democratic Party passed an emergency resolution calling for the re-naming of John Wayne Airport in Santa Ana and condemning Wayne's statements. The airport was named after him in 1979.

The decision at USC comes just a month after the university removed the name of its fifth president, Rufus Von KleinSmid, a eugenics leader, from one of its prominent buildings on campus. President Carol Folt said Von KleinSmid's beliefs were "at direct odds with USC's multicultural community and our mission of diversity and inclusion."

https://www.latimes.com/california/story/2020-07-10/usc-to-remove-john-wayne-exhibit-nearly-a-year-after-student-protests

Petition aims to remove Frank Bogert Statue in Palm Springs

By Taylor Martinez June 22nd, 2020

A petition is aiming to remove a Frank Bogert statue outside of the Palm Springs City Hall. Frank Bogert was an American actor, author and politician. He was also a longtime former Mayor of Palm Springs after being elected to the Palm Springs City Council in 1958 and becoming mayor soon after. He served eight years and was elected to the position for two more two-tear terms in 1982.

The petition states:

Frank Bogert was one of the "founding fathers" of Palm Springs, a Hollywood actor who moved to the Desert oasis and became one of its bigger boosters, starting around 1930. In 1958, Bogert was elected to the Palm Springs City Council and served as mayor from 1958-1966.

It was during this time that Palm Springs had one of its greatest failures to the non-White residents of the City, particularly in Section 14, a

square mile of land next to downtown that was part of the Agua Caliente Indian Reservation. Through a series of schemes that he operated with attorneys, some tribal members and the Bureau of Indian Affairs, Mr. Bogert and the City Council evicted many lower income and almost exclusively Black residents of Section 14. The homes they rented were torched with the assistance of the Palm Springs Fire and Police Departments, and many were "relocated" to Desert Highland Estates on the north end of town.

There is much more to this history, but the bottom line is that Frank Bogert, who was instrumental in these atrocities against Palm Springs residents, has been memorialized by a prominent statue of him in front of Palm Springs City Hall that was installed in 1990. We, the residents, citizens and visitors of Palm Springs, California, believe it is time to remove the statue to a man that only represented White Palm Springs during his time as a booster and politician.

The petition on change.org has over 700 signatures.

https://nbcpalmsprings.com/2020/06/22/petition-aims-to-remove-frank-bogert-statue-in-palm-springs/

Australian family claims son's headstone was removed without knowledge over 'offensive' picture: report

By Paulina Dedaj February 22nd, 2020

A family in Australia says they were "devastated" when they learned that their son's headstone was removed from a local cemetery without their knowledge because some had objected to an "offensive" photo, according to a report.

Peter Bridge, 33, died on April 4 last year after succumbing to a lifelong battle with cystic fibrosis. His father, Arthur Bridge, described his son as a "lovable character" with a "wicked sense of humor," a memory he hoped to capture in choosing the proper headstone, nine.com.au reported. "'Why so serious?' was one of his favorite sayings, so we made sure we wrote that on the headstone."

In addition to that, Bridge told the outlet that they included a small photo of Peter sticking up his middle finger. "Pete would have loved it because that was who he was," Bridge said. "He would be driving along and he would see a mate and the finger would be up to them, just joking around."

But at the end of January this year, Bridge found out from a friend who was visiting the Enfield Memorial Park in Clearview that Peter's headstone had been removed.

"I went straight down there to find out what was going on and they said the photo art was offensive," he told the outlet. In an online petition to bring the headstone back, Bridge said that the reasons for removing the stone "are ridiculous."

"First and foremost, we were not even notified of his headstone's removal - there was absolutely no regard for the memory and resting place of our boy. Secondly, the picture of Peter is so small, you'd have to be standing right in front of it to even see it properly." He continued: "If his picture did offend someone, why is it anyone's problem but theirs? That is our son's personal resting space."

Adelaide Cemeteries Authority Chief Operating Officer Michael Robertson told nine.com.au that the cemetery did reach out to the family by phone and left messages regarding the matter after receiving several complaints about the picture.

Roberston said they have offered to replace the photo without the hand gesture or have offered to have the picture covered by a plaque that can be moved by the family for viewing whenever they want - all of which the Bridge family have refused.

"It's morally wrong, there is just nothing right about it. You don't do that," Bridge told the outlet. "My other son, he is devastated, and my partner, she is devastated. It's taken her back to day one. She goes down to see his gravesite and there is nothing there."

https://www.foxnews.com/world/australia-family-headstone-offensive-picture

Statue of "Star Spangled Banner" Writer Francis Scott Key Toppled in San Francisco by protesters

Submitted by MAGA June 20th, 2020

Activists toppled the statue of Francis Scott Key, who wrote the lyrics to the "Star Spangled Banner" Friday evening in Golden Gate Park in San Francisco.

Per nbcbayarea.com , protesters tore down statues of people in history across the country, condemning them for their ties to slavery, all on Juneteenth, the day to celebrate the freeing of enslaved people over a century and a half ago.

Several videos surfaced on social media Friday of statues of St. Junípero Serra, Ulysses S. Grant and Francis Scott Key being torn down in San Francisco's Golden Gate Park. Police say about 400 protesters arrived around 8:30 p.m. Police say they did not engage with them.

http://redstateobserver.com/article.asp?id=167704

'Kill Whitey': Rioters Topple Statues Of George Washington, Saint Junipero Serra, Francis Scott Key, Ulysses S. Grant And Albert Pike

By Chris Menahan Jun. 20th, 2020

The Red Brigade is carrying out a Cultural Revolution in the streets while the deep state is carrying out a Color Revolution to oust our democratically elected president.

Never lose sight of the fact this is all being done with explicit government approval and only Americans stepping up to try and stop this lawlessness are being arrested and prosecuted. "KILL WHITEY" and "KILL ALL COCLINIZERS [sic]" was spray-painted on the statue of Francis Scott Key in Golden Gate Park.

The statue in Raleigh was "lynched." Remember how Trump said after Charlottesville that next they'd be tearing down statues of George Washington and Thomas Jefferson and the GOP laughed at him and threw him and their own voters under the bus? As Tucker Carlson noted in his show Friday night, the GOP is a group of feckless cowards who have surrendered to the mob.

http://www.informationliberation.com/?id=61544

Rioters In California Tear Down Statue Of Ulysses S. Grant. He Defeated The Confederacy, Devastated KKK.

By Daily Wire News Jun 20th, 2020

Rioters in California destroyed a statue of Ulysses S. Grant (not the one featured in the image above) on Friday night as far-left activists continue to destroy statues across the U.S.

Grant, a Republican who served as America's 18th president, played a key role in helping then-President Abraham Lincoln win the Civil War.

History reports:

Ulysses Grant (1822-1885) commanded the victorious Union army during the American Civil War (1861-1865) and served as the 18th U.S. president from 1869 to 1877. An Ohio native, Grant graduated from West Point and fought in the Mexican-American War (1846-1848). During the Civil War, Grant, an aggressive and determined leader, was given command of all the U.S. armies. After the war he became a national hero, and the Republicans nominated him for president in 1868. A primary focus of Grant's administration was Reconstruction, and he worked to reconcile the North and South while also attempting to protect the civil rights of newly freed black slaves.

Politico reporter Marc Caputo tweeted out a video of the incident, writing: "Lost Cause meet Crazy Cause: using Juneteenth to tear down of [sic] the San Fran. statue of Ulysses S. Grant —who won the Civil War that led to emancipation, long before had freed the 1 slave he had been given & who was later eulogized by Frederick Douglass."

Grant also aggressively went after the Ku Klux Klan, whose founder Confederate General Nathan Bedford Forrest was a Democrat. History reported that the KKK terrorized blacks and Republicans in the South during the era of Reconstruction:

Most prominent in counties where the races were relatively balanced, the KKK engaged in terrorist raids against African Americans and white Republicans at night, employing intimidation, destruction of property, assault, and murder to achieve its aims and influence upcoming elections. In a few Southern states, Republicans organized militia units to break up the Klan. In 1871, passage of the Ku Klux Act led to nine South Carolina counties being placed under martial law and thousands of arrests. In 1882, the U.S. Supreme Court declared the Ku Klux Act unconstitutional, but by that time Reconstruction had ended, and much of the KKK had faded away.

Congress responded to the violence by passing a series of bills that allowed Grant to use military force to protect the rights of blacks. "The Third Force Act, also known as the KKK or the Civil Rights Act of 1871, empowered President Ulysses S. Grant to use the armed forces to combat those who conspired to deny equal protection of the laws and, if necessary, to suspend habeas corpus to enforce the act," Politico reported. "Grant signed the legislation on this day in 1871. After the act's passage, the president for the first time had the power to suppress state disorders on his own initiative and suspend the right of habeas corpus. Grant did not hesitate to use this authority."

Politico added, "Shortly after Congress approved the law, nine counties in South Carolina, where KKK terrorism was rampant, were placed under martial law and thousands of persons were arrested."

https://www.dailywire.com/news/rioters-in-california-tear-down-statue-of-ulysses-s-grant-he-defeated-the-confederacy-devastated-kkk?utm_source=facebook&utm_medium=social&utm_campaign=mjk

Petition calls for St. Louis to be renamed, removal of statue on Art Hill

By Sam Masterson June 19th, 2020

A petition has been made with hopes of changing the city's name in St. Louis and taking down a statue of its namesake, Saint Louis IX in Forest Park. The creators say the city's name is "outright disrespect" to Jewish and Muslim residents and they're asking for support.

The petition on Change.org was started this week, after the statue of Christopher Columbus in Tower Grove Park was taken away. Local writer Umar Lee is a co-signer of the petition.

"For those unfamiliar with King Louis IX he was a rabid anti-semite who spearheaded many persecutions against the Jewish people. Centuries later Nazi Germany gained inspiration and ideas from Louis IX as they embarked on a campaign of murderous genocide against the Jewish people. Louis IX was also vehemently Islamophobic and led a murderous crusade against Muslims which ultimately cost him his life," the petition states.

The statue of Louis IX, which now sits on top of Art Hill in front of the St. Louis Art Museum, was unveiled in 1906. It served as the symbol of St. Louis until the Gateway Arch was completed in 1965. Louis IX is the only King of France to be canonized in the Catholic Church. He became king when he was 12-years-old and is credited with changing the judicial process in France, with trials no longer being settled by combat, but instead by evidence and Roman law.

He was also known as a devoted Catholic, who ordered the burning of some 12,000 manuscript copies of the Talmud and other Jewish books. "I ask all people of good faith committed to the modern values of equity and coexistence to sign this petition to rename the City of St. Louis to something more suitable and indicative of our values," the petition states. The petition has 133 signatures as of Friday morning, with a goal of 200.

https://kmox.radio.com/articles/news/petition-calls-for-st-louis-to-be-renamed-statue-removed

Young Americans support removing statues, renaming buildings....even for Founding Fathers and recent Dem politicians

By Eduardo Neret June 18th, 2020

As the movement to remove statues and rename buildings named after historical figures continues to grow across the country, *Campus Reform* Digital Reporter Eduardo Neret asked young Americans and students for their thoughts on the matter.

Questions first focused on confederate monuments, which most individuals agreed should be taken down. “I don’t know why they have them to begin with,” one individual said. “Like why would you support someone who has a racist past?”

“I feel like that’s a dark part of our past,” another added. Neret then asked if there should be a limit on what is removed, or if statues of Founding Fathers like George Washington and Thomas Jefferson should also be removed, since they were slaveholders.

“I don’t think [removing Washington and Jefferson is] far enough to be honest,” one individual said.

"It's not really for my opinion...it's supporting the people who have been oppressed by this ideology and what their voices say. And if it's part of their healing process, then I'm supportive of it," another said. *Campus Reform* then turned the attention to modern political figures. Without naming any specific politician, Neret questioned whether politicians who have a negative history with women or working with segregationists during the Civil Rights Movement should also have their statues removed and their names scrubbed from buildings.

Some initially agreed. "For more modern figures, it's more okay to clear them from our statues and our names," one individual noted. Neret then mentioned Bill Clinton and Joe Biden by name. "I'm not too sure about that one," the same person said, walking back their previous remarks.

Others were more consistent. "If you've ever sexually assaulted anyone, then you have no right... [to] have your name anywhere."

"I also think that Biden is also like a horrible person, in the sense that we're talking about, you know, current politicians that--he has issues with sexual assault, working with segregationists, all those things," another individual added. "Politicians like him that are currently still in power that have embodied those things throughout history and throughout their political career, they should be investigated more."

The University of Arkansas is home to the Clinton School of Public Service, named for former President Bill Clinton, who has been accused of sexual assault. The University of Delaware is home to the Biden School of Public Policy and Administration, named for former Vice President and presumptive Democratic presidential nominee Joe Biden. Biden has also been accused of sexual assault and has been criticized for siding with segregationists in the 1970s to oppose the practice of busing, an effort to desegregate schools.

https://www.campusreform.org/?ID=15070&utm_campaign=CampusWire&utm_medium=email&_hsmi=89856791&_hsenc=p2ANqtz--455ZhGzy59BMEqWeNvPXAv6-IMt8hmWeQP-

NUrHjs41JuQ4Rffm_ObTc7yljovwkHjVTLPcy4NKgN3-npB37IJP L1lkA&utm_con-
tent=89856791&utm_source=hs_email#.Xu0BEmo0zDw.facebook

Rioters Set American Flag On Fire On Top Of George Washington Statue, Tear It Down

By Ryan Saavedra Jun 19th, 2020

Rioters burned an American flag on top of a statue of George Washington in Portland on Thursday night before destroying the statue by tearing it down. The statue was pulled down by a group of rioters who reportedly converged on NE Sandy Boulevard and NE 57th Avenue at around 10 p.m.

"Some wrapped the statue's head in an American flag and lit the flag on fire," KOIN News reported. "Their numbers grew over the next hour until there were enough people to pull the statue to the ground. They quickly scattered."

A news crew from the outlet "found the statue face down and covered in graffiti." Shortly after it was toppled, Portland police arrived on the scene, KOIN reports. Journalist Andy Ngo tweeted out videos of the destruction of property, writing: "Antifa rioters on Sandy Blvd. in Portland draped a US flag over a George Washington statue [and] set it on fire. They then toppled the statue. 'Genocidal colonist' [and] 'f— cops' are sprayed on monument. Rioters have began to build another autonomous zone nearby."

Ngo continued: "The nearly 100-year-old statue of George Washington in NE Portland has been pulled down. There are no police in the area." Left-wing rioters have destroyed monuments and statues across the country in recent weeks after the death of George Floyd, which follows violent riots and looting that broke out in inner cities across the country.

Last week, rioters destroyed a Christopher Columbus statue in Minneapolis that was created by an Italian immigrant as a gift from the state's Italian-Americans. The Daily Wire reported:

"The 10-foot bronze statue was pulled from its granite base by several dozen people led by a Minnesota-based Native American activist outside the state Capitol," Reuters reported. The destruction of property comes as riots have erupted in inner cities amid a wave of protests over the death of George Floyd. Some of the rioters have started to tear down historical monuments that they deem to be offensive.

According to a Minneapolis government web page, "The 10-foot tall bronze sculpture of Christopher Columbus was dedicated on October 12, 1931 and was presented as a gift from Minnesota's Italian-Americans. The sculpture sits on a red granite base embellished with carvings of sea shells and fish around the top and on either sides are eagles with spread wings atop globe-shaped spheres. Sculptor: Carlo Brioschi, dedicated on October 12, 1931; restoration and preservation efforts in 1992."

Earlier this week, reports surfaced that Boston was weighing taking down a statue of Abraham Lincoln that featured a freed slave rising to his knees while holding a broken chain. The statue is a replica of the Emancipation Memorial in Washington, D.C., which was purchased by freed slaves as a tribute to Lincoln.

https://www.dailywire.com/news/watch-rioters-burn-american-flag-on-fire-on-top-of-george-washington-statue-tear-it-down

Cancel Culture Comes for Junipero Serra. Here's His Real Legacy.

By Katrina Trinko June 20th, 2020

Finally, the mob has realized the need to be inclusive: now they've torn down a statue of one of America's great Hispanics.

In San Francisco (no one let the mob know the city itself is named after another Catholic saint!) Friday night, a group of activists tore down a statue of St. Junipero Serra, a Spanish Catholic missionary in the late 1700s. Of the 21 Spanish missions in California, Serra founded nine of them. The missions—where native Californians lived with Spanish missionaries and learned to farm—played a critical role in California's history and development.

Their spree of toppling statues wasn't limited to Serra: statues of Ulysses S. Grant (the general who Abraham Lincoln relied on to win the Civil War) and Francis Scott Key (author of "The Star-Spangled Banner") were also taken down.

And, of course, no arrests have been made. Seriously? I have no problem with having a debate about statues, and other ways we honor our history, from road names to school names. (Key and Grant had both owned slaves.) But there is a thoughtful, democratic way to have this debate: a way that allows the span of viewpoints to be heard and respected and that honors our legal system.

And there are more options than simply keeping up or destroying statues. Other choices include adding historical context through plaques, or moving statues to museums. But that slower method won't satisfy the tyranny of certain social justice warriors, who prefer to dictate what the rest of us can do (and what statues we may see).

Across the country, mobs are tearing down statues in recent days, and not only of confederate figures. In addition to three torn down in San Francisco, a statue of George Washington was also torn down in Portland. So far as I'm aware, no one has been arrested for any of these actions.

Serra, who was apparently deemed woke enough in 2015 to have California Democrat Gov. Jerry Brown defend him, and House Speaker Nancy Pelosi and then-Vice President Joe Biden join Pope Francis in a visit to the statue of Serra in the Capitol, is now apparently blacklisted.

Activists scrawled "stolen land" on the former base of the Serra statue—an ironic charge from a group of law-breaking thieves who just stole from locals a public statue no one had voted to take down nor had any legally-elected lawmaker opted to remove.

Between the statue of Serra in the U.S. Capitol and news that city of Ventura, home to one of Serra's missions, is considering removing a statue of him, there's no doubt this debate will continue to rage. So let's look at Serra's actual life and legacy—which shows he was hardly some monster who sought to hurt California natives.

Serra, like many religious people, genuinely believed he knew the path to salvation and eternal life—and that was something he dedicated much of his adult life to sharing with Californians. That may not "make sense" to our increasingly secular mindset, where we seem to worry endlessly about everything and anything *except* whether we have an eternal destiny, and if so, what we need to do to work toward that.

But because it is unfathomable to some does not mean that it was rooted in cruelty.n Msgr. Francis Weber, author of "Blessed Fray Junipero Serra: An Outstanding California Hero," wrote about Serra's treatment of native Californians in a 2015 article published on the website of the Knights of Columbus, a Catholic fraternal organization.

"Serra showed himself to be a defender of the Indians' human rights in 1773, when he journeyed from California to Mexico City to personally present to the viceroy a Representación. This document, which is sometimes termed a 'Bill of Rights' for Indians, was accepted and implemented," wrote the archivist emeritus of the Archdiocese of Los Angeles. Weber also disputed that Serra was an enthusiastic participant of Spain's political goals for California, writing:

Junípero Serra, for example, did everything he could to keep the military from having direct contact with the Indians. In many cases, he and other friars concentrated their energies on doing what they could to alleviate a difficult situation. In short, the natives were destined to change for better or worse; the missionaries strove to assist them in changing for the better.

It is sometimes assumed that the Indians in California had been living in some sort of idyllic lifestyle, akin to that of Eden. Contrary to this and related myths, the Indians were attracted to the food and quality of life that the missions provided, when compared to their original state.

When Mission San Diego was burned down and destroyed and the chief priest brutally murdered—stoned and clubbed—Serra called for mercy for those involved. "Let the murderer live so he can be saved, which is the purpose of our coming here and the reason for forgiving him," Serra wrote in a letter to a political leader, according to the 2015 book "Junípero Serra: California, Indians, and the Transformation of a Missionary."

"Help him to understand, with some moderate punishment that he is being pardoned in accordance with our law, which orders us to forgive offenses and to prepare him, not for his death, but for eternal life," Serra added. In that same letter, he made it clear that if he ever faced the same death as the priest at Mission San Diego, he did not want death for his killers. "If the Indians were to kill me, whether they be gentiles or Christians, they should be forgiven," the priest wrote.

Or take the story of Ruben Mendoza, an archaeologist and professor at California State University-Monterey Bay. Growing up, Mendoza hated the California missions to such an extent he requested permission from a grade school teacher to make another project instead of constructing a diorama of a California mission, as his classmates were doing.

In 2015, Mendoza told the Los Angeles Times he inherited his attitude from his father: "Over and over, he claimed Catholic missions were cancers that Spain brought to the New World," Mendoza recalled. But as the years passed, Mendoza found himself having a change of heart. The Los Angeles Times reported:

"Serra endured great hardships to evangelize Native Californians," [Mendoza] said. "In the process, he orchestrated the development of a chain of missions that helped give birth to modern California." Flogging and shackling were common punishments for Indians in Serra's missions, Mendoza said. But documentation also shows that Serra felt Indians stood a better chance of surviving depredation by Spanish soldiers and colonists if they were brought into the fold of the missions.

"The missions were not slave plantations like those of George Washington or Thomas Jefferson," Mendoza said. "They were communes in which friars and Indians worked side by side and consumed the products of their labor."

Ultimately, Mendoza told the Times, "Serra was far from perfect ...Yet we are beneficiaries of this man who believed that poverty, chastity and obedience would open the gates of the kingdom of heaven to Native Californians." Now this is speculation, but would you guess that any of the statue destroyers of Serra knew any of this about him?

I'd suspect not. No person is perfect. But Serra was hardly some cartoonish villain. He was a man who genuinely loved the native Californians he ministered to, and who choose to honor his faith's tenets of forgiveness even when tested. He left his home country in order to be a missionary, driven by the desire to bring salvation to others.

As the first saint canonized on American soil, during Pope Francis' 2015 visit, Serra holds a special place among the United States' approximately 70 million Catholics. A small group of rogue criminals should not be allowed to dictate the fate of statues in America's parks and cities. It's time for law enforcement to enforce the law. For those who wish to tear down statues, use the legal process—and if you're as much on the right side of history as you seem to assume, no doubt others will support you.

"Father Serra had a motto which inspired his life and work, not just a saying, but above all a reality which shaped the way he lived: *siempre adelante!* Keep moving forward!" said Pope Francis during the 2015 canonization ceremony for Serra in Washington, D.C.

"For him, this was the way to continue experiencing the joy of the Gospel, to keep his heart from growing numb, from being anesthetized," the pope continued. "He kept moving forward, because the Lord was waiting. He kept going, because his brothers and sisters were waiting. He kept going forward to the end of his life." Americans might have something to learn from that attitude of Serra's. More and more we seem fixated on the past, not the future. While we should grapple with our history, and especially the sin of slavery, that does not mean such grappling should come to the exclusion of looking forward. If the activists believe there are real wrongs in today's America, they should focus on fixing those, not destroying statues.

https://www.dailysignal.com/2020/06/20/cancel-culture-comes-for-junipero-serra-heres-his-real-legacy/

Nikole Hannah-Jones Endorses Riots And Toppling Statues As A Product Of The 1619 Project

By Allison Schuster June 20th, 2020

Nikole Hannah-Jones, staff writer at The New York Times and lead essayist in The New York Times Magazine's 1619 Project, just endorsed the nationwide destruction of statues as a product of her historically inaccurate work.

The 1619 Project debuted in 2019 on the 400th anniversary of the arrival of African-Americans in the United States as slaves, as an ongoing look into the history of U.S. slavery. Although the project has been taught in schools and applauded by elites, even winning Hannah-Jones a Pulitzer Prize this May despite having to issue major corrections, the project's influence truly revealed itself in the recent removal of historical symbols in nearly every major city across the U.S.

Claremont's Charles Kesler wrote a column in The New York Post Friday, titled "Call them the 1619 riots," blaming the indignation and utter lack of regard for the nation's greatest men on the misinformation stemming from The 1619 Project. Hannah-Jones responded to the article on twitter saying she would be honored to claim responsibility for the defamation of American heroes and Founding Fathers such as George Washington.

"America is burning," Kesler writes. "Rioters set fire to police stations and restaurants. Looters have ravaged shops from coast to coast. And now they're coming for the statues — not just of Confederate generals, but the republic's Founders, including George Washington, whose statue was torn down in Portland, Ore. Call them the 1619 riots." The essence of Hannah-Jones' project, as argued by her editor, Jake Silverstein, is that the emergence of slavery in this country isn't merely a stain on an otherwise honorable U.S. founding, but rather that slavery is the entirety of the founding. Slavery came before the American Revolution and therefore preceded any ideas of liberty and equality.

"In other words, 1619 is not 'as important' as 1776; it is far more important and more revealing," Kesler wrote. "American slavery is the deeper truth of American freedom. It doesn't get more systemic than racism being in 'the very DNA of this country,' as Hannah-Jones claims."

Prominent American historians fiercely denounced the project after its initial release for its glaring inaccuracies. Even "impeccable liberals" voiced their objections, Kesler wrote, including Sean Wilentz, Gordon Wood and James McPherson. Five historians even wrote a letter to The New York Times outlining its errors.

Seventh months after its publication, the Times printed a correction for what they admitted was a significant mistake in one of Hannah-Jones' essays. After being taught in schools for over half a year, the essay was then clarified to show that maintaining slavery wasn't every colonist's motivation to forge the American Revolution, but merely that of some.

The project's scope, however, had already reached young Americans. As evidenced by the mayhem of recent weeks, so many Americans were taught an altered form of history, one riddled with mistruths that discounted the value of the Founders' work. Kesler's article accusing The 1619 Project of inciting this type of defamation with its wrong portrayal of American history divulges truth to those who already saw the project's inherent dishonesty. Hannah-Jones' proud ownership of the accusation, however, is far more telling of her own motivation for the project.

https://thefederalist.com/2020/06/20/nikole-hannah-jones-endorses-riots-and-toppling-statues-as-a-product-of-the-1619-project/

National Park Police in DC Nowhere to Be Found as Mob Takes Down Federal Govt Owned Statue

By Kristinn Taylor June 19th, 2020

The statue toppled by a mob in Washington, D.C. Friday night was federal property owned by the National Park Service just blocks from the Capitol, yet for hours as protesters gathered around the statue trying to pull it down Park Police were apparently not on scene. Park Police Officer Webster who answered a phone inquiry by TGP around 11:19 p.m. EDT said officers were on their way to the statue. When informed a minute later that Park Police were too late and that the statue had been taken down and set on fire Officer Webster snapped that the Park Police had other things going on tonight.

The statue of Albert Pike was located next to the headquarters of D.C.'s Metropolitan Police at 300 Indiana Avenue, NW. MPD had officers on the scene who did not intervene to protect federal property from the mob and no arrests were made. One officer reportedly put out the fire.

The Pike statue has a controversial history in D.C. because even though it was erected by Masons in honor of Pike's service to the Masons, he also served as a Confederate general in the Civil War and there were unproven rumors Pike had been a member of the KKK. The statue was approved by Congress in 1898 with the understanding Pike would be honored as a civilian and not a soldier. The statue was dedicated in 1901 and was relocated in 1977 after highway construction.

https://www.thegatewaypundit.com/2020/06/national-park-police-dc-nowhere-found-mob-takes-federal-govt-owned-statue/

New York City Museum Taking Down Statue Of President Theodore Roosevelt

By Ryan Saavedra June 21st, 2020

The American Museum of Natural History in New York City announced on Sunday that it is going to remove a statue of former President Theodore Roosevelt that has been located on the property for 80 years.

The museum made the call to take down the statue and New York City, which owns the building and property, agreed with the museum's decision, according to The New York Times. The bronze statue features Roosevelt on horseback and flanked on both sides by an African man and a Native American man.

"The statue was meant to celebrate Theodore Roosevelt (1858-1919) as a devoted naturalist and author of works on natural history. Roosevelt's father was one of the Museum's founders, and the Museum is proud of its historic association with the Roosevelt family," the museum said in a statement. "At the same time, the statue itself communicates a racial hierarchy that the Museum and members of the public have long found disturbing."

The statue's removal comes after left-wing activists have destroyed statues across the country in recent days, including statues of George Washington, Thomas Jefferson, Ulysses S. Grant, Francis Scott Key, and Junipero Serra. The museum said that it was going to rename its Hall of Biodiversity after Roosevelt to honor his legacy as a conservationist.

The New York Times added:

[The museum's president, Ellen V. Futter] also made a point of saying that the museum was only taking issue with the statue itself, not with Roosevelt overall, with whom the institution has a long history.

His father was a founding member of the institution; its charter was signed in his home. Roosevelt's childhood excavations were among the museum's first artifacts. The museum was chosen by New York's state legislature for Roosevelt's memorial in 1920. The museum already has several spaces named after Roosevelt, including Theodore Roosevelt Memorial Hall, the Theodore Roosevelt Rotunda and Theodore Roosevelt Park outside.

"It's very important to note that our request is based on the statue, that is the hierarchical composition that's depicted in it," Ms. Futter said. "It is not about Theodore Roosevelt who served as Governor of New York before becoming the 26th president of the United States and was a pioneering conservationist."

The museum noted in its statement that New York City Democrat Mayor Bill de Blasio had created a commission in 2017 to "evaluate a number of controversial monuments around the city, including the Roosevelt statue, which sits on city-owned land. The City determined that the Roosevelt statue would remain in place but that more information should be provided." The movement to remove statues across the country was recently triggered by the death of George Floyd in Minneapolis last month.

https://www.dailywire.com/news/breaking-new-york-city-museum-taking-down-statue-of-president-theodore-roosevelt

Protesters try to pull down Andrew Jackson statue in DC

By Associated Press June 22nd, 2020

WASHINGTON (AP) - Protesters tried to pull down a statue of President Andrew Jackson near the White House Monday night before being dispersed by police.

WUSA-TV in Washington reported that police used pepper spray to move protesters out of Lafayette Square, where the Jackson statue is located. Videos posted on social media showed that the protesters had climbed on the statue and tied ropes around it, then tried to pull it off its pedestal. The statue shows Jackson in a military uniform, riding a horse that is rearing on its hind legs. The 19th century president's ruthless treatment of Native Americans has made his statue a target of demonstrators protesting the United States' legacy of racial injustice.

The Jackson statue remained on its pedestal Monday night. President Donald Trump tweeted late Monday that "Numerous people" had been arrested for "the disgraceful vandalism." He added: "10 years in prison under the Veteran's Memorial Preservation Act. Beware!"

Interior Secretary David Bernhardt was at the scene Monday night, and issued a statement saying: "Let me be clear: we will not bow to anarchists. Law and order will prevail, and justice will be served."

https://www.wsaw.com/content/news/Protesters-try-to-pull-down-Andrew-Jackson-statue-in-DC-571434531.html?ref=531

Texas Ranger Statue Removed At Dallas Love Field

By DFW CBS Local June 4th, 2020

A new book on the Rangers, "Cult of Glory," offered chilling details about dark chapters of the Rangers' history. The book by former Pulitzer Prize finalist Doug J. Swanson, a longtime reporter for The Dallas Morning News who is now on the University of Pittsburgh faculty, says the statue depicts Capt. Jay Banks. The captain was in charge of a Ranger contingent dispatched in 1957 by then-Gov. Allan Shivers to keep black students from enrolling in Mansfield's high school High School and a Texarkana community college despite court rulings that should have prevented Shivers from doing so.

Swanson told his former newspaper that "Banks became sort of the face for that because there's a famous picture of him leaning against a tree in front of Mansfield High School while a black figure hangs in effigy above the school, with Banks making no effort to take it down.

"And Banks sided with the mobs who were there to keep the black kids out. So, he was the face of that and of a statue that welcomes people to Dallas," he said.

Swanson also noted the title "One Riot, One Ranger" came from a Ranger's report of a scene at the Grayson County Courthouse in Sherman in 1930, when a black man stood trial for assaulting a white woman. The mob eventually set fire to the courthouse and roasted the black man alive after he sought refuge in a courthouse safe. Officials said the decision was made by the Office of Arts and Culture and the airport to remove the statue and put it in storage "until a broader community dialogue about its display in a prominent location can take place."

Pictures from the city show the statue being put into a harness and being lifted onto a cart earlier in the day. According to the city, it received the statue before policies on extensive review of public art donations were in place.

https://dfw.cbslocal.com/2020/06/04/texas-ranger-statue-removed-dallas-love-field/

Statues, Buildings and Monuments

Tearing down statues and monuments is what happened in Nazi Germany, Soviet Russia, Venezuela, and China. From Marxism to Nazism (which in my opinion are the same), breaking down one's culture and history by tearing down statues and monuments is just one more step into preparing to turn a civilization into a utopian hell on earth. Why would someone want to tear down an Abraham Lincoln statue? He helped free the slaves. Why would someone want to tear down a Winston Churchill statue, a George Washington statue, or any other war hero? It's simple... These social justice warriors are trying to erase our history. One of the best ways of erasing history is to tear down statues and monuments. In fact, it's only a matter of time before the following are banned, censored, and cancelled:

The Washington Monument
The Lincoln Memorial

The MLK Memorial
Mount Rushmore

You wait... These totalitarian Nazi's (led by the racist BLM and Antifa groups) will be attacking the monuments listed above as well as almost every other statue and monument in America and throughout the world.

12

The War on Toys

Michigan lawmakers push fast-food restaurants to stop offering gender-based toys

By Janine Puhak November 30th, 2018

Receiving a free children's toy at Michigan fast-food joints may soon require restaurants to ask the kids which ones they'd prefer, at least if lawmakers successfully go through with a petition to stop "gender classification" of kids' meal toys at fast-food franchisees.

Earlier this week, the state House of Representatives introduced a motion requesting that chains stop offering "boy toys" and "girl toys" on the grounds that such classifications "limit children's imagination," going so far as to argue that such restrictions can prevent young girls from taking an interest in the STEM (science, technology, engineering, math) fields, KWCH reports.

Instead, the lawmakers want children to be offered a "choice" of toy without traditional gender labels. Rep. Leslie Love (D-Detroit) is the primary sponsor of the House Resolution No. 429, which has 14 co-sponsors, the Detroit Free Press reported.

According to the resolution, many food establishments in the Wolverine State still currently offer gender-classified complimentary toys, despite multiple studies citing the harmful effects of such actions.

"Food establishments often offer a toy with their meals marketed to young children, and in some cases the customer is asked if they prefer a 'girl toy' or a 'boy toy.' Often, the designated 'boy toys' are action figures or building toys, typically, in primary colors, whereas 'girl toys' are often stuffed animals and are usually in a pastel color scheme," the resolution states, as per KWCH. "This is a significant issue as billions of these meals are sold every year and this practice can influence and limit children's imaginations and interests by promoting some toys as only suitable for girls and others only for boys," it continues. "While some food establishments claim to have abandoned this practice, many stores in Michigan continue to offer gender-classified options to customers."

"Numerous studies have highlighted the harmful effects of gender-classified toys," the resolution adds.

"If a customer desires a toy, it should be one of his or her choice without classification by gender. Customers should simply be offered the choice of toy," the statement reads. "(Example: Would you like a Transformer or a My Little Pony?)" The motion goes on to cite a 2015 study from the Association for Psychological Science, which reported that "boys are more likely to play with toys that develop spatial intelligence and reasoning than girls. These skills are especially important for success in academic and professional domains, including science, technology, engineering, and math (STEM)."

As noted by the Free Press, this is hardly a new issue. In 2008, a Connecticut girl questioned the policy of being receiving a "girl" versus a "boy" toy with her McDonald's happy meal, and a 2016 petition on the same topic made headlines as it gained traction. Some critics on Twitter, meanwhile, weren't too happy with news of the resolution, largely calling for Michigan state reps to focus their attention elsewhere and pour their energies into resolving more pressing issues.

"This is what they're spending time and money on? Flint still doesn't have safe water," one wrote. "Seems like there are more important things for them to do, maybe address our crumbling roads, the poisoned wells up north, flint water, poor public schools....just a thought," another agreed.

"God help us," one mused. "Tax dollars hard at work," another chimed in.

https://www.foxnews.com/food-drink/michigan-lawmakers-push-fast-food-restaurants-to-stop-offering-gender-based-toys

Black rag dolls meant to be abused are pulled from stores

By David Porter July 16th, 2019

NEWARK, N.J. (AP) — Black rag dolls that came with instructions to "find a wall" and slam the toy against it have been pulled from three stores after customers and a lawmaker said they were offensive.

The "Feel Better Doll" featured instructions to "whack" the doll "whenever things don't go well and you want to hit the wall and yell." The president of One Dollar Zone said roughly 1,000 dolls were pulled this week from its store in Bayonne and two others also in New Jersey.

The dolls were made of black fabric with yarn hair of red, green, black and yellow in the style of dreadlocks, and featured large white eyes and a white smile. State Assemblywoman Angela McKnight, a Democrat whose district includes Bayonne, called the dolls "offensive" and "inappropriate" after seeing a post on social media.

Bayonne Mayor Jimmy Davis said in a Facebook post that the dolls were "insensitive" and "can certainly be considered racist." One Dollar Zone President Ricky Shah apologized for the dolls' appearance in the stores and said they were pulled Monday after someone posted images online. The Paterson-based company didn't adequately check a large lot of items it had received before distributing them to stores, he said.

"This somehow slipped through the cracks," he said. The dolls were included in a shipment of about 35,000 pieces of closeout merchandise, Shah said, mostly with an "I Love NY" theme, including mugs and picture frames.

The supplier that shipped the order offered to credit One Dollar Zone for the cost of the dolls, Shah said. The dolls' manufacturer, the Harvey Hutter Co., couldn't be reached at several phone numbers and email addresses at its location just north of New York City. Shah forwarded an email from supplier Global Souvenir Marketing stating that the company is no longer in business. Global Souvenir Marketing did not respond to an email seeking comment Friday. One Dollar Zone operates more than two dozen stores in the northeastern U.S. from Massachusetts to Pennsylvania.

https://apnews.com/9a9dad8649c3445ea7c206dbc3bdd05d

Girl power: Hasbro brings gender pay gap debate to game night with new Ms. Monopoly

By Kelly Tyko September 10th, 2019

Addressing the gender pay gap comes down to changing the rules of the game. *That's exactly what Ms. Monopoly brings to the table.* Hasbro is launching a new version of the iconic board game that celebrates female trailblazers and is the first "where women make more than men," officials shared exclusively with USA TODAY.

The new game – which includes several modern updates including ride shares instead of railroads and Wi-Fi instead of water works – goes on sale this month at major national retailers for a suggested price of $19.99. The game is available for preorder at Walmart.com.

Jen Boswinkel, senior director of global brand strategy and marketing for Hasbro Gaming, said the game is designed for today's kids and highlights a subject they may not know about yet.

"With all of the things surrounding female empowerment, it felt right to bring this to Monopoly in a fresh new way," Boswinkel said. "It's giving the topic some relevancy to everyone playing it that everybody gets a turn, and this time women get an advantage at the start."

Wage debate at game night

The debate over equal pay starts before shuffling the cards, choosing a token and rolling the dice. The banker doles out $1,900 in Monopoly

Money to each female player and $1,500 to each male. The gap continues every time a player passes go with women collecting $240 and men $200.

Instead of investing in real estate properties like the classic game, players invest in inventions and innovations made by women, including chocolate chip cookies, bulletproof vests, solar heating and ladies' modern shapewear.

"We made sure that this felt authentic and was a fun game families could play and learn about these things that they love and are a part of their life that they didn't know were invented by women," Boswinkel said.

Other updates to the game include new tokens including a white hat, a watch, a barbell, a glass and a jet plane. While the white hat might conjure up thoughts of Olivia Pope from "Scandal," Boswinkel said it's to symbolize Mr. Monopoly passing his top hat to his niece. The watch is to symbolize that it's "about time for some changes," she added.

Families can choose to give everyone the same amount if they choose, Boswinkel said. It's also possible that a boy wins the game. "It's a way that families can talk about what is happening around them, and it's an easy way to explain to their kids, boys or girls, what has maybe happened to them over the years and what they've been experiencing," Boswinkel said.

Young inventors

To celebrate the new game, Hasbro surprised three young female inventors with $20,580 in real – not Monopoly – money: 13-year-old Gitanjali Rao, of Denver, and Sophia Wang from Connecticut and Ava Canney from Ireland, both 16. A high school freshman, Gitanjali has created a few inventions including the Tethys, a device that detects lead in drinking water.

"There are so many big things that most people think are created by men, but they're actually created by women," said Gitanjali, who was included on Forbes' 2019 30 under 30 list for science. "It really expanded my knowledge and was so empowering to me." An avid Monopoly player, Gitanjali also said she was "appalled" to learn more about the gender pay gap. "I never put the dots together and realized it was that much of a gap," she said. "I think it's super important to talk about equal pay and that there's no such thing as boys' subjects and girls' subjects."

https://www.usatoday.com/story/money/2019/09/10/ms-monopoly-hasbro-brings-gender-pay-gap-debate-game-night/2201160001/

Mattel launches gender-inclusive doll line

By: John Lynch and Rob Sneed September 25th, 2019

COLUMBUS, Ohio (WCMH) – New dolls are hitting the shelves that give kids more options other than the typical hyper-feminine barbie. Mattel launched a line of dolls called "creatable world". It's a new gender neutral doll. Some said they aren't necessary. However, members of the LGBTQIA community say they wish the dolls were around during their childhoods.

You can make the dolls whatever you want them to be. Short hair or long hair, Mattel is giving kids more options with its new line of neutral gender dolls. Briden Schueren loves the new dolls. He a man who's trans, and recalls his life as a child. "It is exciting to know that the world is finally going to a direction to help the younger generation to feel like they can fully be themselves," said Schueren.

The dolls are a far cry from the long pink ball gowns Barbie with Blonde shinny hair Schueren used to play with as a child. The 31-year-old says the gender-neutral dolls would have helped him not be so body conscience as a child. "My experience with Barbies was chopping off all their hair . I didn't get a really great connection with Barbies because it was not something I could see myself looking at or looking like," said Schueren.

He says he didn't identify with G.I Joe's either. A dilemma he says some kids still battle with today. All who are not in support of the dolls.

They felt the dolls will only confuse children. Barbie enthusiast Ryan Richmond also heard these arguments in person and on social media.

"I think a lot of the issues I have wit adults who have problems with this and say I'm never buying this for my kid. That's fine but they don't see it as something threatening. They see it as a toy. A toy size representation of who they are in the moment. And if you take that away from them they have a far more limited of resources to explore that," said Richmond.

https://www.nbc4i.com/news/mattel-launches-gender-inclusive-doll-line/

New York children encouraged to swap toy guns for educational gifts in community 'buyback'

By Hollie McKay December 19th, 2019

For the fourth year in a row, a community on Long Island, New York, encouraged children to swap their toy guns for substitute goods – all in the quest to curb gun violence.

On Thursday afternoon, around 80 to 100 children handed over their imitation firearms and water pistols to members of law enforcement for something fluffier, colorful, or sports-oriented with the kickoff of the Toy Gun Exchange. "Long Island youth can exchange guns for non-violent toys. This year we have several hundred toys to be exchanged and more than in years' past. It keeps growing every year," LaMont Johnson, a trustee of Hempstead Village and the Hempstead Board of Education, told Fox News ahead of the event.

Johnson was joined by Mayor Don Ryan and the program's co-chair, Sean Acosta Jr., to kick off the annual event, pegging its importance on the "recent shooting tragedies that have occurred nationwide." Acosta, a former NYPD officer, launched the program in 2016, aiming to protect youth from gun-related violence, noting that many of the toys – from water pistols to plastic replicas – posed real threats. He noted that police officers in the heat of the moment may not be able to distinguish between the real and the fake.

"The message 'guns are not toys' is critical to teach every child. Whether it means staying away from violence and crime, or teaching to never play with a firearm, it's initiatives like these that save lives and help children learn a lifesaving message," he said. According to the event's news release, the Long Island Toy Gun Exchange Program was "the first of its kind in the region... the new toys are donated by Mr. Acosta Jr. to stop gun violence - before it starts."

Organizers urged children to visit the village offices and trade their toy weapons for sporting equipment or educational toys. Kids who visited the offices without gun-like toys were still issued items such as water pistols and then invited to "turn them in" to be part of the movement.

Nonetheless, some gun-rights advocates said they were skeptical.

"This is being done in good spirit, but I don't think it is a good strategy. I am a physician, and I practice evidence-based medicine. We know early exposure to firearms and firearms safety together reduces gun accidents in children. Keeping guns secured and unloaded also protects children," contended Dr. Matthew Tipton, a Mississippi-based father of three and Alcorn County SWAT team member. "Making guns 'forbidden' adds to the allure for kids. My children are all are being taught to respect weapons." Dennis Santiago, a global-risk analyst and California-based firearms instructor, argued, "imposing toy exchanges is a form of child cruelty."

"It triggers unnecessary stigma for children who would otherwise be unaffected by their elder's phobias. It's a form of passing on fear and prejudice from one generation to the next," he said. "It's a particularly intrusive form of civil rights violation when done by authority figures like the police or school officials because it disrespects the family values of the child whose parents did, in fact, provide the child with the toy in the first place."

And, from the lens of Dianna Muller, a competitive shooter and former Tulsa, Okla., police officer, the toy gun exchange program was "totally inappropriate and irresponsible."

"The anti-gun crowd has irresponsibly focused the conversation on the firearm, a tool, that neither wishes to do harm or good. Removing the opportunity to have a conversation and teach firearms safety makes no one safer," she added. "They are and have been indoctrinating our children that firearms are 'bad,' disguising it under the cloak of safety as opposed to disarmament. Moreover, access to toy guns is nothing new. As opposed to the recent trend in shootings happening in gun-free zones, toy guns are nothing new. You used to be able to buy a real gun from the Sears catalog and have it shipped to your home. School shootings were not a problem during that time, but they are now, so it makes no sense to me to blame firearms on shootings."

https://www.foxnews.com/us/new-york-toy-guns-buyback-gifts-long-island

'Gender neutral' plan for toys would get rid of boys' and girls' aisles in California stores

By Andrew Sheeler February 26th, 2020

California department stores that sell children's products such as toys and clothes would be prohibited from segregating them by gender, under a bill now being considered by lawmakers.

Assembly Bill 2826, by Assemblyman Evan Low, D-Campbell, would apply to all retail department stores with 500 or more employees. The bill would do away with so-called "boys aisles" and "girls aisles," by requiring that children's products be offered in a single, gender neutral section, according to Low's office. If passed into law, the bill would apply to children's clothing, toys and childcare items, "regardless of whether a particular item has traditionally been marketed for either girls or for boys," according to the bill language.

Going into effect in 2023, the bill would make retail stores that fail to comply with its provisions punishable by a fine of $1,000. A spokeswoman for Low's office said that inspiration for the bill came from the 9-year-old daughter of one of Low's staffers. The child told Low that she didn't like how boy and girl sections were separated and that he should make a law against that.

Lawmakers also are considering a bill that would eliminate the "pink tax," the discrepancy in pricing that sees women paying more for female-marketed products than men pay for male-marketed ones. That bill is sponsored by Sen. Hannah-Beth Jackson, D-Santa Barbara.

https://www.sacbee.com/news/politics-government/capitol-alert/article240601601.html

LEGO stops marketing police-themed toys 'in light of recent events'

By Breck Dumas June 3rd, 2020

Toy company Lego requested Tuesday that marketing affiliates immediately cease advertising several of its law enforcement-related products and to even pull them from websites "in light of recent events," as protests rage nationwide over the death of George Floyd.

In an email obtained by The Toybook trade magazine sent on behalf of the Danish company, affiliated partners were notified that "In light of recent events, LEGO has requested the below products to be removed from sites and any marketing ASAP." To be clear, the items are still available for purchase. It was only promotions for such products that were stopped.

More than 30 products were on the list, with a large majority containing the word "Police" in the name, including the Police Station, Police Patrol Car, Police Helicopter Transport, and even the Donut Shop Opening — which, according to The Toybook, "includes Police Officer 'Duke DeTain' and 'Crook' minifigures."

Lego responded to The Toybook's request for comment on the email, saying in a statement: "We requested that our affiliate partners refrain from posting promotional LEGO content as part of our decision to respect #BlackOutTuesday and pause posting content on our social media channels in response to the tragic events in the US. We regret any misunderstanding and will ensure that we are clearer about our intentions in the future." But all of the products Lego stopped marketing were either associated with law enforcement or firefighting, with the exception of one: "The White House" set was also pulled.

Gaming critic Alex Donaldson noted on Twitter, "Wow, Lego has now gone a step further and is pulling down all the marketing for any sets they have that are based around the Police theme or include Police characters. That's a decades-long staple being stepped off." He added, "This includes the Lego Architecture White House set, which pretty much spells out where they stand politically."

https://www.theblaze.com/news/lego-stops-marketing-police-themed-toys-in-light-of-recent-events

Toys

We went from masculine, muscular, and tough *He-Man*, *Thundercats*, *Voltron*, *Transformers*, *Ninja Turtles*, and *GI Joe* toys into nameless, faceless, bland, gender-neutral, and anti-masculine toys for boys. Barbie is under attack. Girls' cooking sets are being cancelled and easy bake oven is now considered sexist. In fact, some states (California) are trying to BAN "boys toy sections" and "girls toy sections" in stores. Boys are not allowed to play with "boys toys" because it's sexist. Girls can't play with "girls toys" because it's sexist. The people who are trying to ban, dominate, and control toys and who plays with them are seriously psychologically damaged individuals.

13

The War on Religion

University Promotes Event to 'Root Out Racism' Among 'White Christian Folks'

By Kyle Reynolds February 5th, 2021

Tufts University promoted an event intended to "Root Out Racism" among "White Christian Folks."

The event, titled "Rooting Out Racism: An Online Retreat for White Christian Folks," was marketed as a "retreat about white supremacy." The event's host, Spiritual Grounding, which does not appear to be directly affiliated with Tufts, insisted upon the necessity of the retreat as"George Floyd's murder has highlighted once again the need for white folks to do their work." Spiritual Grounding stated that the event prompts "White people to search their souls" and to "understand how Christianity has contributed to racial inequity." The organization invites participants to "repent, lament, and uproot racism from [their] own heart."

After *Campus Reform* reached out to Spiritual Grounding, some of the phrasing on its website was removed.

However, *Campus Reform* obtained screenshots prior to the changes. Tufts University's event page lists the contacts for the retreat as the university's Protestant Chaplain, Daniel Bell, and the university's Catholic Chaplain, Lynn Cooper. Tufts also lists the event's sponsors as the university's Protestant and Catholic Chaplaincies.

Spiritual Grounding also has other notable links to higher education. The organization's two founders, Lauren Schwer and Oliver

Goodrich, both serve as university administrators. Schwer is the Associate Director of Campus Ministry at Loyola University Chicago, where she "is responsible for developing and implementing a campus-wide retreat program..."

Goodrich is the Associate Dean of Students for Spirituality and Meaning-Making at Cornell University, where he "provides oversight and support to Cornell United Religious Work, Cornell's long-running chaplaincy program that facilitates the campus engagement and community building of 24 spiritual and faith leaders." National Association of Scholars spokesman Chance Layton told *Campus Reform* that the event is "unnecessary."

"A retreat about 'white supremacy' is unnecessary. A retreat on racism, and the problems we face in our personal lives, the way we treat others, and the means by which we achieve 'equity' ought to suffice," Layton said. "Of course, I can't speak for the journeys some students find themselves on, but I'd bet they aren't 'white supremacists' if they're partaking in this retreat. Religion, especially Christianity, has a lot to offer in the intellectual pursuit. It helps us find the humility to engage with others respectfully (we don't know everything!), to have empathy for the feelings of others, and ultimately to understand (in broad terms) that our intellectual or ideological others are likely seeking the same ends–seeking to do good."

Layton also said that while American Christianity should acknowledge its past, they can do that without Critical Race Theory. "I believe American Christianity has a place to acknowledge its past, distance itself from the theology that upheld slavery and segregation as a natural right, and have a seat at the table today. It can do that without dabbling in the cult of Critical Race Theory," Layton said. Tufts University declined to comment and Spiritual Grounding did not respond to *Campus Reform's* request for comment in time for publication.

https://www.infowars.com/posts/university-promotes-event-to-root-out-racism-among-white-christian-folks/

Christian university absolutely shreds claim that Christianity is a 'platform for white supremacy' in scathing rebuke

By Benjamin Zeisloft January 24th, 2021

Grand Canyon University stood up against a "racial reconciliation workshop" on campus that portrayed Christianity as a "platform for white supremacy."

On January 4, the university released a statement declaring that "Christianity is absolutely NOT a platform for White supremacy or White privilege," stating that "the teachings of Jesus Christ are clearly the exact opposite." The university placed two dance department instructors on a "corrective action plan" after their "lack of civil discourse and the use of profane and abusive language" during a November 12 racial reconciliation workshop.

The "rampant" use of profanities, which "is not an example of the civil discourse and respectful dialogue that faculty members are expected to uphold in classroom settings," forms the basis of the instructors' discipline. In accordance with the school's expectations for instructors, faculty must "provide a positive example to students" even if they do not agree with every notion within the school's doctrinal statement.

"The vast majority of families send their young adults to GCU with the expectation they will be taught from a Christian worldview perspective, and faculty are expected to uphold that expectation," said the statement. "GCU recognizes that critical thought, open dialogue and a fair presentation of all major views are vital to higher education but are indispensable for genuinely Christian instruction."

Additionally, the workshop "included many statements that portrayed Christianity as a platform for White privilege and White supremacy." In response, the university outlined the New Testament's teachings on race and ethnicity, proving that "Christ alone was capable of living a life of sinless perfection and He alone is able to guide individuals and communities toward renewal, reconciliation and restoration."

"Jesus' embrace and inclusion of non-Jewish men and women comported perfectly with the clear teaching of Genesis that all human beings have been created in the image and likeness of God and are therefore worthy of dignity, respect and value," said the statement. "The resolve of Christ to include all races and ethnicities in God's Kingdom enables His followers to grasp more clearly the breadth and depth and height of God's love."

The university likewise decried the "defamatory comments" published in a "one-sided" *Arizona Republic* article about a faculty member whose contract "was not renewed in the aftermath of that profanity-laced workshop."

"We won't address specific comments the *Arizona Republic* chose to publish that portray GCU as a 'bigoted' community 'upholding White supremacy,'" said the statement. "Frankly, those are ridiculous and do not line up with the facts. The story also painted the picture that difficult conversations regarding racial inequality do not occur on campus, which could not be further from the truth." In a phone interview, Grand Canyon University President Brian Mueller told *Campus Reform* that professors who are not Christians — representing roughly ten percent of the faculty — must sign statements promising that "they will not speak against the Christian worldview."

Mueller said that he met with the chairs of the fine arts department, who made clear that "this was an issue that evolved in the dance department" that was "not supported by the institution."

Mueller explained that Jesus' teachings "broke through all of the barriers that existed historically in the world," making it "pretty obvious" that the workshop was promoting "completely the opposite of what the truth is." Grand Canyon University student Kenna Deters told *Campus Reform* that her campus "is a home to students of all races, backgrounds, and even religions."

"As Christians, the vast majority of the student body and faculty see our fellow students not for what the world has painted them to be, but for how God created them, in His image," she said. "This is evident in our campus culture. A workshop like this has no place on campus, where it does not represent the students. White supremacy is far from encouraged within Christianity; in fact, it is exactly what the Bible and the Christian faith seeks to root out of our society."

"God is a god of real justice, not the shallow, self-righteous version that social justice emboldens," added Deters. "As a Government major at GCU, I have had classmates and even professors of all races and ideologies. GCU is a place where real diversity, the diversity of opinion and experience, are able to thrive."

Another Grand Canyon University student told *Campus Reform* that the school, "as a private institution that happens to be a Christian focused campus, has the right to shut down what they feel is standing against what their core beliefs are."

"Saying Christianity creates a platform for racism goes against what GCU believes in," he explained. "As a university with Christian beliefs, we believe that Jesus is who He says He is. Jesus' core focus was loving people, whether they were like you or not, whether they were your enemies or your friends, whether they looked like you or whether they didn't."

"I think to say that Christianity is a platform for white supremacy is very outlandish and doesn't show what GCU stands for," he added.

https://www.campusreform.org/article?id=16683

Twitter Cancel Culture Targets Chris Pratt: 'Radiates Homophobic White Christian Supremacist Energy'

By Hank Berrien October 19th, 2020

On Saturday evening, a TV writer named Amy Berg decided to play a little game, showing a quadrant on Twitter with four pictures of famous actors: Chris Pratt, Chris Hemsworth, Chris Evans and Chris Pine, captioning it, "One has to go."

Pratt is open about his Christian faith but has not been overtly political in his public statements. Pratt told Men's Fitness in 2017, "I don't feel represented by either side. I really feel there's common ground out there that's missed because we focus on the things that separate us." He was also photographed wearing a T-shirt emblazoned with the Gadsden flag, which was popular with many conservative groups.

The current attacks on Pratt for his conservative leanings are certainly not the first. Actress Ellen Page attacked Pratt in February 2019, tweeting that Pratt's church was "infamously LBGTQ." Pratt responded on Instagram, "It has recently been suggested that I belong to a church which 'hates a certain group of people' and is 'infamously anti –LGBTQ.' Nothing could be further from the truth. I go to a church that opens their doors to absolutely everyone."

Pratt later pointed out after his divorce from his ex-wife Anna Faris, his church was not judgmental, writing:

Despite what the Bible says about divorce my church community was there for me every step of the way, never judging, just gracefully accompanying me on my walk. They helped me tremendously offering love and support. It is what I have seen them do for others on countless occasions regardless of sexual orientation, race or gender.

"My faith is important to me but no church defines me or my life and I am not spokesman for any church or any group of people," Pratt continued. "My values define who I am. We need less hate in this world, not more. I am a man who believes that everyone is entitled to love who they want free from the judgment of their fellow man." He concluded, "Jesus said, 'I give you a new command, love one another.' This is what guides me in my life. He is a God of Love, Acceptance and Forgiveness. Hate has no place in my or this world."

Pratt has proven to be willing to take other unpopular stances, including offering tolerance in an increasingly intolerant era. In July 2018, after "Guardians of the Galaxy" director James Gunn was fired by Disney after some of his old tweets joking about pedophilia came to light, Pratt wrote, "Although I don't support James Gunn's inappropriate jokes from years ago, he is a good man. I'd personally love to see him reinstated as director of Volume 3."

Pratt referenced an open letter from the cast of the film; in the letter, the cast wrote:

There is little due process in the court of public opinion. James is likely not the last good person to be put on trial. Given the growing political divide on this country, it's safe to say instances like this will continue. Although we hope Americans from across the political spectrum can ease up on the character assassinations and stop weaponizing mob mentality.

It is our hope that what has transpired can serve as an example for all of us to realize the enormous responsibility we have to ourselves and to each other regarding the use of our written words when we etch them in digital stone; that we as a society may learn from this experience and in the future will think twice before we decide what we want to express; and in so learning perhaps can harness this capability to help and heal instead of hurting each other.

https://www.dailywire.com/news/twitter-cancel-culture-targets-chris-pratt-radiates-homophobic-white-christian-supremacist-energy

'Christian Privilege' professor's argument ignores reality

By Matt Lamb September 18th 2020

Khyati Joshi is a professor at Fairleigh Dickinson University who recently delivered a presentation at Rutgers University and wrote a book on the topic of "white Christian privilege."

But one of her main arguments, that the legal system favors Christians, falls flat because there's numerous examples to the contrary. Joshi either failed to conduct basic research into the history of religious freedom or simply ignored examples that did not fit her narrative.

Furthermore, Joshi argued that Christian politicians do not face questions about their religion, while non-Christians do. This also falls short.

Joshi argued during her Rutgers presentation that non-Christian religions, such as Judaism and Native American religions, have had to fight for religious liberty. It's an example of Christian privilege, the professor said, because Christians do not have to go to the courts to defend their beliefs.

That is inaccurate.

For example, Joshi did not discuss the 2014 *Hobby Lobby* case concerning the Obamacare birth control mandate. In that case, the Christian owners of the crafts store chain sued to prevent the Obama administration from forcing them to pay for birth control and violate their religious beliefs.

Professor Joshi responded to *The College Fix* today after this article was published with several comments relating to a previous media inquiry on her presentation, including a comment on the *Hobby Lobby* case and on Christian candidates. The original article has been updated with those comments.

Joshi told *The Fix* that she does discuss the *Hobby Lobby* case in her book, but as an example of Christians forcing their religion on others. Joshi ignored two similar cases concerning the Catholic Little Sisters of the Poor, whom the Obama administration first tried to force to pay for birth control. The state of Pennsylvania later took up the fight, even though the Supreme Court had already smacked the mandate down in 2015. Pennsylvania lost that battle in 2019.

She likewise ignored baker Jack Phillips' lawsuit against Colorado's Civil Rights Commission for handing him a punishment after he refused to bake a wedding cake for a gay couple. The professor of education never discussed the 2019 Supreme Court case over the Peace Cross in Bladensburg, Maryland. The American Humanist Association challenged that placement of the cross, which honors World War I veterans, on public lands.

Ignoring counter-examples of Supreme Court cases is not the only way Joshi failed in her argument. She also falsely asserted that Christian politicians do not face the same scrutiny as non-Christians.

An example of personal Christian privilege includes that Christian politicians can run for office without having their faith challenged, Joshi said. But Joshi later discussed during her Rutgers presentation how Mitt Romney's Mormon beliefs were challenged by other Christians in 2012.

Joshi did not bring up recent debates over former Vice President Joe Biden's Catholicism and his support for abortion. She also failed to discuss the attacks Senator Rick Santorum faced in 2012 over his Catholic beliefs and the way his wife and him mourned a miscarriage. She looked the other way at how appointees of President Donald Trump have faced questions, either from the media or from politicians, about the role Catholicism plays in their life.

Not once in her presentation did Joshi talk about California Senator Dianne Feinstein accusing Catholic judicial nominee Amy Coney Barrett of allowing her Catholic beliefs to influence her judicial decisions.

"The dogma lives loudly within you," the liberal Senator told Barrett during the nominee's 2017 hearing. How about judicial nominee Brian Buescher, a member of the Catholic fraternity organization Knights of Columbus? Joshi never mentioned the entirely inappropriate question from Hawaii Senator Mazie Hirono about his membership in that group.

Salon also criticized Attorney General William Barr for being a member of Catholic religious order Opus Dei, falsely portrayed as a cult in the "Da Vinci Code." He's not a member of Opus Dei, but if he was there wouldn't be anything wrong with that either. Not that it would matter to Joshi, since she refuses to consider counter-examples that would undercut her argument. Joshi's argument for Christian privilege is a failed one.

https://www.thecollegefix.com/christian-privilege-professors-argument-ignores-reality/

Swedish Journalist Charged With Hate Crime For Publishing Article About Muslim-Owned Pharmacies

By Paul Joseph Watson September 18th, 2020

A journalist in Sweden was charged with a hate crime and faces two years in prison for publishing an article that questioned whether Muslim-owned pharmacies would fairly distribute drugs if supplies became limited.

Yes, really.

Ingrid Carlqvist and her colleague Maria Celander face a court appearance on November 2 over an article which they didn't even write but published on their website. "About a year ago, a woman contributed an article to the site questioning what would happen if there was a shortage of drugs considering the disproportionate number of Muslim pharmacists in Sweden. The question was based on her knowledge of Islamic law (Sharia), which teaches Muslims to prioritize Muslims. In the case of a drug shortage, would drugs be given to Muslims before others?" reports the RAIR Foundation.

Six months later, police contacted the journalists and said they were being charged with a hate crime because the article constituted an "incitement to ethnic groups," which are a "protected" class under Swedish law. "At first I thought they were just going to drop it, because it's absolutely crazy. We are journalists, for God's sake," said Carlqvist, who added that the charge is intended to "send a signal" to other journalists to remain silent on the perils of mass immigration.

"They let murderers and rapists run loose, but the so-called 'hate crime' police – they have the most resources. That is what our government is focusing on," she added, noting that Sweden was now controlled by an "anarcho-tyranny" that targets citizens who criticize government policy while actual criminals run rampant.

"The Swedish government funds a radical online "hate" monitoring group, "Näthatsgranskaren". The group is headed by Tomas Åberg, a former, disgraced police officer," reports the RAIR Foundation. "The group mass reports Swedes who write critically about migration and Islam online to police officers, who have raided speech offenders home and placed them under arrest. The thought crime team is made up of some 15 people, including police, system developers, lecturers, lawyers and social scientists. The organization refuses to identify the people working for it."

One wonders whether ethnic Swedes, who are set to become a minority in their own country within 40 years, will ever become a "protected" class. Don't hold your breath.

https://www.infowars.com/swedish-journalist-charged-with-hate-crime-for-publishing-article-about-muslim-owned-pharmacies/

UCSB teaching assistant says he would 'assassinate Jesus' if he had a time machine

By Matt Lamb July 29th, 2020

A UC Santa Barbara teaching assistant recently tweeted about killing Jesus Christ.

Tim Snediker, who is also a doctoral student in religious studies at the public university in California, tweeted late Sunday night that he would "assassinate Jesus of Nazareth" if he had a time machine. In a follow-up tweet, he said he would also consider "murdering him before his baptism."

Both tweets have since been deleted along with Snediker's Twitter account. Before deleting his account, he changed his profile to say "Tim has repented, now he wants to save Jesus." The tweets drew quick criticism on social media. Rod Dreher, a conservative writer, tweeted screenshots of the tweet and wrote "If you go to his faculty page, you'll see the department statement backing BLM. It says that the study of religion teaches that 'human life is holy because God is holy.' Hmm..." Taylor Brown, a doctoral student at Baylor, tweeted: "This 'joke' that Tim Snediker made is really gross. Even if you're not religious it's not funny. I'm a Christian and I'd never make a 'joke' about time-traveling to kill Muhammad, or Siddartha Gautama, or the Baal Shem Tov. You don't have to be religious to be respectful or kind."

Snediker did not respond to several requests for comment from *The College Fix*.

UC Santa Barbara did not respond to multiple requests for comment on Snediker's tweets or if it felt that Christian students under Snediker's tutelage could feel alienated by his comments.

Snediker's department profile says he has an interest in psychoanalysis, political theology, and philosophy of religion. While the university did not respond to a request for comment, the religious studies department does take a strong stance on Black Lives Matter. It said the department supports Black Lives Matter and called the killing of George

Floyd another example of institutional racism. "It is both a reminder of the anti-Blackness embedded in our society and an example of the systemic institutional brutality directed towards minoritized communities," its website states. The religious studies department at UC Santa Barbara previously faced criticism from a Hindu group for its portrayal of a Hindu goddess.

https://www.thecollegefix.com/ucsb-teaching-assistant-says-he-would-assassinate-jesus-if-he-had-a-time-machine/

Virginia School Bans Christmas Carols Mentioning 'Jesus'

By Thomas D. Williams Ph.D. November 30th, 2018

To celebrate the birthday of Jesus Christ, the Robious Middle School in Midlothian, Virginia, has banned any Christmas carols that mention the name of Jesus.

School administrators reportedly explained they had made the decision to "avoid singing anything of a direct sacred nature" in order to be "more sensitive to the increasing diverse population at the school." David Allen, the father of a student at Robious Middle School, has expressed his concern over the exclusion of Jesus from Christmas songs to be performed at school Christmas concerts.

Allen said students were forbidden from singing a particular carol "because the word Jesus was in there and apparently someone assumed it was of a sacred nature." According to Allen, it seems as if "everywhere you look everyone's afraid of stepping on someone's toes or everything is being so sensitive." In an email exchange with Allen, the school's choir director said that the Jesus ban stems from problems experienced by students.

"We had a few students who weren't comfortable singing a piece I have done many times in the past, but it is of a sacred nature and does mention Jesus," the choir director wrote. While this exchange was going on, Allen said he had received a "diversity notice" from the school explaining their commitment to diversity and inclusion, which struck him as paradoxical.

"I'm trying to rationalize how you can encourage diversity and yet be exclusionary in one specific area," Allen remarked. Attorney Michael Berry of First Liberty Institute wrote a letter to the Chesterfield County School District, of which Robious Middle School is a part, explaining that that, legally, public schools have no reason to ban Jesus from Christmas concerts or other celebrations. "Federal courts have upheld the constitutionality of public school holiday programs that include the use of religious music, art, or drama," Berry wrote, "so long as the material is presented in an objective manner 'as a traditional part of the cultural and religious heritage of the particular holiday.'"

There has been considerable controversy in past years regarding the placement of Christmas nativity scenes, the use of religious imagery, and even the appropriate choice of Christmas greetings. As part of his campaign for the presidency, Donald Trump told voters that he would bring back "Merry Christmas" in place of the more generic "Happy Holidays."

"So when I started 18 months ago, I told my first crowd in Wisconsin that we are going to come back here someday and we are going to say merry Christmas again," Trump told crowds in Wisconsin a month after his election. "Merry Christmas — so, merry Christmas everyone." At last year's White House tree-lighting ceremony, Mr. Trump went further still, referencing the birth of Jesus Christ and his profound impact on human history.

"The Christmas Story begins 2,000 years ago with a mother, a father, their baby son and the most extraordinary gift of all—the gift of God's love for all of humanity," Trump tweeted. "Whatever our beliefs, we know that the birth of Jesus Christ and the story of his life..."

"Melania and I are full of joy at the start of this very blessed season," Trump said, "the celebration of the birth of our Lord and Savior, Jesus Christ." In 2016, a Washington DC-based research group found that

Democrats overwhelmingly favor the more politically correct expressions of "Happy Holidays" or "Seasons Greetings" over the religiously charged "Merry Christmas" that acknowledges the reason for the festivities. The group found that Democrats oppose 'Merry Christmas' more than 2-1 over Republicans

https://www.breitbart.com/faith/2018/11/30/virginia-school-bans-christmas-carols-mentioning-jesus/

Baby Jesus In Cage As Part Of Dedham Church's Immigration-Themed Nativity Scene

By Beth Germano December 5th, 2018

DEDHAM (CBS) – It's an unconventional take on the nativity scene at St. Susanna's Parish Dedham. The baby Jesus is in a cage, the wise men are closed off by a wall.

For the parish, the crèche is meant to be thought provoking. "We try to take a picture of the world as it is and put it together with a Christmas message," said Pastor Fr. Stephen Josoma. That message this year questions "peace on earth", since Jesus represents migrant children being held at the southern border separated from their parents.

The wise men are the caravan of migrants behind the border wall. They believe it's very much the message of Jesus. "Jesus was about taking care of one another. This is not the way to take care of one another," said Fr. Josoma. "We're not trying to scandalize anyone," said parishioner Pat Ferrone, a member of the Pax Christi committee which came up with the idea for the display. "We're trying to reflect back a reality that has to be looked at."

But mixing politics with religion isn't sitting well with some who believe the nativity scene has crossed a line. "This is where you come to pray not to be preached at what you should think about politics," said Helen Watson who drove to church to see the display.

Fr. Josoma insists the scene is not a dig at Trump administration policies. Instead of political activism he calls it gospel activism. “We talk about Matthew 25 feeding the hungry and welcoming the stranger.” Parishioner Phil Mandeville says Jesus was no stranger to politics. “Christ was political, he was hung on a cross for making political statements and bucking authority and that’s exactly why he died,” Mandeville said. The nativity scene is meant to be a symbol of hope, and at St. Susanna’s the hope is that a conversation has begun.

https://boston.cbslocal.com/2018/12/05/dedham-nativity-scene-saint-susana-parish-immigration/

Michigan Activists Lose Fight to Remove Display of 3 Wise Men From Public School Roof

By Neetu Chandak December 11th, 2018

A Michigan school board decided on Monday to keep Christmas decorations on top of the elementary school’s roof despite activists claiming the display is too religious.

The three wise men, a biblical reference to Jesus Christ’s birth, are displayed on Newaygo Elementary School’s roof. The Michigan Association of Civil Rights Activists argued the Christmas display went against the separation of church and state, 24 Hour News 8 reported Monday.

“We’ve asked the school to remove what is in essence a nativity scene, from the top of the school, and from school property,” Mitch Kahle of the Michigan Association of Civil Rights Activists said, according to Fox 17. “If this were on private property it wouldn’t be an issue.”

The association got involved after receiving a complaint from an individual in the district, though the school district said it did not, News 8 reported. The Newaygo Public Schools board of education held a meeting Monday where many seemed to support keeping the display, according to News 8. Many cited tradition for keeping the wise men.

"Look away if it offends you," parent Michael Burns said at the meeting, according to News 8. The decorations have reportedly been on top of the school during the holiday season for more than 70 years. While the board will not be taking down the display, there are talks about making changes, News 8 reported.

"This community has said loud and clear even before tonight's meeting that they want the display to stay," Superintendent Peggy Mathis said, according to News 8. "So we will look at ways to maybe make that happen, maybe enhance it, so it can stay." Mathis told The Daily Caller News Foundation over email that "no decisions have been made regarding specifically how the display might be changed." The Michigan Association of Civil Rights Activists has been involved with many issues surrounding religion in public spaces around Michigan. The group has helped in efforts to remove a Bible verse on a park's sign and remove Bible study in a school, News 8 reported. "We will reserve comment until we receive the school's formal response," the association told The Daily Caller News Foundation over Facebook Messenger.

https://www.dailysignal.com/2018/12/11/michigan-activists-lose-fight-to-remove-three-wise-men-display-from-public-school-roof/

Complaints prompt Amazon to remove products that are offensive to Muslims

By Alaa Elassar January 8th, 2019

(CNN)Amazon has pulled more than a dozen products off its website after receiving complaints that the items are offensive to Muslims.

The Council on American-Islamic Relations (CAIR), the nation's largest Muslim civil rights and advocacy organization, asked the online retailer last week to remove the products, which included doormats, bath mats and other items imprinted with Islamic calligraphy, references to the Prophet Muhammad and scripture.

The products, which were being sold by independent merchants on Amazon's website, are deemed offensive because they "would be stepped-on or otherwise disrespected by customers," CAIR said in a statement on Thursday. The following day, CAIR issued another statement welcoming Amazon's decision to remove the items from its website and conduct an audit to purge similarly offensive products.

"We thank Amazon for its swift action on this issue and hope it sends a message to manufacturers of such inappropriate and offensive items that they will not profit from Islamophobia or any other form of bigotry," Masih Fouladi, executive director of CAIR's

Washington state chapter, said in the statement. Amazon is based in Seattle, Washington. An Amazon spokesperson confirmed that the products are being removed.

"All sellers must follow our selling guidelines and those who do not will be subject to action including potential removal of their account," the spokesperson told CNN on Monday. "The products in question are being removed from our store." Since the announcement, CAIR has received additional complaints of offensive items -- including toilet covers imprinted with the Quran and Islamic scripture -- listed for sale on Amazon, said CAIR spokesman Ibrahim Hooper. "I don't think it would be appropriate to have a toilet seat with the image of a Bible on it either," Hooper told CNN. "It's just inappropriate stuff."

Hooper said it's likely that not all the products were manufactured with the intent to offend. "My gut feeling is that at least for the bath mats, shower curtains, and stuff like that, it's these companies just slapping these designs on everything without even thinking about it," he said. "But there are others crossing the line into intentional Islamophobia. Some of the companies have things like toilet seats. I mean come on, why else would you do that?"

This is not the first time CAIR has asked a company to remove an offensive product. In 1997, the organization complained to Nike that one of its shoes featured a design that bore a striking resemblance to the word Allah. Nike apologized for any unintentional offense and recalled the shoes. CAIR National Executive Director Nihad Awad said in a statement Friday that the organization would continue working with retailers "to ensure that products are not exploiting or promoting bigotry for commercial gain."

https://www.cnn.com/2019/01/08/us/amazon-cair-offensive-products/index.html

Utah teacher forced student to wash off Ash Wednesday cross on forehead, family says

By Katherine Lam March 7th, 2019

A Utah elementary school teacher apologized to one of her Catholic students Wednesday -- and may still face disciplinary action -- after she forced him to wash off the Ash Wednesday cross on his forehead, the boy's family said.

William McLeod, a fourth grader at Valley View Elementary School, received the ash marking -- made in the shape of a cross and applied by a priest -- for the Catholic religious day that signals the start of the Lenten season and then went to school in Bountiful, Fox 13 reported. He told Fox 13 he was the only student who had ashes.

"A lot of students asked me what it is. I said, 'I'm Catholic. It's the first day of Lent. It's Ash Wednesday,'" William said. William's teacher, who was not identified, later approached him and forced him to wash off the symbol, he said. William reportedly attempted to explain why he wanted to keep the ash cross on his forehead, but he said his teacher wouldn't listen.

"She took me aside, and she said, 'You have to take it off,'" William said. "She gave me a disinfection wipe — whatever they are called — and she made me wipe it off." William's grandmother, Karen Fisher, told Fox 13 she was "pretty upset" by the incident and received a call from the school's principal and the teacher who ordered the cross to be washed off.

"I asked her if she read the Constitution with the First Amendment, and she said, 'No,'" Fisher said. Davis School District's spokesman Chris Williams apologized for the incident and said an investigation is being conducted. "Why that even came up, I have no idea," Williams said. "When a student comes in to school with ashes on their forehead, it's not something we say, 'Please take off.'"

William's family said the teacher apologized with a handwritten note and candy. "I hope it helps somebody and I hope it never happens again," Fisher said. "I don't think it will."

https://www.foxnews.com/us/utah-teacher-forced-student-to-wash-off-ash-wednesday-cross-on-forehead-family-says

Historic Catholic marker deemed 'racist symbol' removed by University of California Santa Cruz

By Paulina Dedaj June 22nd, 2019

A university in California removed a historical symbol from its campus Friday in an effort to be "more inclusive" after a years-long campaign by Native American community members argued the marker highlighted a period of racism in the state.

The El Camino Real Bell was removed from the University of California Santa Cruz after administrators had several discussions with members of the Amah Mutsun Tribal Band and other community members who felt that the bell marker glorified a period of time when Spanish missionaries dehumanized their ancestors and culture and enslaved those who converted to Christianity.

Vice Chancellor of Business and Administrative Services Sarah Latham said the school moved forward with the removal "in support of efforts to be more inclusive." The cast-iron bell, named after the route connecting 21 Franciscan missions, was one of hundreds of displays placed across highways in California in 1906 as a way to honor the state's "Hispanic past" and "expand tourism," UCSC said in a press release.

"The bell marker, which memorializes the California Missions and an imagined route of travel that once connected them, is viewed by the Amah Mutsun and many other California indigenous people as a racist symbol that glorifies the domination and dehumanization of their ancestors," the release continued.

Chair of the Amah Mutsun Tribal Band Valentine Lopez called the bells a "painful" reminder that "celebrate the destruction, domination and erasure of our people."

"It is shameful that these places where our ancestors were enslaved, whipped, raped, tortured and exposed to fatal diseases have been whitewashed and converted into tourist attractions." The university hasn't decided on the bell's fate, but the Amah Mutsun have suggested what the school called the only "two acceptable options" for its future: display it in a museum with the proper context or melt it down and "recycle for peaceful purposes."

The removal comes as college campuses across the country take down symbols deemed racist by some community members. Earlier this year Notre Dame announced it would cover campus murals depicting Christopher Columbus in "an attempt to tell the story of the native peoples."

https://www.foxnews.com/us/university-of-california-santa-cruz-removes-historic-catholic-marker-deemed-racist-symbol

Student barred from handing out 'Jesus loves you' valentines wins case against Wisconsin college

By Caleb Park September 20th, 2019

A federal judge ruled in favor of a Christian student who was told by a Green Bay, Wis., public college that she couldn't hand out religious-themed Valentine's Day cards.

Polly Anna Olsen, who was invited by President Trump to be the face of a free speech on campus executive order earlier this year, told "Fox & Friends" Friday that the victory is being celebrated at Northwest Wisconsin Technical College (NWTC).

Olsen, a paralegal student who said she was carrying on her late mother's Valentine's tradition, was stopped by campus security on Feb. 14 last year after handing out paper cutouts with messages like "Jesus Loves You!" and others with Bible verses on them. She was accused of violating a school policy.

Represented by the conservative law firm Wisconsin Institute for Law & Liberty (WILL), Olsen won her case last Friday after U.S. District Court Judge William Griesbach ruled NWTC violated her First Amendment rights, saying the school "had no more right to prevent [Olsen] from handing out individual Valentines than it did to stop her from wishing each individual to have a 'good morning a blessed day.'"

"Several teachers congratulated me," she said. "They are very proud that I stood up for our rights, because it's not just my rights, it's everyone's rights on campus that have been violated."

Olsen explained it was because of her faith: "Well, when Jesus died on the cross and came back to life, he made it so that there's consequences for sin and he paid them, so now there's accountability." But Jeffrey Rafn, NWTC president, told Fox News in a statement that the ban was because Olsen entered an office without permission, not because of her loving message.

"The ruling talks about common spaces and I think we'll make it clear that students can be in any of the common spaces," Rafn said. "But the offices are like any other office, you don't normally go into a place and you can't just walk into any office that you want to walk into."

The office that the school president appears to be referring to was one that she said she had entered for seven years. And after Friday's ruling she plans to hand out the cutouts not just on Valentine's Day, but every day. "I'll be handing them out any day now," Olsen, who plans to continue to share her story with the Leadership Institute, added. "That's kind of become my calling card."

https://www.foxnews.com/faith-values/school-college-student-wisconsin-jesus-valentines-cards

People of faith aren't out of the woods yet

By Chris Woodward June 22nd, 2020

A trio of Senate Republicans blocked a vote last week on H.R. 5, but House Speaker Nancy Pelosi (D-California) and other supporters of the bipartisan measure are still in favor of the legislation. Passed by the House in 2019, the Equality Act had support from every Democrat, as well as from eight Republicans. If the Democrats retain the House and win control of the Senate, the Equality Act will be made a priority.

"This so-called Equality Act basically removes any basic limitation on government forcing people to violate their own religious liberty," warns Rob Chambers of AFA Action, the politically active arm of American Family Association (AFA). "It eliminates any type of protection that the Religious Freedom Restoration ACT (RFRA) will be able to provide people of faith."

RFRA was passed in 1993 and signed into law by President Bill Clinton. Legislators that support the Equality Act tried to get a vote last week to build off of the U.S. Supreme Court's ruling in *Bostock v Clayton County, Georgia*. In a 6-3 decision, justices said employers cannot fire someone for being LGBT. If they do, then employers would be violating that person's rights under Title VII of the Civil Rights Act of 1964.

Justice Neil Gorsuch, a Trump appointee, wrote the majority opinion. "That was their opportunity to take the public sentiment in support of transgender and sexual orientation rights before the Senate," says Chambers about the supporters of the Equality Act. "Of course, they tried to do this or pass it on unanimous consent, and they failed because Senators Josh Hawley (R-Missouri), James Lankford (R-Oklahoma), and Mike Lee (R-Utah) all basically denied the unanimous consent."

Critics of the ruling in *Bostock* say the word "sex" in Title VII does not include sexual orientation and gender identity. They add that it should not be the role of the judicial branch to amend the law. Others point out that the stated purpose for the Equality Act is to create or include civil rights protections for sexual orientation and gender identity.

Kentucky high school scrubs locker room Bible verse after atheist group complains

By Caleb Parke March 4th, 2020

A public high school in Kentucky removed an inspirational Bible verse from the locker room after a "concerned area resident" complained.

The Freedom From Religion Foundation (FFRF) sent a letter to Letcher County Public Schools in Whitesburg, Ky., in November claiming the message above the lockers, along with two other religious messages at other schools in the district, "violates the Constitution" by displaying "religious symbols or messages."

Bold letters on the wall of the Letcher County Central High School athletic locker room said: "But the Lord is with me like a Mighty Warrior," with attribution to Jeremiah 20:11. But in February, school officials removed it. Also scrubbed was a bulletin board message displayed in Fleming Neon Middle School that said, "Jesus is my savior You can't scare me!" and a prayer for children on the Martha Jane Potter Elementary School's Facebook page at the beginning of the school year.

"Dear God, Thank you for the gift of education in every form. As our children prepare to start a new year may confidence be their foundation, may grace be their guide and may hope be their compass toward a bright future. I pray they would have eyes to see the needs of those around them

and a heart to love well. May they face each day with positivity knowing that no matter what comes their way, they do not have to face it alone. Amen."

"The bulletin board has been replaced, the Facebook post has been removed, and the locker room has been repainted," Superintendent Denise Yonts wrote in a February letter to the FFRF.Yonts' actions were praised by the Wisconsin-based atheist group "We applaud the district for taking action to remedy this violation," Annie Laurie Gaylor, FFRF co-president, said in a statement. "Students in our public schools are free to practice any religion they choose — or none at all." First Liberty Insitute, a religious freedom law firm that successfully defended the Bladensburg Peace Cross at the Supreme Court, said the district may have taken action too soon.

"It is unfortunate that the school took such a drastic step before fully vetting the complaint and doing a proper investigation of the background facts," Hiram Sasser, general counsel for First Liberty, told Fox News. "It may be the case that the school committed a First Amendment violation by erasing the messages, but until a full investigation is done, it's impossible to know the correct legal course."

https://www.foxnews.com/us/kentucky-high-school-bible-verse-atheist-group

Shaun King says Jesus images 'a form of white supremacy' that must go: 'They should all come down'

By Douglas Ernst June 22nd, 2020

Shaun King said Monday it's time for anything resembling "white Jesus" to be expunged from the public square. The staunch Black Lives Matter activist made the comments as online activists continued to debate which statues and monuments were culturally unacceptable in 2020.

The May 25 death of George Floyd, a 46-year-old black man, under the weight of Minneapolis police served as the impetus for activists to tear down statues of historical figures like Christopher Columbus and George Washington.

"Yes," Mr. King said regarding his support for tearing down images of Christ. "All murals and stained glass windows of white Jesus, and his European mother, and their white friends should also come down. They are a gross form [of] white supremacy. Created as tools of oppression. Racist propaganda. They should all come down." The activist doubled down on the matter in response to feedback.

"Yes, I think the statues of the white European they claim is Jesus should also come down," he said. "They are a form of white supremacy. Always have been.

In the Bible, when the family of Jesus wanted to hide, and blend in, guess where they went? EGYPT! Not Denmark. Tear them down."

Mr. King, a stalwart liberal, recently made headlines by spotlighting the political power wielded by Democrats in cities with the most racial unrest. "Democrats, from top to bottom, are running the cities with the worst police brutality in America right now," he said June 5. "STOP generically telling us to VOTE in response to all of the police brutality we have right now. Yes, we should vote. But we have to be VERY specific. Democrats, from top to bottom, are running the cities with the worst police brutality in America right now. We voted for them."

https://m.washingtontimes.com/news/2020/jun/22/shaun-king-says-jesus-images-a-form-of-white-supre/

Religion

It seems that one of the only religions under attack is Christianity. You can see this with the canceling of Christmas through means of political correctness. Notice how if you criticize Islam, you are labeled as an "Islamophobe", but if you attack Christians or Christmas, it is seen as a righteous badge of honor and courage from the social justice warrior trendy Nazis. In fact, there has been a terrible war on Muslims in China. It is estimated that 1.5 million innocent Muslims are in internment camps in Xinjiang China. Notice how the press or mainstream media doesn't talk about this? LeBron James doesn't say anything either since China uses slave labor to make his sneakers. Most people will never hear about this because the optics would show China as bad and cruel. Our rulers (who are owned by China) would never allow this information to get out to the public. Want to talk about "Islamophobia?" Look no further than China.

14

The War on Gender

Nurses advised to swap words such as 'breast milk' for the more inclusive 'human milk'

By Emma Colton February 10th, 2021

Midwives at a hospital in England were directed to no longer use words such as “breastfeeding” and “breast milk” in order to be more inclusive to trans parents.

"Human milk,” "breast/chest milk," or "milk from the feeding mother or parent" are the more acceptable terms for midwives to use at the Brighton and Sussex University Hospitals NHS Trust in lieu of using the traditional “breast milk.” The hospital is the first in the country to use the trans-friendly language within its maternity ward, which will now be known as the "perinatal services” department.

“Gender identity can be a source of oppression and health inequality. We are consciously using the words 'women' and 'people' together to make it clear that we are committed to working on addressing health inequalities for all those who use our services,” the BSUH said in a statement.

"As midwives and birth workers, we focus on improving access and health outcomes for marginalised and disadvantaged groups. Women are frequently disadvantaged in healthcare, as are trans and nonbinary people," the BSUH said. "By continuing to use the term 'woman' we commit to working on addressing health inequalities for all who use our services." The word “mothers” on its own will also be avoided, with midwives told to use "mothers or birthing parents" instead. "Woman" will also be swapped with "people" or other inclusive language.

"We are consciously using the words 'women' and 'people' together to make it clear that we are committed to working on addressing health inequalities for all those who use our services," the document said. About 1% of adults in England identify as transgender or nonbinary, though more people reportedly identify as such in the Brighton and Hove area.

https://www.washingtonexaminer.com/news/england-maternity-human-milk-inclusive

University Professor Calls Heterosexuality 'Very Tragic,' Particularly for Women

By Tre Goins-Phillips January 27th, 2021

A professor at the University of California-Riverside believes heterosexuality is "very tragic," especially for straight women. Professor Jane Ward, who teaches her students about gender and sexual studies, argued in an explicit December article for Insider that the "tragedy" of heterosexuality is it advances misogyny, pushes men toward embracing toxic masculinity, and leaves women utterly unsatisfied.

"It really looks like straight men and women don't like each other very much, that women spend so much time complaining about men, and we still have so much evidence of misogyny," she told the website. "From an LGBT perspective, [heterosexuality] looks actually very tragic." The educator explained to Insider's Julia Naftulin that she feels "sorry" for straight people — particularly straight women, whom she said "typically report some of the lowest sexual satisfaction in society." She does, however, save some of her despair for straight men, whom she suggested "are pigeon-holed into toxic-masculine culture that teaches them they both need, and yet should also demean, women."

Ward, author of the book "The Tragedy of Heterosexuality," went on to argue the pandemic has revealed the calamity of male-female romances.

In her book, the professor said she finds it "depressing to see what my straight female friends put up with regarding treatment from men." She went on to write that she "really sympathize[s] with these women, but, at the same time, it makes me feel alienated from them," according to Campus Reform.

Ward said she interviewed nearly 100 men, women, and "non-binary" people of differing sexual orientations during her research for her book. One of the "common threads" that emerged, according to Naftulin, was that "straight women put straight men on a pedestal, even though it doesn't benefit them to do so." One of Ward's interviewees, who described herself as "queer," told the professor: "Our lives become som different when theirs [the lives of straight women] revolves around attachment to a cruel, insensitive, self-centered, or simply boring man."

Some of that projected phenomenon, Ward explained in her book, is the result of what she dubbed the "misogyny paradox," which she said leads men to struggle to respect and admire women. Men, she reasoned, are seen as "more masculine" by our collective society if they objectify their female counterparts.

"I think that if men could recognize that equity and feminism are actually really central to a health and happy relationship, if that's something they want, then they might be able to more further in that direction," she explained. Ward told Campus Reform she endeavored to write the book because she "loves" the straight couples in her life and wants the best for them. "I wrote this book because I love straight people," she said. "And because the research on heterosexual marital satisfaction over the life course shows that straight couples are struggling to balance work and family obligations and this leads to frustration and resentment for many straight women, in particular."

https://www.faithwire.com/2021/01/27/university-professor-calls-heterosexuality-very-tragic-particularly-for-women/

'Chestfeeding?' Breastfeeding Group Tweets Trans Support

By Matt Philbin October 25th, 2020

Apparently, Sunday was The Day of the Deluded, AKA #PronounsDay on Twitter. As one would expect, the hashtag elicited many stupid and craven tweets from the kind of people that put "she, her" in their Twitter bio, and the kind of organizations that buff their woke credentials on social media.

But there was one tweet so breathtakingly dumb, so besides just about every point one can think of, that it beggars belief. It came from The La Leche League which, by its own description, "helps all families feed their babies human milk. Volunteers provide free support, education & promote a better understanding of breastfeeding." So it's a bunch of people who promote breastfeeding. A noble cause I'm sure (though some moms of my acquaintance are given to calling the group "The Breastapo" -- they're pretty zealous.)

So this tweet seems a bit ... strange (apologies for not linking, but apparently, LLL blocked your humble author before he could do it): LLL USA supports all breastfeeding, chestfeeding, & human milk feeding families, inclusive of race, ethnicity, immigration status, national origin, creed, age, sexual orientation, gender identity, family structure, primary language, ability, or socio-economic status.#PronounsDay

"Chestfeeding?" A graphic included in the tweet showed a gay rainbow flag that rapidly morphed into a number of other flags that probably symbolize marginalized groups or something. Maybe one is for chestfeeders or other "human milk feeding families." Maybe there's one for wealthy transgendered Portuguese-speaking Zororastrian septuagenarians of dubious immigration status whose nontraditional families are a polyglot of races. Unless they're bottle feeders. You use baby formula, you're dead to LLL.

Such pronouncements are, of course, an attempt to get out ahead of the trans bullies. Tampax had a similar tweet, and another company proudly announced last week that it was removing the universal female symbol from its feminine hygiene products. The cost of not denying biological reality is steep. Harry Potter author J.K. Rowling has become a pariah for insisting that humans born with ladies parts are women, and that humans born without them are not. For its part, Twitter played mob enforcer and suspended accounts that came to Rowling's defense.

Rowling and others argue that insisting that dudes pretending to be women *are* women is, in effect, erasing women. But the trans bullies will not be denied, and organizations like LLL and Tampax won't even try. Biology loses. You've had a nice run, ladies.

https://newsbusters.org/blogs/culture/matt-philbin/2020/10/25/chestfeeding-breastfeeding-group-tweets-trans-support

Pregnant supermodel Emily Ratajkowski says she and her husband 'won't know' baby's gender 'until our child is 18' and 'they'll let us know then'

By Dave Urbanski October 27th, 2020

It's become standard fare for leftist celebrities to proclaim they're letting their children choose their genders. And pregnant supermodel Emily Ratajkowski is the latest, writing in Vogue that she and her husband "won't know the gender" of their baby "until our child is 18" and "they'll let us know then."

Ratajkowski added to her essay, "I like the idea of forcing as few gender stereotypes on my child as possible" but that she doesn't like "that we force gender-based preconceptions onto people, let alone babies. I want to be a parent who allows my child to show themself to me. And yet I realize that while I may hope my child can determine their own place in the world, they will, no matter what, be faced with the undeniable constraints and constructions of gender before they can speak or, hell, even be born."

Indeed, the woke pronoun thing is primed and ready to go. Still, she acknowledged that she's asked her husband — actor-producer Sebastian Bear-McClard — if he wants a boy, and that "he refuses to give me an answer, swearing that he doesn't have a preference. But one Sunday as he's watching football he makes a remark about how it'd be fun to have a little boy to watch with."

Ratajkowski said she shot back, "Girls watch football, too!" One thing's for sure, though: The supermodel has fears about raising a son — particularly due to the child's inevitable whiteness. "I've known far too many white men who move through the world unaware of their privilege, and I've been traumatized by many of my experiences with them," Ratajkowski wrote. "And boys too; it's shocking to realize how early young boys gain a sense of entitlement — to girls' bodies and to the world in general. I'm not scared of raising a 'bad guy,' as many of the men I've known who abuse their power do so unintentionally. But I'm terrified of inadvertently cultivating the carelessness and the lack of awareness that are so convenient for men. It feels much more daunting to create an understanding of privilege in a child than to teach simple black-and-white morality. How do I raise a child who learns to like themself while also teaching them about their position of power in the world?"

She then shared a story about a friend's struggle with white males — namely her husband and new baby boy:

My friend who is the mother to a three-year-old boy tells me that she didn't think she cared about gender until her doctor broke the news that she was having a son. She burst into tears in her office. "And then I continued to cry for a whole month," she says matter-of-factly. After a difficult birth experience, she developed postpartum depression and decided that she resented her husband more than she'd ever imagined possible. She told me she particularly hated — and she made an actual, physical list that she kept in her journal, editing it daily — how peacefully he slept. "There is nothing worse than the undisturbed sleep of a white man in a patriarchal world." She shakes her head. "It was hard to come to terms with the fact that I was bringing yet another white man into the world. But now I adore him and can't imagine it any other way." She also eventually learned to love her husband again. The sound of his perfect sleep next to her at night is now tolerable.

Ratajkowski is no stranger to expressing left-wing views. She publicly backed Democratic socialist presidential candidate Bernie Sanders in 2016 and took some heat for partnering with Planned Parenthood a year earlier. But in fairness, Ratajkowski in 2017 said she stood up for Melania Trump after a New York Times journalist called the first lady a "hooker."

https://www.theblaze.com/news/pregnant-supermodel-emily-ratajkowski-baby-gender

Apple rolling out gender-neutral Santa Claus, other emojis

By Ben Cost September 30th, 2020

A gender-neutral Santa Claus is coming to town. In an apparent continuation of their digital-diversity campaign, Apple debuted the new Santa emoji with the iOS 14.2 beta release Wednesday, Emojipedia reports. The non-binary Saint Nick is part of a batch, approved by the Unicode Consortium, of 117 emoticons, many of which aim to make online discourse more inclusive.

The virtual Father Christmas will swap his signature beard for a clean-shaven, more androgynous look. The X-mas mascot's makeover comes in the wake of a survey by logo creator GraphicSprings, which revealed that 19% of Americans believe that the big man in red should in fact be neither man nor woman. However, some view Santa's new identity as part of the so-called War on Christmas, alongside other battles like shaming people for saying "Merry Christmas" and the PC reboots of the Yuletide classic "Baby It's Cold Outside."

In one incident from 2019, holiday traditionalists flocked to the defense of a woman who was doxxed over calling him "Father Christmas" instead of just Santa. "This gender-neutral stuff is way out of hand," fumed one Yule die-hard.

Along with the Santa option, the Apple emoji lineup also features new skin tone variations, a much-hyped transgender flag and tuxedo and bridal gown options for both men and women. The inclusive images drew many positive reactions on Twitter.

"APPLE TRANS RIGHTS LETS GOOO!" tweeted one proponent. Another implored Apple to add a "lesbian, bisexual, pansexual, unlabelled and non-binary flag" to the mix. Last year, meanwhile, the tech giant ruffled some feathers after releasing a "period emoji" as part of iOS 13.2.

Controversial add-ons aside, users can enjoy new pictograms of a beaver, bubble tea, a plunger, feeding bottles, a ninja, an anatomical heart and more. The collection will be available on the iPhone, iPad and watchOS. They may also be part of the launch next month, according to the Daily Mail. If that wasn't enticing enough, the Unicode Consortium also recently announced the launch of emoji version 13.1, whose selection will range from "heart on fire" to "face with spiral eyes" in an apparent homage to the tumultuous 2020. However, they likely won't debut until 2021.

https://nypost.com/2020/09/30/apple-rolling-out-gender-neutral-santa-claus-other-emojis/

Comedian Trevor Noah Offended By Gender Reveal Parties: Child Hasn't Picked Gender Yet

By Amanda Prestigiacomo September 10th, 2020

During a supposedly comedic segment on California wildfires, "The Daily Show" host Trevor Noah railed against "gender reveal" parties as "outdated" celebrations of "a baby's genitalia," particularly given what we're "learning" about "gender" in 2020.

While attempting a humorous bit about a gender reveal party in California that potentially sparked the El Dorado Fire, Noah interrupted the jokes with some Woke knowledge: children don't "know" their gender until they are old enough to choose one themselves.

"This has to stop, right? Or, if you insist on a gender reveal, you have to do something that helps the situation: 'The water's pink! It's a girl!'" the comedian said, as a graphic of a helicopter dropping pink water over fire appeared over his left shoulder. Then Noah got deeply serious: "And aside from all the damage it can cause, celebrating a baby's genitalia is starting to feel very outdated. Like, given everything we're learning about gender, gender reveal parties should only happen when the child is old enough to know their actual gender," he said, adding, "and to pitch in some cash for the fire damage."

Though Noah attempts to disconnect gender from biological sex, the two are inextricably connected, which is why if a person thinks their gender is the opposite of their biological sex, it is called "gender dysphoria."

In very progressive language, the American Psychiatric Association acknowledges this fact: "Gender dysphoria involves a conflict between a person's physical or assigned gender and the gender with which he/she/they identify. People with gender dysphoria may be very uncomfortable with the gender they were assigned, sometimes described as being uncomfortable with their body (particularly developments during puberty) or being uncomfortable with the expected roles of their assigned gender."

Noah has been open about his left-wing views. Last year, for example, the host lost it over Kanye West suggesting black people don't have to be Democrats. Noah argued West's comments about "brainwashing" were insulting and stressed that the Democrat Party is the "best choice" for minorities. The Daily Wire reported:

"OK, let me get this straight. So you're saying that every black person in America is brainwashed? You're saying that 70, 80, 90 percent of black people who are voting Democrat, they're brainwashed?" Noah said. "So you're saying you're the only person who's enlightened and all these black people are stupidly following this Democratic-victim [narrative]?"

Noah went on to claim that blacks overwhelmingly vote for the Democratic Party because it is the "best choice" they have in a two-party system.

"What is more likely? The fact that these people are brainwashed, or the fact that, in America, you have to vote for the system that gives you the best chance?" asked Noah. "You only have two choices ... if you are a black person you go, 'Well, I'm going to vote for the choice that gives me the best chance of success.'"

https://www.dailywire.com/news/comedian-trevor-noah-offended-by-gender-reveal-parties-child-hasnt-picked-gender-yet

Merriam-Webster Dictionary Adds to Definition of Female: 'Having a Gender Identity That Is the Opposite of Male'

By Hanna Bleau September 4th, 2020

The Merriam-Webster dictionary appeared to update its definition of "female" to include "having a gender identity that is opposite of male," effectively erasing the concept of biological sex. The dictionary appeared to add to its primary definition of female, which is defined as, "of, relating to, or being the sex that typically has the capacity to bear young or produce eggs."

However, while the primary definition overtly acknowledges the biological reality of the female sex, which makes it distinct from the male sex, the U.S. dictionary effectively negated its own definition by adding additional explanations to seemingly submit to the radical transgender movement.

Merriam-Webster's sub-definitions, which seemingly erase the reality of biological sex, include:

- Having a gender identity that is the opposite of male
- Made up of usually adult members of the female sex
- Designed for or typically used by girls or women
- Having a quality (such as small size or delicacy of sound) sometimes associated with the female sex

This would not be the first time Merriam-Webster has moved to satisfy the mounting demands of transgender activists. As Breitbart News reported in July, Merriam-Webster updated its definition of "trans woman" to "woman who was identified as male at birth," once again taking another step in erasing the biological reality of women.

As reported at the time:

Notably, the new definition conflicts with the dictionary's official description of "woman," which is defined as "an adult female person." Merriam-Webster defines "female" as "of, relating to, or being the sex that typically has the capacity to bear young or produce eggs" — a function a trans woman is, biologically, incapable of.

Similarly, "trans man" is currently defined by Merriam-Webster as "a man who was identified as female at birth," and the same logical sequence prevails. A "man" is defined as "an adult male human," and "male" is defined as "an individual of the sex that is typically capable of producing small, usually motile gametes (such as sperm or spermatozoa) which fertilize the eggs of a female" — another function biological females, or those who would identify as a "trans man" — are not able to do biologically.

Some feminists have remained at odds with transgender activists, who they contend are gradually erasing women to bend to the "woke" mob. Natasha Chart, a feminist writer at FeministCurrent.org who has openly spoken out against radical transgender ideology and the effects it has on women, told Breitbart News that she is "disappointed" to witness the "fall of important cultural institutions, like dictionary publishers, to woke social media mobs and belligerent, junior employees."

"These very online outrage brigades don't represent either the public at large, or the considered opinions of professionals free to speak their minds," she said, urging employers to "strengthen their backbones against irrational mob pressures, and start enforcing workplace rules against harassing colleagues over their political views."

"Then we'll stop seeing embarrassing nonsense like this," she said.

"Everyone knows what women are, and that we aren't defined by a state of mind that a man can have. I don't have a 'gender identity.' I bore a child by means of my female body, not a state of mind, and it disrespects every mother and child to suggest otherwise," she added.

Author J.K. Rowling has also been at the forefront of this debate, coming under heavy scrutiny from transgender activists over the summer after stating that "erasing the concept of sex removes the ability of many to meaningfully discuss their lives." She has continued to stand her ground, despite radical activists calling for her effective cancellation.

Last month, she returned a 2019 award from the Robert F. Kennedy Human Rights foundation after Kerry Kennedy, president of the organization, accused her of posting "deeply troubling transphobic tweets and statements."

https://www.breitbart.com/politics/2020/09/04/merriam-webster-dictionary-adds-definition-female-having-gender-identity-opposite-male/

TedX Says it Will Refer to Women as "Womxn" to Fight "Discrimination"

By Paul Joseph Watson September 8th, 2020

Conference organization TedX says it has started referring to women as "womxn" in order to fight "prejudice" and "discrimination," prompting a backlash on Twitter. The group announced that it was planning to hold a TEDxLondonWomxn conference this coming Autumn, prompting one user to ask, "what is a womxn?"

"Why we're using 'womxn'...No, that's not a typo: 'womxn' is a spelling of 'women' that's more inclusive and progressive," the organization responded. "The term sheds light on the prejudice, discrimination, and institutional barriers womxn have faced, and explicitly includes non-cisgender women."

Numerous respondents on Twitter pointed out that this was just another example of a leftist organization pandering to extremist woke mobs who are trying to control language. "How do you pronounce Womxn? You dont . Cos its bulshit," tweeted Suzanne Moore.

"It's actually less inclusive, considering no normal person knows what the hell you're talking about," remarked another Twitter user.

"This is the kind of crap that has made it almost impossible to watch Ted Talks anymore. Too many people pandering to the "woke" crowd. Sorry, but no.....that is not inclusive, it's just bs," added another. Ted Talk's embrace of social justice warrior lunacy is nothing new. Over four years ago, they gave a platform to Rachel Dolezal, the white former NAACP chapter president who was exposed and humiliated for pretending to be black.

https://www.infowars.com/tedx-says-it-will-refer-to-women-as-womxn-to-fight-discrimination/

Georgetown Professor: 'Castrate' White Men's Corpses And 'Feed Them To Swine'

By Amber Athey October 1st, 2018

Georgetown Professor C. Christine Fair tweeted over the weekend that "entitled white men" should have their corpses castrated and then fed to pigs. Fair, an associate professor in Georgetown's Security Studies program, tweeted, "Look at thus [sic] chorus of entitled white men justifying a serial rapist's arrogated entitlement."

Fair linked to a video of Republican Sen. Lindsey Graham defending Supreme Court nominee Brett Kavanaugh from allegations of sexual assault from when the judge was in high school. "All of them deserve miserable deaths while feminists laugh as they take their last gasps," Fair wrote. "Bonus: we castrate their corpses and feed them to swine? Yes."

Georgetown University said in a statement to The Daily Caller that they respect Fair's right to freedom of speech but also expect her to keep her classrooms "free of bias." "The views of faculty members expressed in their private capacities are their own and not the views of the University. Our policy does not prohibit speech based on the person presenting ideas or the content of those ideas, even when those ideas may be difficult, controversial or objectionable. While faculty members may exercise freedom of speech, we expect that their classrooms and interaction with students be free of bias and geared toward thoughtful, respectful dialogue."

Fair recently came under fire in 2017 when she sent "hateful, vulgar" messages to a former Georgetown professor, Asra Nomani. Nomani claimed Fair began harassing her after she admitted to voting for Donald Trump for president. "I've written you off as a human being," Fair said in one message. "Your vote helped normalize Nazis in D.C. What don't you understand, you clueless dolt?"

"'F**K YOU. GO TO HELL," Fair wrote in a Facebook post directed toward Nomani. In January 2018, Fair was stopped and detained after allegedly calling German officers "Nazi police" at an airport in Frankfurt, Germany.

https://dailycaller.com/2018/10/01/georgetown-christine-fair-white-men-swine/

Michael Moore Tells "Angry White American Guys" to "Give it Up"

By Paul Joseph Watson November 2nd, 2018

During an appearance on NBC's "Late Night" with Seth Meyers, film maker Michael Moore called on "angry white American guys" to "give it up" because their demographic time is over.

"They are fanatical about this because they know their time is up. And it's sort of the angry white guy, which actually — I'm really Trump's demographic," said Moore. "I'm an angry white guy over 50 with a high school education. So that's me. So if I could just speak to my fellow angry white American guys who are semi-uneducated like me. Dudes, give it up. We've been running the show for 10,000 years. It's like — it's like we've had a long run as men running everything. And, you know, the Yankees could never win as many pennants as we've won in these 10,000 years as men," he added.

"So why don't we just take a break. Let the majority gender run the show," concluded Moore. This is not the first time the film maker has expressed anti-white sentiment. During a speech in New York in January, Moore called for America to be "cleansed" of its "white male privilege".

Back in August last year, he celebrated a future where white men were a minority because America's demographic shift will make it easier for Democrats to win future presidential elections. "The angry white guy is dying out, and the Census Bureau has already told us that by 2050, white people are going to be the minority, and I'm not sad to say

I can't wait for that day to happen. I hope I live long enough to see it because it will be a better country," said the film maker.

Speaking to the hypocrisy of Moore claiming to represent poor working class white men, Jack Posobiec tweeted, "Seth Meyers' net worth is $12 Million and he lives in a $7.5M apartment. Michael Moore's net worth is $50 Million and he has 8 homes." During last night's interview, Moore also urged Democrats to "throw all the bastards out," but was cautious about predicting a "blue wave," having accurately predicted that Trump would win against all odds in 2016.

"Well, I'm not going to make the mistake that someone else made on a late night show a couple nights ago," said the film maker, making reference to Nancy Pelosi's appearance on Stephen Colbert's show, during which she said, "We're going to win!" Moore, who back in June admitted that he cried every day over Trump, then warned that Trump "outsmarted" everyone in 2016 and could do so again. "So don't think for a second that come Tuesday, they don't have every intention of holding on to the House and the Senate. And they are good at what they do," said Moore.

As we previously highlighted, having attacked Hillary Clinton as an establishment warmonger earlier in the campaign, Moore quickly sold out and endorsed her candidacy as soon as she secured the nomination.

https://www.infowars.com/michael-moore-tells-angry-white-american-guys-to-give-it-up/

Mom asks little boy to leave public park because she wants girls-only playtime

By Jennifer McClellan November 2nd, 2018

A girl's mom got a reality check from Washington Post advice columnist Carolyn Hax after she felt justified in excluding a little boy from a public playground. The anonymous mother wrote to Hax about her "playground drama." It seems she and other moms of daughters had unofficially claimed a local playground as their girls-only meetup place at a set time each week.

Until disaster struck and a strange mother brought her son to the public park and dared to let him slide, swing and play during their special time. The girl's mom asked the mom of the boy to leave and was shocked when the other woman seemed upset.

"If she comes back, is there a better way I can approach her? This has been such a sweet time for moms and daughters and having a boy there is naturally going to change things. We live in a world where boys get everything and girls are left with the crumbs, and I would think this mom would realize that, but she seems to think her son is entitled to crash this girls-only time. I know I can't legally keep her from a public park, but can I appeal to her better nature?" the mom asked Hax.

That's when the longtime columnist — and mother of three boys — unleashed. How dare a grown adult justify stomping on the feelings of a child. And using it as some sort of "cosmic correction," in the male-female balance is despicable, she said. The little boy does not feel entitled to anything other than playtime at a PUBLIC park. "If you're going to accuse anyone of being "entitled," then ask yourself who was claiming possession of public space for her own purposes," Hax wrote, adding if the mother wants a girls-only playdate, she can do so on private property. "Goddess help us all," said Hax.

https://www.usatoday.com/story/life/allthemoms/2018/11/02/moms-asks-boy-leave-public-park-because-she-wants-girls-only-playdate/1857475002/

Victoria's Secret Executive: 'Hope' to Include a Transgender Model in Women's Lingerie Show

By Neil Munro Nov 13th, 2018

The Victoria's Secret brand hopes to showcase a 'transgender' biological man in women's underwear, says Ed Razek, the brand's chief marketing officer. Razek's statement came after progressives and transgender activists rallied on social media to complain he was excluding men who live as women from the brand's glitzy idealization of women's sexual power. Razek sparked the dispute when he told *Vogue* that the company uses different fashion shows and different brands to target different groups of women:

I think we address the way the market is shifting on a constant basis. If you're asking if we've ... looked at putting a plus-size model in the show, we have. We invented the plus-size model show in what was our sister division, Lane Bryant. Lane Bryant still sells plus-size lingerie, but it sells a specific range, just like every specialty retailer in the world sells a range of clothing. As do we. We market to who we sell to, and we don't market to the whole world.

But the company is under constant social media pressure to weaken the hugely valuable brand by sharing its feminine glamor with non-targeted groups, he said. "The hate that's on social media, it's extraordinarily toxic ... Where does it end?" he said, adding:

So it's like, why don't you do [size] 50? Why don't you do [size] 60? Why don't you do [size] 24? It's like, why doesn't your show do this? Shouldn't you have transsexuals in the show? No. No, I don't think we should. Well, why not? Because the show is a fantasy. It's a 42-minute entertainment special. That's what it is. It is the only one of its kind in the world, and any other fashion brand in the world would take it in a minute, including the competitors that are carping at us. And they carp at us because we're the leader.

Progressives and men who want to be glamorous women complained bitterly about their being excluded from the brand. In response,

Razek rapidly backtracked and issued a press statement saying he hoped a "transgender model" would be used in a show. But he carefully did not promise to hire a transgender model, saying:

The Tweeted message, however, excluded the "hope" comment from the email statement sent to ModernFashionNews.com:

"My remark regarding the inclusion of transgender models in the Victoria's Secret Fashion Show came across as insensitive. I apologize," Razek said via email. "To be clear, we absolutely would cast a transgender model for the show. We've had transgender models come to castings ... And like many others, they didn't make it ... But it was never about gender. Honestly, I really hope that a transgender model will make the show soon. I admire and respect their journey to embrace who they really are."

So far, many business groups have made cost-free political alliances with transgender advocates, usually via the companies' long-standing support of gay advocacy groups. But some companies — notably Target — have suffered badly when their customers resist the company's imposition of pro-transgender ideology on their preferences. RuPaul, a gay activist, has also been slammed for excluding transgender people from his televised mockery of heterosexual Americans.

In the Victoria's Secret dispute, Razek created a backlash by explaining the brand's business case for avoiding transgender advocacy.

The progressive complaints aimed at Razek and the brand were personal, aggrieved and did not include any business arguments for changing the brand's image. Mic.com suggested Razek is just like President Donald Trump: Doubling down on the hateful speech, Razek used the justification of the show being "fantasy" to excuse the lack of casting of transgender models (whom he called "transsexuals," a term that is often but not always considered pejorative). "Shouldn't you have transsexuals in the show? No. No, I don't think we should," he said. "Well, why not? Because the show is a fantasy. It's a 42-minute entertainment special. That's what it is."

This was a powerful white man — caught on the record — asserting a disregard for truth and an unflappable arrogance toward the livelihood of other human beings. Sound familiar? In reality, Trump is using his authority to clarify that the sex of people involved in sex-discrimination legal fights will be based on their male or female body, not on their claimed "gender identity."

"You know what I'm doing? I'm protecting everybody," Trump said October 22. "We have a lot of different concepts right now. They have a lot of different things happening with respect to transgender, right now."

Jezebel covered the Razek statement by emphasizing the personal:

The 70-year-old Razek, who is part of the casting team that chooses the models for each show, gave some bizarrely out-of-touch answers in the interview, lambasting critics as being "haters" who want too much diversity in the show and describing trans models as "transexuals." He comes off as a complete joke and absolute asshole and is clearly the reason the company is stuck in 2005.

Men who live as women used Twitter to make their voice heard:

However, critics of the Transgender Ideology scoffed at the progressives' demand that Victoria's Secret include a transgender man in their line-up of models:

The transgender ideology is deeply unpopular, especially among women and parents. In 2017, Obama told NPR that his promotion of the transgender ideology made it easier for Donald Trump to win the presidency. Multiple polls show that most Americans wish to help and comfort people who think they are a member of the opposite sex, even as they also reject the transgender ideology's claim that a person's legal sex is determined by their feeling of "gender identity," not by biology.

The transgender movement is diverse, so its different factions have different goals and priorities. It includes sexual liberationists, progressives, feminists who wish to blur distinctions between the two sexes, and people who glamorize the distinctions between the two sexes. It includes high-profile children, people who are trying to live as members of the opposite sex, and people trying to "detransition" back to their sex, men who demand sex from lesbians, masculine autogynephiles, wealthy donors, politicians, political professionals, and medical service providers.

Transgender advocates claim that 2 million Americans say they are transgender, to a greater or lesser extent. But very few people who describe themselves as transgender undergo cosmetic surgery of the genitals. Only about 4,118 Americans surgically altered their bodies in hospitals from 2000 to 2014 to appear like members of the opposite sex, according to a pro-transgender medical study.

Yet the gender ideology is rapidly gaining power, aided by huge donations from wealthy individuals and medical companies. In Ohio, for example, in February, a judge forced parents of a teenage girl to give up custody so she can begin a lifetime of drug treatments and surgery that will allow her to appear as a male.

The progressive push to bend Americans' attitudes and their male and female civic society around the idea of "gender identity" has already attacked and cracked many of the popular social rules that help Americans manage the cooperation and competition among and between complementary, different, and equal men and women.

These pro-gender claims have an impact on different-sex bathrooms, shelters for battered women, sports leagues for girls, hiking groups for boys, K-12 curricula, university speech codes, religious freedoms, free speech, the social status of women, parents' rights in childrearing, children's safety, practices to help teenagers, health outcomes, women's ideals of beauty, culture and civic society, scientific research, prison safety, civic ceremonies, school rules, men's sense of masculinity, law enforcement, military culture, and children's sexual privacy.

https://www.breitbart.com/economy/2018/11/13/victoria-secret-executives-hope-use-a-transgender-model-in-show/

Pro-Abortion Professor Says White Republican Men Should Be Castrated "While Feminists Laugh"

By Henry Rodgers Oct 1st, 2018

A professor at Georgetown University known for making incendiary comments against supporters of President Donald Trump said white Republican men deserve "miserable deaths" for supporting Supreme Court nominee Brett Kavanaugh.

Christine Fair, an associate professor at Georgetown in the School of Foreign Service, tweeted Saturday, saying white Republican men should die and an added bonus would be if women "castrate their corpses and feed them to swine." Her tweet was in response to South Carolina Republican Sen. Lindsey Graham's comments in front of the Senate Judiciary Committee. He defended Kavanaugh against an "unethical sham" and slammed Democrats for not releasing sexual assault allegations against the judge for weeks after they first received them.

In the tweet Fair called Kavanaugh a "serial rapist," although he has never been convicted or even accused of rape. The FBI is currently investigating the accusations of sexual misconduct against Kavanaugh and plans to have its investigation finished by Friday. Fair has previously made offensive comments on social media, telling a Muslim Trump supporter "f— off" and "GO TO HELL."

Georgetown University said Fair's views are her own and "not the views of the University," in a statement to The Daily Caller News Foundation. "The views of faculty members expressed in their private capacities are their own and not the views of the University," the university said. "Our policy does not prohibit speech based on the person presenting ideas or the content of those ideas, even when those ideas may be difficult, controversial or objectionable. While faculty members may exercise freedom of speech, we expect that their classrooms and interaction with students be free of bias and geared toward thoughtful, respectful dialogue."

https://www.lifenews.com/2018/10/01/pro-abortion-professor-says-white-republican-men-should-be-castrated-while-feminists-laugh/

Esquire sparks social media debate with profile of white teen from Middle America

By Brian Flood Feb 12th, 2019

Esquire sparked a heated debate on social media Tuesday when it unveiled an upcoming cover story about a white American boy and what's it's like to grow up "in the era of social media, school shooting, toxic masculinity, #MeToo, and a divided country."

The March issue has angered critics who feel that documenting the experiences of a 17-year-old boy is unnecessary, while others are outraged over the outrage. The story quickly became a trending topic on Twitter as detractors rushed to mock the magazine for, as Out Magazine's deputy editor put it, "radicalizing white mediocrity for the clicks." Former ESPN host Jemele Hill sarcastically tweeted an image of the cover captioned, "Because you know what we don't discuss nearly enough? The white male experience."

Esquire's Editor in Chief Jay Fielden explained his rationale in a companion piece headlined, "Why your ideological echo chamber isn't just bad for you, it's also bad for your kids." Fielden explained that his own son grapples with the complicated world that nowadays includes everything from accusations of privilege to gender fluidity.

Fielden said Esquire staffers huddled to discuss what it's like to be a kid these days and the idea for a series on "growing up now" was born. He said the stories aim to look at America through the eyes of a single kid, with Ryan Morgan being the first in the series. "He's white, lives in the middle of the reddest county in Wisconsin, and, as you will see, he is an unusually mature, intelligent, and determined young man," Fielden wrote.

Coming issues will feature similar stories about other kids, including pieces on black, LGBTQ and female subjects, but critics don't think the magazine launched the series with the proper profile. Some were upset the story was published during Black History Month, while others took it even further — such as author Sarah Weinman, who compared it to a profile of infamous church shooter Dylann Roof.

https://www.foxnews.com/entertainment/esquire-sparks-social-media-debate-with-profile-of-white-teen-from-middle-america

Female students sue Yale to admit women into male fraternities

By Nicole Darrah February 12th, 2019

Three female students at Yale University are suing the Ivy League school and nine of its male fraternities in an attempt to stop the school's social organizations from admitting people on the basis of their gender.

The women, who filed a class-action lawsuit in federal court in Connecticut on Tuesday, want to admit women to fraternities in response to alleged sexual assault, harassment and discrimination. Women, according to the students, are being shut out of social and economic benefits offered by all-male fraternities, including access to their alumni networks that can help land coveted jobs

While there are sororities on the New Haven campus, their power and influence lack in comparison to the school's fraternities, the lawsuit claims. "It's not only breeding a very toxic sexual culture but also is giving undue economic and professional benefits to the male fraternity members," one of the plaintiffs, Ry Walker, a junior majoring in astrophysics and African-American studies, told The Associated Press.

Lawyers for the other two plaintiffs, Anna McNeil, a junior, and Eliana Singer, a sophomore, said they believe this is the first-ever lawsuit by students against a university seeking to "gender integrate" fraternities.

All three plaintiffs said they were denied membership to fraternities, and claimed they were groped at fraternity parties and know other students who were sexually assaulted or harassed at frat parties. The three students said they complained to Yale about sexual misconduct and discrimination by fraternities, but school officials offered them "no meaningful assistance or relief." A spokesperson for Yale did not provide a comment on the lawsuit to the AP. An attorney for the fraternities said the students' accusations are baseless.

https://www.foxnews.com/us/female-students-sue-yale-to-admit-women-into-male-fraternities

'American Political Thought' course at CU Denver removes all white men from curriculum

By Ahnaf Kalam March 22nd, 2019

DENVER — I can clearly recall the first day of class a few semesters ago when I eagerly began a course called "American Political Thought" at the University of Colorado, Denver.

My excitement quickly soured, however, after Professor Chad Shomura explained to the students in the room that most traditional "American Political Thought" courses are too focused on the achievements of white men. As a consequence, he told us he had removed every single white male and their theoretical perspectives from the entire course curriculum.

This is echoed in the syllabus:

"This course aims to develop an understanding of American political life from the margins. Rather than surveying traditional figures of American political thought, it attends to historically marginalized voices at the crossings of race, gender, sexuality, and nation. It explores issues such as intersectionality, antiblack racism and the American Dream, ordinary life, borderlands and migration, public feelings, mental health, and settler colonialism. The materials we examine also exceed the usual genres of American Political Thought. They include, among other things, poems, an ethnography, academic articles, a novel, and a hacked tarot card set."

My disappointment and frustration at this narrow view led me to drop the course after just the first day. But the class continues to be taught at CU Denver by Professor Shomura. Making matters worse, political science majors at CU Denver are required to take two political theory courses in order to fulfill the requirements for the degree, and with very few class options to pick from, "American Political Thought" is taken by most to fulfill this requirement.

But the course that is being offered to hopeful political science students as a survey of American political thought appears to be anything *but.* Perhaps the most striking thing that stands out of the course syllabus is that there is absolutely zero mention of the Founding Fathers (or any other U.S. president or political leader, for that matter) or any of the Western Enlightenment thinkers. Nothing on Washington. Or Jefferson. Or Madison. Or Hamilton. Not a mention of Locke or Rousseau. None of that.

Instead of learning about the political theories that guide American social and political life, students learn about intersectionality from the writings of Professor Kimberlé Crenshaw, who coined the term. Instead of understanding the theoretical principles that allow for a functional republic, students learn about Filipino empowerment in Hawaii.

Instead of coming away understanding the influence of, say, federalism and mercantilism in the American political system, students are endlessly reminded of the alleged racism, sexism, and ethnocentrism that apparently runs rampant in American society. And instead of reading the Constitution or the Declaration of Independence, students must read Ta-Nehisi Coates's *Between the World and Me*, in which the author disgustingly and shamelessly smears the 9/11 first-responders, who sacrificed their lives for their fellow countrymen, as racist oppressors: "They were not human to me. Black, white, or whatever, they were menaces of nature; they were the fire, the comet, the storm, which could — with no justification — shatter my body."

To be fair, this course could readily and easily be offered with a different name and in a different department, or as an elective. Perhaps a course on "American life from the margins." Or "perspectives from under-represented Americans." And frankly, the course would truly be better suited in a sociology or humanities department. No matter how you try to frame it, this class has virtually no semblance to a class on American Political Thought.

Asked this week by *The College Fix* for a response to this critique, Dr. Shomura argued that by naming the course "American Political Thought," he wants students to come away being able to challenge the traditional notions of what – and who – gets to dictate what actually constitutes the subject. "It's a criticism that has been expressed in a lot of my course evaluations," he points out, "but with each semester, I try to modify the course accordingly. This class might very well morph into something very different, whether within the next semester or in ten years."

He also noted that he is open to modifying or possibly expanding the course to include the more "canonical" and traditional ideas of American political thought. But as it currently stands, Shomura is the only professor in the department focused on teaching political theory. The political science department is currently in the process of hiring a new faculty member, and if all goes as planned, Shomura said he hopes that the available options for political theory courses will include more than the current handful of options to satisfy the major's theoretical perspectives requirement.

Professor Shomura has expressed openness and a willingness to adapt to feedback. But nevertheless, a course called "American Political Thought" should put the traditional and canonical understanding of American political thought first and foremost, and it should be the predecessor to any derivative course focused on antithetical, critical, and postmodern theoretical perspectives – instead of the other way around.

But alas, as it currently stands, political science students are paying thousands of dollars expecting to learn the centuries-old foundational political theories of the country they reside in and will likely work in. To pretend that this repackaged social justice class will equip students with those necessary foundations is a deep disservice to students and to the department.

https://www.thecollegefix.com/american-political-thought-course-at-cu-denver-removes-all-white-men-from-curriculum/

Biden criticizes 'white man's culture,' role in Hill hearing

By Steve Peoples March 27th, 2019

NEW YORK (AP) — Former Vice President Joe Biden condemned "a white man's culture" as he lashed out at violence against women and, more specifically, lamented his role in the Supreme Court confirmation hearings that undermined Anita Hill's credibility nearly three decades ago.

Biden, a Democratic presidential prospect who often highlights his white working-class roots, said Hill, who is black, should not have been forced to face a panel of "a bunch of white guys" about her sexual harassment allegations against Clarence Thomas. "To this day I regret I couldn't come up with a way to give her the kind of hearing she deserved," he said Tuesday night, echoing comments he delivered last fall as the nation debated sexual misconduct allegations against Brett Kavanaugh amid his Supreme Court confirmation hearing. "I wish I could have done something."

Biden's role in the 1991 Thomas confirmation hearings is among his many political challenges as he considers making a 2020 bid for the presidency. Should he run, he would be among a handful of white men in a Democratic presidential field that features several women and minorities. His comments about Hill drew swift condemnation on social media, with many noting he was chairman of the Senate Judiciary Committee at the time of the hearing.

"It literally does not matter what else Biden says about sexual assault if he cannot acknowledge his own culpability in putting a sexual assaulter on the Supreme Court and then pretending for years like he was powerless to stop it," tweeted Jessica Morales Rocketto, a former aide to Hillary Clinton's 2016 presidential campaign who now serves as the political director for the National Domestic Workers Alliance. Actress and political activist Mia Farrow called Biden's role in the 1991 hearings "shameful."

"Love you Joe but you were in a position to do better — and you didn't," she said. Biden, 76, delivered the remarks at a New York City event honoring young people who helped combat sexual assault on college campuses. The event, held at a venue called the Russian Tea Room, was hosted by the Biden Foundation and the nonprofit group It's on Us, which Biden founded with former President Barack Obama in 2014.

Biden called on Americans to "change the culture" that dates back centuries and allows pervasive violence against women. "It's an English jurisprudential culture, a white man's culture. It's got to change," he said.

The former vice president also repeatedly denounced violence against women during his remarks, which spanned more than a half-hour. It's a topic he knows well. As a senator from Delaware, he introduced the Violence Against Women Act in 1990. "No man has a right to lay a hand on a woman, no matter what she's wearing, she does, who she is, unless it's in self-defense. Never," he said Tuesday.

He then shared a conversation he had with a member of a college fraternity. "If you see a brother taking an inebriated co-ed up the stairs at a fraternity house and you don't go and stop it, you're a damn coward," Biden said. "You don't deserve to be called a man."

https://apnews.com/73e70d011191490d839683b1fc89363f

Volkswagen and Philadelphia cream cheese ads banned over gender stereotypes

By Rob Picheta August 14th, 2019

London (CNN Business) An advertisement juxtaposing male astronauts with a woman sitting by a stroller, and another depicting two hapless dads, are the first casualties of a British ban on gender stereotypes in advertising.

The ads, for Volkswagen and Philadelphia cream cheese, were investigated by the UK Advertising Standards Agency (ASA) after viewers complained they perpetuated gender stereotypes.

New rules that came into force in June prohibit depictions of gender that "are likely to cause harm, or serious or widespread offense." The Volkswagen commercial shows a number of primarily male people taking part in adventurous activities — two male astronauts in space, and a male athlete with a prosthetic leg doing the long jump — before cutting to a mother sitting on a park bench next to a stroller. It prompted three complaints from viewers, and the ASA found it showed a woman "engaged in a stereotypical care-giving role."

"We acknowledged that becoming a parent was a life-changing experience that required significant adaptation, but taking care of children was a role that was stereotypically associated with women," the body added in its ruling. A second commercial for Philadelphia cream cheese showed two dads looking after their children at a restaurant with a conveyer belt.

The men become so distracted by the food that they lose sight of their babies, who end up circling the restaurant on the belt. "Let's not tell mom," says one, after rescuing his child. Over 125 viewers complained. "We acknowledged the action was intended to be light-hearted and comical and there was no sense that the children were in danger," the ASA said in its decision.

"We considered, however, that the men were portrayed as somewhat hapless and inattentive, which resulted in them being unable to care for the children effectively," they added. "We did not consider that the use of humour in the ad mitigated the effect of the harmful stereotype."

Neither ad can appear in its current form following the ruling. A spokesperson for Mondelez International (MDLZ), which produces Philadelphia, said the company was "extremely disappointed" with the decision. "We take our advertising responsibility very seriously and work with a range of partners to make sure our marketing meets and complies with all UK regulation."

The new rules follow a review by the ASA, published in 2017, which found that harmful stereotypes reinforced by advertising "can restrict the choices, aspirations and opportunities of children, young people and adults." A public furor over a 2015 poster on the walls of London's subway system, showing a woman in a bikini with the words "Are you beach body ready?," prompted the regulator to look into all gender portrayals in advertising.

The ad — for a weight-loss product — was not initially banned by the ASA, as it did not explicitly break any rules, but the regulator eventually took action due to its health claims. "Our evidence shows how harmful gender stereotypes in ads can contribute to inequality in society, with costs for all of us," Guy Parker, chief executive of the ASA, said in a statement in June.

The ASA said commercials will still be allowed to show "glamorous, attractive, successful, aspirational or healthy people or lifestyles." Ads that show men or women carrying out tasks with which their genders are sometimes associated, such as women shopping, will also be permitted.

https://www.cnn.com/2019/08/14/media/uk-adverts-banned-gender-stereotypes-scli-gbr-intl/index.html

Next up, conversion therapy: The new left says you're a bigot unless you have sex with EVERY gender

By Sophia Narwitz July 8th, 2020

It sounds insane to say, but the party that once rallied against gay conversion therapy is coming shockingly close to promoting it themselves. All under the guise of supporting the trans community.

Suck the d**k, bigot. No, really! In today's increasingly strange world, in order to show full allegiance to those who tick the final letter of the LGBT acronym, one must forgo all dating preferences and swallow their pride – or something else – to prove they are true allies.

A fringe belief is gaining traction, and previously well-respected publications such as the BBC are now promoting people who present the idea that 'genital preferences' are transphobic. In an article titled 'The black transgender push to keep the fight alive at LGBT Pride', non-trans gay men are called 'transphobic' for not wanting to date trans men. Aka, biological females.

Only in current times can gays come under attack for not liking vagina, all in the name of progressivism! Elsewhere, on social media, more and more people are screaming to the void that those who don't date trans women are also transphobic. In 2019, Veronica Ivy, formerly known as Rachel McKinnon, the trans cyclist infamous for demolishing records, came out and claimed that any sexuality outside of pansexuality is immoral.

This is conversion therapy for the modern age. Growing up as a gay youth, I always aligned with the left in regards to their fight against conversion therapy and their belief that sexuality isn't a choice. Today I still maintain those views. What gender and genitals someone is attracted to is just what someone is attracted to, it simply will not be forcefully changed. But to the new left, sexuality is akin to bigotry, and one must be open to all genders lest they be seen as hateful.

Have I mentioned that this is insane? Taking it further, it is progressive seppuku. Ideological suicide of the highest order that will only cause backlash and fiery anger in return. It is as if LGBT activists want to be hated, because this newfound push to convert people toward sexualities they don't otherwise identify with is only going to create resentment. Resentment which in the end will diminish the standing of trans people to the public at large.

Nobody wants to be called a bigot, more so if they're, well... not bigoted, and labeling gay or straight people as transphobic because of genital preferences is simply going to create actual bigots as people begin to look down on trans people and avoid any association with them.

As a trans person myself, it sucks to say, but I can't blame them. In recent years everything within this universe has somehow been labeled as transphobic. Missing a space between the words 'trans' and 'woman' so that it reads transwoman? That's transphobic. An 'ed' at the end of 'transgender' so that it says 'transgendered'? Yup, that's transphobic now too. Actors doing their jobs and taking on roles in which they have to act? Uh huh, that's transphobic as well. Just ask Halle Berry.

The left has taken horseshoe theory to its limit, and now if someone doesn't want to guzzle my you know what, well then they're transphobic too. If I was on the outside looking in, I wouldn't want to associate with people like me either.

Another horrifying aspect to this is how close they are veering toward being pro-rape. This is emotional manipulation in order to force people into having sex with others. Please explain how this doesn't fall under that umbrella. So kudos internet progressives, you played yourselves and shot countless others in the foot while doing so. Attraction isn't a choice, but there is one choice you can make, and that is to leave. Politely exit public discourse so that the rational people among us can clean up your mess.

https://www.rt.com/op-ed/494189-trans-community-gender-conversion/

Valentina Sampaio Is the First Transgender Model for Sports Illustrated

By Derrick Bryson Taylor July 11th, 2020

Valentina Sampaio made history on Friday, becoming the first transgender woman to be featured in the Sports Illustrated swimsuit issue, the magazine said. In a personal essay on the magazine's website, Ms. Sampaio, a 23-year-old Brazilian model, said she was honored to be in the publication.

"The team at SI has created yet another groundbreaking issue by bringing together a diverse set of multitalented, beautiful women in a creative and dignified way," she wrote.

While Ms. Sampaio's inclusion in this year's swimsuit edition has earned headlines, it's hardly a first for her: Last year, she became Victoria Secret's first openly transgender model and was hired for catalog work for VS Pink, the company's athletic line. In 2017, Ms. Sampaio was also the first transgender model to grace the cover of a Vogue edition.

In recent years, the Sports Illustrated swimsuit issue has had a number of breakthrough moments. The magazine, which debuted in 1964, put Ashley Graham, its first size 16 model, on the cover in 2016. Last year, it featured the Somali-American model Halima Aden, who was the first woman to wear a hijab and burkini in the magazine.

MJ Day, the editor of Sports Illustrated Swimsuit, said in a statement that Ms. Sampaio had been on her radar for some time and that she had noticed her passion for activism, calling the Sports Illustrated rookie a "true pioneer for the LGBT+ community."

Ms. Sampaio said that she was born in a fishing village in northern Brazil, and that being a transgender woman meant facing doors closed to "hearts and minds" as well as encountering insults and violence "just for existing."

In 2019, Brazil had 130 killings of transgender people, the most of any country, according to the Trans Murder Monitoring program, a database and analysis of reported killings of gender-diverse and transgender people. "Our options for growing up in a loving and accepting family, having a fruitful experience at school or finding dignified work," Ms. Sampaio said, "are unimaginably limited and challenging."

Her inclusion in this year's swimsuit issue comes amid a wide push for transgender visibility, acceptance and rights. In the United States, lawmakers in more than two dozen states have introduced measures that would take away transgender rights, including criminalizing medical professionals who prescribe hormone treatments to minors.

Transgender women have long been a target of violence, and Black transgender women, in particular, are killed so often, the American Medical Association has declared it an epidemic. In 2019, 91 percent of the transgender or gender-nonconforming people who were fatally shot were Black women, according to the Human Rights Campaign. So far this year, there have been at least 16 murders of transgender people.

"I recognize that I am one of the fortunate ones, and my intention is to honor that as best I can," Ms. Sampaio said. "What unites us as humans is that we all share the common desire to be accepted and loved for who we are."

https://www.nytimes.com/2020/07/11/business/media/valentina-sampaio-transgender-sports-illustrated.html

Cafe replaces gingerbread men with 'gender neutral gingerbread person'

By Luke Matthews November 8th, 2019

Gingerbread men often become a staple in our diets at this time of year but one cafe has ditched the traditional treat in favour of a more inclusive biscuit. When a customer at The Tannery in Auckland questioned why the human-shaped snacks were called 'gingerbread men' and not 'gingerbread people', owner Andre Cettina was inspired to make a change.

The label on the jar has now been changed to read 'gingerbread gender-neutral person'. The jar of biscuits on the front counter has caused a stir, with customers taking photos and sharing them on social media, as well as sparking a debate on the cafe's Facebook page.

"It was completely tongue-in-cheek at the start," said Andre, as reported by Stuff.co.nz . "But it's become a really good conversation piece in the cafe.

"We've had a lot of people commenting saying 'stop being so pedantic, it's just a biscuit'. I had to reply to them going, 'did you miss the whole point?'

"It used to be that 90 per cent of the time we sold [the gingerbread biscuits], it was to kids. There's a lot more people buying them now, which is quite funny." Andre added the cafe had received positive feedback from customers who saw 'humour' in the name change. The Tannery posted a photo of the jar on it's Facebook page with the caption 'A little something for everyone' with a winking face.

Not everyone agreed with the change with one saying: "PC gone mad, always been gingerbread man, why change now. It's a biscuit, not a living creature. I find this all so sad!!" Another replied to the comment to say: "Me too! Soon we won't be able to use the term human, we'll all be hupeople."

Arguing against the points, a third replied: "Not sure why people getting so mad. This is a conversation starter, and these issues won't be dealt with until we are open to talking about them. "People getting mad about this completely miss the point of what it could achieve.

"It isn't 'PC gone mad', it's an opportunity to take a good hard look at yourself and your feelings around a sensitive topic and do some real introspective work on why you feel the way you do." It's not the first time retailers have shunned the gingerbread man, with the Co-op last year also baking up its own gender neutral version .

The store gave the gingerbread person a gender neutral outfit and eventually called the character 'Crumbs' after encouraging customers to come up with a name.

https://www.mirror.co.uk/news/world-news/cafe-replaces-gingerbread-men-gender-20839491?utm_source=facebook.com&utm_medium=social&utm_campaign=mirror_main

Transgender Who Sued Over 'Bikini Wax Access' Now Targeting Gynecologists

By Amanda Prestigiacomo December 3rd, 2019

Moving on from suing female estheticians for refusing to wax male genitals, the world of gynecology is the next brave frontier for transgender woman and self-styled "LGBTQIA+ advocate" Jessica Yaniv.

According to Yaniv, transgender "rights" not only include female salon workers being forced to wax male genitals, *even when they don't offer the service*, but also gynecologists being forced to take on transgender patients who do not have female reproductive organs.

On Monday night, the activist ranted via Twitter about allegedly being discriminated against and turned away from a gynecology office because Yaniv is transgender. "Ok so [Fraser Health] needs to stop hiring employees who are discriminatory towards the #LGBTQ and use their bulls*** excuses on why they can't see you even though you have a referral from the emergency department and live in the Fraser Health area!!" Yaniv posted to Twitter. "I want help and can't get it!!"

In follow-up tweets, Yaniv elaborated: "So a gynaecologist office that I got referred to literally told me today that 'we don't serve transgender patients.' And me, being me, I'm shocked.. and confused... and hurt."

"Are they allowed to do that, legally?" Yaniv asked, signaling prospective legal action, particularly since the activist has shown to be extremely litigious in the past. "Isn't that against the college practices?"

Yaniv, a biological male, does not have a uterus or ovaries and it's unclear if the activist has had what is often dubbed in the trans world as "bottom surgery." In other words, it's unclear how a standard gynecologist could provide care to the activist. Also, it remains unclear if Yaniv actually was turned away and for what reason. "Gynaecologists form a part of the multidisciplinary team who engage with transgender and non-binary patients, either as part of the transition stage performing surgery or managing pre- or post-transition gynaecological problems," the activist added.

Yaniv made headlines earlier this year when the activist filed at least 15 human rights complaints against female estheticians in Canada for refusing to wax his male genitals, as noted by The Daily Wire. However, in October, the Justice Centre for Constitutional Freedoms, a group that represented five of the women being targeted by Yaniv, announced that the activist's cases against their clients had been tossed by the British Columbia Human Rights Tribunal. Moreover, Yaniv was instructed to pay $2,000 each to at least three of the women.

"The Justice Centre for Constitutional Freedoms (JCCF) is pleased to announce that the BC Human Rights Tribunal has ruled in favour of home estheticians' right to refuse to handle male genitalia against their will," a press release from JCCF said, as highlighted by The Post Millennial. "According to the group, the tribunal's decision said that 'human rights legislation does not require a service provider to wax a type of genitals they are not trained for and have not consented to wax,'" The Daily Wire noted. "Moreover, it was noted that Yaniv 'engaged in improper conduct' and 'filed complaints for improper purposes.' The activist's testimony, according to the ruling, was 'disingenuous and self-serving,' and Yaniv was 'evasive and argumentative and contradicted herself.'"

https://www.dailywire.com/news/transgender-who-sued-over-bikini-wax-access-now-targeting-gynecologists?utm_source=facebook&utm_medium=social&utm_campaign=benshapiro

Air Force changes service anthem to gender-neutral lyrics

By Associated Press February 27th, 2020

COLORADO SPRINGS, Colo. — The U.S. Air Force changed lyrics in its service anthem by dropping gender references that exclude women.

The change announced Thursday by the Air Force chief of staff, Gen. David Goldfein, is designed to make the service friendlier to women, The Gazette reports. "Our song must reflect our history, the inspiring service and accomplishments of all who've served, and the rich diversity that makes today's Air Force indisputably the strongest and most capable in the world," Goldfein wrote in a message to airmen, cadets and academy alumni.

The change originated when female Air Force Academy cadets asked Goldfein why the anthem's third verse hailed the bravery of men, but not women. The third verse is meaningful to cadets at the academy near Colorado Springs, where it is sung after sports victories, but students took issue with the third line: "To a friend we send a message of his brother men who fly." In the new version, the line is changed to read, "To a friend we send a message of the brave who serve on high." Other gender references in the song remain, including "at 'em boys, give 'er the gun."

https://www.washingtontimes.com/news/2020/feb/27/air-force-changes-service-anthem-gender-neutral-ly/

Gender

Inside of our leftist, utopian hellhole, gender does not exist if it fits their psychotic argument. If it does fit their incoherent babble, then gender does exist. They want to have it both ways. And they do have it both ways because we allow them to control the narrative and language in culture. Saying the words "man," "woman," "boy," and "girl," are considered sexist and insensitive. Even in many schools, saying the words "mother" or "father" are censored and cancelled, because not all children have a mom or dad. Replacing "mother" and "father" on many permission slips are the words "parental guardian," "legal parental unit," or "responsible adult." Boys' sports are being cancelled and girls are now allowed to join. Girls' sports are being banned and now boys can join. Whatever happened to "woman power?" Whatever happened to "girl power?" They're gone like the dodo bird. What we are turning into in society is a group of nameless, bland, and faceless asexual people with no boundaries with regards to gender or gender identity. Some psychotic lunatics on the left are now even saying that men standing to urinate is sexist and promotes male dominance. Gone are gender baby reveals. Gone are boys and girls toy sections in stores. Gone are boys and girls clothing section in stores. Welcome to the new gender nightmare created by bi-coastal, wealthy, elitist, elites who want to run, dominate, and control every single aspect of our society and culture.

15

The War on Education

Oregon Educators: Making Math Students Show Their Work Is 'White Supremacy'

By Thomas D. Williams Ph.D. February 16th, 2021

The Oregon Department of Education is seeking to root out white supremacy in mathematics, manifested by emphasis on "getting the right answer" and making students "show their work."

As reported Monday by the attentive folks at the College Fix, Oregon's progressive Department of Education has furnished educators with an 82-page training manual titled "A Pathway to Equitable Math Instruction: Dismantling Racism in Mathematics Instruction."

The education department mailed the manual to teachers as part of Black History Month. The manual enumerates signs of "white supremacy culture in the mathematics classroom," which include a focus on "getting the right answer," an emphasis on "real-world math," teaching math in a "linear fashion," students being required to "show their work," and grading students based on their demonstrated knowledge of the material.

"In order to embody antiracist math education, teachers must engage in critical praxis that interrogates the ways in which they perpetuate white supremacy culture in their own classrooms, and develop a plan toward antiracist math education to address issues of equity for Black, Latinx, and multilingual students," the manual declares.

The unavoidably racist and thoroughly demeaning implication is that black students are not capable of "showing their work" or "getting the right answers," and so teachers must lower the academic bar or remove it altogether.

An impartial observer might even suggest that assuming that students of color are incapable of competing on a level playing field is a manifestation of the deepest form of "white supremacy." What the manual never succeeds in explaining is how dumbing down mathematics will magically eliminate "mathematical inequity," a proposal that is counterintuitive.

It was not long ago that literature and film celebrated heroic educators who, against all odds, challenged their students to rise above their situations and achieve academic success. If the Oregon Department of Education is any indication, such heroism is a thing of the past.

https://www.breitbart.com/education/2021/02/16/oregon-educators-making-math-students-show-their-work-is-white-supremacy/

Chicago Teachers' Union: Expecting Us to Teach Kids is Sexist and Racist

By Daniel Greenfield Monday December 7th, 2020

Ever since the pandemic, teachers' unions have been coming up with excuses not to teach, and the Democrats they have in their back pocket helped them. But the rebellion has very clearly arrived with even the leftiest parents utterly sick and tired of this state of affairs.

That led Mayor Bill de Blasio, a guy who spends all his time pricking his ears up to hear lefty whistles, to backtrack on closing schools. But in Chicago, the teachers' union decided to go to the mattresses. "The push to reopen schools is rooted in sexism, racism, and misogyny," the Chicago Teachers' Union tweeted.

Did they really need to say both sexism and misogyny? The tweet has since been deleted, but the toxic virtue signaling it contains can't be unseen because, remember, the people who most want kids back in school are mothers, that is to say, women. And in Chicago, that's heavily black women.

So the Chicago Teachers' Union decided to cry that expecting its members to teach black kids and help their mothers get back to work is sexist and racist. But they're still supposed to be paid $100K.

Hundreds of thousands of students are left on their own as their educators "fight for the students" by demanding a 15% raise in 3 years, while Chicago's lefty mayor will only offer them 16% in 5 years.

And that's not counting the annual cost-of-living increases which make it more like 25%. 5 years from now, the starting salary for a Chicago teacher would be $72,000 while the average salary for a Chicago teacher would be $100,000. That's the offer that the union claims isn't good enough.

67% of Chicago's school budget already goes to salaries and benefits. Another 33% is left over for the other stuff. Guess where that $2.5 billion that the union is demanding will come from? Not the 67%. Pointing all these facts out is probably also sexist and racist.

https://www.frontpagemag.com/point/2020/12/chicago-teachers-union-expecting-us-teach-kids-daniel-greenfield/

San Diego Public Schools Will Overhaul Its Grading System To Achieve 'Anti-Racism'

By Robby Soave October 19th, 2020

San Diego's public schools want to be anti-racist, so they're...abolishing the traditional grading system? "This is part of our honest reckoning as a school district," San Diego Unified School District Vice President Richard Barrera told a local NBC affiliate. "If we're actually going to be an anti-racist school district, we have to confront practices like this that have gone on for years and years."

District officials evidently believe that the practice of grading students based on their average score is racist, and that an active effort to dismantle racism necessitates a learning environment free of the pressure to turn in assignments on time. As evidence for the urgency of these changes, the district released data showing that minority students received more Ds and Fs than white students: Just 7 percent of whites received failing grades, as opposed to 23 percent of Native Americans, 23 percent of Hispanics, and 20 percent of black students.

Under the new system, students will not be penalized for failing to complete assignments, and teachers will give them extra opportunities to demonstrate mastery of subjects. The grades they receive upon completion of a course will no longer reflect their average test and assignment scores. "Common grading practices such as averaging a student's grade over time can disadvantage students who started the year behind grade level and can discredit the progress a student has made, experts have said," noted *The San Diego Union Tribune.*

The new approach—which is rather confusingly written—still includes letter grades, but these will reflect student's "mastery" of the subject rather than their completion of homework, quizzes, and tests. What constitutes mastery is left unexplained. Grades "shall not be influenced by behavior or factors that directly measure students' knowledge and skills in the content area," which sounds like a recipe for highly subjective grading. And a great deal of leniency will now be given to students who don't do the work for a course, including those who don't show up at all: Attendance can no longer be a factor in grading.

In any case, ending these kinds of grades doesn't actually eliminate the underlying inequities that produced the disparate Fs. It may actually cover those inequities up: Given that grades are a tool for evaluating students' progress, the district is essentially announcing that it will no longer gather as much evidence about the negative social phenomena it would probably like to address. Better grades do not mean students will suddenly have a better grasp of the material. They certainly won't be better prepared for college (where traditional grades are very much still a thing).

Indeed, this comes perilously close to addressing poverty by no longer tallying the number of homeless people—or, to use a timely example, President Donald Trump's frustration that increasing COVID-19 testing will make the epidemic look worse. Coronavirus cases exist even if they go undetected; similarly, minority students who are falling behind their classmates will be falling behind even if their teachers aren't giving them Fs.

Eliminating grades and standardized testing has become something of a crusade for California progressives. California's public universities, for instance, announced earlier this year that they would no longer require applicants to take either the SAT, a measure on which white students have historically outperformed others. But this elides a serious problem for minority students: Other admissions criteria—such as legacy considerations and extracurricular activities—favor privileged applicants even more dramatically than grades and tests do. The wealthiest (and usually whitest) students have better access to résumé-padding activities; yes, they can also hire tutors and take test prep courses, but there's only so much extra value to be extracted from these things.

At present, San Diego schools are only open for a handful of special-needs students. What district kids need most of all is probably a return to normalcy, as soon as possible. An experimental system that eliminates year-end letter grades seems like an especially bad idea for the current moment.

https://reason.com/2020/10/19/san-diego-public-schools-grades-antiracism/

U. Chicago English Dept. says it will ONLY admit 'Black Studies' grad students this year

By Celine Ryan September 14th, 2020

University of Chicago English Department graduate programs will only be open to applicants who plan to study "Black Studies" this year. According to its admissions information webpage, the department is only accepting graduate applications from those who are "interested in working in and with Black Studies" for this academic year. "For the 2020-2021 graduate admissions cycle, the University of Chicago English Department is accepting only applicants interested in working in and with Black Studies. We understand Black Studies to be a capacious intellectual project that spans a variety of methodological approaches, fields, geographical areas, languages, and time periods," the university's English Department website states.

The department's Black Studies program works "in close collaboration with other departments to study African American, African, and African diaspora literature and media, as well as in the histories of political struggle, collective action, and protest that Black, Indigenous and other racialized peoples have pursued, both here in the United States and in solidarity with international movements."

The program boasts a "commitment" not just to "ideas in the abstract," but also to more concrete action in the form of "activating histories of engaged art, debate, struggle, collective action, and counter-revolution as contexts for the emergence of ideas and narratives."

The university introduced this information by proclaiming "that Black Lives Matter, and that the lives of George Floyd, Breonna Taylor, Tony McDade, and Rayshard Brooks matter, as do thousands of others named and unnamed who have been subject to police violence."

"As literary scholars, we attend to the histories, atmospheres, and scenes of anti-Black racism and racial violence in the United States and across the world. We are committed to the struggle of Black and Indigenous people, and all racialized and dispossessed people, against inequality and brutality."

The Black Studies program boasts a number of working groups available to students, including the "Race and Capitalism Project," an initiative with work focusing on "how processes of racialization within the U.S. shaped capitalist society and economy and how capitalism has simultaneously shaped processes of racialization."

Black Studies courses advertised by the department include "Black Shakespeare," during which students will learn how Shakespeare played a role in "the shaping of Western ideas about blackness," and focus on "Shakespearean plays portraying Black characters."

University Assistant Director for Public Affairs Gerald McSwiggan explained to *Campus Reform* that the school "can accept a limited number of Ph.D. graduate students in the 2020-21 application season due to the COVID-19 pandemic and limited employment opportunities for English PhDs."

"Currently, there are 77 Ph.D. students studying a wide variety of disciplines within the English Department, and the department is admitting 5 additional Ph.D. students for 2021," McSwiggan added. "The English department faculty saw a need for additional scholarship in Black Studies, and decided to focus doctoral admissions this year on prospective Ph.D. students with an interest in working in and with Black Studies. As with other departments in the University, the department's faculty will decide which areas of scholarship they wish to focus on for Ph.D. admissions in future years."

https://www.campusreform.org/?ID=15679&fbclid=IwAR2Z8VFhSA0NpNZ2Blk55mnVkVZARPVIj1pnRcG-WRadreuKmSux3HZGxBD0

Elementary school 'whiteness' lesson: Sympathizing with police is 'racist'

By Dave Huber August 16th, 2020

An elementary school in one of the country's wealthiest districts will require fourth and fifth graders to read a book which asserts sympathizing with law enforcement is "racist."

Students at Gladwyne Elementary School in Pennsylvania's Lower Merion School District will get "Not My Idea: A Book About Whiteness," which also claims it's "racist" to not watch the news and showcases Colin Kaepernick as a hero in the fight against racial injustice. According to *The Washington Free Beacon,* the same curriculum uses "A Kid's Book About Racism" for *kindergartners and first graders.*

It seems the four "cultural proficiency" lessons already in use by Gladwyne were deemed "insufficient" by the school's (aptly named) Cultural Proficiency Committee. Principal Veronica Ellers noted in a June email that the school plans "to continue designing lessons that promote anti-racist actions in the upcoming 20-21 school year and beyond." District spokeswoman Amy Buckman added that Lower Merion "fully supports the ongoing implementation of an anti-racist curriculum in its schools."

"A Kid's Book About Racism" reads in part "[racism] happens all the time. Sometimes it shows up in small ways. Like a look, a comment, a question, a thought, a joke, a word, or a belief.... If you see someone being treated badly, made fun of, excluded from playing, or looked down on because of their skin color call it racism."

One outspoken parent was angry enough about these developments to pull her children out of the school:

Elana Yaron Fishbein, a mother of two boys and a doctor of social work, penned a letter to the district's superintendent, board members, and the school's principal demanding the school remove its new "cultural proficiency" curriculum. "The book teaches kids not only to defy parents but to hate themselves," Fishbein told the *Washington Free Beacon*. "To hate their parents also because they are white. By default, [the kids] are white, and they're privileged, and they're bad. [The school] is teaching this to little kids." ...

If kindergartners can be called racist for asking questions, so can parents who question the "anti-racism" being taught to their children. Fishbein told the *Free Beacon* that parents privately message her echoing their disapproval of the cultural proficiency curriculum, but are scared to speak out for fear of being branded racist.

"If you say anything that's racist according to the school or parent's definition of racism, you're out," Fishbein said. "You're called a racist.

No wonder the parents don't talk." According to Gladwyne's website, the Lower Merion InterSchool Council Committee on Equity & Race will host a Zoom discussion later this month on the book "Just Mercy" by Bryan Stevenson. As founder of the Equal Justice Initiative, Stevenson looks into cases involving "wrongly convicted or harshly punished defendants from marginalized groups including juveniles, the poor, and the mentally ill."

Despite this noble endeavor, the author believes slavery never ended after the Civil War — it "just evolved." He told graduates at the University of Delaware just this four years ago. More worrisome is that Gladwyne suggests Nikole Hannah-Jones' "1619 Project" as "supplemental material" for the Stevenson discussion.

https://www.thecollegefix.com/elementary-school-whiteness-lesson-sympathizing-with-police-is-racist/

'Giant Warning': Iowa State University Instructor Warns Anti-BLM, Pro-Life Views Are 'Grounds For Dismissal'

By Mary Margaret Olohan August 18th, 2020

An Iowa State University instructor's syllabus warned students that anti-Black Lives Matter and pro-life viewpoints are "grounds for dismissal." Instructor Chloe Clark's English 250 syllabus includes a "giant warning" advising students that only certain views would be permitted during her classes. "I take this seriously," she notes at the end of the warning.

"Any instances of othering that you participate in intentionally (racism, sexism, ableism, homophobia, sorophobia, transphobia, classism, mocking of mental health issues, body shaming, etc.) in class are grounds for dismissal from the classroom," Clark wrote in the syllabus, a copy of which was provided to the Daily Caller News Foundation by the Young America's Foundation (YAF).

YAF was made aware of Clark's statement through a whistleblower who submitted the syllabus through YAF's Campus Bias Tip Line. "The same goes for any papers/projects," Clark's statement continues, "you cannot choose any topic that takes at its base that one side doesn't deserve the same basic human rights as you do (i.e. no arguments against gay marriage, abortion, Black Lives Matter, etc.)"

Clark did not immediately respond to a request for comment from the Daily Caller News Foundation. The university told the DCNF in a statement that Clark's syllabus statement is "inconsistent with the university's standards and its commitment to the First Amendment rights of students."

"After reviewing this issue with the faculty member, the syllabus has been corrected to ensure it is consistent with university policy," the university said. "Moreover, the faculty member is being provided additional information regarding the First Amendment policies of the University."

"Iowa State is firmly committed to protecting the First Amendment rights of its students, faculty, and staff," the university statement adds. "With respect to student expression in the classroom, including the completion of assignments, the university does not take disciplinary action against students based on the content or viewpoints expressed in their speech."

YAF Spokesman Spencer Brown told the DCNF that such situations "arise far too often within institutions that are supposed to be encouraging healthy debate and intellectual curiosity."

"While it's good that the university reiterated its support for the First Amendment rights of its students, it is alarming that a faculty member would think openly declaring her intent to silence dissent is in line with the practice of education or the Constitution," Brown said.

He added: "Unless concerned students are willing to stand up to this censorship, higher education will continue to rot away."

https://dailycaller.com/2020/08/18/iowa-state-university-instructor-bans-pro-life-blm/

Student faces suspension for background image of Trump on Zoom virtual classroom call

By Christian Toto August 17th, 2020

A Stockton University student is facing suspension after he included an image of President Trump on a Zoom conference call.

A representative from the Foundation for Individual Rights in Education (FIRE) says the episode is part of a "depressing" trend of university students being punished for politically charged social media posts. Doctoral student Robert Dailyda featured the Trump image as his screen background during a July 1 virtual class session. Several fellow students enrolled at the New Jersey college complained about the visuals in a private GroupMe conversation following the session.

The doctoral student also shared a post on Facebook criticizing Black Lives Matter and saying he'd fight to the death to preserve the United States, a la Patrick Henry. The combination of events sparked a July 22 Code of Conduct Complaint about the "bias incident" filed by the university's director of care and community standards. Some students felt "offended, disrespected, and taunted" by the Trump imagery, according to the complaint report, which did not identify the complaining students. The unnamed students added that the Facebook post in question smacked of racism and potential violence.

Zach Greenberg, a FIRE program officer and author of a letter to Stockton President Harvey Kesselman defending Dailyda, says university administrators asked "intrusive" political questions of the student during a July 10 interrogation.

Dailyda faced six charges, according to FIRE, including cyber bullying, disruptive behavior, discrimination, harassment and creating a hostile environment. The University dropped five of the six charges this week, but Dailyda still faces possible suspension. A university spokeswoman said Dailyda's case remains open and "no disciplinary action has been taken."

"For a university to threaten to derail his academic career is really antithetical to the university's mission statement," says Greenberg, whose group defends the "individual rights of students and faculty members at America's colleges and universities."

"This is quintessential political speech meriting the highest level of protection," he adds. Greenberg says no university faculty or officials, to his knowledge, have rallied to Dailyda's side during the imbroglio. School officials have "created a deeply embedded and systematic environment that squelches the free speech of those who disagree with their radical agenda," said Dailyda in a statement.

Dailyda isn't the only student risking punishment for his conservative views. Marquette University's Samantha Pfefferle, set to start her freshman year this fall, told The College Fix in June that her TikTok video supporting President Trump nearly derailed her college dreams.

The social media clip generated online hate and, much worse, death threats, according to Politifact. An Instagram user saw the video and started an online effort to reverse her Marquette University acceptance, scouring other aspects of her social media profile in the process.

"Marquette received hundreds of emails, social media messages and formal bias-incident reports from current students, alumni and others regarding the incoming student's social media posts and her comments on social media, which some deemed to be 'transphobic and racist' language," university spokeswoman Lynn Griffith told PolitiFact Wisconsin in an email.

The university's dean of admissions, Brian Troyer, met with Pfefferle via Zoom. Pfefferle later told radio host Todd Starnes the university gave her "morality tests" to see how she'd engage fellow students of various backgrounds. That conversation, she added, involved social media posts she had written three years ago when she was 15.

She is expected to attend the university this fall after her story gained online media attention. FIRE is seeing an increase in "rescinded admissions" in recent months, says Greenberg, who suspects this is due to the tense political atmosphere surrounding the 2020 presidential campaign, as well as the fallout from protests over the death of George Floyd in Minneapolis. Students increasingly share their political views on social media and, as a result, face consequences for their opinions. The "problematic" comments cross political lines, Greenberg notes.

The universities in question, Greenberg says, give a variety of justifications for their actions, including fear of "hate speech."Free speech cases tied to President Trump get plenty of attention, though. In 2018, an Oregon high school student settled a lawsuit after his pro-border-wall T-shirt sparked an uproar at his school. Officials asked him to remove the Trump-friendly shirt or leave the premises. He chose the latter and later sued. The school eventually paid Addison Barnes $25,000 for legal fees, and the school's principal wrote a formal apology for the incident.

"I brought this case to stand up for myself and other students who might be afraid to express their right-of-center views," Barnes said in a statement. One prominent university warns that even doing nothing can also lead to punishment. Syracuse University is mulling a new rule where students who refuse to interrupt "bias-motivated" incidents could face unspecified consequences.

https://justthenews.com/nation/free-speech/student-faces-suspension-background-image-trump-zoom-virtual-classroom-call

Syracuse University Will Begin Punishing Students Who Witness 'Bias-Motivated' Incidents And Don't Act

By Ashe Schow August 15th, 2020

A string of alleged racist incidents took place at Syracuse University last fall, prompting school officials to create new punishments for students accused of various offenses.

As Jonathan Turley, an attorney and professor at the George Washington University Law School, explained, the new rules were implemented after a group calling itself NotAgainSU demanded students who witnessed or were present when racial incidents occurred be expelled. The school's first diversity and inclusion officer, professor Keith Alford, didn't accept expulsion as a punishment but did say campus rules would be changed to punish student bystanders.

"The Code of Student Conduct has been revised, based on your input, to state that violations of the code that are bias-motivated—including conduct motivated by racism—will be punished more severely. The University also revised the code to make clear when bystanders and accomplices can be held accountable. The code will be prepared and distributed for students to sign in the fall," Alford wrote in an email to students.

Turley warned that the uncertainty surrounding "how silence or inaction will be judged" will "prompt many to guarantee compliance by speaking or acting to avoid even the chance that they might be subjected to a highly damaging bias charge." In addition to new punishable actions (or, rather, inactions), the school also announced it was installing new cameras throughout campus.

"The concern raised by the Syracuse rule is that there remains controversies over vague universities standards on bias or race motivated violations including microaggressive language or actions. Recently, a student writer at Syracuse was sacked for simply questioning the basis for claims of institutional racism. What is viewed as bias-motivated speech for some is viewed as political speech by others. The new rule would suggest that even students who do not agree that an incident is 'bias-motivated' must still act to avoid scrutiny or punishment. Students could feel an obligation to prove that they are not racist by immediately and openly opposing such acts, lest they could be next to be accused," Turley wrote.

Turley added that punishing those who do not act is a form of compelled speech, as it "would now require speech and action to avoid possible discipline." The new punishments come even though there doesn't appear to be news on the outcomes of any investigations into allegedly racist incidents at Syracuse. One of the allegations came from a black woman who claimed a bunch of fraternity members yelled racial epithets at her. Four students from the fraternity were suspended, yet the fraternity's national chapter confirmed to The Daily Orange that after "hours of voluntary interviews with authorities" along with everything they "have learned, we can confirm that no member of Alpha Chi Rho directed racial slurs at anyone."

The only other incident where we have a potential outcome is of a white supremacist document allegedly sent to students while in a campus library, but that turned out to be a hoax. While there have been hundreds of allegations of racism at colleges and universities across the country over the past decade, most – if not all – have turned out to be hoaxes or misunderstandings.

https://www.dailywire.com/news/syracuse-university-will-begin-punishing-students-who-witness-bias-motivated-incidents-and-dont-act

Brooklyn College Education Prof. Claims Math Is 'White Supremacist Patriarchy'

By Tom Ciccotta August 9th, 2020

Brooklyn College Professor of Math Education Laurie Rubel argued this week on Twitter that the mathematical equation 2+2=4 "reeks of white supremacist patriarchy." Rubel's tweet was retweeted and promoted by several academics at universities and colleges around the nation.

According to a report by Campus Reform, Brooklyn College Professor Laurie Rubel, who teaches math education, tried to make the case this week that basic math is "white supremacist." The tweets are part of a larger trend in recent scholarship by American academics, many of which have argued that "objective truth" is a social construct.

"The idea that math (or data) is culturally neutral or in any way objective is a MYTH. I'm ready to move on with that understanding. Who's coming with me?" Rubel wrote in a tweet. "Along with the 'of course math is neutral because 2+2=4' trope and the related (and creepy) 'math is pure' and 'protect math.' Reeks of white supremacist patriarchy," Rubel added. "I'd rather think on nurturing people & protecting the planet (with math in service of them goals)."

Several academics from institutions around the nation chimed in. Harvard Ph.D. candidate Kareem Carr suggested that math should be reevaluated because it was primarily developed by white men. "People say it's subjectivism to ask if math is Western. I don't get that. It's an objective fact that some groups were more involved in the creation of modern math than others," Carr said. "They may have been *trying* to make it objective but it's not stupid to ask if they actually succeeded!"

A few academics have pushed back. James Lindsay, one of the academics behind a series of hoax papers that were published in "social justice" journals, reminded Rubel and her peers that mathematical truths are objective. "It's certainly the case, and the Woke need to be held firmly to the point, that feats of engineering like space travel and rocketry utterly depend upon accepting stable meanings of mathematical statements like 2+2=4 as objectively true, not mere accidents of culture," Lindsay tweeted.

https://www.breitbart.com/tech/2020/08/09/brooklyn-college-education-prof-claims-math-is-white-supremacist-patriarchy/?utm_source=facebook&utm_medium=social

Chicago leaders call for Illinois to abolish history class until a less 'racist' curriculum is formed

By Nick Givas August 4th, 2020

Local leaders in the Chicago area lobbied to scrap history class in the surrounding schools on Sunday until a less "racist" curriculum can be formed, that doesn't promote "white privilege."

During a news conference in the suburb of Evanston, State Rep. LaShawn K. Ford, a Democrat, argued for a complete overhaul of textbooks and lesson plans in an effort to be more inclusive toward minorities and women, NBC 5 in Chicago reported.

Prior to the event, his staff reportedly distributed a press release to those in attendance outlining his agenda. "Concerned that current school history teaching leads to white privilege and a racist society, state Rep. La Shawn K. Ford, D-Chicago will join local leaders today at noon at the Robert Crown Center in Evanston to call on the state to stop its current history teaching practices until appropriate alternatives are developed," the document began.

"When it comes to teaching history in Illinois, we need to end the miseducation of Illinoisans," Ford said. "I'm calling on the Illinois State Board of Education and local school districts to take immediate action by removing current history books and curriculum practices that unfairly communicate our history." He added, "Until a suitable alternative is developed, we should instead devote greater attention toward civics and ensuring students understand our democratic processes and how they can be involved. I'm also alarmed that people continue to display symbols of hate, such as the recent display of the Confederate flag in Evanston."

Attendees also discussed how Jewish and LGBTQ figures have been ignored and pushed for them to have a more prominent place in the classroom, according to NBC 5. Evanston Mayor Steve Hagerty, also a Democrat, said he didn't feel qualified to make a judgment about classes being halted but did say he supports House Bill 4954, which would establish various commemorative holidays and increase the time teachers spend on the civil rights movement of the 50s and 60s.

"As Mayor, I am not comfortable speaking on education, curriculum, and whether history lessons should be suspended. This is not my area," he said. "Personally, I support House Bill 4954 because I am interested in learning more and believe the history of Black people should be taught to all children and include all groups, Women, LatinX, and Native Indians who helped to build America."

HB 4954 would change the school code to "add as commemorative holidays January 15 (to be known as Humanitarian Day and observed as a day of respect for the principles of human and civil rights and to involve the use of the color white as a visual affirmation to practice these principles) -- April 4 (to be known as Victims of Violence Wholly Day and observed as a day of respect for the principles of nonviolence and to involve the use of the color black as a visual affirmation to practice these principles), and August 28 (to be known as Dream Day and observed as a day of respect for the spiritual and moral principles of peoplehood and to involve the use of the colors black and white as a visual affirmation to practice these principles)."

In addition, it would "provide that the teaching of the history of the United States shall include the study of the American civil rights renaissance, that period of time from 1954 to 1965 called the Movement." If the bill became law it would also set "forth additional areas to be included in the Black History unit of instruction, including the study of the American civil rights renaissance and the study of pre-enslavement history."

https://www.foxnews.com/us/chicago-leaders-abolish-history-class-less-racist

Professors allow students to pick their own grade

By William Nardi August 9th, 2018

A literature class at Davidson College this fall will use "contract grading," allowing students to pick ahead of time their grade for the class and the workload they need to complete to earn it.

The offer is posed by Professor Melissa Gonzalez for her Introduction to Spanish Literatures and Cultures course, SPA 270, at the private liberal arts college in Davidson, North Carolina.

She is one of several professors across the nation who allow this pick-your-own grade method, billed as a way to eliminate the student-professor power differential and give students control of their education. But critics contend it is just another example of how colleges coddle students from the harsh realities of the real world, which includes competition and goal expectations. As for Gonzalez, she argues there is "a strong pedagogical rationale for contract grading" in an Aug. 1 email to students obtained by *The College Fix*. "It can help students focus on learning more than on grades, and therefore make more progress in their learning, with less anxiety."

Gonzalez did not respond to repeated email requests for comment from *The College Fix*. "I aim to foster classroom environments that are radically democratic and empower intellectual risk-taking," Gonzalez states in her profile on the school's website. In her email, Gonzalez urged her former students to sign up for SPA 270, indicating that only two students have enrolled thus far and the class is in danger of being canceled.

"I want to make sure you know about some important innovations I am introducing in the course [contract grading] so that you can decide today or as soon as possible whether you want to take SPA 270 in Fall 2018. If you do, please use ADD/DROP as soon as possible to add it, or the course will have to be cancelled," she wrote.

Gonzalez is a Hispanic Studies professor who also teaches in the Gender and Sexuality Studies department. In her email, she told students they could "sign a contract indicating the work that they will do in order to earn that grade."

"At the end of the semester, if the student completed the specific work they said they would, at the satisfactory level, they receive the grade they planned to receive," her email states. To support her claim that contract grading improves the academic experience for students, Gonzalez cites a 2009 research paper by scholars Peter Elbow and Jane Danielewicz. "The contract helps strip away the mystification of institutional and cultural power in the everyday grades we give in our writing courses," according to the research paper.

"Using the contract method over time has allowed us to see to the root of our discomfort: conventional grading rests on two principles that are patently false: that professionals in our field have common standards for grading, and that the 'quality' of a multidimensional product can be fairly or accurately represented with a conventional one-dimensional grade. In the absence of genuinely common standards or a valid way to represent quality, every grade masks the play of hidden biases inherent in readers and a host of other a priori power differentials," it adds.

In their paper, Elbow and Danielewicz also contend that contract grading is "used frequently, but discussed rarely. A Google search reveals a surprisingly large number of teachers who use some form of learning contract in various disciplines for diverse goals." Along with her email, Gonzalez attached two contract grading templates designed by other professors who also use the method: Cathy Davidson of CUNY and fellow Davidson College Professor Mark Sample.

Davidson, in a blog post on the grading method, refers to it as "an act of community." Contract grading has also been referred to as "specs grading" in a 2016 op-ed in *Inside Higher Ed* by Linda Nilson, director of the office of teaching effectiveness and innovation at Clemson University. She explains that "course grades are based on the bundles of assignments and tests that students complete at a pass/satisfactory level."

"Bundles that require more work, more challenging work or both earn students higher grades. No more points to painstakingly allocate and haggle over with students. By choosing the bundle they want to complete, students select the final grade they want to earn, taking into account their motivation, time available, grade point needs and commitment," Nilson stated.

"If a student chooses a C because that's all he or she needs in your course, you can respect that. Under such conditions, students are often more motivated to learn because they have a sense of choice, volition, self-determination and responsibility for their grade, as well as less grade anxiety." But not all students are convinced it's a good idea, including Davidson College senior Kenny Xu, who is majoring in mathematics.

"It degrades trust in your achievement by outside authorities, including employers, grad schools, scholarships etc.," he told *The College Fix*. "Imagine if an employer saw that you got an A not because you were truly one of the best in the class but because you fulfilled some requirement YOU personally set. Would he really trust that A? I think not."

"Colleges are increasingly viewing themselves as a support system rather than an institution of learning," Xu added. "Learning is not supposed to be easy, or comfortable. Excellence requires that you step out of your comfort zone and compete. Colleges are becoming shelters, which is not what this country nor what this generation needs."

https://www.thecollegefix.com/professors-allow-students-to-pick-their-own-grade/

Schools Ordered to Teach Eight-Year-Olds That 'Boys Can Have Periods Too'

By Virginia Hale December 16th, 2018

Schools in Brighton have been ordered to teach children as young as eight that people "of all genders" can have periods, as well as to install sanitary waste disposal units in every toilet room.

The instructions were included in guidelines published by the local council earlier this month on 'Taking a Period Positive Approach in Brighton & Hove Schools', which assert there is "more work to do across all settings to prevent and reduce stigma related to periods and talking about periods". Under the subheading 'key messages', teachers are told to stress to pupils that "trans boys and men and non-binary people may have periods" as well as that "periods are something to celebrate and we can see this in ceremonies and celebrations across the world".

"Language and learning about periods [must be] inclusive of all genders, cultures, faiths and sexual orientations. For example; 'girls and women and others who have periods,'" according to the document, which also tells schools to ensure that "bins for used period products are provided in all toilets from Key Stage 2 (pupils aged between seven and 11)".

"All pupils and students from year 4 (eight to nine-year-old's) receive age and development appropriate period education within a planned program of relationships and sex education," the guidelines note.

However, in addition to this, the document demands schools also take "a cross-curricular approach to learning about periods, particularly in science and PSHE but also in media studies, PE, math, graphics, and textiles." Commenting on the guidelines, Brighton & Hove City Council said: "By encouraging effective education on menstruation and puberty, we hope to reduce stigma and ensure no child or young person feels shame in asking for period products inside or outside of school if they need them.

'We believe that it's important for all genders to be able to learn and talk about menstruation together... Our approach recognizes the fact that some people who have periods are trans or non-binary," a spokesman told the *Mail on Sunday*. Breitbart London has previously reported on guidelines issued by the left-wing council in October, which advised that schools may need to alert social services if parents are dismissive towards a 'gender questioning' child's demands to change sex.

Schools were also told to dismiss objections to 'trans pupils' sharing the girls' changing rooms and safety concerns around male pupils competing in single-sex sports with females, insisting "it is the responsibility of members of staff to support ... trans pupils and students and cisgender pupils and students to feel comfortable around one another."

With the Green party a strong electoral force in the city, Brighton & Hove City Council, in the south of England, has been something of a trailblazer with regards to introducing "progressive" policies, having started quizzing four-year-old infants about their "gender identity" back in 2016.

https://www.breitbart.com/europe/2018/12/16/schools-eight-year-olds-boys-periods/

Colleges de-stress students for finals: therapy horses, coloring, massages, Fortnite tourneys

By Matthew Pinna December 20th, 2018

Therapy dogs and miniature horses. Coloring books. Massages. Even Fortnite tournaments.

All this and more are ways in which universities across the nation are working to help students de-stress as finals unfold, hosting a plethora of interesting activities or all out "De-stress Fests." One of the most common services provided come in the form of therapy dogs, specifically trained to be as calm and affectionate as possible. Campuses such as the University of Colorado at Colorado Springs and Michigan State are just two out of many that recently offered the friendly puppers to pet and relax with in between study sessions.

Duke University went one step further. On top of bringing in puppies, the school offered what it called a "Stampede of Love" — miniature horses. Students were invited on the Friday before Finals Week to partake in an event led by a Raleigh-based nonprofit, staffed by two of their tiny horses, named "Kiwi" and "Lola."

Not to be outdone, Michigan State allowed its students to use the cows at its Dairy Cattle Teaching and Research Center for "brushing" therapy. The program was advertised as: "Finals Stress mooove on out!" The options for students to "de-stress" go beyond the extent of the animal kingdom, however.

For the artistically minded, schools like Brandeis University recently allowed up to 40 uptight students to "channel that energy into creating a beautiful work of art." In that same creative vein, students who love to de-stress with a good crayon or colored pencil were offered a chance to dig into coloring books, a very popular activity as seen this finals season at Oregon State, University of Minnesota, University of Illinois at Chicago and many others. The events are often paired with jigsaw puzzles, Legos, and even origami.

While some colleges recommend exercise to take the mind away from exams, others turn to the wide world of eSports. Hawaii Pacific, Washington State, and Kent State recommended that students "take a break" from studying to compete in their Fortnite tournaments, with some prizes in store for those who came away victorious.

Too stiff to color between the lines or hold a controller? Hunter College, the University of Pennsylvania, Yale, and more can fix that with complimentary professional massages. At Penn State, its officials ensure that students are properly mellowed with guided meditation and "cloud gazing." The University of Arizona offers yoga. Northern Illinois University provides "Crepes & Cocoa."

Is all of this necessary? *The Washington Post* interviewed American University students on the topic, who said that such snacking amenities are a welcome departure from the stress of finals, particularly for the one who said that they had "just finished crying."

https://www.thecollegefix.com/colleges-de-stress-students-for-finals-therapy-horses-coloring-massages-fortnite-tourneys/

North Carolina considers dropping 'F' grade to 39 percent for state public schools

By Bradford Betz February 27th, 2019

The bar for failing test scores in North Carolina's state public schools may be significantly lowered under proposed new legislation.

House Bill 145, introduced by the North Carolina General Assembly last Thursday, proposes to base grades on a 15- rather than a 10-point scale. In other words, an F grade would constitute anything below a 40 percent score — much lower than the 60 percent mark that is the norm in North Carolina and most other states, WPLG reported.

Under the new scale system, an A would be 100 to 85 percent, a B would be 84 to 70 percent, a C would be 69 to 55 percent, and a D would be 54 percent to 40 percent, according to the bill. The scale system would not affect students who are already performing well. But students who are under-performing in school will be allowed to continue. If passed, the law will go into effect beginning with the 2019-2020 school year, according to the bill.

https://nypost.com/2019/02/27/north-carolina-considers-dropping-f-grade-to-39-percent-for-state-public-schools/

Stunning Survey Shows Half Of Americans Don't Know All First Amendment Freedoms

By Study Finds Mar 21st, 2019

NEW YORK — Nearly 6 in 10 Americans believe the First Amendment is under threat, according to a new survey, yet a large portion of respondents couldn't correctly name what the amendment protects.

Of the 2,000 adults who took part in the poll, half thought that "liberty" is one of the five freedoms protected by the First Amendment, while nearly half (49 percent) believed "the pursuit of happiness" was included. Thankfully, only 3 percent named "life" as one of the protected freedoms. What's more, barely more than a quarter (26 percent) of participants knew how many amendments even comprise the Bill of Rights. In fact, 1 in 5 people wasn't even familiar with the Bill of Rights when asked.

Despite the struggle with what should be common American knowledge, the survey — commissioned by the Samuel Hubbard Shoe Company — revealed that 57 percent of respondents feel the First Amendment is at risk in the nation's current climate. Many people point to bias in the media and the rise of fake news as main reasons for their concern. One in seven admit they have trouble telling the difference between real and fake news, while 31 percent agree the mainstream media struggles to report the news of the day without inserting bias within their coverage.

"The online epidemic of misinformation, false news stories and election disinformation campaigns pose significant threats to democratic rights. The respondents' alarm is well-placed," says Alan C. Miller, founder and CEO of the News Literacy Project, a national nonpartisan education nonprofit that teamed up with Samuel Hubbard to bring awareness to the First Amendment, in a statement.

When it came to how participants valued the five protections under the First Amendment, the vast majority — a whopping 84 percent — agreed that freedom of speech is the most important protection. Respondents ranked freedom of religion as second-most important, followed by freedom of the press, freedom of assembly, and freedom to petition the government. Samuel Hubbard has launched a shoe line called the Freedom Collection in which each shoe has the First Amendment engraved on its sole. The survey was conducted in October 2018 by market researcher OnePoll.

https://www.studyfinds.org/survey-half-americans-dont-know-what-first-amendment-protections/

Online petition calls for teacher's firing over 'pathetic' comment on second-grader's worksheet

By Bradford Betz April 19th, 2019

A viral image of harsh feedback written on a second grader's math assignment has prompted online petition to fire his teacher. Chris Piland, whose son attends Valley View Elementary School in Pennsylvania, posted an image on Facebook Tuesday of his son's math assignment with remarks allegedly written by his teacher that read, "Absolutely pathetic. He answered 13 in 3 min! Sad."

"My son Kamdyn's teacher has been so rude to him and myself all year he comes home with this and I am beyond frustrated that someone would write this on a childs (sic) work such great motivation," Piland wrote on the post.

The post went viral and prompted an online campaign to have the teacher fired. As of early Friday, the "Petition to fire Alyssa Rupp Bohenek from the Valley View school district" has garnered nearly 8,000 signatures and has been widely shared on Facebook. Rose Minniti, the school superintendent, said an investigation was opened after a meeting the teacher and the Valley View School District but cautioned that the outcome would be dictated by "the facts and evidence" rather than "social media."

https://www.foxnews.com/us/online-petition-calls-for-teachers-firing-over-comments-written-on-second-graders-worksheet

George Washington University hides syllabus urging students to read book equating conservatism and racism

By Greg Piper July 16th, 2020

An elite university that charges students nearly $60,000 a year in tuition is urging them to read a book that conflates racism and conservatism.

George Washington University pulled the syllabus that includes the book – *Conservatism and Racism, and Why in America They Are the Same* – shortly after the *Washington Free Beacon* asked about it Wednesday, according to reporter Chrissy Clark.

The Office of Diversity and Inclusion published the "Solidarity Resource Syllabus" to recommend more than 100 books to students on the subject of racism in America. The 2010 book by Robert Smith, professor of political science at San Francisco State University, claims that even blacks who subscribe to conservative beliefs are racist:

"Repeatedly I was asked, 'Are you saying that conservatism is racism, that all conservatives are racist?' Aren't there black conservatives? Are they racist?'.... My answer to most of these questions was a qualified yes." Smith also co-wrote a textbook, *American Politics and the African American Quest for Universal Freedom.* The *Beacon* reported that the university hosted several online programs in the past month on racism in America that drew 5,000 registrations. Subjects include the roles of nonwhites in "anti-blackness" and "white people in racial justice and anti-racism":

The workshops culminated with the July 9 release of a 21-page "#GWinSolidarity" syllabus that links to outside resources on the black experience, white allyship, decolonization, and gender and sexuality. Political Science Prof. Samuel Goldman told the news outlet that recommending Smith's book "as the sole resource on the topic gives the impression that GWU is promoting a specific orthodoxy rather than inviting students to study and reflect." While the syllabus was blocked off, the diversity office still had a copy on its website, according to Clark.

https://www.thecollegefix.com/george-washington-university-hides-syllabus-urging-students-to-read-book-equating-conservatism-and-racism/

University To Mandate 'Race And Ethnicity' Course For All Students

By Steve Watson July 17th, 2020

Emory University in Atlanta, Georgia is to mandate that all of its students take a "Race and Ethnicity Requirement" course from next year, following consistent demands from the university's black student group.

Campus Reform reports that the university wants all students to understand "how racial and ethnic antagonisms and inequality develop historically."

"After careful consideration over the past six years, and in ongoing consultation with faculty, students, and administrators, the Emory College Faculty Senate and the Working Group on the Undergraduate Curriculum concur that Emory University has a particular obligation and opportunity to focus a diversity requirement on the crucial role of race and ethnicity in shaping our institutions, and in furthering students' understanding of current domestic and international political and social relations," a statement reads. Black students at the university have been lobbying for the move for over five years.

Back in 2015 a letter from the group noted that it was "still reeling at injustices made by the University and the lack of adequate action."

The students demanded that officials at the university "understand and then appropriately address the mental stress incurred by Black Students at this institution on a daily basis."

"The Bias Incident Reporting that Emory University has not been efficient because they have not thoroughly tended to the concerns of those who have used the reporting system," the students also declared, adding that "The microaggressions and macroaggressions that Black students experience which lead to our trauma should not be regarded for the sole purpose of data collection." The development comes in the wake of black and native American students at several colleges and universities increasingly demanding action against professors and academics who have expressed opinions not directly in line with their own.

A senior researcher at Michigan State University was effectively fired after sharing facts from a study conducted last year that conclusively proved there is no widespread racial bias in police shootings. At Loyola University New Orleans, students demanded the firing of professor Walter Block over his opinions on slavery, even though he vehemently opposes it.

At UCLA, a professor was suspended for rejecting requests to allow black students to take final exams at a later date as a response to the death of George Floyd and black lives matter protests. Accounting lecturer Gordon Klein was punished for saying that students should not be treated differently according to the colour of their skin. Meanwhile, other academics have been lauded and rewarded for promoting opinions in line with the woke mob that even Twitter removed for being hateful.

https://www.infowars.com/university-to-mandate-race-and-ethnicity-course-for-all-students/

Photo with noose gets California school's principal, 4 teachers placed on leave

By Brie Stimson May 11th, 2019

Four elementary school teachers in Southern California were placed on administrative leave this week after a photo of them smiling while holding a noose circulated on social media. The school's principal who reportedly took the photo is also on leave.

One parent claimed, according to KABC-TV of Los Angeles, that the noose was hung from a tree on the grounds of Summerwind Elementary School in Palmdale earlier this month. She also claimed that someone shot video of the teachers laughing and joking about the noose.

An investigation into the photo and the origin of the noose is now underway, district officials said. Some parents were so upset about the photo that they either temporarily or permanently pulled their kids out of the school Thursday, KABC reported.

"Do you know what they use that for? They use that to hang African-American people -- that's what they do -- and kill them," parent Tierra Harris explained to her daughter, according to KABC. "They still do it to this day. I don't want you going here because I don't want you to feel like that."

"It hurts. It absolutely hurts me to the core. It's disgusting and I'm outraged, and I want to see some action and not just administrative leave," parent Breyan Clemmons said about pulling her child out of the school. "We think that we're sending them to a school; they're safe. Never do we think we're sending them to a plantation where they got nooses hanging up, and holding on to nooses," she told the Antelope Valley Press.

The superintendent of the Palmdale School District issued a statement on Facebook, which read in part: "I am appalled that this incident occurred ... I am committed to the Palmdale Promise's values of equity, integrity, and multiculturalism, and I know that most of the district believe[s] in the same values the Promise upholds."

https://www.foxnews.com/us/4-california-elementary-teachers-on-administrative-leave-after-posing-with-noose

Ohio school superintendent defends decision to eliminate valedictorian, salutatorian honors

By Anna Hopkins May 13th, 2019

The superintendent of an Ohio high school has defended the district's decision to eliminate valedictorian and salutatorian honors in an attempt to improve the mental wellbeing of their students.

Jonathan Cooper said during an appearance on "America's Newsroom" on Monday that a spike in suicides at Mason City high school forced the district to consider the level of unhealthy competition among students and find ways to ease their stress. "As our community looked at some unhealthy patterns the rise in anxiety and depression and suicide," he said. "It's the second leading cause of death in youth today across America, so we started to look at what we can do as school leaders to make a change."

The elimination of valedictorian and salutatorian will be replaced by honors similar to those in college - summa cum laude, magna cum laude, and cum laude. The district also announced they'd be starting classes thirty minutes later.

Apart from the academic changes, Cooper said they've also worked to implement wellness programs, including a peer-to-peer suicide prevention program called "Help Squad." The school's previous model allowed students to tack on 0.3 percent to their grade point average if they made a C or higher in Advanced Placement classes, which led to many kids packing their schedule full of more difficult courses to get the highest possible GPA.

When pressed by host Bill Hemmer as to whether student stress could be reduced by capping the number of classes kids are allowed to take, Cooper said the school didn't want to limit their creative interests.

"Well, you know, we want our kids to pursue what they're passionate about," he said. "We don't want them to chase a magic number or artificial goal here. We want them to pursue what they're interested in."

https://www.foxnews.com/us/ohio-school-superintendent-defends-decision-to-eliminate-valedictorian-salutorian-honors

First ever Maths A-level where getting almost half of answers wrong will get you an A

By Camilla Turner & Ewan Somerville August 14th, 2019

Students who got almost half of the answers wrong in their Maths A-level this summer will get a grade A, it has emerged.

Just 54 per cent is required for an A in this year's OCR exam, according to a leaked copy of the grade boundaries seen by The Daily Telegraph. It is believed to be the lowest amount of marks ever needed to secure a top grade in a Maths A-level. Students with 43 per cent will be awarded a B, those with 33 per cent will get a C and those with 13 per cent will pass their A-level with a grade E. Documents revealing the grade boundaries for Edexcel's A-levels also surfaced online on Wednesday, which showed that pupils need to get 55 per cent for a grade A in Maths, 34 per cent for a C and 14 per cent for an E.

This summer was the first year that pupils of all abilities took the new, reformed Maths A-level which was designed to be more challenging and better prepare sixth form students for university. But the leaked documents reveals that pass marks have been drastically reduced compared to previous years.

It comes as thousands of students prepare to pick up their A-level results on Thursday. Pearson revealed last week that dozens of students face having their Maths grade withheld amid an investigation into an online leak which saw exam questions circulated on social media ahead of the exam. Last summer a small cohort of 2,000 very bright students - who learned the syllabus in one year rather than the usual two - took the reformed Maths A-level with Edexcel. They needed 61 per cent for an A, 42 per cent for a C and 23 per cent to pass the exam with an E.

The majority of Maths students in 2018 took the old A-level, where 80 per cent was required for an A, 70 per cent for a C and 40 per cent for an E. However, Pearson said it is not possible to draw direct comparisons between grade boundaries in the old and the new qualification due to the different format of the exams.

To prevent students from being penalized for taking the new, harder exams, Ofqual fixes the proportions of each grade to make them roughly the same as last year, through a process they called "comparable outcomes".

However, experts have pointed out that artificially lowering the pass marks to ensure consistency between different cohorts would create the illusion that students were doing better than they actually were. Students who took the Edexcel Maths A-level earlier this summer complained that they found the exam exceptionally difficult, with thousands signing a petition to demand "some form of compensation" or "special consideration" since questions were "unlike any specimen, past or textbook questions." A separate petition claimed that students' hopes of attending university have been "shattered" thanks to the Maths exams.

Barnaby Lenon, chair of the Independent Schools Council, said that a new Government policy - where schools are offered a cash incentive of up to £2,400 for every extra student that takes Maths in the sixth form - may have played a role in the lower grade boundaries this year.

"This is the first cohort taking Maths A-level encouraged to do so by the extra money that schools get," he told the Daily Telegraph. "What that means is, you may have a group of weaker students taking Maths A-level than there were in the past." Grade boundaries are usually released on Thursday at the same time as results, but teachers could access them a day in advance through a password protected website.

An OCR spokesman said they do this to "minimize the chance of students feeling anxious", while a Pearson spokesman said that the "vast majority" of schools treat this information confidentially.

https://www.telegraph.co.uk/news/2019/08/14/first-ever-level-getting-almost-half-answers-wrong-will-get/

A new law signed by Gavin Newsom bans schools from suspending disruptive kids

By Andrew Sheeler September 9th, 2019

It is will soon be illegal in California for both public and charter schools to suspend disruptive students from kindergarten through eighth grade

Gov. Gavin Newsom on Monday signed into law Senate Bill 419, which permanently prohibits willful defiance suspensions in grades four and five. It also bans such suspensions in grades six through eight for five years.

The law goes into effect July 1, 2020. A previous law had already banned schools from suspending defiant kids through third grade. Sen. Nancy Skinner, D-Berkeley, who wrote the new law, said it would "keep kids in school where they belong and where teachers and counselors can help them thrive."

"SB 419 puts the needs of kids first," she said. California students missed more than 150,000 days of school because of suspensions for unruly behavior in the 2016-17 academic year, according to a California Senate analysis of SB 419.

Skinner and other supporters of the bill argued that students of color are disproportionately affected by such suspensions. SB 419 "may be one of the best ways to disrupt the school-to-prison pipeline," Skinner said. SB 419 was also praised by civil rights activist Dolores Huerta, who said in a statement that, "I strongly believe that SB 419 will bring justice to California youth by eliminating suspensions for disruption and defiance, putting an end to discriminatory discipline policies and instituting restorative justice practices."

The bill was opposed by the Charter School Development Center, whose executive director argued that SB 419 is a "one size fits all" legislation that is "a fix in search of a problem."

https://www.sacbee.com/news/politics-government/capitol-alert/article234912107.html

Seattle Public Schools Say Math Is Racist

By Ben McDonald October 21st, 2019

The Seattle Public Schools Ethnic Studies Advisory Committee (ESAC) released a rough draft of notes for its Math Ethnic Studies framework in late September, which attempts to connects math to a history of oppression.

The framework is broken into four different themes: "Origins, Identity, and Agency," "Power and Oppression," "History of Resistance and Liberation," and "Reflection and Action." The committee suggests that math is subjective and racist, saying under one section, "Who gets to say if an answer is right," and under another, "how is math manipulated to allow inequality and oppression to persist?" Jason Rantz of KTTH in Seattle noted that, "ESAC is made up of a number of educators and was created due to a legislature mandate to 'advise, assist, and make recommendations to the office of the superintendent of public instruction regarding the identification of ethnic studies materials.'"

It is also stated in the document that Western mathematics is "used to disenfranchise people and communities of color." Under this framework students will be able to "construct & decode mathematical knowledge, truth, and beauty" so that they can contribute to their communities.

Furthermore, under this criteria students will analyze the ways in which "ancient mathematical knowledge has been appropriated by Western culture," and "identify how math has been and continues to be used to oppress and marginalize people and communities of color."

The deadline for the final draft of the curriculum is September 1, 2020. Tracy Castro-Gill, Seattle's ethnic studies director, told *King 5* in Seattle, "The goal is to disrupt the status quo and do something different." The idea of math being problematic has been promoted among academics with a Vanderbilt professor saying that math education is sexist and a high school in Canada last year moved to "Africentric Math" to try and promote more black students.

https://dailycaller.com/2019/10/21/seattle-schools-math-is-racist/

Because Racism: Charter School System to Remove 'Work Hard. Be Nice.' as Its Official Slogan

By Alex Corey Jul 3rd, 2020

On Wednesday the charter school organization The Knowledge is Power Program, commonly know as KIPP, announced that it will be retiring the slogan "Work hard. Be Nice." as school officials believe the phrase is counterproductive to abolishing systemic racism.

Richard Barth, KIPP Foundation CEO, said in a press release that after a letter from KIPP Co-Founder Dave Levin about the ways in which the organization can change its culture, he decided to axe the slogan as it "diminishes the significant effort required to dismantle systemic racism."

"Over the last few weeks, we have all been working hard to turn words into action, recognizing that there is still much more work to be done to eliminate any practice at KIPP that furthers systemic racism, anti-Blackness, and inequities experienced by our students, alumni, families, teachers, and staff," said Barth. Levin's letter was full of white guilt, expressing how he takes blame for not doing enough on behalf of KIPP to stop racial injustice. The practice of disciplining students of color instead of making them feel "affirmed, uplifted, and celebrated" was wrong, he said.

"In recent years, I have come face to face with the understanding that white supremacy doesn't just mean the public and hateful displays of racism; it applies to all aspects of the world that are set up for the benefit of and perpetuation of power for white people at the expense of Black, Latinx, and other People of Color," said Levin.

"Work Hard. Be Nice." certainly has the outward appearance of promoting values that would make life better for every person who chose to espouse them. But to Barth, the idea of being nice and working hard offered too narrow of a future for children who might want to be lazy and mean in order to get what they want.

"[The slogan] places value on being compliant and submissive, supports the illusion of meritocracy, and does not align with our vision of students being free to create the future they want," his statement read. In addition to the removal of the slogan, KIPP also plans to distribute grant money to communities most affected by the novel coronavirus and from racial trauma, eliminating discipline practices in schools that officials determine to be inequitable, providing a senior equity officer, along with countless other actions spurred by the killing of George Floyd.

https://townhall.com/tipsheet/alexcorey/2020/07/03/california-charter-school-system-to-remove-work-hard-be-niceas-its-official-slogan-n2571784

Washington and Lee University faculty demand removal of Robert E. Lee from school name

By Greg Piper July 7th, 2020

The erasure of history continues apace in higher education. Nearly two-thirds of Washington and Lee University faculty voted to remove Confederate General Robert E. Lee from the school's name. The Board of Trustees at the small liberal arts school, where Lee was once president and is now buried, will consider the motion.

Black permanent faculty in the law school want a full renaming of the university, removing George Washington as well, reports the *Richmond Times-Dispatch*. Washington's donated stock kept the school from shuttering in 1796, and it continues to feed the endowment, the university says on its namesakes page.

The Monday afternoon vote was prompted by the faculty affairs committee and scheduled by President Will Dudley. The removal motion drew around 80 percent support of those voting, and more than 80 percent of the 300-plus faculty voted. The board is already considering the "removal of all references to the Confederacy" following an earlier petition signed by more than 200 faculty. The proposal to erase Lee moved at lightning speed, according to the newspaper: Faculty only started "[f]ormal conversations" on June 24.

The executive committee of the student government supports removal. It told the student body in a letter that erasing Lee from the university was "not a call to erase our history, but rather a call to end the exultation of a figure representative of values incongruous with the values of our university."

A student petition from late last year, however, specified that it wanted to literally erase the portraits of Washington and Lee on diplomas. The motion by black law faculty to remove Washington as well failed. They told President Dudley:

It is worth exploring why the faculty has decided to make a collective statement on Lee and why the faculty has not included a demand to drop Washington in their petition. It is no longer acceptable, profitable or convenient to be associated with Lee but it is for Washington.

The erasure of namesakes is just a start for activist faculty:

"A name change is a symbolic gesture, but what we really need to invest our energy in is changing our behavior as faculty and students," [Political Science Prof. Zoila] Ponce de Leon said. "The members of our community who come from diverse backgrounds don't feel comfortable because of how we treat people — it isn't just the name."

While the *Times-Dispatch* notes the university had four previous names, it has had the same name since 1870, when President Lee died. The university, which had unbelievably remained open during the Civil War, asked Lee to take the reins in 1865 with the hope that "his reputation as the leader of the Confederate army could help attract students and funding from both the north and the south, thereby allowing the school to recover from its perilous situation," the namesakes page says. The trustees "believed that his dedication to principle and duty would inspire students and faculty."

For the moment, at least, the university calls Lee's presidency "transformative":

Prior to the Civil War, Lee had been superintendent of the United States Military Academy at West Point. During his five years at Washington College, he proved to be a creative educator whose curricular innovations transformed the classical college into a modern university. He incorporated the local law school; instituted undergraduate courses in business and journalism; introduced modern languages and applied mathematics; and expanded offerings in the natural sciences.

The students calling for his removal actually owe their self-governance to Lee:

Lee also endorsed a lasting tradition of student self-governance, putting the students in charge of the honor system that the faculty had previously overseen. "As a general principle you should not force young men to do their duty," Lee said, "but let them do it voluntarily and thereby develop their characters."

The general showed more grace and humility than those students when he wrote to his wife upon accepting the job:

Life is indeed gliding away and I have nothing good to show for mine that is past. I pray I may be spared to accomplish something for the benefit of mankind and the honour of God.

https://www.thecollegefix.com/washington-and-lee-university-faculty-demand-removal-of-robert-e-lee-from-school-name/

California Faculty Demands Free Studies For All Black Students; Charges That Education Is 'Grounded In White Supremacy'

By Steve Watson July 7th, 2020

Issuing the ultimate woke wish list, The Faculty Association at California State university has demanded that all "Black Native, and Indigenous students" should be given free tuition as a "redress for systemic anti-Black racism in the CSU."

The CFA has also charged that "the historical and longstanding infrastructures of universities" should be dismantled because they are "fundamentally grounded in a white supremacist colonial discourse and culture." *Campus Reform* reports that the CFA also wants to overturn the ban on affirmative action, and is arguing that "racial pay equity" needs to be implemented because "workload is also higher for Black faculty given that CSU faculty are majority-white, and CSU students are majority of color resulting in 'cultural taxation.'"

Without providing corroborating evidence, the faculty also claims that research conducted by Black students is "often not valued at the same level as other faculty." A further demand outlines that there be "Black faculty available to serve as reviewers for Black faculty candidates," so as to counter "white supremacy", as well as "dedicated study space" for Black students only.

The faculty also demands an expansion of curriculum for Ethnic Studies, creating Black Student/Resource Centers, and enforcing "unconscious bias" training for all students.

In addition, the faculty urges support for initiatives toward "the full abolition of the police," claiming that Black, Native, and Indigenous students can "not rely on police for safety," and that law enforcement has "racist roots" enhancing "the dehumanization of Black people." For good measure, the woke demand list also includes a petition for protection of the Black LGBTQIA+ community.

The CFA's statement says that it "recognize[s] that the movement for queer and trans liberation was catalyzed by uprisings led by QTPOC (queer and trans people of color), often against police violence." It concludes that students should continue "building on a radical and beautiful legacy of resistance."

This is indicative of demands from woke student groups across the nation. For example, at UCLA, a Professor was recently placed on leave and subject to threats of violence after he rejected requests to allow black students to take final exams at a later date, purely because of the colour of their skin. Other reports from elsewhere in the country have indicated that black students are demanding they be given leniency, or just better grades, to combat 'systemic racism'.

https://summit.news/2020/07/07/california-faculty-demands-free-studies-for-all-black-students-charges-that-education-is-grounded-in-white-supremacism/

University training teaches students to confront 'personal relationship to white supremacy'

By: Jessica Custodio July 13th, 2020

A student and professor team at the University of Florida teamed up to create a week-long training called "Academics for Black Survival and Wellness." Student Pearis Bellamy and Professor Della Mosley, created the initiative "for academics to honor the toll of racial trauma on Black people, resist anti-Blackness and white supremacy, and facilitate accountability and collective action."

The stated goals of the week were to "deepen" participants' "understanding of the history and deep-rooted nature of anti-Black racism in the U.S.," help them confront their "personal relationship to white supremacy and anti-Black racism," and to reflect on their own "personal impact" on "Black people in your immediate environmental context."

Participants were also asked to establish a "personalized plan to enhance the safety and wellness of Black students, staff, faculty, alums, and community members through your academic roles," as well as to "take action that includes time, energy, financial resources, and accountability until Black liberation is realized."

"All academics in the U.S. are socialized in white supremacy. Because of this socialization, it is imperative you can recognize and lean into the psychological resistance that comes up as it relates to understanding and engaging in work related to anti-Black racism and white supremacy," explains the training description. "We will provide material for reflection to help you understand these processes and how you may contribute to or perpetuate them."

The week-long activities included a separate activity for "Black Folx" and others focused on topics like "White Terror and Anti-Black Violence."

"As our non-Black colleagues engage with anti-racist activities, we want to create space for all Black people to heal. We will email people who are registered with information on healing spaces and opportunities for Black people in and out of academia to come together," the "Black Folx" event description stated. Young Americans for Freedom Chapter Chairman at the University of Florida, Phillip Smith, told *Campus Reform,* "it saddens me to see such racial division stoked on our campus, but it seems that over this past week UF has gone down the slippery slope of intersectionality and wokeness."

"It began with banning a tradition, but now they're blaming students for things that they have no responsibility for. My hope is that we can move past this divisiveness and go back to what made us a top ten public university in the first place." Smith added.

https://www.campusreform.org/?ID=15222

Chattanooga Officials Are on the Prowl for Anyone who Commits Hate Speech

By Chris Butler December 21st, 2019

Chattanooga officials are clamping down on hate speech through a program called Hatebase, but they will not specify what is and is not hate speech. *The Chattanooga Times Free Press* defines Hatebase as "an early warning system that helps identify situations of concern" to stop mass violence before it begins.

But how do city officials define hate speech? *The Tennessee Star* posed that question to the office of Chattanooga Mayor Andy Berke in an email Friday. City spokesman Kerry Hayes responded with this:

"City staff do not define hate speech, as that is not the purpose of the Mayor's Council Against Hate or the Hatebase tool," Hayes said. Hayes also said no city funds or taxpayer dollars pay for the city's use of Hatebase. But what happens to people government officials deem are guilty of hate speech? "We believe that anyone who commits a hate crime should be appropriately charged and adjudicated," Hayes said without specifying what, precisely, happens to people who commit hate speech — not hate crimes.

As *The Times Free Press* reported, the city has a Council Against Hate website where "residents can submit sightings or incidents of hate speech they experience or witness. The city pulls this data nightly from Hatebase and adds it to a dataset used to monitor hate speech in the community."

"The City of Chattanooga is one of the first local governments that Hatebase has partnered with in the U.S.," the paper reported.

"Hatebase originated from the Sentinel Project, an international nonprofit based out of Toronto that works to prevent genocide and mass atrocities through engagement and cooperation with victimized populations across the globe." According to *DigitalJournal.com*, "Hatebase has gathered a growing list of over 3,600 terms considered to be hate speech."

Tennessee has at least one other similar program. As *The Star* reported last month, Williamson County School System officials can, if they choose, monitor students' online activity 24 hours a day, seven days a week, and punish students if they say something unsuitable. School administrators are the ones who decide what is and isn't unsuitable. As of this year, school system officials do this through a program called Gaggle. School system officials set up the program to help with student safety issues. WCS spokesman Cory Mason said Gaggle monitors student accounts "for inappropriate or concerning words and images that have been placed on the WCS server."

"Some of the things it looks for include references to drug and alcohol use, self-harm, threats, etc.; the same student behaviors school administrators have addressed for years," Mason said in an email.

https://tennesseestar.com/2019/12/21/chattanooga-officials-are-on-the-prowl-for-anyone-who-commits-hate-speech/?fbclid=IwAR1rQ0qxnljTQCGcsQ7DzVLFaCdkAiNx2oU6L97JN9pFoBIBWBbRnFwIbCs

School district scraps traditional 'A-F' grading system for kinder, gentler model

By Christian Schneider February 12th, 2020

As a kid, I always kicked into full subterfuge mode on the days I received my report card. In order to keep my report card hidden, I suddenly engaged in secret operations that would be the envy of any World War II-era spy. Hiding secret documents from the Nazis would have been child's play compared to hiding my grades from my parents (who often only found out report cards had been issued weeks after the fact, after talking to other parents from the school.)

In the old days, it was easy for my parents to see that I was slacking off in school. They would simply look at the report card and see five or six subjects with a letter between "A" and "F" next to them. (Legend has it that a century ago, "E" was dropped as a grade, allegedly because some schools thought it would be confused for "Excellent.") Yet after a hundred-plus years of the standard "A-F" grading system, many modern schools have deemed it to be antiquated. Some districts have moved to their own proprietary grade scales in order to alleviate the shame a student may feel when earning a "D" or an "F." This week, I received my second-grade daughter's report card from the Madison Metropolitan School District, on which she was given a grade of "EX," "M," "DV," or "E."

According to the key provided, these abbreviations stand for:

- "Exceeding" – Student consistently exceeds grade-level expectations for the end of the year.
- "Meeting" – Student consistently meets grade-level expectations for the end of the year.
- "Developing" – Student is developing understanding and is approaching grade-level expectations for the end of the year.
- "Emerging" – Student begins to show initial understanding of grade-level expectations for the end of the year.

This grading scale, used district-wide, has been in place for a decade. But as you can see, every grade is dripping with optimism, presuming every child is on the road to excellence – the only thing they are being graded on is the speed at which they are attaining complete world knowledge.

As a kid, I would no doubt love this scale – explaining to my parents that I wasn't lazy, I was simply "Emerging," would certainly have saved my rear end a few unwelcome meetings with a kitchen spoon. (Also, isn't every human being constantly "developing?" If nobody ever developed emotionally past second grade, the only job available to them would be U.S. president.) But as a parent, I have no clue how my child is doing in school. None of these "grades" correspond to the "A to F" scale – further, they are all relative to what is expected by the end of the year, not specifically how well a child did during the time period tested.

In fact (warning: proud parent alert), my older daughter frequently received mixed grades on this scale during elementary school, and now she earns straight "A's" on the standard scale being used in high school. (Lest anyone think the high school deserves credit for sticking with tradition, it is proposing a new "grade floor" to give students an automatic 40 percent credit for not turning in assignments, and allowing them up to 90 percent credit for turning in assignments late.)

The two scales don't match up largely because the new grades assigned don't address a specific class or subject – they deal mostly with behavior. The "Exceeding-Emerging" scale applies to 40 different classifications. Instead of being graded on "math" or "science," my daughter is being graded on "Tells a story or describes an experience," "cooperates with partners and in groups," and "understands and identifies stages in the life cycle of insects."

Of course, none of this gives any indication as to how she's really doing in school. A friend of mine noted that her school had recently moved to a number system, where a "4" was the best and "1" was the worst. "But a 3 meant that your kid is doing fine whether the kid had As or Cs," she told me. "You didn't learn the truth until middle school."

Sure, if your child is receiving a lot of grades of "Emerging," it might be time for you to worry – but the sugar-coated classifications only feed the idea that every child is equally brilliant, and they simply develop at different speeds. This sort of rhetorical gamesmanship recently reared its head in California, where state lawmakers have discontinued use of the term “at risk” to describe students under adverse circumstances (criminal records, substance abuse, etc.) Instead, the state’s penal code now refers to “at promise” students, at least until that term falls out of favor and the state has to invent a new term for kids in tough circumstances.

In the old days, seeing a low grade on a report card was sounding an alarm that the kid wasn’t taking his or her studies seriously. Today, a low grade is just a suggestion that a child might have to wait slightly longer to unleash their immense cognitive abilities on the world. The only question that remains is what options are left for parents who send their kids to school districts that deserve an “F” for honesty.

https://www.thecollegefix.com/school-district-scraps-traditional-a-f-grading-system-for-kinder-gentler-model/

University of Virginia student says 'too many white people' at school's new multicultural center: report

By Edmund DeMarche February 13th, 2020

The University of Virginia on Wednesday reminded those on campus that its newly opened Multicultural Student Center is open to everyone after a viral video emerged of a student making a "public service" announcement that there were "too many white people" using the facility.

The video was posted on Twitter by the Young America's Foundation with a caption that said "leftists" at the school were "dictating who is and who isn't allowed" at the center. The unidentified woman in the video begins by saying "public service announcement."

"If ya'll didn't know, this is MSC and frankly there are just too many white people in here and this is a space for people of color," she said. "So just be really cognizant of the space that you're taking up because it does make some of us POC uncomfortable when we see too many white people in here."

She argued that white students already have plenty of recreational facilities on campus, while minority students have very few. She was cheered by what sounded like a handful of students at the end of the announcement.

The Cavalier Daily, the student newspaper, said it reached out to the student in the video but she did not immediately respond for its report. The school recently opened new student spaces to support a diverse student body, the report said.

The paper reported that the new MSC facility replaced the Center for Cultural Fluency that was located inside a basement on the campus. The old location was created in 2004 after a mixed-race female student running for Student Council was assaulted by a man who made a racial slur.

The report pointed out that the woman in the video had some support online. Her detractors called her comments racist. Brian Coy, a spokesman for the school, told the Washington Examiner that "we need to build a community that is not just diverse, but also inclusive."

https://www.foxnews.com/us/university-of-virginia-student-says-too-many-white-people-at-schools-new-multicultural-center-report

Education

From Kindergarten through college, kids and young adults are being inundated with pro communism propaganda. From Kindergarten through college, kids and young adults are being taught:

- Racial division
- Sexual and gender division
- Class division
- Anti-Americanism
- Social justice
- How to protest

- Microaggressions
- Pro-big government
- Pro-big tech
- Pro-big "Hollywood"
- Pro-big academia
- Pro-big pharma
- Pro-big medicine

Unfortunately, too many Americans are concerned about the size of their trucks, professional sports, their spa days, getting their nails and hair done, and taking vacations rather than fighting and taking down these academic tyrants with the propaganda they are shoving down the throats of today's impressionable youth.

16

The War on Fitness

Cosmo Magazine Runs Series Of Obese Women On February's 'This Is Healthy' Cover

By Marlo Safi January 4th, 2021

Cosmopolitan is featuring multiple "plus-size," "fat" women in a magazine issue that commends every body size as "healthy."

The February 2021 edition of Cosmopolitan features women of various body sizes with superimposed text reading "This is healthy! 11 women on why wellness doesn't have to be one-size-fits-all."

Callie Thorpe, a "plus size" blogger and model is among the featured women, and described to Cosmopolitan her involvement with the "body neutrality movement, which focused on what your body can do rather than how it looks."

"Plus-size people often feel like they can't be part of the wellness space," Thorpe told Cosmopolitan. "We are trolled for being fat, then can feel excluded from exercise because our bodies don't fit the narrative." Thorpe has previously described doctor's recommendations for her to lose weight, and remarks made by strangers about developing diabetes.

"People tell me that my husband is going to be a widower because I'll die of Diabetes before him," she told Not Plant Based in 2018. "And they say they'd rather have cancer than be fat."

Jessamyn Stanley, a yoga teacher who self-describes as a "healthy fat person" and "fat femme," is also featured. Stanley has a significant following on Instagram and runs fitness classes.

"A healthy fat person is an oxymoron to most people. People don't realize that they can't tell anything about someone else's health by just looking at them," she told Runway Riot in a previous interview. Stanley described experiences with "fatphobic comments" to Cosmopolitan. "I've had to accept that's how the mainstream sees me and not try to change," Stanley said. "For me, that's been very therapeutic."

While the magazine's edition aims to celebrate every body size involved in the health and wellness industry, fitness experts who have spoken out against obesity have faced backlash for citing the risk it presents for developing various medical conditions. Former "Biggest Loser" star Jillian Michaels stopped short of calling singer Lizzo healthy during an interview with Buzzfeed, instead pointing to the possibility that Lizzo has of developing diabetes.

"There's nothing beautiful about clogged arteries," Michael said to People magazine soon after the interview. "I'm not saying you are not a beautiful person, I'm not saying you're not physically beautiful, but I'm saying being obese is not a beautiful thing, it's actually a sad thing."

Obesity is associated with an increased risk of some of the leading causes of death including heart disease, stroke, diabetes and cancer, according to the Centers for Disease Control and Prevention (CDC). The obesity rate in the U.S. is roughly 38%, a number that makes Americans the heaviest in the world. According to the CDC, people of any age that are obese are at increased risk of severe illness from COVID-19. The COVID-NET report, published by the CDC in April, also found that of the patients who'd contracted coronavirus, 9 out of 10 of them had an underlying health condition. Of those patients, 48.3% were obese.

https://dailycaller.com/2021/01/04/cosmopolitan-magazine-obesity-healthy-callie-thorpe-jessamyn-stanley/

Being healthy is racist? CBS News promotes argument fat-phobia is rooted in anti-blackness

By Frieda Powers August 22nd, 2020

CBS News just erased all doubt that race can really be injected into nearly every issue facing Americans.

A new CBSN Originals documentary focused on attitudes about weight in America and highlighted the argument of a sociology professor who declared that "fat-phobia is rooted in anti-blackness." Sabrina Strings, a University of California, Irvine, professor later slammed the piece for cutting out much of her anti-blackness and white supremacy narrative.

The documentary titled, "Speaking Frankly | Fat Shaming," is set to air on CBS News Sunday and, in a description accompanying the clip on YouTube, is focused on "those trying to change the narrative and challenge stereotypes as well as those concerned that we are avoiding necessary conversations about health."

"My grandmother is a Black woman from the South, grew up during Jim Crow, and for her, being able to eat regularly was a triumph. One time she told me that she got a basket of oranges one Christmas and it was one of her happiest memories," Sabrina Strings, a University of California, Irvine, professor said in the video.

"But when she decided to move to California in 1960, as a lot of Black people were doing at the time ... she encountered for the first time a lot of White women in her integrated community who were on diets, and she was like, 'What? Why are White women on diets?' This was something that she puzzled over for years, because no one could really provide her a satisfactory answer," Strings said.

She was inspired by her grandmother's stories and went on to research the history of fat-phobia, writing a book published last year called, "Fearing the Black Body: The Racial Origins of Fat Phobia."

Strings explained that "skin color was the original sorting mechanism" in the slave trade initially.

Later, she continued, "they decided to re-articulate racial categories, adding new characteristics, and one of the things that the colonists believed was that Black people were inherently more sensuous, that people love sex and they love food, and so the idea was that Black people had more venereal diseases, and that Black people were inherently obese, because they lack self-control."

"And of course, self-control and rationality, after the Enlightenment, were characteristics that were deemed integral to whiteness," Strings contended in the CBS documentary, going on to say that "to be of the elite race and to be a Christian peoples," it was determined that one had to show "restraint" with food.

"We cannot deny the fact that fat-phobia is rooted in anti-blackness. That's simply an historical reality," Strings claimed. "Today, when people talk about it, they often claim that they don't intend to be anti-black ... they don't intend all of these negative associations, and yet they exist already, so whenever people start trafficking in fat-phobia, they are inherently picking up on these historical forms of oppression." The documentary featured other speakers as well, such as fitness guru Jillian Michaels, and others who spoke on the issues of "body positivity" and more.

But in a series of posts on Twitter, Strings made it clear she was not happy with the end product from CBS News, claiming it did not represent her views fully and that there was a "lack of medical evidence behind such assertions" made by others. "I have a hard time watching or listening to anything I'm in. I just saw the documentary for the first time right now and was very disappointed with what was mostly a traditional obesity science approach," Strings wrote.

https://www.bizpacreview.com/2020/08/22/being-healthy-is-racist-cbs-news-promotes-argument-fat-phobia-is-rooted-in-anti-blackness-963378

College warns students against 'fatphobic' phrases like 'you have such a pretty face'

By Lela Gallery August 17th, 2020

The Mount Holyoke College Office of Diversity, Equity, and Inclusion shared a guide on social media called "Phrases You Didn't Know Were Fatphobic."

Phrases included "you're so brave," "that's so flattering on you," "you have such a pretty face," "you carry yourself well," and "I'm so bad for eating this."

The college informed students on August 10 that calling someone "brave" can imply that "there's a reason" overweight people "shouldn't show off [their] bodies or be proud of them," and that "no one should be considered 'brave' for simply existing in their fat body."

"That's so flattering on you," the college said, implies that dressing oneself is about appearing "smaller" and fitting into "society's outdated thin ideal." Calling someone's face "pretty" is also off-limits, because it suggests that someone's face "is their only redeeming or acceptable" feature and "that fat is not beautiful." Saying someone carries himself or herself well "reinforces the negative stereotype" that plus-sized people are "lazy, sloppy, and not well-kept."

Certain comments about one's own eating habits were also called into question, specifically the phrase "I'm so bad for eating this."

"Not only is this phrase incredibly triggering, but it also feeds into a harmful narrative created by diet culture that teaches 'good' foods versus 'bad' foods," the post stated. "No one should feel embarrassed or guilty for eating sugar, carbs, etc. Food is essential to live, and there's no reason to fear that."

The office acknowledged that the guide was originally posted on the Instagram account The Power of Plus, which, according to the account's description, is "a size-inclusive digital community proving that fashion is for every body..." The Mount Holyoke College Office of Diversity, Equity, and Inclusion Office stated in its Instagram caption that it is "taking time to reflect on these everyday comments/phrases that are microaggressions."

"I think that there are lots of things that people are not aware of that, in general, are actually hurtful," Mount Holyoke College freshman Evelyn Bushway told *Campus Reform*.

She spoke about her own personal experience with losing weight and people complimenting her. "When people say things like that to me I feel so self-conscious of what I looked like before," she added. "Talking about weight in general is really hard to do without offending anyone but questions and statements like that said to the right (or wrong) person could be detrimental to their mental and physical health."

The college's post came during the coronavirus pandemic, which has killed tens of thousands of Americans, many of whom had underlying conditions. One of those underlying conditions, which, according to medical experts, makes one more susceptible to contracting the deadly virus, is obesity.

According to the Centers for Disease Control, "people of any age with the following conditions are at increased risk of severe illness from COVID-19." Among the conditions placing someone at "increased risk" for coronavirus is "obesity." According to the CDC's latest numbers, the prevalence of obesity in the U.S. in 2017-2018 was 42.4 percent, the 12th highest in the world.

Nauru, Cook Islands, Palau, Marshall Islands, Tuvalu, Niue, Tonga, Samoa, Kiribati, Micronesia, and Kuwait were the only countries in the world with adult obesity rates higher than that of the U.S., according to the CIA World Fact Book's most recently published data. Mount Holyoke did not respond to a request for comment from *Campus Reform* in time for publication.

https://www.campusreform.org/?ID=15457

'Peloton Husband' confused by viral fame: 'I'm grappling with the negative opinions'

By Alexandra Deabler December 6th, 2019

By now nearly everyone is familiar with the Peloton exercise bike commercial controversy. The 30-second ad spot has sparked extensive mocking online, a spoof video and even a rally around finding the actress who plays the wife in order to "help" her.Now the man who plays the husband – who has been called "abusive" and "a symbol of the patriarchy" – is speaking out about his role in the commercial, while also seemingly embracing the newfound fame on Instagram by changing his handle to "Peloton Husband."Sean Hunter, an actor and elementary school teacher in Vancouver, Canada, wrote a long response to Psychology Today about his experience with the commercial, which he shot in September, claiming when the clip was posted months later, it was "well received."

"A few comments from my friends came in and the overall consensus was that it was awesome, one even mentioning, 'I always knew you would make the big time.' I appreciated the compliments, but in my eyes it was just a small role. I was simply grateful for the experience."

However, the positive reception was short-lived when the video went viral, he says, and now he fears it will haunt him for the rest of his career.

"I couldn't believe what I was seeing. My 5 seconds of air time created an array of malicious feedback that is all associated with my face," he said in the Psychology Today essay. Those on Twitter began chastising the commercial – and the actors in it – as patriarchal, sexist and "corny."

"As my face continues to be screen shot online, I wonder what repercussions will come back to me. I pride myself on being a great teacher and developing actor, and I can only hope that this affects neither," he wrote. "I'm grappling with the negative opinions as none of them have been constructively helpful."

Hunter shares that he's concerned his students will find the commercial and potentially think differently of him – a worry he hopes does not come to fruition as he writes "this commercial has nothing to do with my ability to teach or who I am."

"Unfortunately, the problem is that viewers can mistake an actor as that person after they've seen them on television instead of a person given a script with no opinion on what they are being told to portray," he wrote. Meanwhile, on Instagram, Hunter posted a screenshot from the commercial one day ago with the caption, "Who would have thought my wife and I would be in so much controversy! Wish I kept the receipt."

https://www.foxnews.com/lifestyle/peloton-husband-speaks-viral-fame

Peloton's holiday ad made some onlookers cringe, but experts say it won't hurt the brand

By Megan Graham December 3rd, 2019

Peloton, the maker of high-end at-home fitness equipment, is getting criticized for a new holiday ad that implores viewers to "give the gift of Peloton." But the flap probably won't hurt the company, despite some onlookers complaining about what they saw as undertones of sexism and classism in the ad.

Indeed, Peloton's stock rose 4.6% on the Monday after the Thanksgiving weekend, when much of the criticism surfaced, and is up more than 25% since the stock's September debut.

In the ad, a woman receives a Peloton as a Christmas gift from her husband, then documents her usage of the bike, which costs $2,245 with a monthly $39 membership fee to access classes. The woman in the ad remarks she didn't realize "how much this would change [her]."

According to iSpot.tv, the ad first ran November 4 and has run more than 6,800 times, accounting for an estimated $13.5 million in TV spend. The ad has 15- and 30-second versions running across networks including Fox, NBC and ESPN 2. On social media, some commented that the woman's "before" and "after" looks were identical, or remarked that it was strange that a spouse seemed to be pressuring his partner with the gift to lose weight.

About two years ago, the company said it intended to shift its branding from targeting an affluent audience to include a wider range of consumers who might be willing to splurge, the Wall Street Journal reported in 2017. But the company was mocked earlier in the year in a viral tweet thread that poked fun at some of its ads, which showed Peloton's bikes in what appeared to be outrageously expensive homes.

Peloton declined to make anyone available for an interview or provide a comment. Advertising agency Mekanism, which has worked with Peloton in the past, had another spot with the "Give the Gift of Peloton" tagline on its website, but didn't respond to a request for comment on whether it worked on this particular spot.

A die-hard fanbase

Love their ads or hate them, Peloton has built a die-hard fanbase.

"It's hard to overstate the power of the Peloton brand," said Tim Calkins, a professor at Kellogg School of Management at Northwestern University. Calkins said a brand like GoPro, which primarily positioned itself as being for "big adventurers," had a hard time appealing to people who didn't feel they fit that mold. "A lot of brands struggle with, how do you be both aspirational and relatable?" he said. "Clearly here they're shooting for the aspirational."

Shelley Zalis, CEO of The Female Quotient and co-founder of #SeeHer, a movement led by the Association of National Advertisers to accurately portray women in media, said those commenting on the weight of the woman isn't the way to think about it.

"It's just about being healthy. I think that we need to not go overboard with micro sensitivity in just assuming because a man gives a woman an exercise bike, that insinuates it's to lose weight," she said. But Zalis did see room for improvement in the ad's portrayal of the woman. For instance, the woman saying "I'm a little nervous, but excited" before riding the bike. Zalis said the nervous portrayal could perpetuate a stereotype of women not believing in themselves or lacking confidence.

Another area for improvement Zalis saw was when the woman turned to her husband as if for validation. "It was just a moment where we could have had her exert her self confidence and her independence -- versus turning to him for validation," she said. At any rate, the ad has certainly gotten people talking about Peloton, which can be one mark of a successful ad.

https://www.msn.com/en-us/money/companies/pelotons-holiday-ad-made-some-onlookers-cringe-but-experts-say-it-wont-hurt-the-brand/ar-BBXGZNv?ocid=spartanntp

Personal Trainers Are 'Nazis,' Thinness is 'White Supremacy,' Says Morbidly Obese Woman at College Speaking Gig

By Peter D'Abrosca April 24th, 2019

An overweight woman who has made a career as a "fat and body positive sex therapist" appeared at St. Olaf's College to spout off about fitness trainers being Nazi's and other social justice nonsense.

"I truly believe that a child cannot consent to being on a diet the same way a child cannot consent to having sex," said Sonalee Rashatwar during her speech. "I experience diet culture as a form of assault because it impacts the way that I experience my body."

"Her speech on 'radical fat liberation' was organized by St. Olaf College's Wellness Center, Women's and Gender Studies Department, and Center for Equity and Inclusion," according to *Gateway Pundit.*

"We should be critical of the use of science and the production of knowledge to continue promoting this idea that certain bodies are fit, able, and desirable...is it my fatness that causes my high blood pressure, or is it my experience of weight stigma?" she asked rhetorically during her talk at St. Olaf's.

She proceeded to call science that suggests thin people are healthier than overweight people "fatphobic," and connect it to Nazism, because everything liberals do not like is a product of Nazism – even science.

"[O]ften actually eugenic science....eugenic science is Nazi science," she said.

For her grand finale, Rashatwar attacked personal trainers

"I do not think it's surprising that the man who shot up Christchurch, New Zealand was also a fitness instructor," she said. She then called the shooting "a clear communication that there's still an idealized body. Nazis really love this idea of an idealized body, and so it makes a lot of sense to me that a fitness instructor...might also think about an idealized body in this thin white supremacist way." In 2018, Rashatwar gave a talk at the University of Vermont where she claimed that "thinness is a white supremacist beauty ideal," which garnered significant attention.

https://bigleaguepolitics.com/personal-trainers-are-nazis-thinness-is-white-supremacy-says-morbidly-obese-woman-at-college-speaking-gig/

California may stop school fitness tests over fears they lead to bullying and body-shaming

By Alicia Lee February 6th, 2020

Push-ups, curl-ups and the dreaded one-mile run are a staple of childhood in US schools. But California may put a stop to the tests.

California Governor Gavin Newsom has proposed suspending the physical fitness tests at the state's schools over concerns that they promote bullying and body discrimination. Under current state requirements, students in grades five, seven and nine are required to take a physical fitness test, which includes the one-mile run, curl-ups, push-ups and a measure of body mass index.While the administration argues the physical assessments can cause students of different body shapes to be body-shamed or bullied, the BMI screening is particularly sensitive because it asks students to select whether they are female or male. A number of school districts have complained to the state that this is discriminatory against students who identify as non-binary, according to H.D. Palmer, spokesman for the Finance Department.

If the proposal, which was included in Newsom's budget bill for next year, passes, physical fitness testing would be suspended for three years. "Dispelling myths, breaking down stereotypes, and improving school climate is one way California is working to keep all students safe and healthy, consistent with the Governor's commitment to a California that respects all students," Palmer said in an email.

During the proposed three-year suspension, the Department of Education would consult with experts on fitness, physical education, gender identity and students with disabilities to determine whether the test needs to be modified or a new assessment should be developed.

The proposal comes as California's annual reports of the fitness test since the 2014-2015 school year show a decline in the percentage of students scoring healthy. The share of students meeting the healthy fitness zone for all six fitness standards (aerobic capacity, body composition, abdominal strength, trunk extension strength and upper body strength) decreased by 3.3 percentage points for fifth graders, 4.3 points for seventh graders and 4.6 points for ninth graders. But Palmer says Newsom's proposal will not affect students' physical fitness. "The pause in administering tests won't affect the amount or level of (physical education) that kids receive from their school," Palmer said, adding that PE classes would still be a graduation requirement. Advocates for gender identity are praising Newsom's proposal as a step forward.

"There is an objective in measuring a student's fitness. The problem is when it's defined by gender," Joel Baum, senior director for professional development at Gender Spectrum, told CNN.

The current fitness test sets different criteria for boys and girls. For example, a 12-year-old girl is considered healthy if she can do more than four modified pull-ups. But a boy of the same age is considered healthy if he can do more than seven pull-ups, according to FITNESSGRAM.

This difference in standards can put transgender and non-binary students in a tough spot, possibly even in danger, Baum said.

"If I'm a transgender boy and nobody knows, and then I don't meet the standards of a boy physically, I'm put in a difficult situation. Either I don't meet the standards and take the according grade or I compromise my own privacy and tell my teacher I was actually born as a girl," Baum said, adding that this can lead to bullying of the transgender student.

When a student who identifies as non-binary is pushed to select male or female on the BMI assessment, Baum says, that forces them to claim an identity that's not their own. "It's simply important that kids feel seen by the school that they go to," Baum said. "By recognizing non-binary people and using the right pronouns, that's a huge acknowledgment of someone's reality and experience, and it's affirming."

BMI is commonly used in the US to measure obesity. You divide your weight (in pounds) by your height (in inches) squared, and multiply that number by 703. If the resulting number is 30 or higher, a person is considered obese. But in recent years, BMI has come under scrutiny because it doesn't distinguish between fat and muscle, which can be an issue for athletic people.

Even former California Governor Arnold Schwarzenegger would be considered obese when he won the top bodybuilding title of Mr. Olympia in 1974, Schwarzenegger's spokesman told the Associated Press. "Whether the state uses fitness tests or not, Governor Schwarzenegger believes that the most important thing is that our students have access to daily physical education classes to promote a healthy and fit lifestyle," Schwarzenegger's the spokesman said.

https://www.cnn.com/2020/02/06/us/california-fitness-test-bullying-trnd/index.html

Fitness

Being in good shape and working out are now considered “sexist” and “racist.” You heard me correctly. The idea of eating clean and going to the gym to work out is being banned because the control freaks want a society of fat, out of shape, sick people. You see, you can’t control a group of well-informed, well-educated, in-shape, healthy people. You can control a group of fat, slow, sick, stupid, lazy, un-informed, under-informed and mis-informed people. Lifting weights promotes “toxic masculinity.” Going to yoga is “racist” and showcases “cultural appropriation.” Attending a spin class is “racist.” Doing CrossFit is “ableist.” Is it starting to sink in yet, folks? We’re all being slowly led to the cultural death chamber. Taking out fitness and health is exactly on the radar from the social justice warrior, terrorist Nazis.

17

The War on Masculinity

The War on 'Manly Men'

By Mark Tapson December 17th, 2020

Amid all the election mayhem and politicized coronavirus hysteria of the past several months, it is easy to lose sight of the fact that the cultural realm, not the political arena, is where the deeper threat to our freedoms and civilization lies, because the culture is where hearts and minds are won or lost. The Left has always known this, but the Right tends to obsess over the political and scorn the cultural as trivial and unserious. If we never grasp how critical it is to engage the Left on that front, we will lose the Long Game. Let's look at a couple of recent examples of one aspect of the Marxist assault on our culture in which the Left is gaining ground – their agenda to subvert our traditional norms of masculinity.

After what was widely touted in the media as a "history-making" appearance, Vanderbilt University female soccer player-turned-football kicker Sarah Fuller was recently named Special Teams Player of the Week by the Southeastern college football conference (SEC), along with Florida University player Kadarius Toney.

What did Fuller do to earn this honor? She "[t]ook the opening kickoff of the second half against the Tigers, as her perfectly-executed kick sailed 30 yards and was downed at the Missouri 35-yard line," the SEC crowed in explanation.

That's it. She was on the field for *one play* – not for a high-pressure, game-clinching field goal, but for a low, line drive of a kickoff that "sailed" a mere 30 yards. In all fairness, this kick was intended to be short in order to prevent a runback, but apparently, as a soccer goalie, longer kicks aren't her strong suit: "[The short kickoff] was designed for her because that's what she's used to striking," the head coach later tried to explain to reporters. And "perfectly-executed"? Perfectly-executed is the standard, not the exception, with kickoffs. One perfectly-executed kickoff is not an award-winning achievement – unless the kicker is a woman.

What would have happened if Vanderbilt's opponents *had* returned the kick? "Football is not a contact sport," the late Michigan State coach Duffy Daugherty is credited with quipping. "It is a *collision* sport." At 6'2", Fuller isn't petite (it's unclear what her weight is; she is the only player on the Vanderbilt roster whose weight is not listed), but it's a fair bet that if one of the male Missouri blockers hurtling downfield at full speed after Fuller's kickoff had targeted her, or if she had tried to tackle the ball carrier, the question of whether women can compete on a truly equal footing with men in a collision sport would have been settled in one single collision. To avoid that very possibility, Fuller jogged to the sidelines immediately after her kick.

Meanwhile, her co-Player of the Week Kadarius Toney returned a punt 50 yards for what proved to be the decisive touchdown of the game as his Florida team defeated Kentucky. And yet Fuller's inconsequential kick in a game in which her team was massacred 41-0 earned her equal billing with Toney. This seems suspiciously like affirmative action and virtue signaling, though her head coach tried to distance himself from it as such: "I'm not about making statements. This was out of necessity," he told the media about his choice to play Fuller, pointing out that COVID and the holiday break had reduced student availability for the kicker position to "almost nil."

The fact is, the SEC named Fuller Player of the Week, and the Left-leaning media trumpeted it as history-making, not because of outstanding play but because she is a woman who took the field for a single play in a man's game (a game which feminists – both male and female – decry as brutal and macho; but apparently it's okay when a woman takes part). She is actually being celebrated for an historic breakthrough *not* in college football, but in social justice. "Making history" is how you spin a narrative – however false – to promote a culture-changing agenda.

This is not to take anything away from Fuller's competitive spirit or her athletic ability as a women's championship soccer player. She likely would excel in a *women's* football league. But under ordinary, non-pandemic circumstances, she doesn't belong on the field alongside men in a collision sport. Affirmation action does not empower anyone; on the contrary, it demeans those it is intended to benefit and breeds resentment, distrust, and division all around. And virtue-signaling to promote a political agenda does not alter the reality that women generally are not physically designed for a game made for hulking men with a degree of upper-body strength that would annihilate the average male, much less woman. It is not misogynistic or sexist to point out what in recent memory everyone still would have considered to be a biological truth. Similarly, hulking men who conveniently "identify" as women so they can dominate women's sports don't belong in them (a growing number of female athletes very vocally agree). Such a formerly commonsense stance is now considered "transphobic" hate speech.

In related news in another cultural arena, pop star Harry Styles was celebrated this month as the first man to appear solo on the cover of *Vogue* magazine. In the cover photo and a fashion spread inside, Styles is decked out in women's clothing. Conservative commentator Candace Owens expressed her disapproval of this expression of dubious manliness on Twitter: "There is no society that can survive without strong men," she tweeted. "In the West, the steady feminization of our men at the same time that Marxism is being taught to our children is not a coincidence. Bring back manly men."

The woke internet mob lost what little it had of its collective mind over this triggering term, "manly men." Celebrities and leftist media personalities, who like to think of themselves as free-thinking individuals but who actually make up the most conformist, lockstep-thinking demographic in the world, piped up to accuse Owens of an unforgiveable lack of cool. "You're pathetic," actress Olivia Wilde shot back. Media critic Carlos Maza said Owens sounded "like the pearl-clutching puritans who've been around since the 50s and 60s. Genuinely impossible for them to be cool for even one second." Even radical Rep. Alexandria Ocasio-Cortez took to Twitter to defend Styles, claiming she got a "James Dean vibe" from his cover photo.

This may seem like a tempest in a teapot, because the fashion world, with its artsy pretentions, is ridiculous and superficial anyway, and pop stars like David Bowie have been toying with androgyny for decades. But the question this *Vogue* cover raises, like the female soccer player supposedly breaking into a man's sport, is actually a deeply significant one: why is the Left so heavily invested in discrediting and dismantling traditional sex roles? Why do woke celebrities and their fans so fervently leap to defend the notions that women can compete right alongside men in a collision sport, that men wearing dresses on the cover of a women's fashion mag is "cool," and that, as actor Kumail Nanjiani tweeted recently, "Traditional masculinity is a disease"?

The answer is that Progressives are at war with anything perceived as normal and traditional. Everything that has made us in the West who we are, and made us the freest, most prosperous, most accomplished, most *civilized* civilization in history – our religious beliefs, our values, our traditions, our art and literature, our history, our heroes, even our science – is now deemed either racist, sexist, classist, homophobic, Islamophobic, colonialist, oppressive, exploitative, or a toxic combination thereof, and must be erased. Our past and any links to it are unacceptably unwoke, and so Progressives seek relentlessly to redefine, or preferably eradicate, every cultural norm in order to remake the world according to their self-righteous, allegedly inclusive, collectivist, utopian vision.

The Left claims falsely that sex distinctions derive almost exclusively from an oppressively patriarchal *nurture*, not *nature*. This is important to their agenda because erasing such distinctions is necessary for the "abolition of the family," which Karl Marx called for openly. Why? Because the bonds of the nuclear family are the last and most resistant line of defense against collectivism and totalitarian control, and masculinity is the warrior spirit of the nuclear family. If you emasculate men by disparaging their aggressive, competitive, high-achieving drive as "toxic," and by denying the hard-wired differences between them and women, then men become neutered, the family unit disintegrates, resistance dissolves, the "community" replaces our family, and the State becomes our parental authority.

Candace Owens was not wrong when she claimed that "the steady feminization of our men at the same time that Marxism is being taught to our children is not a coincidence." True – it is no coincidence. The emasculation of Western men is a direct, intended result of the cultural Marxism that has been poisoning our youth for decades. The goal is to sap the independence and fighting spirit of masculinity and to undermine resistance to the power of the State.

Put women on a men's football team, put men in dresses, celebrate them both as virtuous milestones and mock those who think otherwise, and the distinctions and definitions of the sexes will gradually blur. Masculinity and femininity will begin to have no meaning. This is already happening. Contrary to the Left's claims, though, this doesn't make human beings freer and more evolved; it diminishes both men and women and makes us more confused about our roles and purpose in the world. It leaves us unmoored from our true nature, from God, and from each other – just as the State wants us https://www.frontpagemag.com/fpm/2020/12/war-manly-men-mark-tapson/

Gucci dresses men like little girls in emasculated male fashion show

By Life Site News August 24th, 2020

Fashion leader Gucci revealed its fully feminized, emasculated clothing creations for men during Milan's Fashion Week earlier this year, dressing young, mostly male models in outfits that aped the clothing of little girls and homeless women.

The all-out assault on masculinity took place in Milan's Palazzo delle Scintille in January, showcasing designer Alessando Michele's "deconstruction of masculinity through which he hoped to hint at nontoxic alternatives and the positivity of being strange," according to *Vogue*. If the deconstruction of masculinity were not obvious enough from Michele's designs, one model wore a shirt with the word "impotent" emblazoned across his chest. Another young man wore a pink knitted sweater with "mon petit chou" — a French term of endearment, "my little cabbage" — written in baby blue.

"In a patriarchal society, masculine gender identity is often moulded by violently toxic stereotypes. A dominant, winning, oppressive masculinity model is imposed on babies at birth," suggested fashion reviewer consortium "the skinny beep's" blog, regarding the Gucci men's fashion show.

"It condemns men themselves to conform to an imposed phallocratic virility in order to be socially accepted. In other words, toxic masculinity produces oppressors and victims at the same time," the blogger explains.

"Therefore, it seems necessary to suggest a desertion, away from patriarchal plans and uniforms," the posting continues, "deconstructing the idea of masculinity as it has been historically established."

Gucci has succeeded in that. While none of the outfits displayed at the fashion show is able to be bought off the rack, some of the components can be purchased from Gucci's online catalogue of "clothing and accessories with a gender fluid approach." There a man can pick up a pair of Mary Janes for a little over $900.

https://www.lifesitenews.com/blogs/gucci-dresses-men-like-little-girls-in-emasculated-male-fashion-show

#MeToo Is Making Colleges Teach Toxic Masculinity 101

By Avichai Scher September 27th, 2018
Updated: October 1st, 2018

Garrett Robinson is a senior at Brown University, and a running back for the Brown Bears. Late last month, he co-led a mandatory training for freshman players, but it wasn't about their skills on the football field. He taught them about the dangers of being domineering off the field, that it's OK to ask for help, and to watch the locker room talk. Robinson is a peer educator in the Masculinity 101 program at Brown, which aims to help men lead healthier lives by addressing harmful norms of masculinity.

He has led similar workshops in the past, but this year was different. "There were a few sarcastic responses playing into stereotypes of what you'd expect around this topic," Robinson said, "but mostly, people were more engaged and understood it was serious."

Brown's program is part of a growing trend on campuses to address "toxic masculinity," a term generally defined as elements of masculinity that encourage dominance and prevent men from showing emotion. Some experts identify this as a root cause of #MeToo issues. They say it can lead to self-detrimental, sexist and sometimes violent behavior, including sexual assault.

The behavior and attitudes of young men at educational institutions is under particular scrutiny as prospective Supreme Court justice Brett Kavanaugh faces accusations of sexual impropriety dating back to his high school years.

"For some men, they think if they're not raping anyone, that's enough. But we've seen that it's not. We need to train men on healthy masculinity at a young age." Many of the programs on campuses report new energy since the #MeToo movement began, while some unlikely campuses have addressed the issue for the first time because of #MeToo.

Neil Irvin is the executive director of Men Can Stop Rape, a nonprofit that runs training for men, including on college campuses, on stopping sexual assault. He said it's crucial that men break down harmful norms of masculinity. "For some men, they think if they're not raping anyone, that's enough. But we've seen that it's not. We need to train men on healthy masculinity at a young age," Irwin said.

When Robinson was a freshman at Brown, he attended a masculinity workshop for football players as part of a new effort there to unlearn toxic masculinity. He was shocked by what he heard. "Football is a very masculine sport," Robinson said. "So to hear things that I accepted as normal being challenged, like players insulting each other by saying they 'play like a girl,' made me want to get involved."

The masculinity program is led by Marc Peters, assistant director for campus engagement and community dialogue, whom the university brought on in 2014 to address masculinity issues.

Peters explains to men that treating others well starts in small ways, like how they talk, and that it's worth doing for their own growth and relationships, not just to benefit others. His message spoke to Robinson, who quickly got involved with the program as a peer educator.

In 2016, the masculinity program significantly expanded. Guided by Peters, Robinson and a few other students created a curriculum, Pedagogy Against the Patriarchy, to expand and codify their work in order to educate other men's groups outside of football.

The demand for trainings grew last spring, moving beyond sports teams to other men's groups, like men's acapella and Ultimate Frisbee, but also to co-ed groups. Kiana Phillips, a residential peer leader on campus, brought peer masculinity educators to her dorm to co-lead a training for men and women after she noticed some men being domineering and disrespectful to women, particularly one man touching a female student in unwelcome ways. "Brown is a progressive school, but not everyone here is active in the conversation"

"The workshop had us grapple with, do you ever have to think about walking safely at night, being interrupted, what you should wear to be taken seriously," Phillips said. "It helped men understand privilege, and the women in the room could give feedback." Phillips said she noticed improved behavior from men afterward, but the man who had touched the female student didn't attend. "Brown is a progressive school, but not everyone here is active in the conversation," she said.

At University of Wisconsin-Madison, such peer trainings are run by men and women. Their program, Men Against Sexual Assault, is run by a woman, Colleen Whitley, a senior at the school and a survivor of sexual assault.

"It's really important to have both men and women lead training," Whitley said. "Men need to hear different perspectives. All women have experienced toxic masculinity, whether assault or microaggressions."

She said her group's sessions focus on survivor support, but also discuss the root causes. "We look at how toxic masculinity contributes to sexual assault," Whitley said. "We also look at the continuum of harm, like pornography, which is often violent toward women, or just whistling at a woman on the street," she said.

She said that since #MeToo emerged, she's noticed more interest in the conversation, but also more fear from men, something Peters, the Brown administrator, also reports. "More men are interested in learning what constitutes sexual assault and what toxic behavior looks like," Whitley said. "But there is confusion and anxiety for men about the 'sudden' attention to these issues when in reality this movement is not new."

While the term "toxic masculinity" is largely uncontroversial at liberal schools, it can still be quite polarizing, particularly in right-wing or religious communities who may see it as a threat to traditional gender roles. Biola University, an evangelical Christian school in southern California, which made headlines last year for their dubious treatment of transgender students, held its first ever event discussing toxic masculinity last spring.

Jordan Lansbury, a residence hall director there, was one of two organizers who planned and produced the event. He said that the #MeToo movement helped open up support for the conversation, which wound up being the most well attended event during their sexual assault awareness month.

"We made the point that men have to be kind and compassionate, and we cite examples of Jesus behaving this way," Lansbury said. "It's against Christian values for men to abuse their power, physically or culturally." After the event, students wrote down what they learned on cards. Lansbury relayed some of the messages:

"There is no reason for a woman to be less of a person."

"It was really helpful to think about the lack of hesitancy Jesus had in speaking to the woman at the well."

"I learned that the idea of "being a man" is made up." Lansbury said he's encouraged by the response to the event and sees no reason why religious schools can't address these issues. "The conversation will continue," he said. "The #MeToo movement has made it impossible to ignore."

https://www.thedailybeast.com/metoo-is-making-colleges-teach-toxic-masculinity-101

John Mayer We Need a New 'Male Contract' ... Screw This Alpha Male BS

By TMZ October 8th, 2018

John Mayer wants to can the idea that men must be alpha males and take what they want -- including women -- and replace it with a new doctrine focused on respect and sensitivity.

The guitar-slinging crooner was doing a cancer benefit show Sunday night at the Modell Performing Arts Center in Baltimore when he went off on a tangent about toxic masculinity, which he called a "bulls**t" alpha male contract that's nailed into boys' heads from a young age.

He says the sentiment that a man should get an erection at the sight of every woman he wants is crap. John added the so-called "trauma" men might feel when a woman turns them down ... is something men just have to get over. His new idea on how to raise boys ... teach 'em that the world isn't theirs, and they're not definitely not entitled to every woman. It's worth noting this rant came right after John performed "Daughters."

He never calls him by name, but it's pretty clear John's referring to newly sworn-in Supreme Court Justice Brett Kavanaugh. There was some awkward silence as he made his point, but eventual applause once he got it all out. He later apologized for talking about such a sensitive subject during the concert.

https://www.tmz.com/2018/10/08/john-mayer-alpha-male-toxic-masculinity-women/

Millennial Men Ditching Traditional 'Masculine' Values, More Likely To Embrace 'Emotional Strength'

By Ben Renner December 1st, 2018

VANCOUVER — As the famous Village People song declares, "*Every man wants to be a macho macho man / To have the kind of body, always in demand.*" But are "macho macho" mindsets becoming a thing of the past? A new study finds that male millennials are drifting away from stereotypical masculine values.

The research, led by the University of British Columbia, showed that younger men tend to value selflessness, social engagement, and health over traditional male ideals like physical strength and autonomy.

Of course, physique and independence were still prominent values for the 630 Canadian men aged 15 to 29 who took part in the survey, just not as important to participants as selflessness. In fact, selflessness was by far the top-rated male value. Nine in 10 respondents said that men should should help others, and 88 percent of the respondents agreed that men should be open to new ideas, new people, and new experiences. Eight in 10 felt it imperative that a man gives back to his community.

"Young Canadian men seem to be holding masculine values that are distinctly different from those of previous generations. These values may run counter to long-standing claims that young men are typically hedonistic, hypercompetitive, and that they risk or neglect their health," notes lead author John Oliffe, nursing professor and head of the men's health program at UBC, in a news release.

Maintaining tip-top health was also important to the vast majority of men, but that didn't mean having chiseled abs and twenty-four inch biceps, or "pythons," as Hulk Hogan would often say. Three-quarters of participants did feel that physical strength was important, but that finding was still notably less than the 87 percent who agreed a man should embody intellectual strength or the 83 percent who viewed emotional strength as highly important. Similarly, only 78 percent of men listed autonomy as a defining "male" characteristic.

"As a millennial myself, I can see these values reflected in the lives of men around me," says study co-author Nick Black, managing partner at Intensions Consulting, a research firm that helped carry out the survey. "They want to be both caring and strong, both open to others and self-sufficient, and they see no contradiction in these values."

The researchers believe millennial men are widening their value structure and questioning what it truly means to be masculine. The study was published April 16, 2018 in the journal *Psychology of Men and Masculinity.*

https://www.studyfinds.org/millennial-men-ditching-masculine-values-embracing-altruism/

'Traditional masculinity' deemed harmful, could lead to sexual harassment, medical group says

By Lukas Mikelionis January 9th, 2019

It's all your fault, men.

For the first time in its history, the American Psychological Association (APA) released guidelines concerning men and boys, saying that so-called "traditional masculinity" not only is "harmful" but also could lead to homophobia and sexual harassment.

"The main thrust of the subsequent research is that traditional masculinity – marked by stoicism, competitiveness, dominance and aggression – is, on the whole, harmful," reads the news release by the famed association.

"The main thrust of the subsequent research is that traditional masculinity – marked by stoicism, competitiveness, dominance and aggression – is, on the whole, harmful." — The American Psychological Association. It notes that research shows "traditional masculinity is psychologically harmful and that socializing boys to suppress their emotions causes damage that echoes both inwardly and outwardly."

The 36-page document goes on to coin "masculinity ideology," which stems from traditional masculinity, and claims that it harms boys and men. "Traditional masculinity ideology has been shown to limit males' psychological development, constrain their behavior, result in gender role strain and gender role conflict and negatively influence mental health and physical health," the report warns. The "masculinity ideology" is defined by the APA as "a particular constellation of standards that have held sway over large segments of the population, including: anti-femininity, achievement, eschewal of the appearance of weakness, and adventure, risk, and violence."

The research goes on to suggest that masculine boys may put their energy toward disruptive behaviors such as homophobia, bullying and even sexual harassment rather than strive for academic excellence.

"Though men benefit from patriarchy, they are also impinged upon by patriarchy," said Ronald F. Levant, EdD, a professor emeritus of psychology at the University of Akron and co-editor of the APA volume "The Psychology of Men and Masculinities." The new paper also advises clinicians how to address the problems of their own bias when treating boys and men, and urges to address how "power, privilege, and sexism work both by conferring benefits to men and by trapping them in narrow roles."

https://www.foxnews.com/health/american-psychological-association-deems-traditional-masculinity-harmful-could-lead-to-sexual-harassment

P&G Challenges Men to Shave Their 'Toxic Masculinity' in Gillette Ad

By Alexandra Burell January 14th, 2019

One of the manliest brands in men's products has hit on an unusual strategy for divided times: questioning "toxic masculinity."

Gillette, the Procter & Gamble Co. brand that for three decades has used the tagline, "The Best A Man Can Get," is building a new campaign around the #MeToo movement, a risky approach that will be the latest test of how successfully big consumer brands can navigate tricky social movements. The ad, created by the brand's ad agency Grey and titled "We Believe," opens with audio of news about the #MeToo movement, bullying and "toxic masculinity." A narrator goes on to dispute the notion that "boys will be boys," asking, "Is this the best a man can get? Is it? We can't hide from it. It has been going on far too long. We can't laugh it off, making the same old excuses."

"This is an important conversation happening, and as a company that encourages men to be their best, we feel compelled to both address it and take action of our own," said Pankaj Bhalla, Gillette brand director for North America, in an emailed statement. "We are taking a realistic look at what's happening today, and aiming to inspire change by acknowledging that the old saying 'Boys Will Be Boys' is not an excuse."

But in a sign of the risks Gillette is taking, the ad quickly provoked passionate rebukes online.

"The video is sad and depressing while putting ALL men in a bad light," one Twitter user wrote. "Men aren't just waking up to bad things that are going on. There have always been good men. Bad ones too, yes, but the same can be said about women." The new Gillette ad was meant to inspire positive behavior but spends too much time exposing the behavior that men have been criticized for, said Susan Cantor, chief executive of branding firm RedPeak. "Men are saying, we feel marginalized, criticized and accused rather than feeling inspired empowered and encouraged."

P&G said it has no plans to pull the spot in the face of some negative reaction. "We recognize it's sparking a lot of passionate dialogue—at the same time, it's getting people to stop and think about what it means to be our best selves, which is the point of the spot," Mr. Bhalla said. P&G is among the companies that in recent years have used advertising as a platform to promote their stance on topics such as gender equality, immigration and gun control. The company is perhaps best known for its lauded "Like a Girl" ad campaign for feminine-care brand Always and "Stress Test" for deodorant brand Secret.

But brands diving into charged social issues risk turning off customers who don't agree with their stance, don't believe it is authentic or consider it poorly handled. Last year, many Twitter users slammed Dodge Ram Trucks for using audio of a Martin Luther King Jr. speech in a Super Bowl ad for its Ram pickup truck that promoted public service, seeing it as a sales stunt. Dodge has said it was celebrating Dr. King's words and had the approval of his estate.

The new Gillette ad is risky, said Dean Crutchfield, CEO of branding firm Crutchfield + Partners. It "creates a credible, believable, and upfront conversation that takes brutal honesty and tough decisions," he said. As a result, it could appeal to millennials who care about what companies stand for, he said. "There's a demand for this, for purpose, for brands to be tackling tough issues in the moment."

But the ad could backfire and alienate Gillette's base, Mr. Crutchfield cautioned. "Does the customer want to be told they're a naughty boy? Are you asking too much of your consumer to be having this conversation with them?"

Nike Inc.'s ad campaign featuring former NFL quarterback Colin Kaepernick, who had led player protests for racial justice during pregame national anthem ceremonies, generated both praise and boycott threats when it debuted last September.

Nike appeared to weather any backlash from the effort, which was part of the 30th anniversary of the footwear giant's "Just Do It" campaign. The company last month reported sales rose 10% in the latest quarter, driven by growth in both shoes and apparel. Nike Finance Chief Andrew Campion said in a conference call with analysts that the campaign "reignited brand heat in North America." The Gillette ad takes a different approach, according to Ms. Cantor. "The difference between this ad and Nike's controversial ad is that Nike is saying, 'Believe in something even if it means sacrificing everything,'" Ms. Cantor said. "It's an endorsement of conviction, but not telling you what to believe. They weren't explicitly supporting a certain behavior or admonishing a certain behavior."

While misfires could hurt brand reputations in the short term, they don't usually have long-term effects. A 2017 commercial in which Kendall Jenner joins a protest march and hands a Pepsi to a cop was accused of trivializing the Black Lives Matter movement. PepsiCo Inc. pulled the ad from its official YouTube channel and stopped running it on TV. "Pepsi was trying to project a global message of unity, peace and understanding," a PepsiCo spokesman said then. "Clearly we missed the mark, and we apologize."

But the ad didn't have an evident impact on sales. In subsequent quarters, PepsiCo blamed sluggish demand for its sodas in North America on the company's focus on healthier drinks. The company's soda sales have improved in recent quarters after the company ramped up advertising and returned more shelf space to its sodas.

In October, P&G reported its strongest quarterly sales gains in five years, snapping a stretch of lackluster growth during which the maker of products from Pampers diapers to Crest toothpaste has struggled to adapt to rising competition, higher costs and a consumer shift toward smaller brands. Sales in the grooming business that includes Gillette rose 10% in the U.S. But Gillette has been losing market share to online upstarts like Dollar Shave Club and other smaller brands. To compete, Gillette has been cutting prices and coming up with new ways to attract customers, such as personalized 3-D printed razor handles.

https://www.wsj.com/articles/p-g-challenges-men-to-shave-their-toxic-masculinity-in-gillette-ad-11547467200

Professors Claim Marine Corps Suffers from 'Toxic Masculinity,' 'Fraternity' Culture

By Craig Bannister May 30th, 2017

Marines are so masculine it's "toxic," a Marine college professor declared in an interview with Vox.com.

"Women are more unwelcome in the Marines than in any other branch of military service," Vox writes:

"The Obama administration opened the door for women to serve in combat roles. The unhappiest service about that order? The Marine Corps."

Prof. James Joyner of Marine Command and Staff College blames the problems arising from the introduction of females into the Marines on the Corps' 'toxic masculinity culture." Another professor faults Marines for acting like frat boys:

"The corps acts like a fraternity, according to Emerald Archer, an expert on women's advancement at Mount St. Mary's University in California. Many Marines, she said, believe that integrating women would ruin that brotherhood." Even advertising for female recruits has reinforced the fraternity mindset, Vox claims:

"The ad, titled 'Battle Up,' was meant to let women know they're welcome in the Marine Corps. But it also inadvertently refocused attention on the service's well-earned reputation for being a fraternity that often marginalizes or mistreats female troops." The struggle to integrate women into the Marine Corps in nothing less than a battle for the institution's very "soul," Vox concludes: "So as the service tries to win battles around the world, the most important fight may be the one closest to home: the battle for the soul of the Marine Corps."

https://www.cnsnews.com/blog/craig-bannister/professors-claim-marine-corps-suffer-toxic-masculinity-fraternity-culture

Men's cuddling group aims to redefine masculinity and heal trauma

By Aneri Pattani March 25th, 2019

Twice a month, half a dozen men gather in Plymouth Meeting to help each other work through past traumas. Their chosen method of healing? Cuddles. It may seem odd, but members of the Men's Therapeutic Cuddle Group say the practice has helped them cope with everything from childhood sexual abuse to the loss of family members when they were young.

The two-year-old group draws men from various backgrounds: a 37-year-old Mormon who works as an airport gate agent, a 57-year-old married father of three, a 62-year-old retiree. There is a range of sexual orientations. At a time when traditional ideas of manhood are facing scrutiny and such terms as toxic masculinity are becoming more widely known through the MeToo movement, the group aims to provide new ways for men to express themselves.

"So often, we're taught that to be an emotional stoic is the mark of manhood," said Scott Turner, a 46-year-old interior designer and co-founder of the group. "If you show any emotional weakness or vulnerability, that's a failure to your title of a man."

But "if we expect men to be emotionally sensitive to the needs of others, they first need to be able to build an emotional vocabulary," he said. Part of that involves learning that physical touch extends beyond aggression or sex. Platonic affection can be a doorway to emotional closeness. "It's not the ends of what we're doing," Turner said. "It's part of a larger toolbox of healing."

Unlike professional cuddling services, which are gaining popularity in cities across the United States, the group charges no fees and members are not required to undergo training. Although the meet-ups are not open to the public (members must be interviewed and approved), the group held a demonstration for The Inquirer.

At the beginning of the session, everyone agreed not to engage in sexual touch and to ask for consent before each action. They gathered in a huddle and breathed meditatively.

The cuddling started with men pairing up to do "the motorcycle hold," in which one man sits with his back against another man's chest, as if they were riding together on a motorcycle. Some massaged their partner's shoulders or hands, while others stroked the other person's beard. Many closed their eyes as the room fell into silence. After 15 minutes, they switched to a new partner.

For the second half of the session, the men cuddled as one large group in what they call a "puppy pile." Men lay with their heads in each other's laps, chatted, and joked. It's meant to be a space where men feel safe sharing their innermost thoughts, said Kevin Eitzenberger, 57, who founded the group with Turner. That can be challenging in other areas of their lives, where they're expected to be "the strong provider."

In the group, "they learn it's OK to be a little fractured," Eitzenberger said.

The importance of vulnerability

As a child, TJ McDonnell was molested by a neighbor. He didn't tell anyone, ashamed he'd done something wrong. For years, he kept his distance from others. "I never connected with people very well, even my siblings," said McDonnell, now 62 and living in Montgomery County. Getting therapy and attending a support group helped, but McDonnell credits the men's cuddling group for teaching him that emotional intimacy and physical touch aren't always abusive.

"It allowed me to experience what good friendships are, what brothers are," he said.

Another member, Ryan Hancock, has become like a son to McDonnell. Hancock's children even call McDonnell grandpa. "These types of groups can be healthy and helpful for men and women," said Chris Liang, a licensed psychologist and associate professor of counseling psychology at Lehigh University. Liang researches the effect of masculinity on health and was part of a board that helped the American Psychological Association (APA) formulate new guidelines on working with boys and men.

The guidelines highlight ways in which traditional views of masculinity — such as men are tough and never cry — harm their emotional and physical health. Studies show that men who strongly believe in masculine norms are less likely to get preventive health care, more likely to drink heavily and use tobacco, and more likely to hold negative attitudes toward seeking mental-health services.

Many men never learn healthy ways to deal with stress, Liang said. Then, it can emerge in harmful ways. According to the APA, men commit 90 percent of homicides in the U.S. and represent 77 percent of homicide victims. They're also more than three times as likely as women to die by suicide, and their life expectancy is nearly five years shorter, largely because of both violence and the health impact of stress.

Liang hopes that such groups as the cuddling meet-up can help men move beyond one restrictive definition of masculinity. Although those with more serious concerns may want to seek therapy, he said, "if this is something that's more comfortable for men ... then it can do a whole lot of good."

A growing movement of men's support groups

When Kevin Eitzenberger was 11, his 7-year-old brother died. Growing up, Eitzenberger didn't spend much time with his father. The two had little in common. Both experiences left Eitzenberger without a role model to show him what it meant to be a man. "It led me to believe I was less than," he said. "That I wasn't manly."

In 2008, he discovered a group called the ManKind Project (MKP), which would help him overcome that feeling. Founded about 30 years ago, MKP is a nonprofit focused on building male community through more than 900 men's support groups in dozens of countries.

"We want men to come in and figure out what their ideal of manhood is," said Boysen Hodgson, communications director of MKP in the U.S. "It's not something that can be imposed or prescribed to you."

The group doesn't focus on cuddling, but it does promote the idea of being open and vulnerable with other men.

"Asking for affection, asking for time, asking for help from other men is scary," Hodgson said. "But it's a very important skill for men to learn."

Studies published in 2010 and 2014 found that participating in MKP programming improved men's psychological well-being for up to two years.

For Eitzenberger, MKP helped him realize that wanting a connection with other men and seeking their acceptance was OK. It led him to start the cuddling group.

Now he receives about two requests a week from people looking to join the meet-up.

A man among men

At the cuddling group demonstration, Ryan Hancock absentmindedly touched TJ McDonnell's ear. Later, McDonnell squeezed in between Turner and Eitzenberger lying on the floor, calling himself "the cream in the cookie." In this setting, touch was no more notable than asking about someone's day. Some men teared up as they discussed their regrets as fathers. Others were playful. At the end of the session, the group huddled and took turns completing the phrase, "As a man among men, I feel..."

"Grateful to be with all of you," Turner said.

"Worthy of connection," Hancock said.

McDonnell, going last, said, "Loved, accepted, and included."

https://www.inquirer.com/health/men-cuddling-group-healing-trauma-mental-health-20190325.html

TYRANNY ALERT: Virginia to OUTLAW Krav Maga, Brazilian Jiu Jitsu, kickboxing, Tai Chi, firearms instruction and self-defense training under proposed law SB64

By Mike Adams November 27th, 2019

The State of Virginia, now entirely run by truly insane Democrats who support infanticide and child murder, is proposing a new 2020 law known as SB64 which will be taken up by the Democrat-run Senate beginning January 8, 2020.

The law would instantly transform all martial arts instructors into criminal felons. This includes instructors who teach kickboxing, BJJ, Krav Maga, boxing and even Capoeira. It would also criminalize all firearms training classes, including concealed carry classes. It would even criminalize a father teaching his own son how to use a hunting rifle.

Specifically, the law says that a person "is guilty of unlawful paramilitary activity" (a class 5 felony) if that person:

"Assembles with one or more persons for the purpose of training with, practicing with, or being instructed in the use of any firearm, explosive, or incendiary device, or technique capable of causing injury or death to persons..."

The phrase "technique capable of causing injury or death to persons" covers all forms of martial arts and self-defense training, including Krav Maga, BJJ, boxing and other contact martial arts such as Tae Kwon Do or Tai Chi. Under the proposed law, all forms of self-defense training — including hand-to-hand martial arts training — would be considered "paramilitary activity," even if the training consists of private classes involving just one instructor and one student. That's because every form of martial arts training imparts skills which could be used to cause injury to other persons. In fact, according to the language of the law, just "one" person learning such arts is a felony crime, which means that watching a DVD on Krav Maga would be a felony crime.

https://www.naturalnews.com/2019-11-27-tyranny-alert-virginia-to-outlaw-krav-maga-brazilian-jiu-jitsi-kickboxing-firearms-instruction-sb64.html

Female Driver Says Gas Pumps Are Sexist Because They're Designed For Men And Hurt Her Small Hands

By Ellie Kildare No Date

A London woman has accused gas stations of being sexist since the pumps are designed for men and are therefore too big for her hands, causing her pain. The problem is so serious that she now has to have her male partner pump gas for her. Does she have a point?

1. **Melanie Morgan struggles to squeeze the pump.** The 31-year-old snapped photos of herself trying to grip the pump at her local gas station to prove to her partner, Jared Griffiths, that there's a problem. It's clear she was struggling since her hands are small, but are gas stations really guilty of "everyday sexism," as she accused them of on Twitter?
2. **Her partner initially laughed off her pain.** When Melanie first told Jared what she was experiencing at the pump, he thought it was a bit of a joke. "I'd come back to the van having got out and filled up and when I got back in I was flexing my hand, like when you've been writing a lot, and I was like 'ooh actually that quite hurts," Melanie said. "I said this to my partner and he kind of laughed it off and I said 'no really it hurts, you have to grip it really hard when you've got smaller hands.' It's ridiculous that that's something I have to think about."
3. **The best dating/relationships advice on the web - Sponsored** If you're reading this, check out Relationship Hero, a site where highly trained relationship coaches get you, get your situation, and help you accomplish what you want. They help you through complicated and difficult love situations like deciphering mixed signals, getting over a breakup, or anything else you're worried about. You immediately connect with an awesome coach on text or over the phone in minutes.
4. **She never realized what a serious issue this was until recently.** "I have fairly small hands. I'm short, I'm 5ft 3, so I'm fairly small generally but I imagine there aren't many men who have the same size hands as me," Melanie said, according to The Daily Mail. "When I was younger I remember thinking 'ooh this is difficult' but then it's also something you're new to doing. But as an adult now who does it regularly it suddenly occurred to me one day that I don't think most people find filling up the car painful, most people don't have to think 'this doesn't work'."

5. **While not intentional, Melanie believes the issue needs to be looked into.** "I'd assume there's some kind of reason that it needs to be the broadness it is around that point and you have to pull it in tight, of course, but I think it's a classic overlooked issue," she said. "No one's going to complain about it and those who tend to design things like that I assume are typically male engineers. My partner fills the van up now, and started doing it in October, so I don't have to deal with it."
6. **She wants to buy an electric car to avoid the problem.** Having an electric car would mean Melanie no longer has to fill up at the pump, eliminating the issue altogether. However, electric cars are still pretty expensive, it may be awhile before the private tutor can make that happen.
7. **Are gas stations sexist?** Probably not, but it's an interesting debate, I suppose...https://www.bolde.com/female-driver-gas-pumps-sexist-designed/

Employers Should Censor 'Sports Talk' Among Male Workers, Says 'Gender Balance Expert'

By Dan Lyman January 27th, 2020

Male colleagues discussing sports in the workplace create an unwelcoming environment for women, according to a 'gender balance expert' who believes the practice should be curbed by employers.

Ann Francke, CEO of the Chartered Management Institute, claims sports banter makes many women feel excluded and that it can devolve into sexually explicit conversation. "A lot of women, in particular, feel left out. They don't follow those sports and they don't like either being forced to talk about them or not being included," Francke told the BBC. "I have nothing against sports enthusiasts or cricket fans – that's great. But the issue is many people aren't cricket fans."

"It's a gateway to more laddish behavior and – if it just goes unchecked – it's a signal of a more laddish culture."

"It's very easy for it to escalate from VAR (video assistant refereeing) talk and chat, to slapping each other on the back and talking about their conquests at the weekend," she said. Francke's comments drew a wave of ridicule on social media, with Piers Morgan calling her suggestions "utter twaddle."

"We've got to stop these virtue-signaling cretins sucking all the fun out of life," Morgan tweeted. Many netizens pointed out that women often in engage in similar conversations about reality TV and celebrity gossip, and also that many women also enjoy sports. Francke's author biography describes her as an "expert on gender balance in the workplace." She has written a book on the subject and has held senior executive positions at Mars, BSI, Boots, and Yell.

https://www.newswars.com/employers-should-censor-sports-talk-among-male-workers-says-gender-balance-expert/

Masculinity

One of the most horrible and disgusting atrocities from the woke and cancel culture club is the attack on men and masculinity. Men are not allowed to be muscular, fix things around the house, grow facial hair, shoot a gun, drive a big truck, or build anything constructive. All these activities promote "heteronormativity" and "toxic masculinity" according to our psychotic rulers. Men have been under vicious attack and assault from the hard-core left for a long time. The notion of a dad being involved in their children's lives is also under attack in society. All we hear about is toxic masculinity and the need to ban dads from being around their children (you can see this in many divorce and custody cases throughout the world). The fact is, that MORE kids need to be exposed to a strong, father or male influencer in their lives, not less. Since big muscles are now banned and cancelled, the attack on men and masculinity is being increased and promoted across the board.

18

The War on Art

'You thought it would stop at statues?' Darwin exhibits at UK's Natural History Museum may be canceled for being 'offensive'

By RT September 7th, 2020

The UK's Natural History Museum is reviewing options for its Charles Darwin exhibits, including possible removal, after an internal review ordered amid Black Lives Matter protests found that they could be deemed "offensive."

The museum's directors are scrutinizing collections that may be considered *"problematic,"* which could lead to removal or lesser remedies, such as renaming, The Telegraph reported, citing internal documents. Artifacts from the father of evolutionary theory are among the suspects because Darwin's voyage to the Galapagos Islands on HMS 'Beagle' was one of the UK's *"colonialist scientific expeditions."*

"In light of Black Lives Matter and the recent anti-racist demonstrations around the world," the museum is re-evaluating room names, collections and statues to root out any that *"could potentially cause offense."* A large wing of the museum is named after Darwin, and a statue of the naturalist stands in the museum's main hall.

One of the documents cited by The Telegraph was a paper written by a curator arguing that *"museums were put in place to legitimize a racist ideology."* And because *"covert racism exists in the gaps between the displays,"* collections must be *"decolonized."* The journey by Darwin and Captain Robert Fitzroy to South America served to *"enable greater*

British control" – sinfully offensive in the eyes of some. A statue of Thomas Henry Huxley also could be axed, given the late scientist's racial theories. The contributions of Sir Joseph Banks could be at risk because the botanist traveled on Captain James Cook's 'Endeavor' voyage.

A sharp-eyed curator also found that the ceiling in Hintze Hall has images of cotton, tea and tobacco, *"the plants that fueled the British Empire's economy."* Collections from Swedish scientist Carl Linnaeus, who created the Latin naming system for species, and Sir Hans Sloane also are under review. Linnaeus might offend because his system led to renaming of specimens, replacing indigenous terms. Sloane was a founding father of the museum, but he profited from slavery in Jamaica.

"The Black Lives Matter movement has demonstrated that we need to do more and act faster," museum director Michael Dixon told staff in one of the documents. *"We want to learn and educate ourselves, recognizing that greater understanding and awareness on diversity and inclusion are essential."* Twitter users were taken aback by the thought of collections from Darwin and other major historic figures being canceled. *"They're decolonizing museums now,"* conservative social media pundit Ian Miles Cheong said Sunday. *"You thought they would stop at the statues?"* Other observers likened current events to George Orwell's '*1984,*' saying that 'leftists' are trying to *"completely rewrite history to suit their egos."* A New Hampshire writer said: *"They literally want to erase history, not store it somewhere so we don't repeat it."*

https://www.rt.com/uk/500027-darwin-museum-colonialist-offensive/

American flag mural at pizza shop vandalized, protested in small town

By Caleb Parke November 7th, 2018

An American flag mural in a small town in New York was vandalized after several protesters started calling for a boycott, claiming it is a symbol of hate and oppression. The town of New Paltz rallied together a few weeks ago to help raise funds and show support for the patriotic painting proposed by La Bella Pizza Bistro owner Maria Lisante to cover a rundown brick wall on the side of her building, which is across the street from an elementary school. Just days before the mural was completed, it was defaced.

Luitenant Robert Lucchesi told Fox News that police are still actively investigating the case after the graffiti allegedly appeared Monday night. Joey Garcia, a New York state corrections officer and Army National Guard veteran who organized the rally to support the flag, told Fox News he believes the perpetrator is not only disrespecting the flag but the military and country as well.

"I'm saddened and disappointed," said Garcia. "It's one thing to disagree with something but it shouldn't mean that...you must destroy it. I feel bad for the artist who has put so much time and effort into this painting." Although there has been pushback, Garcia said La Bella's has received a lot of support from across the nation since the pro-flag walk. One is Lisa McGovern, who fell victim to a yard sign-stealing SUNY professor.

"I felt like it was a little over-the-top that people were saying it is offensive," McGovern said. "It's a symbol of our country. It's non-political and for people in a small town trying to get a small business shut down is a little outrageous. People should be supporting small business, not trying to get them shut down."

The owner's GoFundMe page for the mural was originally set at $8,000 but was increased to $12,000 "due to the overwhelming support and patriotism of our community and country" to "help fun paint, materials, future maintenance and display lighting to increase visibility," Lisante wrote. As of Wednesday afternoon, they have raised more than $7,500.

https://www.foxnews.com/us/american-flag-mural-at-pizza-shop-vandalized-protested-in-small-town

University of Notre Dame to cover Christopher Columbus murals

By Shelby Copeland January 22nd, 2019

More than 130 years after their debut at the ceremonial entrance to the University of Notre Dame's Main Building, murals illustrating the life of Christopher Columbus will soon be covered up. To many, the 12 murals were "blind to the consequences of Columbus' voyage," university President Rev. John Jenkins said in a letter Sunday announcing his decision. At their worst? "Demeaning."

Italian artist Luigi Gregori painted murals that show various stages of Columbus' voyage to America. The paintings were created in the 1880s after the building's reconstruction. They were painted directly on the wall of the Main Building, which is called the "centerpiece of Notre Dame's past and present." Since the 1990s, students, faculty and guests who view the murals can read a university-provided brochure meant to give historic context to art many depict as affirming stereotypes. Jenkins now is saying that because the building is so busy, it's not an appropriate place for contemplation about the art.

Jenkins is ordering that the murals be covered with a woven material that will allow them to be occasionally displayed. The focus now is designating another area on campus to showcase high-resolution photographs of the original work -- offering more context than a brochure.

Notre Dame spokesman Dennis Brown told CNN officials are discussing many ideas for the new display of the photographs, such as adding descriptive memos on iPads and videos. "This is a good step towards acknowledging the full humanity of those Native people who have come before us," Marcus Winchester-Jones, president of the Native American Student Association of Notre Dame, said in reaction to the decision. Sex, consent, and the ancient city: A closer look at Pompeii's erotic mural of 'Leda and the Swan'

Students, alumni, staff and representatives of the Native American community have long debated whether the murals should stay or go. The president's statement said he recognized the "catastrophe" Columbus' arrival was for native people and acknowledges what he called the "darker side of the story."

"We wish to preserve artistic works originally intended to celebrate immigrant Catholics who were marginalized at the time in society, but do so in a way that avoids unintentionally marginalizing others," Jenkins wrote. The murals depict Columbus as a pioneer devout in Catholic faith. But, critics say, the realities of his exploration under the auspices of Spanish monarchs told a much less heroic narrative. Many local governments and states have recognized Indigenous Peoples Day to replace Columbus Day. St. Joseph County, Indiana -- where the university is located -- has removed Columbus Day from its official holiday schedule.

Some groups have insisted that those who criticize the 15th-century Italian explorer miss his contribution to American society. "We Knights celebrate his holiday, knowing Columbus gave voice and representation to generations of Catholics, helping pave a path for the diverse society we have today," the Knights of Columbus, a fraternal benefit society, says on its website. An article on the site says Columbus "was a man of faith and courage, not a monster." Jenkins writes the solution will respect Gregori's murals in context and the reality of what happened to Native Americans in the aftermath of Columbus' arrival. The president's announcement came "deliberately" in celebration of Martin Luther King Jr. Day, his office told CNN.

https://www.cnn.com/style/article/university-of-notre-dame-christopher-columbus-murals-trnd-style/index.html

High school may erase mural of George Washington: 'traumatizes students'

By Graham Piro May 2nd, 2019

A Northern California public school district may remove a mural of George Washington from the halls of George Washington High School due to concerns that it's offensive and demeaning to Native Americans and African-Americans.

The controversy comes after a working group determined the mural, made up of several panels, "traumatizes students and community members." But advocates for keeping the 83-year-old mural say that removing it ignores the intent of the artist and represents an attempt to erase history. In 1936, Victor Arnautoff painted the 13 panels that make up the "Life of Washington" mural at the San Francisco Unified School District campus. Arnautoff was a prominent Russian-American painter who created the murals as part of a Works Progress Administration project undertaken during the New Deal.

But a working group that met in recent months determined the artwork is highly problematic and should be archived after being removed from the walls of the school. "SFUSD convened a 'Reflection and Action Working Group' that was comprised of members of the local Native American community, students, school representatives, district representatives, local artists and historians," Laura Dudnick, spokeswoman for the district, wrote in an email to *The College Fix.*

The group held four public meetings between December 2018 and February 2019 during which it received input on what to do with the mural. The group's recommendation? Archive the mural to protect the experience of students. "At its conclusion the group voted and the majority recommended that the 'Life of Washington' mural be archived and removed because the mural does not represent SFUSD values," Dudnick's email to *The Fix* continued, adding that the group considered the legacy of the artist when deciding whether or not to keep the mural up.

However, concern for the experience of students won out. Two of the 13 panels are coming under fire for containing objectionable images, according to the *Richmond District Blog*. One of the images involves involves Washington gesturing toward a group of explorers who are walking by the body of a presumably deceased Native American depicted in the color gray. Another depicts Washington next to several slaves performing various types of manual labor, a YouTube video of the murals showed.

The *Richmond District Blog* reports the group's conclusion:

We come to these recommendations due to the continued historical and current trauma of Native Americans and African Americans with these depictions in the mural that glorifies slavery, genocide, colonization, manifest destiny, white supremacy, oppression, etc. This mural doesn't represent SFUSD values of social justice, diversity, united, student-centered. It's not student-centered if it's focused on the legacy of artists, rather than the experience of the students.

But Fergus M. Bordewich, a historian, wrote in *The Wall Street Journal* that the intention of the artist should be taken into account when considering the intent of the images:

The mural's painter, Victor Arnautoff, was a protégé of Diego Rivera and a communist. He included those images not to glorify Washington, but rather to provoke a nuanced evaluation of his legacy. The scene with the dead Native American, for instance, calls attention to the price of "manifest destiny." Arnautoff's murals also portray the slaves with humanity and the several live Indians as vigorous and manly. Bordewich, in a phone interview with *The Fix*, said there "is a deeply wrongheaded habit to project today's norms, values, ideals backwards in time to find our ancestors inevitably falling short."

"It betrays a very troubling intolerance of art and the ambiguity of art and the aspirations of art," he said. The mural's future is up in the air, according to Dudnick. "The superintendent and staff are now reviewing the recommendation and considering the best course of action," she wrote. "At this time there hasn't yet been any recommendation put forth before the SF Board of Education on this matter."

This is not the first time the murals have come under fire. In the late 1960s, protesters called for its removal, which the school responded to by installing another set of murals titled "Multi-Ethnic Heritage: Black, Asian, Native/Latin American." These murals display more positive images of ethnic minorities, the *Richmond District Blog* reported.

"One of the main reasons why it is controversial is because back in the [1930s] when it was painted, George Washington was the saint of the people," one student at George Washington High School told the *Golden Gate Express*. "I've talked to a bunch of students here and I honestly think that they agree it is the true depiction of history and that we all have to know who George Washington really was." Bordewich added that the "mural is not a celebration of genocide, it's a challenge to westward expansion."

"It's incredibly stupid if we try to erase history," he said. "It still happened, and you should argue about its meanings.

https://www.thecollegefix.com/high-school-may-erase-george-washington-murals-traumatizes-students/

Famed San Francisco Art Curator Out After Refusing to Ban White Artists

By Staff July 16th, 2020

Gary Garrels, a senior curator at the San Francisco Museum of Modern Art for painting and sculpture, resigned from his post Saturday after backlash from saying that the museum would continue to collect work from white artists. Garrels was confronted over the comments during a Zoom meeting after he said that banning white artists would basically be "reverse discrimination." *Breitbart* reported that a petition was launched over his "violent language" and called for his job.

The petition read, "Considering his lengthy tenure at this institution, we ask just how long have his toxic white supremacist beliefs regarding race and equity directed his position curating the content of the museum?" Garrels apologized for the "reverse discrimination" comment (which, today, is apparently reverse-reverse discrimination, an even worse offense).

"I do not believe I have ever said that it is important to collect the art of white men," he said, according to artnet.com. "I have said that it is important that we do not exclude consideration of the art of white men."

He said due to the current climate he "can no longer effectively work" there and would resign by the end of the month.

KQED.com reported that Garrels is the fifth staff member at the museum to step down in recent weeks and said the museum has been under some fire over allegations of "racial inequity from both internal and external critics."

The San Francisco Chronicle reported in 2016 that only six percent of the art displayed at the museum was produced by people of color. The museum, according to KQED, has made an effort to start showcasing more works by minorities and women. Last year, the museum announced 11 acquisitions in an effort to "strategically diversify the collection."

"This is just the beginning of what we will be able to accomplish with this fund, which allows us to broaden the scope of the stories we are able to tell in our galleries," said *Neal Benezra*, Helen and Charles Schwab director of SFMOMA. Robby Soave, a senior editor at *Reason* magazine, pointed to Garrels' apology and said that is "not the language of a white supremacist."

"Those who say otherwise—that Garrels is guilty of racism—have stripped the word of its potency," he wrote.

https://www.toddstarnes.com/values/famed-san-francisco-art-curator-out-after-refusing-to-ban-white-artists/

TRENDING: Universities nationwide remove historical artwork deemed offensive

By Graham Piro May 8th, 2019

A major nationwide trend on campuses is the removal of historic artwork depicting prominent figures or scenes that are deemed offensive or racist by today's standards.

The censorship is getting wider in scope. Controversial historical figures like Christopher Columbus and Woodrow Wilson have consistently drawn student outrage and protest, as have Confederate monuments, but other more beloved figures like George Washington and Thomas Jefferson are also beginning to attract controversy. There are many examples in recent years of universities removing or censoring artwork that has been accused of being derogatory, disrespectful, hurtful or racist, according to a survey by *The College Fix*.

Campus activists have aimed their protests at a variety of murals, statues, and other forms of artwork, demanding that they be taken down or covered up because their presences represent some sort of danger to students on campus. Oftentimes, administrators agree.

Perhaps the most prominent example has been the ongoing controversy over the Silent Sam statue at UNC. The statue was torn down at the beginning of this school year by a group of protesters. Subsequent protests also saw violence and an increased police presence on campus. The school's compromise plan to create a history center was shot down by the Board of Governors, and it now appears that the statue will remain off of the school's campus.

Additionally, a student at North Carolina Central University toppled a Confederate statue on campus, and the University of Louisville moved a Confederate statue to a Civil War site in Brandenburg, Ky. In 2017, *The College Fix* reported on more than a dozen universities that took action to censor Confederate-era artwork But beyond Confederate controversies, two consistent themes concern the depiction of African Americans and Native Americans, and how prominent figures in American history are portrayed.

Notre Dame recently made headlines for the school's decision to cover up murals of Christopher Columbus on campus. The movement to get the murals covered began in earnest in 2017, when more than 340 members of the school's community signed a letter asking the university's president Rev. John Jenkins to censor the murals. Jenkins agreed.

"Whatever else Columbus's arrival brought, for these peoples it led to exploitation, expropriation of land, repression of vibrant cultures, enslavement, and new diseases causing epidemics that killed millions," Jenkins said of Columbus's legacy, adding that the explorer's arrival was a catastrophe for native people.

Pepperdine University removed a statue of Columbus in early 2017 in the face of calls to remove the explorer from campus. As a compromise, the school said that the statue would be moved to the school's campus in Florence, Italy. Despite multiple inquiries by *The College Fix*, university officials refuse to say whether the statue has been set up, as promised, at its new location. For now, the statue looks like it's been wiped off the map.

Similarly, Dartmouth University made the decision to remove a set of murals that "depict Dartmouth founder Eleazar Wheelock bringing a cask of rum and educational books to Native Americans, including topless women, one of whom is shown trying to read an upside-down book..." The murals were described as "disturbing" and "incompatible with Dartmouth's mission and values," and were moved to an off-campus storage facility. Several controversial and prominent American historical figures have also come under fire.

A "Reflection and Action Working Group" recommended that George Washington High School in San Francisco remove a mural of

George Washington due to concerns over potentially traumatizing students despite the nuanced intentions of the mural's artist. Two panels showed Washington interacting with Native Americans and slaves.

Princeton University removed a picture of Woodrow Wilson from a dining hall, Yale removed a photo of John C. Calhoun from its Calhoun College dining hall, Duke University removed a statue of Robert E. Lee from a chapel entrance, and the University of Texas took down statues of Jefferson Davis and Woodrow Wilson from campus. Florida State University took down a statue of a descendant of Thomas Jefferson after students brought up the descendant's history of racism.

Yale censored a work of art deemed "hostile" that showed an armed Native American and Puritan standing next to one another. UW-Stout moved frontier paintings of Native Americans canoeing in a river with French trappers to "controlled" campus rooms due to potentially harmful effects on students, and the University of Kentucky also censored a mural of African Americans workers in a tobacco field and a Native American wielding a tomahawk because of concerns over microaggressions against students.

Saint Louis University, a Catholic university, removed a statue that depicted a Jesuit priest praying over two Native Americans. Universities do not only react to left-leaning complaints, though. Marquette University removed a mural of Assata Shakur after a professor spoke out about Shakur's conviction of killing a cop and presence on the FBI's Most Wanted List. The Republican governor of Kansas also called for the removal of an art display at the University of Kansas of an American flag with a striped sock in its upper left corner intended to symbolize the detention of children at the border.

"The disrespectful display of a desecrated American flag on the KU campus is absolutely unacceptable," Gov. Jeff Colyer said. "I demand that it be taken down immediately." The university removed the flag, *Inside Higher Ed* reported. The trend shows no end in sight. Cal State Maritime was recently forced to delay a decision to paint over student murals on campus after the school faced fierce backlash from students angry at the unilateral decision to censor the murals. And right now, students are demanding a Thomas Jefferson statue be removed from its location at Hofstra University.

https://www.thecollegefix.com/trending-universities-nationwide-remove-historical-artwork-deemed-offensive/

Australia: Sculpture of Man's Chest Banned From Art Exhibit Because it May Offend Immigrants

By Paul Joseph Watson July 31st, 2019

A sculpture of a man's bare chest was banned from an art exhibit in Australia because the organizers feared nudity may offend people from other cultures and religions.

Yes, really.

Sculptor Alan Goedecke, who describes the piece as "traditional" and "tame," was told by organizers of the Melbourne event that the bust "has nipples on it, you can see what gender it is so therefore it's banned."

"No one can believe it, I can't believe it, it's staggering," said Goedecke.

The owner of Collins Square, where the work would have been exhibited, said it was banned because, "More than 20,000 workers and families from a wide variety of cultures and religious beliefs visit Collins Square every day" and that "the association agreed to no nudity, no political statements, no racism."

Works by seven other artists were also banned from appearing at the exhibition.

"Ridiculous. Issues of excessive multicultural offense are shackling Western art & expression to the point of absurdity," commented Alexandra Marshall.

- Better tear down Michelangelo's David because someone might be offended.
- Better tear down Dontaello's David because someone might be offended.
- Better tear down the Venus De Milo because someone might be offended.
- Or better yet, why not just cover them all with giant burkas?

https://www.infowars.com/australia-sculpture-of-mans-chest-banned-from-art-exhibit-because-it-may-offend-immigrants/

One Of The World's Most Controversial Artworks Is Making Catholics Angry Once Again

By Katherine Brooks May 13th, 2014

There's nothing more entertaining than when a controversial cultural relic resurfaces to incite anger all over again. Such is the case this week (albeit on a much milder scale) with "Piss Christ," Andres Serrano's infamous artwork from the 1980s, set to hit the Sotheby's auction block Thursday.

You may or may not remember the powerful piece of contemporary artwork that riled devout Catholics and grumpy fiscal conservatives nearly three decades ago. (If not, we suggest you knock on the door of your angriest and oldest neighbor. You know, the one with six or seven "No Soliciting" signs taped to his or her glass door. *That* guy or gal, (s)he'll know.)

If you need a refresher history lesson, here's the jist: The work dates back to 1987, when the American artist Serrano submerged a plastic crucifix in a jar of his own urine, photographed it, and exhibited the image publicly in New York. As you might imagine, a certain subset of Christians were nonplussed at the idea of their deity being dunked in someone's bodily fluids, but outrage didn't hit an apex until another exhibition in 1989, when a few politicians expressed dissatisfaction at the fact that the offensive work was funded in part by the National Endowment for the Arts.

Senator-turned-art-critic Jesse Helms offered a concise summary of his opinion toward the "Piss Christ" creator at the time. "Serrano is not an artist. He is a jerk." The attention "Piss Christ" received continued well after the 1989 show. In 2011, protesters in France attacked and destroyed a print of the "blasphemous" work when it went on display in Avignon on Palm Sunday. And in 2012, the Catholic League got all hot and bothered about a retrospective of Serrano's career that featured the submerged Jesus photograph. Fox News predictably followed suit.

Now, in 2014, Sotheby's *dares* (read with a healthy dose of sarcasm, please) to sell the artistically significant objet d'art as part of its Contemporary Art Day Auction on May 15. With an estimated price of between $100,000 and $150,000, the nearly four-foot tall piece joins the ranks of masterpieces by Roy Lichtenstein, Mark Rothko and Andy Warhol. The Catholic League is, again, peeved. "The Catholic League will not make a bid [on the 'Piss Christ' auction]," it exclaimed to no one everyone aching to know what's on the mind of today's foremost authority on art. "But we are interested in interviewing the sucker who buys it. If you know who the lout is, please have him give us a call."

Oof.

In the end, Serrano, himself a spiritual man, has been unduly forced to defend the piece for over 25 years, despite the fact that his prolific and influential body of work stretches far beyond the one photograph. "The thing about the crucifix itself is that we treat it almost like a fashion accessory. When you see it, you're not horrified by it at all, but what it represents is the crucifixion of a man," Serrano told The Guardian in 2012. "And for Christ to have been crucified and laid on the cross for three days where he not only bled to death, he shat himself and he peed himself to death. So if 'Piss Christ' upsets you, maybe it's a good thing to think about what happened on the cross."

"Piss Christ" sold for $277,000 back in 1999 at Christie's, so there's cause to think the lot will surpass the $150,000 estimate. While we shake our heads until this dramatization of normal auction world activities passes, let's remember Bill Donahue, head of the League, and his own "artwork."

https://www.huffpost.com/entry/piss-christ-sale_n_5317545

Art History Department to scrap survey course

Margaret Hedeman & Matt Kristoffersen January 24th, 2020

Yale will stop teaching a storied introductory survey course in art history, citing the impossibility of adequately covering the entire field — and its varied cultural backgrounds — in one course. Decades old and once taught by famous Yale professors like Vincent Scully, "Introduction to Art History: Renaissance to the Present" was once touted to be one of Yale College's quintessential classes. But this change is the latest response to student uneasiness over an idealized Western "canon" — a product of an overwhelmingly white, straight, European and male cadre of artists.

This spring, the final rendition of the course will seek to question the idea of Western art itself — a marked difference from the course's focus at its inception. Art history department chair and the course's instructor Tim Barringer told the News that he plans to demonstrate that a class about the history of art does not just mean Western art. Rather, when there are so many other regions, genres and traditions — all "equally deserving of study" — putting European art on a pedestal is "problematic," he said.

"I believe that every object I discuss in ["Introduction to Art History: Renaissance to the Present"] (with the possible exception of one truly ghastly painting by Renoir) is of profound cultural value," Barringer said in an email to the News. "I want all Yale students (and all residents of New Haven who can enter our museums freely) to have access to and to feel confident analyzing and enjoying the core works of the western tradition. But I don't mistake a history of European painting for the history of all art in all places."

Instead of this singular survey class, the Art History Department will soon offer a range of others, such as "Art and Politics," "Global Craft," "The Silk Road" and "Sacred Places." Barringer added that in two or three years, his department will offer a substitute class to "Introduction to Art History." But the new class "will be a course equal in status to the other 100-level courses, not the introduction to our discipline claiming to be the mainstream with everything else pushed to the margins," Barringer said.

While concerns about the class's singular focus in Western art has led to its cancellation, student enrollment in Barringer's course skyrocketed this semester after the department's plan was announced. Over 400 students shopped the class last week, though the course is capped at 300 due to constraints in the number of sections that the YUAG can host.

Phoebe Campbell '22 — who was among the lucky 300 to enroll in Barringer's course — said student interest likely stems from positive reviews, as well as the fact that the class is being offered for a final time. According to Barringer, the class will still cover Western art chronologically from 1300 to the present and hopscotch across European art movements under the roof of the Yale University Art Gallery. Students in sections will still examine objects directly from Yale's vast collections.

In his syllabus note to potential students on Canvas, an online course management tool, Barringer wrote that the emphasis would be placed on the relationship between European art and other world traditions. The class will also consider art in relation to "questions of gender, class and 'race'" and discuss its involvement with Western capitalism, Barringer wrote. Its relationship with climate change will be a "key theme," he wrote.

Barringer has also focused attention on the course's written assignments. He said that he will invite students to write an essay nominating a work of art that has been left out of the course's curriculum or its textbook. Like the changes to the course itself, this essay is designed to challenge long-held views of art history.

"I'm really looking forward to seeing what works the students come up with to counteract or undermine my own narratives," he wrote. In an interview with the News, Campbell said she appreciates Barringer's efforts to point out the limited scope of the course.

"The class title is 'Introduction to the History of Art: Renaissance to the Present,' but in lecture and on the slides, [Barringer] calls it 'Introduction to Western Art' because he is aware, while teaching it, that it is not a comprehensive introduction to the global history of art, and that everything we talk about is from a Western perspective," Campbell said.

Campbell added that while is supportive of the changes, she hopes that the pre-modern Western course material will not be lost amongst the shuffle.

But other students expressed certain dissatisfactions with the Art History Department's decision to get rid of Barringer's class. "My biggest critique of the decision is that it's a disservice to undergrads," Mahlon Sorensen '22 said. "If you get rid of that one, all-encompassing course, then to understand the Western canon of art, students are going to have to take multiple art history courses. Which is all well and good for the art history major, but it sucks for the rest of us, which, I would say, make up the vast majority of the people who are taking [HSAR 115]."

The decision to get rid of this survey art history course resembles the English Department's move to "decolonize" its degree requirements in 2017. At the time, the department made a sequence titled "Major English Poets" optional for majors.

For years, the Directed Studies program — a six-credit sequence for first-year students focusing on philosophy, literature and political philosophy — has also fielded criticisms about its exclusive focus on the Western canon. But in an interview with the News in 2018, humanities professor and then-Director of Undergraduate Studies of the program Kathryn Slanski said while many of the authors discussed in the program are "dead white men," everyone can learn from their texts as long as they perform nuanced and analytical readings. While concerns regarding the diversity of texts taught in Directed Studies are perennial, the University is "up-front that Directed Studies is an introduction to the Western tradition and its influence," Slanski said.

Political science professor Steven Smith, who teaches a Directed Studies class in the fall, agreed that there is no course that can address everything and that Directed Studies already covers plenty. Still, some students are pushing to increase minority and female representation among authors in the DS curriculum.

Over the past several years, structural changes in the art history major have come largely in part to the department's active response to similar student suggestions. According to the Director of Undergraduate Studies Marisa Bass, students motivated the creation of courses like "Global Decorative Arts," "Sacred Art and Architecture" and "The Politics of Representation."

"Yale's History of Art department is deeply committed to representing the intellectual diversity of its students and its faculty, and we believe that introductory surveys are an essential opportunity to continue to challenge, rethink and rewrite the narratives surrounding the history of engagement with art, architecture, images and objects across time and place," Bass said. "These surveys and those that we will continue to develop in the future are designed in recognition of an essential truth: that there has never been just one story of the history of art."

https://yaledailynews.com/blog/2020/01/24/art-history-department-to-scrap-survey-course

Art

When an exhibit showing Jesus Christ on a cross soaking in urine is considered "art", you know we are doomed as a society. Gone are the days when classical artists like Davinci, Michelangelo, Picasso, Rembrandt, Van Gogh, and Monet ruled the art world. Now, a banana duct taped to a wall in an art gallery is considered "art." A bunch of ugly squiggly lines any alcoholic with the shakes can make on a piece of used napkin from a coffee shop is considered "art." Even random nonsensical paint splashes on a canvas is considered "art." Bob Ross would be turning over in his grave from the artwork of these modern "artists." When you start attacking art and taking it down and replace it with deviant, disgusting, confusing, and arbitrary "art", society is in its last days. Making art ugly, arbitrary, disgusting, and confusing is a goal from our mastermind ruling class. When they can try to ban and cancel The Mona Lisa due to "sexism", you know we are completely fucked as a society.

19

The War on Housing

Democrats Seek To Outlaw Suburban, Single-Family House Zoning, Calling It Racist And Bad For The Environment

By Luke Rosiak December 23rd, 2019

Democrats in Virginia may override local zoning to bring high-density housing, including public housing, to every neighborhood statewide — whether residents want it or not. The measure could quickly transform the suburban lifestyle enjoyed by millions, permitting duplexes to be built on suburban lots in neighborhoods previously consisting of quiet streets and open green spaces. Proponents of "upzoning" say the changes are necessary because suburbs are bastions of segregation and elitism, as well as bad for the environment.

The move, which aims to provide "affordable housing," might be fiercely opposed by local officials throughout the state, who have deliberately created and preserved neighborhoods with particular character — some dense and walkable, others semi-rural and private — to accommodate people's various preferences.

But Democrats tout a state-level law's ability to replace "not in my backyard" with "yes, in your backyard."

House Delegate Ibraheem Samirah, a Democrat, introduced six housing measures Dec. 19, coinciding with Democrats' takeover of the state legislature in November.

"Single-family housing zones would become two-zoned," Samirah told the Daily Caller News Foundation. "Areas that would be impacted most would be the suburbs that have not done their part in helping out."

"The real issues are the areas in between very dense areas which are single-family zoned. Those are the areas that the state is having significant trouble dealing with. They're living in a bubble," he said.

He said suburbs were "mostly white and wealthy" and that their local officials — who have historically been in charge of zoning — were ignoring the desires of poor people, who did not have time to lobby them to increase suburban density. In response to a question about whether people who bought homes in spacious suburbs have valid reasons, not based on discrimination, for preferring to live that way — including a love for nature and desire to preserve woods and streams — he said: "Caring about nature is very important, but the more dense a neighborhood is, the more energy efficient it is."

He said if local officials seek to change requirements like setbacks to make it impossible to build dense housing in areas zoned to preserve a nature feel, "if they make setbacks to block duplexes, there'd have to be a lawsuit to resolve whether those zoning provisions were necessary."

He wrote on Facebook, "Because middle housing is what's most affordable for low-income people and people of color, banning that housing in well-off neighborhoods chalks up to modern-day redlining, locking folks out of areas with better access to schools, jobs, transit, and other services and amenities."

"I will certainly get pushback for this. Some will call it 'state overreach.' Some will express anxiety about neighborhood change. Some may even say that the supply issue doesn't exist. But the research is clear: zoning is a barrier to more housing and integrated communities," he continued.

He tweeted Sunday that that would include public housing. "Important Q about new social/public housing programs: where are we going to put the units? Under current zoning, new low-income housing is relegated to underinvested neighborhoods, concentrating poverty more. Ending exclusionary zoning has to be part of broader housing reform," he said.Tim Hannigan, chairman of the Fairfax County Republican Committee — in one of the areas Samirah represents — said that urban Democrats were waging war on the suburbs.

"This could completely change the character of suburban residential life, because of the urbanization that would develop," he told the DCNF. "So much of the American dream is built upon this idea of finding a nice quiet place to raise your family, and that is under assault."

"This is a power-grab to take away the ability of local communities to establish their own zoning practices ... literally trying to change the character of our communities," he said. He said suburbs were not equipped to handle the increased traffic, and "inevitably it will just push people to places where they feel they'll get away from that, they may move to West Virginia to get their little plot of land."

Minneapolis became the first city to eliminate single family zoning in December 2018, after a push by progressive advocacy groups promoting "equity." Austin, Texas, and Seattle soon followed suit. But those cities were amending zoning codes that have always been the domain of local governments. Oregon passed state legislation blocking local governments' single-family zoning in July, CityLab reported.

It quoted Alex Baca, a Washington, D.C., urbanist with the site Greater Greater Washington, saying that single-family zoning is a tool for wealthy whites to maintain segregated neighborhoods and that the abolition of low-density neighborhoods is necessary for equity.

CityLab acknowledged that "residents might reasonably desire to keep the neighborhoods they love the way they are," but said that implementing the law at the state level makes sure that those concerns can be more easily ignored.

"By preempting the ability of local governments to set their own restrictive zoning policies, the state policy would circumnavigate the complaints of local NIMBY homeowners who want to block denser housing," it wrote.m While he implied that suburbs are prejudiced, Samirah himself has a history of anti-Semitic comments. "I am so sorry that my ill-chosen words added to the pain of the Jewish community, and I seek your understanding and compassion as I prove to you our common humanity," he said in February.

He interrupted a speech in July by President Donald Trump in Jamestown, Virginia, and said, "You can't send us back! Virginia is our home." His father is Jordanian refugee Sabri Samirah, who authorities banned from the U.S. for a decade after the Sept. 11, 2001 attacks, in part because of his membership in the Muslim Brotherhood, the Chicago Tribune reported in 2014.

https://dailycaller.com/2019/12/23/virginia-house-zoning-environment/

Housing

Single family homes in the suburbs are under attack. Owning property on several acres in the country is being banned and cancelled. Using a heater or air conditioner in your home is also being controlled and regulated to appease the environmental Marxists in society. These people don't want us living in houses. They don't want us living on acres of land. They want us living in single, studio, 300 square feet coffin apartments in big city high-rises managed, monitored, supervised, and controlled through video surveillance and electronic passports to come and go as you please. You can't have a backyard with grass because that is against the plan our elite masterminds have in store for us. If you want to see where we are heading as a society, please read and reference George Orwell's *1984* and Aldous Huxley's *Brave New World*.

20

The War on the Military

Navy SEALs Now "Gender Neutral" Under New Mission Statement

By Kit Daniels September 29th, 2020

The U.S. Navy SEALs changed its mission statements to be more "gender neutral," including even dropping the phrase "brotherhood."

This despite the fact there's no female operators in the SEALs or the related Navy Special Warfare Combatant-craft Crewmen (SWCC). In a recent memo, Rear Adm. Collin P. Green, the commander of the Naval Special Warfare Command, approved the changing of pronouns throughout the SEALs ethos and creed statements to be less male-oriented. The memo was brought to light by retired SEAL Eddie Gallagher, who was cleared last year of charges alleging he murdered an ISIS fighter in Syria, charges of which were spearheaded by Green.

"What a joke," Gallagher wrote. "Note the names that signed off at the bottom, [including] Adm. Colin Green (part of the hierarchy that tried to use the system to put me away). Let's remove all male pronouns & BROTHERHOOD from the SEAL ethos."

"To be honest I thought the ethos was always BS," Gallagher added. "Now I know it is. A creed or ethos is supposed to be written in stone, obviously ours is not and will sway to whatever political agenda is being put out." As mentioned, the memo changes the term "brotherhood" to "group of maritime warriors." Additionally, the memo also modified one sentence in a creed which states "I challenge my brothers to perform, as I expect them to challenge me" to now read "I challenge them to perform, as I expect them to challenge me."

Naval Special Warfare spokesman Lt. Cmdr. Matthew Stroup said the changes were made to conform with new rules allowing women to serve as operators in Naval Special Warfare, although the barriers of entry remain the same.

"The changes do not in any way reflect lowering standards of entry, rather they ensure that all those who meet the requirements to train to become a SEAL or SWCC are represented in the ethos or creed they live out," he said, adding that "to date, no women completed the SEAL or SWCC qualification training pipelines."

In 2013, a veteran SEAL revealed the Obama administration was purging top brass from the military who didn't agree with full-blown political correctness and the roll-back of posse comitatus policies, including the disarming of US citizens during a declared emergency. This would explain this fixation on political correctness by some military leaders over the years despite warnings from critics that it would have no practical use and that it could even disrupt combat readiness.

https://www.infowars.com/navy-seals-now-gender-neutral-under-new-mission-statement/

Navy, Army probes find no racism intent in hand gestures

By Lolita C. Baldor December 20th, 2019

WASHINGTON (AP) — Hand gestures flashed by West Point cadets and Naval Academy midshipmen during the televised Army-Navy football game were not racist signals, military investigations have concluded.

A Navy probe of the event found that the students were participating in a "sophomoric game" on Saturday and had no racist intent.

An Army statement Friday also rejected any racist overtones, saying the hand gestures were "not associated with ideologies or movements that are contrary to the Army values."

The Navy said officials are, however, disappointed in the immature behavior of the students and "their actions will be appropriately addressed." There were no details about their exact punishment, but a Navy report on the investigation said the two midshipmen should face "administrative action" for "failure to use good judgment."

Clips of the hand gestures by the students went viral on social media and immediately raised questions about whether they were using a "white power" sign. But others suggested it was part of what's called the "circle game," in which someone flashes an upside-down OK sign below the waist and punches anyone who looks at it.

The Navy said that reviews of the footage, more than two dozen interviews and background checks by the Naval Criminal Investigative Service and the FBI determined that the two freshmen midshipmen were participating in the "circle game" with West Point cadets.

The investigation added that the two naval academy students "exhibited genuine shock" and said they were not aware of the racist connotation of the hand gestures. It said interviews with friends, roommates and other commanders also found no links to the white power movement. Navy Adm. Mike Gilday, chief of naval operations, said sailors are expected to conduct themselves with integrity and character at all times.

"To be clear, the Navy does not tolerate racism in any form," said Gilday. "And while the investigation determined there was no racist intent behind these actions, our behavior must be professional at all times and not give cause for others to question our core values of honor, courage and commitment." The Navy investigation also made a number of recommendations to better coordinate and screen midshipmen who may be in high visibility areas for major events such as the game day. And it said there should be more training for the students on how they should conduct themselves.

The U.S. Military Academy at West Point reached similar conclusions. Lt. Gen. Darryl Williams, West Point superintendent, expressed disappointment in the cadets' immature behavior. The cadets involved also will receive "appropriate administrative" or disciplinary actions, West Point said. No details were provided.

"The American people trust our Soldiers to do the right things the right way," said Gen. James McConville, chief of staff of the Army. "We must be mindful of behavior which brings that trust into question and ensure our actions meet the high ethical and professional standards our nation expects the American Soldier to uphold."

The circle game, around for generations, was featured in the early 2000s sitcom "Malcolm in the Middle" and has made a resurgence as a photo bomb prank in sports team photos--along the same line as "bunny ears" fingers. In more recent years, it became an internet meme in a online game of "gotcha."

But the Anti-Defamation League said the gesture, with the thumb and forefinger touched in a circle and the other fingers outstretched, has also been appropriated as a signal for white supremacy. That started as a hoax perpetuated on the online message board 4chan. The original idea was to take an innocent and common gesture and arbitrarily transform it into something that would enrage liberals.

The campaign was so successful that the gesture came to be used semi-sincerely by Neo-Nazis, Ku Klux Klansmen and other white nationalists to signal sympathizers in public places. In 2018, the U.S. Coast Guard suspended an officer who appeared to be making the hand sign during a Hurricane Florence television broadcast.

https://apnews.com/df543c8d86f550e1b979f022bc9bca90

Military

Attacking the military accomplishes many goals for the totalitarian left.

- It demonizes masculinity.
- It attacks patriotic nationalism.
- It cancels guns, weapons, and firearms.

If a country can't have its own military to help, support, protect and unite the people of the country, then you do not have an independent country. The globalist elites want nothing more than to ban every country's military and replace it with a one-world government and United Nations "peace keeping" squad. In the United States, our military is being dismantled from within by these globalist tyrants. If our military can be banned, censored, and cancelled, we don't have much of a chance to get through the cultural assault we are under.

21

The War on Holidays

'F*** Thanksgiving!': Antifa Topples Statues of George Washington, Veterans to Fight 'Colonization'

By Tyler O'Neil Novemberm 28th, 2020

A group organizing under the Pan-Indigenous People's Liberation (PIPL) network took credit for the vandalism, which they said was part of a "national decolonial day of action."

A few miles away from the Washington statue, vandals also targeted a large granite monument to pioneers in the city's B.F. Nelson Park. Vandals spray-painted the messages, "no thanks," "no more genocide," decolonize," and "land back" on the statue, the Minneapolis *Star-Tribune* reported. Park Board spokeswoman Dawn Sommers promised, "We will start removing the paint as soon as we can."

"Land back" seemingly refers to The LANDBACK campaign, a Native American movement supposedly fighting "white supremacy." The campaign calls for the dismantling of the "white supremacy structures" supposedly responsible for removing Native Americans from their lands, including the Bureau of Land Management and the National Park Service; for the defunding of "white supremacy" in the forms of the police, the military-industrial complex, Border Patrol, and ICE; a "return" of "all public lands back into Indigenous hands"; and a policy of "consent."

This iconoclasm is nothing new. While it began with Confederate monuments, this summer vandals progressed to targeting America's heroes, such as George Washington, Thomas Jefferson, and Abraham Lincoln. Then came Mahatma Gandhi, Union General Ulysses S. Grant, black Union soldiers, and freed slave Frederick Douglass. Vandals even attacked a monument to 9/11 firefighters and painted a statue of Jesus black.

However, targeting patriotic symbols just before Thanksgiving seems particularly disgusting. Early on Wednesday morning, police prevented vandals from toppling a statue of President William McKinley in a Chicago park. The vandals tethered a rope to a police car and spray-painted the statue with the words "Land Back," NBC 5 Chicago reported. Activists have condemned McKinley, who served as president from 1897 to his death in 1901, as a racist because he championed westward expansion.

Vandals in Spokane, Wash., spilled red paint on a statue of Abraham Lincoln in an attack that may or may not have been related to the "Land Back" campaign. In Portland, the antifa group Youth Liberation Front called for "a decentralized, anti-colonial day of action on Thanksgiving eve," with the message, "F**k Thanksgiving, F**k Black Friday!"

An antifa mob broke windows and sprayed graffiti, including the phrase "Land Back." Portland police arrested three suspects. The antifa radicals targeted a veterans' monument at Portland's Lone Fir Cemetery. Vandals spray-painted, "F**k USA," and "Eat sh*t, colonizers!" on the Soldiers Monument Statue, unveiled in 1903 to honor soldiers of the Civil War, the Spanish-American War, the Mexican-American War, and the Indian Wars.

Antifa rioters also spray-painted, "F**k Thanksgiving" underneath an ATM. Such Thanksgiving attacks on national symbols make perverse sense in light of the Black Lives Matter riots this past summer, the Marxist critical race theory promoted by *The New York Times*' "1619 Project," and the impact of organizations like the far-left smear factory the Southern Poverty Law Center (SPLC). Just before Thanksgiving, the SPLC published an article entitled, "Indigenous Slavery and the Thanksgiving Difference." In that article, Harvard University professor

Tiya Miles argues that "Thanksgiving is a holiday long past due for an overhaul."

Miles claims that the mythology of the first Thanksgiving "is based on a misunderstanding of the early relationships between Wampanoag residents and the English newcomers at Massachusetts Bay." She notes that Tisquantum (popularly known as Squanto) served as a translator between the Wampanoag and the Pilgrims, having learned English during his capture and enslavement in England.

She also notes that the Wampanoag leader Pumetacom allied with the Narragansetts and Nipmucks in a war against the colonists that ended in the natives' defeat. "Thousands would be killed or sold into slavery in the conflict, which ended Indigenous independence in New England. It is no wonder that some Native American families see Thanksgiving as a day of mourning," she writes.

Much of the history between Native Americans and European settlers is indeed tragic, but leftist narratives often deprive the victims of their agency. Tisquantum, for instance, appears to have been plotting to overthrow the Wampanoag leader before Tisquantum's untimely death, and his machinations likely contributed to the ultimate Puritan victory. History is far messier than the simple narrative of evil European colonialism and "white supremacy" suggests.

Americans should reexamine our history, but the nefarious message of Marxist critical race theory suggests we should upend society in order to satisfy historical grievances in the name of racial justice. This toxic vision undermines the very real progress America has made in terms of establishing civil rights regardless of race and in terms of securing broad prosperity through a free market economy. Americans have a great deal for which to be thankful, even in the midst of a pandemic. Rather than railing against the supposed oppressors who established and celebrated Thanksgiving, these vandals should consider just how indebted they are to the system that provides peace and prosperity to the United States.

https://pjmedia.com/news-and-politics/tyler-o-neil/2020/11/28/f-thanksgiving-antifa-topples-statues-of-george-washington-veterans-to-fight-colonization-n1179358

The 2020 Stupid, Politically Correct, Atheists Fighting Christmas Season Has Started

By Jeff Dunetz November 18th, 2020

It happens every year at this time: the atheists fighting Christmas season—A community puts up a Christmas tree, and one of two things happen. Either there is an ACLU battle to take it down, or someone fights to get a Chanukkiyah (that's its real name, not Menorah) placed right next to it. That can be followed by the ACLU representing some atheist group, suing any town whose mayor has a Christmas tree in the living room of their personal residence.

Hey, ACLU, give it up. America is a majority Christian country. And as a Jew, that doesn't bother me one bit because I am free to practice my faith (and I like some of the food). The First Amendment isn't supposed to stop Americans from celebrating their faith. It's supposed to stop the majority from infringing on the other faiths.

As Americans, we are all different. We must celebrate those differences, not merge them into one hodgepodge of progressive mediocrity, celebrating everything simultaneously, while the truth is it celebrating absolutely nothing. America is a great country. It is great not because everyone celebrates the same, but because we can all celebrate our differences.

In Florida a few years ago, threatened lawsuits didn't force the state to remove a nativity scene t from the capitol rotunda, two atheist-themed messages, a "Festivus Pole" and a rendering of the Pastafarian Flying Spaghetti Monster were added. A year later Americans United for Separation of Church and State sent a letter to the Florida Department of Management Services on behalf of the Satanic Temple and their diorama of Lucifer falling into the flames of hell was added.

ENOUGH! The people who see the end of the year as the opportune time to celebrate politically correct multicultural nonsense have to stop! One particularly disgusting part of the 2020 atheist effort is an attack on holiday-themed charity efforts. It's Charity!!! Mark Tapscott details an example of this idiocy in his must-read post, Atheist Group Goes Full Grinch, Steals Christmas From Hundreds Of Poor Kids Around The World. Give it a read no matter what your faith, it will anger any lover of freedom.

https://lidblog.com/atheists-fighting-christmas/

Kansas Middle School Ends Operation Christmas Child After Atheist Complaint

By CBN News November 17th, 2020

A Kansas middle school has decided to stop its participation in a popular Christmas program that collects toys, school supplies, and hygiene products for needy children after an atheist organization told the school such an effort was unconstitutional.

Liberty Middle School located in Pratt, Kansas was to participate in Operation Christmas Child, an annual program of the Christian nonprofit Samaritan's Purse, an international relief agency led by Franklin Graham. The shoeboxes are filled with gifts and distributed by the charity to children around the world. In addition to the gifts, they receive a small booklet that tells of the gospel message of Jesus Christ.

Earlier this month, the Wisconsin-based Freedom from Religion Foundation (FFRF) notified the superintendent of the Pratt school district that a concerned staff member complained to them about the middle school's Christmas project. "The District must cease participation in Operation Christmas Child or taking any other actions promoting

Christianity like including religious references over morning announcements," the FFRF said in their Nov. 3 letter.

"While it is laudable for a public school to promote student involvement in the community by volunteering and donating to charitable organizations, the school cannot use that goal as an avenue to fund a religious organization with a religious mission," FFRF wrote in their letter. Founded in 1978, the FFRF claims to represent 33,000 members across the country. It describes its members as "free-thinkers (atheists and agnostics)."

On Nov. 7, Superintendent Tony Helfrich responded to the group, writing the district was discontinuing its students' participation in Operation Christmas Child. In addition, the FFRF also alleged in its letter that a school vice principal had promoted Christianity and had invited students to participate in the annual "See You at the Pole" event.

"District staff must also be instructed not to in any way participate in, promoting, or endorse religious events like 'See You at the Pole'," the FFRF wrote.

This is not the first time an atheist organization has targeted Operation Christmas Child. In 2016, the American Humanist Association filed a federal lawsuit in Denver to stop Colorado students from putting together Christmas gift boxes for children in need. The organization also fought the program in South Carolina schools in 2013.

Founded in 1993, Samaritan's Purse has collected and distributed more than 178 million shoebox gifts to children in 160 countries, according to the Operation Christmas Child's website.

As CBN News reported last November, one teenage girl had started her own shoebox club when was 8 years old. At the age of 19, Evilyn Pinnow's club was celebrating her 10,000th shoebox for a child in need.

In 2012, Operation Christmas Child asked Pinnow to deliver the organization's 100 millionth shoebox to a girl in the Dominican Republic. "Every box is an opportunity to reach a child with the Gospel of Jesus Christ. It's about telling children around the world and their families that God loves them. God hasn't forgotten them," Franklin Graham said.

https://www.faithwire.com/2020/11/17/kansas-middle-school-ends-operation-christmas-child-after-atheist-complaint/

Pinterest bans "cultural appropriation" Halloween costumes

By Cindy Harper October 2nd, 2020

Pinterest is trying to re-educate users on what it calls "cultural appropriation" when it comes to Halloween costumes.

Pinterest is the go-to app for Halloween costume ideas. Even though the celebrations this year will be different due to coronavirus restrictions, people are still planning to make a statement with unique costumes. "Costumes are consistently a top-searched term, but many people may not know that certain costumes are appropriations of other cultures," Pinterest said in a post in their newsroom.

Pinterest isn't happy with people celebrating Halloween with elements from another culture and has made several changes over the years. In 2016, the company banned ads featuring culturally "inappropriate" costumes. That same year they introduced a feature allowing users to report costumes.

This year, they have taken further measures, including reducing the appearance of costumes that have "appropriated" other cultures. Additionally, when users search culture-specific terms such as "Day of the Dead costumes," the first result will be a pin directing a user to a post by "experts" "on how to celebrate thoughtfully and respectfully."

"Cultures aren't costumes. Halloween should be a time for inspiration — not a time for insensitivity," the company said.

https://reclaimthenet.org/pinterest-bans-cultural-appropriation-halloween-costumes/

Sexy 'Handmaid's Tale' Halloween costume pulled after sparking online outrage

By Cydney Henderson Sept 20th, 2018 Updated: September 21st, 2018

It turns out maybe oppression isn't sexy after all. Online retailer Yandy listed a "Brave Red Maiden" Halloween costume for nearly $65, referencing the garb women forced into surrogacy wear in Hulu's series "The Handmaid's Tale." The provocative rendition includes a red cape, mini dress and white bonnet.

"An upsetting dystopian future has emerged where women no longer have a say," the description reads. "However, we say be bold and speak your mind in this exclusive Brave Red Maiden costume." The Halloween costume instantly sparked outraged across social media.

One Twitter user shared a screenshot of the costume and asked "why," sarcastically adding "nothing like a sexy rape victim for Halloween fun." Another user said, "This is so far from the point I can't even," while another added, "Our society doesn't take the rape of real women seriously, why should they take the rape of fictional women seriously?"

Yandy responded to the brewing controversy by removing the listing from its site. The Phoenix-based company issued an apology in place of the previous link to the costume.

"Over the last few hours, it has become obvious that our "Yandy Brave Red Maiden Costume" is being seen as a symbol of women's oppression, rather than an expression of women's empowerment," the clothing retailer said. "This is unfortunate, as it was not our intention on any level."

The statement continued: "Given the sincere, heartfelt response, supported by numerous personal stories we've received, we are removing the costume from our site."

The iconic red cloak from Margaret Atwood's "The Handmaid's Tale" has become a feminist symbol of protest against women's oppression around the world. Recently, demonstrators donned the costume outside Brett Kavanaugh's Supreme Court nomination hearing. In fact, Yandy revealed the symbol of resistance influenced the Halloween costume many have deemed distasteful. "Our initial inspiration to create the piece was through witnessing its use in recent months as a powerful protest image," the statement said.

Yandy continued: "We support our customers being comfortable in their skin, regardless of who they are or what they choose to wear. Our corporate ideology is rooted in female empowerment, and gender empowerment overall."

https://www.usatoday.com/story/life/tv/2018/09/20/sexy-handmaids-tale-halloween-costume-sparks-outrage/1375851002/

The Five Most Triggering Halloween Costumes of 2018

By Debra Heine October 30th, 2018

With Halloween nearly upon us, it's time again to talk about costume do's and don'ts. It is *imperative* that Americans heed the whims of the SJW community while celebrating this festive fall holiday or risk suffering the social embarrassment of committing a politically incorrect costume faux pas.

Good Housekeeping compiled a list of fifteen problematic costumes that they say are not funny and you should never, *ever* wear. A few of the costumes on their list really *are* wildly inappropriate and not funny — like the burning Twin Towers costume, the "Anne Frank" costume, "anything involving blackface," and of course anything depicting human genitalia. Also, dressing up as dead celebrity zombies is apparently a thing — and that is gross and very wrong. (Remember when Bill Maher dressed up as Steve Irwin, complete with a bloody stingray barb hanging out of his chest for Halloween 2006, less than two months after Irwin's death? Yeah, that was truly depraved). I've not included these on the list because I know most of us would never consider wearing these truly offensive and obscene costumes.

However, most of the costumes that made their list, while arguably in poor taste, are really in the eye of the beholder. What makes them problematic is they might offend people who love to be offended. Which is why the list of costumes to avoid grows every year and the list of permissible costumes gets smaller.

For instance, the costume police say it's wrong to dress up like a hobo — a Halloween favorite for decades that made our list last year — because it makes fun of the homeless. Come on. I suspect if you took a poll, most people would still view hobo costumes as an inoffensive and cost-efficient way to dress up for Halloween. (Most hobos are probably fine with it too.)

The truth is, these PC scolds want to be the arbiters of what we can and can't make fun of. And you know what? It's the job of every patriotic American to tell them to stick it where the sun don't shine.

Once again, as a public service, I've whittled the number down to the top five politically incorrect costumes we should avoid this year if we don't want to trigger the snowflakes and cause a scene on Halloween.

1. Crazy psycho in a straitjacket

Because the risk is just too great that someone who has actually worn a straitghtjacket in a mental institution is actually going to see your costume and be offended? No, "wearing a straightjacket, as well as any other equipment typically associated with the institutionalization of someone with a mental illness, trivializes how devastating these conditions can be," Good Housekeeping chides.

Sigh. I guess if you wear a straightjacket costume for Halloween, that means you and your friends are incapable of taking mental illness seriously, unlike the serious, intelligent, progressive people who always take mental illness seriously and would never dress up in a straightjacket for Halloween. Be shmart and don't dress like a crazy person!

2. Cultural stereotypes

"Cultural appropriation" is a permanent fixture on the Halloween trigger list, so you knew this was coming. "When someone dresses up as a member of a culture that isn't their own, particularly in an exaggerated or 'humorous' way, it can be hurtful to those who *do* belong," Good Housekeeping scolds. "Even if it's a beloved Disney character" (hint: Moana). Yes, Disney pulled the Moana costume after the perpetually offended complained. Whatever happened to "imitation is the sincerest form of flattery"?

3. Body-shaming and objectifying costumes

Since when are these not funny? "When it comes to disrespecting women, this costume is a double whammy of awful. It not only reduces women to sex objects, but it makes a woman's weight into a joke," Good Housekeeping explains. "In the age of body positivity, haven't we grown past this?" (the answer is yes).

Okay but what if the fat suit is for a guy (like the one above). Is it okay then? Aren't we gals supposed to be empowered or something when the roles are reversed?

4. Terrorist Halloween costume

Oh come on!

Yeah, I'm not sure we all agree. It's not for everyone, obviously — but that kid makes a really cute Osama bin Laden.

5. Transphobic costume

Back by popular demand:

"This 'tranny granny' costume was pulled from Walmart after facing a backlash from consumers who pointed out that it mocks and satirizes transgender women — in addition to using a transphobic slur," Good Housekeeping says, meaning "tranny." Oops. When did "tranny" become a slur? It was the perfect catch-all phrase for boomers who can't remember all the different "trans" categories, including transgender, genderqueer, transsexual, transvestite, genderfluid, transitioning, etc. Now we have to worry about getting the various pronouns wrong, which in some areas of the country is actually considered hate speech. For this reason, unless you don't mind being the focus of negative attention, it's probably best to avoid this costume in mixed company.

https://pjmedia.com/culture/debra-heine/2018/10/30/the-five-most-triggering-halloween-costumes-of-2018-n173268

MSU FLOWCHART helps students decide if costumes are 'racist'

By Sergei Kelley October 30th, 2018

A Michigan State University department debuted Halloween posters titled, "A Culture is not a Costume" and included a guide called, "Is Your Halloween Costume Racist?"

MSU's Residence Hospitality and Services department featured the signs, which included a heavily detailed "Cultural Appropriation vs Appreciation" section, as spotted by *Campus Reform*. The boards are found throughout many of the university's dorms. One poster brands the addition of a sombrero to a taco costume as "racist."

The poster contains a flowchart, which asks students whether their costumes use blackface, swastikas, or have "literally a name of a minority (that you are not) in the title of your costume." At one point, the poster suggests that if students are "still asking yourself the question 'is this costume racist?'" that they should not wear it. "A space that is so diverse, tensions arise when certain things happen through costumes," MSU Inclusion and Intercultural Initiatives Director Paulette Russell told *Campus Reform*. "[The] poster is to help students in residence halls to understand why certain depictions might be offensive...and if someone takes offense they have a reason."

But Russell, when asked about possible consequences for students who violate statements on the bulletin boards, suggested that wearing any given costume "certainly is the student's right." Donna Kaplowitz, MSU's faculty associate of the Intercultural Dialogues program, told *Campus Reform* that she was not aware of the boards across campus. She presumed the boards "are not instructing not [sic] what should be worn, but educat[ing] on how certain costumes are perceived by others."

The university continued its cultural appropriation crusade on October 19.

"I'm being asked by my department to talk about a particular topic: cultural appropriation," a Holmes Hall dormitory resident assistant (RA) said in his floor-wide email, which was obtained by *Campus Reform*.

"I didn't want to send the email." the RA, who preferred to stay anonymous, said during an interview with *Campus Reform*. "The cultural appropriation notion is problematic. In discussion with other peers, we found everyone has different definitions of cultural appropriation." The RA said that a proper college environment should allow "for you to learn and think. You might be offensive or become offended."

"The university goes against their own beliefs [...] that during this time of year it is okay (for students) to make assumptions about their peers," MSU College Republicans Finance Chair Alex Overholser told *Campus Reform*. A 2017-2018 event schedule shows that the university held "MRULE (Multi-Racial Unity Living Experience) Cultural Ap-

propriation & Halloween event" and "Cultural Appropriation Campaign" within campus residence halls.
https://www.campusreform.org/?ID=11462

Cultural appropriation turns Halloween into a nightmare

By Jonathan Turley December 30th, 2018

Halloween is again upon us. Across the United States, the prospect of frightening images have some pledging to skip the holiday or closely shield their children. It is not the scary decorations or costumes but "cultural appropriation" that has triggered a tradition of recrimination and anger. Colleges and universities have warned students not to dress as Indian chiefs or Mexican bandits, while parents have publicly debated whether they can allow their children to dress as the Black Panther or Moana without being accused of cultural appropriation or racism.

"Cultural appropriation" has become a common term on campuses and is receiving broader meaning with each passing year. In Utah, a high school student was denounced for wearing a Chinese dress to her prom. White students wearing hoop earrings or dreadlocks have been denounced, while there have been protests over serving sushi at Oberlin College, holding yoga classes at the University of Ottawa or having a "Mexican food night" at Clemson University. The reason behind such limitless forms of cultural appropriation is its limitless meaning. Fordham University law professor Susan Scafidi has defined the term as encompassing the "unauthorized use of another culture's dance, dress, music, language, folklore, cuisine, traditional medicine, religious symbols" and more.

That makes Halloween a nightmarish orgy of cultural appropriation. Colleges and universities now post warnings not to dress as Native Americans, geishas, samurai, or other images. Syracuse University even threatened a few years ago to have its campus police force students to remove "offensive" costumes. There is remarkably little debate over such directives because many faculty members fear being labeled as racist or insensitive. What is increasingly rare is any dialogue or willingness to accept that people can hold good faith views on both sides.

CNN political analyst Kirsten Powers dismissed the concerns of white people who object to being labeled racist over Halloween costumes, tweeting, "Dear white people who are upset that you can't dress up as another race or culture for Halloween: your feelings don't matter." She went on to add that the only feelings that matter are of those who feel disrespected or mocked by appropriating their culture. Similarly, in an Everyday Feminism article a few years ago, Kat Lazo advised that people who do not see the inherent racism or cultural appropriation in costumes are "very privileged" individuals who "never had the misfortune of experiencing or witnessing acts of racism." That of course is a common conversation stopper if someone says any objection to cultural appropriation means you are ignorant and likely a racist in denial.

There is another possibility that reasonable people can disagree. There are clearly racist costumes that most of us join in denouncing, such as blackface or other raw portrayals. However, the cultural appropriation movement opposes any depiction of another culture. Indeed, what constitutes a social norm can be hard to discern. A New York Times column gave a tortured account of whether parents could allow their children to dress as Black Panther. The article included advice on sitting down with kids to discuss racial implications of their choices and, as Texas Woman's University professor Brigitte Vittrup warned, "by not mentioning it, by not talking about it, we're essentially preserving the status quo."

An article by Sachi Feris explored her struggle with her young daughter who wanted to dress like Moana or Elsa last year. She wrote, "I had some reservations regarding both costume choices" and about cultural appropriation, noting the "power" and "privilege" carried by "whiteness" and the standards of beauty that go along with it. Elsa did not reflect cultural appropriation but rather discomfort over how her character "sends the message that you have to be a certain way" to look "beautiful" or to be a "princess" and that you have to have blonde hair and blue eyes. Feris disliked the message. Moana was portrayed as a perfect nightmare for a white girl to adopt, since she told her daughter she is white like Elsa. She instead encouraged her daughter to be Mickey Mouse because this way she would not be "making fun of anyone or dressing up as a culture different from our own because Mickey Mouse is a pretend mouse!"

Ironically, under the standard definition, Halloween itself could be denounced as a raw cultural appropriation. The precursors to Halloween can be traced to the old Celtic tradition of Samhain that explores the line between the living and the dead. However, there has long been a fantasy tradition around the world of using Halloween festivities to pretend you are someone else, as shown by the British tradition of "fancy dress" balls.

Despite the dismissal by Kirsten Powers, there are legitimate concerns on both sides and legitimate questions of whether common cultural images should be viewed as owned or controlled by a group. There also is the debate over who decides in limiting such free expression. Last week, Aulii Cravalho, the actress who played Moana in the Disney movie, declared it "absolutely appropriate" for kids to dress up as the Polynesian princess if it is "done in the spirit of love" and "for the little ones who just want to dress up as their favorite heroine." Is it enough for a native Hawaiian teenager, with a financial interest in the Disney movie, saying it is okay?

Cultural foods and images are shared in society and the arts, particularly in a pluralistic nation like the United States. Adopting a cuisine or a costume is not "appropriating" a culture. Those are part of the mosaic of shared influences and images in a diverse free society. Dressing as a bandit from the movie "Treasure of Sierra Nevada" is not appropriating the Mexican culture. It is mimicking the character of Alfonso Bedoya.

Notably, motivation or message seems irrelevant to the definition of cultural appropriation. It does not matter if such symbols were viewed as celebrating the purity or bravery of a group. Certainly, many costumes incorporate cultural images that have exaggerated or oversimplified elements. But when children dress up as princesses, they are fantasizing, just as they do in dressing as cowboys or soldiers or samurai. They often are portraying positive elements like courage or grace in wearing those cultural images. Is it necessary to dump all our adult anxieties on our children or draw connections to our existing social problems?

The alternative is that we accept that cultural icons like Moana are shared and become part of a broader cultural tradition and dialogue. That little girl in the Indian outfit just might be a little girl who wants to be like Pocahontas, a heroine who is strong and unafraid, nothing more. By the way, it is pretty cool to see kids still pretending and dressing up without having to carry all of our problems, from rapes to racism, as they file down our streets on Halloween. We somehow forget how to do that along the way to adulthood. Maybe, just maybe, we have something to learn from that samurai or princess who comes knocking on our door on Halloween.

https://thehill.com/opinion/civil-rights/413813-cultural-appropriation-turns-halloween-into-a-nightmare

Idaho teachers suspended for border wall, Mexican Halloween costumes

By Reuters November 3rd, 2018

Fourteen staff at an Idaho primary school who dressed up as a border wall and as Mexicans for Halloween were put on administrative leave on Saturday for the "insensitive" and "inappropriate" costumes, a school superintendent said. Photos of the group wearing stereotypical U.S. and

Mexican costumes appeared this week on the Idaho school district's Facebook page, drawing complaints from parents, civil rights groups and members of the state's large Hispanic population.

One photo showed seven staff from the Middleton Heights Elementary School dressed as characters, including the Statue of Liberty and an American eagle, holding a cardboard wall with "MAKE AMERICA GREAT AGAIN" on it. Another showed staff shaking maracas and wearing sombreros, ponchos and fake mustaches.

The incident came at a time of heightened tensions over immigration in the United States as President Donald Trump seeks to use the issue to boost Republican support ahead of congressional elections on Tuesday. Middleton is a town of around 5,500 located about 23 miles northwest of the state capital, Boise.

The suspensions were decided at a meeting of the Middleton School District board on Saturday, Superintendent Josh Middleton told reporters. The district appointed a member of its crisis team to take over temporarily as school principal, he said. "We are better than this. We embrace all students," Middleton said in a Facebook Live video posted on Friday in which he apologized for the costumes. "We have a responsibility to teach and reach all students, period." The costumes were part of an after-school "team-building activity" among the teachers, who were competing to come up with the most stereotypical outfits, board Chairman Tim Winkle told the Idaho Press, adding that this did not justify the actions.

An open letter to the superintendent from 12 advocacy groups, including Immigrant Justice Idaho and the American Civil Liberties Union of Idaho, said the state's climate "continues to grow more harmful against specific groups and identities," including Hispanics.

"The intent or misjudgments of the individuals involved does not undo the trauma experienced by students, families and communities," the letter said. Hispanics are the largest minority group in Idaho at about 11 percent of the population, according to the 2010 census. Around 12 percent of Middleton Elementary School's students were

Hispanic in the 2015-2016 school year, according to the National Center for Education Statistics.

https://ca.news.yahoo.com/idaho-teachers-suspended-border-wall-mexican-halloween-costumes-215414399.html

'Modern Santa:' More than a quarter of people tell survey Santa should be female or gender-neutral

By Ann Smajstrla December 14th, 2018

Some respondents to a survey about Santa Claus say the legendary figure could use an image update -- including going female or gender-neutral.

"We all imagine Santa as the bearded old man in his iconic white and red suit, black belt, matching boots and reindeer-drawn sleigh. But what if Father Christmas was rebranded for today?" Logo design company GraphicSprings asked in a survey detailed in a blog post.

GraphicSprings surveyed more than 400 U.S. and United Kingdom residents on how Santa should be changed. It then used the top suggestions to survey 4,000 people on how they envision a 2018 version of Santa. When it came to Kris Kringle's gender, 10.6 percent responded that Santa should be female, while 17.2 percent said Santa should be gender-neutral. That left just over 70 percent saying Saint Nick should stay male.

In other fields, survey-takers were largely in favor of keeping Father Christmas as-is. More than 90 percent of respondents said Santa shouldn't drink beer, be younger or shave his beard. About 20 percent said he should have tattoos, go on a diet and get a new hairstyle. Regarding Santa's method for distributing gifts, about 55 percent thought Santa should keep his sleigh. Popular alternatives were using a flying car or Amazon Prime -- both received just over 20 percent of responses. Twenty to 25 percent of those surveyed said Santa should be modernized in other ways: having an iPhone, wearing sneakers and being "hipster."

https://www.fox23.com/news/trending-now/modern-santa-more-than-a-quarter-of-people-tell-survey-santa-should-be-female-or-genderneutral/888880199/

Santa Claus Will Be A Gay Black Man In A New Children's Book

By Curtis M. Wong April 4th, 2017

Get ready to see Santa Claus in a new (and refreshingly diverse) light this holiday season, courtesy of a forthcoming parody children's book.

On March 28, publisher Harper Design announced plans to release *Santa's Husband,* which re-casts Kris Kringle as a black man in an interracial, same-sex relationship. Slated for an October release, the book will follow Santa's life in the North Pole, except in this version, he'll have a white husband who fills in for him at shopping malls around the world.

It will be written by Daniel Kibblesmith, a comedy writer on "The Late Show With Stephen Colbert," and feature illustrations by A.P. Quach. Kibblesmith, who co-wrote 2013's *How to Win at Everything: Even Things You Can't or Shouldn't Try to Win At* with Sam Weiner, told The Huffington Post that he got the idea for *Santa's Husband* last Christmas, after the Mall of America faced a backlash when it introduced a black Santa (played by Larry Jefferson).

"My fiancée [author Jennifer Wright] and I joked privately, and then on Twitter, that since every house has its own traditions and lore surrounding Christmas, we would tell our child that the black Santa Claus was the 'real' Santa," he said. "If they saw a white Santa at the mall, we'd explain that this was his husband." After his tweet garnered over 3,300 retweets and 8,300 likes and was featured on parenting blogs, the writer-comedian said he realized “there was genuine interest in this book becoming a reality.”

As to what he’d like readers to take away from *Santa’s Husband*, Kibblesmith said, “warm Christmas-y feelings and a good night’s sleep,” noting that he hopes the book will ultimately become a yuletide favorite “for couples and new families who are looking to begin their own kinds of holiday traditions.” To prospective critics who may be angered at the prospect of a black Santa, Kibblesmith would like to remind them that “everything is OK.”

“Some people — not me — even believe that Santa Claus is just your parents, which would mean that there are as many interpretations of Santa Claus as there are different kinds of families,” he quipped. “But again, this is only a theory, because Santa Claus *is* real, and we have written a book about him.”

https://www.huffpost.com/entry/santa-claus-gay-children-book_n_58e2a35be4b0f4a923b0fa79?guccounter=1

Washington Post ponders if kids should sit on Santa’s lap amid #MeToo movement

By Brian Flood Dec 25th, 2018

Bah humbug.

The Washington Post published a story this week questioning whether or not children should be forced to sit on Santa Claus’ lap amid the #MeToo movement.m WashPost gender and family issues reporter Samantha Schmidt penned the feature headlined, “Should crying children sit on Santa’s lap for photos? Here’s why some parents are saying no.” The story appeared in the Social Issues section of the paper’s website.

Schmidt opened the piece by painting a picture of a two-year-old girl who was reluctant to sit on Santa’s lap during a recent trip to the mall –

which frustrated the toddler's mother. Schmidt asked, "If her daughter was crying and resisting a photo on Santa's lap, should she make her go through with it?"

The reporter notes that a "photo with Santa is still a childhood rite of passage for many Americans," but some parents have "begun questioning the way the culture approaches photos with Santa amid the #MeToo movement and a national conversation over how to teach young children about consent and physical boundaries."

Schmidt pondered what kind of message it sends to girls later in life if they were forced to sit on Santa's lap as a child.

"Some say it's a matter of simply listening to children and not forcing them to follow through with photos if they are scared or uneasy. Others have opted out of taking their children to meet Santa in the first place," Schmidt wrote before detailing various accounts of parents who object to forcing children to sit on Santa's lap. However, Schmidt acknowledged that many people will still partake in the holiday tradition.

"For many parents, merely putting Santa in the same sentence as #MeToo is an absurd overreaction and an attempt to politicize an innocent, beloved holiday ritual," she wrote. Schmidt also cited a developmental psychologist who feels "lessons about consent and unwanted touching should start early, and parents could use the holiday tradition as an opportunity to teach children that they are in control of their bodies." The reporter added that most "Santas are taught to make sure their hands are always visible" during the holiday photo shoots.

https://www.foxnews.com/lifestyle/washington-post-ponders-if-kids-should-sit-on-santas-lap-amid-metoo-movement

Activist pushes politically correct plan to rename Father's Day

By Staff Writers August 25th, 2017

An early childhood activist has been labelled "offensive" after suggesting Father's Day be renamed 'Special Person's Day' so kids without dads wouldn't feel left out. Dr Red Ruby Scarlet, an activist with a doctorate in early childhood studies, is pushing for the name change to the annual holiday. During an interview on *Today Tonight* Dr Scarlet denied it was case of excess political correctness.

"Why are we calling this political correctness when in fact it's about our rights?" Dr Scarlet told host Rosanna Mangiarelli. She went on: "There's a lot of Australian research that has actually informed a lot of international research ... that has demonstrated children's capacity to be really inclusive once they know about these ideas and they think, 'Wow, why are people seeing this as a controversy?"

Dr Scarlet, who insisted that was her real name, said that many families without fathers supported the idea. "We have single parent families, satellite families, extended families, lesbian and gay families," she said.

Her ideas were met with a stern rebuke from New South Wales Liberal minister David Elliott, who called them "rubbish".

"Can't believe that someone who professes to be 'enlightened' would advocate such crap," Mr Elliott wrote on Facebook. "People still celebrate fatherhood even after their father and grandfathers have passed away, in fact for many people Father's Day is a wonderful time of reflecting and remembering."

He went on: "Dr Red Ruby Scarlet — you are the offensive one. Maybe we should start a campaign to address that."

https://www.news.com.au/lifestyle/real-life/wtf/activist-pushes-politically-correct-plan-to-rename-fathers-day-special-persons-day/news-story/354e0c4f6309ef0452b14936a14391e4

New Mexico state Senate votes to replace Columbus Day with Indigenous Peoples' Day

By Paulina Dedaj March 16th, 2019

New Mexico's state Senate voted Friday to replace Columbus Day with Indigenous Peoples' Day. The Senate voted 22-15 in favor of the proposal, which had already passed in the state House, and if Gov. Michelle Lujan Grisham signs the bill, New Mexico will become the fourth state to do away with the holiday that pays homage to Christopher Columbus, The Albuquerque Journal reported. Critics of the bill argue that the measure only serves to further divide the community.

"I think this bill is more about dividing us than bringing us together," Sen. Mark Moores, R-Albuquerque, said, according to nmpoliticalreport.com. A proposal to honor the state's Native American communities on a separate day in February was reportedly shot down.

The celebration of Columbus Day, held on the second Monday of every October, has become an increasingly fractious affair in recent years. Some cities opt to honor the nation's indigenous people with their own day, which has been recognized by the United Nations since 1994. The explorer's history is a divisive one. Some historians assert that Columbus committed atrocities against the Native Americans he encountered as he came to America.

https://www.foxnews.com/us/new-mexico-state-senate-votes-to-replace-columbus-day-with-indigenous-peoples-day

Michigan State University bans 'racially, culturally, or ethnically based' costumes for Halloween

By Victor Skinner October 10th, 2019

Students at Michigan State University are getting an education in how they can avoid offending people with culturally inappropriate Halloween costumes in what's becoming a new tradition that undermines the university's own identity.

The unsolicited advice on what to wear on fright night appeared on message boards in campus residences this week to help students answer the question "Is your Halloween costume racist?" according to The Morning Watch, the school's conservative news site.

What's become an annual reminder from MSU's Residence Education and Housing Services spells out the difference between "cultural appropriation vs. appreciation." When students are selecting a Halloween costume, REHS wants them to ask themselves, "do you belong to that group of people?" If the answer is "no," then it's racist, according to MSU officials. It doesn't matter if the get-up is humorous or sexy, because it's offensive to use "those peoples' human elements ... for the sake of bringing us laughter or making us feel more exotic," REHS advises.

"These are people's lives ... they are not stereotypes," according to the posters. "They can't take off a costume."

"How would you like it if someone turned you into a costume?" MSU questions, according to The Morning Watch. It's the third year MSU officials pushed the program on students in the weeks ahead of Halloween. The boards offer numerous examples of "hypersexualized racism," like women in two piece Native American costumes, as well as other "costume fails" depicting Mexican and Japanese cultures that should be off limits.

Sombreros and mustaches, Nazi gear, Rastafarians, illegal aliens, Middle Eastern attire, and other "racially, culturally, or ethnically based" costumes are also a no-no, REHS advises.

The posters claim it's also racist to dress up as Jay-Z and Beyonce, or Kanye and Kim West. According to MSU, students should understand that cultural appropriation involves "Western appropriations of non-Western or non-white forms" that carries with it "the connotation of exploitation and dominance," The Morning Watch reports.

Cultural appreciation, MSU explains, is "learning about another culture with respect and courtesy." Steve Bertolini, a senior International Relations major, offered a different definition for cultural appropriation at MSU: "A dangerous term that undermines free speech and expression of ideas."

It also undermines MSU's own identity, he argued.

"Suppressing any costume idea because it reflects a culture is ridiculous," Bertolini said. "Should we abandon Sparty as to not offend those of Greek origin?"

Sparty, the MSU Spartans' wildly popular mascot, is a muscular male Spartan warrior dressed in stylized, cartoonized Greek battle gear.

Other MSU students, like freshman Clara Peters, think it's wrong for the university to label students who mimic popular culture or television characters as racists. "I do not think MSU has a role in determining what students should avoid wearing for Halloween," Peters told The Morning Watch. "Just because a student chooses to wear a costume based on a race or culture does not mean that they lack respect for diversity and inclusion."

https://www.theamericanmirror.com/blog/2019/10/10/michigan-state-u-bans-mustaches-sombreros-aliens-in-orange-suits-mexicans-japanese-hypersexualized-racism-for-halloween/

University BANS 'acts of intolerance'

By Adam Sabes October, 18th 2019

With Halloween approaching, college students may be thinking about what type of party they should host or what costume they should pick. However, at Furman University, students might be restricted in their plans. Free speech nonprofit the Foundation for Individual Rights in Education (FIRE) highlighted Furman's "Acts of Intolerance" policy for its October speech code of the month.

The policy states that "an act of intolerance" can be defined "as any conduct that serves no scholarly purpose appropriate to the educational experience and demonstrates bias against others," based on their sex, national origin, age, etc. Under the policy, certain costumes and theme parties can "prompt additional investigation" and are discouraged by the school. "Theme parties that encourage people to wear costumes or act in ways that reinforce stereotypes or are otherwise demeaning," the policy lists as one item that can lead to "additional investigation." Additionally, "culturally offensive gestures," vandalism, and the use of slurs can all be considered "Acts of Intolerance."

"When an Act of Intolerance is targeted toward a specific person, it may rise to the level of discriminatory harassment. It may also constitute a hate crime for the purposes of local, state, or federal law," the policy states.

The same student policy handbook that has the "Act of Intolerance" policy also guarantees the freedom of expression. "Students are guaranteed freedom of inquiry and expression," the handbook reads.

Laura Beltz, senior program officer for FIRE, told *Campus Reform* that the policy could stifle speech on campus. "If you're a student and you're reading this policy and you see that you could be investigated or even punished over expression like this," Beltz said. "[Students] may self-censor because [they're] so concerned that any sort of subjectively controvers[ial] or offensive expression could be investigated. [You're] going to be a lot less likely to engage in conduct that could go up to that line. So, it's a problem really either way whether they're investigating the surface expression or not and that's why they need to revise this policy to make it clear." Beltz also said that since Furman does promise to its students that it will respect freedom of expression, "they should be living up to that promise."

Similarly, in 2018 at Gonzaga University, students received a campus-wide email warning them about being "culturally inappropriate" in their costumes, as reported by *Campus Reform*. "Halloween has also become known for more dangerous and damaging traditions like binge drinking, sexualized or culturally inappropriate costumes, and vandalism," the administrator and student body president wrote to students. "We urge our community to be aware of the potentially harmful impact insensitive behavior can have on fellow students, other members of the Gonzaga community, and our Logan neighbors." During an event, a University of Utah administrator even called cultural appropriation "the baby of racism and capitalism," as reported by *Campus Reform*. *Campus Reform* reached out to Furman University but did not receive a response in time for publication.

https://www.campusreform.org/?ID=13877

Colin Kaepernick calls Independence Day a 'celebration of white supremacy' and REJECTS it because black people have been 'dehumanized, brutalized, criminalized and terrorized' in the US for centuries

By Matthew Wright July 4th, 2020

Colin Kaepernick issued a fierce rebuke of Independence Day, slamming the 'celebration of white supremacy' and calling out America for 'centuries' of abuse against black people.

The star athlete and activist took to **Twitter** to share the powerful rejection, along with a video of actor James Earl Jones reciting Frederick Douglass's renowned speech 'What to the Slave Is the 4th of July?' The video showed a series of shocking visuals, including photos of slave auctions, Ku Klux Klan members, lynchings, videos of officers brutally beating black inmates and of police brutality, racist caricature drawings and the works.

'Black ppl have been dehumanized, brutalized, criminalized + terrorized by America for centuries, & are expected to join your commemoration of 'independence', while you enslaved our ancestors,' Kaepernick said in his tweet. 'We reject your celebration of white supremacy & look forward to liberation for all.' Kaepernick's tweet comes as Americans across the United States take part in historic demonstrations following the death of Ahmaud Arbery, Breonna Taylor and George Floyd.

Roughly 15 million people to 26 million people have been a part of demonstrations to protest against systemic racism and police brutality in the United States.

Recent surveys show that more than 4,700 demonstrations have happened in the United States since May 26, averaging out to roughly 140 per day. Douglass was a prolific abolitionist who often called out the hypocrisy of the Founding Fathers while also applauding their ideals of freedom. He made the patriotic speech the day after the 4th of July in 1852.

https://www.dailymail.co.uk/news/article-8490247/Colin-Kaepernick-calls-Independence-Day-celebration-white-supremacy-REJECTS-it.html

Pamela Anderson's Native American Halloween costume gets her accused of cultural appropriation

By Tyler McCarthy November 4th, 2019

Pamela Anderson is catching serious backlash over her2019 Halloween costume with many on Twitter calling out the 52-year-old model for cultural appropriation.

The former "Baywatch" star and animal rights activist took to Twitter on Thursday to share a pair of images to celebrate Halloween. The first image shows Anderson in high-waisted underwear with what appears to be white paint covering her breasts. In her left hand, she's holding a Native American headdress. In the other photo, Anderson poses topless on a staircase with her back to the camera. This time, she's wearing the full oversized headdress and tipping it to the camera. The post almost immediately caught people's attention on social media, with several users noting that it seems the actress is appropriating Native American culture.

"I hate to break the news to u Pamela but this is the quintessential cultural appropriation that people are not liking. The Native head dress. Not so cool," one user on Twitter wrote. The star didn't directly respond to her detractors' claims of cultural appropriation other than to share an article titled "The Illogic of Cultural Appropriation." However, that doesn't mean she hasn't engaged with her own backlash. Several users claim to have been blocked by Anderson's account after calling out her Halloween costume.

"I'm blocked from Pamela Anderson's account because I, like many others, told her what I thought about her ugly Native-insulting Halloween photos," one user write. "Jail her." #Pamelaanderson blocked me on twitter because she got called out for being a hypocrite and posting her Halloween costume head dress. So celebs can get away with what ever they want?" another user claimed.mA rep for Anderson did not immediately return Fox News' request for comment.

https://www.foxnews.com/entertainment/pamela-anderson-cultural-appropriation-halloween-native-american-headdress

New Hampshire Town Removes Christmas From Its Christmas Ceremony After Two People Complain About Being Offended

By Paul Joseph Watson November 19th, 2019

The town of Durham, New Hampshire announced it was removing several Christmassy elements from its annual "holiday celebration" because two people complained about being offended.

Yes, really.

According to CBS Boston, the town's Annual Tree Lighting Ceremony will undergo changes "in an effort to remove religious overtones." The event will be renamed 'Frost Fest' while the formal tree lighting ceremony itself will be abolished and Santa will not arrive in a town firetruck as he has in the past.

Christmas wreaths that were placed on lamp posts on Main Street will also be absent.

According to councilor Town Councilor Sally Tobias, the changes were made after one person "said that he had always had a problem with the Christmas tree."

"There were a couple of people that did express some concerns about how they felt being included," Tobias said. So in other words, because two weak-minded idiots complained about being offended, the town voted to take Christmas out of its Christmas celebrations, undoubtedly angering the vast majority of residents. "To stop cultures and faiths from practicing publicly would be very un-American. I think that's the beauty of our country," said Rabbi Berel Slavaticki, who was refused when he asked the town to display a Menorah during the eight days of Hanukkah last year.

https://www.infowars.com/new-hampshire-town-removes-christmas-from-its-christmas-ceremony-after-two-people-complain-about-being-offended/

Students say it's NOT Okay to Celebrate Thanksgiving

By Kyle Hooten November 26th, 2019

As Thanksgiving draws near, *The College Fix* visited Macalester College in Minnesota to ask students if it's acceptable to celebrate the holiday.

Most of the students said no, and several gave a qualified yes, that being it's okay to celebrate Thanksgiving as long as one keeps in mind the oppression it represents or that it's more about spending time with family than honoring the past.

For those who said no, they mainly focused on themes such as oppression and colonization. "I think that Thanksgiving has been misconstrued a lot, especially in textbooks," one student told *The College Fix*. "It's kind of just based off of the genocide of indigenous people and I don't really think that we actually give thanks on Thanksgiving, we just eat a bunch of food and it's just a bunch of capitalist bullshit." A few students took this a step further, explaining how they believe most American holidays are rooted in oppression.

"What do Americans do except for celebrate unethical holidays," one student said. Another student interviewed outside the campus chapel said that no holidays with religious connotations should be observed. After spending several hours speaking with students, *The College Fix* found only a handful who unabashedly supported Thanksgiving.

https://www.thecollegefix.com/video-students-say-its-not-okay-to-celebrate-thanksgiving/

Millennials want to ban 'Secret Santa' because it 'gives them anxiety'

By Yael Halon November 25th, 2019

Some millennials want to bring an end to the "Secret Santa" office holiday tradition because it "gives them anxiety," a recent study found. British job-hunting website Jobsite reported that millennials find the "Secret Santa" gift exchange to be anxiety-inducing -- and Dr. Ashley Weinberg, a psychology lecturer at the University of Salford in Manchester, believes it is the fear of appearing "stingy" that makes the holiday tradition "stressful."

The study found that 78% of millennials felt they contributed "more than they should" to an office party gift compared to 58% of the rest of the workforce, while 26% of millennials admitted to dipping into savings or over-drafting their accounts to fund an office gift. Nearly 17% reported that they "felt judged" by their co-workers for their choice of gift. Discussing the study's findings on Fox Nation's "After the Show Show," the "Fox & Friends" hosts had mixed opinions about the holiday gift swap.

"I hate it... I hate it so much," said co-host Jillian Mele in a recent episode of the show. "People spend too much money as is around the holidays so why are we adding to it? Maybe you should have the conversation with your co-workers... 'let's not do it.'"nAsked whether the practice gives her anxiety, Mele, 37, was quick to respond."It does, I'm already figuring out what to get everyone," she said.

Guest host Emily Compagno suggested a $10 maximum, addressing financial concerns, but Mele still wasn't sold on the idea. "Even if it's $10, those are sometimes the hardest because you want to get a really good gift but it's hard to find," she said. "I don't know, I just hate it."

"You can't go wrong with a gift card to a coffee place," Compagno responded.

"Go to the dollar store and just get some crazy stuff," co-host Steve Doocy chimed in.

Asked why nearly 1 in 3 millennials want to boot the holiday tradition, Weinberg said it was the pressure from social media that contributed to the reported anxiety. "If you've grown up in a world where social media is at your fingertips and those kinds of social judgments are being made fairly constantly, suddenly you're even more aware of what others might be thinking. Naturally, that's going to spill over into all kinds of areas, particularly something that can be a social taboo when you think about maybe not giving, or maybe questioning why people are giving," Weinberg said.

https://www.foxla.com/news/millennials-want-to-ban-secret-santa-because-it-gives-them-anxiety

People Are Calling 'Rudolph, The Red-Nosed Reindeer' Racist

By Sethuraman S November 27th, 2019

Rudolph The Red-Nosed Reindeer might be a holiday classic but it's certainly whipping up some controversy with time. The 1964 stop motion television special is a regular feature on TV every holiday season but those that watched it as kids are finding it be problematic on many accounts ranging from marginalization, racism, and homophobia, according to a report by Huffington Post. Many Twitter users commented on the cartoon and found underlying problems with it. One Twitter user labeled Santa "a bigoted exploitative prick." The holiday classic certainly hasn't aged well.

Viewers saw a pattern of bullying and shaming throughout the cartoon. Rudolph's father, for example, often lambasts the poor baby reindeer to cover up his shiny nose, oblivious to Rudolph feeling targeted and shamed. The pattern continues for most of the cartoon with many users pointing out that the school coach encourages the bullying of Rudolph for looking different from the others.

One Twitter user wrote: *Yearly reminder that #Rudolph the Red-Nosed Reindeer is a parable on racism & homophobia w/Santa as a bigoted exploitative prick. The exploitative use of elves, which is problematic in the legend of Santa Clause, is prevalent in the stop motion classic as well.* Another user wrote: *Has anyone else noticed that within the first five minutes of #RudolphTheRedNosedReindeer two characters get bullied?* Right beneath the tweet, a disapproving Twitter user wrote: *Don't care. It's a cartoon.*

One user wrote: *Watching Rudolph the Red-Nosed Reindeer. The moral of the story I've learned since watching it as a kid: People are dicks until they need something from you.* Not everyone enjoyed watching their childhood classic being criticized. Many requested the holiday cartoon to be left alone and argued that it preached acceptance and Rudolph's triumph at the end is a reflection of that. One user tweeted: *This 54yr old children's movie teaches lessons of acceptance, equality, forgiveness, perseverance. It teaches people not to be judgmental, it teaches it's ok to be and to accept those different from themselves. All lessons people could still learn today.* That's hardly problematic IMO. Donald Trump Jr. had his own take on the debate and tweeted: *Liberalism is a disease.*

While the discourse surrounding the cartoon is starkly divided, perhaps it might be good to reflect and understand that a film made over 50 years ago wasn't racist and problematic by design but just didn't age well. One thing is for sure, the debate surrounding the stop motion classic isn't going anywhere and is likely to resurface every holiday season.

https://life.shared.com/people-accusing-holiday-classic-rudolph-red-nosed-reindeer-being-racist-bigoted?utm_medium=Social&utm_source=Facebook#Echobox=1574859532

People say Santa should now be female or gender neutral - sparking debate

By Robyn Darbyshire December 18th, 2019

Many will always think of Father Christmas a jolly white-bearded fellow with a penchant for wearing red and eating treats left beside the chimney.

But now people are wondering whether Santa needs an update for modern times, as one company has offered the possibility of Father Christmas becoming a gender neutral person. GraphicSprings , a logo creation company, polled 400 people from the US and UK about potential ways to modernise Santa, using the top suggestions to poll a further 4,000 people on how they envision him.

In total over one quarter (27%) of respondents reckon he should be rebranded as female or gender neutral, according to 6 ABC . Over on social media the results of the survey have had mixed reactions, with some claiming the idea is "ridiculous", while others don't understand the point in arguing over a made up character.

But given Santa Claus is a fictional character designed simply to make Christmas fun for the kids, does it really matter what's underneath his signature red outfit? The issue of what gender Santa should be has taken on a new significance in recent times, as people on social media and even politicians are taking a stance on the issue. Arun Chandran, an Independent councillor for Newton Aycliffe in County Durham, moved to ban female Santa Claus impersonators from taking part in an annual winter parade last month, after two women volunteered for the job.

He said that the concept of a female Santa Claus was "a form of political correctness," adding that it was "a male role", according to Metro . Piers Morgan also chimed in on the subject, saying on Good Morning Britain in response to the story last month: "He's called Father Christmas! ... The world's gone nuts."

Negative opinions on the matter hasn't stopped some people moving forward with a different take on the traditionally male character. Ponsonby Central, a shopping complex in Auckland, New Zealand, unveiled a Santa Claus modelled on Mary Poppins, complete wearing knickers and fishnet stockings last month.

According to Stuff.co.nz , the staff at Ponsonby Central and Blunt said their representation of Santa can be Mary Poppins or whatever race/gender/persuasion they prefer.

https://www.mirror.co.uk/news/weird-news/people-say-santa-should-now-13733947?fbclid=IwAR1znrt8BM-t133hLsT3hRImgKxl-wrImpEmSAUvSHaQ964vDm6812EAL6U

'Rudolph the Red-Nosed Reindeer' Bullying Scenes Blasted by Viewers

By Kyle Phillippi December 2nd, 2019

It's December which means all your favorite Christmas specials are set to be broadcast. On Monday, *Rudolph the Red Nosed Reindeer* will find itself in primetime. The 55-minute long special will air at 8 p.m. ET on CBS. As many know, the film spotlights Rudolph and his journey from an outsider to being the hero of Christmas and leading Santa's sleigh. It's what happens in between, though, that causes some viewers to feel uneasy.

Early on in the episode, Rudolph finds himself needing to wear a fake black nose to hide his "different" red nose per his parent's request. He does so to avoid embarrassment, and ultimately is the center of the joke when it feels off and the other reindeer, besides Clarice, make fun of him. The scenes of bullying strike a chord with some home viewers.

"Between Rudolph and Hermie...The North Pole seems like the most toxic work environment to ever exist. Ruthless bullying and then banishment to the Island of Misfit Toys," another user wrote. In 2018, one of the special's voice actors, defended the show in an interview with *TMZ*.

"I don't think that by getting sensitive to bullying that you want to copy it... you want to get rid of it!" Conley said. "And certainly in *Rudolph The Red-Nosed Reindeer*, everyone is reconciled happily at the end of the movie and let's hope in today's society, the things that people are bullying about can also be rectified." *Rudolph The Red-Nosed Reindeer* premiered in 1964. It was followed up a decade later by *Rudolph's Shiny New Year* in 1976.

https://popculture.com/tv-shows/news/wheel-of-fortune-vanna-white-reveals-rare-photo-with-dad/

Holidays

The "War on Christmas" has been occurring for a very long time. It seems that it started somewhere in the late 1990s and has got worse every year since then. Christmas songs are being cancelled and "Christmas Break" in school is now "Holiday Break." Christmas movies are under attack as well. The "War on Christmas" is essentially a "War on Christians." The Christians are not alone in their persecution. Also, under attack is Thanksgiving for being "racist" and promoting "colonization." Halloween is also under fire from these authoritarian control freaks as they want to dictate what costumes are "appropriate" and "acceptable." Gone are the days of dressing like a cowboy or Indian. Gone are the days of dressing up like a farmer or hillbilly. Gone are the days of dressing up as an army man, sexy pirate, or any "cultural appropriation" outfits. The 4th of July is also being cancelled and labeled as "racist." Mother's Day and Father's Day are too being taken out for being "exclusionary" and "sexist" by the tyrannical mob. Columbus Day is now Indigenous People's Day. Valentine's Day is under assault as a form of "heteronormativity." Memorial Day is being booted because (according to the psychopaths), it promotes western military expansion and colonization. In the radial world of leftist utopia, every holiday must be banned, censored, controlled, modified, renamed, or cancelled.

22

The War on Guns

12-year-old suspended after teacher spots toy gun during virtual class

By Frank Miles September 7th, 2020

A 12-year-old boy in Colorado got a five-day suspension for flashing a toy gun across his computer screen during an online art class, according to a report. The El Paso County Sheriff's Office said although the teacher thought it was a toy gun authorities still did a welfare check on Isaiah Elliott without parental notification. "It was really frightening and upsetting for me as a parent, especially as the parent of an African-American young man, especially given what's going on in our country right now," Curtis Elliott, Isaiah's father, told KDVR.

He said his son, who has been diagnosed with attention deficit hyperactivity disorder (ADHD) and has learning disabilities, wasn't aware the gun was shown on screen in his distance learning. "He was in tears when the cops came. He was just in tears. He was scared. We all were scared. I literally was scared for his life," said Curtis Elliott.

"The virtual setting is not the same as the school setting," the dad added. "He did not take the toy gun to school. He's in the comfort of his own home. It's a toy." The toy gun was neon green and black with an orange tip featuring the words on the handle: "Zombie Hunter."

Reports said the school district, the Widefield District #3, refused to give the Elliott family the recording of the online class, but authorities showed the family a video of the class from a recording from a police body camera. The boy's mother said the punishment didn't fit the crime. "For them to go as extreme as suspending him for five days, sending the police out, having the police threaten to press charges against him because they want to compare the virtual environment to the actual in-school environment is insane," said Dani Elliott.

She said she wishes the teacher had reasoned with the parents before condemning the boy. "If her main concern was his safety, a two-minute phone call to me or my husband could easily have alleviated this whole situation to where I told them it was fake," said Dani Elliott.

The school won't apologize for its discipline. The Grand Mountain school said in a statement: "We follow all school board policies whether we are in-person learning or distance learning. We take the safety of all our students and staff very seriously. Safety is always our number one priority." The parents are looking to enroll their son in a charter or private school. "I definitely feel they crossed the line," said the mom. "They were extreme with their punishment, especially sending the police out and traumatizing my son and my family."

https://www.foxnews.com/us/12-year-old-suspended-after-teacher-spots-toy-gun-during-virtual-class

Fordham University Student Banned from Campus, Punished by School For Lawful Gun Photo

By Richard Moorhead July 20th, 2020

New York City's Fordham University is punishing a rising senior at the school for little more than posting a legal rifle picture on social media to express his support for the Second Amendment.

Dean of Students D. Keith Eldredge banned Austin Tong from even appearing on campus for two Instagram posts. In the rifle picture in question, Tong is holding his legally owned AR-15 rifle, which is modified to be fully compliant with New York's gun laws. The picture is captioned with 'Don't Tread on Me,' and #198964, a reference to the

Chinese government's persecution of political dissidents at Tiananmen Square.

Tong also shared a picture of murdered Saint Louis retired police captain David Dorn, who was shot and killed by a criminal looter while trying to secure a friend's small business during the area's George Floyd riots.

Tong was confronted with a letter from Eldredge informing him that he was being investigated for alleged "*violation of university regulations relating to bias or hate crimes, threats/intimidation, and disorderly conduct.*"

Tong was later adjudicated to be "guilty" of supposed university crimes, on the mere basis of his two slightly conservative and milquetoast Instagram posts, after declining to attend a formal interrogation hearing at the University. He's hence been banned from so much as appearing on campus, representing Fordham in any capacity until his graduation, and holding any leadership role in a campus club.

Tong has described his support of gun rights and the Second Amendment as inherent to his experience as an immigrant from China. Speaking to Campus Reform, he's describing Fordham's arbitrary sanction as 'Soviet-style interrogation and punishment.' "*I want to honor the memory of an important Chinese Democracy Movement and the appreciation of the right to bear arms in America... As an immigrant, a big beauty of America to me is the right it gives its citizens to bear arms, not only to protect themselves but also to keep the government in check.*"

The Foundation for Individual Rights in Education has reached out to Fordham, demanding that the university rescind its ridiculous punishments against Tong for little more than gun pictures and memorializing David Dorn.

"*America is under attack. Americans are being silenced. I hope to use my punishment as a milestone and reflection of the constitutional crisis we are facing today as a society. Coming to this country as an immigrant, one would think that America is a nation of law and free speech. Yet that is no longer the case...Not simply did Fordham University break its promise and punish me, but it signaled to students nationwide that free speech is a political trap that will destroy you,"* Tong told Campus Reform.

https://bigleaguepolitics.com/fordham-university-student-banned-from-campus-punished-by-school-for-lawful-gun-photo/

Pointing a finger gun lands 12-year-old Johnson County student in handcuffs

By Mará Rose Williams By October 9th, 2019

A 12-year-old Overland Park girl formed a gun with her fingers, pointed at four of her Westridge Middle School classmates one at a time, and then turned the pretend weapon toward herself. Police hauled her out of school in handcuffs, arrested her and charged the child with a felony for threatening.

Shawnee Mission school officials said they could not discuss the case, citing privacy laws, but did say it wasn't the district that arrested the child. "We don't do that," said spokesman David Smith. "That is not our job." He said the role of the district police is "not to enforce the law but to keep kids and adults safe." A school resource officer, employed, by the Overland Park Police Department, would have handled the arrest, Smith said. The department said it could not discuss the case.

But according to Johnson County District Court documents, on Sept. 18, the girl "unlawfully and feloniously communicated a threat to commit violence, with the intent to place another, in fear, or with the intent to cause the evacuation, lock down or disruption in regular, ongoing activities ..." or created just the risk of causing such fear.

The Overland Park Police incident report provided to The Star included no details of what happened, only the date, time and place. A person familiar with a more detailed incident report spoke to The Star on condition of anonymity. The person said that during a class discussion, another student asked the girl, if she could kill five people in the class, who would they be? In response, the girl allegedly pointed her finger pistol — like the ones many children use playing cops and robbers.

Because of that gesture, The Star was told, the girl was sent to Principal Jeremy McDonnell's office, and the other students involved were also talked to. The school resource officer recommended that she be arrested, the source said. She was detained by police and later released to her mother. A hearing in the Juvenile Division of the District Court of Johnson County is set for Tuesday. "I think that this is something that probably could have been handled in the principal's office and got completely out of hand," said Jon Cavanaugh, the girl's grandfather in California, where the girl is now living. He said his granddaughter has no access to a real gun and she had no intent of harming anyone. "She was just mouthing off," he said.

Smith said that in general, pointing a finger pistol might violate the district's policy against intimidation and bullying. "I might not have anything in my hand but I might be so clear that the individual definitely feels threatened," Smith said.

Following the many school shootings across the country, such as last year's Feb. 14 mass killing at Marjory Stoneman Douglas High School in Parkland, Florida, many states have adopted zero-tolerance polices for bullying and threatening. School officials are sensitive to any gesture or language that could threaten the safety of students, teachers or school staff. In 2015, a Colorado first-grader was suspended from school after forming his fingers into the shape of a gun, pointing toward a classmate and saying, "You're dead." School officials there said they have a zero-tolerance policy when it comes to threats.

A year earlier, in Columbus, Ohio, a 10-year-old boy was suspended for three days for pretending his finger was a gun. He reportedly pointed it at another student's head. Last month in the Shawnee Mission district, two 13-year-old students at Hocker Grove Middle School showed up with guns — the real thing — found stashed in their backpacks. Both were charged as juveniles in possession of a firearm, a misdemeanor that carries a penalty of up to one year in jail, a fine of up to $2,500 or both.

It's a felony only if a kid commits the same crime a second time. The principal of Hocker Grove said there was no evidence suggesting the teens had planned to use the guns at school.

According to district policy, having a gun at school results in expulsion for up to 186 days, but it wasn't clear how the two students were disciplined. Threatening is a felony. Shawnee Mission's policies define intimidation as "any intentional written, verbal, electronic, or physical act or threat which is severe, persistent and pervasive enough that it may be expected to: Harm a student or damage a student's property. Create fear of harm to a student or fear of damage to a student's property. Interferes with a student's education or participation in a school-sponsored activity or event. Create an intimidating or threatening educational environment."

The policy states that "conferencing, corrective discipline, and/or referral to law enforcement" could occur in such cases. A felony charge could hurt a student's chances of being accepted into certain colleges or the military. "I'm really worried about my granddaughter's future," Cavanaugh said. He said he was told the child could face as much as a year at a juvenile detention center.

https://www.kansascity.com/news/local/crime/article235891762.html

Judge Refuses to Dismiss Terror Charges Against Young Conservative Who Posted Rifle Pic on Social Media

By Shane Trejo June 28th, 2020

20-year-old Lucas Gerhard, who faces up to 20 years in prison for posting a picture of his rifle on social media, was denied his motion to dismiss charges on June 11 in a Chippewa County court in Sault Ste. Marie, Mich.

Big League Politics broke the story earlier this year of how Gerhard was banned from continuing his studies at Lake Superior State University dorm and charged with making terroristic threats because he posted an image that triggered a far-left student on campus. Because the student was scared by a picture of a firearm with text making fun of liberal snowflakes, Gerhard is facing decades in prison as a result.

The Court repeatedly denied a request made by Gerhard's lawyer, Nick Somberg to record the proceedings and broadcast them on the internet. They are determined to keep the railroading of an outspoken conservative under the cover of darkness, particularly now that the story has gone viral. Many supporters of Gerhard were denied entry into the courthouse as well, with the COVID-19 pandemic used as an excuse to keep them out.

The prosecutor made the argument that because Gerhard posted a picture of his rifle along with a comment regarding how the firearm would offend campus snowflakes on Snapchat, this was adequate to proceed with terror charges and a jury trial. Circuit Court Judge James Lambros ultimately concurred with the argument from the prosecution and denied Gerhard's motion to dismiss. The case will likely head to trial as a result of Lambros' decision.

"My opinion is that the judge had no choice but to take the safe approach, as many of the unorthodox and contextually misleading arguments that the prosecution introduced were simply bells that could not be unrung at that point," said Gerhard's father, Mark, a retired Marine Colonel, to Big League Politics.

Despite the judge commenting positively on Gerhard's demeanor and complimenting the young man for his composure while facing the charges, Gerhard was ultimately kept on a tether because of highly irregular behavior from the prosecution. They inexplicably produced a video of a Mosque shooting in Christchurch, New Zealand from 2019 and played it in the courtroom for several minutes to bias the proceedings.

"As a Marine, I've been exposed to some incredibly traumatic events [to include combat], and even so, it was entirely sickening watching the violent video. It was one of the most horrifying things I've ever seen in my life. The point of a tether is to prevent someone from fleeing bond. How the prosecutor was allowed to play this for seven or eight minutes, without any real contextual value linking the reasoning as to why Lucas should remain tethered, was both mystifying and disturbing," Col. Gerhard said to Big League Politics. "I feel it was borderline unethical and certainly inappropriate for the prosecutor to introduce something so inflammatory, knowing full well the Judge would not know the basis of how and where it was derived from," he added.

Because Lucas was in a Snapchat group in which the video was shared, he was deemed a threat by the courts, and his strict confinement was upheld – in yet another egregious violation of his 1st Amendment rights by the state of the Michigan. The video was not listed as evidence beforehand, and this footage completely unrelated to the case was improperly used to manipulate the hearing.

The prosecution was adamant to Gerhard's attorney that they will not give up the case because they wish to strip Lucas of his 2nd Amendment rights forever and send a message to conservatives nationwide. They are pulling out all the stops to make an example that there are no more core freedoms, only privileges that can and will be yanked away in a moment's notice, in the new Soviet-style regime being instituted nationwide.

The Gerhard family has also yet to receive a written order from the state in order to appeal the court's rejection of the motion to dismiss. They have 21 days to file the appeal, and they fear that the state will send them the order after their window has expired – yet again using coronavirus as the rationale to stack the deck even further against Lucas.

The Gerhard family is also concerned that the state may be dragging the case out in an attempt to bleed them dry of funds. After the family is made financially destitute by the system, a guilty plea could more easily be coerced, which would set a precedent used to deprive outspoken conservatives of their constitutional rights. These are the same tactics that the feds tried to use on General Michael Flynn before he was ultimately vindicated and exonerated.

Right now, the Gerhard family is asking for support as they continue their fight for the Bill of Rights and to keep Lucas out of prison. A defense fund has been set up in Lucas' name via GoFundMe to defray the incredibly high cost of his substantial legal expenses, as the family hopes to escape the horrifying ordeal and prevent an incredible injustice from taking place. Big League Politics will continue to provide updates on the Gerhard case as it proceeds.

https://bigleaguepolitics.com/judge-refuses-to-dismiss-terror-charges-against-young-conservative-who-posted-rifle-pic-on-social-media/

University of Virginia ending 21-gun salute over potential 'panic' by students

By John Gage November 11th, 2019

The University of Virginia announced it would be eliminating the 21-gun salute from its Veterans Day ceremony because they did not want to cause any trauma to students who might hear the gunshots.

"One is that it would be disruptive to classes and two unfortunately with gun violence in the U.S., there was some concern that we would cause a panic if someone heard gunshots on grounds," Jim Ryan, the college's president, told NBC29. The decision was made by the provost's office along with UVA's ROTC program. The Veterans Day program at UVA has included a 21-gun salute for over a decade.

Veteran Jay Levine, who was in UVA's ROTC program, said he was unhappy with the decision and planned to recruit other veterans to protest the school's decision. "I am very disillusioned, very upset, and very surprised that they would make such a decision," Levine said. UVA's Veterans Day ceremony is held for 24-hours from Monday at 4 p.m. until Tuesday. The 21-gun salute typically follows the conclusion of the event.

https://www.washingtonexaminer.com/news/university-of-virginia-ending-21-gun-salute-over-potential-panic-by-students

Guns

Toy guns? Banned. Nerf-type guns? Cancelled. Handgun emoji? Replaced with a green water pistol. Elmer Fudd's shotgun? Cancelled. Yosemite Sam's six shooters? Banned. The assault of guns and firearms is occurring in every country. Specifically in America, guns are under attack from the very dangerous, authoritarian control freaks. The main problem is this... We know what happens in countries when the guns are confiscated from the people:

Mao - China
Hitler - Germany
Stalin - Russia
Castro - Cuba
Chavez - Venezuela

In each one of these countries, once the guns were taken and banned, hell on earth occurred. Millions of innocent people were either murdered or put into internment camps. Also, once the government had control over the guns, they had control over the people, their freedom, food supply, gas supply, imports and exports, and their day-to-day lives. Guns are under attack because the people that want to ban them have very sinister, insidious, and nefarious ideas on what they plan to do to us.

23

The War on Comedy

School Threatens to Exclude Students Who Make Jokes About Coronavirus

By Paul Joseph Watson September 2nd, 2020

A school in the UK has vowed to exclude students who make jokes about coronavirus.

Yes, really.

Pupils at the Ark Alexandra Academy in Hastings, East Sussex, "could be excluded for "malicious coughing or sneezing" or making "inappropriate" jokes about the coronavirus pandemic," reports the Independent. In a letter sent out to parents, the school said that any student caught violating the rules will not be allowed to return "until a risk assessment and we can be assured that the student will adhere to all our expectations."

An affiliated school, Ark Byron Primary Academy in Acton, west London, has also said that students who refuse to follow social distancing rules will "immediately be moved to a separate area."

"Worth remembering that Milan Kundera's satirical novel The Joke about a man whose life is destroyed after he makes an inappropriate gag on a postcard to his girlfriend was set in Soviet-controlled Czechoslovakia," writes Toby Young. Under new rules, students in Scotland above the age of 5 are mandated to wear a face mask in every area of the school apart from classrooms.

In England, face masks are mandatory in communal areas in schools situated where regional lockdowns are in place. All this despite the fact that just six children under 18 have died in the UK with COVID-19 and all of them had a serious comorbidity. Meanwhile, this is the "new normal" students are currently experiencing. Nothing less than prison training.

https://www.infowars.com/school-threatens-to-exclude-students-who-make-jokes-about-coronavirus/

John Cleese: Woke People Have "Zero Sense Of Humour"; They're Killing Comedy

By Steve Watson August 5th, 2020

Legendary British comedian John Cleese has hit out at permanently offended woke people, insisting that they have no sense of humour and are contributing to the death of comedy. In an appearance on the Daily Beast's The Last Laugh Podcast, Cleese noted that woke people simply do not understand the intricacies of comedy.

"There's plenty of people who are PC now who have absolutely zero sense of humour. I would love to debate, in a friendly way, a couple of 'woke' people in front of an audience. And I think the first thing I would say is, please tell me a good 'woke' joke," Cleese urged.

"What they don't understand is that there's two types of teasing," Cleese continued, noting that "There's really nasty teasing, which is horrible, and we shouldn't do it, full stop. But the other type of teasing is affectionate. You can tease people hugely affectionately and it's a bonding mechanism."

"All humour is critical. You cannot get laughs out of perfect human beings," Cleese continued, adding that "If you've got someone up on the screen who is perfect, intelligent and kind and flexible and a good person, there's nothing funny about that. So we only laugh at people's frailties, but that's not cruel. You can laugh at people's frailties in very funny and generous ways."

Cleese was recently at the centre of a 'woke' storm when his Fawlty Towers show, made some 40 years ago was temporarily canceled after complaints that it featured a 'racist' character. Cleese called the BBC "cowardly and gutless" for removing an episode of the show, pointing out that the racist character in question was the target of ridicule in the show. Cleese has previously warned that political correctness will lead to the death of comedy, noting that "If you start to say we mustn't, we mustn't criticize or offend them then humor is gone. With humor goes a sense of proportion. And then as far as I'm concerned you're living in 1984."

https://www.infowars.com/john-cleese-woke-people-have-zero-sense-of-humour-theyre-killing-comedy/

SNL Comedian Nimesh Patel Kicked Off Columbia University Stage by Offended Students

By Alana Mastrangelo December 4th, 2018

Saturday Night Live writer and comedian Nimesh Patel was kicked off stage by Columbia University students on Friday night halfway through his performance because students found his jokes "offensive."

Patel's comedy skit was cut short after the students who organized the event interrupted him and demanded that he end his performance early. The students got on stage, took the comedian's microphone, and denounced his jokes in front of the audience, as first reported by The Columbia Spectator.

The event was called cultureSHOCK: Reclaim, a charity performance showcase hosted by the university's Asian American Alliance. The goal of the event was to provide "a platform for a diversity of Asian American artistic expression," as well as seeking to break through "stereotypes and challenges."

According to The Columbia Spectator, members of the student group found Patel's skit offensive, specifically when the comedian joked that being gay cannot be a choice, adding that if a man is both black and gay, "no one looks in the mirror and thinks, 'this black thing is too easy, let me just add another thing to it.'"

When told to leave, the comedian protested, explaining that his performance was simply familiarizing students with the "real world." The student organizers, however, remained insistent that Patel end his skit. "We deeply apologize for inviting [Patel] in the first place and bringing these comments into a space for inclusion and acceptance," the student group posted to its Facebook page following the event, "We apologize for the hurt his words caused members of the community." The student group added that members were "still processing" what had happened. A few students who attended the event told PJ Media that audience members did not boo or shout during Patel's performance, and therefore, they felt that ending the event early was unsolicited.

"I was very surprised. Either that means I'm not as sensitive as I should be, or the whole thing was just dramatic," said one student. Not all students felt the same way, though. "I really dislike when people who are older say that our generation needs to be exposed to the real world," said another student, Sofia Jao, to The Columbia Spectator, "Obviously the world is not a safe space but just accepting that it's not and continuing to perpetuate the un-safeness of it — is saying that it can't be changed."

"When older generations say you need to stop being so sensitive, it's like undermining what our generation is trying to do in accepting others and making it safer," added Jao. It seems as though it was not too long ago when the opposite was true, and younger generations were the ones calling for older generations to loosen the constraints on comedy.

https://www.breitbart.com/tech/2018/12/04/snl-comedian-nimesh-patel-kicked-off-columbia-university-stage-by-offended-students/

Patriots star Rob Gronkowski's suggestive remark to female reporter draws backlash

By Ryan Gaydos January 30th, 2019

New England Patriots star Rob Gronkowski drew backlash Tuesday after making a sexually suggestive remark to a female reporter during Super Bowl Media Day. Gronkowski, 29, was asked what were the chances he would return next season after playing in Sunday's Super Bowl LIII against the Los Angeles Rams. "You guys know my favorite number. You know what I'm talking about. She knows what number I'm talking about," Gronkowski said as he pointed to a female reporter. "Ask her. That's the answer."

He then tried to break down his answer with a math problem, according to the New York Post. "I'll give you a math problem: What's six times nine plus six plus nine?" he said.

Many in attendance seemed stunned by Gronkowski's comments -- and some expressed their displeasure. "That one is a crossing the line. I think there has been a pass that's been given to Rob Gronkowski for a really long time," New York City radio host Maggie Gray said on WFAN. "I think part of the pass that he gets comes with the fact he is doing this and really doesn't have anything in his past or in his private life that would indicate he actually has an issue. It just seems like an act."

Gray's co-host, former New York Jets linebacker Bart Scott, also appeared to be offended by the tight end's comment. "Workplace etiquette, right?" he said. "He has to understand that this is business time, it's workplace time, that you can't go that route. It's not the time or the place." A Twitter user asked if the episode would have "a lasting impact."

"If you REALLY want the #MeToo movement to have a second wave that will have a lasting impact? Suspend @RobGronkowski for what he said to the female reporter about what his favorite number is. Great football player, complete idiot, not cool. Apologize or don't play," the person wrote. Gronkowski has been making the same joke for a while, including a more cringe-worthy version at the Daytona 500 auto race in 2017. It appears some are not too happy about it this time.

https://www.foxnews.com/sports/new-england-patriots-rob-gronkowski-receives-backlash-over-sexually-suggestive-remark-at-female-reporter

Hyundai Made Fun of Vegans in Its Super Bowl Spot and PETA Is Furious

By Brandon Friederich February 4th, 2019

Sandwiched between plays of the lowest-scoring Super Bowl ever and an admittedly lackluster halftime performance by Maroon 5, there were the customary multimillion-dollar commercials.

Nearly everyone agrees that brands played it safe with this year's Big Game spots. Well, everyone except PETA. It seems People for the Ethical Treatment of Animals took issue with Hyundai implying that eating vegan "Beetloaf" sucks more than than getting a root canal, showing up for jury duty, or taking the middle seat on an airplane. Watch it above. Actor Jason Bateman plays a bellhop on an elevator that travels down, visiting floors filled with universally disliked experiences along the way. At the very bottom is "Car Shopping" which is where the South Korean automaker plugs their "Hyundai Shopper Assurance" service.

PETA's problem was with the "Vegan Dinner Party" floor. The organization voiced its displeasure on Twitter and suggested that viewers by a Mercedes-Benz Smart car instead of a Hyundai. "The trend of 2019 is taking the elevator UP to vegan dinner parties (and an Earth, heart, & animal-friendly lifestyle)," read the organization's tweet, "Instead of buying a car from people with outdated ideas, we suggest a vegan Smart-car by Mercedes. Great mileage & acceleration, turns on a dime."

Responses to PETA's tweet poured in, with many users claiming that animal rights group has no sense of humor. Someone at Hyundai

USA went into damage control mode and posted a recipe for the "Beetloaf" seen in the ad with the words, "We actually love vegan food and are glad it's going more mainstream." For what it's worth, PETA recommends seven different Hyundai models with leather-free interiors on its website.

Maybe a bite of "Beetloaf" will help those angry vegans get the bad taste out of their mouth.

https://www.maxim.com/news/hyundai-super-bowl-commercial-upsets-peta-2019-2

Making jokes at Portland State gets you reported to its bias response team

By Christian Schneider March 20th, 2019

Members of the campus community at Portland State better think twice about making a joke on campus — it could very well lead to their names being reported to the university's bias response team.

Two bias reports filed at the public institution last fall were against people making jokes or similar off-hand comments on campus, according to documents obtained by *The College Fix* through a public records act request. In one case from last September, a student overheard someone in their classroom making a comment about sometimes feeling like they having schizophrenia.

"She then stated she was not trying to make fun of schizophrenia," the student reported, "but that sometimes she can be 'schizophrenic.' ... She stated this in a joking manner and even laughed about it." The student reported the incident to the PSU Bias Review Team, keeping his or her identity a secret. But the person who allegedly made the offending remark, however, was named in the complaint to the administration.

In the second instance, last October a student settled into a seat in the front row of a lecture when they heard the instructor telling another student he knew a lot of "insensitive jokes" he couldn't tell in class. "He proceeded to describe one he like [sic] about Native Americans where he called the characters racist names like chief running water and other names in that style," the student complained. "He did not tell the whole joke, but he said it ended with one of the chief's sons killing someone or being killed," the student said, adding "I did not hear his exact words because he was trying to be quiet." According to the student, the instructor said he knows many more jokes he could not tell in class.

"I am worried he may have impacted any Native students' ability to learn safely in his class by taking advantage of stereotypes created by people to dehumanize Native people after taking their land and committing genocide and the generational trauma they face from that," the student added.

Once again, the complaint was submitted anonymously, but the instructor's name was reported to the university. According to the PSU Global Diversity and Inclusion department's website, making an online report "does NOT initiate an employee discrimination and harassment or a student conduct investigation." In the documents provided to *The Fix*, all personal identifying information was redacted.

According to the university's website, "Any person who has experienced, witnessed, or heard of a bias incident" is encouraged to file a complaint electronically. Students and faculty members are allowed to file a complaint of discrimination against "any PSU student, staff, or faculty member who you believe is engaging in discrimination, discriminatory harassment, or retaliation."

According to the university, "bias" is "a state of mind, tendency, or inclination that impacts our behaviors and perceptions of others (either positively or negatively) based upon preconceived notions." Bias can be "directed toward an attitude, an individual, or group regarding their protected class, including (but not limited to) race, color, religious ideology, national origin, veteran status, sex, sexual orientation, gender identity, gender expression, physical or mental ability, or political affiliation."

During the fall of 2018, four total complaints were filed with the bias response team. In addition to the ones involving jokes, on October 14 a university employee was pulling into the Shattuck Hall parking lot on campus when they saw a white male walking near the entrance to the lot. While the employee waited for the man to pass so they could pull in, the man allegedly looked into the windshield, made his hand into the shape of a pistol and "pulled the trigger." The man then turned away and began to walk south along Broadway.

In the final complaint filed, the student simply reported the place of the incident as "poo" and described the incident with the words "pee pee." Portland State has long been a hotbed of progressive activism. In just the past few weeks, psychology student Lesley Guerra attempted to testify before the university Board of Trustees in favor of armed police officers on campus, but was repeatedly shouted down by protesters.

Earlier in March, pro-gun activist Michael Strickland came to speak on campus but was prevented from doing so by a bell-ringing activist who stood next to Strickland as he attempted to speak. Campus police later said they were unable to do anything to restrain the disruptive bell-ringer.

According to Portland State professor Peter Boghossian, Bias Response Teams create a "chilling" atmosphere on college campuses. Boghossian has been a staunch free speech advocate on the PSU campus following his publication of a nationally famous "Grievance Studies Hoax," in which he and his coauthors successfully published a number of phony "studies" in prestigious academic journals.

"Students and faculty are afraid to have honest conversations—or even joke around with each other—out of fear of being reported for a faux pas," said Boghossian in an email to *The College Fix.* "Bias Response Teams also prevent authentic relationships from emerging because you're never sure if the people you're speaking to believe what they're saying." In an email to *The Fix*, Portland State's communications office said the campus Bias Review Team "communicates and meets regularly to respond to a reported bias incident, and to support students, employees and community members who experience or witness an act of bias."

"When we are informed of bias incidents, we will work hard to get to the root causes and to improve the culture and climate at PSU," said the administration in the statement.

https://www.thecollegefix.com/making-jokes-at-portland-state-gets-you-reported-to-its-bias-response-team/

Southwest passenger allegedly kicked off flight over joke about vodka

By Alexandra Deabler May 14th, 2019

A passenger on a Southwest Airlines flight from Sacramento to Los Angeles was reportedly removed from the plane after he made a joke about vodka, which upset the attendant. According to witness Peter Uzelac, who spoke to FOX40, the Wednesday flight was bound for Austin, Texas, with a layover at LAX. However, while on the tarmac, a maintenance light came on and the plane was forced to return to the gate to check it out.

While the plane was working on the maintenance issue, the flight was delayed again due to a need to refuel. At this point, Uzelac said the attendant started handing out water to passengers since the flight had been delayed for a few hours – and a man sitting near him made a joke. "He said something [like], 'They should be passing out vodka because we've been waiting so long,'" Uzelac said to FOX40.

"[The flight attendant] came by and was like, 'I don't think that and I didn't like your joke,'" he continued. "Then my wife tried to butt-in there and say, 'Look, we've been on this plane for hours.' And [the attendant] says, 'Well, so have I, so get used to it.'" Uzelac said other passengers were shocked by the woman's behavior but dropped it.

"Then all of a sudden, I see her on the telephone up in front," he said. Uzelac told FOX40 the plane returned to the gate again after that, and several Sacramento County sheriff's deputies boarded the flight and removed the man from the plane. "And people started yelling then. In fact, people stood up. I stood up. People were saying this man didn't do anything," Uzelac said.

Police reportedly did not charge the man with a crime, but Uzelac has filed a complaint against the flight attendant with Southwest, the outlet reported. Southwest Airlines told Fox News in a statement that they have contacted the Customer Relations Team over the incident. "We regret any less-than-positive experience a customer has onboard our aircraft. We welcome over 100 million customers each year, and we aim to maintain the comfort of all while delivering Southwest hospitality," the statement said.

https://www.foxnews.com/travel/southwest-kicked-off-flight-joke-vodka

Students triggered by Steve Martin's 'King Tut' on 'SNL'

By Richard Raps November 15th, 2017

Comedian Steve Martin's rendition of "King Tut" is triggering social justice warriors at Reed College because they see it as a form of cultural appropriation.

The song, originally performed on "Saturday Night Live," actually criticizes the commercialization and trivialization of Egyptian history and presents a caricature of the Treasures of Tutankhamun traveling exhibit that toured seven United States cities from 1976 to 1979. However, the context to the SNL skit eludes students who are upset. They are now calling the song a form of "blackface."

The video and song was brought to students' attention when it was played in a humanities class at Reed to spur discussion. Students became so worked up over the video, however, that they have demanded the course be made optional until alternative coursework can be created.

The group primarily upset about the video being played in class, Reedies Against Racism, is comparing Martin's comedic song to the use of the N-word. The Atlantic spoke to members of Reedies Against Racism to get a better idea as to why they are upset about the King Tut song from 1978.

One member of Reedies Against Racism told the Atlantic the song is "like somebody ... making a song just littered with the N-word everywhere." She went on to say that the Egyptian clothing that the backup dancers wear is racist as well. "The gold face of the saxophone dancer leaving its tomb is an exhibition of blackface," she said.

Reedies Against Racism also released a lengthy list of demands which includes a paid day off for Reed staff to boycott the very college they're making demands to. Another demand was that the university host "mandatory conferences for building race sensitivity for staff and faculty." Reedies Against Racism also demanded "the creation of particular scholarships for black students." Students also want the school to host an "Annual anti-oppression workshop for all students, faculty, staff, and administration."

According to the Atlantic, Reedies Against Racism commit to political activism on campus like sit-ins to achieve their goals. The protests associated with the group are described as "visually striking" and reportedly included signs that say things like: "We demand space for students of color," "We cannot be erased," "F*ck Hum 110," and "Stop silencing black and brown voices; the rest of society is already standing on their necks."

Assistant professor Lucía Martínez Valdivia at Reed College, who describes herself as a gay mixed-race woman, wrote an op-ed for t he Washington Post where she talked about how she is afraid to host classes talking about sensitive subject matter due to these protests.

"Some colleagues, including people of color, immigrants and those without tenure, found it impossible to work under these conditions. The signs intimidated faculty into silence, just as intended," wrote Martínez Valdivia.

Reed College has reportedly been attempting to revise their Humanities course to the Reedies Against Racism group's liking but students stopped showing up to the meetings designed to do so. "Hum 110... perpetuates white supremacy—by centering 'whiteness' as the only required class at Reed," according to a Reedies Against Racism statement.

https://www.washingtonexaminer.com/students-triggered-by-steve-martins-king-tut-onsnl?fbclid=IwAR1zU8HGKp9MrNoT-dbI3dCTeFlINp7g4EOFzS7rZT_vP4isiRorPIfr7eW4

Comedy's Civil War: How an 'SNL' Firing Exposed a Growing Rift in Stand-Up

By Seth Abramovitch September 26th, 2019

When *Saturday Night Live* fired Shane Gillis on Sept. 16 — just four days after he was cast as one of the latest Not Ready for Prime Time Players — the news was greeted with high-fives in much of the comedy community. Dana Gould tweeted that Gillis should strive to "be a better comic," while *Silicon Valley* actor Jimmy O. Yang posted that Gillis deserved to go because he was "just plain racist."

But not all comedians were rejoicing. On the contrary, the Gillis controversy — which began hours after his hiring, when podcasts surfaced of the 30-year-old Philadelphia comic calling presidential candidate Andrew Yang a "Jew chink" and spewing other racist and homophobic jokes — has become a flashpoint revealing a deep and widening rift in the comedy world. Like every other aspect of American life in the Trump era, stand-up is turning polarized, pitting comic against comic in an escalating civil war over what's acceptable humor and what's unfunny hate speech. "You millennials, you're a bunch of rats, all of you," Gillis defender Bill Burr snarled on David Spade's Comedy Central show. "None of them cares. All they want to do is get people in trouble."

If the pro-Gillis faction has a rebel base, it would be Gas Digital, a subscription streaming network (it charges $8.50 a month) based in New York's East Village and catering to alt-right sensibilities — or what others see as envelope-pushing, "anything goes" comedy in the vein of Lenny Bruce or Sam Kinison. Gillis was a regular on its airwaves (it's where he cracked his Andrew Yang jokes, as well as another in which he referred to Judd Apatow and actor Chris Gethard as "white faggot comics").

Says Gas Digital co-founder Luis J. Gomez, "It's funny, because when you said one side is very tolerant and inclusive, I was like, 'Yes, that's the side I'm on.' " Gomez, who co-hosts the service's popular *Legion of Skanks* podcast (it tallies half a million downloads per episode), insists any characterization of his network as "alt-right" is wildly off base. "We are on the side of funny," he says. "We're just trying to create freely. I think when you get off Twitter and Reddit and YouTube, you find people who aren't super sensitive about jokes."

But if Gomez — who is Puerto Rican and grew up surrounded by drug abuse and gun violence — distances himself from the alt-right label, he hasn't distanced himself from alt-right ideas or stars. In May, he invited the movement's poster-boy provocateur Milo Yiannopoulos on his *Skanks* podcast, which led to a firestorm of protests and a change of venue after members of the left-wing Antifa movement threatened to storm the Long Island comedy club (The Creek and the Cave) where it was to be taped. "I don't pay attention to politics," Gomez says of booking Yiannopoulos, who's infamous for singing "America the Beautiful" to a roomful of *sieg heil*-ing Nazis and leading a vicious Twitter attack on *SNL*'s Leslie Jones. "I just know that he's a flamboyant gay guy. He was married to a black guy. When people call the guy a Nazi, I'm like, that is the silliest thing I've ever heard."

Gomez has also engaged in freewheeling podcast talk with Gavin McInnes, the Vice Media co-founder turned right-wing leader of the neofascist Proud Boys. But he's also put his arms around some (slightly) less controversial personalities, like Louis C.K., who, in June, performed a surprise set at Skankfest, a three-day comedy festival mounted by Gas Digital in Brooklyn. "The energy when Louis C.K. walked into the building [was intense], everybody from the bartenders to the security guards to the fans. Everybody was stoked," says Gomez.

That *Skanks* festival (which began three years ago, around when Trump got elected) isn't exactly Woodstock — only about 3,600 attended this year — but it is a growth industry (it started with 600). Next year, Gomez will be expanding with one in Houston, and he says he's "in talks" to bring another to L.A. in 2021. Meanwhile, his various Gas Digital podcasts are getting about 1.5 million downloads a week (he won't reveal how many subscribers the company has). It's all part of Gomez's master plan to build a self-sustaining *Skanks* ecosystem insulated from outside forces. "I wanted to create a reverse safe space to create freely," he says, "a platform where [comics] can take chances without backlash."

Not that *Skanks* fans aren't adept at creating backlash of their own: They have made their objections to Gillis' firing extremely clear on Twitter and Reddit. Nor is it the first time Skankers and those like them have marched into battle over what they see as snowflake oppression: In late 2016, Adult Swim canceled *Million Dollar Extreme Presents: World Peace*, a sketch comedy show with alt-right leanings, four months after its premiere amid complaints from some of the network's comedy stars, including Brett Gelman and Tim Heidecker. Heidecker later revealed that he received death threats after the cancellation.

For now, the battle lines remain somewhat porous. (See *THR* columnist Kareem Abdul-Jabbar's take.) Between Gillis' defenders ("To all the 'comedians' who wanted this to happen to Shane ... you are the lowest scum on Earth," tweeted L.A. comic Tony Hinchcliffe) and his detractors ("Fuck that piece of shit," posted *Crazy Rich Asians'* Nico Santos), there's a neutral zone inhabited by comics like Dave Chappelle, who continues to poke at the transgender community (in his latest Netflix special, he likened their plight to being a Chinese man stuck in a black man's body) even as a central pillar of his act has always been identifying racial injustice. Even Janeane Garofalo, the pioneering alt-comedy feminist, performed at Skankfest this year. "She's a real free-speecher and she's also of the generation where 'boys will be boys,' " explains her longtime manager, Dave Rath. "She's thinking about how artists express themselves. Any restrictions to that is what she is reacting to."

Still, it's getting harder to play Switzerland. One well-known comic who asked to remain anonymous because he fears Heidecker-style retribution worries that the Gillis backlash is leading to further divisions and widening the civil war. "They really enjoy these online fights and have started making that the focus of their comedy and podcasts," the stand-up says of Gillis' supporters. "It's a growing rift, and it's a problem." Agrees Rath, "I think we're in this for a while."

https://www.hollywoodreporter.com/features/shane-gillis-snl-firing-comics-mixed-reactions-exposes-growing-rift-stand-up-world-1242739

Director Todd Phillips Says He Made Joker Because "Woke" Hollywood Killed Comedy

By Paul Joseph Watson October 1st, 2019

Joker director Todd Phillips says that "woke" Hollywood and Twitter mob outrage culture has killed comedy. In an interview with Vanity Fair, Phillips said he turned to other themes because he found it increasingly difficult to make comedies in a new "woke" Hollywood that scrutinizes every joke through the lens of identity politics.

"Go try to be funny nowadays with this woke culture," said Phillips. "There were articles written about why comedies don't work anymore—I'll tell you why, because all the fucking funny guys are like,

'Fuck this shit, because I don't want to offend you.' It's hard to argue with 30 million people on Twitter. You just can't do it, right? So you just go, 'I'm out.' I'm out." This is reflected in the script of the Joker, the plot of which centers around "an alienated white guy whose failure to be funny drives him into a vengeful rage."

Indeed, many have expressed concerns that the media's new found obsession with treating the Joker as a white incel propaganda movie will lead to actual incel violence on the day of its release. But aside from this, Phillips is right. Just like numerous other forms of art and entertainment, most comedians have eschewed actually being funny to pursue the amplification of social justice and identity politics narratives in an effort to receive a pat on the head from the new "woke" establishment. Phillips began trending on Twitter after making the comments to Vanity Fair, prompting the outrage mob to come after him and thereby proving his point.

https://www.infowars.com/director-todd-phillips-says-he-made-joker-because-woke-hollywood-killed-comedy/

Comedy writer permanently banned from Twitter for saying "men aren't women"

By Adam Ford June 28th, 2020

Irish comedy writer Graham Linehan has been permanently banned from Twitter after he tweeted "men aren't women tho" in response to a tweet by a women's group wishing men who identify as women a happy Pride Month.

Lineman, who had hundreds of thousands of followers on the social network, is the creator or co-creator of the sitcoms Father Ted, Black Books, and The IT Crowd. Twitter said Linehan "has been permanently suspended after repeated violations of our rules against hateful conduct and platform manipulation."

https://disrn.com/news/comedy-writer-banned-from-twitter-for-saying-men-arent-women

University Athletes Try to Force Expulsion of Student Who Joked About George Floyd's Drug Use

By GQ Pan June 28th, 2020

A group of student athletes at Kansas state University, including the university's football and women's basketball teams, said they would not play or practice until a student who joked about George Floyd on Twitter is expelled. At the center of the controversy is Jaden McNeil, a junior at Kansas State and the founder of nationalist student organization "America First Students." On Thursday afternoon, McNeil wrote "Congratulations to George Floyd on being drug free for an entire month!"

George Floyd, who had an extensive criminal history, died in the custody of four Minneapolis police officers on May 25. A forensic report (pdf) indicates that Floyd had fentanyl and methamphetamine in his system when he died, but doesn't link the drugs to the death. McNeil's Twitter post led to social media backlash resulting in Twitter locking his account until he deleted the tweet.

In a statement posted online, black student athletes from several sports said they they will not play in their respective seasons, unless the Kansas State establishes a policy of expelling students who "openly display racism" on social media. "Due to recent insensitivity from Kansas State students, collectively as Black student athletes we will NO LONGER accept these types of actions. If we do not see any change, we will not participate in any donor or recruiting events," the statement reads. "We also need to see student Jaden McNeil receive strong consequences of [sic] his insensitive actions."

In response, Kansas State President Richard Myers issued a statement on Friday, condemning McNeil of "racism and bigotry" and promising to launch an "immediate review of the university's options."

"Black Lives Matter at Kansas State University and we will continue to fight for social justice," said Myers. Kansas State in 2017 endorsed the "Chicago Statement," a free speech policy statement adopted by many universities that wish to show their commitment to freedom of speech. The university says "it is not the proper role of the University to attempt to shield individuals from ideas and opinions they find unwelcome, disagreeable, or even deeply offensive."

McNeil previously led the Kansas State chapter of Turning Point USA (TPUSA), a conservative youth organization. He parted the TPUSA in 2019 because of his disagreement over the handling of the Lincoln Memorial controversy and founded America First Students as an opposing organization. On America First Students' Twitter profile, McNeil describes it as an organization defined by "support for closed borders, traditional families, the American worker, and Christian values."

https://www.theepochtimes.com/university-athletes-want-student-who-joked-about-george-floyds-drug-use-expelled_3404749.html

Comedian Calls Out Liberal Victims of Cancel Culture: 'This Is What You Idiots Wanted!'

By Brodigan June 30th, 2020

It's clear that cancel culture is starting to come back to bite the leftists who started cancel culture in their smug little heinies. You can tell by the way the woke mafia is trying to gaslight those who use outrage culture against them. But according to satirist Jonathan Pie, what did these idiots expect? This is the world they created.

I'm not sure what set off this rant. Something about the Labour Party and anti-Semitism. Honestly? Instead of doing research, I was more concerned with trying to work "perma-offended woke twats" into the headline, but determined it would run afoul of Facebook's new algorithm changes.

It's what you've always wanted: People losing their jobs for retweeting the wrong opinions. Exactly the same people that have their pitchforks primed for any careless slip of the the tongue or unthinking moment online, they're up in arms. Well, you f***ing shouldn't be. Because this is the world that YOU created. You can't have it both ways.

The brilliance of this and many of Pie's other rants is twofold. One, without even knowing the original news story he's talking about, everything he says here easily applies to the exciting ways leftists are trying the cancel everyone and everything here. The other requires some homework. Go to a YouTube or Twitter search and check out the comedian's thoughts on Donald Trump or Nigel Farage. My dude isn't exactly on our team politically. Far from it. Issue by issue, I'm fairly certain he disagrees with us on all of it. But the far left has even turned him off.

Cancel culture exists because of a small minority of people talking the loudest on Twitter, the social media platform used by the smallest number of people. I hate the term "silent majority," but there are more of us than there are of them. We need to do a better job of working together and pushing back against the perma-offended woke twats.

https://www.louderwithcrowder.com/comedian-calls-out-liberal-victims-of-cancel-culture-this-is-what-you-idiots-wanted

Comedy

George Carlin, Rodney Dangerfield, Andrew Dice Clay, Jerry Seinfeld, Dave Chappelle, Sam Kinison, Richard Pryor, Lenny Bruce, Eddie Murphy, Chris Rock, Larry the Cable Guy, Jeff Foxworthy, and Bill Burr are all being censored, cancelled, and banned. Gone are the days when people went to comedy clubs WITHOUT politically correct sticks stuck up their asses. Gone are the days of racial and sexual jokes. Gone are the days of "politically insensitive language." What we have now is a group of new "WOKE" comedians who have their own new authoritarian rules that they can play by in order to do stand up on stage and tell a joke. Today's soft, social justice warrior snowflakes can't handle the comedy from the 1970's-2000's. In fact, some colleges and universities have banned comedians from performing on their campus to combat a comic's anti-political correctness. Some college students have reported needing therapy, safe spaces, coloring books, and stuffed animals to deal with a "controversial" (aka: not political-correct) comedian performing . What we have now, are a group of bland, dull, dry, nameless, faceless and pointless comedians who are going around telling horrible jokes that subscribe to their new set of comedy rules as to what's is considered acceptable.

24

The War on Social Media

'Mute White People' button appears on Instagram stories

By Emma Colton July 13th, 2020

A new button appearing on Instagram reads, "mute white people." The *Washington Examiner* confirmed the button on Instagram Monday, following a tweet bringing attention to the GIF by conservative commentator Katie Pavlich. "Instagram has a 'mute white people' button in stories," Pavlich tweeted Monday.

Called the "unbothered sticker," it was uploaded to online database GIPHY by *Refinery29*, a media outlet aimed at a female audience, GIPHY's website shows. GIPHY moderates which GIFs are approved to be shared in its library and, subsequently, platforms, such as Instagram. "To ensure that GIPHY stickers will always be fun and safe no matter where you see them, we have an enhanced moderation process for approving stickers into our library. This is a permanent part of our moderation process and may impact the turnaround time for uploaded content to appear within the Sticker API (which powers partners such as Instagram)," GIPHY's website states.

Refinery29 has uploaded more than 500 buttons and GIFs to GIPHY, its profile shows. Some of the GIFs include, "Pay Black Women," "Reparation$$$," and "Afro-Latina Magic," and the outlet has received more than 3 billion views on its GIF uploads. In March, the Heritage Foundation's social media manager, Lyndsey Fifield, claimed the *Daily Signal's* verified status on GIPHY "mysteriously disappeared" after posting anti-abortion and pro-capitalism GIFs. "Just hours after tweeting this, our verified status on @GIPHY mysteriously disappeared—stripping our gifs and stickers from the gif banks on Twitter and Instagram. The only pro-life & pro-capitalism gifs on IG. I'm hopeful this was a mistake and that their team will resolve it," Fifield tweeted after saying one of the GIFs she created garnered 39 million views.

The verified status was reinstated soon after, according to Fifield. "And they admitted they were wrong and reinstated our account without me taking any action. I replied to their email a month ago and (according to them) they just never checked our account again or saw my email before revoking it today," she tweeted. The button comes as a renewed conversation surrounding race has been sparked by the death of George Floyd in Minneapolis on Memorial Day weekend.

In addition to peaceful protests and riots, social media campaigns to fight police brutality and racism have also been launched. Blackout Tuesday, on June 2, for example, swept across the nation and was intended for social media users within the entertainment industry to remain silent that day in an effort to reflect on the Black Lives Matter movement. Other users shared solid black photos as a way to signify their solidarity with the movement. Instagram, GIPHY, and *Refinery29* did not immediately respond to requests for comment.

https://www.washingtonexaminer.com/news/mute-white-people-button-appears-on-instagram-stories

Social Media

Facebook (Fascistbook), Instagram (Instascam), Twitter (Tweaker) and other social media platforms will ban you or suspend your account for arbitrary "hate speech" posts. "Hate speech" posts are nothing more than posts that the rulers at these tyrannical platforms use to control information from the masses. There is no such thing as "hate speech." It's an arbitrary phrase created, invented, and used by people who want to control your language and exterminate your free speech. "Hate speech" is protected speech under the 1st Amendment to the US constitution (See also: Cohen v. California 1971). Who and what entity is the arbiter, controller, ruler and decider on what constitutes as "hate speech?" If you post something that goes against their radical, authoritarian agenda, you are banned, censored, cancelled, and controlled. When we allow these social media platforms to control the narrative, abuse our language and stifle information, we all lose. Remember folks.... You don't live in a free country and your vote doesn't count anymore. Time to wake up and be big boys and big girls.

25

The War on America

Parents fight back after school drops Pledge of Allegiance for student-authored oath to 'global society'

By Victor Skinner August 24th, 2018

Atlanta Neighborhood Charter School Principal Lara Zelski decided students will no longer recite the Pledge of Allegiance during the school's morning meeting agenda, which she described to parents as "an effort to begin our day as a fully inclusive and connected community."

"Over the past couple of years it has become increasingly obvious that more and more of our community were choosing to not stand and/or recite the pledge," she wrote, according to the Atlanta Journal Constitution. The statement, posted to the school website, promised parents students could recite the Pledge of Allegiance later in the day, if they felt like it, and vowed to create better pledge specifically for the school.

"Teachers and the K-5 leadership team will be working with students to create a school pledge that we can say together at morning meeting," Zelski wrote, adding that it "will focus on students' civic responsibility to their school family, community, country and our global society." "I'm really looking forward to what our students create," she wrote, according to TheBlaze.

The move infuriated parents and quickly gained the attention of Georgia House Speaker David Ralston, gubernatorial candidate Brian Kemp, and others who denounced the decision. "I'm sure our House

Education Committee will examine whether taxpayer funds should be used to instill such a divisive ideology in our students," Ralston posted online, the AJC reports.nIn less than a day, school officials reversed course. Zelski's announcement was wiped from the school's website and replaced with a statement from Lia Santos, chairwoman of the school's governing board.

"In the past, the Pledge of Allegiance was recited during our all-school morning meeting, but at the start of the school year, the daily practice was moved to classrooms. This change was done in compliance with state law ... and aligned Atlanta Neighborhood Charter School with most her schools in the state who also say the Pledge of Allegiance in individual classrooms. "However, it appears there was some miscommunication and inconsistency in the rollout. Starting next week, we will return to our original format and provide our students with the opportunity to recite the Pledge during the all-school morning meeting," Santos wrote.

According to the AJC:

The state DOE policy demands that schools set a time for the pledge, each school day, at the beginning of the school day or during the homeroom period. But students may not be compelled to recite the pledge, it adds.

Districts across metro Atlanta abide by both aspects of the policy – doing the pledge and giving the right to not participate.

Janice Crouse, conservative analyst and author of "Children at Risk," told One News Now the situation serves an important lesson for parents. "I think parents should take heart ... in that the administration was forced to change their minds and go back to having the Pledge of Allegiance," she said. "And I think parents can learn from this that they do need to speak out, and they do need to know what's going on so that they can speak out."

https://www.eagnews.org/2018/08/parents-fight-back-after-school-drops-pledge-of-allegiance-for-student-authored-oath-to-global-society/

Campus discourages Sept. 11 memorial citing 'bias' against Muslims

By Lauren Cooley August 30th, 2018

Administrators at Ripon College in Wisconsin have ruled that a Sept. 11 memorial cannot take place on campus because it may offend Muslim students. The private school cited bias reports that were filed during last year's Sept. 11 memorial project, a project that was a part of Young America's Foundation's iconic patriotism initiative which takes place across the country on campuses every year.

The school's Bias Protocol Board said the project creates an "environment" where "students from a Muslim background would feel singled out and/or harassed." As a result, Ripon students will not be allowed to hang flyers as part of their vigil to remember the victims of Sept. 11. According to YAF, administrators claimed that one of their objections is "because radical Islamist terrorism 'represents a small percentage of the terrorist attacks that happened to this country, and they don't represent the full gamut, and they show a very small picture of a specific religion or nationality instead of the larger viewpoint.'"

"This attempt by Ripon College's 'bias protocol board' to sanitize the truth out of remembering the anniversary of September 11 proves the necessity of YAF's iconic 9/11: Never Forget Project, as well as the need for bold YAF activists," Young America's Foundation Spokesman Spencer Brown told Red Alert Politics. "YAF's leadership in creating meaningful memorials on this important date in our nation's history ensures that the rising generation remembers the 2,977 innocent lives lost. The administrators' reliance on feelings rather than facts betrays their intention to cower from the truth rather than highlight the scourge of radical Islamist terror for what it is: evil."

The Ripon handbook states that the college is "committed to the free speech and open exchange of ideas and views, as reflected in the institution's Core Values" but this commitment "requires the confrontation of challenging issues in the context of civil discourse and intellectual inquiry." Students can combat bias by "participating in on-campus programming around multiculturalism, diversity and social justice."

"We offered up alterations to the poster that would also show non-Muslim terrorist attacks," said Hannah Krueger, a Ripon student and member of YAF. The bias protocol board told the students their suggested changes would look like an afterthought and instead suggested they make new posters of just the twin towers, she said. "I would say it was heavily implied that we are not allowed to put the posters up and that we would face potential penalties," Krueger said.

The Ripon Center for Diversity and Inclusion boasts of its programming surrounding International Month, Black History Month, Women's History Month, Hispanic Heritage Month and LGBT History Month, and "Culture Week," yet bans the "social activism" of a patriotic event remembering the deadliest terrorist attack on U.S. soil.

The handbook goes on to explain and vaguely define a "bias Incident" as a "behavior or act—verbal, written, or physical—which is personally directed against or targets an individual or group based on perceived or actual characteristics."

While hate crimes should be punished and bias generally creates a negative environment for learning and living, Americans should absolutely be biased against our enemies, especially terrorist organizations like al Qaeda or the Islamic State. Ripon's censorship of YAF's memorial is a chilling example of speech suppression, where a bipartisan, patriotic event is being shut down due to the anonymous objections of a few. It's also an example of the shocking anti-American sentiment taking place in U.S. higher education.

https://www.washingtonexaminer.com/red-alert-politics/campus-bans-sept-11-memorial-for-bias-against-muslims

Don't call the Alamo's defenders 'heroic,' Texas school curriculum panel urges

By Rebekah Allen September 7th, 2018

AUSTIN — A panel advising the State Board of Education on what seventh-graders should learn in their social studies courses has urged deleting the label "heroic" from a curriculum standard about the Alamo's defenders.

The proposed tweak to a directive about what teachers should teach about Texas history and the state's most iconic battle infuriated several state politicians, including Gov. Greg Abbott, who characterized the nonbinding advice as political correctness run amok. "Stop political correctness in our schools," Abbott, a Republican, tweeted Thursday in response to the story, first reported by *Texas Monthly*. "Of course Texas schoolchildren should be taught that Alamo defenders were 'Heroic'! I fully expect the State Board of Education to agree. Contact your SBOE Member to complain."

The recommendation, made in a report issued last month, was one of several hundred tweaks, additions and deletions offered up by the advisory group reviewing state curriculum standards for social studies. The panel said "heroic" was a "value-charged word." But Barbara Stevens, president general of the Daughters of the Republic of Texas, said the word is critical to giving Texas history its proper context.

"Words like 'heroic' to describe such men are indeed 'value charged,' and it is because anything less would be a disservice to their memories," Stevens said. "To minimize the study of the Republic of Texas is to fail to teach a pivotal portion of the state's history." Current seventh-grade social studies curriculum standards include the "siege of the Alamo and all of the heroic defenders who gave their lives there." The advisory committee recommended cutting the phrase "and all of the heroic defenders who gave their lives there."

Travis' letter

The advisory committee, made up of educators and historians, also suggested removing the requirement that students explain "the Travis Letter," sometimes referred to as the "Victory or Death" letter. It was written by Lt. Col. William Barrett Travis during the Alamo battle. In it, he declared, "I shall never surrender or retreat" from the thousand or more Mexican soldiers besieging the Alamo.

"I am determined to sustain myself as long as possible and die like a soldier who never forgets what is due to his own honor and that of his country — victory or death," Travis wrote in 1836. The recommendations say the letter can be explained by teachers within the context of the battle rather than requiring a separate discussion. Land Commissioner George P. Bush, whose office oversees the Alamo historical site, said the proposed changes were a nonstarter for him.

"This politically correct nonsense is why I'll always fight to honor the Alamo defenders' sacrifice. His letter & the defenders' actions must remain at the very core of TX history teaching," Bush tweeted Thursday, referring to the Travis letter. "This is not debatable to me." Responding to the outcry, State Board of Education Chairwoman Donna Bahorich tweeted Friday that she didn't support the removal of the letter. Hers is one of 15 votes on the board. "Our @TXSBOE work committees have done an excellent job of streamlining TX social studies standards, however, I do not support deleting one of the most iconic letters in US History for 7th grade. #HeroesAll #txed," Bahorich wrote. She did not return a phone call Friday.

SBOE rationale

Debbie Ratcliffe, spokeswoman for the Texas Education Agency, said the recommendation was made in response to complaints that curriculum standards are too long. The advisory group has been reviewing curriculum requirements subject by subject to streamline instruction. This will be the first time social studies standards have been updated since 2010.

"Could this be reduced by either deleting information, combining standards or clarifying? That was the goal," Ratcliffe said. "They suggested deleting the Travis letter because they think when teachers talk about the Alamo they will absolutely mention it, but not having it outlined specifically just meant teachers would spend less time on it." The State Board of Education will meet next week to discuss the matter. A public hearing on all of the curriculum changes will be held Tuesday, and the board could take a tentative vote on Friday. A final vote won't be taken until the board's November meeting.

Walter Buenger, a historian who specializes in Texas history at the University of Texas at Austin, said he could understand why there may be a desire to remove as subjective a descriptor as "heroic" from discussions of those involved in the battle. "Many times the Alamo gets boiled down, as it often does in movies, to the Mexicans are the bad guys and the good guys are good Anglos in coonskin caps," Buenger said. He noted that many Mexicans fought alongside Texans in the siege.

"Part of the problem with the word *heroic* may be that it's too simplistic," he said. But Thomas Lindsay, director of the Center for Innovation in Education for the free-market-oriented Texas Public Policy Foundation, said it's appropriate and necessary for educators to teach students who the good guys and bad guys are in history books.

Lindsay, a longtime college educator, said he has often referred to Frederick Douglass and Martin Luther King Jr. as "heroic" in his history lessons. "To intentionally deprive our students of such powerful lessons about human dignity and principled courage is the moral equivalent of child psychological abuse," Lindsay said. "This twisting of history deprives our students of the truth. If courage in the defense of liberty and equality is not heroic, what, precisely, is?"

https://www.dallasnews.com/news/politics/2018/09/07/don-t-call-the-alamo-s-defenders-heroic-texas-school-curriculum-panel-urges/

Stanford administrator 'told fraternity to remove American flag to improve its image on campus' - so defiant students responded by flying an even bigger one

By Keith Griffith December 4th, 2018

A Stanford administrator once told a fraternity to remove an American flag flying out front in order to 'improve its image on campus,' according to a new report.

Stanford graduate Pablo Lozano says a residential education liaison made the suggestion in fall of 2017 while the Sigma Chi fraternity was on probation, the Stanford Review reports. During a meeting with the fraternity members, the administrator 'insinuated not only that the flag made others uncomfortable but that its being flown tainted Sigma Chi's reputation and, presumably, worsened its chance of survival,' the student publication reported. In a statement to DailyMail.com, Stanford University said it could not verify the incident, adding: 'Students are free to fly an American flag outside their residences if they so choose.'

'We have been reviewing the question regarding Sigma Chi, and thus far we have not been able to verify such a conversation during the timeframe described in media reports,' a university spokesman said. The spokesman said there had been a conversation about what to do with the flag after the Sigma Chi chapter was disbanded earlier this year, as it was believed to be the property of fraternity members.

According to Lozano, the students discussed the administrator's suggestion that they remove the flag and became incensed, wondering why displaying the U.S. flag at an American institution would be offensive or alienating, as the administrator seemed to imply.

Instead of removing the flag, the fraternity members decided to get a larger one, said Lozano. The house's three-by-five-foot flag was removed and placed on framed display inside the house, and in its place was flown a four-by-six-foot flag as a 'silent but visible protest,' said Lozano. The probation process did not go well for the Sigma Chi chapter, for reasons that are apparently unrelated to the flag. In January of this year, a non-Stanford student attending a party at Sigma Chi allegedly drugged five sorority members and two members of the men's rowing team.

The chapter was put under further sanction by Stanford, and in May of this year, the fraternity chapter's charter was revoked by Sigma Chi International. The parent group said it had conducted a membership assessment of the Stanford chapter and 'determined there were few members who would carry the chapter forward in a positive manner'.

https://www.dailymail.co.uk/news/article-6459119/Stanford-administrator-told-fraternity-remove-American-flag-improve-image.html

Pennsylvania school drops 'God Bless America' after complaint, district says

By Paulina Dedaj May 8th, 2019

A Pennsylvania elementary school principal will no longer say "God Bless America" following the Pledge of Allegiance after the district received a legal complaint on behalf of a parent who claimed that doing so broke the law.

Peter Brigg, the principal of Sabold Elementary School in Springfield, would say the phrase after reciting the pledge over the loudspeaker. At least one parent filed a complaint to the Freedom From Religion Foundation. An attorney from the group sent a letter to the district complaining that publicly announcing the expression violated the U.S. Constitution's prohibition of government sponsoring religious messages.

"'God Bless America' is a prayer ... A Prayer hosted by a publicly supported school does not pass constitutional muster," the foundation said. The district released a statement Friday confirming that it received a complaint that reciting the words "God Bless America" over the loudspeaker "violated the law" and that it would stop the practice immediately.

"In accordance with District protocol, this complaint was forwarded to our District Solicitor's Office. Based upon the Solicitor's legal research and recommendation, we ceased this practice. Continuation of any practices that may be unlawful would only expose the District to litigation, which the local taxpayers would have to financially support," the statement read. The district went on to say that the administration never altered the recitation of the pledge and that students would still be able to say "God Bless America" after if they choose to do so. "We understand that this is an important topic for many of our constituents; however, please understand that the District does not make the law. We follow it."

https://www.foxnews.com/us/pennsylvania-school-drops-god-bless-america-after-freedom-from-religion-foundation-complaint

The L.A. Times Proclaims the Anthem Is Racist, Their Suggested Replacement Will Have you Laughing Out Loud

By Bonchie July 14th, 2020

Here's a quick hitter for you before bed, but be warned. It may cost you some sleep because you'll be too busy laughing out loud after reading this. Enter The Los Angeles Times. You see, they've decided that the Star Spangled Banner is racist (insert squeaky Tucker Carlson inflection here) and that it's time to seek a replacement. While this isn't a new suggestion, as crazed destruction of American history has become a left-wing sport at this point, the Times takes it a bit further with perhaps the dumbest replacement suggestion yet.

The writer begins by noting that Francis Scott Key's statue in San Francisco was torn down, as if that's some kind of evidentiary point to his evil nature. At least this is how the monument used to appear. Today, Francis Scott Key is no longer in Golden Gate Park. On June 20, protesters lassoed the statue with ropes, heaved and hoed, and down came Key, somersaulting off the pediment, head o'er heels. Key was a slave owner, like many of the historical personages whose statues have been defaced and destroyed in the Black Lives Matter uprising that followed the May 25 killing of George Floyd by Minneapolis police. But it was also Key's role as a songwriter — his famous ode to the land of the free and the home of the brave — that made him a target for protesters.

Yes, I'm sure the "protestors" were really concerned about the intricate arguments surround the Star Spangled Banner and not, you know, just tearing stuff down. After all, it's not like they also destroyed monuments to Catholic Missionaries in the same riot. Oh wait, yes they did. Later, we get to the meat of the article, which is to proclaim that the National Anthem itself is racist.

A petition posted on Change.org advocated dropping the song as the national anthem, pointing to "elitist, sexist, and racist" verses in Key's poem, "Defence of Fort M'Henry," from which "The Star-Spangled Banner" was adapted. The poem, written by Key on Sept. 14, 1814, after he witnessed the bombardment of an American fort by British ships in Baltimore Harbor, includes the lines: "No refuge could save the hireling and slave/From the terror of flight, or the gloom of the grave."

As is noted, the scholarly interpretation of that line is that the term slave is referring to subjects of the British Crown at the time. Of course, even if he was talking about literal slaves, it's still a stretch to call it "racist." In the end, he was simply noting what he saw. Slavery was a reality in 1814 whether those that want to rewrite history are comfortable with discussing it or not. But it was the suggestion of what to replace the country's anthem with that was the best part of the write-up. Did they research and find some alternative soaring song that denotes the national greatness of The United States of America? Nah, this is their suggestion.

But if we must have an anthem, it should be far different than the one we've got now, positing another kind of patriotism, an alternative idea of America and Americanness. It would also be neat if it was, you know, a decent song, which a citizen could sing without crashing into an *o'er* or a *thee*, or being asked to pole vault across octaves. In fact, there is such a song. The song is "Lean on Me."

Yes, Lean On Me is what the writer believes should be our new National Anthem. This is real life. Here's their reasoning. It doesn't march to a martial beat or rise to grand crescendos. The lyrics hold no pastoral images of fruited plains or oceans white with foam, no high-minded invocations of liberty or God. "Lean on Me" is a deeply American song — but it's not, explicitly at least, a song *about* America.

Well, we wouldn't want any lyrics which espouse the best parts of America, nor anything that invokes that icky God character, right? Heck, let's have an anthem that's not even about the country it's supposed to be honoring. Instead, we can just sing a 70s soul ballad to each other. Makes sense.The media have lost their minds, and while I find this entire thing hilarious, I also find it disturbing. These people aren't going away and every day they continue to spread this drivel is another chip taken out of the current culture. Progressivism never stops by it's very definition. It just keeps taking and taking. Yesterday it was Confederate generals. Today it's the Star Spangled Banner. Tomorrow it'll be book burning parties in Times Square. There is no end game, only subjugation of whatever form their secular ideology takes today. Americans can fight back or they can wake up a decade from now and ask what in the world happened.

https://www.redstate.com/bonchie/2020/07/14/the-la-times-proclaims-the-anthem-is-racist-their-suggested-replacement-will-have-you-laughing-out-loud/

America

American flags are being banned, censored, and cancelled throughout the United States. The rulers who want to control everything in our lives claim that the flag represents "racism," "sexism," and "colonialism." Singing "The Star-Spangled Banner" is also being censored and cancelled in all types of sporting events. The country who helped liberate Europe twice and who started the ending of slavery is now being banned by the woke police. Through free market capitalism, America produced the richest country in the world and the biggest and most successful middle class the world has ever seen. And now, it is being demonized. If America falls, the entire planet will fall. Which is why our social justice warrior rulers are targeting America.

26

The War on Food

Dreyer's announces new name for 'derogatory' Eskimo Pie months after pausing production

By Alexandra Deabler October 5th, 2020

After more than 100 years, Dreyer's is changing its popular Eskimo Pie ice cream bar to Edy's Pie. The new name was announced by the brand Monday. The new name was a long time coming. Back in June, the company stated its intention to rename its "derogatory" product name. "We are committed to being a part of the solution on racial equality, and recognize the term is derogatory," said Elizabell Marquez, head of marketing for its parent Dreyer's Grand Ice Cream, the U.S. subsidiary for Froneri, in a statement to FOX Business in June. "This move is part of a larger review to ensure our company and brands reflect our people values."

Since then, Dreyer's has paused production of the ice cream bars while coming up with new branding and packaging for the treat.

After months of discussion, the brand decided on Edy's Pie, named after one of the company's founders, Joseph Edy. The chocolate-coated ice cream bar will be available under its new name early next year, according to the company. "We anticipate Edy's Pie ice cream bars to be on shelf in early 2021. Our mission at Dreyer's Grand Ice Cream is to bring joy to everyday life with ice cream and we look forward to our Edy's Pie ice cream bars continuing to do just that," Marquez said in a statement to Fox News.

In June, in the wake of Black Lives Matter protests following the death of George Floyd during an arrest by Minneapolis police, several brands underwent name or logo changes in an effort to eliminate racially-insensitive branding. Among them were Aunt Jemima, Mrs. Butterworth's and Uncle Ben's.

https://www.foxbusiness.com/lifestyle/dreyers-new-name-eskimo-pie

New York Times Spoils the Party: 'History of Tiki Bars and Cultural Appropriation'

By Clay Waters December 29th, 2020

Did you realize that "Tiki bars are a beverage industry mainstay – with a painful and underexamined past" requiring "reclaiming" and "repair"? That's the sour message on the front of the *New York Times* Sunday Business section, written and researched by Sammi Katz and illustrated in mock-retro-advertising style by Olivia McGiff. An online headline actually read "History of Tiki Bars and Cultural Appropriation."

On its eternal quest to ruin innocent pleasures, the *Times* is suffering a social justice hangover and is passing the headache to its readers. Meanwhile, 99% of the population will remain blissfully unaware they should beware of sipping on a Mai-Tai from a "particularly racist mug."

It is an unquestionably difficult time for the hospitality industry. Every day, another restaurant shutters, one more bar pulls its steel gate down for good. Since its invention, one kind of watering hole has seen America through its most grueling times: the tiki bar. So the *Times* decided to make things just a little harder for the industry -- by accusing one sector of it of long-standing racism and cultural appropriation. Taste the prejudice behind the paper umbrellas:

Decorated with bamboo and beach-y lights, with bartenders in Aloha shirts serving up mai tais, tiki bars were a booming part of America's hospitality industry. "Put down your phone and put on this lei," say the tiki bars. "Here's something delicious in a silly mug." They offer an intoxicating escape from the weight of the world.

But the roots of tiki are far from the Pacific Islands. A Maori word for the carved image of a god or ancestor, tiki became synonymous in the United States and elsewhere for gimmicky souvenirs and décor. Now a new generation of beverage-industry professionals are shining a light on the genre's history of racial inequity and cultural appropriation, which has long been ignored because it clashes with the carefree aesthetic. Let's peel back the pineapple leaves to examine the choices that created a marketing mainstay.

Katz offered some tiki bar tick-tock, starting with the "Don the Beachcomber" bar, which opened in Southern California in 1933 and began serving the first tiki drinks, elaborate concoctions with fresh juices and lots of ingredients. Then came Trader Vic's. And then came the *New York Times* to ruin it all with a sour mix of white guilt and leftist puritanism.

At its heart, tiki is about fun, creative drinks in a transportive environment. A new wave of industry professionals is reimagining these delicious contributions to cocktail culture, looking to shed the appropriation and racism that have accompanied tiki since its inception. We spoke to a few of them about the ways they're working to shake up the biz for the better.

The region has "higher rates of poverty, lack of access to essential services and more burden from climate change," Kunkel adds. [Bartender Chockie] Tom also reinvests in the groups whose cultures have been historically appropriated. "There's a beautiful opportunity to use what drew people to the aesthetic to help some of these communities," Tom says. "Frankly, if you've been profiting off their imagery, it really is time to give back."

"Spirits specialist and educator" Kelvin Uffre lectured:

To go into a bar and see mostly white guys in Hawaiian shirts presenting this fetishization of a culture, when the people of that country can't even escape what's happening to them. That's dark," he said. But, he added, "I just had a Mai Tai last night, that's a good drink!

Leave it to the *Times* to make anything fun a problem to be worked out:

It's not "last call" for tiki. But the work for those in the industry is just beginning to make these tropical oases inclusive to all, which will benefit both businesses and consumers.

https://www.newsbusters.org/blogs/nb/clay-waters/2020/12/29/new-york-times-spoils-party-history-tiki-bars-and-cultural

The Whiteness Problem of White Wine

By Daniel Greenfield August 26th, 2020

In the Black Lives Matter era, everything is too problematically white, including white wine. As every single industry from cereal to dental supplies engages in its own ritual reckoning with a country so systemically racist that every part of its system is hysterically confessing to racism the way teenage girls in Salem confessed to witchcraft, the hangover is hitting wine country.

The whining about the whiteness of wine is overflowing at every high end publication. "Too White Wine," moaned the *Financial Times*. The column by Jancis Robison, who received an Order of the British Empire for writing about wine, began by tweeting her, "shame at the lack of ethnic diversity in the world of wine."

Perhaps Jancis could give her FT column and her OBE to a more deserving minority. Articles warn, The Wine Industry is Overwhelmingly White." and they frantically urge, "It's Time to Decolonize Wine" and "It's Time: Diversity in Wine". Wine is actually very diverse. Not only does wine come from all over the world, but it comes in different colors and shades, it originates from different cultures and exists in different languages. It's mentioned in the Bible, in ancient Chinese poems, and in 2,000 year old verses from India.

But now wine, the universal solvent of cultures across human history, is not diverse enough. At least not once George Floyd's death while high on fentanyl cast light on the whiteness of wine. "In the two months since the June George Floyd protests, some Black winemakers have called out the racism in their industry," *Mother Jones* exclaimed. What does Floyd have to do with wine? Not a whole lot.

But Julia Coney, who writes about wine and racism, posted an Instagram video titled, "Racism and the Wine Industry: Your Silence is Betrayal." Coney, who described herself as a leader on "race and wine", jabbed one finger at her webcam, "Wine industry, shame, shame on you!" The other appeared to be holding a glass. Then Coney insisted that those members of the wine industry who hadn't been supporting her shouldn't rest because black people killed by the police were not resting in peace.

It was enough to make a man turn to strong drink. In the months since Floyd's death, this warmed-over race-baiting had hijacked every industry. The wine industry, which caters to and includes wealthy lefties, and had been laboriously trying to diversify by ushering in the likes of Coney to indict them as racists, was feeling the squeeze.

It didn't take long for the whining about the whiteness of wine to turn into political witch hunts. A survey contended that 84% of professionals in the wine industry are white, while only 2% are black. And the American Association of Wine Economists (AAWE) claimed that "In terms of $$$, the U.S. wine industry overwhelmingly supports Trump." The targets were a few industry figures, notably Marvin Shanken, the Jewish publisher of *Wine Spectator* and *Cigar Aficionado*, who has raised a fortune for children with autism.

But he also donated to President Trump. The American Association of Wine Economists did not seem very interested in the fact that Speaker Nancy Pelosi's vineyard makes her the fourth-richest Californian in

Congress or that Governor Newsom has his own winery which stayed open for tastings even as he ordered wineries in much of the state to shut down. And then there's John Legend, a black leftist celebrity and Biden fundraiser, who owns the LVE–Legend Vineyard Exclusive wine label.

The point of this viniter witch hunt was spreading accusations of conservative politics, racism, and generating wine boycotts against the enemies of the politically correct people. "It's important that we share values with people and businesses we support... and purchasing decisions will be impacted by this list," a San Francisco winery replied.

Wineries whose owners had donated to President Trump were put on the defensive, forced to plead their support for diversity, even as an elitist white lynch mob accused them of racism. Concern for the opposed minorities of the wine industry had given way to the true agenda. And how oppressed are those minorities, some of whom own vineyards in Napa Valley where an acre can cost a quarter of a million dollars, by the white man of the white wine trade? "The wine industry has long been enigmatic, cloaked in whiteness, wealth and privilege," *Style Weekly* bleated.

The wealth and privilege part is just as true of the black participants in the industry. "But the problem with racism? Add another 30-pound bag, at least. Instead of carrying three, I have to carry four." Dan Johnson, a San Francisco lawyer who boasted of winning a $265 million verdict against Verizon, complained. Johnson has his own winery and three acres in Napa. Quite a few Americans of all races would like to carry what he's carrying.

Turning Black Lives Matter into Black Wineries Matter and the death of George Floyd into the dearth of black millionaires with their own vineyards exposes the privileged position of corporate black nationalism which exploits the deaths of poor black people for black and white elites. The absurdity of mobilizing a witch hunt in George Floyd's name in the wine industry ought to have brought down the entire Black Lives Matter shakedown industry in gales of laughter.

But everyone's too afraid to laugh. Instead the Court of Master Sommeliers was browbeaten into no longer having its members be addressed as, "Master." At some point the Court will also be forced to drop the full name. And the Hue Society was promoted as a safe space for black wine drinkers. There are scholarships, diversity initiatives, and statements of fealty from the wine industry.

"The team and directors at the Oregon Wine Board have been processing, reflecting on and discussing our responsibility in the fight for racial equity in America. We must recognize the power of our platform and our potential to help build a just, equitable and thriving Oregon wine industry that in turn contributes to a just, equitable and thriving Oregon," the aforementioned organization declared in its BLM statement.

What does the Oregon Wine Board have to do with George Floyd, or Black Lives Matter, or race? Nothing. But in Communist China, rocket scientists were required to quote Mao, in the Soviet Union, they had to quote Lenin, and now in what used to be America, every undertaking must begin with a tribute to BLM and a vow to embed "anti-racism" into the organization.

The wine industry is being warned that, like all else, it must get on the right side of history. "Wine is pretty much an upscale beverage for white people of European heritage," Steve Heimoff, a former editor for *Wine Enthusiast Magazine,* claimed. "I don't see Latino or Hispanic people drinking wine, and the same goes for Asians and Blacks."

This would have come as news to everyone from Omar Khayyam to Christopher Columbus. The crews of the maligned discoverer of America imbibed wine heavily. And brought Hispanic people from their European origins to a new world where they became indigenous people of color. When Joseph was entombed in an Egyptian prison with the Pharaoh's wine steward, we are reminded that wine played an important role in ancient Egypt and its North African precincts.

But admittedly beyond there, wine did not play much of a role in ancient Africa. And by the bigoted illogic of Black Lives Matter, there must thus be something wrong with wine. Despite its use by nearly every ancient civilization across history, wine is not diverse enough. It's only something that upscale people of European heritage drink. Like Heimoff's ancestors. China is the world's fourth biggest wine importing country. Japan is in sixth place, Hong Kong, on its own, is in eleventh, and Singapore is in fifteenth place.

But the Asians, as usual, don't count when it comes to diversity. The United States exports millions of dollars a year in wine to Mexico. Mexicans actually do drink wine just to spite progressives. And despite demographic changes, wine consumption in the United States continues to increase. Either white people are drinking more wine, or everyone's drinking more wine.

Wine consumption nearly doubled between 1995 and 2017. Not only isn't wine doomed, but it's more popular than ever. And in a country where wine is being accused of lacking diversity, you can understand why. After reading through the latest episode of the madness with which leftists have afflicted yet another pleasant element of human life, you may be in the mood for a drink. And hopefully you won't mind if I join you.

https://www.frontpagemag.com/fpm/2020/08/whiteness-problem-white-wine-daniel-greenfield/

Politically correct animal crackers hitting the shelves (but not the cages)

By Journal-Courier staff August 21st, 2018

After more than a century behind bars, the beasts on boxes of animal crackers are roaming free. Mondelez International, the parent company of Nabisco, has redesigned the packaging of its Barnum's Animals crackers in response to pressure from People for the Ethical Treatment of Animals.

PETA, which has been protesting the use of animals in circuses for more than 30 years, wrote a letter to Mondelez in the spring of 2016 calling for a redesign. "Given the egregious cruelty inherent in circuses that use animals and the public's swelling opposition to the exploitation of animals used for entertainment, we urge Nabisco to update its packaging in order to show animals who are free to roam in their natural habitats," PETA said in its letter.

Mondelez agreed and started working on a redesign. In the meantime, the crackers' namesake circus — Ringling Brothers and Barnum and Bailey — folded for good. The 146-year-old circus, which had removed elephants from its shows in 2016 because of pressure from PETA and others, closed down in May 2017 due to slow ticket sales. The redesign of the boxes, now on U.S. store shelves, retains the familiar red and yellow coloring and prominent "Barnum's Animals" lettering. But instead of showing the animals in cages — implying that they're traveling in boxcars for the circus — the new boxes feature a zebra, elephant, lion, giraffe and gorilla wandering side-by-side in a grassland. The outline of acacia trees can be seen in the distance.

"When PETA reached out about Barnum's, we saw this as another great opportunity to continue to keep this brand modern and contemporary," said Jason Levine, Mondelez's chief marketing officer for North America, in a statement. Mondelez is based in Illinois, which passed a statewide ban on circuses with elephants that went into effect in January. More than 80 U.S. cities have fully or partially banned circuses with wild animals, according to Animal Defenders International.

PETA Executive Vice President Tracy Reiman says she's celebrating the box redesign for the cultural change it represents. "The new box for Barnum's Animals crackers perfectly reflects that our society no longer tolerates the caging and chaining of wild animals for circus shows," she said.

Nabisco has been making Barnum's Animals crackers since 1902. It has redesigned its boxes before, but only for limited-time special editions. In 1995, it offered an endangered species collection that raised money for the World Wildlife Fund. In 1997, it offered a zoo collection that raised money for the American Zoo and Aquarium Association. And in 2010, it worked with designer Lilly Pulitzer on a pastel-colored box that raised money for tiger conservation. The company won't say how many boxes it sells each year. Canadian boxes already had a different design and aren't affected.

https://www.myjournalcourier.com/news/article/Politically-correct-animal-crackers-hitting-the-13171203.php

Coon Cheese Dumps "Racist" Name After Complaints From Men Who Share Names With the Two Largest Slaveholders in the U.S.

By Ben Davis July 24th, 2020

The owners of Coon Cheese have decided to dump the brand name in a bit to help "eliminate racism in all its forms" following complaints that its branding is "racist." Aboriginal activist Stephen Hagan and actor Josh Thomas called out the company earlier this year for their use of the word "Coon", a historically racial slur that's been used against people with dark skin.

Despite the brand being originally named after its founder, Edward William Coon, parent company Saputo made the announcement today that the company would "retire the Coon brand name" in order to align with "current attitudes and perspectives." Ironically, the two Australians who complained about the branding share names with two of the largest slaveholders in U.S. history, Joshua John Ward and Stephen Duncan.

Joshua John Ward, also known as the "King of the Rice Planters", was the largest slave owner in the United States, holding more than 1,100 blacks on his Brookgreen plantation in South Carolina. The second-largest slaveholder was said to be Stephen Duncan, who collectively enslaved more than 2,000 blacks during his time as a cotton producer. Duncan held 858 slaves in Issaquena at one time and owned more than 15 plantations in Mississippi and Louisiana. Can we expect Joshua Thomas and Stephen Hagan to follow Coon's example and change their "racist" names, immediately?

https://caldronpool.com/coon-cheese-dumps-racist-name-after-complaints-from-men-who-share-names-with-the-two-largest-slave-holders-in-the-u-s/

Swedish primary school bans children from wearing racist 'gingerbread' men dress

By ANI December 11th, 2012

Schoolchildren in Sweden have been banned from dressing up as gingerbread men for a Christmas parade because their teachers fear the costumes could be considered racist. Youngsters from a primary school in Laxa told their parents they had been ordered not to wear the outfits for the St Lucia celebrations on Thursday.

Traditionally, children dress as either St Lucia, or gnomes, stars, or gingerbread men for the candle-lit parade, the Daily Mail reports. But heartbroken 10-year-old Mio Simiv was told he could not wear his gingerbread man costume to the celebration because it might be seen as 'offensive'.

"I thought he had to have got it wrong so I called the school and they said people might find a brown gingerbread character offensive," his angry mother Jenny Simic told local media. "I said, well then my son won't participate. He won't support some Ku Klux Klan procession - because that's what the little Lucias look like when they all come in with white hoods and white dresses," she added.

According to the report, she later sent a text message to Mio's teacher to see if the ban still stood. "I know what you think and what you're writing. Unfortunately we have no gingerbread men or songs in our procession! We cannot offer gingerbread cookies because of allergies among pupils," she received the response.

A school spokesman blamed the row on a 'misunderstanding'. "The children and their teachers chose the songs for the parade and they didn't chose the gingerbread boy song, so there will be no gingerbread boys," district schools head Marghareta Zetterlund claimed. "We don't serve gingerbread cookies because of possible nut allergies. I can't comment on who might find the costumes offensive," she added.

https://www.bignewsnetwork.com/news/211303190/swedish-primary-school-bans-children-from-wearing-racist-gingerbread-men-dress

LA City Council Plan To Require Vegan Protein Options To Fight Climate Change

By CBSLA December 5th, 2018

LOS ANGELES (CBSLA) – A Los Angeles city councilman wants to require all movie theaters, large-scale entertainment venues, and other locations in the city to provide at least one vegan protein option in order to combat climate change.

A motion introduced by Councilman Paul Koretz pointed to several studies which suggest a link between the meat and dairy industry and the environment, including a University of Oxford study that found if more people in the United States adopted plant-based eating it could cut greenhouse-gas emissions from food sources by 70 percent.Under the proposal, various city departments would be asked to report on ways to make sure at least one vegan protein option is available at all concessionaire locations at city-operated venues, parks, the Los Angeles Zoo,

Meals on Wheels programs, Los Angeles International Airport restaurants, movie theaters and large-scale entertainment venues.

"I want to make it easier for us to do better around the city, as well as provide more options for people who are already following a plant-based diet," Koretz said, adding that while the motion would need to be examined by the City Attorney's Office, he believes the move would be legal. A spokesperson for People for the Ethical Treatment of Animals (PETA) hailed the plan and linked the dearth of vegan dietary options to a string of wildfires that have devastated parts of both Northern and Southern California.

"Vegan eating is booming, but good laws like this do not come soon enough," said Ben Williamson, senior international media director for PETA. "Natural disasters such as the wildfires that this great city recently suffered are a terrible reminder that we must do more to protect our planet and its inhabitants. Animal agriculture is one of the most, if not they most, significant contributor to the world's very serious environmental problems."

https://losangeles.cbslocal.com/2018/12/05/la-city-council-vegan-option-climate-change-wildfires/

Principal bans candy canes, says 'J shape' stands for Jesus

By Nicole Darrah December 7th, 2018

An elementary school principal in Nebraska was placed on leave after telling teachers to avoid decorating their classrooms with Christmas-themed ornaments so as not to offend those who don't celebrate the holiday.

The principal at Manchester Elementary School, identified by Fox affiliate KPTM as Jennifer Sinclair, sent out a memo earlier this week with guidelines as to what is considered appropriate for classroom decorations and assignments. Teachers reportedly were told that generic winter-themed items, such as sledding and scarves, and the "Frozen" character Olaf, were acceptable.

Decorations that included Santa, Christmas trees, reindeer, green and red items and even candy canes, however, were not acceptable for the elementary school. The candy canes, according to KETV, were prohibited because Sinclair deemed them to have religious significance. "Historically, the shape is a 'J' for Jesus. The red is for the blood of Christ, and the white is a symbol of his resurrection," she reportedly wrote. "This would also include different colored candy canes."

"I feel uncomfortable that I have to get this specific, but for everyone's comfort, I will," Sinclair reportedly wrote in the memo. The Elkhorn School District told Fox News in a statement that "the memo does not reflect the policy of Elkhorn Public Schools regarding holiday symbols in the school."

The district's policy states that "Christmas trees, Santa Claus and Easter eggs and bunnies are considered to be secular, seasonal symbols and may be displayed as teaching aids provided they do not disrupt the instructional program for students." Sinclair was placed on administrative leave as of Thursday morning.

https://nypost.com/2018/12/07/principal-bans-candy-canes-says-j-shape-stands-for-jesus-report/

HopCat to rename "Crack Fries" because 'drug addiction is not a joke'

By Robert Allen December 11th, 2018

Signature French fries — served with a drug reference — are getting a name change at gastropub Hopcat's 17 locations.

"While the name Crack Fries was intended to be tongue-in-cheek, drug addiction is not a joke," Mark Gray, CEO of BarFly Ventures,

HopCat's parent company, said Monday in a Youtube video and blog post. "The drug crack has devastated many of the communities that we serve." Menus, signs and posters are being redesigned, with a yet-to-be announced name change in January. The more-than 11-year-old recipe for the beer-battered fries, with salt and pepper among a secret blend of seasonings, is to remain intact.

Besides tap lists ranging to more than 100 different curated beers, Crack Fries are what HopCat is known for. When it opens a restaurant, HopCat has a tradition of offering many of its first customers free Crack Fries for a year. Food Network named them one of "America's 10 Best French Fries."

"People love Crack Fries, a lot of people love the name, but we thought it was time to make a change," BarFly Ventures spokesman Chris Knape said. "Frankly, I've been thinking about it for years and getting different feedback through the years — including through some of our partners in Detroit." He said they're making sure the new name doesn't cause any trademark issues, and the change is expected to be made in time for HopCat's anniversary fry-eating contest in January.

HopCat's footprint has grown with the rise of craft beer, as its locations offer beers from smaller, more local breweries on a menu offering a wide range of styles from across the country and world. The first location opened in January 2008 in downtown Grand Rapids, and HopCat now has seven Michigan locations, including one that opened in Midtown Detroit in 2014 and another in Royal Oak in 2017. Other HopCats are in Florida, Kentucky, Chicago, St. Louis and more.

https://www.freep.com/story/entertainment/2018/12/11/hopcat-crack-fries-menu-detroit/2274876002/

Pho restaurant with 'offensive' sign claims city officials signed off on pun-filled name months ago

By Michael Bartiromo Jan 8th, 2019

Pho Keene Great isn't going down without a phight. The French-Vietnamese restaurant, which is scheduled to open on March 1, is accusing city council members in the town of Keene, N.H., of "spreading a false narrative" after asking the owner to remove a temporary sign displaying the name.

Pho Keene Great had originally removed the sign in late December at the request of City Manager Elizabeth Dragon, who told restaurant owner Isabelle Jolie that the establishment hadn't gotten the correct permit to post it. Pho Keene Great also claims Dragon found the name of the restaurant – which is a play on the word pho (pronounced "fuh") and the name of the town (Keene) – offensive, leading to complaints from Keene residents.

In a Sunday post on Facebook, Pho Keene Great says city officials are also accusing the restaurant of violating a lease with the city – the eatery will be housed in the same building as Keane city hall, according to New Hampshire Public Radio – and suggesting that Pho Keene Great had considered using another name altogether at the time the contract was signed.

"Keene City councilor, Randy Filiault, is creating and spreading a false narrative," reads a statement posted by Pho Keene Great's team to Facebook on Sunday. "In his statement... he indicates that our lease agreement was conditional and 'one of the conditions was that a different name would be used.'"

Pho Keene Great instead claims they had never offered to use another name, and furthermore, that the name was on the paperwork that the city and state approved as of April. "We have reviewed our contract and studied the sign ordinance regarding temporary signs and do not believe we violated ordinance or the contract," the restaurant wrote. "As for the permanent sign, which we have never placed on the building, inside or outside, the permit submission is pending resolve of this controversy."

In a statement to Fox News, however, Dragon claims Jolie had not yet received a permit to put outward facing signs on the restaurant, something that Dragon claims Jolie and her lawyer agreed to long ago. Dragon further says Jolie negotiated "under her food truck name — Bon Vivant Gourmet Street Food," and "entered the lease as Pho Keene Great, LLC."

"Lots of businesses own LLC's which aren't necessarily the same of name of the restaurant, store, apartment building, etc.," said Dragon. Dragon alleged that Jolie is also postponing a meeting with city management, despite the restaurant's claims to the contrary in Pho Keene Great's latest Facebook post.

Prior to Sunday post, Pho Keene Great had also been polling social media users, asking if they think the name of the restaurant is offensive. A representative for Pho Keene Great was not immediately available to comment.

https://www.foxnews.com/food-drink/pho-restaurant-with-offensive-sign-claims-city-officials-signed-off-on-pun-filled-name-months-ago

College students slammed for photo advertising 'Taco Tuesday' event: 'Y'all should know better'

By Alexandra Deabler Jan 16th, 2019

The Ballard Center at Brigham Young University (BYU) has apologized after two students were called out for a photo advertising a Taco Tuesday event at the center that some have found offensive.

The Instagram post, which has since been deleted, featured two male BYU students dressed as tacos, wearing sombreros and holding flags for

Bolivia, Argentina and the United States in their mouths. Students were quick to call out the Utah school's center for being "insensitive" and "dumb" over its promotion, which advertises tacos – a food not typically associated with either of those South American countries.

Some, however, felt the outrage was too much and that the school did nothing wrong. After the backlash, the school released an apology on their Instagram offering "sincere apologies." This is not the first time a university campus has been called out for being culturally unaware in regards to its menu choices. In February of last year, NYU was accused of being "racially insensitive" and "ignorant" after serving a menu of ribs, collard green, cornbread, Kool-Aid and watermelon-flavored water in honor of Black History Month.

https://www.foxnews.com/food-drink/college-students-slammed-for-photo-advertising-taco-tuesday-event-yall-should-know-better

Trader Joe's Changing "Racist Packaging" on Ethnic Foods

By Dan Lyman Monday July 20th, 2020

Trader Joe's has announced plans to change packaging for many items after a petition calling their branding "racist" garnered media attention.

A Change.org petition with less than 3,000 signatures at the time of this writing has been cited in a variety of mainstream publications, prompting the grocery chain to reveal the rebranding effort, which they say has been in the works for some time.

"We demand that Trader Joe's remove racist branding and packaging from its stores. The grocery chain labels some of its ethnic foods with modifications of 'Joe' that belies a narrative of exoticism that perpetuates harmful stereotypes," the petition states. "For example, 'Trader Ming's' is used to brand the chain's Chinese food, 'Arabian Joe' brands

Middle Eastern foods, 'Trader José' brands Mexican foods, 'Trader Giotto's' is for Italian food, and 'Trader Joe San' brands their Japanese cuisine."

"The Trader Joe's branding is racist because it exoticizes other cultures – it presents 'Joe' as the default 'normal' and the other characters falling outside of it – they are 'Arabian Joe,' 'Trader José,' and 'Trader Joe San.'" The company, which has hundreds of locations nationwide, addressed the 'concerns' of those demanding changes, saying they have been in the works for years and will be complete "very soon."

"While this approach to product naming may have been rooted in a lighthearted attempt at inclusiveness, we recognize that it may now have the opposite effect — one that is contrary to the welcoming, rewarding customer experience we strive to create every day," Trader Joe's spokeswoman Kenya Friend-Daniel said in a statement.

https://www.newswars.com/trader-joes-changing-racist-packaging-on-ethnic-foods/

White people's diets are killing the environment: study

By Hannah Sparks March 28th, 2019

White people are already accused of hogging the majority of jobs, film roles, and housing — and now they're getting blamed for eating up Earth's natural resources, too. Caucasian populations are disproportionately contributing to climate change through their eating habits, which uses up more food — and emits more greenhouse gases — than the typical diets of black and Latinx communities, according to a new report published in the Journal of Industrial Ecology.

Researchers tracked information from multiple databases to identify foods considered "environmentally intense" by requiring more precious resources such as water, land and energy to produce — and, as a result, releasing more greenhouse gases such as carbon dioxide through production and distribution.

Potatoes, beef, apples and milk are some of the worst offenders. "The food pipeline — which includes its production, distribution and waste — contributes significantly to climate change through the production of greenhouse gases and requires significant amounts of water and land, which also has environmental effects," says Joe Bozeman, a student at the University of Illinois at Chicago, who helped author the study.

The EPA provided data on per capita food consumption rates for more than 500 foods groups, including water, plus estimates from the NIH on individual diets. Data showed that whites produced an average of 680 kilograms of the CO2 each year, attributable to food and drink, whereas Latinx individuals produced 640 kilograms, and blacks 600.

They also found the diets of white people required 328,000 liters of water on average per year. Latinx used just 307,000 liters, and blacks 311,800. Both black and Latinx individuals used more land per capita with 1,770 and 1,710 square meters per year, respectively, than white people with just 1,550. Nevertheless, white people still made the greatest overall contribution to climate change. "While the difference may not be enormous, these numbers are per individual, and when you add up all those individuals, it's very clear that whites are responsible for the majority of greenhouse gases emitted as a result of their food choices," says Bozeman.

https://nypost.com/2019/03/28/white-peoples-diets-are-killing-the-environment-study/

Store withdraws chocolate ducklings over racism complaint

By Jack Guy April 9th, 2019

(CNN) UK grocery chain Waitrose has apologized after being accused of racism over the names of three chocolate ducklings. The "Waitrose Trio of Chocolate Easter Ducklings" contains a white, milk and dark chocolate version, which were named "Fluffy," "Crispy" and "Ugly" respectively.

A Twitter user questioned why Waitrose had chosen to call the darkest duckling "Ugly."

"Overheard women saying 'this is not right,' I agree, doesn't look good at all," wrote Livia A. Aliberti on March 7. Waitrose has since apologized in a short statement seen by CNN.

"We are very sorry for any upset caused by the name of this product, it was absolutely not our intention to cause any offence," reads the statement. "We removed the product from sale several weeks ago while we changed the labeling and our ducklings are now back on sale." One possible explanation for the naming is a reference to the Hans Christian Andersen fairytale "The Ugly Duckling." The story features an unfortunate young duckling who is bullied by all of those around him before turning into a swan. Aliberti thanked Waitrose for changing the packaging in another tweet Tuesday.

https://edition.cnn.com/2019/04/09/uk/waitrose-ducklings-scli-intl-gbr/index.html

Oreo Promotes "Pronoun Packs" to Celebrate Trans Agenda

By Dan Lyman July 2nd, 2019

Oreo cookies announced the release of special edition treats which celebrate the LGBT agenda and 'trans pronouns.'

"We're proud to celebrate inclusivity for all gender identities and expressions. In partnership with NCTE, we're giving away special edition Pronoun Packs and encouraging everybody to share their pronouns with Pride today and every day," Oreo wrote on its social media accounts. The National Center For Transgender Equality (NCTE), "advocates to change policies and society to increase understanding and acceptance of transgender people," according to its website.

"Pronoun Packs" were given away at the New York City Pride Parade on Sunday, along with Oreo cookie pins reading, "Ask Me My Pronouns."

"Three different packs—'she/her,' 'he/him,' and 'they/them'—had pronouns written on the cookies themselves, with blue, pink and purple packaging reminiscent of the transgender flag," *Newsweek* reports. The limited run cookies will apparently not be available for sale.

"It appears it wants to get all the cred from LGBT politics without alerting the majority of their customers, who probably won't see their Facebook post and/or this offensive product in any store to tip them off. In other words, this is a big, blaring anti-virtue signal," notes Joy Pullman of *The Federalist*. Introduced in 1912, Oreo is the best-selling cookie in the United States and is now owned by multinational food and beverage company Mondelez International.

https://www.newswars.com/oreo-promotes-pronoun-packs-to-celebrate-trans-agenda/

Macy's pulls plates advocating against 'mom jeans' portion sizes

By Brian Ries July 22nd, 2019

(CNN) Macy's may have bitten off more than it could chew. The retail giant announced late Sunday that it would pull a line of porcelain plates advocating for smaller portion sizes after a wave of criticism that began -- and ended -- on Twitter. The decision came in response to a customer's tweet criticizing the plates' message Sunday night.

The $9.50 plates, designed by a company called Pourtions, feature three circles of increasing sizes in which one might place their food. The circles are labeled "skinny jeans," "favorite jeans" and "mom jeans." Two of them had just been featured in a display at Macy's flagship Herald Square location in New York -- a milestone celebrated on the Instagram page for the small company -- which is where writer Alie Ward saw them, rolled her eyes and took out her phone.

She tweeted a photo and asked: "How can I get these plates from Macy's banned in all 50 states?" That was all it would take. The tweet spread. The outrage grew. And within hours, Macy's responded: "Hi, Alie -- we appreciate you sharing this with us and agree that we missed the mark on this product. It will be removed from all STORY at Macy's locations."

And that was that. Macy's told CNN on Monday, "We apologize to our customers for missing the mark on this product. After reviewing the complaint, we quickly removed the plates, which were only in our STORY at Macy's location in Herald Square." Ward said Monday afternoon that she didn't intend for plate-gate to be national news: "I just saw it, rolled my eyes, got sad for the people it would impact and used my voice on a public platform," she explained, calling the plate's message "a pointless joke with a cheap punchline." She added that it wasn't her tweet that did them in but "a chorus of others echoing that it was ignorant and in poor taste." Pourtions' "Mom Jeans" plates can still be purchased on its website.

A representative of Pourtions, which is still selling the plates online for wholesale customers, said the company heard about the decision when a reporter called to ask for her reaction. "We feel very strongly about the positive, light hearted message conveyed by our glasses & plates. The response today has been overwhelmingly positive, including more interest in Pourtions & sales today than ever before," President Mary Cassidy wrote in an email.

"As the creators of Pourtions, we feel badly if what was meant to be a lighthearted take on the important issue of portion control was hurtful to anyone. Pourtions is intended to support healthy eating and drinking. Everyone who has appreciated Pourtions knows that it can be tough sometimes to be as mindful and moderate in our eating and drinking as we'd like, but that a gentle reminder can make a difference."

https://www.cnn.com/2019/07/22/us/macys-plates-mom-jeans-trnd/index.html

University bans burgers to help save the planet

By Alison Kershaw August 12th, 2019

Beef burgers have been banned by a university as part of efforts to tackle the climate emergency. Goldsmiths, University of London said it is to remove all beef products from sale from next month as the institution attempts to become carbon neutral by 2025.

Students will also face a 10p levy on bottles of water and single-use plastic cups when the academic year starts to discourage use of the products. The college's new Warden, Professor Frances Corner, said staff and students "care passionately about the future of our environment" and that "declaring a climate emergency cannot be empty words".

But the National Farmers' Union (NFU) told PA the move was "an overly simplistic approach" and said there was a "lack of understanding or recognition between British beef and beef produced elsewhere." Goldsmiths Students' Union has backed the ban with president Joe Leam saying that the university has a "huge carbon footprint" and that the promise to eradicate this in the next few years is needed.

As well as the beef ban and 10p levy on single-use water bottles and plastic cups, there are plans to install more solar panels across the college's New Cross campus in south-east London and switch to a 100% clean energy supplier as soon as possible.

Officials said Goldsmiths will also continue to invest in its allotment area and identify other places where planting could help to absorb carbon dioxide, and will review how all students can access modules which cover climate change and the role of both individuals and organizations in reducing carbon emissions. Prof Corner said: "The growing global call for organizations to take seriously their responsibilities for halting climate change is impossible to ignore.

"Though I have only just arrived at Goldsmiths, it is immediately obvious that our staff and students care passionately about the future of our environment and that they are determined to help deliver the step change we need to cut our carbon footprint drastically and as quickly as possible. "Declaring a climate emergency cannot be empty words. I truly believe we face a defining moment in global history and Goldsmiths now stands shoulder to shoulder with other organizations willing to call the alarm and take urgent action to cut carbon use."

NFU vice-president Stuart Roberts told PA that the union has been encouraging public bodies, such as universities to back British farming and source locally-produced food. "Tackling climate change is one of the greatest challenges of our time but singling out one food product is clearly an overly simplistic approach," he said.

"The main issue with this is the lack of understanding or recognition between British beef and beef produced elsewhere. Our standards of beef production in the UK are among the most efficient in the world, with British livestock grazing in extensive, grass-based systems – meaning a greenhouse gas footprint 2.5 times smaller than the global average. "Anyone wanting to play their part in helping our planet amid the current climate change challenge we're all facing should buy British, locally produced beef reared to some of the highest and environmentally sustainable standards in the world.

"The NFU has for years been encouraging public bodies such as schools and universities to back British farming and source their produce locally wherever possible. This makes more sense and keeps the choice to eat tasty, sustainably-produced meat firmly on the menu." Figures show that Goldsmiths emits around 3.7 million kg of carbon emissions each year, the college said. Referring to the statistic in a blog, Mr Leam said: "It is clear our university has a huge carbon footprint. The promise to have ended this by 2030 at the latest, with the hope of doing so by 2025, is one which is needed.

https://uk.news.yahoo.com/university-bans-burgers-help-save-114859056.html

Burger King Removes "Ham" From "Hamburger" to Avoid Offending Muslims

By Paul Joseph Watson September 12th, 2019

Burger King in South Africa is dropping the word "ham" from "hamburger" to avoid offending Muslims.

Yes, really.

The "Double Spicy Hamburger" will now become just a "Double Spicy Burger," while the "Triple Hamburger with Cheese" becomes the "Triple Burger with Cheese," and a "Hamburger King Jr" on the children's menu will now be just a "Kids Burger." The company, whose headquarters are based in Miami, Florida, said the word was being eliminated in order "to be more respectful of Muslim customers."

The change is being made despite the fact that the "ham" in hamburger has nothing to do with pork and relates to the German city of Hamburg, where the patties were first made. However, the company admitted that its outlets in South Africa would be losing their "halal" certification because of popular demand for some sandwiches to include bacon. This all appears to be a very awkward, or you could say – ham-fisted – attempt to be politically correct.

https://www.infowars.com/burger-king-removes-ham-from-hamburger-to-avoid-offending-muslims/

New York City schools want to ban chocolate milk

By Selim Algar September 15th, 2019

Holy cow.

The city Department of Education wants to ban chocolate milk from public schools, The Post has learned. Citing health concerns, including sugar content, Schools Chancellor Richard Carranza and his underlings are pushing for a white-milk-only policy, DOE sources said.

"The thinking is that these kids are already getting too much sugar, why are they getting it in their milk?" one DOE source said, adding that higher-ups "are discussing what to do and how to do it."

Other school districts, from San Francisco to Washington, D.C., have banned flavored milk, and concern over dairy has come up before in New York City, where students' milk options were limited to low-fat and nonfat in 2006. But the city has resisted putting the kibosh on the chocolate variety — at least until now.

The moo-ve is already dividing parents and kids. "It would be awful to take away people's chocolate milk," said Caterina Ditommasa, a 10-year-old at PS 58 in Carroll Gardens, Brooklyn. Her mother, Joanna, argued that removing chocolate milk won't solve schools' dietary problems.

"The schools serve other sugary drinks that are no better — juices and sodas," she said. "The real problem is that New York City lunches are unhealthy in general, all prepackaged and full of preservatives."

Caterina's dad, Luke, was more open to a chocolate-milk ban. "Not to be a health nazi," he said, "but it's not the worst idea." Upstate dairy farmers got wind that something was ahoof in the city and are having a cow about it.

They say taking away chocolate milk will lower kids' milk intake, which would hurt their health, not to mention farmers' bottom lines.

A group of dairy farmers enlisted the help of their local Congress members, who fired off a letter to Mayor Bill de Blasio last week. "Over two-thirds of milk served in school is flavored, which represents an essential way that kids get the nutrients they need for healthy growth and development," the letter said.

One of the politicians, Rep. Anthony Brindisi (D-Utica), told The Post: "This is a very large school system. This is a time when dairy farmers are already struggling and facing a lot of uncertainty." The DOE stressed that a final decision has not been made. "Our priority is the health and well-being of our students, and every day, we offer a variety of healthy, delicious, and free meal options that exceed USDA standards," it said in a statement.

"We look forward to discussing our menu with these members of Congress." The San Francisco Unified School District, which Carranza previously led, banned flavored milk shortly after he left in 2016. While Los Angeles eliminated chocolate milk in 2011, it brought it back in 2017 after finding kids were rejecting milk altogether. According to the city Health Department, 8 ounces of local public schools' chocolate skim milk has 120 calories and 20 grams of sugar, 8 grams of which are added sugar.

The same amount of skim white milk has 90 calories and 12 grams of sugar, none added.

https://nypost.com/2019/09/15/new-york-city-schools-want-to-ban-chocolate-milk/

How the Government Made You Fat

By Bret Scher September 23rd, 2019

Ever since the introduction of the Food Pyramid in the early '90s, the average American has gotten fatter and sicker. Has this government-approved nutritional guideline — the basis of the modern "healthy diet" — led us astray? If so, how did this happen, and what can we learn from it? Cardiologist Dr. Bret Scher offers some food for thought on this very weighty issue.

Here's a riddle:

How is it that ever since the government began telling us what to eat, we have gotten fatter and sicker? In 1977, when the government first set dietary guidelines, the average American male weighed 170 pounds. He now weighs 197. It's not any better for women —145 to 170. And you don't need an academic study to know the same thing is happening to kids. Just look around.

The weight gain has real-life consequences: the percentage of Americans diagnosed with type 2 diabetes—a condition that can lead to severe medical issues—has risen from 2% in 1977 to over 9% in 2015. In hard numbers, that's five million people to over *30* million people.

How did this happen? It all started innocently enough in the 1950s, when President Dwight Eisenhower had a heart attack while in office. Suddenly, the issue of heart health became a national obsession.

Keep in mind this was an era when scientists had harnessed the power of the atom, unlocked the secrets of DNA, and cured once incurable diseases like polio. Surely, there *had* to be a scientific solution to heart disease.

There was. And a charismatic medical researcher from the University of Minnesota named Ancel Keyes had it. Cholesterol, Keyes claimed, was the villain of the heart disease story. His now famous "seven countries study" determined conclusively—in *his* mind, at least—that people who consumed high amounts of fat—specifically, saturated fat—had higher cholesterol levels and thus, higher rates of heart attacks.

Lower your fat intake, and you would lower heart disease risk. The ever-confident Keyes spread the gospel. As an influential member of the American Heart Association, he was in a very strong position to do so. There was only one problem: Keyes's study was bad science. The sample size was so small, the data collection integrity so shoddy, and the life-style variables between the countries he studied so great, that his research had no scientific validity. In other words, he asserted a conclusion he couldn't prove.

When other scientists questioned Keyes's conclusions, they were invariably met with stern responses like: "people are dying while you're quibbling over data points." And, "there are great benefits and no risks" to adopting this new way of eating.

In 1973, the American Heart Association set the dietary limit on saturated fat at 10%, and in 1977, the US government followed suit. Where did the 10% value come from? It didn't come from any scientific data. It was merely a government committee's best guess.

This was despite contrary evidence like the 1957 Western Electric Company employee study showing no difference in heart attacks in those who ate more or less saturated fat. A longer-term study of the same Western Electric subjects in 1981 reached the same conclusion. But again, no one wanted to hear it.

To make this all easier to understand and to spread the message to schools, "the food pyramid" was created. That's the chart you first saw in third or fourth grade with all the supposedly good foods at the bottom—meaning, "eat a lot of those," and the bad foods at the top—"eat those ones sparingly."

What our kids are fed in school, what our military troops are fed on bases, what sick people are fed in hospitals; what crops we plant and how we raise our cattle, are all predicated on this deceptive nutritional concept.

As Americans ate less saturated fat—margarine instead of butter, processed oils like corn oil instead of olive oil, low fat milk, low fat yogurt and so on— they also started to eat more "heart healthy" grains—exactly what the food pyramid, and the updated version called MyPlate, advise you to do.

As the consumption of saturated fat decreased by almost 40%, the consumption of refined grains—carbohydrates that convert to sugar in the body—increased substantially. Total intake of calories also began to increase.

This happened, in no small part, because food companies took advantage of the low-fat craze. They lowered fat and increased sugar. Suddenly, supermarkets were full of supposedly healthy low fat, high sugar foods. It remains that way today. Foods that are high in sugar stimulate reward centers in the brain and leave us wanting more. Thus, the famous line about potato chips: "Betcha can't eat just one!"

The end result is a fatter population with greater and greater health issues—like type 2 diabetes, a problem that's getting worse, not better. How do we get ourselves out of this spiral? There are many answers: for some, it's a low-carb, high fat diet; for others, it's a Mediterranean diet; for some, it's vegetarianism; for others, it might be something else.

You need to find the best solution for *you*. And that's really the point: we need to take responsibility for our own health. If the food pyramid has taught us one thing, it's this:

Don't rely on the government to take care of you.

https://www.prageru.com/video/how-the-government-made-you-fat/

Corporate Wokeness Continues: Kellogg's Launches LGBT Cereal

By Infowars.com October 19th, 2019

Kellogg's has announced the rollout of its new LGBT-themed cereal to celebrate diversity and inclusion.

The company launched its "All Together" cereal to promote "Spirit Day," a day for LGBT awareness, despite the fact there's an entire month now dedicated to the LGBT community. "As part of #SpiritDay we are launching a new "All Together Cereal" and donating $50,000 to support GLAAD's anti-bullying and LGBTQ advocacy efforts. Get your limited edition box of ALL TOGETHER cereal at http://kellogg-store.com," the company tweeted Thursday.

Gay website PinkNews couldn't contain its excitement for the LGBT breakfast, saying that now "you can start your day with maximum gay. If you're a fan of breakfast and being gay, we have grrrrreat news for you!" The $20-a-box cereal is an amalgamation of six of Kellogg's most popular cereals, including Corn Flakes, Froot Loops, Frosted Flakes, Frosted Mini Wheats, Raisin Bran, and Rice Krispies.

The company's website explains their social justice cereal further:

"We all belong together. So for the first time in history, our famous mascots and cereals are offered exclusively together in the same box for All Together Cereal. It's a symbol of acceptance no matter how you look, where you're from or who you love. We believe that all people deserve an environment where they can be their best selves."

Great! It's not like we have enough corporations virtue-signaling their social justice wokeness, do we?

https://www.infowars.com/corporate-wokeness-continues-kelloggs-launches-lgbt-cereal/

Food

Eating the following foods are now considered "racist" by the thought and victimhood police:

Chinese food
Italian food
Mexican food
Vietnamese food
Thai food
Japanese food
Korean food
Indian food
French food

You can't even get drunk off your ass on Cinco De Mayo by drinking an endless supply of margaritas at happy hour unless you want to be considered a "racist." Gone are the days you can order a steak because eating cows causes "climate change." The people who are attacking every single aspect of culture won't stop until we are all eating bugs and worms in internment camps.

27

The War on Fashion

SF School Teacher Says Bernie Sanders' Mittens Are a Symbol of "White Privilege"

By Paul Joseph Watson February 3rd, 2021

In an article published by the San Francisco Chronicle, a public school teacher asserts that Bernie Sanders' inauguration mittens are a symbol of "white privilege."

The article begins with Ingrid Seyer-Ochi revealing how she conducted a lesson on the Capitol building breach, telling her high school students, "This is white supremacy."

"Across our Zoom screen, they affirmed, with nods, thumbs-ups, and emojis of anger and frustration," she writes. Seyer-Ochi, a former UC Berkeley professor, then explains that she oversaw a similar study of the inauguration (why a teacher is spending so much time analyzing current affairs through her obviously demented far-left bias isn't explained, but this is San Francisco).

"What do we see?" I asked again. We've been studying diversity and discrimination in the United States; my students were ready. What did they see? They saw a white man in a puffy jacket and huge mittens, distant not only in his social distancing, but in his demeanor and attire." She then expressed how upset she was that the next day, Bernie was "everywhere."

"A wealthy, incredibly well-educated and -privileged white man, showing up for perhaps the most important ritual of the decade, in a puffy jacket and huge mittens." Still fuming at the onslaught of Bernie memes, Seyer-Ochi whines, “He manifests privilege, white privilege, male privilege and class privilege, in ways that my students could see and feel.”

“I don’t know many poor, or working class, or female, or struggling-to-be-taken-seriously folk who would show up at the inauguration of our 46th president dressed like Bernie. Unless those same folk had privilege. Which they don’t,” she concludes. The point of her argument seems to be that Bernie didn’t try hard enough when choosing his attire, therefore disrespected “diversity” and is therefore exhibiting “white privilege.”

Utterly demented and perhaps peak ‘performative woke’. And remember, this individual is teaching your kids. Meanwhile, elsewhere in the city, the San Francisco Unified School District Arts Department has announced that “acronyms are a symptom of white supremacy culture” because non-English speakers find them hard to understand.

The department responded by changing its name from “VAPA”, short for “Visual and Performing Arts’, to SFUSD Arts Department – which is still an acronym. You’d think they’d all have bigger problems to worry about...

https://summit.news/2021/02/03/sf-school-teacher-says-bernie-sanders-mittens-are-a-symbol-of-white-privilege/

Lena Dunham slams Revolve for featuring her controversial sweatshirt design on 'thin white women'

By Michelle Gant September 14th, 2018

Lena Dunham says she no longer supports the controversial collection of sweatshirts she helped create with brand LPA that are being slammed for their fat-shaming message.

Online retailer Revolve released one of the sweatshirts on its website earlier this week. The gray crewneck, worn by a slender, light-skinned model, reads: "Being fat is not beautiful it's an excuse." Many people online were outraged by the clothing item's perceived message, calling it "gross," "judgmental" and "damaging."

In an Instagram post featuring a close-up of a Peter Paul Rubens painting of feminine curves, Dunham explained she no longer wants to be involved with the sweatshirts. "Without consulting me or any of the women involved, Revolve presented the sweatshirts on thin white women, never thinking about the fact that difference and individuality is what gets you punished on the Internet, or that lack of diversity in representation is a huge part of the problem (in fact, the problem itself.) As a result, I cannot support this collaboration or lend my name to it in any way," she wrote. LPA noted the sweatshirt was meant to be modeled by Dunham.

Dunham also expressed her "deep disappointment" for the way Revolve handled "a sensitive topic and a collaboration rooted in reclaiming the words of Internet trolls to celebrate the beauty in diversity and bodies and experiences that aren't the industry norm." Both LPA and Revolve have since put out statements apologizing for the sweatshirt and explaining that the collection was conceived in collaboration with Lena Dunham, Emily Ratajkowski, Cara Delevingne, Suki Waterhouse and Paloma Elsesser as a way to spotlight online bullying with proceeds benefiting Girls Write Now, a charity aimed at empowering girls.

"The prematurely released image featured on Revolve.com was not only included without context of the overall campaign but regrettably featured one of the pieces on a model who's size was not reflective of the piece's commentary on body positivity," the Revolve statement read. Revolve has since donated $20,000 to Girls Write Now. Dunham said she would also be making donations "to the charity of every woman's choice who was wronged with me."

https://www.foxnews.com/lifestyle/lena-dunham-slams-revolve-for-featuring-her-controversial-sweatshirt-design-on-thin-white-women

Forever 21 Upsets Fans After Using White Model to Promote 'Black Panther' Sweater

By Nicole Drum December 21st, 2018

With *Black Panther* being one of the most successful films of 2018 it's no surprise that merchandise celebrating the Marvel film and character would be a big part of the holiday season. However, it's the marketing of some of that merchandise that leaves little to be celebrated as Forever 21 discovered on Tuesday.

The fast-fashion retailer shared a photo and link for their Wakanda Forever Fair Isle Sweater to Twitter today. Nothing wrong with that, it's a common way retailers advertise their offerings. The problem? Well, just take a look at the now-deleted tweet below.

As you can see, Forever 21 opted to use a blonde-haired, blue-eyed, very white man to model the *Black Panther*-themed sweater complete with the "Wakanda Forever" slogan and Black Panther mask adorning the front. Now, this isn't to say that there is anything wrong with a white person appreciating *Black Panther*-related merchandise. Both the blockbuster film and the Marvel Comics character the film is based upon have wide appeal to readers of all races, genders, and identities. It just feels like something that, considering the film is about a black superhero, probably should have been featured on a black model -- which Forever 21 does feature on their website. In fact there is a black sweater with a yellow panther print currently on the website that is modeled by a black model.

This isn't the first time *Black Panther* merchandise has gotten some negative attention thanks to what some might term "whitewashing".

Earlier this year, Disney came under fire when a collectible *Black Panther* pin available at Disney theme parks were revealed by The Disney Pin Blog to have a remarkably light-skinned appearance than one might expect for Chadwick Boseman's heroic King T'Challa. In that case, the pin appeared to have some sort color variation possibly due to paint differences or even lightning in photos, though fans were troubled by the pin's lighter-appearing coloring.

As for Forever 21's sweater issue, while the tweet may have been deleted, sweater -- as worn by the white model -- remains on the website at the time of this article though clicking on it redirects you to the yellow and black sweater option instead and social media plenty to say about it. Read on for a sampling of the reactions to Forever 21's *Black Panther* sweater snafu and be sure to let us know your thoughts in the comments.

https://comicbook.com/marvel/news/forever-21-black-panther-sweater-white-model/

San Francisco area restaurant bans 'Make America Great' hats, compares to white hoods and swastikas

By Associated Press January 31st, 2019

SAN MATEO, Calif. (AP) - An award-winning cookbook author and California restaurant owner says anyone wearing a red "Make America Great Again" baseball cap will be refused service at his restaurant. Kenji Lopez-Alt is a chef-partner of the Wursthall restaurant in San Mateo and says in a tweet Sunday that he views the hats as symbols of intolerance and hate.

The San Francisco Chronicle reported Thursday that Lopez-Alt's decision was met with mixed reaction by restaurant clients. Diners interviewed by the newspapers said they understood Lopez-Alt's stance but questioned the hat ban and said he could have found a way to start a dialogue on the issue. On Twitter, many criticized the so-called tolerance of the liberal Bay Area. Lopez-Alt wrote the 2015 book "The Food Lab: Better Home Cooking Through Science." He says his restaurant received threatening emails following the tweet and declined further comment.

https://www.fox5ny.com/news/san-francisco-area-restaurant-bans-make-america-great-hats-compares-to-white-hoods-and-swastikas

Student Forced to Remove 'Fake News' Shirt During Field Trip to CNN

By Mike LaChance November 18th, 2017

A seventh grader in Georgia made the hilarious decision to wear a 'fake news' t-shirt on a field trip to CNN with his middle school. His teachers failed to see the humor and made him change his shirt.

Jessica Chasmar reports at the Washington Times:

A Georgia county commissioner and her school board member husband are crying foul after their seventh-grade son was ordered to change out of his "FNN – Fake News Network" T-shirt before going on a school field trip to CNN's Atlanta headquarters. Jaxon Jester, a student at Peachtree Charter Middle School who is the son of DeKalb County Commissioner Nancy Jester and DeKalb County Schools board member Stan Jester, reportedly complied with his teacher's request to change out of the shirt before touring the CNN studios, but his parents say his First Amendment rights were violated." This year when the CNN tour was announced, my 7th grade son Jaxon asked me if he could purchase an FNN-Fake News Network shirt to wear for his field trip," the boy's father wrote in a blog post. "As an advocate for the First Amendment, I agreed to his request. He picked out the shirt he wanted and and ordered it from Amazon. His mother cautioned him that he might cause a controversy and needed to be prepared for that. He was fully aware of the implications of his decision and made the affirmative choice to wear his shirt. "We received a phone call from the principal at the middle school this morning informing us that he was forced to change his shirt," he wrote. "I'm disappointed by the hypocrisy of this decision."

This was the reasoning the school gave:

"The teacher involved said that she told Jax to change his shirt because she thought his shirt said 'F-CNN,'" she wrote. "I told her that it absolutely did NOT say that. She apologized and said that she now realizes that the shirt has no profanity or suggestion of profanity on it. The principal stated that he should have been made aware of the situation before Jax was made to change his shirt. He apologized for the incident.

The local CBS News affiliate has a full statement from the school:

"An incident occurred at a DeKalb County school last week in which a teacher asked a student to change his shirt prior to leaving the school for a field trip. The request was out of concern for the student's safety in accordance with the district's Student Code of Conduct, which states . . . . " the wearing of clothing, tattoos or other adornments which show offensive and/or vulgar words, pictures, diagrams, drawings or includes words or phrases of a violent nature, a disruptive nature, a sexual nature, politically/socially controversial words or graphics or words or phrases that are derogatory regarding a person's ethnic background, color, race, national origin, religious belief, sexual orientation or disability is prohibited." The parent of the student was contacted by the principal and informed that the student was being asked to change his shirt. The student complied with the request made by the teacher. The safety of all DCSD students and staff is paramount.

You have to admire this kid's sense of humor and his parents for supporting him. You also have to wonder if the teachers would have reacted the same way if he was wearing an anti-Trump shirt.

https://legalinsurrection.com/2017/11/student-forced-to-remove-fake-news-shirt-during-field-trip-to-cnn/amp/

High School Student Suspended for Posing With Pro-Trump MAGA Flag and Sweatshirt

By Tyler O'Neil March 7th, 2019

Last Friday, Perry High School in Gilbert, Ariz., suspended student Logan Jones after a security officer reprimanded her as she posed for photos in a "Make America Great Again" (MAGA) sweater while holding a pro-Trump "Make America Great Again" flag. On Wednesday, Alliance Defending Freedom (ADF) sent a demand letter warning of legal action unless the school dropped the suspension. The school agreed to allow Jones to return to school that day but it refused to remove the suspension from her record.

"Public schools have a duty to respect the legitimate free expression of students that the First Amendment guarantees to them," Tyson Langhofer, ADF senior counsel and director of the Center for Academic Freedom, wrote in a statement Thursday. "While it's good that the school is allowing Logan to return to school, it isn't acceptable that this unjust suspension will remain on her record."

ADF will not accept this state of affairs. "As we continue discussions with the school, we are also consulting with Logan and her mother to determine what our next steps will be if the school doesn't do the right thing and remove the suspension," Langhofer added. According to the demand letter, Jones and her friends had dressed in patriotic and USA-themed clothing for a "Party in the USA Day" on Friday of Spirit Week.

"Immediately after school was dismissed at 2:14 p.m., [Jones] and a few of her friends went to one of the outdoor common areas of campus to take pictures together before they went home," the letter reads. "This is a common practice for [Jones] and many other students and it happens virtually every day after school without any interference by school officials. Less than five minutes after they arrived, while [Jones] and her friend were taking a picture in their MAGA sweatshirts and holding a flag that said 'Trump' and 'Make America Great Again,' a School Resource Officer approached and ordered [Jones] and her friends to leave."

Jones immediately obeyed and started packing up to leave. The officer took photos of her and her friends with his phone, began following her as she left campus, and then ordered her to give him her name. Jones asked why he needed her name, as she was complying with his order. At that point, the officer told her to speak with Vice Principal Heather Patterson.

Jones called her mother and told her about the situation. Her mother said she would come to the school herself and told Jones not to speak with anyone until she arrived. At the office, Jones was again asked to give her name. She "politely replied that her mother was on her way to the office and that her mother had instructed her not to answer any questions until she arrived."

Once the mother arrived, a brief discussion ensued between the mother, Principal Dan Serrano, Vice Principal Patterson, and the officer. Principal Serrano left, saying, "I am tired of hearing this. Logan Jones, you are suspended for 10 days. Get off of school property." Jones was allegedly suspended for failing to identify herself to school officials, yet ADF argued that "this reason was mere pretext."

"Contrary to the stated reason, there is ample evidence to establish that you imposed the suspension against [Jones] based on a disagreement with the viewpoint of [Jones's] message," the letter states. "Multiple videos demonstrate the hostility that School officials displayed towards the messages expressing support for President Trump and his MAGA slogan. And it is our understanding that other students have been punished as well for expressing similar viewpoints."

"This blatant censorship of [Jones's] speech violates the First Amendment," the letter declares. In dropping the suspension, the school seems to have recognized that punishing Jones for her pro-Trump and MAGA demonstration was a violation of her free speech. Even so, the school reportedly is refusing to drop the suspension from the girl's record.

No school should suspend a student for expressing a political viewpoint. Sadly, many liberals have stigmatized Trump's "Make America Great Again" slogan as hateful, and it appears these school officials consider MAGA unacceptable. This school should have learned from the backlash and lawsuits after the media ran with the story that the MAGA hat-wearing Covington High School boys were haters. The school's action violates the First Amendment. Students have the right to wear MAGA sweaters and hold Trump flags. This is outrageous.

https://pjmedia.com/news-and-politics/tyler-o-neil/2019/03/07/high-school-student-suspended-for-posing-with-pro-trump-maga-flag-and-sweatshirt-n64283

Calvin Klein apologizes to LGBT community for ad of Bella Hadid kissing female robot

By Sara Moniuszko May 18th, 2019

Calvin Klein is apologizing after the fashion label came under fire for a video campaign showing model Bella Hadid kissing female robot Lil Miquela. The 30-second ad drew backlash since Hadid identifies as heterosexual, with critics commenting, "There are plenty of real LGBTQ Models that could have been used." In a statement posted to their social media late Friday, the company said they "welcome all types of constructive feedback from our community."

"The concept for our latest #MYCALVINS campaign is to promote freedom of expression for a wide range of identities, including a spectrum of gender and sexual identities," the statement read. "This specific campaign was created to challenge conventional norms and stereotypes in advertising. In this particular video, we explored the blurred lines between reality and imagination."

The statement continued, "We understand and acknowledge how featuring someone who identifies as heterosexual in a same-sex kiss could be perceived as queer-baiting. As a company with a longstanding tradition of advocating for LGTBQ+ rights, it was certainly not our intention to misrepresent the LGTBQ+ community. We sincerely regret any offense we caused."

In the ad, a female voice is heard. "Life is opening doors," the voice says as Miquela approaches Hadid, who then caresses the robot's face before kissing her. "Creating new dreams that you never knew could exist." It is unclear whether the voice is Hadid's or Miquela's.
https://www.usatoday.com/story/life/people/2019/05/18/calvin-klein-apologizes-lgbt-community-bella-hadid-lil-miquela-kissing-ad/3718939002/

Woman wearing see-through top kicked off plane for 'disruptive behavior': 'I was in shock'

By Michael Hollan June 30th, 2019

A woman was kicked off a flight after passengers complained about her revealing outfit, but the airline says it was her behavior, not her outfit, that got her in trouble.

The woman reportedly became "disruptive" after being asked to change her top, which other passengers on the EasyJet flight found too "revealing." While the woman agreed to wear a new top provided by the airline, witnesses said she continued to act in a disruptive manner. Harriet Osborne was originally wearing a sheer top which left her nipples "clearly visible," MSN reported. Other passengers on the flight from Malaga, Spain, to London Stansted Airport, complained to the flight crew about the outfit, and the woman was offered an additional top to wear, which she reportedly obliged.

But Osborne apparently continued to act disruptive toward a member of the crew, leading to her being removed from the flight. EasyJet says that had she not behaved in that manner, she would have been allowed to travel, Independent.co.uk reports.

A spokesperson for EasyJet told Fox News, “We can confirm that a passenger traveling from Malaga to Stansted on 23 June was unable to travel due to behaving disruptively. Following concerns about her clothing crew politely requested that the customer wear an additional top for the flight which the customer agreed to. However, she then proceeded to act disruptively towards a member of our crew.

“Our cabin and ground crew are trained to assess all situations and to act quickly and appropriately. We do not tolerate abusive or threatening behavior towards our staff.”

Osbourne, however, tells a different story. She told The Sun, “The crew were horrible and made me feel cheap. This air hostess confronted me in front of the whole plane and said I wasn’t allowed on in that top. She said to me, ‘Oh no, move to the side,’ and tried to cover me up with my hands. She said, ‘You’re not coming on my plane like that — you need to put a top on’. Then she ordered me off the plane, so of course, I put a top on.

"When I tried to get back on she turned to the ground crew and said, ‘She’s not coming on my plane.’ I was escorted away from the aircraft," Osbourne continued. "I was in shock. It was so sexist. I just burst out crying. We had to walk back through the terminal where Spanish police stopped to question us. They were baffled when I told them why we’d been kicked off.”

https://www.foxnews.com/travel/easyjet-revealing-outfit-kicked-off

Lululemon apologizes after art director promotes 'bat fried rice' T-shirt during coronavirus

By Frank Miles April 21st, 2020

New details about efforts to find out how the coronavirus pandemic began; Gillian Turner reports. Fitness apparel brand Lululemon is apologizing after a senior staffer promoted a T-shirt design for "bat fried rice" during the coronavirus pandemic.

Senior global art director Trevor Fleming, whose social media accounts now have all been deactivated, posted the design featuring a Chinese takeout box and pair of chopsticks with bat wings on his Instagram on Sunday. The design was created by California artist Jess Sluder who was selling it digitally for $60. "Where did COVID-19 come from? Nothing is certain, but we know a bat was involved," the artist wrote in a post of the design online.

Lululemon later announced that Fleming "is no longer an employee." Neither Fleming nor Sluder responded to requests from Fox News for comment.

A scientific consensus is still evolving, but the World Health Organization said the virus originated in bats in the wild. Sources have told Fox News that there is increasing confidence the naturally occurring virus was being studied in a Wuhan lab and escaped – as opposed to claims it originated instead in a nearby wet market.

Critics took to social media with their outrage, calling the T-shirt racist. "There have been 100+ daily attacks on Asian Americans since the start of #COVID19," wrote one user on Twitter along with photos of the T-shirt. "To see people adding to the hurt & racism hurts my heart." Lululemon apologized for the shirt, noting the image didn't align with the core values of its athletic brand "We take matters like this extremely seriously. The T-shirt design is not a Lululemon product. We apologize that an employee was affiliated with promoting an offensive T-shirt, and we take this very seriously. The image and the post were inappropriate and inexcusable and we do not tolerate this behavior. We acted immediately, and the person involved is no longer an employee of Lululemon," a company spokesperson for Lululemon said in a statement.

https://www.foxnews.com/lifestyle/lululemon-coronavirus-tshirt-art-director

Hawaiian Shirts Have Become an Unlikely Symbol of White Supremacy

By Samantha Sutton April 25th, 2020

We've known for a while that clothes can be used to send a message, sometimes overtly (we're looking at you, Melania's Zara coat), and other times as a kind of subtle nod (like when Kate Middleton channels Princess Diana). We've mined celebrity outfits for clues about their personal lives, and have come to spot rainbows as a proud representation of the LGBTQ community. Sometimes, a symbolic bit of style could be marching right in front of you, speaking a sinister meaning you'd never expect.

Take Hawaiian shirts, for instance. Did you know that they're being used as a dog whistle for the white supremacist movement? Reece Jones, PhD, a political geography professor at the University of Hawaii who is currently writing a book on anti-immigrant groups, exposed this culture clash in a now-viral Twitter thread, which explains how the typically happy, casual, 'dad-shirt' of the Polynesian islands has become associated with the alt-right. Unfortunately, the shirt style, along with other "far right iconography" you'd glance right past if you didn't know (such as igloos), keep popping up at protests, and it's important to be aware of what it's being used to represent. Especially if you, like us, had just become convinced Aloha shirts were the laidback style to live in for Summer 2020. (Our bad.)

"Part of the strategy of white supremacists is to disguise themselves behind new names and seemingly innocent symbols," Jones explains to

InStyle via email. "No one identifies as KKK or a Nazi. Instead, they use terms like alt right, groyper, or boogaloo, that mean the same thing but do not yet have the same negative connotations. Similarly, everyone recognizes a swastika, so modern day racists co-opt other symbols like the OK sign, Pepe the Frog, and now, unfortunately, aloha shirts."

Here's a bit of backstory on how the latter came to be.

Breakin' 2: Electric Boogaloo

So many movies that were initially panned somehow end up with cult followings, and such was the case with this 1984 flop about breakdancing. Fans of this sequel eventually connected through message boards on Reddit, 4chan, and 8chan, sharing jokes and memes about the film, but, as Jones pointed out in his thread, the radical far right gathers on those sites as well. They use boards like /pol/ to discuss politics, and there are ones dedicated to being "politically incorrect," where they use racial slurs and hate speech. Niche memes flourish here, which is how Pepe the Frog got involved. One major idea they discuss — and especially on 4chan's /k/, a gun worship board — is how the government is coming to take their guns away. Seemingly the weird movie fandom and gun fanaticism have nothing to do with one another, but wait.

The Second Civil War

Obviously, people have a lot of thoughts about gun control, and the radicals that we mentioned are very much against it. In 2012, when California's then-lieutenant governor Gavin Newsom addressed the National Rifle Association in a Facebook post, saying he was "coming for your guns," they latched onto that — and were ready to fight back. There was a lot of talk about a second Civil War, and infamously inflammatory host Alex Jones kept pushing the idea.

Those who believe this war is imminent do not always share the same overall ideas, and they're not all white supremacists. Some are intense gun rights activists and are associated with the militia movement. As CNN points out, many are anti-government extremists. However,

Jones (Reece, not Alex) stated in another tweet that for others, it *is* about race. "They believe immigration is leading to the great replacement," he said. They are white nationalists, and a Tolerance.org article further explains this, saying that these people believe there is a white genocide happening.

So the main thing that needs some explaining is how these two ideas — a supposed second Civil War and a random breakdancing movie — merged. Jones briefly mentions this in his thread, and it basically boils down to weird Internet word play. Over time, *Breakin' 2: Electric Boogaloo* was shortened to just "the Boogaloo" on chat boards and — likely due to the way the word boogaloo sounds — later became "Big igloo." Another term that was derived from boogaloo was "Big Luau," which directly connects to the attire one would wear to a luau, aka Hawaiian shirts.

An *Anti-Defamation League* article also notes that, at one point, people began putting different things in front of the first part of *Breakin' 2: Electric* Boogaloo, interchanging the "Breakin' 2" part with random phrases or titles. Someone came up with *Civil War 2: Electric Boogaloo*, and connected it with the Gavin Newsom quote, which tied the two worlds together.

Hawaiian Shirts

Once "Big Luau" merged with Civil War 2, Hawaiian shirts (and, sometimes, igloos) became symbols representing the ideas of this alt-right group. Remember when crowds were protesting for the states to re-open, even though people were and are still dying from Covid-19? Many were wearing Hawaiian shirts. And, it's not just shirts, either; there are also guns with aloha patterns now, which some of those anti-government, anti-shutdown protestors carried with them. Because, did we mention, they love their guns?

The Current Protests

Once protests began following the death of George Floyd, these radical 'Boogaloo bois' (another name for the group) saw it as an opportunity to further their agenda, too. They began showing up to the protests wearing Hawaiian shirts, as *Esquire* reports, which can now mean one of two things. Some of these Hawaiian-shirt-wearers actually *are* calling for justice for George, because they were already against the police, the military, and the government. They see this man's murder as proof of why they need to fight back, to take power away from the police (and, no less frighteningly, put it in their own hands). But, there are the white supremacists in the mix, who are ready for their supposed race war to begin. In both cases, the Boogaloo bois are willing to incite violence to reach their desired outcome, and there are plenty of photos of white men in Hawaiian shirts destroying property and touting rifles.

Clearly, this radical group is taking advantage of the situation in order to further their cause of destruction and harm. This presents a challenge for Black Lives Matter protesters: to be louder than they are, shut down their racist and violent plans with data and facts, and continue to educate them on the many ways they are wrong.

"Thankfully more people know what to look for now and are asking them to leave," Jones says. "The FBI also arrested three people, who identify as part of boogaloo [and were armed with Molotov cocktails], for terrorism in Las Vegas."

As for whether you can keep wearing Hawaiian shirts, Jones says yes. "As long as you do not accessorize it with body armor and a long gun, it is fine." And we get it — we just got into this trend, and we don't want to let the few bad actors take it away. That said, just to be safe, maybe choose something else to wear to a protest.

https://www.instyle.com/fashion/hawaiian-shirts-alt-right-white-supremacy-protestors

Is political correctness killing fashion? Designers are speaking up against the 'tyranny' of the woke

By RT Oct 3rd, 2019

The fashion industry has come under increasing pressure to be as politically correct and "woke" as possible in recent years, but some designers have had enough and are speaking out against social "tyranny."

Scandals have rocked the fashion world, with brands like Dolce & Gabbana, Gucci, Prada, and Saint Laurent all coming under fire for varying social sins; too sexy, too racist, too white, too colonial, too skinny, too much cultural appropriation. Too much sensitivity?

"Demagogic political correctness has become a kind of tragic tyranny of the literal," Hedi Slimane of luxury French brand Celine said in an interview last month. Slimane described the movement as *"disguised neo-conservatism"* and said *"it feels [like] tolerance has switched sides."*

Admittedly, some of the fashion industry's biggest controversies have been avoidable and self-inflicted. D&G, for instance, should have been able to predict the backlash at having an Asian woman clumsily attempt to eat pasta and spaghetti with chopsticks. Gucci could also have anticipated the uproar sparked over its *"blackface"* sweater this year.

But the demands go much further than simply avoiding outright racism. Some have called for racial quotas on the catwalks. Others have called for more body shapes and sizes to be represented in *"real"* fashion shows. Brands have faced uproar online for expressing the 'wrong' political views; D&G, for example, felt the wrath of the 'Resistance' when it endorsed Melania Trump as a #DGWoman in 2017. Then there's Saint Laurent, which was slammed for its apparently overly sexy ads, dubbed *"porno chic."* Slimane's fashion at Celine has been described by the Financial Times as *"super-skinny and near exclusively white."*

In this culture war, it seems there are two camps, those who believe fashion has a deep responsibility to espouse the edicts of modern liberal society, always furthering the 'correct' political causes with slogans and awareness campaigns, and those who believe that fashion should be more frivolous and, similar to comedy and art, should not be afraid to offend or find itself constrained by the boundaries of modern political correctness.

Saint Laurent's Anthony Vaccarello told AFP on the eve of Paris fashion week that a *"witch-hunt atmosphere"* has taken over the industry, making it *"impossible"* to even have an opinion that goes against the mainstream.

Indeed, there's even a full-time Instagram watchdog account just waiting to pounce on any brand that makes an unacceptable fashion faux pas or political misstep. Dubbed *"the most feared Instagram account in fashion,"* by Business of Fashion, Diet Prada was founded by Tony Liu and Lindsey Schuyler and began with the goal of calling out copycat designs in the industry. Yet, Diet Prada quickly appointed itself arbiter of right and wrong in the fashion world and now polices the industry for real or perceived sexism, racism, and cultural appropriation. The account boasts 1.6 million followers and while some hail the founding duo as modern-day heroes, others say they are promoting censorship.

Right or wrong, Diet Prada fits perfectly into the *"cancel culture"* world where one professional misstep or questionable comment made ten years ago can threaten to ruin a public figure's career today. Dior was recently forced to pull an ad for its 'Sauvage' perfume which featured Native Americans performing a traditional dance. Critics jumped on the brand, accusing it of promoting the idea that Native Americans are *"savages"* only to discover that 'sauvage' in French actually means *"wild."* The outrage police also accused the brand of *"cultural appropriation"* and harmful stereotyping. The ad only survived a few hours on social media before Dior chopped it. Diet Prada called it *"triggering imagery."*

So, is all of this PC pressure stifling creativity and innovation? Italian fashion journalist Angelo Flaccavento recently slammed the suffocating nature of these *"violently moralistic times"* which he said are *"destroying freedom of expression and invention."* He is clearly not alone in his assessment. More and more fashion industry figures are daring to challenge the liberal authoritarianism of the mainstream. *"You can't say or do anything anymore,"* Richard Rene of Guy Laroche told AFP after his show last week during Paris fashion week. Not everyone feels totally stifled by the demands of these woke times, however.

Some brands have capitalized on the latest social trends. Michael Kors, Coach, Chanel, Gucci, and Burberry, among others, have all gone fur-free. Stella McCartney and Vivienne Westwood have also won fans for their eco-conscious stances and promotion of climate activism. McCartney even hosted a roundtable discussion on climate change before her recent Paris show. Westwood's husband and design partner, Andreas Kronthaler, told AFP that he includes male models in all his shows because men *"can be just as beautiful as women in a dress."* Meanwhile, male model Leon Dame became a viral internet meme after he dramatically strutted down the catwalk in black shiny high-heeled boots last week.

That kind of thing might not be everyone's cup of tea, but that's the point really, isn't it? Each fashion statement does not need to be universally loved and appreciated by everyone. While woke, eco-conscious, liberal designers will appeal to some, others will be drawn to the anti-PC types who take bigger social risks. That's diversity, after all.

https://www.rt.com/news/470096-fashion-industry-woke-pc/

Fashion

Fashion shows previously showcased the up-and-coming fashion trends by having smoking hot models walk the runway in the newest garb. Now, fashion designers want to dumb down our entire wardrobes and our culture by promoting obese "models" wearing shower curtains as a dress. In every conceivable way, our wardrobes are being attacked and are becoming gender fluid. Men are no longer allowed to wear nice suits. Now, men must wear tight suits with high-water, tapered trousers and "Connecticut-style" yacht boating shoes with no socks to be considered "trendy" and "cool." Wearing American flag clothing is banned. Women wearing short, cut off, daisy duke jean shorts are cancelled because it shows "sizeism" and "sexism." When what we wear is under attack, society is now in a downward spiral free-for-all.

28

The War on Free Speech

Study: "Cancel Culture" Decimating Free Speech At World's Leading Universities

By Steve Watson December 17th, 2020

A study by leading education focused think tank Civitas has found that free speech at the world's leading universities is being eroded at an alarming rate owing to the rise of "cancel culture".

The study found that within the past three years, more than 68 per cent of universities in the UK have seen free speech severely restricted, with academics unable to meaningfully discuss the nuances of issues such as race and gender. The report notes that universities including Oxford, Cambridge and St Andrews, three of the world's premiere institutions are among those that have fallen into a "red" category for free speech following instances of "no platforming" of scheduled speakers.

The study warns that the situation has gotten so severe that it requires government legislation to stop campus censorship at 48 universities, the equivalent of at least 35 per cent of institutions. Civitas noted that a further 70 institutions, over half, placed into a "amber category", have experienced restrictions on freedom of expression that should be looked into by university watchdog The Office for Students.

Researchers noted that freedom of speech "could be curbed by perceived transphobic episodes" in an alarming number of institutions, and that a "cancel culture" of open letters and or petitions from "external pressure groups" is eroding free speech. Lead researcher Jim McConalogue noted "Our findings suggest that 86 per cent of universities faced either severe or moderate free speech restrictions which need to be addressed."

"The fundamental issue must be dealt with because students and academics find themselves in educational institutions in which they cannot speak freely of the leading subjects of their day including on race, gender, the outcomes of elections, their views on religion, or on discrimination itself for fear of judgements that lead to eventual penalty or censorship," McConalogue explained. A previous Civitas report, published last month, found that "The racialisation of campus relations is driving a wedge between students and undermines any sense of our common humanity".

The report also noted that there is no statistical evidence that 'ethnicity' determines the educational attainment of higher education students:

The latest Civitas study was undertaken before another prominent incident at Cambridge University, with dons rejecting 'authoritarian guidelines' from the university that decreed opinions should be "respectful of the diverse identities of others". Academics instead said they will promote 'tolerance' of differing opinions, and are backing amendments to make it more difficult for public speakers to be 'no-platformed' based on their beliefs and opinions.

In one particular incident, some students at Clare College, Cambridge, attempted to get a city councillor (who is also a porter at the college) fired for refusing to support a pro-trans motion. The decimation of free speech at universities has become so severe that the Education Secretary Gavin Williamson announced earlier this year that stamping out 'no platforming' was a top priority.

https://summit.news/2020/12/17/study-cancel-culture-decimating-free-speech-at-worlds-leading-universities/

Kareem Abdul-Jabbar: Crack down on conservative celebrities' speech – and even left-wing luminaries who aren't woke enough

BY Dave Ubanski December 18th, 2020

NBA legend-turned-cultural commentator Kareem Abdul-Jabbar said social media companies aren't doing enough to silence "irrational and harmful" posts from conservative celebrities — and even from fellow left-wing luminaries who don't check every woke box.

In his column for the Hollywood Reporter this week, Abdul-Jabbar said that "no matter their previous achievements, celebrities deserve legacy-killing backlash when they spread ignorance."

He first pointed his finger at Rudy Giuliani — the personal lawyer of President Donald Trump — saying that his legacy of "calm authority" in the wake of the 9/11 terror attacks in New York City has been overshadowed by his Trump alliance and last month's "cringeworthy news conference about unproven conspiracies while black streaks streamed from his hair." Abdul-Jabbar also ripped Giuliani for being on a "hidden camera in the latest *Borat* movie with his hand down his pants while lying on a bed in the presence of a teenage girl." (Giuliani insists he was tucking in his shirt.)

Problem for Abdul-Jabbar is that the female in question is a woman, and Giuliani said "at no time before, during, or after the interview was I ever inappropriate. If Sacha Baron Cohen implies otherwise he is a stone-cold liar."

Abdul-Jabbar then turned his attention to conservative actors, saying "Roseanne Barr had achieved the near impossible, sabotaging her career not once but twice. After she left her top-rated sitcom, she faded into irrelevance with out-of-left-field political musings. Seeking to connect to the Trump demographic, ABC gave *Roseanne* new life, but her character was killed off after she went on a racist rant. James Woods, winner of a Golden Globe and Emmy, was once considered a dynamic actor. Now, after his caustic social commentary tweets, he's viewed as the cranky geezer who won't let you get your ball from his yard. Jon Voight, once a shining star among actors, recently posted a rambling video calling the political left "Satan" and promoting conspiracies about the election, reducing him from brilliant Oscar winner to cultural dumpster diver."

Abdul-Jabbar also found fault with Christian actress Letitia Wright, who starred in "Black Panther," because she "posted a link to a YouTube video questioning the COVID-19 vaccine and vaccines in general. After a tsunami of social media backlash, she wrote: 'My intention was not to hurt anyone. My ONLY intention of posting the video was it raised my concerns with what the vaccine contains and what we are putting in our bodies. Nothing else.'" But Abdul-Jabbar said "at best, that's naive, and at worst, disingenuous. If someone wants to raise concerns — that's legitimate — they need to do basic research: Find facts, statistics and qualified authorities. Because the reality is that when she posts, readers believe she endorses the false conclusions — and that can't be undone."

The former NBA great pointed out that famed author J.K. Rowling, a left-winger by just about every measure, took a "stumble from grace" due to her "anti-trans tweets" which "could end up tainting her entire literary legacy." But Rowling doesn't appear to be backing down an inch, most recently declaring that the "climate of fear" around the trans debate needs to end. "Many are afraid to speak up because they fear for their jobs and even for their personal safety," Rowling said in an interview with Good Housekeeping magazine. "This climate of fear serves nobody well, least of all trans people."

He also ripped John Cleese's "tone-deaf defense of Rowling," saying it "left many fans bitterly disappointed, tarnishing his reputation." But like Rowling, the former Monty Python legend doesn't seem to care about what others think — and unabashedly thinks for himself. In fact, Cleese accused the rage mob of "wokery, humorless posturing, and moral self-promotion."

"If you can't control your own emotions, you're forced to control other people's behavior," Cleese said of Twitter users who've attacked Rowling and demanded that she shut up. "That's why the touchiest, most oversensitive and easily upset must not set the standard for the rest of us." Concluding his piece, Abdul-Jabbar said social media giants "have begun slapping warnings on some messages that are false, incite violence, or cause harm to society. But this needs to be done with more consistency and vigilance. Studies indicate that when readers see these warnings, they are less likely to read or believe things. However, as another study showed, there can be a backfire effect in which content that *isn't* flagged, even when inaccurate, is perceived as true."

He added: "The irresponsibility of tweeting irrational and harmful opinions to millions, regardless of the damaging consequences to their country or people's lives, proves that those stars deserve the harsh backlash."

https://www.theblaze.com/news/kareem-abdul-jabbar-crack-down-conservative-speech

'Flatten the hate': Penn launches task force to address 'China Virus' hashtag

By Benjamin Zeisloft August 17th, 2020

The University of Pennsylvania recently launched a task force to address potential anti-Asian and anti-Asian American racism arising due to the coronavirus.According to UPenn, the university launched the "Task Force on Supporting Asian and Asian American Students and Scholars at Penn" in April. The group will take "an active stand to affirm its commitment to diversity and anti-discrimination," mainly through a variety of panel discussions. The university said it is "working to support all of its community members in meeting the challenges of the COVID-19 pandemic, including those who may experience bias, discrimination, abuse, and/or violence as a result."UPenn refers to the hashtags #WuhanVirus and #ChinaVirus, which trended on Twitter in mid-March, as justification for the task force. It also cited an article from the *New York Times* that criticized President Donald Trump's continued use of the monikers "Chinese Virus" and "Kung Flu," further asserting that "inflammatory statements from leaders can exacerbate racist behavior."The University of Pennsylvania pointed students to the University of Pennsylvania Division of Public Safety, which is equipped to investigate hate crimes, as well as the university's "bias incident reporting form" within the Office of Diversity and Inclusion.Students, however, are not satisfied with the anti-Asian Task Force, expressing their dissatisfaction on the university's Instagram page.

"If you're so committed to tackling racism, let's start by paying PILOTs so that Black kids in Philly can go to safe schools with teachers, nurses, librarians, and social workers," said one student. "Where is the support for ethnic studies if you support students of color," inquired another.

One Asian-American student who asked to remain anonymous told *Campus Reform* that there is no "significant anti-Asian racism at Penn." The student said they have never personally experienced racism at Penn, but believes the university can reduce prejudice against Asians "by not discriminating against Asians in college admissions." The task force is planning a series of lectures and seminars about anti-Asian bias, dubbed "multilingual restorative practice circles."

The first one, hosted in June, was called "Stopping the Hate and Starting to Heal: Living With and Through the COVID-19 Pandemic." The group is slated to host a documentary screening and discussion in August centered around the film "9066 to 9/11: America's Concentration Camps, Then... And Now?" which "focuses on the parallels between the post-September 11 treatment of Arab Americans and Muslims in this country with treatment of Japanese Americans after the start of World War II," according to the Japanese American National Museum.

https://www.campusreform.org/?ID=15442

Lieu: 'I Would Love to Be Able to Regulate the Content of Speech' but First Amendment Stops Me

By David Rutz December 12th, 2018

Rep. Ted Lieu (D., Calif.) said he would "love to be able to regulate the content of speech" during an interview Wednesday, noting he was prevented from doing that by the First Amendment.

Lieu got attention a day earlier when Google CEO Sundar Pichai testified at a House Judiciary Committee hearing, assailing conservative claims of the tech giant's bias against them by reading positive and negative stories about Republican Reps. Steve Scalise (La.) and Steve King (Iowa), the latter of whom has repeatedly courted controversy with racially charged remarks.

After CNN host Brianna Keilar praised Lieu for the "clever" stunt, she wondered if Democrats should have used more of their time to question the Google leader about how it and other tech companies can work to prevent the spread of conspiracy theories and other online trolling. "It's a very good point you make," Lieu said. "I would love if I could have more than five minutes to question witnesses. Unfortunately, I don't get that opportunity. However, I would love to be able to regulate the content of speech. The First Amendment prevents me from doing so, and that's simply a function of the First Amendment, but I think over the long run, it's better the government does not regulate the content of speech."

He added he would urge private companies to regulate their platforms more themselves but repeated the government shouldn't play that role. Lieu blasted the hearing as a waste of time perpetrated by Republicans and backed the right of corporations to free speech. He backs a constitutional amendment to overturn the Supreme Court decision *Citizens United*, however, which confirmed that right. Lieu tweeted Tuesday he would like to regulate Fox News but said the fact that he couldn't was "a good thing in the long run."

https://freebeacon.com/politics/lieu-i-would-love-to-be-able-to-regulate-the-content-of-speech-but-the-first-amendment-stops-me/

Is the PC culture dictated by white elites?

By Michael Brown, August 3rd, 2020

In today's woke culture, it is politically correct to expose white supremacy everywhere in our culture. But wouldn't it be ironic if the ones driving PC culture were actually white elites? According to a major study released in October 2018, most Americans share an aversion to PC culture, with certain groups of Americans demonstrating an extreme aversion to this toxic culture. (I just became aware of the study last week and found it extremely relevant, leading to this article.)

The study was titled "Hidden Tribes: A Study of America's Polarized Landscape," and, as explained by Prof. Yascha Mounk in *The Atlantic*, the study was "based on a nationally representative poll with 8,000 respondents, 30 one-hour interviews, and six focus groups conducted from December 2017 to September 2018." The "Hidden Tribes" report is 160 pages long, so I can only summarize some of the findings here. But, as outside groups (like Antifa) increasingly dominate the current protest-riot movement, it's worth revisiting this study.

Our goal will be to answer the questions: Who is bothered most by PC culture? Who is advocating for radical change? Who are the ones setting the tone for what is acceptable and what is not? According to the study, as of 2018, while 25 percent of Americans were traditional or devoted conservatives, only 8 percent were progressive activists. As for the 67 percent who did not fall into either of these categories, they were dubbed the "exhausted majority."

As Mounk wrote, "Among the general population, a full 80 percent believe that 'political correctness is a problem in our country.' Even young people are uncomfortable with it, including 74 percent ages 24 to 29, and 79 percent under age 24. On this particular issue, the woke are in a clear minority across *all* ages." Since the study was completed, the BLM movement has risen to greater prominence and the Democratic party as a whole has lurched further left, raising the bar all the more for political correctness. So, one might think that less Americans find the PC culture offensive, since much of the country is heading in a more PC direction.

On the other hand, because that culture has become so extreme, finding its expression in the cancel culture, there is an increasing pushback even from very liberal circles. In the words of Bill Maher, addressing Bari Weiss, who recently resigned from the *New York Times*, "Bari, the fact that you — they call you a centrist or right-winger! I mean, if a hip, millennial, Jewish bisexual girl living in San Francisco is not a liberal ... who is these days?"

As Weiss explained, "What cancel culture is about is not criticism. It is about punishment. It is about making a person radioactive. It is about taking away their job." And then, with tremendous insight, she said, "It's not just about punishing the sinner, it's not just about punishing the person for being insufficiently pure. It's about this sort of secondary boycott of people who would deign to speak to that person or appear on a platform with that person. And we see just very obviously where that kind of politics gets us. If conversation with people that we disagree with becomes impossible, what is the way that we solve conflict?... It's violence."

Exactly. And if liberals like Maher and Weiss feel this way, how about the rest of America? How much larger and more exhausted is the "exhausted majority" today? Turning back to the study, Mounk noted that, "Whites are ever so slightly *less* likely than average to believe that political correctness is a problem in the country: 79 percent of them share this sentiment. Instead, it is Asians (82 percent), Hispanics (87 percent), and American Indians (88 percent) who are most likely to oppose political correctness." Who would have guessed? Among all ethnicities surveyed, American Indians have the biggest problem with the PC culture. It appears that many woke people know what matters to these Native Americans more than they do themselves.

As for African Americans, while they were not as strongly opposed to PC attitudes as the other groups listed, still, "Three quarters of African Americans oppose political correctness." Who, then, is driving the narrative? Who, then, is pushing the PC ideas? Who, then, is creating the feeling that America, as a whole, has thoroughly embraced PC culture and that only a minority oppose it? Mounk summarizes the findings of the report: "Compared with the rest of the (nationally representative) polling sample, progressive activists are much more likely to be rich, highly educated — and white. They are nearly twice as likely as the average to make more than $100,000 a year. They are nearly three times as likely to have a postgraduate degree. And while 12 percent of the overall sample in the study is African American, only 3 percent of progressive activists are. With the exception of the small tribe of devoted conservatives, progressive activists are the most racially homogeneous group in the country."

Put another way, these are "the kinds of people, in other words, who are in charge of universities, edit the nation's most important newspapers and magazines, and advise Democratic political candidates on their campaigns."

I say that we expose *this kind* of white supremacy — this, rich, highly-educated, elitist supremacy — joining together as a nation to push back against a tiny minority attempting to impose its will on everyone else.

https://www.christianpost.com/voices/is-the-pc-culture-dictated-by-white-elites.html

Argentinian shock jock ordered to co-host show with feminists after sexism accusations

By Samantha Beniac-Brooks December 24th, 2018

An Argentine radio presenter has been ordered to host a feminist guest every week for five months as part of his probation, after being accused of sexism.

The punishment will start in March, with Angel Etchecopar ordered to not interrupt his guests for 10 minutes - he's also not allowed to criticise them after they finish. The air time will also be free of advertising. It comes after prosecutors accused him of discrimination and gender-based violence.

Local media reports he used his program on Argentina's Radio 10, *El Angel Del Nodia* to attack feminists. According to French newspaper Le Monde, he referred to the group as "feminazis" and "disgusting people." Prosecutor Federico Vilalba Diaz told Argentine daily newspaper La Nacion that Etchecopar had been charged with "disrespectful, insulting, denigrating and discriminatory" outbursts against women.

But it's reported Etchecopar was able to convince authorities of his remorse and a female judge agreed to drop the case against him in favour of a probation-based solution. "Etchecopar came to the inquiry with a repentant attitude and showed himself to be very different from the personality I had seen in the media," Mr Diaz told La Nacion. Under the terms of the agreement, prosecutors will provide a list of gender specialists and Argentina's special gender violence prosecutor Veronica Guagnino will come up with the topics for discussion.

"It seemed important to me that the listeners of Baby Etchecopar could listen to other voices and other explanations, different from the ones they are used to, " Mr Diaz said. "It is a non-punitive idea, but one that aims to improve tolerance." For a year, Etchecopar - nicknamed "Baby" - will also have to avoid making offensive remarks against women, while he will also have to donate 15,000 pesos (approximately

$AUD1,070) to the Catholic Charity Association Caritas. If he breaks the terms of the agreement, it will be terminated and he will be re-prosecuted.

https://www.sbs.com.au/news/argentinian-shock-jock-ordered-to-co-host-show-with-feminists-after-sexism-accusations

Jordan superintendent reviewing display of Trump banner at basketball game

By Paul Walsh January 17th, 2019

Michael Walker posted on Facebook a photograph of fans in Jordan with a Trump flag draped over the legs of four front-row spectators.

The boys basketball coach for Minneapolis Roosevelt High School questioned on Wednesday why young fans at his team's road game in Jordan prominently displayed a flag promoting the re-election of President Donald Trump during Tuesday night's contest. Michael Walker posted on Facebook a photograph of fans on the Jordan side of the gym with the flag draped over the legs of four front-row spectators.

The message read: Trump 2020 Keep America Great! Several other young fans sitting nearby were wearing clothing patterned after the American flag. "I coach a predominantly black inner city high school team," Walker wrote on his Facebook posting. "We go out to a rural area in Jordan, MN and this is there. Please explain how and why this is appropriate at a high school basketball game?"

Walker included a slew of hashtag phrases, among them #critical questioning, #blackandproud and #blackmenmatter. Walker, who is black, also is the director of his district's Office of Black Male Student Achievement. School District Superintendent Matt Helgerson released a statement Wednesday afternoon expressing "regret that Roosevelt players and their coaching staff, fans and community were made to feel uncomfortable, as it is always our intent to graciously host our opponents."

Helgerson said district personnel are "reviewing this matter and collecting information [and] working cooperatively with the Minneapolis School District and Roosevelt High School in our review and response to this event." Bridget Kahn commented on the Roosevelt coach's Facebook posting wrote that the flag belonged to her and was used by students as part of a long-planned USA blackout theme night.

Kahn told the Star Tribune later that her son and others took two of the flags with them to the game and "left with them wrapped around them like capes. I didn't see anything wrong with that." She said this was nothing more than young people wearing "a bunch of red, white and blue, supporting their president. They don't have a racist bone in their body."

Kahn also pointed out, and the superintendent confirmed, that the Roosevelt team remained in the locker room during the playing of the national anthem before tipoff. The Roosevelt team has been carrying out this action at both home and away games, and "the Jordan team was made aware of that practice before the game," Minneapolis schools spokesman Dirk Tedmon said.

Helgerson said he arrived to the gym in the second half and saw the spectators in U.S. flag-inspired garb for what he said was not a school-sponsored theme night. He added that he didn't see the Trump flag by the time he arrived. As for whether the presence of the flag during a school event violated any district policy, Helgerson said, "We're in the process of reviewing all our policies as it relates to this particular situation. This is a new one for me."

Tedmon said that the Minneapolis district's policy is "to not allow political advertising" at games it hosts. Jeanna Orris, who has three children in district schools, was at the game Tuesday and said, "I have no issues with a Trump flag at our game last night in regards to racism. It could be seen as 'It's actually pretty cool [young people] are paying attention to things going on in our country.'"

Joining the Roosevelt coach in concern about the flag's presence during the game is Crystal Flint, who coached the Minneapolis North girls team from 2005 until early 2018. "You got freedom of speech, but would that remotely be appropriate?" said Flint, who now coaches the girls team at Cretin-Derham Hall in St. Paul. "No, it would not." Flint said she wants to know whether the flag was displayed because Roosevelt's team is mostly black or has it been brought to previous Jordan home games.

In any event, she continued, "Why is politics being represented at sports? Is there an intimidation factor? ... I think it's divisive in this racial climate that we have." Orris defended the intentions of those who brought the flag to the game, saying it was there merely as part of one of a series of theme nights at Jordan athletic events. "They were not trying to be offensive," she said. "Our little town is the least racist ... I just don't understand how this got turned into a race thing."

https://www.startribune.com/minneapolis-roosevelt-high-school-basketball-coach-questions-fans-displaying-pro-trump-flag-at-game-in-jordan/504437562/

Students say offensive speech is not free speech

By Jon Street & Cabot Phillips March 21st, 2019

Campus Reform's Cabot Phillips, ahead of President Donald Trump signing an executive order Thursday that is intended to address free speech on college campuses, talked with students at Marymount University in Virginia to ask them their thoughts on what type of speech should be allowed and the type of speech they think crosses a line.

A number of students suggested that hateful, offensive, or rude speech should not be considered free speech. "I think if it's, like, hateful and disrespectful to specific groups, then that's not OK," one student said.

Another student suggested that "I think that you can be rude but not saying anything discriminatory and...you know..." while another stated, "I understand you have free rights to say what you want about people but when it's, like, negatively impacting our school as a whole and other students around you, that's crossing the line." Trump, on Thursday, will sign an executive order that will require colleges to certify they are complying with First Amendment protections in order to receive federal research dollars, according to a senior administration official.

The official declined to provide any more details of what exactly is in the order. Trump previously stated at CPAC that the order would "require colleges and universities to support free speech if they want federal research dollars." In anticipation of what the president initially said, *Campus Reform* compiled a report, based on publicly available data, showing how much colleges and universities receive in federal research funding. The White House did not respond in time for publication to *Campus Reform*'s request for further comment when asked if the order will, in fact, tie federal research dollars to colleges' support of free speech, as the president initially that said it would.

https://www.campusreform.org/?ID=12003

Florida man arrested after refusing to remove 'obscene' sticker from window

By Associated Press May 8th, 2019

LAKE CITY, Fla. (AP) — Authorities say a Florida man was jailed after refusing to remove an obscene sticker from his vehicle's window.

A Columbia County Sheriff's Office report says 23-year-old Dillon Shane Webb was arrested Sunday and charged with misdemeanor counts of violating Florida's obscenity law and resisting an officer without violence. It says a deputy stopped Webb in Lake City because of a sticker crudely describing a sexual appetite. The sticker said "I eat ass," according to the Lake City Reporter.

The deputy initially cited Webb for obscenity with a notice to appear in court. Officials say the deputy told Webb to alter the sticker to change the derogatory part but Webb refused, citing his First Amendment free speech rights. The deputy then charged Webb with resisting and took him to jail. Webb was later released on $2,500 bond. Jail records didn't list an attorney.

https://www.wfla.com/news/florida/florida-man-arrested-after-refusing-to-remove-obscene-sticker-from-window/1988430814/

Disturbing number of students say hate speech is not free speech, report says

By Adam Sabes May 20th, 2019

A new report has revealed that support of the First Amendment among college students seems to be decreasing, as nearly half of students believe that hate speech should not be protected.

Conducted by the Knight Foundation, the survey reveals that 41 percent of college students believe hate speech should not be protected under the First Amendment, while 58 percent believe that it should be protected. While the majority of students believe that hate speech should be protected, 53 percent of college women contend it should not be protected, as well a majority of black students.

Over half of college students agree that shouting speakers down is "always" or "sometimes" acceptable. At the same time, 83 percent of college students agree that using violence to end an event is "never acceptable." According to the survey, there seems to be a disconnect on how individuals of various races look at the issue of free speech.

More than six in 10 black students believe that inclusivity is more important than free speech, while 49 percent of Hispanic students believe the same thing. Just 42 percent of white students believe that inclusivity is more important than free speech, according to the survey. Multiple colleges around the country have implemented mandatory "diversity" and "inclusion" classes for all students, including Tulane University, Georgia Southern University, and Clemson University. Syracuse University mandated a diversity course for all incoming students in fall 2018, but later admitted it "didn't hit the mark."

The survey comes after a heated semester for free speech issues on campus. In late April, a Canadian professor argued that "vile little sh*tlords" who are passionate about free speech should be fired and harassed. A New York college president even wrote an op-ed titled "A Campus Is Not the Place for Free Speech," in which he explained his opposition to free speech on college campuses. Students' views on the importance of free speech may be declining, but more than half of all states have now passed or introduced campus free speech bills.

https://www.campusreform.org/?ID=12243

Florida Democrat says those 'making fun' of members of Congress online should be 'prosecuted'

By Lukas Mikelionis July 3rd, 2019

Democrat Rep. Frederica Wilson said people who are "making fun" of members of Congress online should be "prosecuted."

The Florida congresswoman made the comments on Tuesday outside of the Homestead Temporary Shelter for Unaccompanied Children in her home state.

"Those people who are online making fun of members of Congress are a disgrace, and there is no need for anyone to think that is unacceptable [sic]," Wilson said.

"We're gonna shut them down and work with whoever it is to shut them down, and they should be prosecuted," she added. "You cannot intimidate members of Congress, frighten members of Congress. It is against the law, and it's a shame in this United States of America." Wilson's comments came amid a controversy over a Facebook group that includes Border Patrol agents and where they allegedly mocked and posted graphic content about members of Congress, including New York Rep. Alexandria Ocasio-Cortez.

The website ProPublica posted a story Monday headlined "Inside the Secret Border Patrol Facebook Group Where Agents Joke About Migrant Deaths and Post Sexist Memes." In addition to showing indifference toward the deaths of migrants, members made vulgar jokes about Ocasio-Cortez and other members of the Congressional Hispanic Caucus ahead of their visit a Border Patrol facility in Texas on Monday, the story alleged.

Wilson also blamed President Trump for people losing respect for Congress and the White House, saying he has "taken this country to its knees." She once accused Trump of being "hateful towards black people" and declined to participate in the State of the Union address in 2018.

The congresswoman also rose to prominence in 2017 after she leaked the conversation Trump had with the Gold Star widow whose husband died in Niger and criticized the president for being "so insensitive" after he said that the slain soldier "knew what he signed up for...but when it happens, it hurts anyway."

https://www.foxnews.com/politics/florida-democrat-making-fun-congress-should-prosecuted

Free Speech

Every small thing you say is being controlled, monitored, censored, cancelled, regulated, and manipulated by the speech police arm of our rulers. One of my favorite all-time comedians, the late and great comic genius, George Carlin once said:

"There's a lot of groups, a lot of institutions in this country want to control your language, tell you what you can say and what you can't say. Government wants to control information and control language, because that's the way you control thought. And basically, that's the game they're in."

I can't really say it any better than he did. He is 100% spot on. When you can start controlling language, verbs, nouns, pronouns, figure of speech, metaphors, analogies, and hypotheticals, that's when you can start totally dominating and controlling an entire society.

Quote Reference: https://www.vulture.com/2016/06/in-2016-george-carlins-political-nihilism-is-becoming-the-only-sensible-opinion.html#:~:text=%E2%80%9CGovernment%20wants%20to%20control%20information,game%20they're%20in.%E2%80%9D

29

The War on the Family

'Disrespectful': Google Employees Melt Down Over The Word 'Family'

By Peter Hasson Jan 16th, 2019

A Google executive sparked a fierce backlash from employees by using the word "family" in a weekly, company-wide presentation, according to internal documents obtained by The Daily Caller News Foundation.

Many Google employees became angry that the term was used while discussing a product aimed at children, because it implied that families have children, the documents show. The backlash grew large enough that a Google vice president addressed the controversy and solicited feedback on how the company could become more inclusive.

TheDCNF received the documents from a source who insisted upon anonymity in order to share them. One employee stormed out of the March 2017 presentation after a presenter "continued to show (awesome) Unicorn product features which continually use the word 'family' as a synonym for 'household with children,'" he explained in an internal thread. That employee posted an extended rant, which was well-received by his colleagues, on why linking families to children is "offensive, inappropriate, homophobic, and wrong."

He wrote:

"This is a diminishing and disrespectful way to speak. If you mean "children", say "children"; we have a perfectly good word for it. "Family friendly" used as a synonym for "kid friendly" means, to me, "you and yours don't count as a family unless you have children". And while kids may often be less aware of it, there are kids without families too, you know. The use of "family" as a synonym for "with children" has a long-standing association with deeply homophobic organizations. This does not mean we should not use the word "family" to refer to families, but it mean we must doggedly insist that family does not imply children.

Even the sense, "suitable for the whole family", which you might think is unobjectionable, is totally wrong too. It only works if we have advance shared conception of what "the whole family" is, and that is almost always used to mean a household with two adults, of opposite sex, in a romantic/sexual relationship, with two or more of their own children. If you mean that as a synonym for "suitable for all people" stop and notice the extraordinary unlikelihood of such a thought! So "suitable for the whole family" doesn't mean "all people", it means "all people in families", which either means that all those other people aren't in families, or something even worse. Use the word "family" to mean a loving assemblage of people who may or may not live together and may or may not include people of any particular age. STOP using it to mean "children". It's offensive, inappropriate, homophobic, and wrong."

Roughly 100 other Google employees upvoted the post, signaling their agreement. Other Google employees also echoed their displeasure with the term. "Thanks for writing this. So much yes," one wrote.

"Using the word 'family' in this sense bothers me too," wrote another employee, who felt excluded by the term because she was neither married nor a parent.

"It smacks of the 'family values' agenda by the right wing, which is absolutely homophobic by its very definition," she wrote, adding: "[I]t's important that we fix our charged language when we become aware of how exclusionary it actually is. As a straight person in a relationship, I find the term 'family' offensive because it excludes me and my boyfriend, having no children of our own."

"My family consists of me and several other trans feminine folks, some of whom I'm dating. We're all supportive of each other and eventually aspire to live together. Just because we aren't a heterosexual couple with 2.5 kids, a white picket fence, and a dog doesn't mean we're not a family," another employee added in agreement. Another employee wrote that "using 'family' to mean 'people with kids' is also annoying to me as a straight-cis-woman who doesn't have or want kids. My husband, my parents, and my pets are my family."

Google vice president Pavni Diwanji joined the conversation and acknowledged that use of the term "family" had sparked "concerns."

"Hi everyone, I realize what we said at tgif might have caused concerns in the way we talked about families. There are families without kids too, and also we needed to be more conscientious about the fact that there is a diverse makeup of parents and families," Dwiwanji wrote.

"Please help us get to a better state. Teach us how to talk about it in inclusive way, if you feel like we are not doing it well. As a team we have very inclusive culture, and want to do right in this area. I am adding my team here so we can have open conversation," Dwiwanji concluded. Google did not return a request for comment on the controversy, which is yet another example of left-wing Google employees bringing their politics to work with them.

https://dailycaller.com/2019/01/16/google-family-triggered-meltdown/#:~:text=Brightbulb-,'Disrespectful'%3A%20Google%20Employees%20Melt,Down%20Over%20The%20Word%20'Family'&text=Google%20employees%20melted%20down%20after,which%20they%20argued%20was%20homophobic

Family

Having a family is offensive to people who don't have families. Having a mother is offensive and sexist to people who don't have mothers. Having a father is considered sexist and offensive to people who don't have fathers. One of the main attacks from the woke culture club is attacking the family. When you can't use the words "momma" or "daddy" in schools because they are deemed “exclusionary”, you know society is going down the shitter.

30

The War on the Environment

Brothers face $450,000 in penalties for removing trees from their property

By Dana Afana October 22nd, 2018

CANTON TWP., MI -- Brothers Gary and Matt Percy could face nearly half a million dollars in penalties for removing more than 1,400 trees from their property without permission from Canton Township. The two own a 16-acre property off of Yost Road, east of Belleville Road in Canton Township with the intention of creating a Christmas tree farm on the plot, according to their attorney, Michael J. Pattwell.

The land was filled with "invasive plants like phragmites, buckthorn and autumn olive," he said. But the township requires land owners to gain permission and promise new tree plantings before cutting down existing forestry, especially for landmark or historic trees. The township had an arborist compare the parcel to an adjacent property with the similar forestry to estimate how many trees were removed. Township attorney Kristin Kolb said "it was all part of a forest."

"They identified certain plots," Kolb said. "They identified the number or type of trees and did some math to figure out approximately how many trees." The arborist estimated 1,385 trees with trunk diameter of six inches or more were removed. That could mean $225 to $300 per tree in penalties. Anther 100 landmark trees were also removed, the township estimated, meaning another $450 each.

"Canton Tree Police showed up," said Pattwell. "Canton Township's tree removal ordinance prohibits landowners from removing trees from private property without government permission, which may be obtained by either payment into the township's so-called tree fund or on-site replacement with trees of certain designated trunk diameters.

"Canton Township defines 'trees' as 'any woody plant with at least one well-defined stem and having a minimum diameter at breast height of three inches.' The Percy parcel was used historically by a local farmer for dairy pasture, so much of the vegetation on the parcel was invasive buckthorn, scrub brush and dead ash trees."

Pattwell disputes the township's method of estimating the number of trees removed by studying what he called "nearby property with a different land history and distinguishable characteristics." He also points out an exemption in the township ordinance, which states "all agricultural/farming operations, commercial nursery/tree farm operations and occupied lots of less than two acres in size, including utility companies and public tree trimming agencies, shall be exempt from all permit requirements of this article."

Although the land is zoned "heavy industrial," Pattwell said, the brothers believed they were in the clear under the farming exemption when they removed the trees. "The Percy brothers believed they were exercising a state and local exemption for farming when they cleared the land, but city officials arrived on-site and signaled immediately their intention to levy big fines in excess of $700,000," Pattwell said. "But that's not what this case is about. We are talking here about a parcel of former pasture land surrounded entirely by industrial activity.

"This case is about misguided overreach. It is unavoidably about whether people who own property are allowed to use it ... We contend the Percy brothers exercised a farming exemption in the local tree removal law to clear the historic pasture behind their business and develop a Christmas tree farm."

But Kolb said the brothers were "specifically told at least twice last year" that if they were to remove the trees, they needed a permit. "(They) never came and got one," Kolb said.

The brothers have not yet been fined, but Pattwell asked the township for a settlement figure, Kolb said. The township's settlement offer is roughly $450,000. Under the ordinance, the Percys could have received a credit to reduce the fees by paying into the township's tree fund and planting new trees, Kolb said.

The two own a commercial trucking company in Canton Township, as well as Montgomery Farms, a tree specialization company that operates in Albion and Hillsdale, Pattwell said. The trucking company, A.D. Transport Express, has been in the township since the late 1980s. The Percys' options include: Paying money into the tree fund to plant trees across the township, planting replacement trees or a combination of both, Kolb said.

The Percys are working to resolve the matter, Pattwell said, but are prepared to take it to court. Additionally, they are moving forward to plant 2,500 Christmas trees on the property they cleared, with 1,000 planted thus far.

The ordinance states:

"Landmark tree replacement: Whenever a tree removal permit is issued for the removal of any landmark tree with a (diameter at breast height) of six inches or greater, such trees shall be relocated or replaced by the permit grantee. Every landmark/historic tree that is removed shall be replaced by three trees with a minimum caliper of four inches. Such trees will be of the species from section

Replacement of other trees: Whenever a tree removal permit is issued for the removal of trees, other than landmark/historic trees, with a (diameter at breast height) of six inches or greater (excluding boxelder (acer negundo), ash (fraxinus spp) and cottonwood (populus spp)), such trees shall be relocated or replaced by the permit grantee if more than 25 percent of the total inventory of regulated trees is removed."

https://www.mlive.com/news/detroit/2018/10/brothers_could_pay_nearly_half.html

Johnnie Walker whisky to be sold in paper bottles

By BBC July 13th, 2020

Johnnie Walker, the whisky which traces its roots back 200 years, will soon be available in paper bottles. Diageo, the drinks giant that owns the brand, said it plans to run a trial of the new environmentally-friendly packaging from next year.

While most Johnnie Walker is sold in glass bottles, the firm is looking for ways of using less plastic across its brands.Making bottles from glass also consumes energy and creates carbon emissions. To make the bottles, Diageo will co-launch a firm called Pulpex, which will also produce packaging for the likes of Unilever and PepsiCo.

Diageo's paper whisky bottle, which will be trialled in spring 2021, will be made from wood pulp and will be fully recyclable, the company said. The idea is that customers would be able to drop them straight into the recycling.

Drinks companies have been developing paper bottles to try to cut down on pollution and make products more sustainable.

Carlsberg in the process of developing a paper beer bottle. UK firm Frugalpac produces paper wine bottles which it says are made from recycled paper with a "food grade liner". However, drinks giant Coca-Cola in January said it would not ditch single-use plastic bottles because consumers still want them. Diageo said its bottles will be made by pressurizing pulp in molds which will then be cured in microwave ovens.

The bottles will be sprayed internally with coatings that are designed not to interact with the drinks they will contain. Many cartons made out of paper have a plastic coating inside to stop the drinks leaking out. Diageo, however, said its drinks bottles will not have that plastic coating.

Companies are coming under increasing pressure to reduce the amount of plastic in packaging as consumers increasingly focus on damage to ecosystems.

In Europe, 8.2 million tons of plastic were used to package food and drink in 2018, according to ING analysts. Diageo, which also makes Guinness and Smirnoff vodka, said it uses less than 5% of plastic in its total packaging. However, while glass bottle manufacturers are striving to make production more efficient, they still have a significant carbon footprint. It takes a lot of energy to power glass furnaces, many of which use natural gas to melt raw materials such as sand and limestone.

https://www.bbc.com/news/business-53392949

Environment

If you didn't agree with the notion of "global warming" in the 1970's-1990's, you were labeled as a "conspiracy theorist" and were considered and uneducated moron. Now that it's been proven that the earth is not heating up, the social justice warrior tyrants changed the title from "global warming" to "climate change." And according to our rulers and masters, "climate change" is affected by everything we do in life. The real war on the environment is the war on all aspects of your day-to-day life. These psychopaths actually think that farting cows are destroying the planet...

31

The War on Everything

Cancel culture infects mommy blogging community as women turn on and boycott mother who donated to Trump

By Cindy Harper January 22nd, 2021

A parenting blogger has faced backlash online and threats to boycott her business after screenshots were posted suggesting her family donated to the Trump campaign.

Someone shared screenshots showing she and her husband had made several donations to President Donald Trump's reelection campaign. Fellow mommy bloggers and other influencers on Instagram have criticized and distanced themselves from her, campaigning against her and telling millions of followers not to buy any of her products.

The motherhood niche is quite big on Instagram. Many accounts are dedicated to motherhood; sleeping tips, toddlers' activities, and other topics related to mothers and small kids. One such account is TakingCaraBabies, whose founder, Cara Dumaplin, is a Neonatal Nurse and Certified Pediatric Sleep Consultant. Her account has more than 1.3 million followers, including other mommy bloggers, Instagram influencers, and real-life celebrities, many of whom enjoy her content.

However, people seemed to forget how much of an expert she was after she was exposed for being a Trump supporter. Fellow motherhood-focused account, @mamabirdlosangeles, shared screenshots showing Dumaplin and her husband had made multiple donations to the Trump campaign. MamaBird encouraged her followers to unfollow Dumaplin's account.

Some of her followers or fans were outraged by the revelation. Others, particularly fellow mommy bloggers, distanced themselves from Dumaplin, many were even encouraged to stop doing business with her.

https://reclaimthenet.org/cancel-culture-mothers/

Rock Bottom: Boulder To Be Removed After Students Complained It Is Racist

By Steve Watsion November 19th, 2020

A large rock in the campus of Wisconsin-Madison University is to be removed after the student's union there declared that it is racist.

Not content with removing statues of actual people, the woke mob has now seemingly turned its attention to inanimate objects. It appears that some bright spark unearthed a news clipping from the 1920s that referred to the large rock as a "n***erhead," and all hell broke loose.

The *Wisconsin State Journal* reports:

UW-Madison is moving forward on a plan to remove a boulder from Observatory Hill after calls from students of color who see the rock as a painful reminder of the history of racism on campus. The 70-ton boulder is officially known as Chamberlin Rock in honor of Thomas Crowder Chamberlin, a geologist and former university president. But the rock was referred to at least once after it was dug out of the hill as a "n***erhead," a commonly used expression in the 1920s to describe any large dark rock.

The Wisconsin Black Student Union called for the rock's removal over the summer. President Nalah McWhorter said the rock is a symbol of the daily injustices that students of color face on a predominantly white campus.

McWhorter also faulted the Wisconsin State Journal for printing the vulgarity in a 1925 news article. The report notes that the press clipping from 95 years ago was the only time that anyone has ever referred to the rock using the term. As Def Leppard famously posited in their 1992 number one hit, 'Let's get the rock outta here!'

The university's campus planning committee voted unanimously that the boulder should be removed, but has not worked out what they are going to do with it. Perhaps they should put it in a museum along with other racist horrors including (but not limited to) The US Constitution, Any term with the word 'black' in it, Chess, Vikings, Clowns, SpongeBob Squarepants, and time itself.

https://www.infowars.com/posts/rock-bottom-boulder-to-be-removed-after-students-complained-it-is-racist/

Why White People Owning Dogs is Racist

By Cayde-6 August 1st, 2020

Way back in time, almost 12,500 years ago, the first canines were becoming domesticated. Through toil and hardship, people had earned the trust of our now beloved best friends.

The symbiotic relationship between dog and woman was very groundbreaking, as humans had never been this close to an animal before. Humans would provide shelter and care for the dogs, and in turn, the dogs would hunt and fetch firewood for humans. The reason I am detailing this history for you is so everyone understands the importance of the events that took place all these years ago.

According to bio-archaeologist Gregor Larson, the domestication of dogs started in 2 places: Eastern and Western Eurasia. The Eurasian people worked non stop to gain and maintain the trust with these gorgeous creatures, but it was all stolen from them.

The greedy actions by white people stained the history books forever.

What actually happened?

Shortly after the Eurasian people worked so hard to train and bond with wolves, most of them were shipped off and given to Europeans. These filthy white savages took the work and credit from the Eurasian people and branded these magnificent creatures as their own.

The need for white people to claim premade or pre-discovered things is not isolated to just this incident. Countless times in history, whites have been caught stealing the work and talent of POC for their own success. Honestly speaking, we shouldn't be surprised that white people would steal the domestication of dogs as well. Based on historical knowledge, this behavior will not slow down within the white community.

How does this affect us right now?

If you are white and own a dog, you are openly participating and advocating for cultural appropriation and colonialism. Reinforcing this culture is NOT acceptable and will come with its repercussions.

Dogs are and always will be the living reminder of how tainted our history is as a whole. POC deserve to exclusively own dogs as a form of restitution for their stolen ancestor's work. Supporting the idea of white dog ownership is spitting on the grave of past POC generations. With International Dog Day coming up, it is important we remember and advocate for the work of POC, and never let this unbalanced history be forgotten. If you are white and own a canine, please consider donating them to a local POC family or non kill shelter so it can truly find the perfect home.

https://unitedwildlifeunion.com/2020/08/01/why-white-people-owning-dogs-is-racist/

Hair salon had to remove job ad for 'happy' stylist because it is 'discriminatory' against unhappy people

By Fox News September 4th, 2020

A hair salon says it was told by a job center it couldn't run an advertisement recruiting a "happy" stylist because the word is "discriminatory" against unhappy people.

Alison Birch listed a job ad looking for a part-time qualified hairdresser at her AJ's Unisex Hair Salon in Stroud, England. The position called for someone with five years' experience of working in a salon, who is "confident in barbering as well as all aspects of hairdressing."

And the advertisement stated, "This is a busy, friendly, small salon, so only happy, friendly stylists need apply." But on Wednesday, Birch says she received a call from her local job center informing her they could not run her ad because the word "happy" is considered "discriminatory."

Birch claims the job center told her that the advertisement may make some people feel they cannot apply if they do not consider themselves to be a "happy" person. Birch shared the conversation she had with the job center on the salon's Facebook page. She claims the man at the job center said to her: "I'm sorry, but the word happy is a discriminatory word and we aren't allowed to use it, as somebody who is not happy will be discriminated against."

According to Birch, he then asked: "Should we change the word in case somebody thinks that they can't apply for the job because they are not a happy person?"

Birch said she was questioning herself. "Was I being a bit sensitive, and is the word happy discriminative? Or has this whole world all gone mad?" Birch said. And plenty of Birch's customers agreed with her outrage over the job center's "ridiculous" stance on her advert.

Karen Evans commented: "The world has gone absolutely mad. "Does this mean that every descriptive word is discriminative... happy, tall, smart, elegant? Good luck with your search." Julie Thickins added: "I thought this was a joke, realizing it clearly isn't has left me absolutely speechless... what has the human race come to?" And Charlie Brown wrote: "You cannot make it up, how ridiculous are they being. "Stick to your guns Ali, you are a happy salon and if some numpties cannot deal with that wording then tough."

https://www.foxnews.com/lifestyle/hair-salon-job-posting-happy-hairdresser-discrimanatory

Hospitals Are Racist, Says Actress Who Gave Birth at Home

By James Macpherson August, 16th, 2020

Actress Jodie Turner-Smith gave birth at home rather than in a hospital because of "systemic racism", according to a report in the New York Post last week. The black British actress told the Post: "We had already decided on a home birth because of concerns about negative birth outcomes for black women in America."

"According to the Centre for Disease Control, the risk of pregnancy-related deaths is more than three times greater for black women than for white women, pointing, it seems to me, to systemic racism." Turner-Smith could have given birth by a river to be more culturally attuned. But I digress. Frankly, I'm surprised it's taken two months since the death of George Floyd for someone to finally bring systemic racism in the maternity ward to public attention.

I say that because I well remember the day after I was born and placed in the recovery room with the other newborn babies. The "N" word was just flying around the room. Of course, I only heard it because I was in the front row. All the minority babies were made to lay in cribs up the back.

I'll never forget lying on the white sheet they had provided for me and thinking, "Wow. They're not even trying to disguise it." But before we defund hospitals we might want to consider that the pregnancy-related death rate for black women may be due to factors other than white supremacist nurses lurking menacingly in post-natal suites.

Asthma related deaths are three times greater for African Americans than for whites. Does this mean asthma is racist? Perhaps the inhalers discriminate. Diabetes-related deaths are also more common in blacks than in whites. Defund insulin. Blacks have a much higher rate of teen pregnancy which is a factor in higher rates of death during childbirth. But rather than call attention to this social problem, it's much easier just to make stuff up.

I once had a bad case of indigestion bought on by systemic racism and eating too fast. But mostly I blame systemic racism. What exactly is Jodie Turner-Smith, who is married to former Dawson's Creek star Joshua Jackson, suggesting when she says systemic racism in hospitals is responsible for black women dying in childbirth?

Are hospitals turning away black women? Are midwives targeting black mums for death? If we want to talk about blacks dying in pregnancy, we might have a conversation about the fact that blacks represent 13% of the American population and yet account for five times as many abortions as whites. Abortionists, who typically set up in poor black neighbourhoods, kill 1000 black babies every day. This is the one form of actual systemic racism in America and the only form of systemic racism no-one wants to talk about.

It's not Planned Parenthood killing black babies every day but hospitals assisting black children to be born in a safe, professional environment that is the real race problem in America. Just don't tell Beyonce, who reportedly took over an entire hospital floor when she last gave birth.

As for home births, a report published in the American Journal of Obstetrics and Gynecology in February found that nearly 14 newborns per 10,000 live births died following planned home births – more than four times the rate for babies born in hospitals. When you endanger the life of your newborn in order to engage in post-natal virtue signalling, you've done nothing to end imagined systemic racism, but you've certainly proven that endemic stupidity is a thing.

https://caldronpool.com/hospitals-are-racist-says-actress-who-gave-birth-at-home/

Ryan Reynolds Apologizes For 2012 Wedding At A Former Slave Plantation

By Paul Bois August 4th, 2020

Actor Ryan Reynolds has publicly apologized for hosting his wedding at a former slave plantation.

In 2012, the "Deadpool" actor, and his now-wife, actress Blake Lively, tied the knot at Boone Hall in South Carolina, and the venue offered the kind of idyllic scenery fit for such an occasion, its checkered past as a former slave plantation was not so pleasant. Now, eight years and one massive Black Lives Matter movement later, Reynolds has apologized. Speaking with Fast Company, Reynolds said that choosing Boone Hall for their wedding venue was a "giant f***ing mistake."

"It's something we'll always be deeply and unreservedly sorry for," he said. "It's impossible to reconcile. What we saw at the time was a wedding venue on Pinterest. What we saw after was a place built upon devastating tragedy. Years ago we got married again at home—but shame works in weird ways. A giant f***ing mistake like that can either cause you to shut down or it can reframe things and move you into action. It doesn't mean you won't fuck up again. But repatterning and challenging lifelong social conditioning is a job that doesn't end."

At the time of the wedding, the press mostly focused on the glamour of the event. It wasn't until 2018 that Reynolds caught flack for the locale when he publicly praised Marvel's "Black Panther." As the Black

Lives Matter movement picked up steam, he and Lively have donated considerable money to the NAACP and other charitable causes. "It's a topic he's reluctant to talk about, in part because he worries that white celebrities too often drown out non-white voices, even if that's not their intention," reported Fast Company of Reynolds philanthropy.

In late May, Lively and Reynolds issued a statement about systemic racism and their desire to become better educated on the subject: We've never had to worry about preparing our kids for different rules of law or what might happen if we're pulled over in the car. We don't know what it's like to experience that life day in and day out. We can't imagine feeling that kind of fear and anger. We are ashamed that in the past we've allowed ourselves to be uninformed about how deeply rooted systemic racism is.

We've been teaching our children differently than the way our parents taught us. We want to educate ourselves about other people's experiences and talk to our kids about everything, all of it... especially our own complicity. We talk about our bias, blindness and our own mistakes. We look back and see so many mistakes which have led us to deeply examine who we are and who we want to become. They've led us to huge avenues of education.

We are committed to raising our kids so they never grow up feeding this insane pattern and so they'll do their best to never inflict pain on another being consciously or unconsciously. It's the least we can do to honor not just George Floyd, Ahmaud Arbery, Breonna Taylor and Eric Garner, but all the black men and women who have been killed when the camera wasn't rolling.

https://www.dailywire.com/news/ryan-reynolds-apologizes-for-2012-wedding-at-a-former-slave-plantation?utm_source=facebook&utm_medium=social&utm_campaign=benshapiro&fbclid=IwAR0-mip8RAwju5i7TT60J53U4kR9epn6XP2iMFiruUvy5UlkA-upJh2iwMUY

Walmart Yanks State Flag From Mississippi Stores

By Tauren Dyson June 23rd, 2020

Walmart stores in Mississippi will no longer hang the state flag above their stores because the flag contains a design that has components of the Confederate flag. The Mississippi flag is the only state flag in the country with an "X" pattern, resembling the flag of the Confederate States of America.

Walmart spokesman Lorenzo Lopez said the company would stop flying the Mississippi flag on top of its stores throughout the state due to the part because of the reference to the Confederacy. "We know the design of the Mississippi state flag is being discussed by various stakeholders," Lopez said in a statement to CNN Business. "While the issue continues to be discussed, we've made the decision to remove the Mississippi state flag from display in its current form from our stores." Lopez said removing the flag from atop Walmart stores in the Southern state was the "right thing to do."

"We believe it's the right thing to do, and is consistent with Walmart's position to not sell merchandise with the confederate flag from stores and online sites, as part of our commitment to provide a welcoming and inclusive experience for all of our customers in the communities we serve," Lopez said.

https://www.newsmax.com/politics/walmart-mississippi-flag-confederate/2020/06/23/id/973800/

'Pimples are in' – the rise of the acne positivity movement

By Laura Barton September 18th, 2018

It was on a family holiday that Kali Kushner discovered, abruptly, just how others viewed her skin. "At the end of the day I washed off my makeup," she recalls. "My nephew said: 'Why is your face so dirty?' It took me a minute to realise he saw my foundation as a 'clean face' and acne as dirt."

Soon after, Kushner, 23, from Cincinnati, Ohio, began documenting her struggle with acne on the Instagram account @myfacestory – her experience with the drug Accutane, dermarolling, makeup, scarring, hyperpigmentation, alongside all the ways people have responded to her acne, from her husband, who has been steadfastly supportive, to the traffic police officer who assumed she was a junkie. To her surprise, people began following. Today, with more than 50,000 followers, she makes up part of the growing acne positivity movement.

After years of oppressive aesthetic perfection, acne positivity is a drive for people to be more open about their skin problems, from the occasional spot to full-blown cystic acne. It joins recent moves to celebrate the many and varied appearances of our skin – from vitiligo to freckles and stretch marks – but also seeks to educate those who still believe that acne is a problem for the unwashed and unhealthy.

Many trace the movement back to the British blogger Em Ford, who in 2015 posted a YouTube video called You Look Disgusting. It showed her both in full makeup and bare-faced with her acne visible, as a succession of comments people had posted about her skin sprung up around her: "WTF is wrong with her face?", "I can't even look at her", "Ewww, gross, horrible, ugly ...". In the first week alone, it amassed 10 million views. Ford, whose YouTube channel My Pale Skin now has more than one million subscribers, will shortly launch You Look Disgusting 2.0.

Others have followed, including the Colorado Instagrammer Hailey Wait and the British beauty blogger Kadeeja Khan, as well as a host of celebrities – from Kylie Jenner promoting her favourite spot treatment to Justin Bieber's Instagram post that claimed "Pimples are in" and Lorde's sardonic replies to people giving her unsolicited skincare advice. Last year, Teen Vogue launched the inaugural Acne awards.

Kushner developed acne in high school. "Whiteheads, blackheads, the usual stuff." It was around the age of 20 that she developed adult cystic acne. "It was hard. And extremely painful. I had no idea what was going with my skin. Nothing worked. Or if it did, it didn't for long."

She grew increasingly socially anxious, certain that everyone she met was staring at her skin. "One time I remember I was talking to my friend in class and started laughing at a joke she told me. As I was laughing, a cyst burst open and started bleeding down my face. It was horrifyingly embarrassing. I ran out of the classroom and didn't come back for the next two weeks."

Dr Bav Shergill of the British Association of Dermatologists says that acne "often affects people without much power in society, such as adolescents". He tells of a US study in which participants were shown a selection of photographs of high-school students with skin problems, as well as photographs of the same students with their acne airbrushed out, and asked for their impressions. The results, Shergill says, showed that "as soon as you have any disfigurement on your face, you get viewed as an introverted nerd".

While many regard acne as a teenage affliction, it can evolve into adulthood. An estimated 25% of all women over 30 still have the condition. "I see so many women – adult, professional, intelligent women – who have had their lives ruined by acne," says Shergill. Women often find that their breakouts are tethered to the hormonal shifts associated with their menstrual cycles. "Female hormonal acne is miserable," Shergill says. "You may not get many spots a month, but each one will leave a scar. And every scar has both an emotional and a physical component."

Corrinne, an educational psychologist from Folkestone, turned 40 in August. To celebrate, she visited the Mac Cosmetics counter for a makeover. Sitting before the makeup artist, she felt horribly, painfully exposed. "I couldn't make eye contact," she says. "To sit there with my face naked, I felt so vulnerable."

Every morning, Corrinne dedicates an hour to the process of getting ready, with the bulk of that time set aside for makeup. She will use a base, foundation, concealer, then more foundation, then powder, then a spray to fix it. It is not an attempt to look unfailingly glamorous: "I'm just trying to get myself to a baseline to face the world."

It has been like this since she was 14. At school, she would wear makeup so thick it was "almost a mask". She hated to be seen in daylight and would use a tiny vanity mirror rather than something that showed her whole face or full length. She spent an hour and a half getting ready for school each morning, and at lunchtime she would go home to reapply her foundation. At breaktimes, she would head straight to the toilets to check her concealer. Comments were made that she says shaped her. "I remember someone said I'd put so much make-up on, it looked like Polyfilla.

"Without social media, it was isolating, lonely, secretive. I thought I was acne. I thought I wasn't bigger than that." In her 20s, she met a friend who had also suffered from severe acne. To find someone who understood so fully, who would discuss it openly and felt no shame, was hugely helpful to Corrinne – it was a taste, perhaps, of today's acne positive attitude. "I wish we'd had that movement when I was 14," she says. "I think it's a fantastic thing."

When Kushner began her Instagram account in 2015, it was solely for herself – a private page to track her progress on Accutane. "I wasn't really interested in sharing my journey at first because I didn't realise that others were going through the same thing," she explains. "I wanted to document my skin and side-effects so that I could look back on it and see how far I've come."

When she made her page public, it was an act of defiance. "If anything, my account was a rebellion against the typical beauty blogger accounts at the time," she says. "There was no curation taking place, no filters, angles, and certainly no Photoshop. I would take out my phone, take a picture, think of a caption within four or five minutes and post it. It was and always has been about keeping it real. It was a call against stereotypical standards of beauty, saying that you don't need X/Y/Z to be beautiful. All you need is you."

This attitude has now spread to other previously flawless areas of social media. Jessica Olie is a fitness guru known for her Let's Start Yoga ebook and an Instagram account in which she is often photographed holding yoga poses in charming locations around the globe. A year or so ago, Olie's account broke its carefully calibrated perfection in favour of a new kind of honesty, documenting her divorce, her father's illness and her problems with her skin.

Olie suffered from teenage acne, exacerbated by the constant exposure to chlorine as a competitive swimmer, and in her late teens was prescribed the pill. Five months after she stopped taking the contraceptive last year, her skin went "haywire" – worse, she says, than when she was a teenager.

For someone who makes a living out of looking enviably, radiantly healthy, posting honestly about her skin problems came with a degree of risk. "If someone said: 'You're supposed to be healthy, why is your skin bad?', I'd tell them just because you're healthy it doesn't mean your skin is good, and just because your skin is good it doesn't mean you're healthy."

And the pursuit of perfection can be wearisome. "I think I was fed up of not feeling pretty or beautiful enough because I had a few pimples. I looked at my friends who didn't wear makeup and I realised when they had pimples they still looked beautiful." Today, she posts pictures and videos of herself makeup-free, her skin mid-flare or masked by splodges of spot cream. "People put you on a pedestal, they think everything in your life is perfect, so it's nice when people on social media reveal there are things they don't feel confident about."

The niceness seems to be spreading. Last year, the photographer and activist Peter DeVito was surprised to find the supermodel Cara Delevingne had reposted a picture of the words "Acne is normal" emblazoned across his acne-marked face. He had recently come to the conclusion that "it was dumb to retouch an image [on social media] for hours, just to post it where people would forget about it in minutes". These days, he says: "It makes me happy when people accept themselves for the way they look and learn to stop comparing themselves to other people on social media all the time."

Kushner, too, has felt a shift in attitudes. "Honestly, there hasn't been as much backlash as you would think," she says. "At first, definitely. People will always have something negative to say no matter what you do or post or say, so that's important to keep in mind. But now I feel like our little community has been able to educate those who were once ignorant on the subject. It feels like a more understanding and accepting place than it was four years ago. I only hope that it continues to grow and the community continues to shine its light."

https://www.usatoday.com/story/life/tv/2018/09/20/sexy-handmaids-tale-halloween-costume-sparks-outrage/1375851002/

Kleenex to rebrand 'man size' tissues after gender complaints

By WTVQ Admin October 18th, 2018

Kleenex will re-brand its "Mansize" tissues after consumers complained the name was sexist — touching off a social media conversation about what's in a name. The company behind Kleenex, Kimberly-Clark, said Thursday that the product, which is sold only in the U.K., will now be called "Kleenex Extra Large." Packages for the tissues describe them as "confidently strong" and "comfortingly soft."

Kimberly-Clark told Britain's Daily Telegraph that it in "no way suggests" that being both soft and strong was "an exclusively masculine trait, nor do we believe that the Mansize branding suggests or endorses gender inequality."

"We are always grateful to customers who take time to tell us how our products can be improved, and we carefully consider all suggestions," the company said in a statement. The tissues, which had been on shelves for 60 years, were launched at a time when large cotton handkerchiefs were still very popular and the brand offered "a unique disposable alternative," the company said. It remains one of their most popular products, with over 3.4 million people buying the tissues every year.

Kimberly-Clark is not the first company to run into a branding issue forced by changing social views. Among the more memorable casualties was stationery maker BiC, which ran into disparaging comments when trying to market pink and purple pens "for her." Amazon was flooded by reviews poking fun at the strategy and the notion that it was "designed to fit comfortably in a woman's hand."

In another example, the British grocery chain Waitrose on Thursday said it will be changing the name of its Gentleman's Smoked Chicken Caesar Roll because of complaints the name was sexist. The roll, which is part of celebrity chef Heston Blumenthal's range, contains anchovy mayonnaise, similar to a classic product called Gentleman's Relish created in the 19th century. Amy Lame, who was appointed by London Mayor Sadiq Khan as the capital's first Night Czar in 2016, posted an image of the product on Twitter with a smirking emoticon.

"I never knew sandwiches were gender specific," she said. "I'm female but thankfully Waitrose let me purchase this anyway." The post touched off some spirited replies, with some noting that Pink Lady apples, Lady Grey tea and lady fingers could be subjected to name changes. Waitrose, for its part, said it was changing the name of the sandwich. "It's never our intention to cause offense — we're not dictating who should eat this sandwich," the company said in a statement. "We hope anyone who tries it will love the distinctive flavors."

https://www.wtvq.com/2018/10/18/kleenex-to-rebrand-039man-size039-tissues-after-gender-complaints/

'Healthy' Is Now Racist

By Robert Stacy McCain July 22nd, 2020

How "woke" are you? No matter how attuned you may be to social-justice ideology, you're probably not as woke as Maxine Ali. She is the kind of young feminist who spells "women" as *womxn* while slinging around academic jargon about "normative gender binaries." Ms. Ali does most of her "activism" on her Instagram account, which, until a few years ago, was a typical sort of "influencer" account about food and exercise. But that was before Ms. Ali got herself a master's degree from King's College London, where critical theory is a central component of the curriculum. Critical theory is to cultural Marxism what a hammer is to carpentry; Ms. Ali is now qualified to identify systemic oppression wherever it may be found, which is to say, *everywhere*.

"The social construction of the 'healthy' body promotes norms that preserve white supremacy," Ms. Ali proclaimed last month in an Instagram post, which detailed at length how BIPOC (black, indigenous, people of color) are oppressed by the "white normativity" involved in "discourses of health."

When people talk about health and refer to a "healthy body," Whiteness is often assumed because it is what we have always seen in visual representations and performances of health.... The prevailing dietary and lifestyle practices that constitute "healthy living" glorify White middle-class standards of food consumption and living as the singularly correct standard. Within this is also an inferentially racist logic that only by embodying White norms, and by downplaying ethnic difference, can BIPOC achieve a state of health and success.

White dominance is bolstered by healthism. The strategy of charging individuals with a moral duty to stay well obscures the effects of structural racism that underpin society and produce health inequity. Discourses of health function to re-secure white privilege. The conflation of the thin, white "healthy" body with beauty, morality and desirability aims to preserve racial hierarchies. Health discourses position Whiteness as "good" and "pure," whilst simultaneously devaluing Brown and Black bodies and framing them as "bad," deviant and pathological.

We cannot use the term "health" uncritically. We cannot have conversations about Wellness without acknowledging how its structures and performances facilitate the exclusion, marginalisation and harm of BIPOC. It's time to call it out. [Emphasis added.] As with most critical-theory writing, it's difficult for a casual reader to discover exactly what is meant by all that academic gibberish. Perhaps our "inferentially racist logic" prevents us from understanding it. But Ms. Ali appears to be saying that the adjective "healthy" is a racist code-word signifying an effort to "preserve white supremacy" by promoting norms that assume whiteness and thereby *facilitating harm* to BIPOC. Thus, to the lengthy indictment of historic evils that white people are accused of perpetrating, we can now add the sin of bolstering "white dominance" by "healthism."

Readers may be tempted to dismiss Ms. Ali's rant as the silly ramblings of a young fanatic with too much time on her hands, but our universities are producing quite a lot of these fanatics nowadays. The anarchist mobs besieging major cities with "mostly peaceful" protests are sufficient evidence that such silly ramblings have an impact, and who knows where the pursuit of social justice may lead them next? In fact, the claim that "discourses of health" are oppressive to minorities has already gained traction in the mainstream media.

The *New York Times* in May published an op-ed column by Sabrina Strings, a sociology professor at the University of California-Irvine who is author of *Fearing the Black Body: The Racial Origins of Fat Phobia*. Noting that obesity had "surfaced as an explanation" for the above-average death rates of African-Americans from the COVID-19 pandemic, Professor Strings harrumphed, "The cultural narrative that black people's weight is a harbinger of disease and death has long served as a dangerous distraction from the real sources of inequality, and it's happening again." After some discussion of the data, Professor Strings then got to her main theme:

Promoting strained associations between race, body size, and complications from [COVID-19] has served to reinforce an image of black people as wholly swept up in sensuous pleasures like eating and drinking, which supposedly makes our unruly bodies repositories of preventable weight-related illnesses.... My research showed that anti-fat attitudes originated not with medical findings, but with Enlightenment-era belief that overfeeding and fatness were evidence of "savagery" and racial inferiority.

Well, far be it from me to question the validity of a professor's research, but it's a rather long leap from (a) identifying a statistical disparity in health outcomes, and (b) claiming that the source of this disparity is "anti-fat attitudes" dating back to the 16th century. Perhaps I've misunderstood her argument, which later references "the centrality of systemic racism in current racial health inequities," but her field of academic expertise is not viral epidemiology or public health. Nowhere does Professor Strings explain what fighting "anti-fat" attitudes (racist or otherwise) has to do with reducing "health inequities." Her argument is a *non sequitur*, in terms of protecting black people from COVID-19 or any other disease.

Of course, much of the "research" emerging from our universities is at best useless, in terms of solving real problems, and is often mischievous, in that the critical-theory obsession with "systemic" injustice is a distraction from practical approaches to social problems. Critical theory ultimately amounts to a denial of individual agency, portraying people as members of categorical castes trapped in collective roles as either "privileged" oppressors or victims of various forms of oppression. Only from such a warped perspective can it be claimed that the obese are being collectively victimized by what Ms. Ali terms "healthism."

Like so much of social-justice rhetoric, these claims are focused on the consequences of emotion, the belief that *hurt feelings* are the root cause of social problems. We need not argue with Professor Strings about racial attitudes that were prevalent three or four centuries ago to ask, what difference does that make to any African-American in 2020? Black people are dying from coronavirus, not from prejudice, and yet every attempt to discuss disparities in the COVID-19 pandemic keeps returning to racism as the automatic one-size-fits-all explanation.

Opinion columns in the *New York Times* will not solve "health inequities," any more than rants about "whiteness" on Ms. Ali's Instagram account will improve the health of her 20,000-plus followers. This is what I mean by describing critical theory as analogous to a carpenter's hammer. When the only tool you've got is a hammer, every problem looks like a nail. When the only tool you've got is critical theory, every problem looks like systemic oppression. Social justice ideologues are very good at finding problems by defining everything as racist, sexist, homophobic, etc., but when it comes to solutions, they offer nothing useful. Now excuse me while I finish eating my pizza. No one can accuse *me* of "healthism."

https://spectator.org/healthy-racist-healthism-white-normativity/

University lecturers told DON'T USE CAPS as it frightens students

By Eugene Henderson Nov 20th, 2018

Staff at Leeds Trinity's school of journalism have also been told to "write in a helpful, warm tone, avoiding officious language and negative instructions". Some blasted the move as "more academic mollycoddling" of the snowflake generation. An "enhancing student understanding, engagement and achievement" memo lists dos and don'ts - with "do" and "don't" among words frowned upon.

Course leaders say capitalising a word could emphasise "the difficulty or high-stakes nature of the task". The memo says: "Despite our best attempts to explain assessment tasks, any lack of clarity can generate anxiety and even discourage students from attempting the assessment at all. Generally, avoid using capital letters for emphasis and "the overuse of 'do', and, especially, 'DON'T'." The memo also says that staff must be "explicit about any inexplicitness" in their assignment briefs.

And it warns that when students are unsure of an assessment, "they often talk to each other and any misconceptions or misunderstandings quickly spread throughout the group (usually aided and abetted by Facebook).

This can lead to further confusion and students may even then decide that the assessment is too difficult and not attempt it." One staff member said they use capitals to emphasise the importance of a particular point so students do not miss it.

The lecturer said: "We have some excellent students but it's a constant battle against a system that wants to treat them like little kids. We are not doing our students any favours with this kind of nonsense." The university said the guidance was sharing "best practice from the latest teaching research", adding: "We take pride in supporting our students to be the very best they can be." Students at Manchester have voted to ban clapping over fears noise could trigger anxiety and suggest using "jazz hands" to show appreciation.

https://www.express.co.uk/news/uk/1046977/university-lecturers-not-to-use-cap-letters-student-failure

University Educator: Mowing Your Lawn & Acting Respectable Is Racist

By Tim Brown December 29th, 2018

Earlier this month, a university educator told the Madison Board of Education why things like civility, time limits and mowing your lawn indicates you are racist. Seriously, I truly wonder how someone completed higher education courses and is teaching students with this kind of mental defect in their thinking. The University of Wisconsin – Madison "educator" said that she teaches her students the alleged "connection" between white liberalism and white supremacy.

In doing so, she sought to provide "working definitions." According to this "enlightened" individual, "white liberalism" means "valuing law and order and protocol above the lives of people."

No, seriously, I don't know how those things are inseparable. Law and order does value the lives of people, but to this person, they are at odds with one another because she does not know how to think logically or clearly. "In this room, we see white liberalism and this is just from my students reflections," she said.

Some of what she claims is white liberalism are things like a "timer" and the calls to "please finish up" when someone's time is up. Other things include numbers, the sign up process, the stage, the barrier. "All of these signs suggest that the law and the decorum and the civility of this conversation is actually more important than what is being said," this white "educator pontificated.

"Another aspect of white liberalism is policing people's tones of voice," she continued. "The obsession with civility, refusing to hear black and brown people when they aren't following white cultural norms of communication."

"For young people speaking today to you, what they're saying is a matter of life and death," she said without providing a shred of evidence for what she is claiming. "I'm not sure what it means to you, but I imagine it's a combination between a sense of duty, being able to put a line on a resume, feeling like someone needs to take charge, and feeling like you're the best person for the job."

"That's actually where the connection lands between white liberalism and white supremacy because it's by maintaining law and order and by maintaining civility by keeping your front lawn nice and tidy and by putting that 'all are welcome in our communities' sign on your front lawn, you are denying the fact that all the while you are with the other hand passing money to a deadly institution that polices with great disparity and causes tragic, tragic harm to the communities that are our neighbors and the communities that we actually should be building forward with."

What? What in the world does having a nice lawn and law and order and a sign that welcomes people have to do with any of this? It's like me saying that this woman took a shower and fixed her hair and put on makeup is somehow racist and detrimental to other ethnic groups. It's stupid! Who gave this woman a diploma?

"So telling black and brown people to please wrap up suggests that their voices, their pain and their stories are less important than rules and that in and of itself is the place where white liberalism turns into white supremacy is because white supremacy is the accumulation of these aggressive messages that say 'stay off the grass,' 'mow your lawn,' 'act respectable,' 'pull your pants up,' right?"

"So, if I was to raise my voice and start using god forbid some swear words to you, I don't believe that it would be received in quite the same way as it would be if a black or a brown youth were using those swear words so here's what I have to say 'fuck white liberalism and fuck white supremacy.'" Of course, she got applause, but not for the idiocy she just uttered, but for her vulgar use of words at the end because it's clear from those in the background that they have no idea what she is talking about.

I suppose this "educator," if she lived according to her own rules would wear hear pants hanging off her rear end, keep a messy house, not abide by the law, fail to act respectable (ooops, she just did that in her last line) and a host of other things. I'll bet when a crime is committed against her, she calls the police and wants that law she is belligerent against to be enforced. She wants order and justice no matter what ethnicity the person is who committed the crime. However, my guess is that she follows, for the most part, the very things she is berating. So, what would that make her? Yep, a white supremacist.

https://freedomoutpost.com/university-educator-mowing-your-lawn-acting-respectable-is-racist/

Charcoal Face Masks Deemed an Example of 'Racism' and 'Blackface'

By Katherine Timpf February 2nd, 2019

Crying racism where none exists makes people a lot less likely to listen to real accusations of racism. Apparently, wanting to draw toxins out of your skin using a charcoal mask is actually pretty problematic — because the masks resemble blackface and are therefore "racist."

Thankfully, there were also a lot of people who replied to Oliver's original tweet, saying that her point of view was utterly ridiculous. This is, no doubt, a good thing — because it is. Charcoal has some unique properties that other substances don't have. It can absorb pollutants and toxins and unclog your pores. It also happens to be black, which means that if you want to get these benefits for your face, you're going to have to put something that is black on your face — and I don't see why that should be a problem. After all, the reason that actual blackface is offensive is because it has historically been intended to demean people with black skin. Wearing a charcoal facemask, however, has none of this history nor this intention. No, the intention of a charcoal facemask is simply to improve your skin, and there's absolutely nothing offensive about that.

https://www.nationalreview.com/2019/02/charcoal-face-masks-deemed-an-example-of-racism-and-blackface/

Handshakes could be BANNED under new workplace rules to avoid expensive sexual harassment claims

By Alahna Kindred April 24th, 2019, Updated: April 25th, 2019

HANDSHAKES could be banned under new workplace rules to avoid expensive sexual harassment claims, an expert has said. Kate Palmer, an associate director of advisory at HR consultancy Peninsula, said employers may ban all forms of physical contact to avoid confusion about what kind of touch is appropriate.

Ms Palmer added the #MeToo movement has forced employers to think about implementing more "black and white" policies. She told the Metro: "Some employers may put a complete ban on physical contact.

"Whether that's going too far or not is a question I would pose, because it's contextual. Does shaking someone's hand go too far?

"They may just say 'no contact at all' because there's no grey area." She said a handshake is "probably safe" unless an employer bans it, then it is a rule that needs to be followed. It comes as three out of four people want a complete ban on physical contact in the workplace, according to a recent survey of 2,000 adults by Totaljobs.

Ms Palmer added putting a hand on someone's back or giving them a hug when they are upset could be "too personal" and staff should be "mindful" of that kind of touch. She said the level of appropriate contact varies from person to person but also from industry to industry. For example, patting someone on the back on a construction site may be more acceptable than if it was an office.

The associate director said employers should make it clear what their policies are. She said added the workplace does extend outside the office – including leaving drinks or the Christmas party. Ms Palmer said employers should remind staff to "be sensible, but don't cross the line".

https://www.thesun.co.uk/news/8930608/handshakes-banned-workplace-rules-sexual-harassment-claims/

New From Teen Vogue: Sleep Is Systemically Racist

By Hank Berrien Jul 16th, 2020

Teen Vogue, in its imperishable desire to act as the spearhead for political correctness, published an article titled "Black Power Naps Is Addressing Systemic Racism in Sleep," in which they plugged an artistic initiative entitled "Black Power Naps," which argues that blacks have had shorter lives than whites because blacks were not permitted to sleep, and thus reparations must be given in the form of time off from work.

Teen Vogue writes of Fannie Sosa and Navild Acosta, who created Black Power Naps, that they "were tired, but it wasn't just any old fatigue. Yes, they experienced a lack of sleep, but they were specifically experiencing a generational fatigue familiar to Black people and people of color." Teen Vogue says Black Power Naps is "also a recognition of the hundreds of years of sleep deprivation that Black people and people of color have experienced as a result of systemic racism, a way to pushback against the false stereotype that Black people are lazy, and an investigation of the inequitable distribution of rest."

Acosta posited, "We're dealing with an inheritance of sleep deprivation. Sleep deprivation was a ... deliberate tactic of slave owners to basically make the mind feeble. That same tactic has only evolved." Sosa added, "Slavery is a regime of stealing and extraction: Stolen wages, stolen life, stolen land, but stolen time was one of the main things. We need time. We need time off; we need time out. Our ancestors never got to take a month off for holidays; they never got to take a sabbatical; they never got to take a nap. When you pile all of those together, you see the reparations that need to happen are monetary, but they're also time and space."

Teen Vogue writes, "Acosta and Sosa are calling for rest as reparations. Yes, they're looking for an ease to the many burdens that might prevent Black people and people of color from sleeping like systemic racism, socioeconomic struggle, and more." Teen Vogue adds, "This conversation about rest is particularly pertinent now, as people take to the streets to say Black Lives Matter. If Black people keep having to fight for their humanity, how can they ever rest knowing they could be in danger?"

Sosa said, "We are having to go out in the streets during a pandemic, expending our energy in really huge amounts in order to ask for reparations and rest and energy. It is a ... double edged sword to navigate as an activist or organizer. You are putting your body on the line to reclaim it. That creates a lot of burnout. We have people who are 20, 21, they are burnt out. They need time off. They need not only to sleep, but to know their people are going to be ok, to know they're going to be ok, to know they can take a break."

https://www.dailywire.com/news/new-from-teen-vogue-sleep-is-systemically-racist

Liberal's Tweet Goes Viral: 'White People Love Dogs Because They Miss Owning Slaves'

By Michael van der Galien Jul 17th, 2019

Scientific research has shown that a great and fascinating — perhaps even mysterious — bond exists between dogs and human beings. They even understand human language. The love story between dogs and humans goes back tens of thousands of years, the results of which can still be seen everywhere, every single day. Families going out with their dogs, which are carefully groomed, looking extremely healthy and happy. The pet is a real member of the family. His needs are as important to his owners as their own. Because of this close relationship, dogs have developed the ability to perfectly understand us.

Dogs are capable of understanding the emotions behind an expression on a human face. For example, if a dog turns its head to the left, it could be picking up that someone is angry, fearful or happy. If there is a look of surprise on a person's face, dogs tend to turn their head to the right. The heart rates of dogs also go up when they see someone who is having a bad day, say Marcello Siniscalchi, Serenella d'Ingeo and Angelo Quaranta of the University of Bari Aldo Moro in Italy. The study in Springer's journal Learning & Behavior is the latest to reveal just how connected dogs are with people. The research also provides evidence that dogs use different parts of their brains to process human emotions.

Considering these abilities, it's not so strange that we love dogs so much.

Liberal Twitter-user Danielle (@ladypalerider) has a different explanation for people's love for dogs, however. Wait. I should've written: for *white* people's love for our canine comrades. According to her, "white people love dogs so much because deep down they miss owning slaves. They love the owner and master dynamic, desperate for something to control."

Silly me, here I was thinking that slave owners generally treated their slaves very badly indeed. But, according to Miss Liberal, slave owners cuddled their slaves, took them for regular walks, groomed them, hugged them regularly, showered them with love, bought them all kinds of gifts, and even made sure that when they went on holiday, their slaves would be treated well. After all, that *is* how we dog-owners treat our dogs.

Calling Danielle's tweet "ridiculous" would be the understatement of the century. It goes without saying that many Twitter users (rightfully) took offense to Danielle's tweet. "What about cats, gerbils, birds, snakes, horses, ducks..." @MadonnaMadsen asks, after which she says she gives Danielle "the STUPIDEST TWEET award." And what about African American people who own dogs? Do they miss slavery too? Or do they love dogs because they like taking care of others (which, according to Danielle's reasoning, could also be constructed as a result of slavery)?

Yet another Twitter user comments sarcastically that he sure does miss owning slaves, but that he hopes he'll get new ones "for my next birthday when I turn 170 [explicit] years old": @B_Rad_ikal calls Danielle's tweet "the quintessential example of pseudoscience." Joel points out that he actually adopted his dog from the pound. "I couldn't stand that pup being well taken care of in a cage 100% of the time," he adds cynically, "given crap food, and seemed traumatized. I just had to exert my control to allow her to roam my yard, while spending hundreds on her."

Human Events Managing Editor Ian Miles Cheong is quite happy with Danielle's tweet, though. "Listen, I just wanted to thank you for driving more people towards the right," he writes. "Trump wouldn't be president without people like you." A very good point indeed. The more radical leftists repeat such silly accusations, the more voters are driven in the arms of Trump and other conservatives. So, who knows? Perhaps us dog owners *should* thank Danielle for her tweet.

https://pjmedia.com/news-and-politics/michael-van-der-galien/2019/07/17/liberals-tweet-goes-viral-white-people-love-dogs-because-they-miss-owning-slaves-n67313

Newsweek: Time to Rethink Taboo on Cannibalism?

By Thomas D. Williams, Ph.D. August 22nd, 2019

Since cannibalism is found throughout the animal kingdom and therefore is something natural, perhaps it is time for humans to rethink the "ultimate taboo" against eating human flesh, *Newsweek* proposes in an article Wednesday.

There is nothing necessarily unethical or unreasonable about eating human flesh, declare psychologists Jared Piazza and Neil McLatchie of Lancaster University, but careful reasoning over the merits of cannibalism is often "overridden by our feelings of repulsion and disgust." While not going so far as to recommend cannibalism, saying "there is no need to overcome our repulsion for the foreseeable future," the two authors suggest that humans could master their aversion for human flesh if they needed to.

"Many people develop disgust for all kinds of meat, while morticians and surgeons quickly adapt to the initially difficult experience of handling dead bodies," they note. "Our ongoing research with butchers in England suggests that they easily adapt to working with animal parts that the average consumer finds quite disgusting." Moreover, the psychological revulsion experienced over the prospect of consuming human flesh is not the product of reason and may even contradict reason, they argue in Wednesday's article, which originally appeared last week in The Conversation.

"Survivors of the famous 1972 Andes plane crash waited until near starvation before *succumbing to reason* and eating those who had already died," they propose. All sorts of animals eat members of their own species, from spadefoot tadpoles and Australian redback spiders to gulls and pelicans, they state. And cannibalism can even be found among mammals, they add, such as with many rodents as well as bears, lions, and chimpanzees.

Yet humans seem entrenched in their conviction that anthropophagy is simply wrong, no matter how many conditions are placed on hypothetical scenarios. Human revulsion toward cannibalism stems from our tendency to associate "personhood and flesh," the authors propose, even when the flesh in question is no longer living.

Even if we can bring ourselves to deem cannibalism morally acceptable, they contend, "we can't silence our thoughts about the person it came from" and so our "bias" against eating human flesh persists. "The way we interact with animals shapes the way we categorize them. Research shows that the more we think of animals as having human properties—that is, as being 'like us'"—the more we tend to think they're gross to eat," they note.

While noting in passing that "philosophers have argued that burying the dead could be wasteful in the context of the fight against world hunger," the authors ultimately do not propose breaking this taboo "for now," saying that "we're as happy as you are to continue accepting the 'wisdom of repugnance.'"

https://www.breitbart.com/the-media/2019/08/22/newsweek-time-to-rethink-taboo-on-cannibalism

'OK' hand gesture added to hate symbols database

By Associated Press September 26th, 2019

COLLEGE PARK, Md. - The "OK" hand gesture, a mass killer's bowl-style haircut and an anthropomorphic moon wearing sunglasses are among 36 new entries in a Jewish civil rights group's online database of hate symbols used by white supremacists and other far-right extremists.

The Anti-Defamation League has added the symbols to its online "Hate on Display" database, which already includes burning crosses, Ku

Klux Klan robes, the swastika and many other of the most notorious and overt symbols of racism and anti-Semitism.

The New York City-based group launched the database in 2000 to help law enforcement officers, school officials and others recognize signs of extremist activity. It has grown to include nearly 200 entries. "Even as extremists continue to use symbols that may be years or decades old, they regularly create new symbols, memes and slogans to express their hateful sentiments," Anti-Defamation League CEO Jonathan Greenblatt said in a statement.

Some of the new entries started as trolling campaigns or hateful memes on internet message boards such as 4chan, 8chan and Reddit, before migrating to Facebook, Twitter and other mainstream platforms, and to public forums and fliers. The ADL has updated its database to include the "OK" hand symbol, which became fodder for a 4chan trolling campaign to dupe viewers into thinking the fingers formed the letters "W" and "P" to mean "white power." But the ADL says extremists also are using it as a sincere expression of white supremacy.

Brenton Tarrant, the Australian man charged with killing 51 people at mosques in Christchurch, New Zealand, in March, flashed the "OK" symbol during a courtroom appearance after his arrest. Tarrant also had the number 14 written on his rifle, a possible reference to the "14 Words," a white supremacist slogan, according to the Southern Poverty Law Center. Oren Segal, director of the ADL's Center on Extremism, said context is key to interpreting whether an "OK" symbol is hateful or harmless. He said the ADL had been reluctant to add it to the database "because 'OK' has meant just 'OK' for so long."

"At this point, there is enough of a volume of use for hateful purposes that we felt it was important to add," Segal said. An earlier addition to the database was Pepe the Frog, a cartoon character that became hijacked by online extremists who superimposed the frog with Nazi symbols and other hateful imagery. The ADL branded Pepe as a hate symbol in September 2016 and supported cartoonist Matt Furie's efforts to reclaim the character he created.

The "Happy Merchant," one of the new database entries, is an anti-Semitic meme that depicts a stereotypical image of a bearded Jewish man rubbing his hands together. Another addition, the "Moon Man" meme, is derived from "Mac Tonight," a character in a McDonald's advertising campaign during the 1980s. Internet trolls transformed the sunglasses-wearing cartoon moon into a vehicle for rap songs with racist and violent lyrics. The ADL also added the "Dylann Roof Bowlcut," an image of the hairstyle worn by the white supremacist who shot and killed nine black people in 2015 at a church in Charleston, South Carolina.

Roof's bowl-style hair became an avatar for extremists, including a Washington, D.C., man whose relatives contacted the FBI to report concerns about his behavior and far-right extremist rhetoric after last year's Pittsburgh synagogue massacre . Jeffrey Clark's username on the Gab social media platform was "DC Bowl Gang," an FBI agent wrote in a court filing for gun charges against Clark.

Logos of white nationalist groups including the Rise Above Movement and the American Identity Movement also are among the new ADL database entries. The recently formed American Identity Movement is the successor to the now-dissolved Identity Evropa, which frequently plastered its white nationalist propaganda on college campuses and is one of the groups that has been sued over the violence that erupted at a white nationalist rally in Charlottesville, Virginia , in August 2017. Four members of the California-based Rise Above Movement pleaded guilty this year to attacking counterprotesters at the Charlottesville rally. A federal judge sentenced three of them to prison terms ranging from 27 months to 37 months.

https://www.fox2detroit.com/news/ok-hand-gesture-added-to-hate-symbols-database

California Democrats pass resolution calling for John Wayne Airport to be renamed

By Adam Shaw June 27th, 2020

California Democrats in Orange County are demanding that the county's John Wayne Airport be renamed and all likenesses of Wayne be removed from the airport, over "racist and bigoted statements" made by the American icon decades ago.

"The Democratic Party of Orange County condemns John Wayne's racist and bigoted statements, and calls for John Waynes' name and likeness to be removed from the Orange County airport, and calls on the OC Board of Supervisors to restore its original name: Orange County Airport," the resolution, passed Friday, says. The resolution, first reported by the Los Angeles Times, calls on the Orange County Board of Supervisors to reverse the 1979 decision to rename it after Duke, and cites remarks he made in a 1971 interview with Playboy.

"I believe in white supremacy until the blacks are educated to a point of responsibility. I don't believe in giving authority and positions of leadership and judgment to irresponsible people," he said in that interview nearly 50 years ago. "I don't feel guilty about the fact that five or 10 generations ago these people were slaves," he said at another point in the interview.

There have been a number of pushes to rename the airport as a result of those comments after they resurfaced. Wayne's defenders have said it is unfair to judge him based off remarks made nearly 50 years ago, and when he is no longer alive to defend or even retract them. The latest push comes amid a movement across the country to tear down monuments and rename buildings and institutions that are named after people deemed to have held racist views or committed racist acts.

The Democratic resolution hails a "national movement to remove white supremacist symbols and names is reshaping American institutions, monuments, businesses, nonprofits, sports leagues and teams, as it is widely recognized that racist symbols produce lasting physical and psychological stress and trauma particularly to Black communities, people of color and other oppressed groups, and the removal of racist symbols provides a necessary process for communities to remember historic acts of violence and recognize victims of oppression."

According to the LA Times, Wayne lived a good portion of his life in Newport Beach in Orange County, was a political power broker in the county and was buried in the city after his death in 1979.

https://www.foxnews.com/politics/california-democrats-resolution-john-wayne-airport-renamed

L'Oreal to Remove Words Like 'Whitening' From Skin Products

By Associated Press June 27th, 2020

French cosmetics giant L'Oreal said Saturday that it will remove words like "whitening" from its skincare products, a move that comes amid global protests against racism sparked by the death of George Floyd in the United States. The company said in a statement Saturday that it "has decided to remove the words white/whitening, fair/fairness, light/lightening from all its skin evening products."

L'Oreal's decision follows a similar move by Anglo-Dutch firm Unilever on Thursday. It is among a number of companies that have been the target of criticism in the wake of Floyd's death following his arrest in Minneapolis. Earlier this month, L'Oreal tweeted that it "stands in solidarity with the Black community and against injustice of any kind. ... Speaking out is worth it." The post drew a negative reaction from people who see the company's business model and advertising as focused on white consumers.

English model Munroe Bergdorf notably accused the beauty brand of hypocrisy for having fired her three years ago. Bergdorf was sacked as

L'Oreal UK's first openly transgender model in 2017 for decrying "the racial violence of white people."

https://www.nbclosangeles.com/news/national-international/loreal-to-remove-words-like-whitening-from-skin-products/2387213/

Think the 'Cancel' Mobs Can't Get Any Worse? Think Again

By Harlan Hill June 27th, 2020

America is in the midst of one of the great moral panics in our nation's history. If we don't stand up for our nation's core values, the situation could get even worse – and soon. If you've spent any time on social media in the last three weeks, you've probably noticed the organized campaigns to get college and even high school students expelled or denied admission based on their political views. You've also seen gleeful mobs celebrating as Americans lose their jobs for running afoul of someone's momentary political obsessions.

In every sector of American society, people are having their careers destroyed to the pitiless baying of the "woke" masses. It's happening in business. CrossFit CEO Greg Glassman spent 20 years building the fitness brand into a multi-billion dollar company, only to be thrown out of the empire he built for declining to go along with the "racism is a public health crisis" dogma.

It's happening in journalism. New York Times editor James Bennet, a liberal, was fired for publishing an op-ed by a sitting Republican senator advocating for a military response to nationwide rioting -- a position the majority of Americans agreed with. The same fate befell Philadelphia Inquirer editor Stan Wischowski, who was terminated for approving an article that condemned looting and arson.

It's happening in entertainment, in academia, and pretty much anywhere someone can be found who is not sufficiently supportive of the

Black Lives Matter movement. It's even happening to people who didn't do anything at all. An L.A. Galaxy soccer player was forced to resign because *his wife* tweeted that rioters should be shot. A lawyer in San Francisco was fired because *his wife* was rude to a man she thought was spray-painting BLM propaganda on a building that wasn't his (it was). On Thursday, this Stasi-esque trend reached another level when a company called Equity Prime Mortgage fired the *stepmother* of the officer charged in the controversial shooting of drunk driver Rashad Brooks after he fought with and fired a taser at police. The stepmother was apparently fired for no reason other than family loyalty.

On Monday, the panic reached what one can only hope will be its peak when a San Diego Gas and Electric employee lost his job for "making a white supremacist hand gesture." We've long since debunked the notion that the OK sign is somehow racist -- that was just a fiction perpetrated by internet trolls -- but in this case, this man lost his livelihood despite the fact *he wasn't even making an OK sign*. He was apparently cracking his knuckles as he drove.

What America is going through right now is not merely another, more intense round of "cancel culture." We're now in the midst of a full-force, totalitarian remolding of our society, one that seeks to place the petty resentments of an outraged minority of leftist activists above everything else in American life. Because of their willingness to riot, loot, and assault anyone they perceive to be insufficiently sympathetic to their cause, leftists are able to bully ordinary people into submission. As a result, television shows such as "Cops" and "Live PD," classic films such as "Gone With the Wind," and iconic brands such as Aunt Jemima, Mrs. Buttersworth, and Uncle Ben's rice are consigned to the "dustbin of history."

I used to speak frequently to nervous conservatives who were convinced that if we only allowed the left to tear down Confederate war memorials, they would be satisfied. How quickly events have disproved that wishful thinking. From Christopher Columbus, George Washington, Thomas Jefferson, and the western pioneers, activists are now coming after cartoon sports mascots and college fight songs. *Everything* -- from the core of our country's history to the values and norms undergirding American culture -- must be uprooted to appease the mob.

They are tearing down dozens of statues and facing no consequences whatsoever for vandalizing our public spaces -- including memorials to our nation's greatest heroes. When private citizens try to do the job the government won't and protect our culture, our history, and our public property from destruction, local officials step in and remove the statues on behalf of the vandals, lest they injure themselves while imitating Iraqis celebrating the fall of Saddam Hussein.

These people are not seeking change at the margins. They are demanding a total cultural revolution, and cowardly public officials are giving it to them. If you look at this national outpouring of hatred and recrimination with horror verging on despair, I assure you that you are not alone. Tens of millions of Americans feel exactly the same way.

President Trump is doing exactly what an American president should do in a crisis like this. He is working to maintain law and order and prevent cowed local officials from allowing political violence to flare again. He issued an executive order to add to his legacy of reform and address legitimate concerns about law enforcement in this country. He also issued a separate executive order targeting the systemic bias in Silicon Valley's censorship offices, which has allowed our social media platforms to become echo chambers for left-wing extremism and "cancel culture."

The only thing that could make the situation worse at this moment would be handing the White House to a doddering and unprincipled establishment politician beholden to the "cancel culture" mob. Presumptive Democratic nominee Joe Biden would immediately delegate *de facto* control over the vast justice, civil rights, and regulatory apparatus of the federal government to the loudest voices in his coalition: the woke activist class.

At this moment, there is a veritable army of lawyers and bureaucrats who have spent the last three and a half years subsisting on resentment and salivating at the prospect of regaining power. Things are bad enough now, but conditions will become much worse if the "cancel culture" born on social media is augmented with the force of law and given the full attention of Biden appointees imbued with the sweeping powers of the federal bureaucracy. Dark forces have been unleashed in this country. Even now, we are only seeing the tip of the iceberg. If we don't want to find out how much damage it can inflict on the ship of state, we must prevent those forces from taking control of the federal government.

https://www.realclearpolitics.com/articles/2020/06/27/think_the_cancel_mobs_cant_get_any_worse_think_again.html

Liberal's All-Out Assault On Free Speech

By Derek Hunter Jul 12th, 2020

In 1964, comedian Lenny Bruce was convicted in New York City on obscenity charges. It wasn't for anything he did, it was for what he said...while doing stand-up comedy. It seems absurd now that an American could face jail time, as did the owner of the comedy club where he'd uttered the offending words (he was sentenced to four months in prison but died of an overdose while appealing the case).

What destroyed Lenny Bruce has ultimately destroyed itself - those words are now commonplace on basic cable television, and sometimes broadcast networks. The words were "banned" by social conservatives at a time when nearly everyone in power was what would have been called a social conservative. Societal norms were that you not only shouldn't say those words in public, but you couldn't. There was no real push-back, by politicians anyway, against the restrictions. "Liberal" celebrities spoke out in support of Bruce, but his conviction stood until he was posthumously pardoned by then New York Governor George Pataki in 2003.

While the "conservatives" at the time were the ones imposing penalties on speech, it's now the liberals seeking to do the same, and worse. The idea of criminalizing so-called "hate speech" has been popular with college-aged liberals for a while now. While normal people laughed at those stupid college kids needing safe spaces when someone was on campus saying things they didn't agree with and requiring "trigger warnings" before engaging in normal human conversations on subject that might cause them to need a diaper change, liberals were busy looking for an opportunity to use this childishness to their advantage. They found it...by becoming them.

Adults, chronologically anyway, began embracing what they should have grown out of and joined the outrage mob. Ideological corporations like CNN and MSNBC took up the cause of being the nation's tattletale, tracking down people who'd posted things deemed impure of thought by the progressive left and exposing them, leaving it to the mob to inform employers in the hopes of ruining lives.

This Nazi tactic has been institutionalized by groups like Media Matters (which is somehow a tax-exempt non-profit) and Sleeping Giants. Sleeping Giants exists explicitly to enforce conformity of speech in public. They go after websites publishing unacceptable words and have damaged many by getting cowardly corporations to block out their ability to sell ads. While it seems like these fascists are on the ascension, and in many quarters they are, they are also suffering from what always plagues leftists – greed and jealously.

Who would've thought there was so much money in advocating for the poor and oppressed? There is. The admitted Marxists who run Black Lives Matter are raking in the cash. ANTIFA leaders aren't missing any meals. Al Sharpton has a TV show in addition to his race-baiting extortion racket. All manner of grievance grifters are starting organizations and milking moneyed liberal suckers hoping to prove their purity, show that they're "allies," to avoid the rage for anything they may have said or done in the past that could be deemed unacceptable now. It's a profitable scam, with tens, if not hundreds of millions of dollars sifting through the hands (bank accounts) of these "leaders."

But with money and power comes the greed to control it and the source of its power (the mob), and jealously over who gets that control and the attention that accompanies it. A group of leftists signed a letter this week begging for permission to continue to speak their minds. They weren't seeking approval to disagree in the way normal people think of the word -- they all agree with progressive dogma -- they just differ on tactics and degrees of government control. These "intellectuals" even framed their letter as an attack on President Trump, in the hope that their show of solidarity with purists would give them some leeway and forgiveness should they ever run afoul of the mob. It didn't work.

The signatories were denounced as "rich, mostly white" apostates. In the tradition of begging for mercy, shown during the Maoist purge called the Cultural Revolution, the slightest pushback was met with denunciations. Some signatories renounced their own actions, which were little more than a pleading to be able to think.

Nothing in that letter was a defense of conservatives who experience violence when invited to speak on college campuses. None of it could have remotely be read as an embrace of free and open debate or a defense of the concept of free speech guaranteed by the First Amendment. It was the equivalent of asking to be allowed to support a "public option" in Obamacare rather than a full government takeover of health care – simply a matter of degrees. That wasn't good enough. If you are a 99.9 percent ally of the left, you are their 100 percent enemy. Even asking for the leeway to possibly, at some point in the future, be allowed to deviate on a potential issue (which was what the letter was really doing) was not good enough.

There were calls for firings, public pressure brought to silence signers, and a second letter, this one by other liberals arguing that the first letter deserves scorn because it wasn't woke on the right issues. Here are a few choice passages from this second, much longer, letter denouncing the ability to disagree, marginally, with fellow leftists:

"In truth, Black, brown, and LGBTQ+ people — particularly Black and trans people — can now critique elites publicly and hold them accountable socially; this seems to be the letter's greatest concern."

"The letter reads as a caustic reaction to a diversifying industry — one that's starting to challenge institutional norms that have protected bigotry. The writers of the letter use seductive but nebulous concepts and coded language to obscure the actual meaning behind their words, in what seems like an attempt to control and derail the ongoing debate about who gets to have a platform."

"The signatories claim that "books are withdrawn for alleged inauthenticity." This could be a reference to American Dirt, a book by Jeanine Cummins — a non-Mexican white woman who recently began identifying as Puerto Rican — about a Mexican bookseller, which was roundly criticized by Latinx writers and authors like Myriam Gurba and Los Angeles Times writer Esmeralda Bermudez."

These are just a few, but the whole thing is worthy of mockery. It ends the way every progressive declaration does – in a woke-off, with participants trying to out-victim each other. "Their letter seeks to uphold a 'stifling atmosphere' and prioritizes signal-blasting their discomfort in the face of valid criticism. The intellectual freedom of cis white intellectuals has never been under threat en masse, especially when compared to how writers from marginalized groups have been treated for generations. In fact, they have never faced serious consequences — only momentary discomfort." Over at Sleeping Giants, a woman named Nandini Jammi announced she was leaving the fascistic sect she cofounded not because she suddenly realized they were everything they'd claimed to be campaigning against, she quit to form her own group because she wasn't getting enough credit for their group's "successes."

The subtitle of her resignation column is, "How my white male cofounder gaslighted me out of the movement we built together." Jammi's beef is about attention and power, probably money too. Someone's funding this stuff. With her own group, she controls all of it.

Each of these intrasquad slap-fights are akin to the fight between the Bolsheviks and Mensheviks – two sides of the same coin hoping to be the ones wielding the sword of power over everyone else. They want to be the arbiters of what is acceptable and what isn't and be able to punish accordingly. They want to decide what can and cannot be said, and what happens if you cross their blurry, ever-moving line of conformity.

These are dangerous people, all of them. Their impulses and ideology are totalitarian. That they demand and obtain the ruination of heretics without the power government under their control, just imagine what they'd do with it.

People never believed Hitler, Stalin, Mao, and other leftists were as fanatical as the signs indicated they were or that they'd go as far as they did in the last century and were horrified to learn they were wrong. When someone tells you who they are, believe them – especially when it's horrible.

Lenny Bruce would still be arrested today, not because his words were obscene, but because they offended the sensibilities of leftists. That they're eating their own now, when they expect to obtain power in the fall, think about how hungry they'll be if they win and the rest of us are the only meal around.

https://townhall.com/columnists/derekhunter/2020/07/12/liberals-allout-assault-on-free-speech-n2572324

Celebrating Adele's weight loss isn't a compliment – it's fatphobia

By Adwoa Darko November 28th, 2019

This week, pictures emerged of a slimmer looking Adele, as the singer arrived at rap star Drake's birthday party.

Instantly people were tweeting and sharing the photos, congratulating her on her "revenge body" – a reference to her ongoing divorce with

Simon Konecki. Across my social media feeds, it seemed that everyone was sharing headlines that discussed her "sensational new look", posting her "before and after" snaps. The resounding reaction was: "She looks so good now!"

For me, this was far from unexpected. It merely confirmed that we live in a society which idealises thinness and celebrates weight loss as inherently positive. The underlying premise behind the reaction to Adele's photos was a) the assumption that her "old" body was "wrong" and b) that she made a deliberate and "healthy" choice.

In reality, this reaction is just a series of backhanded compliments. Saying that she looks good *now,* is just a more subtle form of body shaming that masquerades as a compliment. By glamourising this terrible concept of the "revenge-body", we are saying that fitness and eating well are tools to be weaponised against a former relationship as opposed to a positive choice we should all be making. It centres our value in our physical appearance, and the idea that bigger bodies are not worthy of a fulfilling relationship.

At its worst, the fixation on Adele's post separation "glow up" reveals our deep rooted societal fatphobia, in which skinniness is valued at any detrimental cost and equated with attractiveness.

We have reached a stage in which we are well versed in the health implications of obesity, which can be a positive thing. After all, it is important that we all make steps to eat well and exercise for our mental and physical wellbeing. However, why do we rarely acknowledge that weight loss, especially at a rapid rate, can be a cause for concern?

Quick weight loss can be the unintended result of a mental or physical condition. It is common knowledge that Adele is in the process of a divorce – a deeply traumatic and stressful experience for anyone, let alone someone in the public eye. Yet, when these photos were released, there was a distinct lack of concern for her welfare. Studies have shown that stress can cause a whole range of digestion problems, including loss of appetite. While many of us respond to mental health challenges by comfort eating, some people struggle with disordered eating as a response to depression or anxiety.

Adele's mental and physical health is, of course, her own business. She could be happy, healthy and intentionally trying to lose weight. If this is the case then I truly wish her every success. But why do we continue to comment on people's bodies without knowing context? How can we be sure that a 'compliment' is not fuelling or validating a potential crisis?

It is an uncomfortable truth that, although packaged as support for the person's health, in general these "compliments" speak to the fact that our celebration of weight loss is not always about welfare. Society just cares that you're slim, no matter how objectively harmful the journey was to get there.

Adele always has been and always will be beautiful. She is more than a before and after picture, she is an immense talent and national treasure – this, not her body, should be the focus.

https://www.independent.co.uk/voices/adele-weight-loss-picture-drakes-birthday-party-fatphobia-mental-health-a9174976.html

Everything

There is one thing to take away from this book and this section... Everything can be arbitrarily banned, censored, and canceled from groups of nameless and faceless, politically correct psychopaths who want to run, dominate and control every single aspect of our lives.

32

Conclusions

Whew.... That was exhausting, wasn't it? You probably need a moment to catch your breath, shotgun a few beers, down a couple of shots of whiskey and smoke some pot in order to fully understand and comprehend all of the news stories and articles you just read.

The sad part of all of this politically correct and authoritarian nonsense is that these social justice, snowflake, language and thought police control freaks, ARE. DEAD. SERIOUS. These people are not messing around.

It's only a matter of time before Panda Express gets cancelled and shut down because they perpetuate "racist stereotypes" and "cultural appropriation" against China and other Asian countries. I could go on and on about what could be shut down, banned, censored and cancelled but this book would be over 10,000 pages long. The point of bringing this all to your attention is simple... You need to wake up. If you don't put your foot down now and say "no" to all of this authoritarian control and management, these vile people are not going to stop. Below, I will give you an example of how easily EVERYTHING in life can be banned, censored, cancelled and shut down.

Popeye. Remember him? The swashbuckling NAVY sailor man cartoon man that started in the 1920's? NORMAL people see Popeye and enjoy watching him eat his spinach and beat up Brutus who is always bullying him. However, let me show you how easy it would be to ban, censor, cancel and shut down Popeye by taking the same approach as these self-righteous Nazi's do...

Popeye is "ableist"- Think about how Popeye looks. He has a collapsed eyeball, a broken jaw, misshaped head and no teeth. How dare Popeye exist. He perpetuates hate against the freak community, the disabled community and the transabled community.

Popeye showcases eating disorders and anti-climate change- He's addicted to spinach. This is an eating disorder. How dare Popeye shape the minds of young girls out there by force feeding himself spinach in order to get strong and be healthy? Furthermore, Whimpy is addicted to hamburgers. With Whimpy eating hamburgers, he clearly does not believe in climate change caused by consuming more meat products.

Popeye is anti-woman- Why is it that Popeye always saves the poor, helpless FEMALE Olive Oil? This is male chauvinist sexism and must be banned.

Popeye promotes white male colonialism- Popeye is offensive because he in a white male in the NAVY. The NAVY is part of the US military. Popeye represents conquering indigenous people's lands through colonialism.

Popeye is sexist- First, Olive Oil clearly has an eating disorder. Look at how sickly, thin and gangly she is. No one can look like that unless they are binging and purging. She also seems to have an illegitimate son, Swee'Pea. This shows the sexism as a white male has to "save the day" of the single mom every single episode.

Popeye is fatphobic- Look at Whimpy. He is constantly eating hamburgers. This is not only promoting eating disorders, it shows what body shaming truly is. Whimpy probably has diabetes due to his horrendous hamburger habit and how does he get around in each episode? By bartering and gambling those very same hamburgers in order to get through life.

Popeye is anti-children and promotes bastardization of children- Swee'Pea is the neglected son of Olive Oil who constantly tries crawling away from his mother. Olive Oil also promotes Heteronormativity by forcing her "son" to wear little boy's hat. How do we not know that he is asexual or a trans baby?

Popeye promotes violence against women- Brutus basically walks around always trying to steal or hurt Olive Oil. This type of sexual aggression cannot stand. He also displays the offensiveness of being an alpha male macho man. This also is unacceptable.

So, let's look at what Popeye promotes. Popeye has taught us that it is full of:

- Food Addictions
- Drug Abuse
- Freak Deformity Discrimination
- Sexual Assault
- Poor Parenting
- Gambling
- Eating Disorders
- Military Imperialism
- Heteronormativity
- Reinforcing Gender Roles
- Sexism
- Racism
- Ableism
- Fat Shaming

Now most of these politically correct, virtue signaling, self-righteous and sanctimonious social justice warriors would probably think that I make some valid points up here! Instead of people enjoying and liking a cartoon series and cartoon character, they take it many steps to far. Remember this... **If Popeye can be banned, then literally everything else can be banned.**

So, who are the arbiters and judges as to what is considered offensive, racist, sexist, etc.? Who or what entity determines what is offensive and needs to be banned, censored and cancelled? What are the criteria in measuring these campaigns of destruction? The truth is that these are arbitrary judgements passed down by bi-costal elite, wealthy, virtue-signaling, sanctimonious, self-righteous, ivory tower, self-serving, guilty, radical fascists.

These people have a goal; to tear down the existing society and replace it with their "Brave New World" meets "1984" meets Plato's "Republic" utopian hell hole. They are systematically dismantling our entire culture because they want to control the narrative of the future and rewrite history. The question here is simple. Are there more of us than there are of them? We must stop banning, cancelling, censoring and dismantling all of our culture, or our children and grandchildren will grow up in a horrible, bland, non-free world.

It's time to tell these control freaks to go fuck themselves. Resist, disobey and be free again.

Love,
Steven

www.ingramcontent.com/pod-product-compliance
Lightning Source LLC
Chambersburg PA
CBHW070824020826
48982CB00014B/456
9780578873091